Prisons and Jails

A Reader

FIRST EDITION

Richard Tewksbury
Dean Dabney

Boston Burr Ridge, IL Dubuque, IA New York San Francisco St. Louis
Bangkok Bogotá Caracas Kuala Lumpur Lisbon London Madrid Mexico City
Milan Montreal New Delhi Santiago Seoul Singapore Sydney Taipei Toronto

The McGraw·Hill Companies

Published by McGraw-Hill, an imprint of The McGraw-Hill Companies, Inc., 1221 Avenue of the Americas, New York, NY 10020.

This book is printed on acid-free paper.

1 2 3 4 5 6 7 8 9 0 DOC/DOC 0 9 8

ISBN: 978-0-07-338002-5
MHID: 0-07-338002-4

Editor in Chief: *Michael Ryan*
Publisher: *Frank Mortimer*
Sponsoring Editor: *Katie Stevens*
Editorial Coordinator: *Teresa Treacy*
Marketing Manager: *Leslie Oberhuber*
Production Editor: *Regina Ernst*
Manuscript Editor: *Barbara Hacha*
Cover Designer: *Margarite Reynolds*
Production Supervisor: *Louis Swaim*
Composition: *10/12 Palatino by Aptara®, Inc.*
Printing: *45# New Era Matte Plus, R. R. Donnelley & Sons/Crawfordsville, IN*
Credits: The acknowledgements section for this book begins on page 599 and is considered an extension of the copyright page.

Library of Congress Cataloging-in-Publication Data

Prisons and jails : a reader / [edited by] Richard Tewksbury, Dean Dabney. —1st ed.
p. cm.
ISBN-13: 978-0-07-338002-5 (alk. paper)
ISBN-10: 0-07-338002-4 (alk. paper)
1. Prisons—United States. 2. Jails—United States. 3. Prisoners—United States.
I. Tewksbury, Richard A. II. Dabney, Dean A.
HV9471.P786 2008
365'.973—dc22 2008039060

www.mhhe.com

TABLE OF CONTENTS

Preface ix

PART I: MODERN CORRECTIONS—PHILOSOPHICAL UNDERSTANDINGS 1

READING 1: Franklin E. Zimring: *Imprisonment Rates and the New Politics of Criminal Punishment* 3

READING 2: Richard Tewksbury and Matthew T. DeMichele: *The Good, the Bad, and the (Sometimes) Ugly Truths: American Penal Goals and Perspectives* 9

READING 3: Jonathan Simon: *From the Big House to the Warehouse: Rethinking Prisons and State Government in the Twentieth Century* 21

PART II: LEGAL ISSUES IN CORRECTIONS 39

READING 4: Christopher E. Smith: *Prisoners' Rights and the Rehnquist Court Era* 41

READING 5: Frank A. Zeigler and Rolando V. Del Carmen: *Constitutional Issues Arising from "Three Strikes and You're Out" Legislation* 59

PART III: THE PSYCHOLOGY OF IMPRISONMENT 75

READING 6: Thomas J. Schmid and Richard S. Jones: *Ambivelent Actions: Prison Adaptation Strategies of First-Time, Short-Term Inmates* 77

READING 7: Chris Sigurdson: *The Mad, the Bad, and the Abandoned: The Mentally Ill in Prisons and Jails* 95

PART IV: INMATE MISCONDUCT 109

READING 8: *Nancy Wolff, Cynthia L. Blitz, Jing Shi, Jane Siegel, and Ronet Bachman: Physical Violence Inside Prisons: Rates of Victimization* *111*

READING 9: Christopher Hensley, Mary Koscheski, and Richard Tewksbury: *The Impact of Institutional Factors on Officially Reported Sexual Assaults in Prisons* *121*

READING 10: Stephen E. Lankenau: *Smoke 'Em if You got 'Em: Cigarette Black Markets in U.S. Prisons and Jails* *129*

PART V: MANAGING AND RESPONDING TO MISCONDUCT 147

READING 11: David R. Eichenthal and Laurel Blatchford: *Prison Crime in New York State* *149*

READING 12: Mark Fleisher and Scott H. Decker: *Gangs Behind Bars: Prevalence, Conduct, and Response* *159*

READING 13: James W. Marquart: *Prison Guards and the Use of Physical Coercion as a Mechanism of Prisoner Control* *175*

PART VI: CORRECTIONAL STAFF 191

READING 14: Mary Ann Farkas: *A Typology of Correctional Officers* *193*

READING 15: Peter Finn: *Correctional Officer Stress: A Cause for Concern and Additional Help* *207*

READING 16: Francis T. Cullen, Edward J. Latessa, Velmer S. Burton, Jr., and Lucien X. Lombardo: *The Correctional Orientation of Prison Wardens: Is the Rehabilitation Ideal Supported?* *221*

READING 17: Richard Tewksbury: *Reasons for Professors to Teach in Prison* *237*

PART VII: INSTITUTIONAL PROGRAMMING 247

READING 18: Richard Tewksbury and Elizabeth Ehrhardt Mustaine: *Insiders' Views of Prison Amenities: Beliefs and Perceptions of Correctional Staff Members* 249

READING 19: Carl G. Leukefeld and Frank R. Tims: *Drug Abuse Treatment in Prisons and Jails* 263

PART VIII: HEALTH CARE ISSUES 275

READING 20: James W. Marquart, Dorothy E. Merianos, Jaimie L. Hebert, and Leo Carroll: *Health Condition and Prisoners: A Review of Research and Emerging Areas of Inquiry* 277

READING 21: Mark Blumberg and J. Dennis Laster: *The Impact of HIV/AIDS on Corrections* 291

READING 22: Dean A. Dabney and Michael S. Vaughn: *Incompetent Jail and Prison Doctors* 305

PART IX: INMATE FAMILIES 333

READING 23: Jeremy Travis: *Families and Children* 335

READING 24: Megan L. Comfort: *In the Tube at San Quentin: The "Secondary Prisonization" of Women Visiting Inmates* 351

PART X: AGE-SPECIFIC ISSUES IN CORRECTIONS 365

READING 25: Wilson R. Palacios, Ph.D.: *Moving Beyond the "Pepsi Generation": The Contemporary Inmate Subculture in Juvenile Correctional Settings* 367

READING 26: Frances P. Reddington and Allen D. Sapp: *Juveniles in Adult Prisons: Problems and Prospects* 379

READING 27: John J. Kerbs and Jennifer M. Jolley: *Challenges Posed by Older Prisoners: What We Know About America's Aging Prison Population* 389

PART XI: GENDER ISSUES IN CORRECTIONS 413

READING 28: John D. Wooldredge and Kimberly Masters: *Confronting Problems Faced by Pregnant Inmates in State Prisons* 415

READING 29: Eric D. Poole and Mark R. Pogrebin: *Gender and Occupational Culture Conflict: A Study of Women Jail Officers* 423

PART XII: DEATH ROW 445

READING 30: Bruce A. Arrigo, Carol R. Fowler, and Kristie R. Blevins: *The Death Row Community Revisited: Lessons Learned from Community Psychology* 447

READING 31: Michael L. Radelet: *Humanizing Death Row Inmates* 473

PART XIII: UNIQUE CHALLENGES 481

READING 32: James L. Williams, Daniel G. Rodeheaver, and Denise W. Huggins: *A Comparative Evaluation of a New Generation Jail* 483

READING 33: Bonnic L. Green, Jeanne Miranda, Anahita Daroowalla, and Juned Siddique: *Trauma Exposure, Mental Health Functioning, and Program Needs of Women in Jail* 495

READING 34: Eileen M. Luna-Firebaugh: *Incarcerating Ourselves: Tribal Jails and Corrections* 505

PART XIV: CORRECTIONS IN THE COMMUNITY 517

READING 35: Edward J. Latessa and Lawrence F. Travis III: *Residential Community Correctional Programs* 519

READING 36: Brian K. Payne and Randy R. Gainey: *A Qualitative Assessment of the Pains Experienced on Electronic Monitoring* 533

READING 37: Joan Petersilia: *Prisoner Reentry: Public Safety and Reintegration Challenges* 545

PART XV: FUTURE DIRECTIONS IN CORRECTIONS 559

READING 38: Doris Layton MacKenzie: *Corrections and Sentencing in the Twenty-First Century: Evidence-Based Corrections and Sentencing* 561

READING 39: Hans Toch: *The Future of Supermax Confinement* 573

READING 40: Anne Larason Schneider: *Public-Private Partnerships in the U.S. Prison System* 583

PREFACE

Contemporary criminal justice is an evolving institution that reflects philosophical, technological, and managerial changes and developments coming from a variety of sources. As a result, concerns and attention to the practice and planning of tasks is of paramount importance. For our justice system to achieve "justice", and be viewed as a legitimate institution, it is imperative that the public understands how the agencies and actors of the system function.

The goal of this book is to provide students with exposure to a variety of perspectives about the operations of the largest and most expensive component of the American criminal justice system—institutional corrections. Prisons and jails today house more than 2 million Americans, and the numbers continue to grow. Attempts to control the rapid growth in the number of inmates, as well as the number of institutions, staff, and the expense of operating a correctional system, necessarily require understandings of how these systems operate, the challenges created and faced by rapid growth, and insights regarding how both inmates and staff experience incarceration. Exposing students to these issues is the goal of this book.

Through the readings presented in this book, it is our hope that readers—both those who will move on to work in, with, and near the correctional enterprise and those who may not be directly involved but will bear the costs of corrections as citizens of the United States—can see the realities of living and working in corrections. As can be quickly and easily seen by glancing through the table of contents, institutional corrections involves much more than simply locking people up for a period of time. Operating a correctional institution is a broad and diverse task, requiring a range of skills, perspectives and understandings. Similarly, being an informed member of American society that comprehends the ways that prisons and jails impact society also requires a range of skills, perspectives, and understandings.

Hopefully, the readings contained in the following pages will help students gain these skills, perspectives, and understandings. If this is achieved, our work in editing this book has been a success.

Richard Tewksbury
Dean Dabney

I

MODERN CORRECTIONS—PHILOSOPHICAL UNDERSTANDINGS

READING 1

Imprisonment Rates and the New Politics of Criminal Punishment

Franklin E. Zimring

This article provides commentary on the increases in American imprisonment rates that occurred during the last quarter of the twentieth century. Particular attention is paid to the period of 1993–2000, when crime rates plummeted while imprisonment rates skyrocketed. The author attributes this paradoxical relationship to a political climate oriented toward heightened punishment for offenders and increased attention to victim needs. The symbolic messages of the day are criticized for carrying a false implication that punishing offenders automatically translates into a benefit for crime victims, and a shift in punitive authority away from judicial discretion, and toward legislatively mandated punishment initiatives. The author forecasts a continued reliance on a punitive crime control agenda and predicts increased incarceration rates of the future.

ONE GROWTH ERA OR THREE?

Figure 1 divides the last 75 years of the 20th century into two discrete segments. Between 1925 and 1973, there was very little fluctuation from a mean level, that averages between 110 and 120 per 100,000 and never varies by more than 30 percent up or down from that. After a low of 93 per 100,000 in 1972, the rate of imprisonment has increased in 26 consecutive years, growing during this time from 93 to 452 per 100,000, or just under fivefold in a quarter century. What had been a non-volatile and cyclical phenomenon becomes very volatile and non-cyclical.

The visual evidence suggests that the acceleration of prison populations was a unitary phenomenon, a process that starts in the early or middle 1970s, picks up steam in the early 1980s, and just keeps going. And history may very well regard the last quarter of the 20th century in unitary terms. But it seems that three

FIGURE 1 Imprisonment rate per 100,000 population, United States, 1925–98.

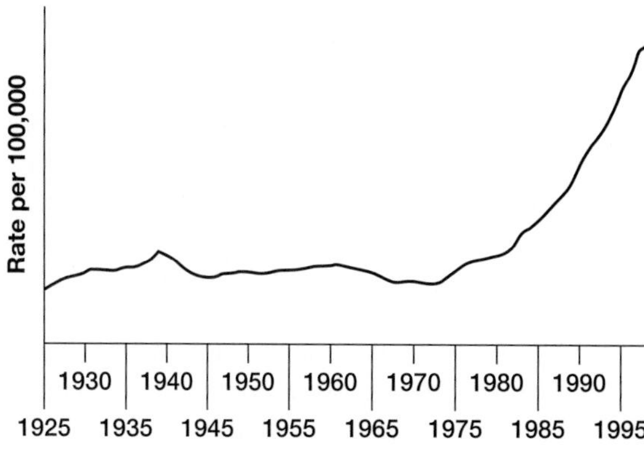

different patterns of substantive emphasis have accompanied this steady upward progression at different times in the 26-year push. From 1973 to the mid-1980s, the emphasis was on general increases in the commitment of marginal felons to prison, with few clear patterns by type of crime or by type of offender (Zimring and Hawkins, 1991: Ch. 5). During the period from about 1985 to 1992, the substantive emphasis shifted to drugs, and the growth of drug commitments and drug sentences far outpaced the rate of growth of other offense commitments.

The third period is the subject of my focus in this article, the period of time when imprisonment rates defy gravity and continue to grow even as crime rates are dropping. This is the high point of what I shall call the new politics of punishment, of Megan's Law and Three Strikes and You're Out and Truth in Sentencing. Here the shift in emphasis is from "lock 'em up" to "throw away the key," and I believe (without currently sufficient evidence) that lengthening of sentences has begun during this period to play a much larger role in sustaining the growth of prison population. In the six years from 1992 to 1998, the imprisonment rate grew from 313 to 452 per 100,000, or 139 per 100,000. To put that in context, the total prison population was 139 per 100,000 as recently as 1981. So what we have added in a six-year period is another United States prison system the size of the 1981 total to the 1992 mass which was already a United States high.

I believe a new politics of criminal punishment has played a major role in the events of the past eight years in the United States and will play an important part in determining future policy. In this article, I want to highlight three characteristics of the new political attitudes and then make some guesses about how the new political landscape might limit the range of decarceration.

THREE CHARACTERISTICS OF THE NEW POLITICAL LANDSCAPE

Three characteristics of the recent politics of punishment that deserve special attention are: (1) the loose linkage between the symbolic and operational content of punishment laws, (2) the zero sum rhetoric supporting punishment proposals, and (3) the paradoxical politics of distrust in penal legislation.

Loose Linkage

First, the matter of loose linkage. There are two quite different public purposes served when legislation concerning criminal punishment is enacted. One purpose is the symbolic denunciation of crime and criminals, a statement of condemnation that enables the political community to make its detestation of crime manifest in legal form. A second and distinct public purpose is to effect change in the operations of punishment systems—to change the behavior of courts, prisons, or parole authorities. For most members of the public, the symbolic functions of penal legislation are the most important aspect of new legislation. For this reason, there need not be any profound linkage between symbolic legislation and large changes in the punishment output of operating criminal justice systems.

This loose linkage between symbolic and operational impacts has traditionally allowed new criminal laws to bark much louder than they bite, to satisfy the need for symbols of denunciation without making much difference in the penalties meted out to most offenders. But recent events have shown that the loose connection between symbolic and operational impact can work both ways. Both the United States federal system and California passed laws labeled "Three Strikes and You're Out" in 1994. By late 1998, the United States federal statute had resulted in 35 special prison sentences while the California law had produced more than 40,000 sentences under its terms (Zimring et al., 1999). Laws serving the same symbolic functions can have vastly different operational impacts in different settings.

The federal law was traditional in that it barked louder than it bit. The California law actually bit louder than it barked because 90 percent of its enhanced prison sentences were given not to people with two prior strikes convictions, but to offenders with only one prior strike. The law was 10 times as broad as its label.

When citizens are more concerned with the symbolism than with the operational impact of penal laws, the same rhetorical appeals can lead to very different operational law reforms. In such cases, the practical impact of new penal laws will be determined more by who controls the planning and drafting process and what they want than by the level of public support for labels like three strikes. And those who wish to maximize impact can ride slogans a long way. The California version of Three Strikes has resulted in nine times as many prison terms as all of the 26 other three strikes laws in the United States combined. The chronically loose linkage between symbolic and operational impact will lead to high stakes competition for control of legislative drafting as a recurrent phenomenon in the politics of modern criminal justice.

The Zero Sum Fallacy

A second feature of the recent politics of punishment also concerns the relationship between the symbolic and the operational aspects of penal law. The rhetoric in support of new punishment proposals in current politics often seems to assume that criminals and crime victims are engaged in a zero sum contest. If the criminal justice process is imagined as a zero sum game, anything that hurts offenders *by definition* helps victims. If the competition between victims and offenders is really like a football score, then any detriment to the offender team helps the victim's score.

The zero sum assumption is a convenient method of avoiding questions about exactly how (and how much) measures that hurt criminal offenders might also help their victims. In a zero sum universe, there is a law of equivalent benefit. Anything that hurts the other team by definition helps the competition in equal measure. In a zero sum setting, all a citizen must do to choose punishment policy is decide whether she prefers victims or offenders. The zero sum assumption is open-ended and seemingly universally applicable.

The problem here, of course, is the non-logic of the assumption. If victims of violent crime are given public funds to compensate their economic losses, does that benefit automatically hurt criminal offenders? Of course not, because there is no real zero sum relationship. But assuming such a relationship generates a justification for endless cycles of increased infliction of suffering on counterfeit utilitarian grounds. I suspect that what happens here is that the symbolic aspects of a status competition where the denunciation of offenders might be seen as supporting the social standing of crime victims is carried over to assumptions that the actual hurt of punishment creates equal and opposite reactions in victims.

The Paradoxical Politics of Governmental Distrust

The punishment of criminals is at root an exercise of governmental power. It might therefore seem reasonable to suppose that citizen support for harsh measures against criminals would increase with increasing levels of citizen trust in government, and that citizen support for excessive punishments would decline when levels of confidence in government fall off. In this reading, support for harsh punishment would be a disease of excess confidence in state authority. But support for mandatory penalties and Truth in Sentencing actually increases with additional distrust of parole officials, distrust of judges, and with distrust of the governance of punishment by professionals.

Distrust in government can raise the stakes in criminal punishment. Citizens worry that judges will identify with offenders and treat them with inappropriate leniency. A bad judge in this view is one prone to coddle criminals and thus act against the interests of the citizenry. The way to guard against such governmental weakness is to force the imposition of stern penal measures. What makes the government untrustworthy in this rhetoric is the danger that it might side with the criminals and thus against the interests of the ordinary citizen.

The mandatory punishment term is the way to insure against such weakness. But the mandatory term is a huge expansion of punishment, rendering excessive outcomes in many cases to assure sufficiency of punishment in a very few that might otherwise escape their just deserts. Such huge inefficiency is the hallmark of Three Strikes and You're Out in California and of Truth in Sentencing generally. What links Megan's Law (where citizens rather than police get information on sex offender addresses) to Three Strikes and to Truth in Sentencing is the politics of distrust. Megan's Law is distrust of police, Three Strikes and mandatory sentences are distrust of judges, and Truth in Sentencing is distrust of parole authorities.

POLITICAL LIMITS ON DECARCERATION

The independent power of this new political cast on prison populations is difficult to determine in the 1990s. The counterfactual control we would need is a United States from 1992 onward without a political climate aimed at increasing imprisonment. But there is nothing evanescent about this new political emphasis, no reason to expect it to spend itself in the near future, and every reason to believe that political pressures that have added to hyper-incarceration will also provide resistance to downward movements in prison populations. How great a counter-pressure this political climate will amount to is not something that can be precisely measured.

My current guess is that undoing even this last six years of the United States incarceration boom will be more than difficult, more than improbable, under the political conditions that currently determine punishment policy. In one respect, this gloomy prediction contradicts the common-sense physics of prison population. Surely what went up so very recently can come down as well. How can it be that even 1992 levels of incarceration seem out of reach? This is not a prediction based on statistical study of any long-standing dynamic processes associated with prison populations. It is instead a guess about the politics of the matter, about links that have been created between political processes and imprisonment levels, and that cannot be easily undone. In six years, the United States has grown a second prison system with an extra incarceration rate per 100,000 larger than the United States had at any time between 1900 and 1980. This run up was a policy change but I would not want to say *only* a policy change.

Just as the American incarceration explosion was unprecedented, so too would be the reduction in prison rates and numbers that we would need to get back to 1992 levels. Cutting a prison system by 139 per 100,000 in times of governmental stability has never ever been done. To imagine any such policy reversal can be achieved sailing into the political winds of recent years is difficult indeed.

A decade ago Gordon Hawkins and I wrote a book on the scale of imprisonment and there was no chapter in it on politics (Zimring and Hawkins, 1991). Perhaps this was not an oversight. It is probable that the politics of criminal punishment now play a much more important role in determining prison populations than in earlier eras. Here, too, however, there is no obvious path to reversing the political momentum that has created closer links between politics and rates of imprisonment. Putting distance between state politics and the creation of state level imprisonment policy should obviously be a high priority in efforts to restrain and to reverse the growth of incarceration.

REFERENCES

Zimring, F.E. and Hawkins, G. (1991) *The scale of imprisonment.* Chicago, IL: University of Chicago Press.

Zimring, F.E., Kamin, S. and Hawkins, G. (1999) *Crime and punishment in California: The impact of three strikes and you're out.* Berkeley, CA: Institute of Governmental Studies, University of California, Berkeley.

REVIEW QUESTIONS

1. What underlying social factors account for the shift toward a heavier reliance on incarceration as the primary response to criminal offending?
2. What role does the media play in the loose linkage between symbolic and operational realities of the recent crime control agenda?

3. Identify and discuss 3–5 policy initiatives that increase punishment of offenders but have no measurable impact on crime victims.
4. The current political landscape is quick to point to the negative outcomes that follow from the discretionary leniency of liberal judges. Identify and discuss 3–5 examples of negative outcomes that follow from the routinized decision-making of punitive conservative judges.

READING 2

The Good, the Bad, and the (Sometimes) Ugly Truths

American Penal Goals and Perspectives

Richard Tewksbury

Matthew T. DeMichele

The evolution of correctional goals and the assessment of these goals is the focus of this reading. The authors present the strengths and weaknesses of a variety of views of what prisons are about, why they exist, and what they should and should not emphasize as a means of highlighting problems that scholars and administrators face when trying to define the concept of "success." It is noted that a lack of consensus exists regarding what the goals of corrections should be and that this disagreement often impedes the effective and efficient operation of a prison or a prison system. This lack of consensus is attributed to numerous sources, including the rapid turnover in who works in corrections. Although concrete proposals for resolving this problem are not proposed, this reading points out issues that contribute to the lack of uniformity in beliefs about the goals of corrections.

INTRODUCTION

Currently, the criminal justice system is caring for and supervising, in some capacity, nearly 7 million adults. This represents more than a three-fold increase in adult correctional supervision since 1980. This growth should not surprise any of us working in, with, or around the criminal justice system. In order to meet the growing organizational demands this scope imposes, we are scrambling to create innovative strategies and practices and, therefore, hopefully influencing changes in both the formal and informal goals of the criminal justice system. To be sure, most criminal justice practitioners and scholars are familiar with the ongoing philosophical debate regarding correctional goals; on the simplest level pitting rehabilitation against retribution. This philosophical debate reaches to the heart of correctional processes as policy is shaped around such thought and translates into everyday practices for correctional staff.

Interesting about this recent correctional population growth are consequences of policies geared toward expanding the reach of the criminal justice system. These include: how the police must arrest more people, the courts process larger numbers, prisons and jails incarcerate ever more Americans, and community correctional agencies that are both over-worked and under-funded. According to the *Sourcebook of Criminal Justice Statistics* (2001), law enforcement officers made slightly less than 14 million arrests in 2001, the U.S. District Court terminated 60,991 cases in 2002, more than doubling the 29,297 terminated in 1980, and nearly 2 million adults were incarcerated. The 6.7 million American adults under some form of correctional supervision represents 3% of the U.S. adult population with nearly 2 million of them being housed, fed, clothed, cared for, and released back into society at a greater rate than ever before (see Christie, 2000).

As state and federal governments continue to cut already tight budgets, criminal justice decision makers continue to scramble to contend with growth in the raw number and rates of imprisonment. One result is that programs and policies must be, and are being developed, implemented, and evaluated—or at least sometimes evaluated—to determine the most effective and efficient techniques for meeting the public demands of protecting and reintegrating offenders within communities. Obviously, it is important for the criminal justice system to reach its stated goals in the most resource conscious fashion. This usually means attempting to hold programs accountable through the creation of standardized and uniform criteria ensuring adequate delivery of services. This evaluative agenda is made all the more difficult, however, due to a lack of an overarching criminal justice goal(s) and a lack of a shared vision for correctional systems, practices, and policies.

The criminal justice system presents government with a unique moral obligation with its responsibility to administer justice. One of the clearest ways we have seen this obligation dissected and explicated is in Shichor's (1995) argument for limiting the expansion of private prisons. Simply stated, the criminal justice system differs from other public works and responsibilities with its ability to impose fines, restrict liberty, and, in extreme cases, inflict death. Therefore, as researchers, practitioners, and policymakers struggle to locate better ways to process the growing number of criminal justice consumers efficiently and effectively—with a necessarily vigilant eye toward managing scarce resources—we are faced with the question of what we are pursuing and whether our pursuit of whatever goals we happen to set for ourselves are in fact done in a "fair" manner. Supposedly, fairness is a key goal of all criminal justice agencies (Dilulio, 1993). For these reasons, it is necessary for crime and justice scholars to work with practitioners to uniformly assess and evaluate criminal justice system, agency, and actor performance. This is clearly not a new idea, nor anything in the least bit innovative. . . .

As is commonly known, academics writing in the correctional literature have traditionally recognized the importance of recidivism and incarceration rates as the two key performance indicators for our institutions, agencies, and systems. It is also common criminological knowledge that supra-individual characteristics preceding criminal activity have more to do with the frequency by which crimes are committed than other indicators (see Christie, 2000; Dilulio, 1993; Garland, 2001). Nevertheless, this does not preclude criminal justice agencies and officials from working toward the utopian goal of diminishing—or potentially "eliminating"—criminal opportunities and activities.

In order to enhance efforts to better develop, implement, and evaluate correctional policies, it is suggested that criminal justice scholars would do well to scrutinize recidivism and other fundamental correctional performance indicators. This, however, must be done in a socially contextualized framework—most notably taking into account political and economic trends. . . .

This is not to necessarily question the use of recidivism as an optimal indicator of community reintegration, or true and absolute correctional "success," but rather suggests that need exists to highlight and deconstruct the many ways this often reified concept of "recidivism" has been both operationalized and reported. Therefore, it is suggested that criminal justice scholars should work toward developing, refining, implementing, and testing correctional performance indicators.

CORRECTIONAL GOALS AND STRATEGIES

Initially, it might appear as a simple or common sense task to develop correctional goals and performance indicators, and to both share them, and agree on their shared use with other criminal justice scholars and practitioners. Sadly, though, this is not necessarily the case. Criminal justice scholars and practitioners have yet to develop complete, or even near, consensus regarding what does and should constitute correctional success. The debate over correctional goals and the purposes of punishment has waged on for centuries. More than two centuries ago, for instance, Classical criminologists such as Beccaria (1764) argued for a utilitarian model fond of deterrence and punishment. In the 19th century, Bentham (1843) suggested a corrective or transformative agenda to positively balance our inherent hedonistic propensities. In more contemporary times, organizational changes brought about by overwhelming caseloads given to correctional, in fact all criminal justice, staff elevates the need for practitioners, policymakers, and scholars concerned with the system to combine efforts and collaborate to develop, disseminate, and evaluate correctional programs and practices (Gist 1997, 2000; Logan, 1993).

This lack of a clear evaluative agenda and strategy for achieving a shared vision is in sharp contrast to much of the world of private industry where multiple measures of success are incorporated in any discussion of performance. Private sector administrators are known in some circles to look toward us in the public sector and basically dismiss us as amateurs lagging far behind them in establishing and using standardized accountability measures. The corporate world is pretty much on target when dismissing us for failing to even know "what counts" or what we are really hoping and trying to achieve. It is not simply that researchers and academics have failed to find the one goal or definition of success; corporate America has found it possible to employ multiple indicators of success and still focus on the ultimate goal of profit realized in the bottom line. In the case of the criminal justice system, things are not so parsimonious when determining success.

The criminal justice system, more so than other public services, is clearly and painfully ambivalent about overall goals (Garland, 1996; Pratt, 2000) and specific and sufficient performance indicators (Dilulio, 1993; Petersilia, 2001a; Travis, 2001). After all, what is it the correctional system is trying to accomplish? Is the system most concerned with changing offenders? Is the system most concerned with punishing and making offenders suffer? Does the system alternatively want to demonstrate to others that certain criminal behaviors are not tolerated? And, if consensus develops regarding one of these goals, what evaluative measures are needed to determine if and when success is achieved?

It could be argued that the recent incarceration boom is an indication of improved efficiency in detection, apprehension, court processing, and post-release supervision (Feeley & Simon, 1992). Indeed, that more people are arrested, tried, convicted, and supervised suggests that the system is becoming more efficient, organized, and in general incorporating a business-like ethos. The police, quite simply, arrest more because they are better able to detect crimes, courts process more cases due to improved efficiency, prisons and jails only need space and minimal amenities to accommodate offenders, and community corrections effectively recognize violators that are returned to custody.

Unfortunately for criminal justice administrators, this growth does not necessarily signal a successful system. An alternative argument could be made, as many have with relative ease, that the incarceration boom of recent decades is a clear indication of large-scale failure in the American criminal justice, and corrections in particular, systems. The near explosion in correctional populations could be seen as evidence of a political system that has become over-zealous and overly concerned with warehousing and incarcerating offenders with little thought given to post-release conditions and the likelihood of warehousing, producing a law-abiding citizen from a wayward or vicious social outcast. A quick glimpse indicates that our bulging prisons signal a failed attempt at reintegration or failed rehabilitation—after all, it was suggested nearly three decades ago that "nothing works," or does it? (Martinson, 1974) Prisons and jails are bursting at the seams, so clearly we have failed to deter too many from crime.

In a social institution where rehabilitation remains an important stated goal and an almost-always present agenda item, one would hope to see less recidivism than what is currently being experienced. Just last year, the Bureau of Justice Statistics reported that within one year of being released 44.1% of prisoners were rearrested, and this grew to two of every three (67.5%) within three years after release (for a felony or serious misdemeanor) (Langan & Levin, 2002). One in every four released inmates were convicted and received a new sentence within three years of release (Langan & Levin, 2002). Clearly, this is failure, is it not? Actually, that depends. Without having clearly established goals and objectives, it is difficult to determine appropriate performance indicators; hence, it is unclear whether correctional programs are successful.

In response to increased burdens on the whole of our criminal justice system, Logan (1993) proposed a confinement model stressing just desserts and emphasizing a punishment oriented correctional agenda. In this model, the essential purpose of corrections is to incarcerate offenders proportionate to their criminal offense and encourage correctional facilities to develop mission statements that move away from abstract values and normative criteria in favor of one that details ultimate goals of operation. Again, however, identifying what these "ultimate goals" are and should be is an as-of-yet unresolved task. Yes, there is one largely accepted official mission in corrections, to keep prisoners—to keep them in, keep them safe, keep them in line, keep them healthy, and keep them busy in as efficient a way as possible. Evaluating whether our prisons and jails achieve success then can be fairly simple. All we need to do is review our institutional records and administer a few staff surveys to evaluate medical services, religious services, counseling, education, work training, and other aspects of our daily operations. Determining these factors would reveal whether the correctional system is successful. Or, would they?

Despite the attraction for some, the confinement model neglects the potential backlash of aggressively punitive measures. By suggesting that prisons should focus solely on punishing and warehousing offenders, such an approach is all but guaranteeing that little, if any, inmate changes will occur. That is, if the correctional system ignores the potentially positive effects of substance abuse programs, religious based programs (Kennedy, 2003), educational opportunities (Brooks, 1992), anger management (Wang, Owens, Long, Diamond, & Smith, 2000), drug courts (Spohn, Piper, Martin, & Frenzel, 2001), and work release programs (Turner & Petersilia, 1996)—as well as numerous other innovative and granted sometimes "odd" programs and initiatives—then researchers and practitioners are failing to develop and implement research-based initiatives that can potentially facilitate the reintegration of offenders. In turn, such efforts may also diminish unintended negative consequences of incarceration—namely social disorganization worsened by turnstile-like reimprisonment (Petersilia, 2001a, 2001b).

A second significant problem with a strict confinement model approach is that this "get tough on crime" philosophy is precisely what has been driving our explosive population growth and has intentionally resisted efforts to seek social improvements or offer even the slightest hint of opportunity for real offender change. As a result, our "get tough" approach has generated outrageous costs for local, state, and the federal government. These costs, especially now as states and the federal government are forced (in the face of budgetary shortfalls) to find cost cutting avenues, are becoming an ever important reality when discussing the corrections system. Throughout the last two decades, criminal justice spending has skyrocketed for all levels of government. In 1982, for example, municipalities, state, and federal direct expenditures totaled $35.8 billion and by 1999 it reached $146.55 billion, a four-fold increase (Bureau of Justice Statistics, 2002a).

These figures represent massive increases in all direct spending for the criminal justice system. A four-fold increase in both state (396%) and federal (419%) spending is, of course, going to decimate our budgets. Local government spending on criminal justice activities, however, is much more reasonable. These expenses have increased only about 300% (Bureau Justice of Statistics, 2002b).

The irony here is that, regardless of financial allocations to the criminal justice system, all the while there has yet to be a clear understanding of what end(s) the criminal justice, and corrections systems specifically, are to achieve. It is logical to assume, similar to other industries, that fields requiring such large financial expenditures, and given the unique power of the corrections system, should have stated uniform purposes. As this paper has stressed, the correctional field needs to reach a consensus on what is the goal or goals to be pursued. There are several options to choose from—rehabilitation, punishment, social transformation, or simple warehousing. Understanding how correctional staff members, administrators, and the public view the organizational mission is instrumental in working toward developing standardized correctional goals.

CORRECTIONAL OPINIONS

The lack of clear correctional goals raises the question of how correctional staff members, policy makers, and even the public envisions the correctional system's place in society. Gaining a more complete understanding of how those involved in structuring and delivering correctional services perceive their organizational missions and goals provides important insight and tools for moving toward the development of shared correctional goals and performance criteria.

Several attempts have been made to identify the foundational values and beliefs that guide correctional workers' tasks, but no one thought to address such issues until a mere 25 years ago. From that earliest foray into the quest to identify what corrections is really all about, one theme has remained consistent. Correctional staff largely and strongly believe that rehabilitation is, or at least should be, among the main purposes of incarceration.

The precise degree of support expressed for a rehabilitative goal varies across time, place, individual, and methodology in the research. Perhaps most clear in the variation is that the beliefs of frontline correctional officers are those most likely to stray from a belief that efforts can and should be targeted on change for offenders. Correctional officers, instead, often express views more closely aligned with ideals of incapacitation, deterrence, and retribution. This, however, does not mean that officers disfavor treatment programs, nor does it presuppose that they favor the assertion that prisons should simply "sleep 'em, feed 'em, work 'em" (Cullen, Cullen, & Wozniak, 1989, p. 37). Rather, on the contrary, one thing that this research is telling us is that officers favor, a mixture of correctional agendas including both order maintenance and the potential for treatment programs.

However, the divergence in beliefs and views about what our tasks are supposed to be achieving needs to be viewed in the context of the economic and structural realities of today's prisons in order to be fully understood. It is true that correctional officers express a mixed view of what the purpose of prisons and incarceration is and should be. However, these views are "mixed" only when looking across the board at correctional officers as one unified group. Research in Kentucky has revealed that central to the views of what correctional officers believe incarceration should be about is the individual officer's length of job tenure (Tewksbury & Mustaine, 2003). There are very strong beliefs in retribution and incapacitation among our newest correctional officers. However, as officers gain experience, moving even into their second year on the job, their views begin to modify. "Experienced" correctional officers, defined here as someone with four or more years on the job, are not strong advocates of incapacitation or retribution. Rather, a belief in pursuing rehabilitation becomes primary.

It is important to ask why does the aggregated data from correctional staff, especially correctional officers, not show this tilt in favor of rehabilitation? One plausible answer is that the system cannot and does not keep staff in our prisons. Turnover rates of 20%, 30%, even 50% are not uncommon in correctional institutions. Turnover is highest among security staff. This means that fresh, new correctional staff members largely populate our institutions. Or, said a bit differently, the correctional system is operating prisons not only with fewer staff members today than in the past, but staff members are in large part new to the job and tend to possess views and values different than their more seasoned colleagues.

There are several reasons accounting for this turnover, most notably, corrections' pay is extremely low. Starting salaries in numerous state correctional systems throughout the South are at or below $20,000. And that is for the "good paying" jobs in a state-operated facility; our private facilities typically pay even less. Second, the public and policymakers expect a great deal, and yet a lack of precise long term expectations do not exist. Therefore, the correctional system hires new correctional guards, and in an average of one year and three months in Kentucky, they tend to leave. Correctional administrators are then faced with the daunting task of recruiting, training, and financing another correctional officer only to see him or her quit in less than one and a half years. This process continues at an alarmingly high expense to the correctional system (Tewksbury & Mustaine, 2003).

What this should begin to point toward, rather clearly, is that any discussion of corrections and criminal justice by necessity must consider external political and economic forces that saturate any public organization and the internal managerial decisions and strategies (although some of these decisions really are without options) that shape the day-to-day activities around these political forces. Organizational research, in fact, identifies the vacillating nature of social service institutions as they struggle to maintain legitimacy in the face of external pressures. This line of research argues that managers, and in corrections wardens and higher ranks are included, tend to shift emphasis on performance indicators to internal bureaucratic control issues. This suggests support for what Garland (2001) and others (Feeley & Simon, 1992) contend is the emergence of a correctional field embracing managerial ethos—not concerned with altering, reintegrating, training, or other positive correctional ends. Correctional system goals are shaped not by what can or should be done about crime and criminals, but rather by budgetary allowances and the need to maintain a quiet institution that avoids attracting political or public attention.

Still, some assert that much of this punitive, managerial, warehouse style of corrections is developed less out of a desire for punishment or from a belief that "nothing works" (Martinson, 1974) and born more of limited resources. As the American correctional population has grown (and continues to grow), budgetary allocations are in danger of being yet further reduced, or more optimistically, maintained. This means that some programs or staff positions will likely need to be cut in order for the financial resources to adequately cover housing and punishing and/or rehabilitating more inmates, and supervising more upon release. What is usually among the first items to be cut? Programs, and anything that does more than keep 'em in, keep 'em safe, keep 'em healthy, and keep 'em quiet.

While recognizing what policymakers and administrative officials define as indicators of success is important for understanding what presently serves, by default, as central objectives. It is also important, especially politically, to know what the public views as central to the mission of correctional agencies and institutions. Few criminal justice policymakers and administrators are unaware of the potential influence of the public on political decisions. Central to public opinion is the recognition of the public's desire to punish inmates. Most research suggests that there is strong public support for capital punishment, three-strikes laws, mandatory minimums, and other purely punitive strategies (see Beckett, 1997; Pratt, 2000). However, less prominent in both public and political discourse is the bifurcated nature of public opinion that simultaneously favors and supports both punishment and rehabilitative ideals. Cullen, Fisher, and Applegate (2000) have highlighted the strange coupling of get-tough and transformative policies, manifesting in public support of punishment and rehabilitation and wanting "the correctional system to achieve the diverse missions of doing justice, protecting public safety, and reforming the wayward" (p. 79) (also, see Applegate, 2001; Bouley & Wells, 2001). On its face, meeting these goals might appear as a simple task. Why wouldn't the public expect public servants to be able to quickly, easily, and affordably both punish and rehabilitate offenders?

What appears to be happening, we argue, is a general sense of ambivalence coupled with the expected volatility that typically accompanies times of rapid social and political changes (see Fceley & Simon, 1992; Garland, 1996, 1997, 2001; O'Malley, 1999; Pratt, 2000; Rose, 2000). This volatility creates a disjuncture between official policy and rhetoric and actual correctional practices. Also, it has fostered a climate in which traditional correctional strategies are pitted against one another. Indeed, O'Malley (1999) suggests that the correctional field is currently faced with a debate featuring "disciplinary obedience versus incapacitation, warehousing versus correctional reform, punishment and stigmatization versus reintegration, [and] formal criminalization versus informal victim/offender settlements" (p. 176). Although this theoretical argument is insightful for better understanding contemporary punishment, there is nonetheless a need to develop correctional goals, programs to realize these goals, and evaluative strategies to closely monitor correctional success. In the final portion of this paper, a brief summary of current evaluation strategies is offered.

PROGRAMS, MEASURES, AND EVALUATION

Designing, developing, implementing, refining, and sharing programs that both effectively and efficiently address the needs of offenders and lead to a safer community are essential for those of us who believe that the correctional system can and should be more than a mere dumping ground and warehouse for society's castoffs. The official rhetoric of at least some of our nation's highest-ranking justice officials also reflects this view. In a 1997 report by the U.S. Department of Justice, Director Nancy Gist states clearly that "building safer, less violent communities is a major challenge being faced" by correctional administrators. She goes on to mention, "real progress can only be achieved if [researchers] demonstrate and confirm 'what works'" through a commitment "to evaluating and publicizing those programs and activities . . . [to make them] more accessible to planners and practitioners alike" (iii).

This yet again highlights the need to define clear correctional goals. How can and do practitioners know "what works" if researchers do not know the goal(s) of the correctional system? For some, the important focus is not necessarily identifying "what works," but rather approaching the issue from the other side, and seeking to weed out what does not work. More than two decades ago, Harris and Moltra (1978) suggested applying failure rate methods to evaluate correctional outcomes and to contribute to more cost-effective management of correctional practices. Identifying failures is also easier than identifying successes. Often times, it is relatively easy to point to things that do not work, for the consequences and implications of failures are more obvious than the consequences of succeeding. If the central focus of correctional goals is to reduce or eliminate crime, how can practitioners know their efforts led an offender to desist from crime, and similarly, if crime rates decline (as they have tended to for nearly two decades) for a community, what administrative program is responsible? Interestingly, and this reaffirms the earlier assertion of identifying failures, the repeat offender is continually offered as an example of poor correctional services. But, is it really possible to identify when correctional efforts are successful? This approach of identifying failures and making judgments about a program, initiative, institution, agency, or overall paradigm has essentially always characterized correctional evaluations.

A look at correctional failures usually means looking at recidivism and crime rates. That is, given the lack of consensus regarding what constitutes correctional success, researchers have traditionally fallen back on the relatively easy to identify issues of recidivism and crime rates. The question then becomes: is this really such an easy approach? It might be, again, if shared definitions and perspectives regarding correctional performance indicators existed. However, they do not. For instance, what is recidivism? This is a very difficult question to answer as it has been operationalized in many ways. Researchers, policymakers, politicians, and laypersons are often unable to agree on simple definitions of success and fail to speak the same language. When considering recidivism, some may define a person as a recidivist, while others will argue that he/she is an "at risk" individual, and still others could suggest this person is a correctional "success." If researchers and practitioners do not come together to speak the same language (i.e. agree on definitions of success), how can we share our ideas and how can we ever hope to draw together to pursue a common goal? Our problems and shortcomings are rather clear, and they begin with a lack of shared vision, mission, and purpose. If we cannot know where we are going, how can we expect to know how to get there? And, how can we ever provide directions to our peers and colleagues? If we do find something that "works," will we be able to tell others about it in a meaningful way, and in a way that we can trust that our conclusions are valid?

CONCLUSION

Identifying correctional objectives and evaluative criteria is essential to facilitating smooth operational functioning of the correctional system. Complicating this necessity is the tremendous growth and responsibilities of the correctional system as budgets continue to suffer reductions or stagnations. Traditional evaluative studies producing valuable insights, have yet to, for the most part, move beyond recidivism and incarceration rates as performance indicators. This is due mostly to the fact that criminal justicians—scholars and practitioners—and the general public lack consensus regarding correctional goals. Instead, what we are experiencing is an ambivalence placing an unfair burden upon the correctional system to create and maintain effective rehabilitative programs, devise punitive strategies, and fulfill these countervailing missions with decreased financial resources than in the past (relative to case load). To be sure, wardens and correctional administrators are called upon today to do more with drastically fewer dollars.

The correctional system, we argue, given its unique task of incapacitating people, demands that scholars, practitioners, and policymakers combine efforts to develop correctional goals. These goals once defined, however, are not to become fixed static categories. Instead, they must remain flexible and imitate or adapt to social and cultural conditions, which is not to say merely reflect public opinion. Rather, correctional goals must consider legal, normative, and other structural changes affecting the correctional system—as many scholars recognize these variables having greater impact on incarceration (see Christie, 2000; Dilulio, 1993; Garland, 2001). This joint effort should take advantage of research-based knowledge and examples of best practices to identify the good aspects, weed out the bad, and climinate the ugly in the U.S. penal system.

REFERENCES

Applegate, B. (2001). Penal austerity: Perecived utility, desert, and public attitudes toward prison amenities. *American Journal of Criminal Justice, 25*(2). 253–268.

Beccarin, C. (1764 [1963]). *On crimes and punishments.* Indianapolis: Bobbs-Merrill.

Beckett, K. (1997). *Making crime pay.* New York: Oxford University Press.

Bentham, J. (1843). *The works of Jeremy Bentham, volume 1.* Edinburgh: William Tait.

Bouley, E., & Wells, T. (2001). Attitudes of citizens in a southern rural county toward juvenile crime and justice issues. *Journal of Contemporary Criminal Justice, 17*(1). 60–70.

Brooks, J. (1992). Addressing recidivism: Legal education in correctional settings. *Rutgers-Law-Review, 44*(3), 699–742.

Bureau of Justice Statistics. (2002a). *Key facts at a glance: Direct expenditure by level of government, 1982–1999.* Washington DC: U.S. Department of Justice.

Bureau of Justice Statistics. (2002b). *States spend more on criminal justice than municipalities, counties, or the federal government.* Washington DC: U.S. Department of Justice.

Christie, N. (2000). *Crime control as industry: Towards gulags, western style.* New York: Routledge.

Cullen, F., Cullen, J., & Wozniak, J. (1989). Sanctioning ideology and the prospects for reform: Is rehabilitation really dead? Paper presented at the annual meeting of the Illinois Sociological Association, Chicago. Illinois.

Cullen, F., Fisher, B., & Applegate, B. (2000). Public opinion about punishment and corrections. In M. Tonry (Ed.). *Crime and justice: A review of research, volume 27* (pp. 1–79). Chicago, IL: University of Chicago Press.

Dilulio, J. (1993). Rethinking the criminal justice system: Toward a new paradigm. In J. Dilulio, G. Alpert. & M. Moore (Eds.), *Performance measures for the criminal justice system* (pp. 143–156). Washington, DC: U.S. Bureau of Justice Statistics.

Feeley, M., & Simon, J. (1992). The new penology: Notes on the emerging strategy of corrections and its implications. *Criminology, 30*(4), 449–474.

Garland, D. (1996). The limits of the sovereign state: Strategies of crime control in contemporary societies. *British Journal of Criminology, 36*, 445–471.

Garland, D. (1997). Governmentality and the problem of crime: Foucault, criminology, sociology. *Theoretical Criminology, 1*, 73–214.

Garland, D. (2001). *Mass imprisonment: Social causes and consequences.* London: Sage.

Gist, N. (1997). *Improving the nation's criminal justice system: Findings and results from state and local program evaluations.* Washington, DC: Bureau of Justice Assistance.

Gist, N. (2000). *Creating a new criminal justice system for the 21st century: Findings and results from state and local program evaluations.* Washington, DC: Bureau of Justice Assistance.

Harris, C., & Moltra, S. (1978). Improved statistical techniques for the measurement of recidivism. *Journal of Research in Crime and Delinquency, 15*(2), 194–213.

Kennedy, S. (2003). Redemption or rehabilitation? Charitable choice and criminal justice. *Criminal Justice Policy Review, 14*(2). 214–228.

Langan, A., & Levin, D. (2002). *Recidivism of prisoners released in 1994.* Washington, DC: Bureau of Justice Statistics.

Logan, C. (1993). Criminal justice performance measures for prisons. In J. Dilulio, G. Alpert, & M. Moore (Eds.). *Performance measures for the criminal justice system* (pp. 19–60). Washington, DC: U.S. Bureau of Justice Statistics.

Martinson, R. (1974). What works? Questions and answers about prison reform. *The Public Interest, 35*, 22–54.

O'Malley, P. (1999). Volatile and contradictory punishment. *Theoretical Criminology, 3*, 175–196.

Petersilia, J. (1993). Measuring the performance of community corrections. In J. Dilulio, G. Alpert, & M. Moore (Eds.), *Performance measures for the criminal justice system* (pp. 61–86). Washington, DC: U.S. Bureau of Justice Statistics.

Petersilia, J. (2001a). Prisoner reentry: Public safety and reintegration challenges. *The Prison Journal, 81*(3), 360–375.

Petersilia, J. (2001b). When prisoners return to the community: Political, economic, and social consequences. *Corrections Quarterly Management, 5*(3), 1–10.

Pratt, J. (2000). The return of the wheelbarrow men; or, the arrival of postmodern penalty? *The British Journal of Criminology, 40*(1), 127–145.

Rose, N. (2000). Government and control. *British Journal of Criminology, 40*, 321–339.

Sourcebook of Criminal Justice Statistics. (2001). *Persons under correctional supervision.* [On-line]. Available: www.albany.edu/sourcebook/1995/tost_6.html#6_a.

Shichor, D. (1995). *Punishment for profit: Private prisons/public concerns.* Thousand Oaks, CA: Sage.

Spohn, C., Piper, R., Martin, T., & Frenzel, D. (2001). Drug courts and recidivism: The results of an evaluation using two comparison groups and multiple indicators of recidivism. *Journal of Drug Issues, 31*(1), 149–176.

Tewksbury, R., & Mustaine, E. (2003). *Staff members' perceptions of institutional environments in the Kentucky department of corrections: Views on amenities, definition of purpose, and factors influencing inmate victimization risks.* LaGrange, KY: Kentucky Department of Corrections.

Travis, J. (2001). But they all come back: Rethinking prisoner reentry. *Corrections Management Quarterly, 5*(3), 23–33.

Turner, S., & Petersilia, J. (1996). Work release in Washington: Effects on recidivism and corrections costs. *The Prison Journal, 76*(2), 138–164.

Wang, E., Owens, R., Long, S., Diamond, P., & Smith, J. (2000). The effectiveness of rehabilitation with persistently violent male prisoners. *International Journal of Offender Therapy and Comparative Criminology, 44*(4), 505–514.

Wilcox, P., Land, K., & Hunt, S. (2003). *Criminal circumstance: A dynamic multicontextual criminal opportunity theory.* New York: Aldine de Gruyter.

REVIEW QUESTIONS

1. What are the goals of American corrections? How are these goals measured?
2. What are the positive and negative aspects of a confinement model of corrections?
3. What do correctional staff persons generally believe is the goal of corrections?
4. What are some of the likely disconnects that exist between the viewpoints of upper- and lower-level correctional staff when it comes to penal goals and operations?

READING 3

From the Big House to the Warehouse

Rethinking Prisons and State Government in the Twentieth Century

Jonathan Simon

In this essay, Simon uses his review of four books on the growth and development of state-level prison systems in California and Michigan to provide some general observations about the evolving role of prisons in twentieth-century American culture. The central premise of the discussion is that imprisonment is as much a function of the way that states are governed as it is a function of national politics and established social conditions. Beginning with the turn of the twentieth century, the author argues that the boom in prison construction and management of the first three decades of the century were an outgrowth of a pervasive political Patronage State model that rewarded privileged interest-group members and organizations. Simon argues that the Roosevelt administration ushered in an alternative political era, known as the New Deal style of governing, whereby government officials reached out to the mass public and academics to generate a scientifically informed model of activist government that confronts head on the social ills of the day. Under this regime, which remained prominent from the 1940s through the 1970s, correctional practice was driven by therapeutic and rehabilitative reform ideals. Rising violent crime rates and the broken promises of the rehabilitation era led to another ideological shift in the early 1980s. Conservative principles coupled with a segmented population organized along class and racial lines resulted in the emergence of what Simon dubs the Initiative State model, wherein an organized, white middle class incrementally gained control over the penal agenda. Driven by a goal of reducing taxes while simultaneously increasing levels of punishment, politicians during the last two decades of the twentieth century ushered in an era of punitive sentencing and mass incarceration.

The long lead-time required by complexly empirical research almost guarantees that the interpretive work of researchers will have a troubling theory gap. By the time such work is published, read, reviewed, responded to, chances are good that theoretical developments will call into question not just its conclusions, but even the choice and construction of objects. The existentially positive side of this for the researcher is the opportunity sometimes occasioned to look again at a subject of research and through the lens of subsequent scholarship, see it again as for the first time.

In my case the subject was the phenomenal growth of the California prison system in the 1980s. My study argued that prison growth was being driven in large part by the collapse of the internal narratives which had historically permitted parole to serve as an exit from prison and as an alternative to further imprisonment (Simon, 1993). These narratives sustained parole agents in taking the risk of keeping known felons in the community by linking the agent to both sources of justification and to real deposits of power in the community. Both of these faculties were undermined starting in the 1970s, making parole far more vulnerable to political pressure for intensive use of imprisonment, pressure that grew dramatically in the 1980s.

In analysing this process my explanatory framework identified two key variables associated with venerable social science traditions, changes in the conditions of the working classes and changes in the mode of rationalizing state power. The growing gap between a relatively affluent working class and an underclass increasingly separated from the disciplines of labor, made it more and more difficult for parole to provide an account of how its parolees were to be kept secure in the community. At the same time, transformations in the legal context of parole increased the demand for rationality and transparency in the working of the control system. The combination of fewer social resources, and greater performance demands, forced the transformation of parole itself from a mechanism of community surveillance into a mechanism for returning parolees to prison. . . .

Developments in the 1990s have only made these gaps more significant. Two consecutive decades of rapid growth in American penal populations and steady decline in public support for the federal government have made state governments and their penal practices a vital question for American government. State prison populations have produced the highest incarceration rate in the history of the United States and any other liberal democracy. The scale of the penal population, magnified greatly for some communities, makes the norms being promulgated in prison culture even more critical to the future governability of our society than before.

In both respects it has become important to rethink the relationship between the enormously extended power to punish in the United States over the last two decades and the political problem of government at the state level in the United States. . . .

THE BIG HOUSE AND THE PATRONAGE STATE

Charles Bright's *The Powers that Punish* (1994) is an in-depth historical analysis of one prison over three decades and two quite distinct regimes of political power. Through a careful parallel reading of the history of the prison and the history of state government the study pursues the "interconnection between the constitution of the political realm and the construction of carceral regimes" (Bright, 1994: 1). Drawing on prison records, memoirs, and newspaper accounts, Bright reconstructs the framework of power inside the prison, and then carefully traces the circuits that linked carceral power to this political field.

> The prison is constituted in and by these relations, and it retails them upon others. It is one position of power formed up in a field of combinations, rivalries, and alliances that make some more powerful than others and frame the terms of dominant discourse. (1994: 2)

The 19th century firmly established the centrality of the penitentiary to the constitution of the state. Existing states built penitentiaries, taking over functions long served by county institutions. New states entering the union recognized immediately that having a state penitentiary was part of being a state, much like having a constitution, a court system, and a flag. Once constructed, the prisons became an embodiment of the state. Building and operating a prison historically provided one of the larger enterprises under the control of state government. Counties typically paid for schools and courts. State universities were small affairs. Even state police were not common until the 1900s. In short, prisons were a big piece of the whole material body of the state.

Going beyond the typical history of political administrations, Bright identifies a fundamental shift in the style of state power during the period of his study. The earlier period was dominated by competition among territorially based (and small town dominated) party committees brought together in unstable alliances through the distribution of patronage. The activities of the state were most useful politically, for their potential to create jobs and public spending with which to cement solidarity. In the 1940s a new approach shaped by the influence of the federal New Deal changed the way Michigan governors sought election and how they governed in order to be re-elected. The New Deal style linked politicians directly to urban masses through media and the new forms of public spending unleashed by the federal "New Deal."

Bright argues that there is a strong relationship between the formation of these distinct political fields and the account that penal institutions give of how they exercise power:

> The process of constituting a public sphere . . . a formal framework that disciplines discourse, contains the possibilities and congeals alliances for governing, is also simultaneously, the process of forging normative standards, deploying disciplinary forces, and bringing things to order behind the walls in an articulation of control strategies and correctional goals that offers a coherent account of what prisons are doing to whom and with what results. (1994: 2)

If Bright is correct, then we need to look for more than an ideological relationship between state power and the prison. Rather than a question of whether a particular governor or party embraces a more punitive or rehabilitative approach to punishment, it is a question of how they exercise power, what kind of discourses and forms of expertise do they invest with judgment; and how they construct their subjects.

When construction on Jackson prison began in 1924 Michigan was dominated by the Patronage State. The Republican Party had once had a strong enough state-wide network to effectively reproduce itself by handing political power from one generation of candidates to the next. By the 1920s, that state-wide network had decayed leaving Michigan governors to personally hold together a highly uneven balance between population and revenue heavy Detroit, and the portion of the rest of the state necessary to a stable majority in the legislature. The growing body of state public works provided the key to holding such networks together.

The main currency of reward inside this political machine was patronage. Controlling the office of governor guaranteed the candidate and his partisans access to a large number of state jobs and state supply contracts. The distribution of this patronage sustained a chain of loyalty leading from individual activists, to local party bosses, up to the successful governor.

The prison was well situated to produce numerous effects capable of being distributed at this local political level. Like highways, demand for which grew rapidly with the popularity of the automobile, prisons were a popular form of public spending in the 1920s. Jackson, the largest prison in the world when built, would provide a rich treasure to be divided for many years of construction, and then for jobs and supplies into the future. While Bright points out that several smaller prisons might have made it easier to distribute the patronage largesse across a wider variety of territorially based local political machines, the very scale of the project assured that there would be larger flows of capital from which to draw off rewards for political supporters and greater opportunity to hide the kinds of petty corruption that kept patronage systems together. It also represented an opportunity to cluster a great deal of patronage resources together, relatively close to all-important Wayne County, with its thriving automobile industry in Detroit. Once in operation, Jackson's numerous farms and manufactories produced an endless supply of goods and services that could be provided to political supporters of the governor. The darker side of this circulation of benefits from prison to political system may have even included assassination. Bright investigates the unresolved rumors that gangsters imprisoned at Jackson may have been deployed to murder a State Senator who was about to open investigations potentially embarrassing to the governor (Bright, 1994: 111).

The prison also provided symbolic goods appropriate to the small town values still prevalent in the Patronage State. At a time when cities like Detroit were experiencing high levels of prohibition fueled violence, much of it associated with immigrants (Eastern European Jews among others), the construction of Jackson signaled an intent to get serious about punishing and containing this criminal class. Its huge size reflected a direct capacity to absorb a burgeoning criminal class, and the staying power to see prohibition through with its indirect promise to discipline this dangerous new urban working class.

In a sense the "Big House" prisons like Jackson were smaller scale versions of the Patronage State. In both cases, the background theme of industrial production served to support a parallel scheme of rackets and patronage. Bright suggests that similar technologies of power operated inside the prison. If Jackson sustained a variety of external rackets, it also contained a whole set of internal ones through which the wide variety of officially proscribed pleasures of life (from sex to food and alcohol). Jobs provided the most important rewards for the internal patronage system. Getting a choice job required cooperation with a prison leader with influence in the warden's office. Such jobs then typically provided access to various goods and services that could circulate in the underground prison economy. This system of interlocking rackets allowed the warden and his staff to assure the appearance of normality, and the smooth operation of industrial work recognized as penologically appropriate and punitively hard, without having to rely constantly on violence and coercion to overcome inmate resistance. This system also promoted stable relations among inmates. The parole system, which had come in at the turn of the century, gave inmates an incentive to work without resistance, while the rackets provided a role in the prison world with at least some promise of pleasure and camaraderie for those who accepted the customs and mores.

The prison was thus both a nodule within the larger patronage economy and a patronage system all its own. When they operated smoothly these systems could produce a more or less reliable order with norms to control the nature of competition both inside and outside the prison. Of course, the Patronage State and the Big House, in addition to providing functional inputs to each other, also produced by-products that were dangerous to each. The prison, for example, inevitably produced scandals as the accommodations among prisoners and staff that produced its working arrangements occasionally came to light. Since prison wardens were so closely associated with governors, such scandals could pose an immediate threat to the governor. The sudden changes and crackdowns that scandals led to undermined order inside the prison as the forms of laxness and accommodation that created its necessary surpluses were withdrawn. The result was sometimes a riot, requiring extraordinary measures, sometimes state police, to suppress. Such riots were, of course, particularly major scandals.

Despite the potential for self-destabilization, the Patronage State and the Big House might have survived occasional cycles of scandal had their basic economic and social anchors remained strong. What truly undermined both regimes was the Great Depression that dried up the public spending surpluses and destroyed the profitability of prison industries that sustain the internal rackets and external petty corruption. When the Depression ended, a new model of power was available, one largely borrowed from the successful national regime of Franklin Roosevelt and the New Deal. By the 1940s Michigan governors could no longer rely on mobilizing party leaders and reached out for a mass constituency through new claims of professional governance and moral leadership promoted through a mass media directly to voters.

THE CORRECTIONAL INSTITUTION AND THE NEW DEAL STATE

Bright's study ends as the New Deal style of state government is being established in Michigan in the late 1940s and early 1950s. Although initially associated with the Democratic Party, ultimately both parties engaged in competition to promote new programs designed to solve social problems by mobilizing expertise and resources. Local machines continued to decline in significance and governors increasingly mobilized the state directly. This approach dominated politics at the national level until the 1980s, and in a good many states until the 1990s. Since then a new breed of politicians (first conservatives but more recently liberals as well) began to successfully challenge the structures of New Deal power, especially taxes and government spending and project a new model for governing.

The hallmark of the New Deal federal government was the proliferation of regulatory agencies and federal benefit programs that still dominate the administration of government in many respects. At the state level governors created smaller scale versions of the same sorts of agencies and programs. New Deal oriented governors also invested heavily in public spending, especially on intellectual capital, mainly education at the primary, secondary, and higher levels, including grand research universities.

The old Patronage State had relied on local party networks to mobilize voters who need have no particular interest in the candidate for governor but instead would look for rewards to be made available at the local level through loyalty to a winning electoral alliance. The crucial element of the New Deal style of governing was a direct relationship between the executive political leader (president or governor) and a largely urbanized population. The place of the old networks was taken in part by new mass organizations like unions that could mobilize the voters with respect to their mass interests rather than along geographic lines.

Another part of this relationship between the mass population and the political leadership was dependent on the mass media. Newspapers and later radio and television were critical for establishing a personal relationship between leader and mass public (Lowi, 1985). Media also helped shape the voter into a consumer of government services by relaying a steady stream of information about social problems and governmental solutions.

Science and professional expertise also played a prominent role in the New Deal style of governing along both dimensions. The institutional capacity to be able to access and make use of the best scientific advice in managing social problems was a critical feature of the New Deal style. Scientific discourse was critical to running the regulatory and benefit systems and helping to manage their relationship with the quasi-corporatist collective subjects of this state, unions, large corporations and the like. To some extent these subjects adopted the language of the social sciences as their own internal discourse (certainly economics, at certain high points in the New Deal era even sociology).

Two recent books (Cummins, 1994; Schrag, 1998) shed light on New Deal government in California in ways that permit a parallel analysis to that which Bright (1994) has provided for the start of the New Deal period in Michigan. In many respects California in the 1960s and 1970s was the successor to Michigan. Its economy, driven by the advanced sector of industrial manufacturing from automobiles through aerospace, took industrial society to its highest level of affluence yet. Detroit was the coming city of the 1920s with its relatively high wage auto jobs and its driver friendly neighborhoods. Los Angeles, and its freeways, became that in the city of the 1960s from where it seemed to offer the dominant model of the future. In universities, schools, and freeways, California led a national pattern of heavy investment. Led by a progressive Supreme Court, it also expanded welfare, health, and education entitlements for the poor. And significantly, the California Department of Corrections was clearly the national leader in commitment to a scientific model of expertise and a rehabilitative penology.

California governance in this period reflects many of the features Bright attributes to the New Deal model. The Governors from 1958 to 1978, Pat Brown, Ronald Reagan, and Jerry Brown, were all media oriented politicians, far less dependent on a decentralized state party organization than earlier governors. Their ability to mobilize political support was tied to the masses of voters through images of expert leadership over production of highly popular government services and the mediation of the press, large unions, and big business. The legislature, which in many states remained rooted in earlier structures of local party networks, developed in California along the same New Deal lines with high profile and media savvy members, a large and highly professionalized staff, and an emphasis on popular public spending.

The University of California system, and the even larger systems of state universities and community colleges, were the crowning glory of this regime and reflected all these virtues. By providing nearly free access (at the beginning) to a world class grade of education, higher education offered a highly attractive benefit to the economically mobile and ambitious families that moved to the state in large numbers during those years. The elite schools also provided researchers and graduates for the state's high technology industries.

Administering resources like the university systems bathed state government in the glow of technical competence, economic growth, and scientific progress. Pat Brown oversaw the expansion of the University of California system from two to nine campuses. And while costs began to rise in the late 1960s and 1970s, even conservative governors like Ronald Reagan protected the funding of higher education, a pattern that continued into the 1980s.

In both Michigan and California, New Deal influenced governors saw the prison system as an immediate area to establish the virtues of a scientifically informed activist government. In the 1950s, where Bright leaves his story, Jackson prison's regime was being reconfigured around this new model. The riots at Jackson in 1952 served as an occasion for a major reworking of the official rhetoric and the staffing of Michigan prisons in line with rehabilitation and psychotherapeutic treatment. The physical structure of the Big House remained, but the new model of classification reshaped routines and individualized treatment carried out by a staff supplemented by new corps of treatment professionals. While the talk of rehabilitation had continuities with 19th-century ideas of reform and discipline, it promoted a very different narrative of punishment, and was realized in a distinct practical regime. From the 1950s through the 1970s Jackson's inadequate work supply was supplemented and ultimately displaced by education and therapy.

Prisons in California began to be reshaped as early as 1944 when Governor Earl Warren reorganized the Department of Corrections and placed Richard McGee at its helm (Simon, 1993). While its glory days lay ahead, California prisons in the late 1940s and early 1950s began to feel the changing narrative of punishment toward rehabilitation, and toward a claim to control the prison through individualized management of the offender in the context of his psychological and behavioral needs.

In both Michigan and California, New Deal government very much altered the nature of the state's claims in rehabilitation. The Big House prison promised to reform inmates by submitting them to the discipline of hard labor and a life bereft of distractions. But its legitimacy never depended on reform. It was enough that government kept offenders safely behind bars where they were exposed to deserved hardship. If reform came, it was through the personal transformation invited but not demanded by the routines of industrial life that the prison self-consciously sought to mimic. The "correctional institution" in contrast staked the government's capacities squarely on the rehabilitation of offenders. Routines would not simply scrub rogues clean of their bad habits, but would reach inside with scientific techniques to address deep individual pathologies.

New social science promised not only to provide necessary treatment programs, but to provide monitoring to see whether the state achieved what it promised. The prisons built by the New Deal State in the 1950s and 1960s looked strikingly like the schools and college campuses that New Deal governors were also building at brisk clip to educate the baby-boom generation that was emerging as the prime beneficiary of the New Deal State. . . .

Cummins suggests that the heart of California's new rehabilitative penology was a set of political technologies aimed at increasing the capacity of prisoners to govern their own "self" as an object in the social world including group counseling, education, and "bibliotherapy." Reading and writing were especially important given the relative dearth of treatment professionals. Cummins rediscovers the fascinating history of the San Quentin library which at its peak in the 1950s held over 30,000 volumes (few of them law books) (Cummins, 1994: 28). The librarian of San Quentin in that era noted that 90 percent of his inmates patronized the library compared with a mere 45 percent of the general public, and he calculated that the inmates borrowed from 45 to over 100 books per year (1994: 28). Perhaps more remarkably, prisoners wrote manuscripts they hoped to circulate in the free world with a seriousness more associated with graduate students. In 1947 almost 400 prisoner manuscripts were submitted to the San Quentin librarian in the hope that they could be published—a number that rose to almost 2,000 by 1961.

Cummins' work supports Bright's argument that the rehabilitative era brought new forms of governance to the prison and not just rhetoric. Just as parole had provided the incentive for convicts in the Big House to participate in the official economy of labor (and subordinate their further resistance to the unofficial economy of the rackets), parole provided the key incentive for inmates to play along with rehabilitation. If it was in some sense a "game" to them (Cummins, 1994: 19), like its Big House counterpart rehabilitation provided viable roles and plausible scripts to work toward easily shared goals (getting out, getting some pleasures while in).

Cummins focuses his main attention on a number of convict writers in California, Caryl Chessman, Eldridge Cleaver, and George Jackson, whose celebrity as writers brought them power in the prison, and fame and influence outside of it. For Cummins these figures are the contact points for his primary interest in the circuit between the political Left and the prisons in this era. But Cummins also points to the way that these famous figures operated as real examples for other prisoners and icons of the promise of New Deal governance as penology.

In some sense these writers became for the correctional institutions what racket bosses were in the Big House, the key convicts around which the master narratives of penal control have to fit, and with whom the actual operation of the prison will be negotiated. In the former respect these writers were an enormous success, carrying to millions of baby-boom readers the message that rehabilitation worked (and with it the message that the New Deal state really could wield science to accomplish social progress on demand).

Cummins also suggests that the effort to recast the subjectivity of prisoners through investing in the compulsory production of language was part of the New Deal State's governing strategy. The new language practices were intended to influence the increasingly endangered normative order of inner city poverty communities, undermined by the deindustrialization of American cities that began almost as soon as World War II was over. In this respect, rehabilitative penology was more than just a good ideology for the New Deal style of government to promote its forms of power mainly to be channeled through other means. For an important segment of the urban population, the circulation of prisoners and their new discursive practices would be a direct form of New Deal governance. Rehabilitation was a way of establishing a relationship between the state and what we have now come to call the "underclass."

These new technologies of power inside the prison fit well with a New Deal governmental rationality that emphasized investment in education and the production of academic expertise at research universities for both government and industry. They also began to establish a real circuit of power and knowledge between prisoners encouraged to write and a public eager to read about criminal lives and willing to believe in the possibility of dramatic transformation. This was particularly true of the baby-boom kids who would be the first and only generation to be wholly raised up by New Deal State governments. Exposed to the best capitalized public education system in the world, California youth were quite open to a critical rereading of the moral status of the welfare state that raised them.

THE PRISON AND THE CRISES OF THE NEW DEAL STATE

Between the late 1950s and the 1970s, Cummins shows a spiral of writing and reading between increasingly militant convict writers and an increasingly radicalized youth population that helped shape the dramatic student protest movements of that era. In a very real sense these two groups (both privileged by New Deal forms of governance) would become the threat around which a reaction against the New Deal State would form. Cummins argues that convict writers and their radical student followers led each other into a period of terrorism (both inside and outside the prison) that helped discredit the New Deal State as well as destroying any mass political appeal for the Left.

Crime, especially violent crime by repeat offenders is the greatest possible rebuke to the New Deal style of government. Violent crimes like robbery, rape, and homicide strike at just those places where the New Deal's preferred approaches to social problems, regulation and redistribution are least effective. Insurance (perhaps the most important New Deal political technology) cannot reach the harms most feared from violent crime. The victims of violent crime, and those who empathetically project themselves into that subject position, experience themselves as outside the protections of the New Deal State in this sense. Their own loss is both a complete separation from the common ground of the state, and a condemnation of that state's incompetence in failing to protect you in the most direct possible way. To the extent that people imagine themselves or people they love as likely to experience violent crime they partake of the same distancing.

Violent crime has also become associated with the very populations that *appear* to be the primary beneficiaries of the New Deal State (although this is a gross misrecognition). This is the heart of the neo-conservative critique of the

New Deal State in its 1960s and 1970s versions. State sponsored social policy, e.g. desegregation, entitlement expansion, and due process reforms of criminal justice, unleashed the violent crime wave of the 1960s and 1970s. The maintenance of that culture could be blamed as well for the crime surge in the mid-1980s since "crack" cocaine, widely blamed for the increase, was identified with the violence proliferated in the same populations.

These vulnerabilities began to become critical in the 1970s when a stagnant national economy and inflation made the capital intensive political technologies of New Deal governance increasingly ineffective and costly. In the backlash that followed the very mechanisms by which state government raises revenue and decides to spend it were altered. The attack on the New Deal State was led by New Right politicians, like Ronald Reagan, and took place largely within the Republican Party. In the 1990s, however, both parties have begun to compete to produce post-New Deal governance. Not surprisingly, given the history that Bright has provided, the prison serves as a central resource for shaping a new approach to governing.

It was also fed by a number of popular electoral initiatives introduced into California in the late 1970s that attacked the New Deal State at its source and helped coalesce an alternative politics.

THE WAREHOUSE PRISON IN THE INITIATIVE STATE

California government since 1980 presents a striking case of the transformation in the rationalization of state power in the New Deal State. Peter Schrag describes the new governing approach as a "southward shift" (Schrag, 1998: 95) toward strategies of governance that have long dominated the southern states, which resisted and in good measure avoided the developments of the New Deal (in both state craft and penology). Schrag's (1998) portrait of California politics in the 1990s shows it to be different from the New Deal State on almost every level. The legislature as an organ has been decimated by some of the most severe term limit rules in the country which virtually assure that no elected representative will have the experience to really lead the body. This absence of leadership has only intensified a strong trend toward ideological partisan representatives with little interest in practical programs around which compromises might be struck. Even if the legislature and governor could formulate new policy initiatives their ability to spend money has been fundamentally altered by a series of fiscal initiatives, beginning with the (in)famous property tax initiative, Proposition 13, in 1978. Subsequent measures intended to prevent governments from manipulating around Proposition 13 tied the overall growth of state spending to a formula based on population and inflation. Other measures have reactively sought to guarantee funding for various purposes, including prisons and education, and leaving little room for spending agreed to through representative government.

Proposition 13 directly attacked the capacity of the New Deal State to govern. Its most immediate effect was to impede revenues. As Schrag persuasively argues, its more damaging and longer term effect was to disaggregate California property owners from the body of New Deal constituencies (and even from future property owners). In this sense it also reflected a new kind of political solidarity, one based on a shared fear of the consequences of government itself. The problem of protecting individuals from a state whose revenue needs were fundamentally adverse to the interests of that individual helped establish a new politics based on pervasive mistrust of government.

It took years and many further initiatives for the Proposition 13 effect to really alter the capacity of California's New Deal State government, but as a political technology its effects were much quicker. The success of Proposition 13 helped establish the ballot initiative not only as a primary vehicle for political decision making, but as a model for how to govern. Just as New Deal governors operated through streams of public spending, linked through media attention to election cycles, the initiative process has created its own cycles of fundraising, mass television advertising, and its own networks of pollsters, fundraisers, and political consultants. The role of mass publics like unions, university students, and the other client groups of the New Deal, has been taken by a circuit of direct advertising to a public sliced up into so many small demographic slices; an inert public of individuals moved together in short term bursts of empathy by mass advertising and professionally managed news coverage of the sort politicians now take for granted.

Schrag (1998: 15) suggests that one effect of this Initiative State has been to preserve the power of California's shrinking white non-Hispanic plurality of residents. Because this group continues to be a majority of state-wide voters, initiative politics is ideal for projecting their power. Ballot initiatives are voted on by the state as a whole, and they trump the power of locally elected representatives whose traditional methods of interest group bargaining would predictably transfer more power to the state's growing majority of minorities. The cumulative effect of numerous successful ballot initiatives is to have set sweeping restrictions on the ability of cities and counties, and their local majorities, to set policies (Schrag, 1998: 224).

Criminal justice legislation has been a central example of this. Criminal laws allow state-wide electoral majorities (more suburban, whiter, older, and wealthier than the state's resident majority by a wide measure) to establish and enforce norms for urban populations in cities they long ago abandoned for the suburbs. This allows them to exercise moral authority without having to share other aspects of government with the minority and poor populations of the city, including schools, neighborhoods, or risk sharing systems. Mandatory sentencing legislation of the kind so popular today further exacerbates this by giving county prosecutors enormous power over the fate of inner city community residents whose interests are unlikely to be represented in a winner take all county-wide office as most prosecutors offices are organized.

While California's constitution makes it initiative friendly, Schrag suggests that underlying social changes have sustained the rapid rise of initiative government. Perhaps most important has been the shift of political allegiance from occupational, class, and racial/ethnic solidarities to interests defined by domestic experience. It is not surprising in this respect that it is property tax relief that provided the opening moment of the initiative age in California. The mobility friendly New Deal style government that California elected in the 1950s and 1960s was leveraged in large part on the high wage increases of the aerospace industry, itself a cold-war public subsidy, and the relatively low cost of housing in California. As housing prices began to soar in the late 1960s and 1970s, property tax increases became a real and painful index of social transformation for many middle class property owners, especially those at or near the end of their income growth.

The sheer growth of California's population and urban media markets has driven a segmentation of California into a number of geographically distinct city-states, which themselves fragment into increasingly class defined enclaves. Schrag points to the problem this posed to a New Deal style of politics. Mobilizing support through the prestige of something like the University of California system required a sense of identity at the state level. Even after Pat Brown's massive expansion of the system, it still only had seven comprehensive campuses, and specialized medical and law facilities in San Francisco.

The initiative process has proven itself to be a successful politics in these changing circumstances in part because of more specific political technologies, like direct mail fund raising, political consultants, and advertising. These technologies, now also embedded in campaigns for political office, were capable of finding and linking the complex pattern of identities and solidarities that composed California's voters. The logic of citizenship that has emerged in this new regime is a peculiar one. While initiatives aim at empowering citizens by reflecting directly majority will, they have also helped construct a public that is largely passive and inert, depending on the machinery of initiatives to mobilize them. The new fiscal and political structures have created a series of public concerns that emphasize security for current assets against economic growth and social change.

The Initiative State shares with New Deal government a circuit of power running from mass public to the media and to political figures. Increasingly this circuit moves in such swift cycles that no enduring political forces or collective identities seem to coalesce. At the same time the Initiative State shares with the old Patronage State a significant stake in the distribution of resources, particularly money to run the expansive media campaigns required. Here the prison is playing its old role but on a far larger scale. The California Correctional Peace Officer's Association, the main union for parole agents and correctional officers, has become the second biggest contributor to California state elections, just behind the California Medical Assocation and more than twice as much as the California Teachers Association (Schrag, 1998: 135). The union has aggressively tied its cause to a war-like vision of the crime threat. Prison staff are described as working the "toughest beat in the state" (Schrag, 1998: 136).

The Initiative State has been most effective at mobilizing support around two issues, reducing taxes and regulations and increasing the severity and scope of the criminal law. The selection of these two are no accident, rather, they form the central sources of what Schrag describes as "neo-populist" politics (Schrag, 1998: 18). Like the populist movements that influenced state governments at the end of the 19th century, the new politics is strongly distrustful of expertise and the idea of government efforts to reshape private life. Unlike the traditional populists, however, the new politics is not about permanently empowering citizens to control politics. Instead, the ideal promoted is a kind of abolition of politics where some mythically simple system of rules allows individuals to pursue pure self-interest without any sustained attention to politics. Thus the fascination since the 1970s with legislation providing various kinds of mechanical formulas like property tax caps imposed by Proposition 13 and the whole panoply of mandatory sentencing rules including "Three-Strikes" laws. Schrag describes this new politics as

> A parody of the Newtonian system of checks and balances written by the framers into the U.S. Constitution, a mechanical device that's supposed to run more or less by itself and spares the individual the bother and complexities of any sort of political engagement. (Schrag, 1998: 18)

In this new configuration it is not surprising that punishment has become even more central to political authority. Like property taxes, fear of crime is particularly rooted in a sense of domestic location and the vulnerability to social changes beyond the control of ordinary people. Just as rapidly inflating real estate prices might involuntarily force someone to sell their home, rapidly rising crime by directly threatening the household and family could require flight. At the same time, crime as a subject of extensive mass media coverage lends itself to the kind of virtual or imaginary California (or Florida, or New York) which is where the constituency of the Initiative State lives.

Certain crimes did rise rapidly in California during the 1980s, especially violence associated with young males in the inner cities of the kind that were being savaged by the economic dislocation of the sort that had undermined the New Deal State (Davis, 1998: 400). Most of this crime did not directly threaten suburban white voters who dominate the Initiative State. But the dangers of "breakout" were highlighted in a number of incidents that generated significant media attention. A noteworthy example of the 1993 kidnapping and murder of 12-year-old Polly Klaas from her northern California edge-city home (Schrag, 1998: 227–8). The incident galvanized the electorate in time to re-elect a conservative Republican incumbent in the teeth of California's deepest recession in decades, and found expression in a classic act of the Initiative State, the "Three-Strikes" law which was placed into the California Constitution by initiative despite the fact that the legislature had adopted the exact same law. The Los Angeles riot of 1992 was another breakout event. It was more violent than any of those that haunted the New Deal State at the height of its power in the 1960s and reached farther into the white community (Davis, 1998: 369–77).

But if crime has been a powerful source for mobilizing a voting public for the Initiative State, it also helps sustain a political foundation for imprisonment as a central platform for exercising governmental power in the Initiative State. It is in the context of what Mike Davis calls "the ecology of fear" that we can see how prisons operate as important sources of public order in the Initiative State. Davis's (1998) analysis of the new spatial order of governance in Los Angeles provides us with another angle on the Initiative State. Schrag, a former editorial-page editor of the major newspaper in California's capital city, focuses on formal politics of initiatives, governors, and elections. Davis, a geographer and long-time observer of southern California captures the way initiative government looks from the ground. If the Initiative State replaces politics with mechanistic decision rules, the spatial order of contemporary Los Angeles replaces the functionally integrated order of the industrial metropolis with a quilt of unrelated segregated spaces controlled by private governments and obsessed with security.

In Davis's (1998) analysis, California's many new prisons, a remote "gulag ring" that surrounds the greater Los Angeles metropolis at a great distance, serves as a kind of waste containment facility designed to lower the short term risks of crime in other places. In this sense, prisons provide a public good that is theoretically consumable by the whole state. Each prison cell built adds to the capacity of judges everywhere in the state to send more offenders to prison for longer. Since the 1980s, California has been dominated with conservative Republican governors for whom increasing imprisonment has been essentially the top priority (Schrag, 1998: 94). During this time the legislature adopted more than 400 bills increasing criminal sentences (1998: 94).

Not untypical was Governor George Deukmejian's January 1990, State of the State Address, at the start of his final year in that office after two terms. Deukmejian compared California at the dawn of the 1990s with the state as he found it in 1983. With nods toward the remnant structures of the Patronage and New Deal States, Deukmejian began with some comments on the general condition of things in the state. He mentions recovery from earthquakes and recessions. He mentions the record sums of money in the budget cycle for public expenditures on highways and other "infrastructures." In his very first comment on his government's program, before he gets to anything about the environment, AIDS, homelessness, and highways, Deukmejian says this:

> In 1983, California had just 12 state prisons to house dangerous criminals. Since then, we have built 14 new prison facilities. That has enabled us to remove an additional 52,000 convicted felons from neighborhoods to send them to state prisons.

This logic has helped make growing the prison population a positive project of state power. The size of the prison population was not important to the New Deal State, other than the danger that expensive prisons could prevent other public spending. Transforming delinquents if successful is a powerful source of prestige to the state whether it is being done on tens of thousands or hundreds of thousands. The Patronage State had some interest in growing prisons, as Bright's analysis of Jackson suggests, yet the industrial form of the Big House was also important. The Initiative State has made its capacity to simply hold a large population, or warehouse them, the crucial test of its competence.

The prison's internal regime reflects this new governing mandate of the Initiative State. In Davis's (1998: 364–5) new imaging of urban morphology Park and Burgess's functionally differentiated urban zones (downtown office buildings, zone of transition, working men's rooming house quarter, etc.) has been replaced by zones defined by risk. In this mapping prisons exist on the far end of the risk distribution but with its variation along the same lines. Like other communities, prisons in California vary in the intensity of their security regime. The super-max prisons, with their total isolation and high technology systems resemble the gated suburbs. The intensely overcrowded medium security prisons are more like the badly decayed inner ring suburbs that have become dangerous crime zones as they are denuded of commercial and industrial opportunities.

In place of the rackets of the Big House and the compulsory self-narration of the correctional institution, the public order of the warehouse prison increasingly relies on coercive regimes of total segregation to isolate the most threatening inmates. Ironically the practice of administrative segregation began in the New Deal State where it was used to separate those deemed too threatening to the rehabilitative practice of the prison. Parole release, which played a crucial role in motivating inmate performance in both previous regimes, has been abolished in many states (an especially marked tendency in those governed under the logic of the Initiative State). The warehouse prison lacks the industrial or discursive circuits of power and knowledge that joined prison and community in the Patronage and New Deal States. Its interior no longer reflects any imperative of order other than concentration in space and containment. Because of this it has increasingly come to rely on technology and a militarized guard force to manage a population permanently in what both the Big House and the Correctional Institution would have considered a state of emergency (Haney, 1997; Human Rights Watch, 1997).

It is too early to predict when and if this will become a crisis for the Initiative State. Because penality is a co-producer of public order, the absence of a coherent correctional narrative to requalify the now massive population of prisoners and recently released prisoners for a place in the public order may ultimately endanger the Initiative State. Just as the universities and prisons ultimately weakened the New Deal State that had invested so much in them, the Initiative State may find itself producing political subjects and institutions that it can neither govern nor get rid of permanently. The political vulnerabilities of that strategy should begin to come visible in the next decade as the fiscal costs of aging prison populations and the economic costs of sustaining a criminalized underclass in urban America both grow.

CONCLUSION

When I began studying the growth of the California population in the 1980s it seemed uninteresting to make the point that prison populations were rising because current California governors were seeking to increase the prison population. I was looking for deeper social explanations for this apparently political decision. Political pressure for imprisonment was surely nothing new, even if greater in the 1980s, so why did the rhetoric of law and order now lead to burgeoning prison populations? My efforts at explanation emphasized the collapse of the internal narratives that had supported efforts to supervise felons outside of prison. I argued that the crucial change was not the politics of law and order (Scheingold, 1984), but the internal organizational rationality of corrections whose twin social and epistemological crises had undermined its historic capacity to self-regulate. Later Malcolm Feeley and I, co-reflecting on our independent work on court reform and parole developed the new penology idea to describe the technocratic managerialism that was increasingly organizing criminal justice institutions (Feeley and Simon, 1992, 1994; Simon and Feeley, 1995).

This explanation dramatically diminished the role of governors and their policies in shaping the actual prison population. Was I wrong? In some sense clearly yes. Recent research using multiple regression techniques to look across states and prison populations suggests that in otherwise quite similar states, the views of the governor on prison has a large influence on relative imprisonment rate (Davey, 1998). Recent research also suggests that the war on drugs and its promises of lengthy prison sentences for thousands of small time drug criminals was mobilized primarily by politicians who led rather than followed public opinion on this (Beckett, 1997).

Bright's (1994) framework for thinking about state government and penality offers a way of seeing the relationship between the two accounts. Bright's analysis suggests that penal narratives are not simply the ideological superstructure of some more basic structure of state government or politics, but rather a highly important site for the co-production of successful strategies for governing states in the 20th century. In recent work I have described this as "governing through crime" (Simon, 1997). The new penology in that sense is not simply the penal rhetoric of the Initiative State but part of its governing style. Governors who have openly governed on the numbers of new prison cells built, and the construction by a simple province of a nation state of a world class penal system, have governed through the new penology. Likewise, our new prisons represent many of the same political technologies of segregation and surveillance that are becoming common aspects of American society from gated communities to drug testing in suburban high-schools. Studying this space will call for something which combines the sociology of punishment (Simon, 1993) and political sociology (Beckett, 1997) along the lines that Stuart Scheingold has recently dubbed "political criminology" (Scheingold, 1998).

Seeing that imprisonment is a function of the way states are governed (and not simply the sociology of institutions or elections) underlines the potential for stasis and change in our now historically gargantuan system. State governments present potentially very different perspectives on imprisonment than the national policy debate that has dominated both media and academic thinking about the prison crisis (Scheingold, 1991; Lyons and Scheingold, 1999). Some states have remained remarkably free of massive investment in prison populations, institutions, and cultures. In most states, minority communities (who are typically the most hard hit by the social costs of the Initiative State's penal strategies) have the capacity to bring concentrated political pressure to bear on government in a way nearly impossible at the level of national politics. The works canvassed here suggest that we also need to conduct careful analysis of individual states, not just for the ideology of their governors but for the organization of political power in the state. Not every state is on its way to being an Initiative State as that ideal type has been developed here. Many other political forms operate in states, some remnants of Patronage and New Deal orders, some parts of strategies as yet unrecognized.

REFERENCES

Anderson, Elijah (1999) *Code of the street: decency, violence, and the moral life of the inner city.* New York: W.W. Norton.

Ashcroft, Bill, Griffiths, Gareth and Tiffin, Helen, eds (1995) *The post-colonial studies reader.* London & New York: Routledge.

Beckett, Katherine (1997) *Making crime pay: Law & order in contemporary American politics.* New York: Oxford University Press.

Bourgois, Philippe (1996) *In search of respect: Selling crack in El Barrio.* New York: Cambridge University Press.

Bright, Charles (1994) *The powers that punish: Prison and politics in the era of the "Big House," 1920–1955.* Ann Arbor, MI: University of Michigan Press.

Burchell, Graham, Gordon, Colin and Miller, Peter, eds (1991) *The Foucault effect: Studies in governmentality.* Chicago: University of Chicago Press.

Carleton, Mark T. (1971) *Politics and punishment: The history of the Louisiana state penal system.* Baton Rouge, LA: Lousiana State University Press.

Clemmer, Donald (1940; 2nd edn 1958) *The prison community.* New York: Holt, Rinehart & Winston.

Cummins, Eric (1994) *The rise and fall of California's radical prison movement.* Stanford, CA: Stanford University Press.

Davey, Joseph Dillon (1998) *The politics of prison expansion: Winning elections by waging war on crime.* Wesport, CT: Praeger.

Davis, Mike (1990) *City of quartz: Excavating the future in Los Angeles.* London: Verso.

Davis, Mike (1998) *Ecology of fear: Los Angeles and the imagination of disaster.* New York: Metropolitan Press.

Feeley, Malcolm and Simon, Jonathan (1992) The new penology: Notes on the emerging strategy of corrections and its implications, *Criminology 30*(4): 449–74.

Feeley, Malcolm and Simon, Jonathan (1994) Actuarial justice: The emerging new criminal law, in David Nelken (ed.) *The futures of crimonology,* pp. 173–201. London: Sage.

Foucault, Michel (1977) *Discipline and punish: The birth of the prison,* trans. Alan Sheridan. New York: Pantheon.

Garland, David (1985) *Punishment and welfare.* Aldershot: Gower.

Garland, David (1990) *Punishment and modern society.* Chicago, IL: University of Chicago Press.

Grossberg, Lawrence, Nelson, Cary and Treichler, Paula A., eds (1992) *Cultural studies.* New York: Routledge.

Hall, Stuart, Cricher, Chas, Jefferson, Tony, Clarke, John and Roberts, Brian (1978) *Policing the crisis: Mugging, the state, and law and order.* London: Macmillan.

Haney, Craig (1997) Psychology and the limits to prison pain: Confronting the coming crisis in Eighth Amendment law, *Psychology Public Policy & Law 3:* 499–552.

Human Rights Watch (1997) *Cold storage: Super-maximum security confinement in Indiana.* New York: Human Rights Watch.

Jacobs, James B. (1975) *Stateville: The penitentiary in mass society.* Chicago, IL: University of Chicago Press.

Krakauer, John (1997) *Into thin air.* New York: Vintage.

Lowi, Theodore J. (1985) *The personal president: Power invested, promise unfulfilled.* Ithaca, NY: Cornell University Press.

Lyons, William and Scheingold, Stuart (1999) The politics of crime and punishment. (Unpublished manuscript on file with the author.)

Maguire, Kathleen and Pastore, Ann L. (1998) *Sourcebook of criminal justice statistics 1997.* Washington, DC: Bureau of Justice Statistics.

Messinger, Sheldon L., Berecochea, John E., Berk, Richard A. and Rauma, David (1988) *Parolees returned to prison and the California prison population.* Sacramento, CA: California Department of Corrections, Bureau of Research.

Messinger, Sheldon L., Berecochea, John E., Rauma, David and Berk, Richard A. (1983) "The foundations of parole in California," *Law & Society Review 19*(1): 69–106.

Park, Robert E. and Burgess, Ernest W. (1925) *The city.* Chicago, IL: University of Chicago Press.

Powell, Walter W. and DiMaggio, Paul J., eds (1991) *The new institutionalism in organizational analysis.* Chicago, IL: University of Chicago Press.

Rothman, David J. (1971) *The discovery of the asylum: Social order and disorder in the New Republic.* Toronto: Little, Brown.

Royko, Mike (1971) *Boss: Richard J. Daley of Chicago.* New York: Dutton.

Scheingold, Stuart (1984) *The politics of law and order: Street crime and public policy.* New York: Longman.

Scheingold, Stuart (1991) *The politics of street crime: Criminal process and cultural obsession.* Philadelphia, PA: Temple University Press.

Scheingold, Stuart (1998) "Constructing the new political criminology: Power, authority, and the post-liberal state," *Law and Social Inquiry 23*: 857–95.

Schrag, Peter (1998) *Paradise lost: California's experience, America's future.* New York: The New Press.

Simon, Jonathan (1993) *Poor discipline: Parole and the social control of the urban underclass, 1890–1990.* Chicago, IL: University of Chicago Press.

Simon, Jonathan (1997) "Governing through crime," in Lawrence Friedman and George Fisher (eds) *The crime conundrum: Essays on criminal justice.* Boulder, CO: Westview Press.

Simon, Jonathan and Feeley, Malcolm (1995) "True crime: The new penology and public discourse on crime," in Thomas G. Blomberg and Stanley Cohen (eds) *Punishment and social control: Essays in honor of Sheldon Messinger,* pp. 147–80. New York: Aldine de Gruyter.

Sykes, Gresham (1958) *The society of captives: A study of a maximum security prison.* Princeton, NJ: Princeton University Press.

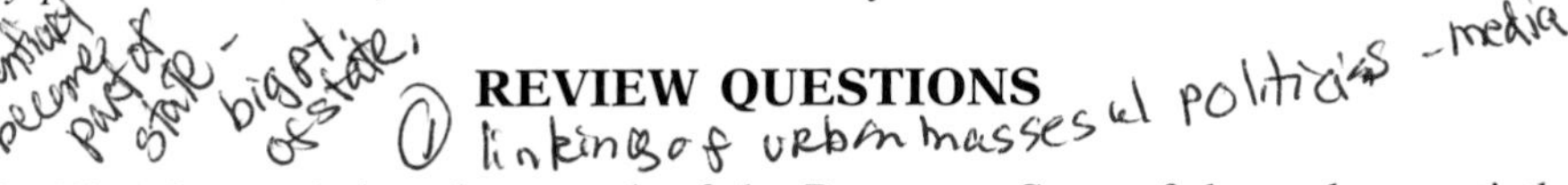

REVIEW QUESTIONS

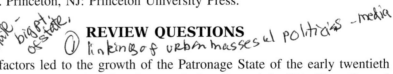

1. What factors led to the growth of the Patronage State of the early twentieth century and the "good ole boys" network that dictated the "Big House" penal policy and practice in the pre-WWII era?
2. Compare and contrast the positive and negative trends in prison policy that emerged under the Patronage and New Deal state models.
3. Are there any policy exceptions to the "winner take all" political climate that Simon describes during the Initiative State era?
4. To what extent do the penal policies of your state embody the principles of the Initiative State model described by Simon?

II

LEGAL ISSUES IN CORRECTIONS

READING 4

Prisoners' Rights and the Rehnquist Court Era

Christopher E. Smith

This article provides a historical overview of U.S. Supreme Court decisions in the area of prisoners' rights, with special attention paid to the precedent-forming actions of the Rehnquist-led Court (1986–2005). The author observes that the Rehnquist Court developed a series of analytical tests to be applied by the lower courts when dealing with cases revolving around prisoners' rights issues. Conservative-leaning analytical tests such as the deliberate indifference standard for Eighth Amendment claims, the deferential test that applies to prison policies, the actual injury standards applied to prisoner access claims, and the atypical and significant hardships test that limits enforceable liberty claims by inmates emerged during this era. The article goes on to analyze the text of decisions written by Justice Stevens on the left and Justices Scalia and Thomas on the right to more fully extrapolate the divisive and pronounced differences in legal philosophy that underlied prisoners' rights cases of the Rehnquist Court.

The death of Chief Justice William Rehnquist in 2005 marked the end of an era on the U.S. Supreme Court. Although Rehnquist served on the nation's highest court for more than 30 years (1971 to 2005), during his 19 years as chief justice (1986 to 2005) he was positioned to exert special influence on the development of constitutional law through his power to lead discussion of cases in conference and make opinion-writing assignments when he voted with the majority (Baum, 1992). Because of the visibility and influence of the chief justice, scholars define Supreme Court eras according to the tenure of a specific chief justice and use the conclusions of those eras as mileposts for assessment of the Supreme Court's performance and impact during discrete periods (Maltz, 2003). As the Supreme Court moves ahead into the new Roberts Court era under the leadership of Chief Justice John Roberts, it is appropriate to evaluate the significance of the preceding era under the leadership of Chief Justice William Rehnquist (Smith, 2006a).

During the Rehnquist Court era, prisoners' rights cases assumed new significance with respect to the breadth of their impact on individual human beings incarcerated in the nation's state and federal corrections institutions. At the dawn of the Rehnquist Court era in 1986, there were 3.2 million people under correctional supervision in the United States, including 526,000 held in prison. By the end of the Rehnquist Court era in 2005, that number had grown to 7 million people under correctional supervision, including more than 1.4 million in prison (Bureau of Justice Statistics, 2006, Table 6.1.2005). Thus, the Supreme Court's decisions defining prisoners' rights significantly affected increasing numbers of Americans during the Rehnquist Court era. In light of the importance of decisions shaping prisoners' rights and affecting the daily lives of prisoners, detainees, parolees, and probationers, it is essential to understand how the Rehnquist Court shaped the law and helped to define the state of American corrections today. This article addresses these issues by identifying and analyzing important themes and developments in the Rehnquist Court's treatment of prisoners' rights cases.

THE REHNQUIST COURT'S ANALYTICAL TESTS AND NEW LIMITATIONS ON PRISONERS' RIGHTS

The most important development from the Rehnquist Court's corrections law decisions concerned the articulation of analytical tests that served to limit the expansion of prisoners' rights and, indeed, diminish some legal entitlements for prisoners. These judicial limitations on the recognition of prisoners' rights coincided with congressional action, in the form of the Prison Litigation Reform Act of 1996, to limit prisoner litigation and district judges' remedial powers in corrections cases. Thus, the Rehnquist Court era can be seen as a period in which lower court judges were directed to limit their remedial interventions into corrections and prisoners faced little likelihood of gaining recognition of new or expanded constitutional rights. The impact of this development was especially far reaching because increasingly punitive sentencing policies subjected hundreds of thousands of additional people to the effects of corrections law as the Rehnquist Court era progressed.

Despite its deserved reputation for expanding definitions of constitutional rights with respect to such issues as equal protection (e.g., *Brown v. Board of Education,* 1954), privacy (*Griswold v. Connecticut,* 1965), defendants' rights (e.g., *Miranda v. Arizona,* 1966), and religious freedom (e.g., *Engel v. Vitale,* 1962), the Warren Court (1953 to 1969) had a relatively modest role in defining and applying constitutional rights for convicted offenders. The Warren Court deserves credit (or blame, depending on one's perspective) for opening the door to civil rights lawsuits by prisoners against corrections officials through its decision in *Cooper v. Pate* (1964). Although that decision opened the door for judicial protection of prisoners' constitutional rights, the actual identification and application of those rights came later, primarily through the initiative of judges in the lower federal courts. With respect to specific Warren Court decisions concerning prisoners' rights, there are only a limited number of examples. Of particular importance was *Johnson v. Avery* (1969), which helped protect prisoners' access to the courts by enabling "jailhouse lawyers" to provide assistance to other prisoners when corrections officials provided no alternative form of legal resources or assistance. Another notable case was *Lee v. Washington* (1968), which affirmed a lower court ruling applying the Equal Protection Clause to prisons and forbidding corrections officials from employing systematic racial segregation.

Two other Warren Court decisions eventually had a significant impact on prisoners' rights. *Trop v. Dulles* (1958) provided the test for defining "cruel and unusual punishments" under the Eighth Amendment by requiring that the constitutionality of punishments be evaluated according to the "evolving standards of decency that mark the progress of a maturing society." A majority of later justices adopted and followed this test throughout the Rehnquist Court era, as evidenced by the reasoning presented to justify the 2005 prohibition on the application of the death penalty to offenders who commit their capital crimes while younger than 18 (*Roper v. Simmons,* 2005). The other Warren Court case, *Robinson v. California* (1962), incorporated the Eighth Amendment prohibition on cruel and unusual punishments and thereby made this constitutional provision applicable to state and local corrections officials. As summarized by Fliter (2001), "The opinions of the [Warren] Court contributed little to the substantive nature of prisoners' rights, but they extended due process protections and access to the courts" (p. 87).

As described in detail by Feeley and Rubin (1998), much of the development of prisoners' rights occurred during the Burger Court era (1969 to 1986) through decisions by federal lower court judges across the country. Individual cases identified constitutional deficiencies in conditions of confinement and various policies and practices in correctional institutions in nearly every state. Judicial involvement in corrections during this period extended as far as the assignment of court-appointed special masters to supervise implementation of detailed and intrusive court-ordered remedies (e.g., Crouch & Marquart, 1989). The Burger Court initially approved and legitimized the judicially directed transformation of many prisons and the identification and definition of various constitutional rights for prisoners. For example, in *Hutto v. Finney* (1978), the Burger Court endorsed the authority of lower court judges to identify constitutional violations and order remedies with respect to conditions of confinement in punishment cells in the Arkansas prison system. The Court also identified some specific rights for prisoners, such as due process rights associated with prison officials' effort to take away "good time" credits as a disciplinary measure (*Wolff v. McDonnell,* 1974). Another example is *Estelle v. Gamble* (1976), which recognized that prisoners possess an Eighth Amendment protection against corrections officials being "deliberately indifferent" to their serious medical needs. In the later years of the Burger Court era, however, the justices made decisions that signaled lower court judges that they should proceed no further in the expansion of rights for prisoners. The Rehnquist Court continued this process, with additional decisions that not only signaled an end to the expansion of judicially recognized rights but that arguably also contributed to a reduction in the scope of rights or in the accessibility of federal courts to prisoners' efforts to seek vindication and protection of rights.

"Deliberate Indifference" and Conditions of Confinement

After prisoner litigation and judicial orders by federal judges in the lower courts had contributed to a transformation of many correctional institutions, the Burger Court indicated that judges should proceed no further in identifying new rights for prisoners. In *Bell v. Wolfish* (1979), the Supreme Court applied a very deferential analysis in approving various policies at a federal jail, including policies for intrusive strip searches and body-cavity inspections of pretrial detainees who had received visitors. In *Rhodes v. Chapman* (1981), the Court rejected claims about the alleged unconstitutionality of double celling in cells designed for only one prisoner. In *Rhodes,* Justice Lewis Powell's majority opinion contained words that were taken by many as a message to the lower courts: "Courts cannot assume that state legislatures and prison officials are insensitive to the requirements of the Constitution or to the perplexing sociological problems of how best to achieve the goals of the penal function in the criminal justice system." Although lower court judges could continue to identify and remedy violations based on rights already defined by the courts, the Supreme Court's decisions in *Bell v. Wolfish* and *Rhodes v. Chapman* were regarded as exhorting judges to be more deferential to prison officials when examining prisoners' rights claims.

During the Rehnquist Court era, the Court's decision in *Wilson v. Seiter* (1991) has been characterized by Feeley and Rubin (1998) as "[signaling] a true retrenchment" because it "appears to raise a substantial barrier to Eighth Amendment suits against state prisons" (pp. 48–49). In *Wilson,* Justice Antonin Scalia's majority opinion borrowed Justice Thurgood Marshall's Eighth Amendment "deliberate indifference" test that had been applied by the Supreme Court only to cases concerning a right to medical care (*Estelle v. Gamble,* 1976) and declared that prisoners must prove officials' "deliberate indifference" to win any Eighth Amendment case concerning conditions of confinement (Smith, 2001). Proving officials' knowledge and intent can be a daunting task for prisoners. Moreover, the test created new opportunities for corrections officials to use various defenses. According to Feeley and Rubin (1998),

> It is conceivable that the case could preclude most conditions of confinement suits on the ground that the conditions are the result of an insufficiently trained staff, an insufficiently funded operational budget, an insufficiently large physical plant, or any of the other insufficiencies that genuinely bedevil state prison systems, (p. 49)

Ultimately, the new standard appeared to make it significantly more difficult to prove Eighth Amendment violations in conditions of confinement cases.

Deference to Prison Officials

The Burger Court's opinions in *Bell v. Wolfish* (1979) and *Rhodes v. Chapman* (1981) used deferential language in rejecting prisoners' claims. Then-Associate Justice Rehnquist's opinion in *Bell v. Wolfish,* in particular, emphasized the need to "[balance] the significant and legitimate security interests of the institution against the privacy interests of the inmates" and thereby emphasized the idea of subordinating prisoners' interests to security claims of the officials to whom judges should show deference.

The Rehnquist Court subsequently provided a more specific articulation of a deferential test to be applied to most constitutional rights claims by prisoners. The Court's influential four-part test from *Turner v. Safley* (1987) calls for an examination of (a) a rational basis for the prison's challenged policy or practice, (b) alternative means of accommodating aspects of the prisoner's asserted rights with the challenged policy or practice in place, (c) potential adverse impacts from modifying the challenged practice or policy to accommodate the prisoner's asserted right, and (d) the existence (or lack thereof) of an easy alternative means to fulfill the institution's objectives in the absence of the challenged policy or practice. In a unanimous majority opinion concerning a prisoner's First Amendment claim, Justice Thomas characterized the *Turner* test and, implicitly, its importance and broad applicability by saying, "In *Turner* we adopted a unitary deferential standard for reviewing prisoners' constitutional claims" (*Shaw v. Murphy,* 2001).

Although the Supreme Court applied the *Turner* test to strike down one prison's overly restrictive policies against prisoners getting married (*Turner v. Safley,* 1987), the test has been applied in a deferential manner in other cases to turn down prisoners' rights claims concerning a variety of issues. For example, in *O'Lone v. Estate of Shabazz* (1987), the Court applied the *Turner* test in a deferential manner to deny minimum-security Muslim prisoners on outside work detail the opportunity to return to the prison on Friday afternoons for a religious service that Chief Justice Rehnquist's majority opinion acknowledged to be based on "sincerely held beliefs [that] compelled attendance at [the service]." In *Overton v. Bazzetta* (2003), the majority applied the *Turner* test to overturn a pro-prisoners' rights decision from the Sixth Circuit U.S. Court of Appeals and thereby uphold prison regulations that barred visits by various categories of individuals, including prisoners' unaccompanied minor siblings and minor nieces and nephews.

The Rehnquist Court's enunciation of the *Turner* test provided a relatively clear and strong articulation of the Burger Court's exhortation for judicial deference to prison officials and their policies and practices. The words of the *Turner* test leave room for judicial interpretation of facts and policy justifications, as evidenced by the reasoning and decision of the U.S. district judge who invalidated prison visitation policies at the trial level in *Overton v. Bazzetta* (see *Bazzetta v. McGinnis,* 2001). However, in the hands of the Rehnquist Court, the *Turner* test was applied in ways that rationalized the presumed importance of policies and practices that clash with prisoners' claims about certain constitutional rights.

Access to the Courts

During the Burger Court era, Justice Thurgood Marshall's majority opinion in *Bounds v. Smith* (1977) imposed an affirmative obligation on corrections officials to provide access to a prison law library or an alternative form of legal assistance to ensure that prisoners had the opportunity to prepare and file legal petitions. As the Supreme Court recognized as early as the 1940s (*Ex parte Hull,* 1941), prisoners' right of access to the courts, which is generally acknowledged to flow from the right to due process, is the linchpin for all other prisoners' rights. Prisoners must be able to gain judicial attention for their habeas petitions and civil rights lawsuits to obtain legal protections against improper policies and practices in the judicial process and in correctional settings. Although Marshall's opinion in *Bounds* represented an expansion of prisoners' rights, its weakness, in practice, as a genuine protection for the right of access to the courts was apparent to many critics, including lower court judges, such as the U.S. district judge who wrote,

> In this court's view, access to the fullest law library anywhere is a useless and meaningless gesture in terms of the great mass of prisoners. . . . To expect untrained laymen to work with entirely unfamiliar books, whose content they cannot

understand, may be worthy of Lewis Carroll [*Alice's Adventure in Wonderland*], but hardly satisfies the substance of constitutional duty. Access to full law libraries makes about as much sense as furnishing medical services through books like: "Brain Surgery Self-Taught," or "How to Remove Your Own Appendix," along with scalpels, drills, hemostats, sponges, and sutures. (*Falzerano v. Collins,* 1982)

In *Lewis v. Casey* (1996), the Rehnquist Court faced a challenge to the adequacy of prison library materials for ensuring access to the courts by prisoners in administrative segregation and by those beset with deficiencies and disabilities that would interfere with their effective use of library materials (i.e., non-English speakers and illiterates). In rejecting an extensive remedial order by the district judge, Justice Scalia's majority opinion seized the opportunity to impose standing requirements (i.e., proof of actual injury) that three of his colleagues found to be more restrictive than necessary (Stevens, Souter, Ginsburg). Scalia's opinion also emphasized the need for deference to prison officials (i.e., "Of course, we leave it to prison officials to determine how best to ensure that inmates with language problems have a reasonably adequate opportunity to file nonfrivolous legal claims challenging their convictions or conditions of confinement."). Scalia also referenced the *Turner* test in admonishing the district judge for "[failing] to accord adequate deference to the judgment of prison authorities." The *Lewis* decision appeared intended to have a dual impact on prisoners' claims concerning their right of access to the courts. First, the case requires a strict examination of standing: Prisoners must make a demonstration of "actual injury" from policies that prevent the filing of nonfrivolous claims that attack their sentences or challenge conditions of confinement but that concern no other legal issues that might affect prisoners (e.g., divorce, custodial rights of parents, property disputes, etc.). The nature of these requirements might constitute an insurmountable catch-22 barrier if prisoners who are, for example, illiterate or unable to speak English must go to court and prove to the court that they are unable to go to court and effectively offer proof of legal issues. Second, the decision gives repeated emphasis to the need for judges to defer to corrections officials and thereby presumably has an additional chilling effect on judges inclined to provide close examination of access-to-the-courts claims by prisoners.

The Rehnquist Court also blocked any additional expansion of rights related to access to the courts by, for example, rejecting any asserted First Amendment right for prisoners to help other prisoners with legal matters (*Shaw v. Murphy,* 2001). The Rehnquist Court has also declined to invalidate congressional impediments to prisoners filing legal petitions as imposed by the Antiterrorism and Effective Death Penalty Act (*e.g., Felker v. Turpin,* 1996) and the Prison Litigation Reform Act (*e.g., Booth v. Churner,* 2001; *Porter v. Nussle,* 2002).

"Atypical and Significant Hardships" and State-Created Liberty Interests

The Burger Court triggered due process claims by prisoners through its identification of "state-created liberty interests" (*Hewitt v. Helms,* 1983). Prisoners were able to look at relevant statutes to see if states had placed legal obligations on themselves. If a statute or regulation affecting prisoners said that the state "will" or "shall" take a certain action, the mandatory language created an enforceable liberty interest for prisoners. Statutory or regulatory language that gave discretion to corrections officials did not create such enforceable interests (Smith, 2000b, p. 148). The Rehnquist Court subsequently diminished prisoners' opportunities to pursue legal protections through this avenue by limiting state-created liberty interests to, in the words of Chief Justice Rehnquist,

> freedom from restraint which, while not exceeding the sentence in such an unexpected manner as to give rise to protection by the Due Process Clause by its own force . . . nonetheless imposes atypical and significant hardships on the inmate in relation to the ordinary incidents of prison life. (*Sandin v. Conner,* 1995)

In the case in question, the Supreme Court permitted a prison disciplinary committee to impose a punishment of 30 days in disciplinary segregation after a hearing in which the committee denied the prisoner's request to present witnesses on his behalf. A lower federal court that was overruled by the Supreme Court had found that a prison regulation requiring a finding of guilt to be based on "substantial evidence" provided the prisoner with a state-created liberty interest that should enable him to call witnesses as part of due process (*Sandin v. Conner,* 1995).

The Rehnquist Court's new test focusing on "atypical hardships" not only diminished the previously existing situations in which prisoners could claim the existence of a state-created liberty interest, but the language of the test was also later applied to examine whether prison policies improperly compel prisoners to incriminate themselves in violation of the Fifth Amendment privilege against compelled self-incrimination. In *McKune v. Lile* (2002), a convicted sex offender faced the prospect of being transferred to a higher security prison where prisoners have fewer privileges and less freedom within the institution as a result of his refusal to participate in a therapy program that would require him to openly admit to all of his past sex crimes—with the knowledge that these admissions could be used against him in future prosecutions. The ruling plurality of justices (Kennedy, Rehnquist, Scalia, Thomas) did not see the threatened transfer to a more restrictive institution as imposing an "atypical and significant hardship" that would cause it to be viewed as a form of compulsion that would violate the Fifth Amendment. In a concurring opinion, Justice. O'Connor believed that the plurality's test was insufficiently protective, although she agreed that no compulsion existed in this case. The four dissenters (Stevens, Breyer, Ginsbug, Souter) strongly objected to the reasoning and result in which "a person who has made a valid assertion of the privilege [against compelled self-incrimination] may nevertheless be ordered to incriminate himself and sanctioned for disobeying such an order."

As demonstrated by the example of *McKune v. Lile* (2002), Rehnquist Court language that was created to limit prisoners' rights in one context can be applied to other kinds of claims to produce similarly restrictive impacts on assertions of rights.

PRO-PRISONER DECISIONS OF THE REHNQUIST COURT

As described in the foregoing sections, the Rehnquist Court created new tests that served to limit any expansion of prisoners rights and, with respect to many issues, arguably diminished rights that existed more broadly under Burger Court doctrines. Although the Rehnquist Court's deference to corrections officials and restrictive impacts on asserted prisoners' rights are clearly dominant elements in the Court's decisions, the Court did not use its authority to extinguish legal protections for prisoners. For example, despite the imposition of the "deliberate difference" test for asserted violations of Eighth Amendment conditions of confinement, the Court held open the possibility for certain kinds of lawsuits by, for example, permitting Eighth Amendment claims for nonsignificant physical injuries from corrections' officers use of force ("minor bruises and swelling of his face, mouth, and lip . . . loosened . . . teeth and cracked partial dental plate"; *Hudson v. McMillian,* 1992) and for risks of future physical harms (risk of future harm from confinement with a chain-smoking cellmate; *Helling v. McKinney,* 1993). In *Johnson v. California* (2005), the Court ruled that strict scrutiny analysis must apply to equal protection claims in prison, yet this decision merely reinforced existing Fourteenth Amendment doctrine and had limited applicability to corrections contexts because only the state of California was practicing systematic racial segregation in its classification center (Marquart & Trulson, 2006).

With respect to corrections officials' susceptibility to lawsuits, the Rehnquist Court denied claims of qualified immunity for corrections officials who chained a prisoner to a post in the prison yard under harsh conditions (*Hope v. Pelzer,* 2002) and denied qualified immunity protection to employees at a private prison (*Richardson v. McKnight,* 1997). The foregoing decisions did not expand any substantive rights and, indeed, left in place the challenging requirements for proving "deliberate indifference" or, in certain use-of-force cases, the more challenging intent requirement from the final term of the Burger Court, "malicious and sadistic" intent (*Whitley v. Albers,* 1986).

If one were to try to identify new or expanded protections that emerged for prisoners during the Rehnquist Court era, the focus must primarily fall on the Court's willingness to accept *statutory* protections provided—either intentionally or inadvertently—by Congress. For example, in *Pennsylvania Department of Corrections v. Yeskey* (1998), Justice Scalia, writing on behalf of a unanimous Court, found that state prisoners were entitled to the accommodations for disabled people mandated by the federal Americans with Disabilities Act of 1990 (ADA). This protective approach continued in the Roberts Court era as it unanimously upheld the application of the ADA to a claim by a prisoner against state officials (*Goodman v. Georgia,* 2006).

In another example, the Rehnquist Court unanimously upheld the Religious Land Use and Institutionalized Persons Act of 2000 (*Cutter v. Wilkinson,* 2005) that mandated a strict scrutiny test for prisoners' free exercise of religion claims instead of the lesser "laws-of-general-applicability" standard required by the Constitution from Justice Scalia's opinion in *Employment Division of Oregon v.*

Smith (1990). These decisions seem to reflect the Court's deferential posture to Congress with respect to these matters rather than any effort by the majority of justices to use their interpretive authority to expand legal protections for convicted offenders.

JUSTICE STEVENS AS ADVOCATE FOR PRISONERS' RIGHTS

One theme that emerges in the prisoners' rights cases of the Rehnquist Court is Justice Stevens's role as the primary advocate for constitutional rights in corrections contexts (Smith, 2006b). At the conclusion of the Burger Court era, scholars noted that Stevens stood out in these cases during his first decade on the Court. According to Canon (1991),

> In no other area of criminal justice did Stevens differentiate himself as much from the Burger Court majority as in prisoners' rights cases. He supported the prisoner in 16 of the 17 cases considered; the Court did so in only 5 cases—and in none after O'Connor's appointment [in 1981]. (pp. 370–371)

Stevens continued this pattern during the Rehnquist Court era.

During the Burger Court era, for example, Stevens was the lone justice to express skepticism about the "deliberate indifference" test that Justice Marshall applied to prisoners' Eighth Amendment right to medical care in *Estelle v. Gamble* (1976). According to Stevens,

> By its repeated references to "deliberate indifference" and the "intentional" denial of adequate medical care, I believe the Court improperly attaches significance to the subjective motivation of the [prison officials] as a criterion for determining whether cruel and unusual punishment has been inflicted. Subjective motivation may well determine, what, if any, remedy is appropriate against a particular defendant. However, whether the constitutional standard has been violated should turn on the character of the punishment rather than the motivation of the individual who inflicted it. Whether conditions in Andersonville [the prisoner of war camp during the Civil War] were the product of design, negligence or mere poverty, they were cruel and unusual. (*Estelle v. Gamble,* 1976, pp. 116–117)

Not surprisingly, he continued to object to the imposition of subjective standards, such as the deliberate indifference standard applied by the Rehnquist Court majority to expanding Eighth Amendment contexts. In *Wilson v. Seiter* (1991), Stevens joined Justice White's concurring opinion that challenged Justice Scalia's application of the deliberate indifference test to all conditions of confinement cases. In *Hudson v. McMillian* (1992), Stevens's concurring opinion urged the use of a "wanton and unnecessary infliction of pain" test instead of the more demanding and subjective "malicious and sadistic" intent test applied by the Court for use of force cases. In *Hope v. Pelzer* (2002), Stevens wrote the majority opinion (in opposition to dissenters Thomas, Scalia, and Rehnquist) that identified an "obvious" Eighth Amendment violation, even when the deliberate indifference test is applied, in the case of a prisoner chained to one spot in a prison yard all day without adequate access to drinking water or toilet facilities.

Writing an opinion concurring in part and dissenting in part on behalf of his colleagues Justices Brennan, Marshall, and Blackmun, Stevens strongly objected to the Rehnquist Court's creation of the deferential test in *Turner v. Safley* (1987). According to Stevens,

> But if the standard can be satisfied by nothing more than a "logical connection" between the regulation and any legitimate penological concern perceived by a cautious warden, . . . it is virtually meaningless. Application of the standard would seem to permit disregard for inmates' constitutional rights whenever the imagination of the warden produces a plausible security concern and a deferential trial court is able to discern a logical connection between that concern and the challenged regulation.

There are a variety of other examples of Stevens's unique role. In *Lewis v. Casey* (1996), Stevens dissented against Justice Scalia's majority opinion concerning standing and access to the courts, even as his next-most-liberal colleagues, Souter and Ginsburg, concurred with parts of Scalia's opinion and only dissented against one section. In *Johnson v. California* (2005), when a six-justice majority on an eight-member Court (Rehnquist was ill and absent) ruled that strict scrutiny analysis should apply to an equal protection claim concerning the use of racial segregation in cells during the first 60 days of incarceration in California's prison, Stevens wrote a solo dissent that urged the Court to go even farther and actually declare that California's segregation practices were clearly unconstitutional. The majority had remanded the cases to see if California had a compelling justification for the segregation. In *McKune v. Lile* (2002), Stevens wrote the dissent, arguing for the protection of prisoners against compelled self-incrimination with respect to sex offender therapy programs. Even when Stevens joined a unanimous majority to overturn a ruling that favored broader visitation rights for prisoners, Stevens took the time to write a concurring opinion to remind lower court judges of the importance and continuing existence of prisoners' rights:

> It is important to emphasize that nothing in the Court's opinion today signals a resurrection of [outdated doctrines that deny the existence of prisoners' rights]. . . . To the contrary, it remains true that the "restraints and the punishment which a criminal conviction entails do not place the citizen beyond the ethical tradition that accords respect to the dignity and intrinsic worth of every individual." (*Overton v. Bazzetta,* 2003)

These examples show that Justice Stevens's role in prisoners' rights cases deserves further, more systematic examination. Moreover, his departure from the Supreme Court in the foreseeable future (Stevens celebrated his 87th birthday in April 2007) will raise questions about the extent to which the Court will contain any justices who strongly advocate for the protection of prisoners' constitutional rights.

THE THOMAS–SCALIA VISION OF PRISONERS WITH A NEAR ABSENCE OF RIGHTS

As indicated in the foregoing discussion, Justice Antonin Scalia played a major role in the impact of the Rehnquist Court on prisoners' rights through his authorship of *Wilson v. Seiter* (1991), the case that took the "deliberate indifference" test from its applicability to medical care issues and mandated that it be applied to all Eighth Amendment conditions of confinement cases. He also wrote *Lewis v. Casey* (1996), the decision that imposed stricter standing requirements for access-to-the-courts claims and that warned district judges away from fashioning broad remedies for cases involving such issues. In both instances, Scalia ingeniously drew from ideas originally put forward by Justice Thurgood Marshall to expand prisoners' rights in *Estelle v. Gamble* (1976; deliberate indifference in medical care cases) and *Bounds v. Smith* (1977; the capability of prisoners to use law libraries to gain access to the courts). However, Scalia appropriated these ideas for the purpose of reducing the scope of prisoners rights (Smith, 2001). For example, when Scalia imposed the deliberate indifference test for all Eighth Amendment conditions of confinement cases, he claimed to rely on precedent. But the precedents he used focused on narrow Eighth Amendment issues of medical care (*Estelle v. Gamble,* 1976) and use of force during a disturbance (*Whitley v. Albers,* 1986). He appeared to overlook or minimize the most comparable precedents concerning general living conditions in prisons (*Hutto v. Finney,* 1978; *Rhodes v. Chapman,* 1981), presumably because those decisions emphasized objective examinations of the nature of prison conditions, and therefore would not advance his apparent goal of switching to a subjective test. Thus, one can argue that Scalia's influence over the Rehnquist Court's direction and impact regarding prisoners' rights has been especially significant. However, these opinions, although effective in changing law and policy, do not reflect Scalia's true views on how the Supreme Court should define prisoners' rights. Those views can be seen in the opinions in which Scalia joins concurring and dissenting opinions written by Justice Thomas.

Advancing the originalist interpretive perspective preferred by both Thomas (Smith & Baugh, 2000) and Scalia (Schultz & Smith, 1996), Thomas has argued that the framers of the Eighth Amendment did not intend to protect prisoners against anything other than "cruel and unusual" sentences announced by a judge. Thomas and Scalia do not see the Eighth Amendment as providing any protection for prisoners in the implementation of the sentence. As Thomas, joined by Scalia, wrote in *Hudson v. McMillian* (1992), "For generations, judges and commentators regarded the Eighth Amendment as applying only to torturous punishments meted out by statutes or sentencing judges, and not generally to any hardship that might befall a prisoner during incarceration." In Thomas's view, the framers "simply did not conceive of the Eighth Amendment as protecting inmates from harsh treatment" (*McMillian* dissent).

In *Helling v. McKinney* (1993), again joined only by Scalia in his dissent, Thomas reiterated his argument by asserting that prison conditions cannot be considered as "punishment" and therefore fall outside of the protections of the prohibition on "cruel and unusual punishments." According to Thomas,

> I believe that the text and history of Eighth Amendment, together with the decisions interpreting it, support the view that judges or juries—but not jailers—impose "punishment." At a minimum, I believe that the original meaning of "punishment," the silence of the historical record, and the 185 years of uniform precedent [that never applied the Eighth Amendment to prisons] shift the burden of persuasion to those who would apply the Eighth Amendment to prison conditions. [That burden of persuasion] was certainly not discharged in *Estelle v. Gamble* [the 1976 case in which the Supreme Court for the first time applied the Eighth Amendment to prison conditions].

Thomas again reiterated this view in *Farmer v. Brennan* (1994), a case in which a prisoner filed an Eighth Amendment lawsuit for corrections officials' failure to protect him against violent sexual assaults, although he had pleaded with them and warned them that such assaults would occur if he were placed in the general prison population at a high-security facility. According to Thomas,

> As an original matter, therefore, this case would be an easy one for me: because the unfortunate attack that befell the petitioner was not part of his sentence, it did not constitute "punishment" under the Eighth Amendment [and therefore does not implicate any constitutional rights under the Amendment].

If one were to ask Thomas and Scalia whether and how prisoners would receive any protection against being starved, beaten, frozen in winter from lack of heat, or otherwise forced to endure horrific, inhumane conditions, Thomas would reply that "primary responsibility for preventing and punishing [abusive practices and misconduct by prison officials] rests not with the Federal Constitution but with the laws and regulations of the various states" (*Hudson v. McMillian,* 1992, p. 28). Thomas and Scalia thus apparently enunciate a vision of prison law in which prisoners do not possess any rights under the Eighth Amendment. Although this viewpoint claims to derive from reliance on history in the form of original intent jurisprudence, it is, in fact, ahistorical in nature. It may be true that the framers of the Eighth Amendment did not intend it to apply to conditions in prisons, but it is also true that those 18th-century framers were not familiar with the use of prisons for long-term sentences as a form of criminal punishment. The development of prisons in the United States primarily occurred during the 19th century (Clear, Cole, & Reisig, 2006). One cannot specifically attribute intentions to individuals who had no knowledge about institutions comparable to contemporary prisons.

In other respects, this vision of prison law is either ahistorical or impervious to human suffering because the government officials whom Thomas and Scalia trust to prevent and correct abusive conditions are exactly the people who permitted such conditions to flourish throughout most of American history and thereby led both Republican and Democrat judges to intervene with remedial orders in institutional reform litigation in the 1960s, 1970s, and 1980s (Feeley & Rubin, 1998). Chief Justice Rehnquist, a frequent ally of Thomas and Scalia, disagreed with their vision because even he acknowledged that "the deplorable conditions and Draconian restrictions of some of our nation's prisons are too well known to require recounting here, and the federal courts rightly have condemned these sordid aspects of our prison systems" (*Bell v. Wolfish,* 1979).

The vision articulated by Thomas and Scalia would, if adopted by a majority of the Supreme Court, negate current legal protections that seek to provide minimum standards for medical care, appropriate use of force by staff, nutrition, sanitation, prevention of prisoner-to-prisoner violence, and conditions of habitability in prisons. Instead, there would apparently be complete federal judicial deference to the decisions of state legislators, governors, and corrections administrators, which would effectively transfer judicial scrutiny of corrections completely to state courts with predictably wide-ranging results.

But what of other rights for prisoners? The lone right for prisoners that Thomas appears to acknowledge as enjoying constitutional protection is the right of access to the courts, which flows from the right to due process. However, Thomas envisions the narrowest possible right of access,

> a right not to be arbitrarily prevented from lodging a claimed violation of a federal right in a federal court. The State, however, is not constitutionally required to finance or otherwise assist the prisoner's efforts, either through law libraries or other legal assistance. (*Lewis v. Casey,* 1996)

It appears that Thomas's conception of the right is merely that the prison officials must have a mail slot into which prisoners can place letters addressed to the courts. Contrary to current law and practice, Thomas would not require prison officials to provide paper, pencils, stamps, envelopes, law books, or anything else that would make it feasible for prisoners to actually prepare for those letters.

With respect to claims of racial discrimination in prisons, Thomas and Scalia would not apply strict scrutiny under equal protection analysis for such claims. Instead, they would apply the *Turner* test and adopt a deferential posture toward corrections officials' rationalizations for discrimination and segregation (*Johnson v. California,* 2005). According to Thomas, "Time and again, even when faced with constitutional rights no less 'fundamental' than the right to be free from state-sponsored racial discrimination, we have deferred to the reasonable judgments of officials experienced in running this Nation's prisons" (*Johnson v. California,* 2005). Similarly, with respect to other rights, such as First Amendment claims by prisoners, Thomas consistently praises the deferential posture of the *Turner* test and appears willing to apply it to all other situations. Because the *Turner* test is essentially a "rational basis" test and Thomas is especially inclined to defer to the asserted interests of corrections officials (e.g., "This Court recognized that experienced prison administrators, and not judges, are in the best position to supervise the daily operations of prisons throughout the country"; *Johnson v. California,* 2005), it is difficult to envision any circumstances in which Thomas would identify a prison policy or practice as violating a constitutional right of prisoners.

CONCLUSION

The Supreme Court's decisions during the Rehnquist Court era had a significant impact on prisoners' rights, primarily by changing key tests for rights violations in ways that either blocked further expansion of rights or resulted in a diminution of existing rights. Of particular importance in this regard were the Supreme Court's decisions in *Wilson v. Seiter* (1991; deliberate indifference test for Eighth Amendment conditions of confinement), *Turner v. Safley* (1987; deferential rational basis test for a variety of rights), and *Lewis v. Casey* (1996; strict standing requirements and barriers to judicially ordered remedies for access-to-the-courts claims). This trend occurred as prison populations rose and hundreds of thousands of additional offenders were affected by conditions of confinement and other rights-related aspects of corrections. Congress complemented and enhanced the Rehnquist Court's judicial diminution of legal protections for convicted offenders by imposing additional barriers to prisoners' petitions and limiting judges' authority to order remedies for certain rights violations (Antiterrorism and Effective Death Penalty Act, Prison Litigation Reform Act).

Throughout the Rehnquist Court era, as he had done during the Burger Court era, Justice John Paul Stevens stood out as a unique and notable voice favoring constitutional protections for prisoners. It remains to be seen how long he will remain on the Court and whether another justice will step forward to assume the role, previously shared by Justices Thurgood Marshall and William Brennan, of advocate for scrutiny of corrections policies and judicial intervention to ensure the protection of prisoners' constitutional rights.

With respect to prisoners' rights issues, Thomas and Scalia were outliers on the Rehnquist Court who could not even convince their usual ally, Chief Justice Rehnquist, to agree with their views on the Eighth Amendment. Although a two-person voting bloc is typically not a locus of power in a nine-member Court, the opinions of Thomas and Scalia have laid the groundwork for potential future decisions that could drastically reduce the scope of prisoners' already-diminishing rights. Moreover, no one really knows yet how Chief Justice John Roberts, the former Rehnquist law clerk, will approach cases concerning prisoners' rights. It is equally uncertain how Justice Samuel Alito would approach such issues on the Supreme Court, although some commentators believe he is more conservative than Scalia on rights issues in criminal justice cases (Gordon, 2005). In addition, there is the question of how long 87-year-old Justice Stevens can continue on the Court, not to mention 74-year-old cancer survivor Justice Ruth Bader Ginsburg, another liberal on prisoners' rights issues. Depending on how changes in the Court's composition affect viewpoints on prisoners' rights, the vision enunciated by Thomas and Scalia could become influential in shaping future law and policy during the Roberts Court era.

In the broad history of corrections law, the Rehnquist Court era will be noted as a period in which the Supreme Court firmly halted the expansion of constitutional rights for offenders. More importantly, the Rehnquist Court enunciated specific legal doctrines to provide precedential power to the Burger Court's earlier exhortations about judicial deference to corrections officials. The Court's tests in *Turner v. Safley* (1987), *Wilson v. Seiter* (1991), and *Lewis v. Casey* (1996) used, respectively, the concepts of a rational basis test, proof of subjective intent, and strict standing requirements to diminish the opportunities for and the likelihood of judicial intervention to identify and remedy rights violations. The advent of professionalized corrections administration and judicially initiated prison reforms during the Burger

Court era may have facilitated the Rehnquist Court's impact on corrections law because fewer patently egregious, systemic policies and practices entered the court system to remind the justices of any need for close judicial supervision of corrections (Smith, 2000a). Because future legal issues in corrections will be affected by societal developments, including economic changes, government budgets, offending patterns, and new technologies, it remains to be seen whether subsequent decisions by the Roberts Court and later Supreme Court eras will reinforce the Rehnquist Court doctrines or subject corrections systems to renewed judicial scrutiny.

REFERENCES

Baum, L. (1992). *The Supreme Court* (4th ed.). Washington, DC: CQ Press.

Bazzetta v. McGinnis, 148 F.Supp.2d 813 (E.D.Mich. 2001).

Bell v. Wolfish, 441 U.S. 520 (1979).

Booth v. Churner, 532 U.S. 731 (2001).

Bounds v. Smith, 430 U.S. 817 (1977).

Brown v. Board of Education, 347 U.S. 483 (1954).

Bureau of Justices Statistics. (2006). *Sourcebook of criminal justice statistics 2005.* Washington, DC: U.S. Department of Justice. Available from University at Albany Web site, http://www.albany.edu/sourcebook

Canon, B. C. (1991). Justice John Paul Stevens: The lone ranger in a black robe. In C. M. Lamb & S. C. Halpern (Eds.), *The Burger Court: Political and judicial profiles* (pp. 343–374). Urbana: University of Illinois Press.

Clear, T. R., Cole, G. F., & Reisig, M. D. (2006). *American corrections* (7th ed.). Belmont, CA: Thomson/Wadsworth.

Cooper v. Pate, 378 U.S. 546 (1964).

Crouch, B. M., & Marquart, J. W. (1989). *An appeal to justice: Litigated reform of Texas prisons.* Austin: University of Texas Press.

Cutter v. Wilkinson, 125 S.Ct. 2113 (2005).

Employment Division of Oregon v. Smith, 494 U.S. 872 (1990).

Engel v. Vitale, 370 U.S. 421 (1962).

Estelle v. Gamble, 429 U.S. 97 (1976).

Ex parte Hull, 312 U.S. 546 (1941).

Falzerano v. Collins, 535 F.Supp. 800 (D.N.J. 1982).

Farmer v. Brennan, 511 U.S. 825 (1994).

Feeley, M. M., & Rubin, E. L. (1998). *Judicial policy making and the modern state: How the courts reformed America's prisons.* Cambridge, UK: Cambridge University Press.

Felker v. Turpin, 518 U.S. 1051 (1996).

Fliter, J. A. (2001). *Prisoners' rights: The Supreme Court and evolving standards of decency.* Westport, CT: Greenwood.

Goodman v. Georgia, 126 S.Ct. 877 (2006).

Gordon, R. (2005, November 1). "Alito or Scalito? If you're a liberal, you'd prefer Scalia." *Slate.* Retrieved November 3, 2005, from http://www.slate.com/id/2129107/

Griswold v. Connecticut, 381 U.S. 479 (1965).
Helling v. McKinney, 509 U.S. 25 (1993).
Hewitt v. Helms, 459 U.S. 460 (1983).
Hope v. Pelzer, 536 U.S. 730 (2002).
Hudson v. McMillian, 503 U.S. 1 (1992).
Hutto v. Finney, 437 U.S. 678 (1978).
Johnson v. Avery, 393 U.S. 483 (1969).
Johnson v. California, 125 S.Ct. 1141 (2005).
Lee v. Washington, 390 U.S. 333 (1968).
Lewis v. Casey, 516 U.S. 804 (1996).
Maltz, E. M. (2003). Introduction. In E. M. Maltz (Ed.), *Rehnquist justice: Understanding the Court dynamic* (pp. 1–7). Lawrence: University Press of Kansas.
Marquart, J. W., & Trulson, C. R. (2006). The first available house: Desegregation in American prisons and the road to *Johnson v. California. Corrections Compendium, 31*(5), 1–5, 12.
McKune v. Lile, 536 U.S. 24 (2002).
Miranda v. Arizona, 384 U.S. 436 (1966).
O'Lone v. Estate of Shabazz, 482 U.S. 342 (1987).
Overton v. Bazzetta, 539 U.S. 126 (2003).
Pennsylvania Department of Corrections v. Yeskey, 524 U.S. 206 (1998).
Porter v. Nussle, 534 U.S. 516 (2002).
Rhodes v. Chapman, 452 U.S. 337 (1981).
Richardson v. McKnight, 521 U.S. 399 (1997).
Robinson v. California, 370 U.S. 660 (1962).
Roper v. Simmons, 543 U.S. 551 (2005).
Sandin v. Conner, 515 U.S. 472 (1995).
Schultz, D. A., & Smith, C. E. (1996). *The jurisprudential vision of justice Antonin Scalia.* Lanham, MD: Rowman & Littlefield.
Shaw v. Murphy, 532 U.S. 223 (2001).
Smith, C. E. (2000a). The governance of corrections: Implications of the changing interface of courts and corrections. In C. M. Friel (Ed.), *Boundary changes in criminal justice organizations* (pp. 113–116). Washington, DC: National Institute of Justice.
Smith, C. E. (2000b). *Law and contemporary corrections.* Belmont, CA: Wadsworth.
Smith, C. E. (2001). The malleability of constitutional doctrine and its ironic impact on prisoners' rights. *Boston University Public Interest Law Journal, 11*(1), 73–96.
Smith, C. E. (2006a). Chief justice William Rehnquist and corrections law. *Corrections Compendium, 31*(5), 6–8, 41–42.
Smith, C. E. (2006b). The roles of justice John Paul Stevens in criminal justice cases. *Suffolk University Law Review, 39*(3), 719–744.
Smith, C. E., & Baugh, J. A. (2000). *The real Clarence Thomas: Confirmation veracity meets performance reality.* New York: Peter Lang.
Trop v. Dulles, 356 U.S. 86 (1958).
Turner v. Safley, 482 U.S. 78 (1987).

Whitley v. Albers, 475 U.S. 312 (1986).
Wilson v. Seiter, 501 U.S. 294 (1991).
Wolff v. McDonnell, 418 U.S. 539 (1974).

REVIEW QUESTIONS

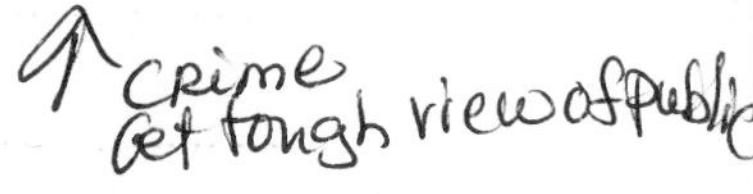

1. What role did the political climate of the 1980s and 1990s play in decision making of the Rehnquist Court? Provide concrete policy examples to illustrate your logic.
2. What, if any, common ground exists between the ideals of Justice Stevens and Justices Thomas and Scalia when it comes to prisoners' rights issues?
3. What are the key prisoner's rights issues that promise to come before the Roberts-led Court in the near future?
4. What is the principal legacy of the Rehnquist Court when it comes to prisoners' rights issues?

R E A D I N G 5

Constitutional Issues Arising from "Three Strikes and You're Out" Legislation

Frank A. Zeigler

Rolando V. del Carmen

This reading depicts "three strikes laws" as being among the most important legislative developments to impact correctional practices in the U.S. over the past century. Originating with the passage of a 1994 California law, three strikes legislation affords the courts the power to single out those repeat felons who commit a disproportionate amount of serious crime and incapacitate them with life in prison without the possibility of parole. This reading considers three strikes legislation in light of the Eighth Amendment to the United States Constitution and its prohibition on cruel and unusual punishment. Four major court cases are used as a means of illustrating the various constitutional issues that surround this extreme public safety legislation.

Seated at counsel table after an adverse jury verdict, the lawyer turned to the defendant to offer consolation. The client, realizing that all that could be done had been done, gave a wan smile and said, "You do the crime, you do the time." With that, the sheriff escorted the convicted felon away to serve a life sentence.

Over the years, that scenario has become familiar and is replayed daily in courts throughout the country. In contemporary language, the above aphorism might be more aptly stated: "You do the third crime, you do a lifetime." This reformulation is derived from the "three strikes and you're out" legislation passed in 1994 in California that is gaining momentum across the United States ("Recent Legislation," 1994).[1] The constitutional limits on these mandatory minimum sentencing schemes are left for the courts to resolve primarily by interpreting the "cruel and unusual punishments" clause of the Eighth Amendment and similar state constitutional provisions.

How the words *cruel and unusual* are defined by the courts reflects an evolving standard based on a developing societal view on punishment for crime. In *People v. Romero* (1995), the first constitutional test of California's new statute, the appellate court's decision reflects this public view in upholding three-strikes punishment. The opinion states that the ultimate test whether the statute is cruel and unusual or disproportionate can be determined by the results of California's initiative referendum (Proposition 184) conducted November 1994, in which the voters approved the new three-strikes law by a 72% to 28% margin. The judicial attitudes appear to be that the public has spoken; the appellate court defers to the will of the public. It is not always that simple, however.

This chapter examines, through decisions of the U.S. Supreme Court, the constitutional conflict presented when habitual offender statutes are challenged on Eighth Amendment grounds as being cruel and unusual. First, a brief historical background traces the origins of repeat offender provisions and the term *cruel and unusual punishment* and tracks their ultimate collision in the landmark case of *Rummel v. Estelle* (1980). Next, the chapter analyzes a trilogy of cases in the decade that followed that found the Supreme Court clearly divided on the constitutionality of three-strikes measures. Another section summarizes current applications of proportionality laws. A final section discusses the emerging constitutional challenge under the doctrine of separation of powers.

It must be noted at the outset that the legislative power to enact habitual offender laws similar to current three-strikes statutes has rarely been rejected by the courts on a constitutional basis, but when they have, it has been on disproportionality grounds. Given this, the main thrust of this chapter is on the proportionality doctrine as it relates to the cruel and unusual punishments clause of the Eighth Amendment. In essence, the proportionality doctrine prohibits a punishment more severe than that deserved by the offender for the harm caused or the acts committed. Over the years, the Supreme Court has woven an uneven tapestry of standards for evaluating three-strikes provisions, as the cases discussed below illustrate.

BACKGROUND

James Madison borrowed the phrase "cruel and unusual" from the English Bill of Rights of 1689 and incorporated these words into the Eighth Amendment to the U.S. Constitution in 1791. It is essentially a term of enlightenment—that government is obliged to respect the human dignity of its citizens. Traditionally, the framers were thought to have been concerned only with torturous punishment methods. The accepted view today, however, is that the framers' intention was to create a right to be free from excessive punishment ("The Effectiveness," 1961). Despite its importance as a constitutional protection, the debate on the inclusion of the phrase "cruel and unusual" at the Constitutional Convention involved just two speakers and featured fewer than 200 words.[2] From such inauspicious beginnings, this clause has evolved to become the major constitutional limitation on today's three-strikes legislation.

Serving as backdrop to the constitutional conflict between cruel and unusual punishment and the enhancement of the length of sentences for repeat offenders are two cases decided by the U.S. Supreme Court almost nine decades ago but whose effect is felt up to the present. These cases are seminal on the issue of cruel and unusual punishment.

Cruel and Unusual Punishment: *Weems v. United States*

The constitutional principle that the punishment should fit the crime was first articulated by the Supreme Court in *Weems v. United States* (1910). As sometimes happens in developing law, unusual circumstances gave birth to precedent. William Weems was convicted of falsifying a public document and was sentenced to 15 years of hard labor. His punishment included shackling at the ankle and wrist and permanent loss of a multitude of civil rights, including parental authority, property ownership, and permanent surveillance for life (*Weems,* 1910, p. 364).

The majority opinion began with unusual candor by admitting that there was no precedent, and little commentary, on the meaning of the words cruel and unusual from which to fashion an interpretation of the Eighth Amendment. Nevertheless, the Court went on to say that justice required that punishment for crime be graduated and proportioned to the offense (*Weems,* 1910, p. 367). Reasoning that the Constitution must be read in light of contemporary social needs, the Court took the course of a broad interpretation of the Eighth Amendment. Thus, the doctrine of proportionality was born. The test used to reverse the conviction was an objective comparison of punishments of similar crimes in other jurisdictions and a comparison with punishments for more serious crimes within the same jurisdiction (*Weems,* 1910, p. 380).

The decision can be read as the first pronouncement by the Supreme Court on the basic conflict between legislative enactment of punishment measures and judicial interpretation of their constitutionality. The power of the legislature to define crime and punishment is vast, but not absolute; therefore, constitutional limits exist. The Court, in sweeping language, recognized the evolutionary potential for humaneness in a broad application of the cruel and unusual punishments clause. *Weems* was a landmark holding in Eighth Amendment law; most scholars commenting on the decision were surprised by the ruling (Fredman, 1910). There had been little prior indication that the Court was inclined to expand the cruel and unusual punishments clause into the area of sentencing—using the proportionality rationale.

The proportionality doctrine enunciated in *Weems* must be viewed as the most important limitation on present three-strikes legislation. This Eighth Amendment protection, however, had to wait more than 50 years to be held applicable to state criminal proceedings. This came about in *Robinson v. California* (1962), where the defendant was given a 90-day sentence by the trial court for narcotics addiction. The Supreme Court nullified the sentence, saying that any imprisonment for merely being addicted, as opposed to being found in personal possession or selling a specific controlled narcotic, was disproportionate. The importance of *Robinson* is twofold: First, it placed limitations on the states to criminalize a person's status (e.g., addiction to drugs or vagrancy, having no money); second, for purposes of this chapter, it made proportionality review of criminal sentences applicable to the states through the due process clause of the Fourteenth Amendment. Prior to this, an Eighth Amendment analysis was used only for federal crimes.

Graham v. West Virginia and Early Habitual Offender Statutes

The Supreme Court's first review of habitual offender laws came in *Graham v. West Virginia* (1912). In that case, the Court traced their beginnings to English statutes that "inflicted severer punishment upon old offenders" (*Graham,* 1912, p. 625). The record does not disclose how "old" John H. Graham was. It does indicate he had previously been convicted of grand larceny and burglary before his final grand larceny conviction resulted in a life sentence under a forerunner three-strikes provision enacted in Virginia in 1796 and later codified when West Virginia was partitioned and entered statehood in 1863.

In the 19th century, a majority of states had statutes that enhanced punishment for previous felons (*Graham,* 1912, p. 622). The Court in *Graham* first disposed of the former jeopardy argument of twice being punished for the same crime (using the former convictions) before indicating that habitual offender laws did not constitute cruel and unusual punishment.

Early repeat offender statutes were cumbersome, requiring the warden of the receiving penitentiary to investigate a person's criminal history and return him for a second indictment and jury trial on his previous convictions. The sole issue at this trial was whether the "convict is the same person mentioned in several records."[3] With the Baumes Act (1926)[4] passed by New York and adopted by other states, the procedure was simplified into one proceeding with the defendant's prior record determined at his initial trial and his sentence enhanced accordingly.

California enacted a forerunner three-strikes provision in 1927.[5] Its purpose was more remedial than deterrent. The theory that a small number of offenders committed a majority of crimes was yet to be known and was not the rationale for the statute. Eleven other states in that era had similar statutes in effect that were designed to sentence nonviolent third offenders to life imprisonment. Criminal punishment at that time did not reflect the public frustration that currently drives three-strikes legislation, hence these early statutes were seldom used to incapacitate a certain category of offenders. California repealed its early version in 1935. By 1980, when the Supreme Court first fully examined the conflict between three-strikes laws and cruel and unusual punishment, only West Virginia, Washington, and Texas still had nonviolent three-strikes statutes in their penal codes (*Rummel,* 1980, p. 296, n. 13).

THE COLLISION: PROPORTIONALITY AND THREE STRIKES

Rummel v. Estelle (1980) was the first of four Supreme Court cases between 1980 and 1991 that yield seemingly inconsistent holdings on proportionality review. These decisions exemplify the struggle within the Court to clarify the parameters of punishment under three-strikes provisions and cruel and unusual punishment. This collision between criminal and constitutional law is discussed in the cases that follow.

Rummel v. Estelle: The Turning Point

William Rummel was convicted in Texas in 1964 of credit card fraud to obtain \$80.00 worth of goods; was convicted in 1969 of passing a forged check for \$28.36; and, in 1973, was convicted of obtaining money (\$120.75) by false pretenses. All three nonviolent offenses were classified as felonies under Texas law. Rummel was prosecuted for his third "strike" offense under the Texas equivalent three-strikes provision. Within the statute, a third-strike conviction would result in a mandatory life imprisonment. Pursuant to the statute, the trial judge imposed the obligatory life sentence (*Rummel,* 1980, pp. 264–266).

Thereafter, an intense constitutional debate ensued within the appellate courts on the proportionality of Rummel's sentence. The Texas Court of Criminal Appeals affirmed his conviction in *Rummel v. State* (1974). A divided panel of the Fifth Circuit reversed his conviction as disproportionate in *Rummel v. Estelle* (1978). On rehearing, the circuit court, sitting en banc, rejected the panel's ruling and affirmed the conviction in *Rummel v. Estelle* (1978). On appeal, the Supreme Court, Justice Rehnquist writing for a 5–4 majority, held that the state of Texas could constitutionally impose a sentence of life imprisonment for three sequential nonviolent felonies.

The Court justified the *Rummel* (1980) result by distancing it from the precedent of proportionality in *Weems* (1910), stressing that recent applications had been limited to death penalty cases such as *Coker v. Georgia* (1977) because of their finality. A "bright line" was thereby drawn between death and imprisonment. The majority reasoned that to do otherwise would invite imprecision in future cases in attempting to draw a clear line on different lengths of imprisonment (*Rummel,* 1980, p. 275). *Weems* was characterized as limited by its particular facts (shackling at the wrist and ankles); the Court emphasized the highly subjective character of legal analysis used in establishing constitutional limits on amounts of punishment. The Court concluded that punishment is traditionally a state instead of a federal concern and is purely a matter of legislative judgment (*Rummel,* 1980, p. 282).

In a dissent, premised on *Weems* and the humanitarian intent of the framers of the Constitution, Justice Powell opined that proportionality analysis is an inherent aspect of the cruel and unusual punishments clause. He felt a constitutional obligation to measure "the relationship between the nature and number of offenses committed and the severity of the punishment inflicted upon the offender" (*Rummel,* 1980, p. 288). Justice Powell laid out three objective criteria, earlier announced in *Weems,* for reviewing proportionality challenges to the length of criminal sentences: (a) the nature of the offense, (b) comparison with sentences imposed in other jurisdictions for commission of the same crime, and (c) comparison with sentences imposed in the same jurisdiction of commission of other crimes (*Rummel,* 1980, p. 295).

Applying these criteria, the dissent concluded that Rummel's sentence violated the Constitution. First, the strike offense of false pretenses was found to be nonviolent. Next, the dissent established that Texas punished repeat offenders dramatically harsher than other jurisdictions. Finally, within the Texas statutory equivalent three-strikes scheme, Rummel's sentence for three nonviolent felonies was harsher than for those first and second offenders who committed more serious crimes, such as murder or rape (*Rummel,* 1980, pp. 295–303). The majority conceded in a footnote that one could imagine extreme examples when the doctrine of proportionality would be an issue (*Rummel,* 1980, p. 274, n. 11).

The *Rummel* decision is best understood in the context of Justice Rehnquist's statement that defendant Rummel had been well informed of the consequences of repeated criminal conduct (two prior prison sentences) and given every opportunity to reform. Therefore, the early three-strikes statute was nothing more than a "societal decision that when such a person commits yet another felony, he should be subjected to the admittedly serious penalty of incarceration for life, subject only to the state's judgment as to whether to grant him parole" (*Rummel,* 1980, p. 278). To the dissenters, however, evolving standards of decency necessitated the Court's exercise of its historic role as the final interpreter of the cruel and unusual punishments clause and felt that under the circumstances of this case, the Court ought to have rejected the punishment as unconstitutional.

The battle to delineate the precise contours of proportionality was fought again 2 years later in *Hutto v. Davis* (1982). The decision exemplifies the intensity of the continuing debate over the three-strikes legislation.

Hutto v. Davis: Anarchy in the Fourth Circuit

In *Hutto v. Davis* (1982), the Supreme Court upheld the power of the states to punish repeat offenders with severe sentences, including first offenders. Although not a three-strikes decision, *Davis* (1982) is instructive because it set the stage for a reversal of *Rummel* (1980) a year later in *Solem v. Helm* (1983).

Roger Davis's first offense in 1976 resulted in conviction on two counts of both possessing with intent and distributing 9 ounces of marijuana. A Virginia jury set his sentences at 20 years on each charge to run consecutively, or a 40-year prison term. *Davis's* procedural history resulted in the Fourth Circuit reversing his conviction on proportionality grounds in 1979 (*Davis v. Davis,* 1979). Two weeks after issuing its mandate in *Rummel* (1980), the Supreme Court ordered *Davis* (1979) vacated and remanded for further consideration in light of *Rummel.*

On remand, the Fourth Circuit reaffirmed its earlier reversal, reasoning that Davis's sentence fell within that narrow group of "rare" cases the majority in *Rummel* had conceded in a footnote that the doctrine of proportionality might apply (*Davis v. Davis,* 1981). In the protocol of the Supreme Court's supervisory powers over the circuit courts, this rejection of *Rummel* was almost unprecedented, prompting the Court to again grant review and state that "unless we want anarchy to prevail within the federal judiciary, a precedent of this Court must be followed by the lower federal courts no matter how misguided the judges of those courts may think it to be" (*Hutto v. Davis,* 1982, p. 375).

In affirming Davis's punishment, Justice Burger defended the bright line drawn in *Rummel* between death penalty cases and varying lengths of imprisonment. *Davis's* major premise was that an Eighth Amendment review should not be subjective; the Court also concluded that the 40-year sentence was beyond the constitutional range of the federal courts (*Davis,* 1982, p. 373). Once again, the Court stressed that federal courts should be reluctant to review legislatively mandated terms of imprisonment, be it within a habitual offender scheme or otherwise. This reluctance is based on the Tenth Amendment, which reserves to each state the power to determine varying lengths of sentences for the same criminal violation. (Using this approach, grand larceny may carry a 10-year maximum for a first offense in one state and 2 years in another.)

Justice Powell concurred and followed the precedent of *Rummel,* perhaps in an effort to quell the uprising in the Fourth Circuit. He pointed out, however, that neither the majority in *Rummel* nor the majority in *Davis* had laid the doctrine of proportionality to rest (*Davis,* 1982, p. 277). In retrospect, Justice Powell's concurrence was the fulcrum for his opinion 1 year later in *Solem v. Helm* (1983), which would reverse an almost identical three-strikes provision in South Dakota.

Three justices dissented in *Davis,* distinguishing *Rummel* as a three-strikes case that was not applicable to the first offense before the Court. The dissent also refused to go along with the Court's criticism of the mischief of the Fourth Circuit Court of Appeals. Moreover, the dissent argued that this was one of those exceedingly rare cases where the disparity of Davis's punishment, in comparison to other sentences in Virginia for marijuana offenders, required reversal on proportionality grounds. To support this, the dissent alluded to an unusual letter from Davis's trial prosecutor, included in the record, which characterized the sentence as "grossly unjust" (*Davis,* 1982, p. 385).

The *Davis* decision resulted in uncertainty in the Eighth Amendment analysis of the length of legislative sentences for both repeat and first offenders. With the majority of the Court demanding objective criteria (while rejecting all proffered criteria as too subjective), the two leading opinions in *Rummel* and *Davis* resulted in legal confusion within various circles regarding the applicability and scope of proportionality review ("The Eighth Amendment," 1982). State courts were equally confused; some chose to disregard Supreme Court interpretation and proceeded instead to decide similar cases under their parallel state constitution's cruel and unusual punishments clause.[6]

Solem v. Helm: Three-Factor Proportionality for Three Strikes

Just three terms after *Rummel,* the Supreme Court, by a 5–4 majority in *Solem v. Helm* (1983), demonstrated that no constitutional precedent is safe from revision. In a dramatic departure, the Court reversed a three-strikes life imprisonment sentence.

Jerry Helm had spent much of his life in the penitentiary and had six previous nonviolent felony convictions. In 1979, he pleaded guilty to writing a bad check for $100. Instead of asking the trial court to sentence Helm under the South Dakota general criminal statute, which carried 5 years for the offense charged, the prosecutor proceeded under an equivalent three-strikes provision. This resulted in a life sentence (*Helm,* 1983, p. 280).

The trial court record reveals that the sentencing judge indicated to Helm that it would be up to him and the parole board when he would be released. Unknown to the judge, a buried provision in the statute provided that Helm was not eligible for parole.[7] This proved crucial to the reversal of the sentence by the Eighth Circuit in *Helm v. Solem* (1982) and provided the rationale for the majority decision in the Supreme Court.

Justice Powell, who dissented in *Rummel* (1980), began the majority opinion by tracing the origin of the cruel and unusual punishments clause and proportionality back to English common law and *Weems* (1910). The opinion stressed the need for deference to both the legislature and the sentencing courts. Such deference meant that successful proportionality challenges would be rare, but no sentence was beyond constitutional scrutiny. As he did in dissent in *Rummel,* Justice Powell opined that when sentences are reviewed under the Eighth Amendment, courts should be guided by three objective factors or the "Helm test": (a) a comparison of the gravity of the offense and the harshness of the penalty, (b) a comparison with sentences imposed for other crimes in the same jurisdiction, and (c) a comparison with sentences imposed for the same crime in other jurisdictions (*Helm,* 1983, pp. 291–292). Although these factors are relative, they are not purely subjective. Judges are assumed competent to make broad comparisons of crime, relative harm, and culpability; moreover, legal line-drawing has always been a standard technique of the judicial art.

Applying the *Helm* test to the facts, the majority concluded that the three-strikes sentence was cruel and unusual. The strike crime of writing a $ 100 check was nonviolent and involved a small amount. The statute carried heavy penalties for two prior convictions that the court also viewed as nonviolent, minor offenses. Life imprisonment without possibility of parole was the most severe punishment available in South Dakota, hence the first factor suggested an imbalance between crime and punishment. Second, the court reviewed punishment for other crimes in the state and found that only a few much more serious crimes were mandatorily punished by life imprisonment without parole. Thus, the Court concluded that Helm's life sentence was more severe than sentences that South Dakota imposed for far more serious crimes. Finally, the majority considered the sentence in the national context and concluded that Helm would have been punished less severely for his third offense in every other state (*Helm,* 1983, pp. 298–300).

Because *Rummel* (1980) and *Helm* (1983) were essentially the same case (involving three-strikes life imprisonment punishment for nonviolent offenders), Justice Powell distinguished the facts by emphasizing the difference between life imprisonment with and life imprisonment without parole. Parole is a regular part of the rehabilitative process, is governed by legal standards, and assuming good behavior, is the normal expectation of a defendant like Rummel. On the other hand, Helm's only possibility of release was executive clemency, which lacked articulable standards (*Helm,* 1983, p. 303).

The dissenters were outraged that the majority would apply the three-factor test that *Rummel* had categorically rejected as imprecise while rejecting the bright-line rule of *Rummel* (proportionality review only for death sentences). Chief Justice Burger's dissent further highlighted the intra-Court dissonance that mandatory minimum sentencing evokes and that would reoccur in *Harmelin v. Michigan* (1991). In conclusion, the dissent reiterated its concern that proportionality review of length of sentences would open the floodgates to lower courts making subjective determinations of excessive sentences.

This prediction proved to be false, however, in the 8 years that followed. Lower courts had little difficulty in applying Eighth Amendment proportionality to cases involving legislative determinations. During this period, only four state cases were reversed on the basis of the *Helm* three-factor test and none in the federal courts. These cases were *Clowers v. State* (1988), in which there was a reduction of a 15-year sentence without parole for a forged check; *Ashley v. State* (1989), in which there was a reduction of sentence for a defendant who burgled a home of $4.00 to pay for food eaten in a store; *Gilham v. State* (1988), in which the court struck down a felony conviction for using a vehicle in a criminal endeavor when the defendant had engaged in the lesser crime of prostitution; and *Naovarath v. State* (1989), in which the court set aside a life sentence without parole for an adolescent who killed an individual who repeatedly molested him.

The Eighth Amendment balance between crime and punishment in *Helm* would again change 8 years later when a divided Supreme Court issued a decision that would result in another reversal of precedent and a narrowing of the constitutional principle of proportionality review.

Harmelin v. Michigan: Proportionality "Strikes Out"

The war on drugs served as the catalyst for a third 5–4 Supreme Court decision on the constitutionality of three-strikes measures and similar mandatory minimum sentencing schemes. In *Harmelin v. Michigan* (1991), the Court again reversed itself on when proportionality review can be applied and returned full circle to principles announced a decade earlier in *Rummel.* The disagreement over the contours of the Eighth Amendment, as applied to legislative punishment, is evidenced by the five separate opinions the decision generated.

Ronald Harmelin was stopped for a routine traffic violation. A search of his vehicle revealed 672 grams of cocaine. Michigan's statute required that Harmelin be sentenced to life imprisonment (for possession of more than 650 grams) with no possibility of parole even though he had no prior felony record. Review was granted by the Supreme Court to consider the issue of whether a mandatory life sentence constitutes cruel and unusual punishment.

Justice Scalia rejected the principle that the Eighth Amendment requires a proportionality review for non-death penalty cases and called for the overruling of *Helm* (1983). Only Chief Justice Rehnquist, however, shared this view. The other three members of the plurality, led by Justice Kennedy, discerned a narrow proportionality doctrine in the Eighth Amendment, even though they agreed with Justice Scalia that there was nothing unconstitutional about Harmelin's sentence (*Harmelin,* 1991, p. 1008). The four dissenting justices argued, in three separate opinions, that mandatory sentences or three-strikes provisions like *Helm* called for more searching analysis.[8]

The decision's balance tilted in the direction of Justice Kennedy's concurrence. It began with a recognition of *Helm's* three-factor test and a narrow proportionality doctrine. To provide guidance in limiting appellate review of sentences, the concurring opinion rejected Harmelin's contention that full comparative analysis under *Helm's* three factors was required. Justice Kennedy stated that under the first prong—severity of the crime and harshness of penalty—Harmelin's sentence was proportionate. With that threshold determination, an analysis of the second and third prongs of *Helm* became unnecessary. This conclusion was rested on the three-part severity of Harmelin's drug offense: (a) A drug user may commit crime because of drug-induced changes in cognitive ability, (b) a drug user may commit crime to buy drugs, and (c) a violent crime may occur as part of the drug culture (*Harmelin,* 1991, p. 1002).

To support its position, the plurality cited results from *Drug Use Forecasting* (National Institute of Justice, 1990), in which a vast majority of arrestees had tested positive for illegal drugs. Therefore, Justice Kennedy reasoned that the Michigan legislature could conclude that because of the link between drugs, violence, and crime, the possession of large amounts of cocaine warranted the deterrence and retribution of a life sentence.

The decision in *Harmelin* (1991) represents a subtle shift in the balance between severity of crime and harshness of punishment from one of disproportionality to that of gross disproportionality. In conceding the harmful effects of drug trafficking on the nation, the Court failed to take into account defendant Harmelin's low position in the drug hierarchy or his first-offense status. In *Rummel* (1980), *Davis* (1982), and *Helm* (1983), the Court examined the nature of the crimes and the history of the individual defendants. In *Harmelin* (1991) the focus was on the abhorrent nature of the drug problem and its current status as "one of the greatest problems affecting the health and welfare of our population" (p. 1002).

THE IMPLICATIONS OF *HARMELIN:* CURRENT APPLICATIONS OF PROPORTIONALITY TO THREE-STRIKES LEGISLATION

Federal Courts

The four cases analyzed above constitute a roller-coaster ride in Supreme Court proportionality review. Seldom has a constitutional amendment generated such closely split decisions as the cruel and unusual punishments clause has in defining the legislative parameters of three-strikes laws and mandatory sentences. Using the antidrug justification in *Harmelin,* the Court stripped the Eighth Amendment of much of its potential to prohibit the lifelong imprisonment of individuals for one offense and, correspondingly, of three-strikes offenders (see, generally, Vandy, 1993).

Under the last-decided-best-decided theory of legal precedent, only the extremely rare case wherein the punishment is grossly disproportionate to the crime will the threshold of *Harmelin* be crossed. Although the Court has not completely retreated to the bright-line rule of applying the Eighth Amendment only to death penalty cases, three-strikes measures similar to the California statute appear well poised to withstand constitutional challenges. Federal courts have cited *Harmelin* as the dispositive case in Eighth Amendment challenges, and three recent circuit court opinions appear to have settled the issue at the federal level at least for now.[9]

California's Three-Strikes Statute and Proportionality

The preceding discussion has highlighted the Supreme Court's view of proportionality under the Eighth Amendment of the U.S. Constitution. The California three-strikes statute has prompted other jurisdictions to implement similar legislation that will likely result in legal challenges.

As proportionality challenges develop, each state must chose between the holding of *Harmelin* under federal law or interpret its three-strikes measure under its own state constitution's cruel and unusual punishments clause. In *Romero* (1995), mentioned earlier, the California Court of Appeals looked to the California Constitution in holding the statute constitutional (*Romero,* 1995, p. 378). In a departure from *Harmelin,* the court applied the three-factor *Helm* test while mandating defendant Romero's sentence of 25 years to life for his third conviction.

In another departure, the Michigan Supreme Court, a year after *Harmelin,* reconsidered its 650-gram "lifer" law and held in *People v. Bullock* (1992) that such sentences for simple possession for first offenders were disproportionate to the crime under the Michigan state constitutional provision against cruel and unusual punishment. The decision used the three-objective criteria of *Helm* to examine the individual circumstances of defendant Bullock and concluded that it would be unfair to impute full responsibility of the defendant for any unintended consequences that might be later committed by others in connection with the seized cocaine (*Bullock,* 1992, p. 876). The decision applied only to those convicted of simple possession, which meant Ronald Harmelin's earlier sentence was reduced to life, with eligibility for parole in 10 years.

Summary of Current Varying Interpretations of the Proportionality Review

In general, federal courts are currently in accord with the "grossly disproportionate" approach announced in *Harmelin* (1991). In contrast, at the state level, *Romero* (1995) retains the objective comparison criteria of *Helm* (1983) in applying a somewhat cursory proportionality review. Finally, *Bullock* (1992) totally rejects *Harmelin* by engaging in extended proportionality review using the three factors of *Helm,* along with the individual circumstances of the defendant, to find Michigan's 650-gram life statute cruel and unusual. *Bullock* represents that rare situation where in-depth analysis favors the defendant (*Helm,* 1983, p. 285).

The difference in the above approaches is central to determining the balance between crime and punishment and the constitutionality of three-strikes laws. Proportionality of the length of sentence is determined by each court's application of the three-step sequence of objective criteria of *Helm* to Eighth Amendment review. As with most balancing analyses, the difficulty remains in identifying important variables, assigning them a weight, and deciding their cumulative effect (*Helm,* 1983, pp. 292–295).

Although *Harmelin* appears to severely limit the three criteria in *Helm,* chances are that most initial state court decisions will follow the extended analysis of *Helm* in reviewing their respective three-strikes legislation. This is evident in the *Romero* and *Bullock* state court decisions. The fact that *Harmelin* was divided on a 5–4 plurality lessens its precedential value. A comparison between the gravity of the offense and the harshness of the penalty is a matter of judicial determination. The other two factors in *Helm*—comparison of sentences for other crimes in the same jurisdiction and comparison with sentences for the same crime in other jurisdictions—induce a deference to preferences expressed by the state legislature. It is within this framework that three-strikes statutes will likely be decided. Rare, then, will be a case that will favor the defendant. Even in that case, a successful proportionality challenge does not set the defendant free; instead, it merely obliges the state to resentence within broad constitutional limits.

PERSPECTIVE: MANDATORY SENTENCING AND THE EMERGING CONSTITUTIONAL ISSUE OF SEPARATION OF POWERS

It is evident from court decisions that currently the Eighth Amendment is a limited source for invalidating three-strikes statutes. *Solem v. Helm* (1983) stands as the only Supreme Court decision declaring a criminal sentence disproportionate. The opinion, however, was based on the nonviolent nature of Helm's three offenses coupled with a no-parole provision within the early South Dakota three-strikes statute.[10]

The new California law,[11] learning well the lesson of *Helm,* requires that prior strike crimes be "violent" or "serious"[12] (the current offense can be any felony). The statute also provides for parole release, but increases the length of imprisonment for offenders with one prior by reducing the "good time" credits prisoners can earn from one half to only one fifth of the total sentence and mandating a minimum of 25 years for those with two or more prior convictions.

At first glance, the California law appears to comport with the essentials of *Helm.* A closer examination, however, reveals an important distinction. The South Dakota trial judge who sentenced defendant Helm had the option to dismiss from the record Helm's previous nonviolent crimes, thereby avoiding the imposition of a life sentence without parole if the court was persuaded that such punishment was not proportionate to the offense of writing a $100 bad check. Under the California three-strikes scheme, this individualized, proportionate review does not exist. Only the prosecution is vested with the power to dismiss a prior strike conviction(s).[13] This legislative change in the balance of power in the sentencing process is emerging as a second constitutional challenge to three-strikes legislation.

In the context of criminal punishments, our system of checks and balances separates the power to punish the offender within three constitutional functions. The legislature has inherent power to define and provide punishment for crime, the executive has the power to prosecute criminal conduct, and the judiciary has the duty to provide a remedy for legislative and executive excesses (*People v. Tenono,* 1970).

Other three-strikes laws in various states include statutory provisions, similar to those in the California law, that abrogate the longstanding historical power of judges to discretionarily impose criminal punishments. Not unexpectedly,

Proposition 184 represents the public's displeasure with the judicial system's "revolving door" and "soft on crime" judges, who use loopholes to reduce punishment (*Romero,* 1995, p. 377).

The emerging separation-of-powers constitutional challenge is exemplified in *Romero* (1995), the first appellate decision on California's three-strikes statute. Jesus Romero had five previous felony convictions when he was arrested for possession of one tenth of a gram of cocaine. Two of the prior convictions were for residential burglary, qualifying Romero with two strikes ("life priors") and a mandatory sentence of 25 years to life imprisonment. The trial judge dismissed from the record Romero's two strikes and imposed a sentence of 6 years, reasoning that the mandatory sentence constituted cruel and unusual punishment under the California Constitution, The trial court further opined that the three-strikes provision that allowed only the executive (prosecutor) to dismiss prior convictions violated separation of powers (*Romero,* 1995, p. 371).

On review, the California Court of Appeals rejected the trial court's determinations and returned the case with instructions to sentence Romero in accordance with three strikes (25 years to life imprisonment). Addressing the issue of separation of powers, the court found the narrowing of judicial discretion to dismiss strike convictions as consistent with the public's pronouncement in Proposition 184 that the judiciary keep its "hands off three strikes" and the certainty of the statute's punishment for repeat offenders (*Romero,* 1995, p. 377).

The decision was also premised on a narrowing of prosecutorial discretion contained within the law. Whereas three strikes grants the prosecutor sole authority to dismiss strike convictions "in the interest of justice," other provisions[14] require the executive to plead and prove all prior convictions available on a defendant, thus eliminating a valuable tool from a prosecutor's plea bargaining arsenal. The appelate court found a balance in the statute because the legislature had placed limitations on the use of discretion on both the judicial and executive branches of government (*Romero,* 1995, p. 373). As this chapter goes to press, *Romero* is pending before the California Supreme Court.

The U.S. Supreme Court has yet to determine the constitutionality of state statutes that curtail the traditional authority of judges in the sentencing process. Interestingly, the Court has previously affirmed prosecutorial discretion on the use of prior convictions in the plea bargaining process. In *Bordenkircher v. Hayes* (1978), the defendant was offered a 5-year sentence by the prosecutor in exchange for a plea of guilty. Hayes did not plead guilty and was charged with being a habitual offender under Kentucky law. He was convicted and sentenced to life imprisonment. The Supreme Court upheld Hayes's conviction and concluded, in a 5–4 decision, that the prosecutor's alleged vindictiveness was within the sound discretion of prosecutorial authority (*Hayes,* 1978, p. 358).

Hayes would appear to be inconsistent with three-strikes limitations on a prosecutor's discretion to use prior strike convictions in the plea bargaining process. The narrowing of both judicial and executive authorities in three strikes, therefore, may result in legal challenges from both branches of government as state legislatures across the nation expand their power to punish offenders who "strike out" for the third time.

CONCLUSION

Over the years, the Supreme Court has struggled with the concept of cruel and unusual punishment as applied to sentencing. The standard is proportionality. The Court has shown deference to punishment choices made by state legislatures, sometimes bowing to political realities when resolving constitutional dilemmas. In *Rummel* (1980), the majority sought to develop havens behind which to retreat. In *Davis* (1982), the majority had difficulty implementing its policy decision. In *Helm* (1983), a new majority of those present at *Rummel* recognized the inability of some state criminal justice systems to guard constitutional rights under the Eighth Amendment. In reaffirming principles of proportionality in sentencing, the *Helm* majority reasserted its role as final arbiter of the Constitution. The emergence of the drug wars brought with it the *Harmelin* (1991) plurality and ushered in three-strikes legislation and a return to legislative deference.

These four Court decisions first clarified and then confused proportionality review. Even if the states retain the objective criteria of the three-factor test of *Helm* after *Harmelin,* it is unlikely that there will be many three-strikes reversals. With mandatory sentencing severely hampering judicial discretion, the appellate courts might assert their authority and reject, under the doctrine of separation of powers, legislative provisions within three-strikes statutes that transfer sentencing discretion to the executive branch. Because the contest is being played in their ballpark and because they make the crucial calls, courts may ultimately find a way to limit three-strikes punishments and the courts' assumption that prior convictions contain all the information needed for justice to be served. Should that happen, the judiciary will then have redefined its role in society's continuing search for a system of justice where the punishment truly fits the crime.

NOTES

1. Seventeen other states have implemented similar three-strikes measures in which the third strike results in a calculated low end (usually 25 years) to life imprisonment, with differing parole restrictions. Five other states are debating similar measures. See also *People v. Romero,* 37 Cal. Rptr.2d 364, 381 (1995) for a list of states with three-strikes laws.
2. *Annals of the Congress of the United States* (J. Bales, Ed., Vol. 1), 754 (1789).
3. Code of West Virginia, chap. 165, sec. 4 (1863).
4. New York Penal Laws, para. 1941 et seq. (1926).
5. California Statutes, chap. 634, para. 1, p. 1066 (1927).
6. See, for example, *State v. MuLally*, 127 Ariz. 92, 618 P.2d 586 (1980); *State v. Fain,* 94 Wash.2d. 387, 517 P.2d 720 (1980).
7. South Dakota Codified Laws, para. 24-15-4 (1979). See also Aked (1984).
8. Justice White dissented, joined by Justices Blackmun and Stevens. Justice Marshall filed a separate dissenting opinion. Justice Stevens also filed a dissenting opinion in which Justice Blackmun also joined.

9. See *United States v. Kramer,* 955 F.2d 479 (7th Cir. 1992); *United States v. Lowden,* 955 F.2d 128 (1st Cir. 1992); *United States v. Hopper,* 941 F.2d 419 (6th Cir. 1991). But compare in *Austin v. United States,* 113 S. Ct. 2801 (1993), the Court reversed a civil forfeiture as disproportionate under the excessive fines clause of the Eighth Amendment.
10. South Dakota Comp. Laws Ann., para. 22-6-1 (1969).
11. California Penal Code, sec. 667(b)–(i).
12. California Penal Code, sec. 667(d).
13. California Penal Code, sec. 667(f)(2).
14. California Penal Code, sec. 667(f)(1) and (g)(1).

CASES

Ashley v. State, 538 So.2d 762 (Miss. 1989).
Bordenkircher v. Hayes, 434 U.S. 357 (1978).
Clowers v. State, 522 So.2d 762 (Miss. 1988).
Coker v. Georgia, 433 U.S. 584 (1977).
Davis v. Davis, 601 F.2d 153 (4th Cir. 1979) (en banc).
Davis v. Davis, 646 F.2d 123 (4th Cir. 1981).
Gilham v. State, 549 N.E.2d 555 (Oh. 1988).
Graham v. West Virginia, 224 U.S. 616 (1912).
Harmelin v. Michigan, 501 U.S. 957 (1991).
Helm v. Solem, 684 F.2d 582 (8th Cir. 1982).
Hutto v. Davis, 454 U.S. 370 (1982).
Naovarath v. State, 779 P.2d 944 (Nev. 1989).
People v. Bullock, 485 N.W.2d 866 (Mich. 1992).
People v. Romero, 37 Cal. Rptr.2d 364 (1995).
People v. Tenono, 473 P.2d 933 (Cal. 1970).
Robinson v. California, 370 U.S. 660 (1962).
Rummel v. Estelle, 568 F.2d 1193 (5th Cir. 1978).
Rummel v. Estelle, 587 F.2d 651 (5th Cir. 1978) (en banc).
Rummel v. Estelle, 445 U.S. 263 (1980).
Rummel v. State, 509 S.W.2d 630 (Tex. Crim. App. 1974).
Solem v. Helm, 463 U.S. 277 (1983).
Weems v. United States, 217 U.S. 349 (1910).

REFERENCES

Aked, J. (1984). Solem v. Helm: The Supreme Court extends the proportionality requirement to sentences of imprisonment. *Wisconsin Law Review,* pp. 1401–1430.

The effectiveness of the Eighth Amendment: An appraisal of cruel and unusual punishment [Note]. (1961). *New York University Law Review, 36,* 846.

The Eighth Amendment: Judicial self-restraint and legislative power [Note]. (1982). *Marquette Law Review, 65,* 434–443.

Fredman. (1910). Comment on recent judicial decisions—Cruel and unusual punishment. *Journal of Criminal Law, 1,* 612.

National Institute of Justice. (1990, June). *Drug use forecasting annual report* (Vol. 9). Washington, DC: Author.

Recent legislation: California enacts enhancement for prior felony convictions [Note]. (1994). *Harvard Law Review, 107,* 2123.

Vandy, K. (1993). Mandatory life sentences with no possibility of parole for first time drug possessors is not cruel and unusual punishment, *Harmelin v. Michigan,* 501 U.S. 957 (1991) [Note]. *Rutgers Law Review, 23,* 883.

REVIEW QUESTIONS

1. What are the origins and original intent of the phrase "cruel and unusual punishment"?
2. From where did three-strikes legislation originate, and what are the legal foundations and background of these laws?
3. What is the concept of "proportionality," and how does it apply to legal challenges to three-strikes laws?

III

THE PSYCHOLOGY OF IMPRISONMENT

READING 6

Ambivalent Actions

Prison Adaptation Strategies of First-Time, Short-Term Inmates

Thomas J. Schmid

Richard S. Jones

A person who is incarcerated for the first time becomes a "prisoner" but does not automatically acquire a meaningful status within the prison world. If the incarceration is short term, the person is unlikely to ever achieve a significant prison status because participation in the prison world will be inhibited by identification with the outside world. This condition of social marginality results in an ambivalence that directly shapes inmates' strategies for survival within the prison world. This article examines the effect of ambivalence on inmates' adaptation strategies. Data for the study were collected through participant observation and focused interviews with inmates at a maximum security prison for men.

This reading describes first-time inmates sentenced to short prison terms as being marginal members of the prison community. Because of their relatively short stay in the correctional environment, it is argued that such inmates both do not develop an identity as a "prisoner" and are never fully integrated to the culture of correctional facilities and populations. As such, inmates hold on to their identities and perspectives established prior to coming to prison; they experience ambivalence—a sense of disconnectedness and noninvestment—regarding their time and experiences in prison. This lack of connectedness to the prison environment has direct effects on the ways that such inmates adapt on a daily basis to prison life.

"DOING TIME" in a maximum security prison is not simply a matter of being in prison. It is, rather, a creative process through which inmates must invent or learn a repertoire of adaptation tactics that address the varying problems they confront during particular phases of their prison careers.

There is an extensive literature on the informal organization of prison life and the socialization processes through which inmates come to participate in this informal organization. Clemmer (1958) defines prisonization as "the taking on in greater or lesser degree of the folkways, customs, and general culture of the penitentiary" (p, 279). Prisonization is thus fundamentally a process of cultural accommodation through which inmates are first initiated into and then made a part of the prison social and cultural system. Neither of the two theoretical models developed to account for inmate adaptations to imprisonment—the "deprivation model" (Goffman 1961; Sykes [1959] 1971; Sykes and Messinger 1960) or the "importation model" (Thomas 1973; Thomas and Peterson 1977)—adequately represent the multiple ambiguities faced by the sociologically distinctive category of inmates who have no prior experience with the prison world and whose imprisonment is relatively brief.

When first-time inmates are sentenced to prison they have already lost their status as free adults but have not yet achieved any meaningful status within the prison world; they are, to older inmates, “fish” (see Cardozo-Freeman 1984; Irwin 1980). They can shed this label through their increasing participation in prison life, but if they are short-term inmates as well as first-timers they are unlikely to ever achieve a significant prison status. Their participation in the prison world will continue to be inhibited by their ties to, and identification with, the outside world. Their social marginality, grounded both in place and in time, is thus parallel to that experienced by immigrants who expect to return to their country of origin within a few years' time (see Morawska 1987; Shokeid 1988) or who otherwise manage to maintain a “sojourner orientation” (Gibson 1988). Immigrant sojourners, however, can typically draw on shared symbols or institutions in their transient adaptations to a new culture. New inmates, in contrast, have little in common with one another except their conventionality (Schmid and Jones 1991) and consequently have fewer collective resources available to resist assimilation into the prison culture.

In this article, we examine how first-time, short-term inmates in a maximum security prison make use of their social marginality, and the sociological ambivalence that results from it, to forge highly delimited adaptation strategies to the prison culture. After describing our methodological approach and fieldwork experiences, we briefly summarize our earlier analysis, which demonstrated that the social marginality of the first-time, short-term inmates we studied shaped their experiential orientations toward the prison world. We then analyze the relationship between ambivalence and inmates' prison strategies and discuss the extended sociological implications of our findings.

METHOD

Ordinarily, one of the most difficult steps in sociological research on prisons is gaining unrestricted access to inmates' day-to-day lives within the prison world. Our study originated with such access, when one of the authors (R. Jones) was serving a year-and-a-day sentence in a maximum security prison for men in the upper midwestern region of the United States. Through negotiations with prison officials, Jones was permitted to enroll in a graduate sociology course in field methods. What began as a directed studies course between professor and former student rapidly evolved, at Jones's suggestion, into a more comprehensive project conducted by co-researchers. At the same time, it evolved from a general observational study of prison life to an analysis of the prison experiences of first-time, short-term inmates.

Jones's prison sentence, our decision to conduct the study together, and our focus on first-time, short-term inmates offered us an unusual strategy for balancing the participant observer's needs for both objective and intimate knowledge about the group or culture being studied (see Davis 1973). This balance can be particularly difficult to achieve in prison research, where suspicions about academic roles often lead researchers to cultivate alternative roles that are more acceptable or better defined (Giallombardo 1966; Jacobs 1977). The circumstances of our study enabled us to examine the prison world for a period of 10 months from the combined viewpoints of both a “complete participant” and a “complete observer” (Gold 1958).

As the "inside observer," Jones had a number of specific advantages. In his interactions with other inmates and with guards, he was not viewed as a sociologist or a student or any other kind of outsider: He was viewed as a prisoner. Moreover, he was not merely assuming the role of a prisoner to learn about the prison world—he *was* a prisoner. He literally shared the experiences of other first-time, short-term inmates, enabling him to contextualize his observations of others with a full measure of sociological introspection (Ellis 1991). Because of his prior training, which included an undergraduate degree in sociology, a university course in participant observation, and a supervised field research project, he was also prepared to document his own experiences and those of his fellow inmates.

Any researcher role closes as well as opens lines of information, and Jones's role had certain limitations as well. As a new inmate, he did not have immediate access to the entire prison world, a limitation that directly influenced our decision to focus on the experiences of first-time inmates. He was also constrained by prison interaction norms, especially those governing relations between members of different racial or ethnic groups. At the prison we studied, these norms were not entirely rigid, but they were sufficiently strong to suggest that Jones's initial observations primarily depicted the experiences of White inmates. (We were able to compensate for this racial selectivity to some extent through a second phase of our fieldwork.) Finally, the most critical question about any "auto-ethnography" (Hayano 1979,1982) is whether researchers will be able to examine their own social world objectively. Jones expressed concerns about his objectivity early in the directed studies course; it was in response to this problem that we agreed to conduct the research together.

As the "outside" observer for the project, Schmid attempted to guide the direction of the fieldwork by placing Jones's observations in a sociological context—suggesting theoretical concepts that could be useful, additional questions that might be asked, methods that could be used to address these questions, and procedures through which we could test the validity of Jones's initial observations. Schmid also supplemented Jones's field notes with his own observations at the prison, and took a primary role in data analysis.

Our fieldwork essentially began with a journal that Jones started keeping several days before the beginning of his sentence. His early entries were predominantly personal expressions, although they included more traditional ethnographic descriptions as well. Once our research project was formally initiated, Jones restricted his journal entries to personal thoughts and impressions and chronology of his daily experiences. Using a process similar to the "diary-interview" method described by Zimmerman and Wieder (1977), these entries provided a framework for extended conversations between the researchers. Schmid's notes on these conversations were then used to derive new observational strategies and to identify potential analytic themes.

In addition to journal entries, Jones also prepared field notes on his participation in prison activities, his conversations with individual prisoners and groups of inmates, and his general observations of prison life. This procedure meant that the journal and the field notes contained different kinds of information, and it had the additional advantage of keeping the field notes more objective than they otherwise might have been. Although these general observations incorporated the experiences of hundreds of prisoners, most of the field notes were based on his repeated, often daily, contacts with about 50 inmates as well as on personal relationships established with a smaller number of inmates.

We were able to discuss our research progress through letters, occasional telephone calls, and regular meetings arranged with the cooperation of prison officials. Shortly after the beginning of the study, we settled on a communication routine that proved to be quite efficient. Jones prepared one to three field observations each week (averaging 8–10 handwritten pages) and mailed them to Schmid for annotation and suggestions. Every other week Schmid would meet with Jones in an office or testing room provided by the prison's education department. At these meetings, we would review the journal entries and observations, plan our research strategy, and piece together our emerging conceptualization of the prison world.

Following Jones's release from prison, we devoted a year to the analysis of our initial data, and then returned to the prison to conduct focused interviews. Using information provided by prison officials, we were able to identify and interview 20 additional first-time, short-term inmates. The fieldwork we had already completed guided our preparation of the interview questions, which addressed inmates' changing prison imagery and adaptation tactics as they progressed through their prison careers. We decided that Jones should do the actual interviewing, on the assumption that inmates would be more willing to talk freely with someone who had only recently completed his own prison sentence. To retain the methodological advantages of having both an "inside" and "outside" observer, Schmid reviewed a tape recording of each interview so that we could continuously refine the interviewing procedures.

Our analysis of the prison experiences of first-time, short-term inmates thus draws on three primary sources of data. Our principal source is the field notes, representing 10 months of participant observation by a "complete participant" in collaboration with a "complete observer." Included in these notes are specific events and interactions, quotations from Jones's fellow inmates, and general observations of the prison world. A second source is Jones's prison journals in which he recorded his own prison experiences. We used these journals throughout our project as a form of research development, and we draw on them to illustrate portions of our analytic model. Our subsequent interviews with other inmates constitute our third source of data; these interviews allowed us to pursue a number of topics in greater depth and provided us with an independent source of data to test our initial findings.

MARGINALITY, PRISON IMAGERY, AND PRISON ADAPTATIONS

Our earlier analysis of experiential orientations to prison (Schmid and Jones 1990) demonstrated that, at the beginning of their sentences, first-time, short-term inmates defined prison from the perspective of an outsider, drawing on the shared public meanings that exist in our society about prison. By the midpoint of their sentences they had not lost their outsiders' perspective completely and still had only a marginal status within the prison world, but they nonetheless defined prison principally in terms of shared subcultural meanings learned from other inmates. This "insider's perspective," however, subsequently gave way to concluding images that again expressed an outsider's point of view. (More precisely, their concluding imagery was a reflection of their marginal involvement in both worlds; it was a synthesis of their anticipatory and midcareer images and hence a synthesis of their outsider's and insider's perspectives.) These changes in prison imagery are summarized in Table 1.

Inmates' subjective understandings of the prison world are important because they provide a basis for action (Blumer 1969). Our earlier analysis also demonstrated, in a general way, how inmates' adaptation strategies followed their shifting prison imagery (as summarized in Figure 1). For example, in response to the violence of their initial outsider's imagery, their earliest survival tactics were protective and defensive in nature. As cultural outsiders, however, new inmates also recognized their need for more information about the prison world, and virtually all of their early survival tactics served as information seeking as well as protective measures. Thus territorial caution, impression management, and their partnerships (a friendship with another prisoner recognized by other inmates and guards) guided their ventures into the cafeteria, the yard, the gym, and other unexplored areas of the prison. Selective interaction with other inmates, impression management, and their partnerships helped them confront such prison experiences as parole board hearings, cell transfers, legal and illegal recreational activities, and participation in the prison economy. The barrage of often conflicting information they received through these tactics was the raw material out of which they continuously revised their prison images. Although they continued to view prison with

TABLE 1 Orientation and Prison Imagery

	Preprison	Prison	Postprison
Inmate perspective	Outside looking in	Inside looking in	Inside looking out
Central concerns	Violence/uncertainty	Boredom	Uncertainty
Specific problems	Survival	Endurance	Re-integration
Orientation to space	Prison as separate world	Prison as familiar territory	Prison as separate world
Orientation to time	Sentence as lost time	Killing time/time as measure of success	Sentence as lost time/ using time
Supportive others	Family and friends	Partners	"Real" family and friends
Perception of sentence	Justified and unfortunate	Arbitrary and unjust	Arbitrary and unjust (intensified)
Predominant emotion	Fear	Detachment	Apprehension (about outside)

ANTICIPATORY IMAGE Outsider's perspective: violence; uncertainty; fear	→	**ANTICIPATORY SURVIVAL STRATEGY** Protective resolutions: to avoid unnecessary contacts with inmates; to avoid unnecessary contacts with guards; not to be changed in prison; to disregard questionable information; to avoid all hostilities; to engage in self-defense if hostilities arise
		↓
		SURVIVAL STRATEGY Territorial caution Selective interaction with inmates Impression management with inmates Partnership with another inmate Redefinition of prison violence as "explained" rather than random events
		↓
MIDCAREER IMAGE Insider's perspective: boredom	→	**ADAPTATION STRATEGY** Legal and illegal diversions Suppression of thoughts about outside world Minimization of outside contacts Impression management with inmates and outsiders Partnership
		↓
CONCLUDING IMAGE Synthetic perspective: revision of prison image and reformulation of outside image	→	**DISSIPATION OF ADAPTATION STRATEGY** Continued diversions Decreasing impression management Decreasing suppression of outside thoughts Disassociation with partner Formulation of outside plan

FIGURE 1 Prison Images and Strategies

essentially an outsider's perspective, their survival tactics allowed them gradually to acquire an insider's knowledge of the prison and to modify their adaptation tactics accordingly.

A common form of prison adaptation is the creation of a survival "niche" (Seymour 1977) that allows inmates some measure of activity, privacy, safety, emotional feedback, structure, and freedom within the larger, hostile environment of the maximum security prison (Johnson 1987; Toch 1977). Because of their inexperience, first-time inmates were particularly ill-equipped for finding such niches (Johnson 1987,114), and new short-term inmates were further handicapped by their continuing marginality in the prison world, which restricted their ability to exert personal control (Goodstein, MacKenzie, and Shotland 1984) and inhibited their acceptance by other inmates. But short-term inmates, in contrast to those facing years of imprisonment, needed only to develop a *transient* niche in prison. The problems they faced were similar—understanding the prison status hierarchy and recognizing their place in it, learning whom to trust and whom to avoid, and determining how to evade trouble in a trouble-filled environment—but their solutions did not need to be as enduring. The men we studied were able to achieve such transient "accommodation without assimilation" (Gibson 1988) within a few months' time. To a casual observer, moreover, they soon became indistinguishable from long-term inmates, relying on such adaptive tactics as legal and illegal diversions and conscious efforts to control their thoughts about the outside world. Their relative integration into the prison world was short-lived, however, and their marginality within this world again became evident as they prepared for their departure from prison. Like more experienced inmates, their preparatory concerns included both practical problems, such as finding a job and a place to live, and existential concerns about how the outside world had changed and how the inmates themselves had changed during their time in prison (see Irwin 1970). Faced with these problems, it became increasingly apparent to inmates that most (though not all) of the adaptation tactics associated with their prison orientation were inadequate for dealing with the outside world.

Based on this general pattern, it is tempting to infer that inmates' adaptations strategies change simply because their reference group changes. In this explanation, suggested by Wheeler's (1961) finding of a curvilinear relationship between institutional career phase and conformity to staff expectations, inmates come to abandon the beliefs, values, and norms of the outside world as they acquire more information about and eventually achieve membership in the prison world. In similar fashion, they abandon the beliefs, values, and norms of the prison world when they are about to regain membership in the outside world. Our earlier analysis (Schmid and Jones 1990) challenged this explanation by focusing on inmates' continuous and active work to *interpret* the prison world. This explanation becomes even more unsatisfactory when we introduce into our analysis the ambivalence that inmates experience throughout their entire prison careers.

AMBIVALENCE AND PRISON STRATEGIES

In its most general sense, ambivalence refers to the experience of being pulled in psychologically different directions; because prison inmates *share* this experience, it becomes sociologically as well as psychologically significant. The ambivalence of first-time, short-term inmates flows directly from their transitional status between the outside social world and the prison's: It is an ambivalence grounded in the marginality of "people who have lived in two or more societies and so have become oriented to differing sets of cultural values . . . [or] of people who accept certain values held by groups of which they are not members" (Merton and Barber 1976, 11–12). Although inmates' ambivalence affects their prison imagery and strategies in various ways, its principal effect is to limit behavioral changes by inhibiting new inmates from becoming fully assimilated into prison culture.

Feelings of ambivalence characterized the thoughts, emotions, and, sometimes, the actions of the inmates throughout their entire prison careers. Their adaptations to prison expressed both the outsider's perspective they preferred and the insider's perspective they provisionally accepted. Because their strategies were guided by their imagery, their outsider's perspective was most apparent in their behavior at the beginning of their sentences, whereas their insider's perspective was most apparent during the middle part of their sentences. Their behavior during the final months of their sentences was a mixture of nonprison forms of interaction and prison adaptive tactics because their concluding imagery was a synthesis of outsider's and insider's perspectives. Yet a closer inspection of inmates' evolving strategies reveals that the simultaneous influence of the outside and inside worlds was not restricted to the end of their sentences. At every stage of their prison careers, their actions were influenced by the underlying ambivalence that resulted from their marginal position in both the outside and prison social worlds. Table 2 presents the various manifestations of this ambivalence that occurred throughout the prison career.

TABLE 2 Experiences of Ambivalence During Prison Career

	Career Experiences	Reported Ambivalence
Preprison	Conviction and sentencing Detention in county jail Transportation to prison	Desire to postpone sentence versus desire to proceed with sentence
Early months of sentence	Holding cell In-processing First night in cell	Desire to insulate self versus desire for sociability
	Orientation classes (first week) Initial correspondence and visits with outsiders	Desire to proceed with new experiences versus relief at security of close supervision during first weeks of sentence
	Transfer to another cell Assignment to caseworker First contacts with general inmate population Job or program assignment Cellblock transfer	Desire for greater mobility within prison versus fear of greater contact with inmates
Middle portion of sentence	Work/program participation Legal and illegal diversions Correspondence and visits with outsiders	Desire to discontinue outside contacts and "do your own time" versus desire to maintain outside contacts
Conclusion of sentence	Application for transfer to minimum security Transfer to minimum security Outside passes	Desire for greater freedom versus willingness to complete sentence in maximum security
	Home furloughs Transfer to reentry program Release from prison	Desire to put prison in past and return to free world versus desire to avoid existential concerns about return to free world

Preprison and Early Career Experiences

Inmates' ambivalence began before they arrived at prison. Like most outsiders, they viewed prison as a world quite different from their own and had difficulty picturing themselves within that world. In the final days of their freedom, they were faced with conflicting desires: They wanted desperately to avoid their sentences—to escape or be forgotten about—but they also wanted their sentences to proceed because they knew this was inevitable. They retained an outsider's perspective but knew that they were no longer full members of the outside world.

Their ambivalent feelings continued throughout their sentences, although the form and emphasis of their ambivalence changed as they progressed through their prison careers. But even in their earliest days in prison, the dominant form of their ambivalence emerged: Their desire to insulate themselves from the surrounding prison world was countered by their desire for human sociability (see Glaser 1969, 18–21). Throughout their careers, but especially during the first half of their sentences, both sides of this fundamental conflict between an outsider's detachment and an insider's participation in the prison world influenced their behavior. Of importance here is that inmates began to *act,* albeit cautiously, on their desire for contact with others during the first week of their sentences. Their initial contacts with others were quite limited, and they did not appreciably alter their images or strategies, but these contacts did indicate that their isolation did not need to be as extreme as they had anticipated. A 23-year-old inmate, convicted of narcotics sales, described his earliest encounter with another inmate:

> There was one guy that they brought in with me, and we sort of talked off and on. He was sort of scared too, and it was his first time too. He was talking to a guard; I overheard him talking to a guard. I heard him say that he was just basically scared as hell. The guard was trying to calm him down. We were all together in a group; we eat at the same table and everything, and I got talking to him. So I had somebody to talk to. (Interview)

During their first week in prison, in which they were housed together with other incoming inmates but segregated from the general inmate population, they were able to express their desire for contact with others through limited interaction with both guards and inmates. They learned that not all guards fit their initial stereotypes, and many new inmates encountered one or more fellow inmates with backgrounds similar to their own. They were still intimidated by the prison, particularly by those aspects of prison life that they had not yet experienced, but they began to reduce their isolation and expand their knowledge of the prison world.

The first week thus enabled new inmates, through passive observations and direct interaction, to modify (but not radically transform) both their images and their strategies. Their segregation during this week also led to yet another variant of their ambivalence: They were relieved at the protection of close supervision, but because they knew that they could not avoid facing the general inmate population indefinitely they were anxious to move on to the next phase of their sentences. Similar feelings of ambivalence resurfaced with each new experience. When they learned that they would be transferred to a different cell, and later to another cellblock entirely, they looked forward to the greater mobility these moves offered, but they feared the increased inmate contact the moves would necessitate:

> After only 2 days they moved me [to another cell]. . . . With this move came more freedom. . . . I could go out in the yard and to the dining hall for meals. I was a little apprehensive about getting out. I had made friends with one guy, so we went into the yard together. We were out for about an hour when we were approached by a black dude. He wanted to get us high. I'm sure that's not all he wanted. . . . It helps to find a friend or two; you feel safer in a crowd. (Field notes)

Their fear mirrored the violence of their prison imagery, whereas their desire to proceed reflected their acceptance that they were now prison inmates.

The evolution of inmates' prison perspectives continued and accelerated through the early months of their sentences. The survival strategies they formulated during these months, like their anticipatory survival strategies, were based on their images of prison. But increasingly their strategies led to modification of these images. This happened because their strategies continued to be influenced by the same motivational factors: (a) their concern for safety but also their recognition that their prison imagery was incomplete and (b) their ambivalence, especially their desire to proceed with new and inevitable prison experiences. The same tactics that gave them new information also reflected the opposing directions of their ambivalence. Their practice of territorial caution and their rudimentary impression management skills expressed their apprehension over contact with other prisoners and their desire for self-insulation, but these tactics also allowed them to initiate or accept limited interaction with others. Their selective interaction with other inmates and their partnership with one other inmate directly expressed their desire for sociability while providing them with a means of maintaining social and emotional distance from the majority of the inmate population.

Midcareer Experiences

Inmates' midcareer adaptation strategies, like their earlier survival strategies, were based on their prison imagery and their ambivalence. Their adaptation strategies differed from their survival strategies because their images changed and because the form and emphasis of their ambivalence changed. Their survival strategies were intended to insulate them from the violence of their anticipatory images but also to allow them to confront new prison experiences and to provide them with new information about the prison world. By midcareer their imagery was dominated by the theme of boredom rather than violence, and they no longer saw a need for more information. But boredom was only one of the problems associated with "doing time" at midcareer: Their relationships with the outside world presented them with other difficulties. As they approached an insider's perspective on the prison world, they came to share the long-term inmate's belief that preoccupation with the outside world could make their sentences more difficult:

> I was talking with [a long-term inmate] and he was telling me that he doesn't usually hang around short-timers because they are so preoccupied with time. He said it took him a long time to get over counting the days, weeks, and months,

> and that he doesn't really like to be reminded about it. (Field notes: conversation with middle-aged inmate convicted of murder)

Intimate relationships were likely to be questioned and might even be curtailed (see Cordilia 1983). As expressed by a 37-year-old convicted thief,

> I think it would be almost impossible to carry on a relationship, a real close relationship, being here for 2 years or a year and a half. It's literally impossible. I think that the best thing to do is to just forget about it, and if the relationship can be picked up again once you get out, that's fine. And if it can't, you have to accept that. (Interview)

Similar concerns were raised regarding all outside contacts. A 26-year-old inmate, convicted of the possession and sale of marijuana, told us,

> When they [the inmate's visitors] left I felt depressed. . . . it's a high when they come, and you get depressed when they leave. I was wondering if that's good. Maybe I should just forget that there is an outside world—at times I thought that, maybe as a survival mechanism to forget that there are good people in the world. (Interview)

Within a few months' time, inmates' adoption of an insider's perspective thus resulted in yet another manifestation of their ambivalence: Their desire to maintain their involvement in the outside world was countered by a temptation to discontinue all outside contacts so that they could do their own time without the infringement of a world to which they no longer actively belonged.

In a matter of months, then, inmates' perspectives underwent a substantial transformation: They were now viewing the outside world from the perspective of the prison world rather than the reverse, and their adaptation strategies, accordingly, were designed to help them cope with their insider's problems of "doing time" rather than their outsider's fears. Their viewpoints were only an *approximation* of an insider's perspective, however, and their insider's tactics were equivocal because they never achieved more than a marginal status within the prison world. During the middle portion of their sentences they may have been tempted to sever all outside contacts to make their time pass more easily, but they did not actually follow through on this temptation. And although the relationships they established in prison, especially their partnerships, might have seemed more important than their outside relationships, they knew that they would not have freely chosen to associate with most of these people on the outside, and they knew that they would not continue most of these relationships once they were released from prison. In this respect, the prison relationships of the men we studied were more cautious than those typically formed by long-term inmates (Cordilia 1983, 13–29; Johnson 1987, 62–63): They acknowledged that they did not fully belong to the prison world in the same sense that long-term or multiple-term inmates do, and they recognized that these other inmates did not fully accept them as members of their world. First-time, short-term inmates, in other words, never completely relinquished their outsider's perspective, even in the middle stage of their prison careers when they were most alienated from the outside world.

Concluding Experiences

Inmates continuing ambivalence was a motivating factor in their decision to apply for a transfer to the minimum security unit in the concluding months of their sentences. Their behavior, once again, embodied both directions of their ambivalence: Their outsider's perspective was apparent in the application itself, which indicated a desire for the greater privileges and outside contacts available in minimum security, whereas their insider's perspective was reflected in their emotional caution about their chances that the transfer would be approved:

> As much as I try to, it is very difficult to keep [minimum security] off my mind. I figure that if I don't think about it, it won't be as agonizing waiting for it to happen. It would be much easier if they would give a date to go, but they won't. (Journal)

If their applications were approved, their ambivalence also influenced their response to the transfer itself:

> I am looking at this transfer a little bit differently from my coming to prison and my transfer to "B" Hall. I don't want to expect too much from [minimum security] because then I won't be disappointed. Also, there is one big difference; if I don't like it out there I can always come back here. (Journal)

They were aware that their transfer marked the final phase of their prison sentences and a first step toward rejoining the outside world, but they were equally aware that they would still be in prison for some time and that they could be returned to maximum security at the whim of prison officials. Consequently, they were reluctant to admit—to themselves or others—that their transfers held great symbolic importance. They armed themselves with an insider's rationalization: If they didn't like minimum security, they could always come back. And if they should be sent back involuntarily, they were now confident of their capabilities to survive the remainder of their sentences in maximum security

Once inmates were transferred to minimum security, they experienced yet another manifestation of their ambivalence, similar to that reported by long-term inmates after they have been placed in halfway houses (Cordilia 1983, 99–100): They wanted to put their prison experiences behind them and prepare for their return to the free world, but they also wanted to avoid the existential concerns raised by this preparation and to complete their sentences by "doing their own time," just as they did when they were in maximum security:

> Doing time is not as easy as it may sound; actually, it is a rather complicated business. For one thing, you must try to keep yourself busy even though there is very little for you to do. . . . You would like to plan for the future, but it seems so far away that it doesn't really seem like it is worth thinking about. Also, thinking about the future tends to make the time drag. You also don't want to think about the past, because eventually you get around to the dumb mistake that got you in here. So, I guess it must be best to think about the present but that is so boring . . . that it can lead to depression. You don't want to think too much about the outside because it makes you realize all that you are missing, which can be somewhat depressing. But then, you don't really want to just think about the prison, because there isn't anything more depressing at all. (Journal)

In the final months and weeks of their sentences they vacillated between directly confronting questions about their futures and avoiding these questions through their continuing tactics of thought control and diversionary activities.

Each of the manifestations of ambivalence itemized in Table 2 reflects inmates' marginality because each involved a conflict between an outsider's and an insider's point of view. At various stages in their careers, inmates might place more emphasis on one or the other viewpoint but they never fully resolved their feelings of ambivalence. During the middle portion of their sentences, for example, they might believe that thoughts about the outside world made their sentences more difficult (an insider's belief) and hence might consciously suppress these thoughts (an insider's tactic), but they did not generally terminate outside contacts and would be severely disappointed if their visitors or letters had ceased to arrive. Thus, even when inmates placed greatest emphasis on an insider's viewpoint, their perspectives (that is, the interdependent relationship between their images and their strategies) expressed their marginality. Similarly, when they placed most emphasis on an outsider's viewpoint, namely, at the beginning and end of their sentences, closer inspection of their perspective again reveals their marginality. Our analysis thus suggests that inmates' changing imagery and strategies did not represent a total conversion to an insider's point of view and a subsequent reversion to a more conventional point of view, as suggested in Wheeler's (1961) cyclical model of prison socialization. Rather, the inmates we studied experienced a subtler transformation in which their movement toward either an insider's or an outsider's perspective was circumscribed by their ambivalence.

Discussion

Using ambivalence in any explanatory scheme can place social scientists in a precarious position. Psychological ambivalence is such a universal condition, and one that can result from such myriad causes and situations, that its use in sociological analysis inevitably leads to charges of reductionism. Moreover, as Room's (1976) critique of this concept in the alcoholism literature has demonstrated, pervasive ambivalence resulting from ambiguous cultural norms is a seductively easy but not very useful causal explanation for deviant (and other forms of) behavior. And yet the very pervasiveness of ambivalence in social life also suggests that its interactional significance cannot be ignored.

The ambivalence experienced by the inmates we studied was derived from a very specific set of circumstances: involuntary but relatively brief confinement in a total institution that was both entirely unknown and absolutely feared. Similar, if less extreme, feelings of ambivalence can emerge whenever human beings become fully immersed in highly demanding but time-limited social worlds or social situations. For example, we would expect ambivalence to characterize the behavioral adaptations of new mental patients, military recruits, ethnographic researchers, or students entering college or graduate school. The nature and effects of ambivalence will obviously be influenced by a host of other considerations: how the individuals involved define and evaluate the social world in question, whether their participation is voluntary or involuntary, whether participants share a previous culture, the extent to which they desire to maintain that culture, and so on. Although acknowledging the importance of such situational variations, we nonetheless believe that our analysis of inmates' prison adaptations may help interpret the experiences of others whose ambivalence results from social marginality.

In his critique, Room (1976) specifically points to three connotations of the term "ambivalence" that result in theoretical difficulties: that it "draws attention away from the content of norms or values and places the emphasis on the fact of a conflict in values," that it implies a continuous state rather than an occasional condition, and that it suggests "an especially excited and explosive state, where irrational behavior is to be expected" (p. 1053). Although we are using ambivalence in a holistic rather than a causal model (Deising 1971), Room's comments are nonetheless helpful for our specification of how sociological ambivalence operates in the prison world.

First, for a new inmate the conflict of value systems was as important, or more important, than the content. The first-time inmates we studied were socially heterogeneous; one of the few characteristics they had in common was their belief that they were different from other inmates and hence did not "belong" in the prison world (Schmid and Jones 1991). To differing degrees they learned (but did not fully accept) the norms and values of the prison world. The prison strategies of new inmates had to acknowledge and deal with the content of prison norms and values, but it was the conflict between this value system and their outside values that resulted in their marginality.

The second connotation noted by Room (1976)—that ambivalence refers to a pervasive social condition—is a temporal one. But time itself was central to the marginality of the inmates we studied: They knew that they would be in prison for a year or two but they hoped (and later expected) to return to the outside world. Although ambivalence pervaded their entire prison careers, their role in prison, as defined by themselves and other inmates, was primarily determined by their status as short-timers. Their ambivalence was thus situational, imposed by the specific circumstances of their imprisonment.

It is the connotation of an excited, explosive state that makes ambivalence such an attractive variable in causal explanation. Yet this connotation, which derives from the use of ambivalence in the psychotherapeutic literature, is not inherent in the concept itself; citing *Hamlet,* Room (1976) notes that the term has traditionally suggested paralysis more than action (p. 1058). In our analysis, inmates' feelings of ambivalence served sometimes to motivate action (for example, to break through their initial isolation or later to apply for transfer to minimum security) and sometimes to inhibit action (not to break off ties to the outside world during the middle portion of their sentences despite a temptation to do so). At some career points, the inmates' ambivalence offered them no real choice in behavior (after orientation, inmates were transferred to another cellblock regardless of how they felt about it); at other points, they did face choices (decisions about continuing outside contacts). The principal effect of their ambivalence, however, was to circumscribe their behavior, keeping it somewhere between the more extreme perspectives of the prison outsider and the long-term inmate.

The traditional model of prison socialization suggests that inmates enter prison with conventional values, become socialized to the values of an inmate culture, and then subsequently become resocialized to the values of the outside world. Our research suggests an alternative model of the prison experiences of first-time, short-term inmates, in which their social marginality continuously shapes both their subjective understanding of the prison world and their adaptations to it. Specifically, we argue that the ambivalence that results from these inmates' transitional status limits the behavioral adaptations they make in prison and inhibits their assimilation into prison culture.

The importance of ambivalence in the prison experiences of the men we studied extended beyond its effect on their prison behavior: It also affected their identities. As we have shown elsewhere (Schmid and Jones 1991), these inmates drew a distinction between their "true" identities (i.e., their preprison identities) and the artificial "prison identities" they created and presented through impression management. This self-bifurcation was itself an expression of both directions of the inmates' ambivalence. Because their prison interactions were based almost exclusively on their shared prison role, conditions existed for a "role-person merger" (Turner 1978). Actual identity change was moderated, however, by the inmates' marginality within the prison world and their consequent ambivalence toward their temporary prison role. In this respect, ambivalence helped to shape not only inmates' adaptations to the prison world but their subsequent adaptations to the outside world. By extension, if the final measure of cultural assimilation is whether a new cultural identity emerges, understanding cultural ambivalence in specific, time-limited social worlds may have larger theoretical implications as well.

REFERENCES

Blumer, H. 1969. *Symbolic interactionism: Perspective and method.* Englewood Cliffs, NJ: Prentice-Hall.

Cardozo-Freeman, I. 1984. *The joint: Language and culture in a maximum security prison.* Springfield, IL: Charles C Thomas.

Clemmer, D. 1958. *The prison community.* New York: Holt, Rinehart & Winston.

Cordilia, A. 1983. *The making of an inmate: Prison as a way of life.* Cambridge, MA: Schenkman.

Davis, F. 1973. The Martian and the convert: Ontological polarities in social research. *Urban Life* 2:333–43.

Deising, P. 1971. *Patterns of discovery in the social sciences.* Chicago: Aldine-Atherton.

Ellis, C. 1991. Sociological introspection and emotional experience. *Symbolic Interaction* 14:23–50.

Giallombardo, R. 1966. *Society of women: A study of a women's prison.* New York: Wiley.

Gibson, M. A. 1988. *Accommodation without assimilation: Sikh immigrants in an American high school.* Ithaca, NY: Cornell University Press.

Glaser, D. 1969. *The effectiveness of a prison and parole system.* New York: Bobbs-Merrill.

Gold, R. 1958. Roles in sociological field observations. *Social Forces* 36:217–23.

Goffman, E. 1959. *The presentation of self in everyday life.* Garden City, NY: Doubleday.

_____. 1961. *Asylums: Essays on the social situation of mental patients and other inmates.* Garden City, NY: Doubleday.

Goodstein, L., D. L. MacKenzie, and R. L. Shotland. 1984. Personal control and inmate adjustment to prison. *Criminology* 22:343–69.

Hayano, D. 1979. Auto-ethnography: Paradigms, problems, and prospects. *Human Organization* 38:99–104.

_____. 1982. *Poker faces: The life and work of professional card players.* Berkeley: University of California Press.

Irwin, J. 1970. *The felon.* Englewood Cliffs, NJ: Prentice-Hall.

_____. 1980. *Prisons in turmoil.* Boston: Little, Brown.

Jacobs, J. 1977. *Stateville: The penitentiary in mass society.* Chicago: University of Chicago Press.

Johnson, R. 1987. *Hard time: Understanding and reforming the prison.* Monterey, CA: Brooks/Cole.

Jones, R. S., and T. J. Schmid. 1989. Inmates' conceptions of prison sexual assault. *Prison Journal* 69:53–61.

Merton, R. K., and E. Barber. 1976. Sociological ambivalence. In *Sociological ambivalence and other essays,* by R. K. Merton, 3–31. New York: Free Press.

Morawska, E. 1987. Sociological ambivalence: Peasant immigrant workers in America, 1880s-1930s. *Qualitative Sociology* 10:225–50.

Room, R. 1976. Ambivalence as a sociological explanation: The case of cultural explanations of alcohol problems. *American Sociological Review* 41:1047–65.

Schlenker, R. 1980. *Impression management: The self concept, social identity and interpersonal relations.* Belmont, CA: Wadsworth.

Schmid, T. J., and R. S. Jones. 1990. Experiential orientations to the prison experience: The case of first-time, short-term inmates. In *Perspectives on social problems,* edited by G. Miller and J. A. Holstein, vol. 2, 189–210. Greenwich, CT: JAI.

_____. 1991. Suspended identity: Identity transformation in a maximum security prison. *Symbolic Interaction* 14:415–32.

Seymour, J. 1977. Niches in prison. In *Living in prison: The ecology of survival,* by H. Toch, 179–205. New York: Free Press.

Shokeid, M. 1988. *Children of circumstances: Israeli emigrants in New York.* Ithaca, NY: Cornell University Press.

Sykes, G. [1959] 1971. *The society of captives: A study of a maximum security prison.* Reprint. Princeton, NJ: Princeton University Press.

Sykes, G., and S. Messinger. 1960. Inmate social system. In *Theoretical studies in social organization of the prison,* by R. A. Cloward, D. R. Cressey, G. H. Grosser, R. McCleery, L E. Ohlin, G. M. Sykes, and S. L. Messinger, 5–19. New York: Social Science Research Council.

Thomas, C. C. 1973. Prisonization or resocialization? A study of external factors associated with the impact of imprisonment. *Journal of Research in Crime and Delinquency* 10:13–21.

Thomas, C. C., and D. M. Peterson. 1977. *Prison organization and inmate subcultures*. Indianapolis: Bobbs-Merrill.

Toch, H. 1977. *Living in prison: The ecology of survival.* New York: Free Press.

Turner, R. H. 1978. The role and the person. *American Journal of Sociology* 84:1–23.

Wheeler, S. 1961. Socialization in correctional communities. *American Sociological Review* 26:697–712.

Zimmerman, D., and D. L Wieder. 1977. The diary: Diary-interview method. *Urban Life* 5:479–98.

REVIEW QUESTIONS

1. In what ways do feelings of ambivalence in prison inmates serve to both motivate and inhibit actions/reactions on their part?
2. How do inmates' psychological reactions to incarceration tend to change over the course of their time in prison?
3. If short-term prison inmates are unlikely to achieve a significant prison status, how could this knowledge/experience be used to further the goals of prisons and the criminal justice system?

READING 7

The Mad, the Bad, and the Abandoned

The Mentally Ill in Prisons and Jails

By Chris Sigurdson

Replacing treatment and hospitalization for the mentally ill with incarceration in prisons and jails is discussed as one of the major challenges facing American corrections. As many as 15 percent of inmates in American correctional facilities have severe mental illnesses, yet our prisons and jails are extremely poorly equipped to treat such inmates. The author notes that a lack of community resources for treatment has made the correctional system the de facto mental health service provider in many communities. As a result, our correctional systems are overwhelmed with providing mental health care treatment, and the future seems to be that the situation will only become more severe and rife with yet more problems and higher costs.

Imagine that our government deliberately began to cut funding for the chronically mentally ill. Instead, prisons and jails were built to provide public psychiatric care. Therapists and hospitals were replaced with police and the criminal justice system. Thirty years ago, I would have dismissed this as an Orwellian fantasy—but I would have been wrong. We currently have alarmingly high numbers of mentally ill men and women in our prisons and jails and exponential growth in the number of people we incarcerate. We also have eliminated more than 90 percent of our former state psychiatric hospital beds.[33] Jails in most major cities contain a larger number of severely mentally ill people than the local mental health hospitals. For example, the Los Angeles County Jail houses the largest single population of mentally ill men and women in the United States.[1] This criminalization of mental illness has become an unrecognized crisis in mental health care.

Two hundred years ago, families cared for their mentally ill relatives. Those whose families were unable or unwilling were housed in prisons and poor houses.[2] Effective treatments were not available. Two centuries of mental health reform eventually led to the development of large public hospitals designed to care for the mentally ill in more humane and effective ways. During the past 50 years, we have radically increased our medical understanding of the causes and treatment of mental illness. We know that severe mental disorders are not the product of moral weakness, poor parenting or demonic possession. They are chronic medical illnesses, such as diabetes, hypertension or asthma.

Following the development of anti-psychotic and antidepressant medications in the 1950s, and the use of lithium in the 1960s, life outside the confines of a mental hospital became possible for the vast majority of men and women with severe mental illnesses. In the current decade, new anti-psychotic and antidepressant medications and the use of anti-convulsant medications for manic depressive illness have further advanced the medical treatments of these illnesses. These newer medications are better-tolerated, have fewer side effects and, in some cases, are more effective than the medicines they replace.

Our most recent mental health "reform" movement, deinstitutionalization, was theoretically designed to improve the lives of severely mentally ill men and women by bringing them, and their care, out of state hospitals and into their communities. This practice has led to important improvements in mental health care. However, there also have been devastating and unexpected consequences. One such result is the incarceration of large numbers of mentally ill individuals. The United States currently has more mentally ill men and women in jails and prisons than in all state hospitals combined.[3,50] Further, mental health professionals familiar with both settings recognize that mentally ill inmates have the same illnesses and symptoms as past and present state hospital patients.[4] We also have seen a large homeless population emerge during the past 40 years, and approximately 30 percent of homeless men and women have severe mental illnesses.[41,46] For many of these people, there is a revolving door between the streets and jail.[34] We have essentially turned the clock back 200 years. We again are housing the severely mentally ill in prisons and poorhouses.

I am a psychiatrist at a federal medical center—one of four psychiatric referral hospitals within the BOP. Ironically, this medical prison occupies the site of a now-defunct state psychiatric hospital. Although I received my psychiatry training within 5 miles of this hospital, I learned nothing about the extent and severity of mental illness in inmates or the challenges prison systems face trying to adequately care for them. My experiences during the past five years have taught me that mentally ill offenders are an easily forgotten and ignored population. They have been effectively removed, not only from their lives in the community, but from public and professional awareness as well.

THE INMATES AND THEIR STORIES

J.J. is a 48-year-old bank robber. She came from a traditional middle-class background and was a senior in college, about to become a teacher, when she developed paranoid schizophrenia. Intermittently hospitalized and homeless through most of the 1970s and 1980s, she first robbed a bank in 1989 to obtain money to flee from a board and care home, where she believed she was being poisoned. She found the safety she needed in prison. Her modus operandi during the past 10 years has been to pass a note demanding money to a bank teller, leave with the money in a paper bag and go to the nearest fast food restaurant to await arrest. When she receives enough treatment to become lucid, she poignantly describes her choice between incarceration and a life of destitution and fear in the community. Even when she is psychotic, she reasons that robbing a bank is the best way for her to obtain the safety she needs.

M.M. is a 22-year-old illegal alien. He legally immigrated to the United States as a child with his family and grew up here. He has no meaningful ties to his country of origin. He became mentally ill in his late teens and developed psychotic delusions of grandeur and invincibility. He got involved with drug dealers and subsequently was arrested and deported. He returned illegally to his family but refused the psychiatric care his relatives arranged for him. The local mental health center determined he could not be committed for care because he was not dangerous, even though he believed he was God and frequently threatened his family for ostensibly hindering him. He began living on the streets. His family was forced to turn him in to the Immigration and Naturalization Service, hoping that in prison, he (and they) would be safe. He subsequently responded well to treatment for bipolar disorder. He will be deported after serving his sentence for illegal re-entry and cannot return to his family even though they continue to be supportive and are involved in the psychiatric care, which he now accepts.

H.H. was a successful computer operator with a major Midwestern university when he developed a paranoid delusional belief that the university was discriminating against him. He began filing lawsuits, his work performance deteriorated and he ultimately was fired. He became obsessed with misconceived wrongdoings by the university and the justice system. His frustration and paranoia grew as his lawsuits were dismissed. He came to believe that he was being followed and that his life was in danger. He was arrested carrying a large knife and a loaded gun into a courthouse in an attempt to get his judge's attention. He was sent to our hospital for treatment before trial, to become rational enough to participate meaningfully in his defense.

S.S. is a 36-year-old male who was stopped for speeding in November 1987 and found to be carrying a sawed-off shotgun. He told police at that time that he was en route to a bank in a major city to obtain $2 billion dollars to develop a flying saucer. He planned to give the saucer to the government for defense purposes. He was charged with a firearms violation. Attempts to treat his mental illness (paranoid schizophrenia) failed to restore his reason enough to make him competent for trial. He was committed to our hospital by a federal court under a statute that allows the indefinite commitment, without a criminal conviction, of an incompetent defendant who has been found to be dangerous due to a mental illness. S.S. has never physically hurt anyone. The finding of dangerousness was based on several potentially violent behaviors in his past that were related to paranoid delusions. He had been hospitalized in his home state following the most dangerous incident—threatening his father with a butcher's knife in response to auditory hallucinations—but was released after a brief stay because he had not carried through with his threat.

S.S.'s mental condition now is greatly improved. He has been receiving medication and treatment for more than 11 years and knows that he will need to take medication for the rest of his life. He could be safely released to his home state with the cooperation of the state's mental health system, but it refuses to accept him. If it would accept him, S.S. could return to his home state with the support of his parents, social security disability payments and lifelong supervision by federal parole officers. The statute under which he was committed also allows for automatic involuntary rehospitalizations (federal, state or private) if local mental health authorities or his parole officer say he needs more supervision or care. The state previously has called him not-dangerous with essentially the same history.

The tragedy is not that he will be voluntarily or involuntarily monitored by the mental health system (this is a necessary precaution), but, rather, that he will spend his life in prison for a relatively minor offense because his state mental health system will not assume his care.

RESEARCH IN PRISONS AND JAILS

Several recent studies have shown that up to 15 percent of incarcerated men and women have severe acute and chronic mental illnesses,[4–5,34] such as schizophrenia, manic-depressive illness and major depression. People with these illnesses have serious impairments in everyday functioning. They can lack foresight, adequate problem-solving skills and motivation to participate fully in the community. Functional impairments can range from problems with appropriate social relationships to disorganized, irrational and, at times, violent, behavior. Moreover, mental illness can be fatal. Approximately 10 percent to 15 percent of individuals with schizophrenia, manic-depressive illness or major depression in the United States die by suicide.[6] The rest suffer mental and physical deterioration, which often is irreversible if not treated adequately.[65] Most of these tragedies are preventable. Our current treatments are extremely effective. When given appropriate care, the vast majority of mentally ill men and women can live productive lives, even in prison, if necessary. This particularly is true when early recognition allows treatment of the illness at an early stage.

Research also shows that jails and prisons are poorly equipped to recognize and treat inmates with mental illnesses.[7,8,9] Estimates are that fewer than 50 percent of men and women with severe mental illnesses receive mental health treatment while incarcerated.[7,9,42] Fewer than 25 percent of inmates with more moderate, but still significant and treatable, forms of mental illness receive care.[7,8] These deficiencies in recognition and treatment exist despite national standards and laws addressing these issues.[10,11,12] Clearly, all of us who work in corrections must find better ways to meet the needs of mentally ill inmates.

To end the discussion of mental health care with a simple indictment of our penal institutions, however, would be superficial, if not hypocritical. The subject is far more complex. Prisons were never designed to be primary providers of mental health care. The rising number of inmates has led to a crisis in mental health care for many prisons. Jails and prisons are dependent on county, state and federal funding. Public funding generally has not kept pace with the increasing number of inmates. Because of changing social attitudes, containment, rather than rehabilitation or treatment, is the primary goal of imprisonment. The identification and treatment of mentally ill offenders is but one of many competing demands for limited resources. Further, mental health professionals and the public generally are indifferent toward correctional health care. Some state medical boards issue licenses restricted to work in corrections. Previously impaired physicians who are considered too unsafe to practice in the community are given licenses to practice in prisons and jails.[13] Gruesome deaths have occurred under the care of such physicians.[14]

It often takes the threat of a lawsuit before enough resources are allocated to correctional institutions to adequately care for mentally ill offenders.[5,15,16,43,44,45] As of November 1997, 67 correctional facilities with mental health issues were under investigation by the DOJ and another 46 were correcting deficits in mental health care to avoid lawsuits.[15] Last year, in response to such an investigation, Los Angeles County had to appropriate more than $8 million to improve mental health care in its jail.[1]

However, we cannot look to legislatures and prison systems alone to correct this complex problem. Our social policies are failing the severely mentally ill in this country. In the name of civil liberty and imagined cost savings, we have moved large numbers of mentally ill men and women from the public institutions designed for their care (hospitals) into public institutions designed for the containment of offenders. We have left another large group of mentally ill people homeless and vulnerable to victimization and incarceration.[46]

ROOTS OF THE PROBLEM

We arrived at our current crisis in mental health care through a combination of factors. When the state hospitals were emptied, the money necessary to care for patients with severe mental illnesses did not generally follow them into their communities.[40,46] Deinstitutionalization became more of a cost-saving measure than a human rights initiative. However, recent studies show that it can cost as much, or more, to care adequately for seriously mentally ill people in the community as it did in state hospitals.[18,19,20]

In many communities, an appropriate level of care is not available, even to patients who recognize their need for it.[17,46] Further, there is a discriminatory lack of parity (equal coverage) in most insurance plans between mental health treatment and other forms of medical care.[36] Hospital stays for both publicly and privately insured patients now are so short that severely ill patients are unable to achieve stable remissions.[21] If brief hospital care is not efficiently coordinated with intensive outpatient programs that include day treatment, residential care and assertive case management, these patients have little chance of sustained improvement.[46] Therefore, for some unfortunate patients and their families, incarceration has become their only reliable "safety net" (J.J. and M.M.).

Scrimping on adequate community care for the mentally ill does not necessarily save money. It is frequently argued that the cost of treating mental illness is recovered by savings in other public service areas and by increased productivity.[26,63] This argument is particularly important regarding mentally ill offenders. Incarceration is an extremely expensive way of housing and treating the mentally ill. . . .

By failing to provide appropriate mental health care in our communities, we do shift the cost in dollars from our communities onto state and federal governments. However, this local cost saving is only an illusion. We seem to forget that we pay for incarceration with taxes. We also take individuals, jobs and resources out of our communities and move them to central facilities (prisons), in which adequate care is very expensive because of the added cost of incarceration. We have not saved money overall; we have only shifted where we spend it—from our community mental health systems to our penal systems. The resultant cost in suffering to patients, families and victims of crime is arguably immeasurable.

There also are many reasons why major mental illnesses themselves leave individuals vulnerable to incarceration (and homelessness). When untreated, these illnesses impair judgment, thinking and mood. Individuals may be incapable of finding and keeping adequate employment or accessing mental health services.[45] Disordered thinking leads to the mistrust of normal support systems, such as families, churches and the mental health system (S.S. and M.M.). Paranoid delusions can lead to criminal behavior when individuals mistakenly attempt to right misconceived wrongs or defend themselves against misconceived threats (H.H.). Since a distortion of reality often is a hallmark of severe mental illness, patients frequently are incapable of making rational assessments of their treatment needs (M.M. and H.H.). Individuals with poor judgment, delusions and disorganized thinking are easily led at times into criminal activity (e.g., as runners or "mules" for drug organizations) (M.M.). Further, there now is easy access to alcohol and illegal drugs in most communities. It is estimated that 80 percent to 90 percent of mentally ill offenders have substance abuse problems (as do 60 percent to 70 percent of all inmates).[22,23]

Law enforcement and judicial practices also contribute to the large numbers of mentally ill men and women in jails and prisons. There is evidence that police arrest mentally ill persons more often than they arrest the general public.[66] In many communities, the police are considered more capable of responding efficiently to a mental health crisis than is the local mental health system.[3,4,48] Police make "mercy bookings" to provide brief safety and shelter for the indigent mentally ill.[4] In other instances, judges incarcerate pretrial defendants for mental health evaluations and/or treatment because of a lack of faith in the civil commitment process or concern about the amount of mental health care available to offenders in the public sector. They also give longer sentences to convicted inmates with mental illnesses for the same reasons.[24,25,34] Recidivism also is a serious problem with mentally ill offenders. They have the highest rates of recidivism of any offenders.[34,49] "Institutionalization" (the loss of the ability to live outside of a very structured environment) always has been a problem for both long-term inmates and state mental hospital patients. This is a double liability for mentally ill offenders—especially in areas in which prison has become the social safety net (J.J.).

A very significant factor in the incarceration of a large number of mentally ill people is our current restrictive civil commitment processes. In most states, involuntary commitment statutes for mental health treatment require that individuals be a serious danger to themselves or others, or so impaired that they are unable to care, even minimally, for themselves.[40] Commitment for dangerousness usually needs to be substantiated by a significant and recent history of violence. Commitment is used more for containment than to ensure needed treatment. Therefore, civil mental health interventions often are too late to prevent harm. Less serious disruptive (and/or illegal) behaviors are not considered grounds for commitment, leaving interventions again to the criminal justice system.

WHERE DO WE GO FROM HERE?

The first step in addressing this crisis in mental health care is to end the stigmatization and discrimination that surround mental illness. We need to make a clear distinction between treated and untreated mental illnesses. The failure to distinguish between these radically different states leads to misunderstandings and fear of the mentally ill. Because untreated severe illnesses are associated with derangements of mood, thinking and behavior in individuals who otherwise appear healthy, untreated mentally ill men and women can be confusing, frustrating, unpredictable and, at times, explosively violent. Appropriate mental health treatment usually can effectively correct the mental distortions that drive these behaviors and return individuals to functional and adaptive forms of behavior. . . .

In the United States, we readily accept the need for appropriate care for individuals with other brain conditions, such as stroke, Alzheimer's disease and mental retardation. We know these individuals need ongoing treatment and, when appropriate, rehabilitation, supportive services and guardianship. Individuals with mental illnesses need and deserve the same level of care and services. The tragic irony is that most mental illnesses are far more treatable than other chronic brain conditions. . . .

We need to prevent harmful delays in the treatment of individuals with severe mental illnesses. For the vast majority of individuals, this simply means making mental health care more accessible. Providing timely care to a small subset of the severely mentally ill will require the rewriting of civil commitment laws in ways that acknowledge the profound cognitive impairments that can accompany mental illnesses. Mentally ill individuals without insight can easily destroy their lives and the lives of others when they resist treatment. We must develop laws that enforce treatment for these individuals before a far more restrictive commitment—to prison—is the only option. Many states currently are attempting to do this.[52]

Freedom from unwanted medical or psychiatric treatment is a fundamental civil right that we need to respect and protect. However, it is blatantly irrational to think that mental and physical deterioration and incarceration and homelessness due to a brain illness are valid expressions of free choice. It also is cruel and irresponsible. Involuntary medical treatment is not unique to mental illness. We currently insist on medical treatment or isolation for people with tuberculosis.[28] We do not require that they first spread the disease to someone else.

Arguments against involuntary mental health treatment raise the important concern that mandated care will be unnecessary or substandard.[53,54,55,56] Due process procedures and professional review requirements need to be carefully delineated to protect the civil rights of individuals with severe mental illnesses and to ensure appropriate care. Mental health systems receiving committed patients must be capable of providing several levels of well-integrated care and supervision, including clinics, hospitals, day treatment, residential programs and assertive case management. Of course, mental health systems that have these services in place most likely will have fewer patients requiring commitment. Improved engagement and access to care alone will prevent many severe deteriorations. Advanced mental health care directives—made when a patient is competent—-also may be useful in avoiding delays in treatment and lengthy civil proceedings.[64]

Many states are implementing outpatient commitment procedures that allow people who otherwise would be committed to hospitals to live freely in their communities, with provisions for rapid intervention if they begin to deteriorate.[57,58,52,33] Outpatient commitment programs are only effective, however (as measured by rehospitalization), if adequate care is provided.[38] The underuse of these programs was tragically demonstrated by the 1998 killing of two policemen in Washington, D.C. The alleged perpetrator was known to be mentally ill and threatening. His family was unable to handle him. Outpatient commitment requiring treatment and monitoring was possible in his state, but it apparently was not used.

Fortunately, many communities are forging new alliances between their mental health and criminal justice systems. Some courts are developing jail diversion programs for the mentally ill, which provide both legal sanctions and appropriate mental health care to mentally ill offenders.[29,59] Mentally ill offenders with nonviolent misdemeanors can be committed for a period of mandatory inpatient or outpatient treatment in lieu of imprisonment. Jail diversion programs have been shown to work with regard to decreasing both subsequent hospitalization and rearrest.[25,39] Similarly, many mentally ill offenders are released from jail or prison with periods of supervision by parole officers and provisions for mandatory mental health care.[61,62] This is another important opportunity to ensure treatment, promote reintegration and decrease recidivism.[25,39] The treatment and supervision of mentally ill offenders present a serious challenge to the limited resources of most community mental health systems.[61] If there is reluctance to recognize shared responsibilities between the mental health and criminal justice systems, important treatment opportunities are lost. Successful programs have formal coordination between police, the courts and mental health officials.[30,39,40,48,63] By supporting and expanding these programs, we will decrease the number of mentally ill inmates and the amount of illegal activity due to untreated mental illnesses.

There will, of course, always be mentally ill men and women who need to be incarcerated. Very serious offenses will continue to be the domain of the criminal justice system. Violent offenders may be best contained and treated, at least initially, in our jails and prisons. When people with mental illnesses commit crimes that are not related to their illnesses, they must receive appropriate judicial sanctions. There also are many individuals who enter prison mentally healthy, only to have mental illnesses emerge while incarcerated. Regardless of the relationship between illness and incarceration, we must recognize that the need for mental health treatment does not disappear with imprisonment.

We need to review our social policies regarding mental illness and incarceration. If, in doing so, we decide that prison is where were want to house a large number of our severely mentally ill citizens, we then must fund our jails and prisons accordingly. The right of inmates to adequate mental health and medical care has been consistently upheld by the Supreme Court.[31,32] The denial of care is not an option. It also is not wise. More than 12 million people are released from jails and prisons each year. At least 10 percent of them will be mentally ill.[13]

SUMMARY

When we stand back and look at the "big picture" of public mental health care today, several striking paradoxes emerge. During the last 30 years, we have combined unprecedented advances in the recognition and treatment of severe mental illnesses with the most regressive practice in 200 years, i.e., returning large sections of public care to prisons and poor houses (homeless shelters). We say that we cannot afford to treat all the mentally ill in our communities, but we imprison many of them at an expense exceeding that of appropriate community care. We generously fund care and treatment for individuals with other, irremediable, brain illnesses but frequently ignore more easily treated human suffering due to mental illnesses. We have both the ability and the obligation to resolve these paradoxes; we now must find the will.

ENDNOTES

1. Grinfeld, M.J. 1998. Nation's 'largest mental institution' hurries reform. *Psychiatric Times,* February, p. 13.
2. *Madness in America: Cultural and medical perceptions of mental illness before 1914,* eds. L. Gamwell and N. Tomes. Cornell University Press, 1995.
3. Fuller, Torrey E. 1995. Editorial: Jails and prisons—America's new mental hospitals. *American Journal of Public Health.* December, 85(12): 1611–1613.
4. Lamb, R. and L. Weinberger. 1998. Persons with severe mental illness in jails and prisons, *Psychiatric Services,* 49(4).
5. Metzner, JL. 1997. Analysis and commentary: An introduction to correctional psychiatry—Part 1. *Journal of the American Academy of Psychiatry Law,* 25(3):375–381.
6. Ghosh, T.B. and B.S. Bictor. 1994. Suicide. In *Textbook of psychiatry*, ed. R. Talbott, S. Hales and S. Yudofsky. The American Psychiatric Press.
7. Steadman, H., B.S. Holohean Jr. and J. Dovoskin. 1991. Estimating mental health needs and service utilization among prison inmates. *Bulletin of the American Academy of Psychiatry and the Law,* 10(3):297–307.
8. Koenig, H., S. Johnson, J. Bellard, M. Denhen and R. Felon. 1995. Depression and anxiety disorder among older male inmates in a federal correctional facility. *Psychiatric Services,* 46(4):399–401.
9. Teplen: L., K. Abram and G.M. McClelland. 1997. Mentally disordered women in jail: Who receives services? *American Journal of Public Health,* 87(4): 604–609.
10. National Commission on Correctional Health Care (NCCHC). 1992. *Standards for health services in prisons.* Chicago: NCCHC.
11. American Psychiatric Association (APA): *Psychiatric services in jails and prisons* (Task Force Report 29), Washington, D.C.: APA, 1989.

12. American Public Health Association (APHA): *Standards for health services on correctional facilities,* second edition, ed. N.N. Dubeer. Washington, D.C.: APHA, 1986.
13. Skolnick, A.A. 1998. Critics denounce staffing jails and prisons with physicians convicted of misconduct. *Journal of the American Medical Association,* 280(16):1391–1392.
14. Skolnick, A.A. 1998. Prison deaths spotlight how boards handle impaired disciplined physicans. *Journal of the American Medical Association,* 280(16):1387–1390.
15. Allegations of poor psychiatric care in county jails prompt increased funding. *Mental Health Economic.* Supplement to Psychiatric Times, November 1997.
16. Candillis, P.J. and K.L. Appelbaum. 1997. Analysis and commentary: Anatomy of a prison commission. *Journal of the American Academy of Psychiatry Law,* 25(3):401–409.
17. Lamb, H.R. 1994. Public psychiatry and prevention. In *Textbook of psychiatry,* eds. R. Talbott, S. Hales and S. Yudofsky, The American Psychiatric Press.
18. Rothbard A.B., A.P. Schinnar, T.P. Hadley, K.A. Foley and E. Kuno. 1998. Cost comparison of state hospital and community-based care for seriously mentally ill adults. *American Journal of Psychiatry,* 155:523–529.
19. Wolff, N., T.W. Helminiak, G.A. Morse, R.J. Calsyn, W.D, Klinkenberg and M.L. Trusty. 1997. Cost-effectiveness evaluation of three approaches to case management for homeless mentally ill clients. *American Journal of Psychiatry,* 154(3):341–348.
20. Hollingsworth, M.S. and J.K. Sweeney. 1997. Mental health expenditures for services for people with severe mental illnesses. *Psychiatric Services,* 48(4):485.
21. Segal, S.P., P.D. Akotsu and M.A. Watson. 1998. Factors associated with involuntary return to a psychiatric emergency service within 12 months. *Psychiatric Services,* 49(9):1212–1217.
22. Chiles, J., E. Von Clere, R.P. Jemelka and E. Trupen. 1990. Substance abuse and psychiatric disorders in prison inmates. *Hospital Community Psychiatry,* 41(10):1132–1134.
23. Regier, D., M.E. Farmer, D.S. Rae, B.Z. Locke, S.J. Keith, U. Judd and F.K. Goodwin. 1990. Co-morbidity of mental disorders with alcohol and other drug abuse. *Journal of the American Medical Association,* 264(19): 2511–2518.
24. Applebaum, K. and W. Fisher. 1997. Judges' assumptions about the appropriateness of crime and forensic commitment. *Psychiatric Services,* 48(5): 710–712.
25. Lamb, R.H., L.E. Weinberger and C. Reston-Parham C. 1996. Court interventions to address the mental health needs of mentally ill offenders. *Psychiatric Services,* 47(3):275–281.
26. *Parity in financing mental health servives: managed care effects on cost, access and quality, office of public information,* National Institute of Mental Health.

27. Camp. C. and G. Camp. *The corrections yearbook 1997,* ed. C. Camp and G. Camp. Criminal Justice Institute Inc.: S. Salem, N.Y. p. 74.

28. For example: "Tuberculosis Health Threat Act?" Minnesota Statutes S 144 4801–144.4813.

29. Steadman, H.J., S.M. Morris and D.L. Dennis. The diversion of mentally ill persons from jails to community-based services. A profile of programs.

30. Jemelka, R., E. Trupen and J. Chiles. 1989. The mentally ill in prisons: A review. *Hospital and Community Psychiatry,* 40(5):481–491.

31. U.S. Statute: *Estelle vs. Gamble,* 1976.

32. U.S. Statute: *Ruis vs. Estelle,* 1980.

33. Rheinstein, Bruce. 2000. True pariety means eliminating Medicaid's IMD exclusion. *Catalyst.* March/April, 2(2): I.

34. Ditton, P.M. 1999. *Mental health and treatment of inmates and probationers.* Bureau of Justice Statistics Special Report. U.S. Department of Justice Office of Justice Programs. July, NCJ (74463).

35. Legal cases.

36. U.S. Department of Health and Human Services, Mental Health Report of Surgeon General—Executive Summary, Rockville, MD: U.S. Department of Health and Human Services, Substance Abuse and Mental Health Services Administration, Center for Mental Health Services, National Institutes of Health, National Institute of Mental Health, 1999.

37. Goldstein, Andrew.

38. Muntez, M.R., T. Grande, J. Kleist and G.A. Peterson. 1996. *Psychiatric Services.* 47(11):1251–1253.

39. Project Link, Department of Psychiatry, University of Rochester, Rochester, N.Y. 1999. Prevention of jail and hospital recidivism among persons with severe mental illness. *Psychiatric Services,* 50(11):1477–1480

40. Jacobs, C. *Not as it seems: To change before tragedy.* A speech to the Washington State AMI Forensic Conference, June 26, 1998.

41. Haugland, G. C. Siegel, Kim Hooper and M.G. Alexander. 1997. Mental illness among homeless individuals in a suburban county. *Psychiatric Services,* 48(4):504–9.

42. Veysey, B.M., I.H.J. Sleadman, J.P. Morrissey and M. Johnsen. 1997. In search of the missing linkages: Continuity of care in U.S. Jails. *Behavioral Science Law,* 15:383–97.

43. Cohen, F. 1998. *The right to treatment in the mentally disordered inmate and the law.* Ink. Kingston, N.J.: Civic Research Institute. 4–1–39

44. Hafemeister, T.L. 1998. *Legal aspects of the treatment of offenders with mental disorders in treatment of offenders with mental disorders,* ed. R.M. Wettestein. New York: The Guilford Press: 44–125

45. Becker, R.E., N. Meisler, G. Stormer and M.J. Brondino, M.J. 1999. Employment outcomes for clients with severe mental illness: A pact model replication. *Psychiatric Services,* 50(1):104–6.

46. Durham, M.L. and J.Q. Lafond. 1996. Assessing psychiatric care settings: Hospitalization vs. outpatient care. *International Journal of Technology Assessment in Health Care,* 12(4):618–33

47. Hutw, Jerrell J.M. 1998. Estimating the cost impact of three case management programs for treating people with severe mental illness. *British Journal of Psychiatry,* 173(suppl 36):26–32.
48. Deane, M.W., H.J. Steadwan, R. Borum, B.M. Veysey and J.P. Morrissey. 1999. Merging partnerships between mental health and law enforcement. *Psychiatric Services,* 5(1):99–101.
49. Harris, V. and T.D. Koepsell. 1996. Criminal recidivism in mentally ill offenders: A pilot study. *Bulletin of the American Academy of Psychiatry Law,* 24(2):177–86.
50. Zdanowicz, M.T. 2000. State updates. *Catalyst*, March/Apri:5–8.
51. Winerib, M. 1999. Bedlam on the streets: Increasingly, the mentally ill have nowhere to go—That's their problem and ours. *New York Times Sunday Magazine.*
52. State Updates in *Catalyst,* November/December 1999:1–2
53. Wettstein, R.M. 1999. The right to refuse psychiatric treatment. *The Psychiatric Clinics of North America,* 22(1):173–8.
54. Engleman, N.B., D.A. Jobes, A.L. Berman and L.I. Langbein.1998. Clinicians' decision-making about involuntary commitment. *Psychiatric Services,* 49(7):941–5.
55. Frese, F.J. III. 1997. The mental health services consumers' perspective on mandatory treatment. *New Directions For Mental Health Services.* 75: 17–26.
56. Olsen, D.P. 1998. Toward an ethical standard for coerced mental health treatment: Least restrictive or most therapeutic? *A Journal of Clinical Ethics,* 9(3):235–46.
57. Geller, J.L., M. McDermeil, A.L. Grudzinskas, T. Lowlor and W.H. Fisher. 1997. A competency-based approach to court-ordered outpatient treatment. *New Directions for Mental Health Services,* 75:81–94.
58. Rubin, W.V., M.B. Snapp, P.C. Panzano and J. Taynor. 1996. Variation in civil commitment processes across jurisdictions: An approach for monitoring and managing change in mental health systems. *The Journal of Mental Health Administration,* 23(4):375–388.
59. Draine, J. and P. Solomon. 1999. Describing and evaluating jail diversion services for persons with serious mental illness. *Psychiatric Services,* 50(1):56–61.
60. Lamb, H.R., L.E. Weinberger and B.H. Gross. 1999. Community treatment of severely mentally ill offenders under the jurisdiction of the criminal justice system: A review. *Psychiatric Services,* 50(7):907–913.
61. Wiederanders, M.R., D.L. Bromley and P.A. Choate. 1997. Forensic conditional release programs and outcomes in three states. *International Journal of Law and Psychiatry,* 20(2):249–257.
62. Hartwell, S.W. Orrk. 1999. The Massachusetts forensics transition program for mentally ill offenders re-entering the community. *Psychiatric Services,* 50(9):1220–1222.
63. Eells, T. 1999. Is there a cost offset to psychotherapy? *Journal of Psychotherapy Practical Research,* 8(3):243–247.

64. Srebnik, D.S. and J.Q. LaFond. 1999. Advanced directives for mental health treatment. *Psychiatric Services,* 50(7):919–925.
65. Stephenson, J. 2000. Delay in treating schizophrenia may narrow therapeutic window of opportunity. *Journal of the American Medical Association,* 283(16): 2091–2092.
66. Teplin, L.A. 1984. Criminalizing mental disorder. *American Psychologist,* 39(7):794–803.

REVIEW QUESTIONS

1. How do the numbers of mentally ill persons in prisons/jails and mental hospitals/treatment centers compare in the United States?
2. What are the reasons that the number of mentally ill prison and jail inmates has increased dramatically in the last three decades?
3. Why does the author argue that it is a good idea to provide involuntary treatment to the mentally ill?

IV

INMATE MISCONDUCT

READING 8

Physical Violence Inside Prisons

Rates of Victimization

Nancy Wolff

Cynthia L. Blitz

Jing Shi

Jane Siegel

Ronet Bachman

Common perceptions hold that prisons are extremely violent places where inmates physically assault each other and staff members, and staff physically assault inmates. This article looks at the rates of inmate assault across one state prison system. Based on anonymous surveys with more than 7,000 inmates, the researchers find that victimization rates vary by gender, institution, and how questions about victimization are asked. The results suggest that prisons are violent places, although not all inmates are at equal risk of being victimized.

Violence is a pervasive feature of prison life (Bowker, 1980; Irwin, 1980; Johnson, 1987). It is not surprising that violence is the leading by-product of prisons because hundreds or thousands of people with antisocial tendencies or behavior are aggregated and confined in close and frequently overcrowded quarters characterized by material and social deprivation (Bowker, 1980; Toch, 1985; Wolfgang & Ferracuti, 1976). Even without assuming a Hobbesian-like character, one would reasonably predict that environments such as these would bring out the worst in human nature. Survival instincts are notoriously primitive and the behavior code of prison life (Clemmer, 1958; Gilligan, 1997; Sykes, 1958), much like the code of the streets in impoverished communities (Anderson, 1999), reflects such instincts.

Recent research on prison violence has focused on explaining variation in prison environments regarding safety, misconduct, and physical assaults by using models of deprivation, importation, and institutional management (Keller & Wang, 2005; Wooldredge, Griffin, & Pratt, 2001), but research that examines the epidemiology and context of physical violence inside prisons is almost nonexistent. Indeed, more attention, although limited, has been focused on measuring and documenting sexual violence (Gaes & Goldberg, 2004) than physical violence in prisons. The limited attention given prison violence is testimony to the societal norms regarding acceptable conditions and behavior inside prisons. Johnson (1987) observed that "the reality of violence [is a fact] of everyday life" (p. 75) in prison and, because violent acts are common occurrences, do not apparently warrant much notice.

Extant research, although limited, supports the notion that violence is an integral part of prison life. At the extreme, violence culminates in homicide. In 2000, 51 deaths (less than 0.1 per 1,000) resulting from inmate assaults were reported among all inmates held in federal or state prisons, down from 82 in 1995

(Stephan & Karberg, 2003). Whereas homicide is a rare event inside prisons, inmate-on-inmate physical assault is more common. According to official statistics, for every 1,000 inmates in federal and state prisons in 2000, 28 were reportedly physically assaulted by another inmate (Stephan & Karberg, 2003).

Official estimates of physical violence inside prison, however, grossly underrepresent the level and type of victimization inside prison. Bowker (1980), in reporting estimates of prisoner victimization rates from Fuller, Orsagh, and Raber (1977), noted that "the assault problem as viewed by prisoners is 11 times as great as the assault problem that is officially recognized by prison administrators" (p. 26). It is well known that victimization in general and violence in particular is underreported inside prison (Bowker, 1980; McCorkle, 1993), as it is outside prison (Myers, 1982), but for different reasons. The threat of retaliation inside prison for "Snitching," a preeminent norm within the code of prison, suppresses the official reporting of assaults, as well as other types of misconduct between inmates. In prison parlance, "Snitches get stitches." This peer-enforced norm creates a strong disincentive to report victimization to officials, thereby reducing the official appearance of inmate-on-inmate victimization behind the walls. A similar disincentive exists for reporting violence perpetrated by custody staff on inmates. Again, the opportunity and motivation for retaliation by staff quiet the voice of inmates (Gilligan, 1997).

No nationally representative surveys have been undertaken to improve on these official estimates of physical victimization inside prisons. Consequently, what is known is based on surveys drawn from small, localized studies (See Bowker, 1980). Based on a survey of 231 inmates (48% sample) at a single prison, 14% of responding inmates reported being a victim of a personal crime over a 3-month period, whereas 20% reported being victims of property crimes (Wooldredge, 1994). In a more recent survey utilizing a sample of 581 inmates (sampling rates varying from 20% to 38% of the prison populations) drawn from three Ohio prisons, Wooldredge (1998) found that approximately 1 of every 10 inmates reported being physically assaulted in the previous 6 months, whereas 1 of every 5 inmates reported being a victim of theft during that same time frame. More inclusively, when all crimes were aggregated together, including physical assault, theft, robbery, and property damage, 1 of every 2 inmates surveyed reported being a victim of crime in the previous 6 months. Using a sample of British inmates (N = 594, 90% response rate), O'Donnell and Edgar (1998) found that roughly 1 in 5 adult inmates had been physically assaulted in the previous month. These self-report estimates, although focusing on nonrandom samples from different states and countries, indicate very high levels of victimization inside prisons.

Other evidence of victimization inside prison comes from research focusing on inmates' fear and reactive behaviors to fear. Toch (1977) observed that inmates are constantly on guard. In reaction, inmates engage in risk-minimizing behavior. McCorkle (1992), based on a sample of 500 male inmates in Tennessee prisons, found that a quarter of the inmates reported carrying protection (e.g., a "shank"). Others engaged in more "passive" precautionary measures such as consciously avoiding areas where victimization is likely to occur (e.g., the shower, the yard, or blind spots) or isolating themselves in their cells (Lockwood, 1980; McCorkle, 1992, 1993). More recent evidence suggests that there is inter-prison variation in terms of inmates' self-reported perceptions of safety. Camp (1999) found that male inmates, housed in medium-, low-, and minimum-security federal prisons, were less fearful of being "hit, punched, or assaulted by other inmates" than those housed in administrative and high-security federal prisons, who were more likely to feel vulnerable to these types of behaviors.

Although this literature has helped illuminate the problem of physical victimization inside U.S. prisons, there has been no attempt to reliably and validly estimate the magnitude and context (e.g., inmate-on-inmate or staff-on-inmate) of this violence with a random sample of prison inmates. This study, to our knowledge, is the first to explore the bid-time (i.e., time served in prison on the index offense) and 6-month prevalence of physical victimization within a state prison system, inclusive of both male and female facilities. It is also the first to use (a) a full population sampling design, inclusive of approximately 21,000 inmates at 14 prisons; (b) multiple general and specific questions to measure physical victimization; and (c) an audio-computer assisted survey instrument (CASI) to administer the survey. In addition, to ensure full participation and reliable reporting, the survey questionnaire included a broader set of questions probing the quality of life inside prison.

METHOD

Participants

The study's population comprised all inmates housed at the 13 adult male prisons and 1 female prison operated by a single mid-Atlantic state ($N = 22{,}898$). . . .

Participants were sampled in two ways. First, all inmates housed in the general population ($n = 19{,}615$) were invited to participate in the study. Response rates by facility ranged from 26% to 53%, with an average rate of 39% ($SD = 0.065$). . . . Second, 10% of inmates held in administrative segregation were sampled. . . .

A total of 7,221 men (M age = 34.2) and 564 women (M age = 35.5) aged 18 or older participated in the study. More than two thirds (68.4%) of the female inmates were non-White, whereas 81.4% of the males were non-White. . . .

Procedure

The surveys were conducted from June through August of 2005. Audio-CASI was used to administer the survey, which was available in English and Spanish. Respondents interacted with a computer-administered questionnaire by using a mouse and following audio instructions delivered via headphones. This method of survey administration is considered most reliable when probing sensitive or potentially stigmatizing information (Gaes & Goldberg, 2004). . . . Completing the English version of the computer-assisted survey took approximately 60 minutes, whereas the Spanish version took approximately 90 minutes. Face-to-face interviews were conducted in cases where participants had restricted movement or when they were apprehensive about the computer. . . .

Survey Instrument The questions regarding physical violence were modified from the National Violence Against Women and Men surveys (Tjaden & Thoenness, 2000). . . . Physical violence was measured in the survey through the use of two general questions for two categories of perpetrator: inmates or staff members. Specifically, the questions were "Have you been physically assaulted by an inmate (or staff member) within the past 6 months?" and "Have you ever been physically assaulted by an inmate (or staff member) on this bid?" Behavior-specific questions about physical victimization were asked as well. . . .

RESULTS

Bid-Time Prevalence Rates

. . . . Approximately 20% of female inmates and 25% of male inmates reported being physically assaulted by another inmate while in prison serving their current sentence. The prevalence rate for inmate-on-inmate physical assault was significantly larger for the male facilities than the female facility (252 per 1,000 vs. 204 per 1,000). In contrast, the comparable staff-on-inmate rate was significantly and substantially larger for males compared with women (292 per 1,000 vs. 82 per 1,000). Younger inmates (25 years old or younger) were significantly more likely than older inmates to report a physical assault during incarceration either by another inmate (310 per 1,000 vs. 227 per 1,000) or a staff member (358 per 1,000 vs. 250 per 1,000).

Six-Month Prevalence Rates

. . . . As seen in Table 1, a comparison of these two prevalence measures revealed that for both inmate-on-inmate and staff-on-inmate physical victimization, estimates based on the general question were lower than those based on answers to the questions focusing on specific types of victimization for both women and men. . . .

TABLE 1 Six-Month Prevalence of Physical Victimization in Statewide Correctional System by Gender and Form of the Survey Question: 2005

Incident	Female (n = 564) Rate per 1,000 Inmates[a] (95% Cl)	Male (n = 7,221) Rate per 1,000 Inmates[a] (95% Cl)
Inmate-on-inmate physical violence		
General question	92 (76–108)	75 (69–81)
Specific question	185 (16–208)	192 (184–201)
Any incidents with weapon[b]	94 (76–110)	141 (134–149)
Any incidents without weapon[b]	149 (128–169)	117 (110–124)
Staff-on-inmate physical violence		
General question[b]	51 (39–64)	156 (148–163)
Specific question[b]	57 (44–71)	206 (198–215)
Any incidents with weapon[b]	23 (14–32)	149 (142–156)
Any incidents without weapon[b]	44 (33–57)	139 (132–147)

Note: Cl = confidence interval.

a. The estimates of rate per 1,000 inmates are based on weighted valid numbers.

b. Statistically significant difference between men and women ($p < .05$).

Estimates in Table 1 were also disaggregated by type of incident (incident with a weapon or without a weapon). Inmate-on-inmate physical victimization prevalence rates were similar for female and male inmates, with approximately 21% reporting being physically victimized by another inmate in the past 6 months. However, women were more likely than men to have experienced an incident of inmate-on-inmate physical violence that did not involve a weapon (149 per 1,000 vs, 117 per 1,000), whereas men were more likely than females to report an incident of inmate-on-inmate physical violence involving a weapon (141 per 1,000 vs. 94 per 1,000). In addition, male inmates were 3 times as likely as female inmates to report any type of staff-on-inmate physical violence, with nearly 1 in 4 male inmates (24.6%) reporting they had been physically victimized by a staff member. This statistically significant between-gender difference held for both incidents involving the use of a weapon and those not involving a weapon.

Table 2 compares 6-month prevalence rates for inmate-on-inmate and staff-on-inmate physical violence against male inmates, by facility size, measured by the size of the facility's inmate population (up to 1,100 inmates; 1,101–1,900 inmates, and more than 1,901 inmates). Prevalence rates varied by facility, ranging from 129 to 346 per 1,000 for inmate-on-inmate physical victimization and 101 to 321 per 1,000 for staff-on-inmate physical victimization. In general, compared to large facilities, small to medium-sized facilities had higher prevalence rates of inmate-on-inmate

TABLE 2 Six-Month Prevalence of Physical Violence in Statewide Male Correctional System Grouped by Perpetrator and Facility Size: 2005

Facility	Inmate-on-Inmate Rate per 1,000 Inmates[a] (95% Cl)	Staff-on-Inmate Rate per 1,000 Inmates[a] (95% Cl)
Average, all male facilities	205 (197–214)	246 (237–255)
Facilities with populations 1,100 or less		
1	216 (182–248)	198 (166–230)
2	172 (129–211)	101 (66–133)
3	248 (201–296)	136 (98–175)
4	264 (206–322)	215 (168–263)
Facilities with populations from 1,101 to 1,900		
5	236 (197–272)	319 (277–361)
6	346 (294–401)	321 (278–361)
7	246 (210–281)	309 (271–347)
Facilities with populations over 1,901		
8	142 (114–172)	192 (160–224)
9	318 (283–352)	316 (280–352)
10	144 (125–164)	268 (244–291)
11	188 (172–204)	280 (262–297)
12	129 (103–155)	179 (149–209)
13	157 (137–178)	192 (170–215)

Note: Cl = confidence interval.

a. The estimates of rate per 1,000 inmates are based on weighted valid numbers.

TABLE 3 Month Prevalence of Physical Violence by Type of Incident in Statewide Male Correctional System Grouped by Perpetrator, Use of Weapon, and Facility Size: 2005

	Inmate-on-Inmate Rate per 1,000 Inmates[a] (95% CL)		Staff-on-Inmate Rate per 1,000 Inmates[a] (95% CL)	
Facility	Violence with Weapon	Violence Without Weapon	Violence with Weapon	Violence Without Weapon
Facility with populations 1,100 or less				
1	145 (116–174)	124 (97–150)	127 (101–151)	126 (100–153)
2	70 (43–98)	125 (86–165)	55 (31–82)	51 (27–74)
3	150 (112–189)	150 (111–188)	64 (34–90)	60 (30–90)
4	174 (132–216)	190 (137–238)	121 (84–157)	142 (105–185)
Facilities with populations from 1,101 to 1,900				
5	138 (109–169)	166 (135–197)	180 (146–217)	197 (161–231)
6	229 (188–272)	210 (167–251)	165 (131–199)	198 (164–233)
7	181 (150–211)	139 (111–167)	176 (143–207)	190 (160–223)
Facilities with populations more than 1,901				
8	108 (84–134)	58 (40–76)	121 (97–148)	88 (66–110)
9	240 (211–268)	173 (143–204)	193 (164–220)	177 (144–209)
10	104 (86–120)	79 (65–95)	167(147–187)	166 (146–186)
11	128 (115–142)	115 (102–128)	172 (158–187)	154 (140–169)
12	100 (76–124)	52 (36–68)	134 (108–160)	88 (64–112)
13	100 (82–119)	83 (67–99)	114 (95–131)	104 (87–122)

Note: Cl = confidence interval.
a. The estimates of rate per 1,000 Inmates are based on weighted valid numbers.

physical victimization, whereas medium-sized and large facilities had higher staff-on-inmate rates of physical victimization, compared to small facilities.

Prevalence rates for inmate-on-inmate and staff-on-inmate physical victimization with and without use of a weapon organized by facility size are shown in Table 3. Rates varied considerably across facilities and by type of incidents, ranging across facilities from 70 to 240 per 1,000 for inmate-on-inmate physical victimization involving a weapon and 52 to 210 per 1,000 for inmate-on-inmate victimization not involving a weapon. A similar pattern was found for staff-on-inmate physical victimization. Here the rate of victimization not involving a weapon varied across facilities by a factor of 3.5 and victimization with a weapon by 3.9.

DISCUSSION

The results of this study confirm the stereotype that prisons are violent places. The rates of physical assault for male inmates is over 18 times higher than assault victimization rates for males in the general population, and rates for female inmates are over 27 times higher than their nonincarcerated counterparts (Catalano, 2005). Rates of victimization within the general population are not representative of the population in prison. It is true that victimization rates are correlated with poverty (Rennison & Rand, 2003) and people inside prison are more likely to be drawn from poor communities. However, Teplin and colleagues, using the National Crime Victimization Survey, weighted victimization rates by race/ethnicity, sex, age, and income and estimated 12-month assault rates of 1.5% for people in poorer communities (Teplin, McClelland, Abram, & Weiner, 2005); these adjusted rates are still more than 10 times lower than the rates for people inside prison.

Over a 6-month period, 20% of inmates reported experiencing some form of physical violence, measured in terms of being hit, slapped, kicked, bit, choked, beat up, or hit with or threatened with a weapon. Overall, such outcomes were equally likely for female and male inmates. However, acts of physical violence against male inmates by other inmates were more likely to involve a weapon than were incidents involving female inmates. Male inmates were also more likely to report incidents of personal violence perpetrated by staff and more likely than not these incidents involved the threat of or use of a weapon.

Physical victimization was not uniform across facilities. Small facilities were associated with above average rates of inmate-on-inmate physical violence, but below average rates of staff-on-inmate physical violence. The opposite was found for large facilities, with lower than average rates of inmate-on-inmate physical violence but higher rates of staff-on-inmate violence. Moreover, in large facilities, incidents of physical violence, whether inmate-on-inmate or staff-on-inmate, were more likely to involve the threat of or use of a weapon. Medium-sized facilities had above average rates of inmate-on-inmate and staff-on-inmate physical victimization, and these incidents were less likely to involve weapons when involving staff but were slightly more likely to involve the threat of or use of weapons when involving inmates only.

The rates of physical victimization estimated here are roughly 40%–100% larger than those estimated by Wooldredge (1994, 1998) for prisons in the Midwest in the 1990s (ranging from 10% to 14%) but are virtually identical to the 1-month estimates of physical assaults (20%) in British facilities reported by O'Donnell and Edgar (1998). Both studies relied on self-report data. Overall, rates of physical victimization are higher when based on information provided through self-report than official reports (Bowker, 1980). Official reports of physical assault over a year in the United States were reported at 28 per 1,000 inmates in federal and state prisons (Stephan & Karberg, 2003), whereas rates based on self-report information for this study were 92 per 1,000 for women and 75 per 1,000 for men and, over an inmate's entire period of incarceration, were 204 per 1,000 and 252 per 1,000, respectively. Another limitation of official reports is that they do not capture information on physical violence against inmates by staff (Bowker, 1980), which often occurs at rates higher than inmate-on-inmate violence, particularly in male facilities.

The results of this research indicate that the risk of victimization varies significantly across institutional setting. This interfacility variation in physical violence is nontrivial and warrants careful attention. In some facilities, more than 25% of inmates reported experiencing an incident of physical violence over the past 6 months.

Even higher rates of physical violence were reported for staff-on-inmate incidents, with rates over 30% reported for 4 facilities (31% of the 13 male facilities). Inmates held in the medium-size and in 3 of the large facilities, on average, reported being at greater risk of experiencing physical violence by staff than inmates at other facilities. Physical violence in male facilities more commonly involved weapons whether perpetrated by inmates or staff. Indeed, nearly 60% of inmates in all medium-size and 3 large facilities reported carrying a weapon for protection from often to all the time. Carrying weapons for protection inside the facility was a commonly reported occurrence, with more than 50% of male inmates and 22% of female inmates reporting that they carried a weapon for protection from often to all the time. Obviously, unchecked violence inside the facility contributes to inmates' perceptions that they need to arm themselves for self-preservation, which in turn helps perpetuate serious violent incidents inside prison. Future research should explore in what way populations inside prisons of different sizes might explain this variation. Variables of interest might include median age, offense distribution, length of incarceration, and racial composition.

This survey underscores the importance of using a variety of behaviorally specific questions to elicit reports of physical victimization. Limiting questions to ones that ask about "physical assaults" will understate the experience of violence inside prisons because respondents may erroneously believe that acts that constitute assaults, such as hitting or slapping, in fact would not be considered assaults. Our estimates of physical violence were more representative when survey questions were more explicit about the behaviors that should be included in estimates of physical victimization, such as being hit, slapped, kicked, or threatened with a weapon. More exact language that explicitly defines the behavior considered violent or threatening provides more valid and reliable estimates of violent behavior.

The estimates presented here focused on physical violence, which is only one form of victimization. These rates of victimization do not include property theft, emotional or psychological victimization, intimidation, or sexual victimization. To accurately and fully characterize the crime environment inside prison, surveys need to probe victimization in all of its forms that is perpetrated by inmates-on-inmates and staff-on-inmates and across multiple facilities within a state system. Bowker (1980) noted the following:

> All of the forms of prison victimization are related so that each becomes a causal factor in the other, forming an insane feedback system through which prison victimization rates are under constant pressure to increase. A similar feedback phenomenon occurs when prisoners feel constrained to take revenge for past victimization and to defend themselves in current victimizations. The interaction takes on the form of a macabre version of the game of musical chairs in which today's aggressor may become tomorrow's victim. (p. 31)

. . . . Crime, violence, and injustice are ubiquitous in prisons (Commission on Safety and Abuse in America's Prisons, 2006), Our research sheds light on this issue in ways that elucidate the level and types of physical violence, as well as their variation among facilities. Surviving prison often depends on the ability to fight, defend oneself with weapons, steal for personal advantage, and manipulate others with threats of violence (Gilligan, 1997; Johnson, 1987). The task of "correcting" inmates in a correctional setting is almost impossible to achieve when inmates are confined in environments where violence is pervasive. Increasing attention is being focused on safety inside prison and its relevance to corrections and community reintegration. The Commission on Safety and Abuse in America's Prisons (2006) recommended improving safety conditions inside prison as well as carefully monitoring these conditions to ensure that people are kept safe while they serve their time. Both inmates and staff must believe that they can interact with each other without fear of physical harm. Only then can a civilizing environment begin inside the walls.

REFERENCES

Anderson, E. (1999). *Code of street, decency, violence and the moral life of the inner city*. New York: Norton.

Bowker, L. (1980). *Prison victimization*. New York: Elsevier North Holland.

Camp, S. D. (1999). Does inmate survey data reflect inmate conditions? Using surveys to assess prison conditions of confinement. *The Prison Journal, 79,* 250–268.

Catalano, S. (2005). *Criminal victimization, 2004* (No. NCJ 210674). Washington, DC: Department of Justice. U.S. Bureau of Justice Statistics.

Clemmer, D. (1958). *The prison community*. New York: Holt, Rinehart and Winston.

Commission on Safety and Abuse in America's Prisons. (2006). *Confronting confinement*. Retrieved June 19, 2006, from http://www.prisoncommission.org/report.asp

Fuller, D., Orsagh, T., & Raber, D. (1977). *Violence and victimization within the North Carolina prison system*. Paper presented to the Academy of Criminal Justice Sciences.

Gaes, G. G., & Goldberg, A. L. (2004). *Prison rape: A critical review of the literature* (Working Paper). Washington, DC: National Institute of Justice.

Gilligan, J. (1997). *Violence: Reflections on a national epidemic*. New York: Vintage Books.

Irwin, J. (1980). *Prisons in turmoil*. Boston: Little, Brown.

Johnson, R. (1987). *Hard time: Understanding and reforming the prison*. Monterey, CA: Brooks/Cole.

Keller, M., & Wang, H. (2005). Inmate assaults in Texas jails. *The Prison Journal, 85,* 515–534.

Lee, E., Forthofer, R., & Lorimer, R. (1989). *Analyzing complex survey data*. Newbury Park, CA: Sage.

Lockwood, D. (1980). *Prison sexual violence*. New York: Elsevier.

McCorkle, R. C. (1992). Personal precautions to violence in prison. *Criminal Justice and Behavior, 19,* 160–173.

McCorkle, R. C. (1993). Fear of victimization and symptoms of psychopathology among prison inmates. *Journal of Offender Rehabilitation, 19,* 27–41.

Myers, S. (1982). Why are crimes underreported? What is the crime rate? Does it really matter? *Social Science Quarterly, 61* 23–43.

O'Donnell, I., & Edgar, K. (1998). Routine victimization in prison. *Howard Journal of Criminal Justice, 375,* 266–279.

Rennison, C. M., & Rand, M R. (2003). *Criminal victimization,* 2002 (No. NCJ 199944). Washington, DC: U. S. Department of Justice, Bureau of Justice Statistics.

Stephan, J. J., & Karberg, J. C. (2003). *Census of state and federal correctional facilities 2000* (No. NCJ 198272). Washington. DC: U.S. Department of Justice, Bureau of Justice Statistics.

Sykes, G. (1958). *The society of captives: A study of a maximum security prison.* Princeton, NJ: Princeton University Press.

Teplin, L. A., McClelland, G. M., Abram, K. M., & Weiner, D. A. (2005). Crime victimization in adults with severe mental illness: Comparison with the National Crime Victimization Survey. *Archives of General Psychiatry, 62,* 911–921.

Tjaden, P., & Thoennes, N. (2000). *Full report of the prevalence, incidence, and consequences of violence against women: Findings from the national violence against women survey* (No. NCJ 183781). Washington, DC: National Institute of Justice & the Centers for Disease Control and Prevention.

Toch, H. (1977). *Living in prison: The ecology of survival.* New York: Free Press.

Toch, H. (1985). Warehouses of people. *Annals of American Academy of Political and Social Science, 478,* 58–72.

Wolfgang, M. E., & Ferracuti, F. (1976). *The subculture of violence.* London: Tavistock.

Wooldredge, J. D. (1994). Inmate crime and victimization in a southwestern correctional facility. *Journal of Criminal Justice, 22,* 367–381.

Woodredge, J. D. (1998). Inmate lifestyles and opportunities for victimization. *Journal of Research in Crime and Delinquency, 35,* 480–502.

Wooldredge, J. D., Griffin, T., & Pratt, J. (2001). Considering hierarchical models for research on inmate behavior: Predicting misconduct with multilevel data. *Justice Quarterly, 18,* 203–231.

REVIEW QUESTIONS

1. How does the way that questions about victimization are asked influence the results of research?
2. What types of inmates are at the greatest risk of being physically assaulted by other inmates?
3. What types of inmates are at the greatest risk of being physically assaulted by staff?

READING 9

The Impact of Institutional Factors on Officially Reported Sexual Assaults in Prisons

Christopher Hensley

Mary Koscheski

Richard Tewksbury

One of the popular assumptions about men's prisons is that sexual deviance and violence is rampant among inmates. This article reviews the research on the rates of sexual violence and characteristics of individuals who are sexually victimized while incarcerated. What this article adds to the literature is a look at whether factors about the institutional structural aspects of an institution are related to the rates of sexual assaults in those institutions. Results suggest that these factors may have some influence, but not as much as individual-level characteristics.

INTRODUCTION

Due to the efforts of the Stop Prison Rape Organization (2001), Amnesty International (1999, 2001), Human Rights Watch (1996, 2001), and numerous researchers who have been permitted to enter various correctional systems in the United States (Davis, 1968; Fuller and Orsagh, 1977; Bowker, 1980; Lockwood, 1980; Wooden and Parker, 1982; Nacci and Kane, 1983, 1984a, 1984b; Saum, Surratt, Inciardi, and Bennett, 1995; Struckman-Johnson, Struckman-Johnson, Rucker, Bumby, and Donaldson, 1996; Struckman-Johnson and Struckman-Johnson 2000, 2002; Hensley, 2002; Hensley, Castle, and Tewksbury, 2003; Hensley, Tewksbury, and Castle, 2003), the once "forbidden" topic of prison sexual assault is becoming a matter of public attention. . . .

Rates of sexual assaults within prisons have fluctuated over the past forty years depending on the type of study conducted, the reluctance of inmates to disclose their assaults, and the terminology used within the studies to define sexual assault (i.e., sexual aggression, sexual coercion). Davis (1968), for example, defined sexual assault as "solicitations accompanied by physical assaults or threats, and other coercive solicitations" (2). Lockwood's (1980) definition of sexual aggression, on the other hand, ranged from imagined sexual overtones by the target to actual incidents of completed rapes. Researchers have also described sexual victimization as a by-product of forced sex and violence (Wooden and Parker, 1982; Saum, et al., 1995). More recent studies concerning sexual victimization have broadened the spectrum of behaviors to include such behaviors as attempted touching of genitals or sexual parts, fondling of genitals, and unsuccessful efforts of sexual intercourse in a threatening manner (Struckman-Johnson et al., 1996; Struckman-Johnson and Struckman-Johnson, 2000, 2002).

Most data concerning inmate-on-inmate sexual assaults have been obtained through surveys and/or interviews with inmates. Unfortunately, few studies have addressed the number of officially reported inmate-on-inmate sexual assaults within prisons. In fact, no study exists which gathers such information on a national scale. Furthermore, no prison sexual assault study has rigorously examined which, if any, institutional factors impact whether inmates who have been sexually assaulted reported their victimization. Therefore, using data from a national sample of prison wardens, the purpose of this study is to examine the effect of these institutional factors on officially reported inmate sexual assaults (attempted or completed inmate-on-inmate rapes).

LITERATURE REVIEW

Although sexual assaults have probably occurred within prisons since their formal development, it was not until the summer of 1966 that the first study was undertaken to measure the rates of sexual assault among inmates. Davis (1968) conducted interviews with 500 staff members and 3,304 male inmates over a 26-month period within the Philadelphia jail system. He found that 97 (or 4.7%) of the inmates reported being sexually assaulted either while incarcerated or while being transported to and from court in the sheriffs' vans. These incidents were not only substantiated through the facility's records, but also through polygraph examinations of the reporting inmates.

Lockwood's (1980) extensive study conducted between 1974–1975 within New York state male prisons focused on the targets of sexual coercion. Results of the study revealed that among the 107 inmate respondents, 28% reported being targets of sexual aggression. Only one inmate, however, reported being raped while in prison.

Fuller and Orsagh's (1977) study included a sample of 400 male inmates in six separate North Carolina state prisons. Interviews with inmates and a review of disciplinary records were used to ascertain the rate of sexual assault. The average reported rate of sexual assault per year was 2.4% within the six correctional institutions.

By examining the broader scope of violence within prisons, Bowker (1980) found that male inmates were more prone to report physically violent assaults than those encounters that included sexual victimization. In 1982, Wooden and Parker conducted their study of prison sexuality by administering a comprehensive survey to 200 male inmates in a medium security California prison. Nearly 14% of the sample reported that they had been sexually victimized.

Nacci and Kane (1983, 1984a, 1984b) led an investigation into the relationship between sexual aggression and violence in 17 male federal prisons. In their two–part study of 330 inmates and 500 correctional officers, it was found that 2% of the sample had been sexual targets, 0.6% had performed an undesired sex act, and 0.3% had been raped while incarcerated in a federal institution.

Saum et al. (1995) focused their one-year study of a Delaware medium security prison on responses of inmates concerning prison sexual experiences and sexual activities that had either been observed, heard about, or experienced by the inmates themselves. The results of the 101 male inmate interviews revealed that 40% admitted to knowing that sexual assaults occurred. Three percent reported that they had witnessed a rape within the past year. One percent reported that they had witnessed two rapes within the past year. Although two inmates disclosed that another inmate had attempted to rape them, only one inmate reported that he had been raped.

Struckman-Johnson et al.'s (1996) study was conducted in the Nebraska prison system in 1994. This study disclosed the highest rate of sexual victimization found in prison sex studies. Twenty-two percent of the 474 male inmates and approximately 1% of the 42 female inmates reported being pressured or forced to have sex against their will. In 1998, Struckman-Johnson and Struckman-Johnson extended their previous research by conducting a more comprehensive study of sexual coercion in seven Midwestern male prisons and three female prisons. Twenty-one percent of the 1,788 male inmates and 11% of the female inmates reported that they had experienced unwanted sexual contact (Struckman-Johnson and Struckman-Johnson, 2000, 2002).

The most recent study of male inmate sexual victimization was conducted in three (one minimum, medium, and maximum security) Oklahoma prisons. Approximately 14% of the 174 male inmates reported being sexual targets and 1.1% disclosed being victims of completed sexual assaults during their incarceration (Hensley, Tewksbury, and Castle, 2003). Finally, in the most recent study of sexual coercion in a female southern prison, Hensley, Castle, and Tewksbury (2003) found that approximately 4.5% of the 245 respondents had been victims of sexual coercion (i.e., attempted and completed rapes).

The majority of these studies have relied on obtaining the rate of sexual assaults in prison through questionnaires and interviews. Rarely have researchers been afforded the opportunity to rely on the official number of inmates who report sexual assaults in order to examine possible factors for explaining such disclosure. The purpose of the current study is to address which, if any, institutional factors effect these reports.

METHODOLOGY

Subjects

Data for the present study come from surveys distributed in August 2001 to 441 state prison wardens. One half of the male facilities in each state were randomly selected to be included in the sample. Furthermore, because of the low number of female prisons, all wardens of women's prisons were surveyed (62 wardens). Wardens located at federal correctional facilities, privately operated correctional facilities, pre-release centers, juvenile detention facilities, and jails were excluded from the study. . . . Five state department of corrections (Delaware, Illinois, Massachusetts, New York, and Pennsylvania) refused to participate in the study due to time and management constraints. . . .

MEASURES

Wardens were asked how many inmates had officially reported being sexually assaulted within their institutions during the past twelve months. Because of the diverse range of responses, the categories were dichotomized so that 0 equals no officially reported sexual assaults and 1 equals one or more officially reported sexual assaults. This item served as the dependent variable.

Data were also collected on the current number of inmates in each institution, overcrowding (if the capacity of the institution was larger than the current number of inmates, no overcrowding existed), sex of institution (male v. other), security level of institution (minimum v. other), ratio of inmates to correctional staff (number of current inmates divided by the number of security staff), and whether the facility had a conjugal visitation. . . .

Results

Of the 226 wardens who responded to the questionnaire, 72% reported that no inmate had officially reported being sexually assaulted within their institution during the past twelve months. Almost 11% of the wardens revealed one officially reported sexual assault within their institution. The remaining 17% of wardens reported between two and 19 officially reported sexual assaults within their institutions. . . .

When examining the correlational relationship between the independent and dependent variables, the most salient variables were current number of inmates, security level, and whether the institution had a conjugal visitation program. Prisons with higher numbers of inmates were more likely to have official reports of inmate sexual assaults. Minimum-security prisons were less likely to have reports of inmate sexual assaults. Finally, institutions with a conjugal visitation program were more likely to have reports of inmate sexual assaults.

TABLE 1 Zero-Order Correlation Matrix

		X_1	X_2	X_3	X_4	X_5	X_6	Y_1
X_1	Current Number of Inmates							
X_2	Overcrowded Facility	.01						
X_3	Sex of Institution	−.12	.03					
X_4	Security Level	.32*	.09	.22				
X_5	Inmate to Staff Ratio	.11	−.14*	.12	−.13			
X_6	Conjugal Visitation Program	.51*	−.12	.09	.03	−.05		
Y_1	Sexual Assault	.38*	.06	−.07	.24*	−.05	.16*	

*Denotes statistical significance at the .05 level. Coding: Current Number of Inmates (range = 36 −6600); Overcrowded Facility (If Capacity of Institution is Smaller than the Current Number of Inmates 0 = No. 1 = Yes); Sex of Institution (0 = Male, 1 = Other); Security Level (0 = Minimum Security, 1 = Other); Ratio of Inmates to Staff (Number of Current Inmates Divided by the Number of Security Staff in the Institution); Conjugal Visitation Program (0 = No, 1 = Yes).

Because the dependent variable is dichotomous, a logistic regression analysis was performed to test if the predictor variables had an effect on the dependent variable. The most salient variables were current number of inmates and security level. Prisons with higher populations of inmates were more likely to have official reports of inmate sexual assaults within those facilities. Additionally, minimum security prisons were less likely to have reports of inmate sexual assaults. . . . Twenty-three percent of the total variance in the analysis was explained by the predictor variables.

DISCUSSION

The research reported here is unique and differs significantly from the existing literature on prison sexual assaults. Previous research has focused on identifying factors associated with individual victimization and perpetration of assaults. This research, instead, looks at institutional factors of prisons, assessing whether or not environmental and staffing variables are related to the officially reported number of sexual assaults. Therefore, the present research presents a more macro-level analysis than currently exists in the literature.

Results show that sexual assaults are more likely to be reported to correctional officials in institutions with larger populations and those with higher security levels. More interesting, and perhaps more important for policy and practice purposes, are the findings regarding variables that are not significant predictors.

Whereas anecdotal evidence and for some, "common sense," has long suggested that institutional overcrowding and a higher inmate-staff ratio are threats to inmate personal security, these variables do not show a statistically significant relationship to the number of officially reported sexual assaults in prisons. Whether an institution is overcrowded, the ratio of inmates to staff is an issue that can be—albeit sometimes at significant financial expense—managed by day-to-day practices. Correctional administrators that seek to establish a community of inmates where sexual violence is minimized may find that directing their efforts at these factors fail to achieve their desired goals. This fact raises the question of whether policies, procedures, and manipulation of institutional variables can effectively address inmate sexual assaults. Where it does appear that efforts may be productive is in the area of controlling the size of the inmate population. Reducing the size of individual institutions' populations may lead to a reduction in inmate sexual assaults. . . .

REFERENCES

American Correctional Association. (2000). *2000 Juvenile and Adult Correctional Departments, Institutions, Agencies, and Paroling Authorities Directory.* Lanham, MD: American Correctional Association.

Amnesty International. (2001). *Broken Bodies, Shattered Minds: Torture and Ill-Treatment of Women.* London: Amnesty International.

Amnesty International. (1999). *Not Part of my Sentence: Violations of the Human Rights of Women in Custody.* New York: Amnesty International.

Bowker, L. (1980). *Prison Victimization.* New York: Elsevier North Holland.

Camp, C. & Camp, G. (1998). *The Corrections Yearbook, 1998.* Middletown, CT: Criminal Justice Institute.

Davis, A. (1968). Sexual Assaults in the Philadelphia Prison System and Sheriff's Vans. *Trans-Action,* 8–16.

Fuller, D. & Orsagh, T. (1977). Violence and Victimization within a State Prison System. *Criminal Justice Review,* 2(2), 35–55.

Hensley, C. (ed.). (2002). *Prison Sex: Practice and Policy.* Boulder, CO: Lynne Rienner Publishers.

Hensley, C., Castle, T., & Tewksbury, R. (2003). Inmate-to-Inmate Sexual Coercion in a Prison for Women. *Journal of Offender Rehabilitation,* 37(2), 67–77.

Hensley, C., Tewksbury, R., & Castle, T. (2003). "Characteristics of Prison Sexual Assault Targets in Male Oklahoma Correctional Facilities." *Journal of Interpersonal Violence,* 18(6), 595–606.

Human Rights Watch. (2001). *United States: No Escape, Male Rape in U.S. Prisons.* Online. Available at: http://www.hrw.org/reports/2001/prison/ report1.html.

Human Rights Watch. (1996). *All Too Familiar: Sexual Abuse of Women in U.S. State Prisons.* New York: Human Rights Watch.

Lehrer, E. (2002). No Joke: Prison Rape is Finally Taken Seriously. On-line. Available at: http://www.nationalreview.com/comment/comment-lehrer062002asp.

Lockwood, D. (1980). *Prison Sexual Violence.* New York: Elsevier Press.

Nacci, P. & Kane, T. (1984b). Inmate Sexual Aggression: Some Evolving Propositions, Empirical Findings, and Mitigating Counter-Forces. *Journal of Offender Counseling, Services, and Rehabilitation,* 9(1/2), 1–20.

Nacci, P. & Kane, T. (1984a). Sex and Sexual Aggression in Federal Prisons: Inmate Involvement and Employee Impact. *Federal Probation,* 48(1), 46–53.

Nacci, P. & Kane, T. (1983). The Incidence of Sex and Sexual Aggression in Federal Prisons. *Federal Probation,* 47(4), 31–36.

Saum, C., Surratt, H., Inciardi, J., & Bennett, R. (1995). Sex in Prison: Exploring the Myths and Realities. *The Prison Journal,* 75(4), 413–430.

Stemple, L. (2002). Stop Prison Rape Accuses FBI of Ignoring Male Rape Victims in New Crime Report. Online. Available at: http://www.spr.org.

Stop Prison Rape. (2001). Wolf-Scott Prison Rape Reform Act of 2001. Online. Available at: http://www.spr.org.

Struckman-Johnson, C. & Struckman-Johnson, D. (2002). Sexual Coercion Reported by Women in Three Midwestern Prisons. *The Journal of Sex Research,* 39(3), 217–227.

Struckman-Johnson, C. & Struckman-Johnson, D. (2000). Sexual coercion rates in seven Midwestern prison facilities for men. *The Prison Journal*, 80(4), 379–390.

Struckman-Johnson, C., Struckman-Johnson, D., Rucker, L., Bumby, K., & Donaldson, S. (1996). Sexual coercion reported by men and women in prison. *The Journal of Sex Research,* 33(1), 67–76.

Wooden, W. & Parker, J. (1982). *Men Behind Bars: Sexual Exploitation in Prison.* New York: Plenum Press.

REVIEW QUESTIONS

1. What institutional structural factors are important in understanding the rates of officially reported sexual assaults in prisons?
2. How common is sexual assault in men's prisons?
3. What other institutional factors that were not looked at in this research might be important influences on the rates of sexual assaults in prison? Why?

READING 10

Smoke 'Em if You Got 'Em

Cigarette Black Markets in U.S. Prisons and Jails

Stephen E. Lankenau

As prisons (like much of society) move toward banning smoking, a number of structural and interactional changes are occurring in prisons. The change from seeing and using cigarettes as a common form of institutional currency to cigarettes (and all tobacco products) being considered contraband creates an underground, illegal economy that has both significant similarities and differences from other contraband economies. The author highlights important influences on the tobacco black market, including physical features of the prison, daily activity routines of inmates and staff, and inmates' abilities to bribe or coerce staff into both ignoring the rules and contributing to the black market economy by smuggling cigarettes and tobacco into the institution. The "simple" change of a prison becoming a smoke-free environment is shown to have far-reaching effects on institutional culture, structures, and daily routines.

Since the mid-1980s, cigarette-smoking policies have become increasingly restrictive in jails and prisons across the United States. Currently, two thirds of U.S. jails and one quarter of U.S. prisons ban inmates from smoking cigarettes or possessing tobacco (Falkin, Strauss, & Lankenau, 1998,1999). In institutions where bans are enforced, inmates are prohibited from smoking any form of tobacco inside the facility or outside on the facility grounds. Despite this trend toward banning tobacco in correctional facilities, virtually no studies have examined the effect of this policy change on inmate culture and prison economies. In particular, no research has focused specifically on cigarette black markets that invariably emerge in jails and prisons where tobacco is prohibited.

We conducted ethnographic case studies of smoking policies in 16 jails and prisons to understand the effects of cigarette bans (the prohibition of tobacco) and restrictions (the sanctioning of tobacco smoking) on the exchange and use of cigarettes among inmates. In the following analysis, we contrast relatively benign cigarette "gray markets," where cigarettes are traded and used as currency in facilities that restrict tobacco, with more problematic black markets, where cigarettes are a highly priced contraband item in facilities that ban tobacco. In particular, our analysis points to several structural factors that affect the development of cigarette black markets in the facilities that we visited: the architectural design of the institution,

This research was funded by the Robert Wood Johnson Foundation (Grant No. 031607) and was directed by Greg Falkin, principal investigator, and Sheila Strauss, coinvestigator, of National Development and Research Institutes, Inc. (NDRI). The points of view presented in this article do not necessarily represent those of the Foundation, NDRI, or participating correctional institutions. I acknowledge Greg Falkin and Shiela Strauss for helpful comments on earlier drafts of this article. In addition, I acknowledge all of the state and county officials, wardens, officers, staff, and inmates at the 16 participating correctional institutions, who assisted me in carrying out this research. Correspondence should be sent to Stephen E. Lankenau, NDRI, Two World Trade Center, 16th Floor, New York, NY 10048; email: stevelankenau@ndri.org.

including the configuration of inmate-housing units; the degree to which inmates move around and outside of an institution; and the vigilance of correctional officers and staff in enforcing the smoking policy and their involvement in smuggling cigarettes to inmates. Although these factors affect the influx of other types of contraband in to correctional facilities, such as illegal drugs, we argue that the demand and availability of cigarettes creates a unique kind of black market.

THE FUNCTION OF CIGARETTES IN A PRISON ECONOMY

The legitimate and illicit exchanges of goods and services occurring inside jails and prisons comprise both a formal and informal economic system (Williams & Fish, 1974). The formal economy constitutes a prison's legitimate economic system that includes prison industries, work release programs, and other licit activities that generate income for inmates (and the correctional facility). This official system includes inmate monetary accounts, which are supplemented through prison employment and deposits made by associates, as well as the commissary, which dispenses goods, such as soap, snack foods, and sometimes cigarettes. For many inmates, however, the formal prison economy does not provide enough opportunities to earn income and offers too few desirable goods and services from the commissary. Consequently, an informal economy develops that is premised on consuming prohibited or contraband items and "hustles" (Gleason, 1978) to earn extra resources to pay for contraband and legitimate commissary goods.

Traditionally, cigarettes have been used by inmates as a standard form of currency in informal prison economies. Radford's (1945) description of a Nazi Germany prisoner of war (POW) camp was the first to discuss the economic and social importance of cigarettes in an inmate economy. Radford, a former POW, indicated that although active trading of other goods and services existed, only cigarettes were transformed from a commodity to a form of currency due to their durability, portability, supply, and demand. Likewise, Williams and Fish (1974) reported that cigarettes functioned as an ideal currency in prison because they were often smoked and replaced by new packs before the old packs became mangled and worn out.

The packaging of cigarettes into cartons, packs, and individual cigarettes creates natural denominations that foster convenient transactions among inmates. Kalinich's (1986) study of one prison economy found that stable prices evolved for contraband items that were expressed in terms of packs and cartons of cigarettes, such as five packs for a joint of marijuana or two cartons for a tattoo. Likewise, Radford (1945) reported that prices evolved for certain commodities and were expressed in number of cigarettes, such as 40 cigarettes for a loaf of bread or 15 cigarettes for a chocolate bar.

Another defining feature of the camp described by Radford (1945) was the development of an embryonic labor market, such as laundrymen earning two cigarettes per washed garment, and the emergence of entrepreneurial services, such as coffee stall proprietors selling coffee for two cigarettes per cup. Labor marketers and entrepreneurs using cigarettes as currency is also commonly found in jails and prisons. One practice, "mushfaking," involves manufacturing contraband items out of available materials in exchange for cigarettes or other goods and services (Foster, 1982). Examples include inmates creating dice from cubes of sugar marked with a black felt pen or making shivs or knives from silverware. Likewise, tattooing (Demelco, 1993), drug dealing (Gleason, 1978), and gambling (Kalinich, 1986) are common hustles that generate illicit income tied to the exchange of cigarettes.

A primary feature of the prison environment is the policing of hustles and the management of contraband problems through occasional or frequent shakedowns. Shakedowns are accomplished by correctional officers searching through an inmate's cell and possessions and ferreting out and seizing unauthorized items (Guenther, 1978). Shakedowns typically focus on more serious contraband, such as weapons, illegal drugs, and escape equipment, rather than on less serious "nuisance contraband," such as pornography, gambling equipment, and personal effects. In prisons that allow smoking, cigarettes constitute contraband only when amassed in large quantities (Kalinich, 1986).

Despite the integral role that cigarettes have traditionally played in the prison economy, both as a commodity and as a currency, no formal research has investigated the effects of cigarette bans on inmate culture. Rather, research examining cigarettes in prisons or jails has focused on housing-unit smoking policies (Falkin et al., 1998; Romero & Connell, 1988; Vaughn & del Carmen, 1992), rates of smoking among inmates (Vaughn & del Carmen, 1992), and legal issues surrounding cigarette bans (Vaughn & del Carmen, 1992). Prison and jail research conducted over the past 10 years, the period during which most bans have occurred, has focused on topics that relate to informal prison economics, such as changes in prison culture (Hunt, Riegel, Morales, & Waldorf, 1993), new generation jails (Jackson & Stearns, 1995), and sex in prison (Saum, Surratt, Inciardi, & Bennett, 1995), without mentioning the recent trend to ban cigarettes.

This article addresses an important gap in the existing literature on the role of cigarettes in informal prison economies. In particular, this research examines how changes in institutional policy, namely, restricting or banning cigarettes in jails and prisons, affects the informal prison economy and inmate culture.

METHOD AND SAMPLE

This research is part of a broader project focused on documenting and understanding the changes in cigarette-smoking policies in jails and prisons. As we describe, our particular focus on cigarette black markets emerged while learning about outcomes linked to jail and prison policies banning cigarettes. We gathered information about cigarette black markets using a case study method.

We began by contacting jails and prisons that were changing their smoking policy (or had recently changed), were viewed as authorities on the subject of banning cigarettes in correctional facilities, or were located in regions of the country where tobacco was an important part of the local or regional economy. Based on these criteria, we selected jails and prisons for qualitative exploration after individually examining hundreds of previously collected surveys (Falkin et al., 1998) or learning about cases while attending jail and correctional association annual meetings. Administrators at prospective jails and prisons were then contacted via phone and probed for additional information regarding their smoking policies. During these initial conversations, the discussion often turned to problems surrounding the enforcement of cigarette bans and the development of cigarette black markets. Consequently, we paid particular attention to the issue of cigarette black markets during site visits.

Following the screening process, 10 jails and 6 prisons in eight states (California, Connecticut, Indiana, Kentucky, Michigan, New Jersey, North Carolina, and Washington) were identified as possessing smoking policies of interest and later visited. All of the site visits were conducted between May 1998 and April 1999. Ten of the case study sites (6 jails and 4 prisons) banned cigarettes for staff and inmates, whereas 6 of the sites (4 jails and 2 prisons) restricted smoking, that is, staff and inmates were permitted to smoke in certain parts of the institution at specific times. Visits lasted 2 days and included touring the facility, interviewing key administrators, conversing with correctional officers and staff at their posts (e.g., medical clinic, control center, jail cell), and talking to inmates.

Interactions with line staff and inmates consisted of informal conversations and formal interviews to obtain information on inmate access to cigarettes and cigarette prices in facilities that permitted smoking and to describe three main aspects of the cigarette black market in facilities that banned smoking: smuggling, dealing, and smoking practices. Inmates were chosen by randomly selecting a housing unit and then interviewing only smokers who agreed to discuss their experiences under the facility's smoking policy. Officers assigned to the same housing unit where also interviewed whenever possible. For both inmates and staff, interviews were conducted privately inside housing units or designated offices and occurred after gaining informed consent. In total, 50 staff and 140 inmates were interviewed. Nearly all of the 140 inmates interviewed were men, a reflection of the fact that we visited exclusively men's prisons and that the jails were dominated by male inmates.

In addition to directly asking administrators, staff, and inmates about cigarette practices and policies, inmates were observed interacting with other inmates and with officers in the jails and prisons. Also, health department officials in four counties were interviewed to gain insights into local public health initiatives toward smoking cessation in the community and inside jails. Finally, department of corrections officials in three states were interviewed to understand smoking policy formulation at the state level and to learn how these officials viewed problems surrounding the enforcement of cigarette restrictions in prisons.

Researchers who investigate clandestine activities, such as cigarette black markets in jails and prisons, have to be particularly attentive to the validity of the information gathered. Inmates and staff often have reasons to lie or withhold facts about black market activities because disclosing any involvement could jeopardize personal safety, relationships with others, and jobs. Although the verification of any particular fact is problematic, we believe our understanding of cigarette black markets in the facilities we studied reflects the reality of the situation at the time we visited the facilities. We independently asked staff and inmates many of the same questions, such as "How much does a cigarette cost?" and "How are cigarettes brought into the facility?" A consensus often emerged in response to these questions, indicating that the individuals we talked to had similar perceptions of these issues. In addition, we were often able to validate these perceptions through participant observation, such as smelling tobacco on inmates or seeing remnants of cigarettes in bathroom stalls.

Given the subterranean nature of the cigarette black market, the relatively brief time we spent inside each institution, and the limited number of inmates and staff that we interviewed and observed, we do not make inferences as to how widespread or problematic the cigarette black market was in each facility. Rather, our primary objective is to describe the principal features of the cigarette economy and cigarette black market as we came to understand them during our 16 site visits.

To provide a context for understanding how and why cigarette black markets emerged and functioned in the facilities that banned tobacco, we first describe the gray market cigarette economy in facilities that permitted smoking.

THE GRAY-MARKET CIGARETTE ECONOMY

Access to Cigarettes

In the six facilities that permitted smoking, inmates purchased cigarettes as well as other commodities, such as snack foods, beverages, personal hygiene products, medication, and clothing, from a commissary or in-house store. Whereas new inmates received basic hygiene items, such as toothpaste and soap, from the commissary on admission, all inmates were responsible for paying for luxury items as well as necessities after admission. In lower security facilities, inmates went to the commissary to buy cigarettes and tobacco, whereas in higher security facilities, purchased items were delivered directly to their cells.

Because U.S. currency was regarded as contraband inside all of the facilities visited, inmates were given personal debit accounts, and the costs of commissary items were deducted from their accounts. Money could be. added to inmate accounts via deposits made by inmates themselves, families, or associates. Inmates also accrued income through institutional jobs, and these earnings were added directly to their accounts. Depending on their level of skill and job responsibility, inmates earned between $ 15 and $35 per month. For instance, an inmate working as a welder earned more than a janitor. In some cases, inmates earned a wage for attending general equivalency diploma classes or drug abuse treatment programs. In addition, inmates who were prohibited from working, chose not to work, or attended classes received "idle pay," a minimal monthly allowance that provided for basic hygiene purchases.

Depending on the facility, inmates ordered commissary items between one and three times per week. Commissary purchases, including cigarettes, were limited to a maximum weekly amount, such as $50 or $60. The commissary was the only source for these products because inmates were prohibited from receiving such items from friends or family. Outside gifts were prohibited because they could serve as conduits for tobacco and other contraband, such as illegal drugs and weapons.

In the six institutions that sold tobacco, the price, quality, and diversity of tobacco products varied from facility to facility. For example, inmates in a small jail could purchase only a generic brand of cigarettes costing $1.25 for a pack of 20 cigarettes, whereas inmates in a large prison could buy cigars, loose tobacco, and name brand cigarettes, such as Marlboro, for $2.25 per pack. Cartons with 10 packs of cigarettes were also sold but typically without any discounted pricing. Loose tobacco, which was sold in 6-oz cans or 1-oz boxes along with cigarette rolling papers, was the cheapest form of tobacco. For instance, in one prison, a 6-oz can of Bugler cost $4, which could then be rolled into 300 cigarettes, the equivalent of 15 packs of cigarettes costing about $0.40 per pack.

Cigarettes as Currency

All of the facilities that allowed inmates to smoke prohibited them from trading cigarettes for other goods and from giving cigarettes to each other as gifts. However, cigarette exchanges among inmates were difficult to police, and sanctions for trading were rarely imposed, according to both inmates and officers at these six facilities. Furthermore, because U.S. currency was prohibited, cigarettes functioned as a local form of currency in these prisons and jails. In particular, a pack of cigarettes stood as the basic unit of exchange and favored form of currency for several reasons. First, compared with other common commissary items, such as candy bars, soups, and soap, a pack of cigarettes cost enough to be a meaningful object of exchange. Second, a pack of cigarettes is a portable, semidurable object that could be conveniently exchanged; however, because trading or giving away cigarettes constituted a rule violation in these facilities, the unit of currency had to be inconspicuous. Third, because the great majority of inmates smoked, a pack of cigarettes served the dual function of acting as currency and as a consumable good. Rather than trading other items for a pack of cigarettes, an inmate could simply smoke up his winnings or earnings.

A pack of cigarettes was used as payment for a variety of services and exchanges. For instance, a visit to the prison barber sometimes required a pack of cigarettes as a tip to ensure the desired haircut. In several facilities, inmates who wanted their laundry properly folded had to tip the laundryman a pack of cigarettes for each load of clothes washed. In some cases, inmates who failed to tip not only received poorly folded clothes but had their belongings subjected to a "state wash," that is, a laundryman washed and dried an inmate's clothes without ever removing them from the laundry bag, which often left clothes still dirty and wrinkled.

Apart from inmates who used their institutional jobs to gain income, such as laundrymen or barbers, other inmates devised various hustles to earn extra income. For instance, one inmate created cards and envelopes that he exchanged for cigarettes. He also ran a "store" where he bought items from inmates at one price, such as a shirt for two packs of cigarettes, and then sold the items later for a higher price, such as three packs of cigarettes for the same shirt. Gambling debts were also frequently paid in packs of cigarettes.

One particular inmate's hustle, to roll loose tobacco into cigarettes, clearly illustrates the value of cigarettes and how cigarettes can circulate within a jail or prison economy. In one prison, a 6-oz can of loose tobacco sold for $4, and the buyer would pass it to an inmate who was highly skilled at rolling cigarettes. Using 4 oz of tobacco, he rolled 200 cigarettes, the equivalent of 10 packs of cigarettes, and he kept the remaining 2 oz as payment for his labor. He then rolled the extra tobacco into 100 additional cigarettes. Because his cigarettes were so skillfully rolled, other inmates were often willing to trade a pack of 20 cigarettes, valued at $2, for his 100 cigarettes. He then traded packs of cigarettes for commissary items. This inmate, who also worked a night job as a janitor, rolled between two and seven cans of tobacco per day. Whereas his janitor job paid only $16.50 per month, he earned the equivalent of $4 to $14 per day rolling cigarettes. Although rolling and exchanging tobacco was forbidden under the institution's rules, this inmate was able to succeed because the dorm officers often looked the other way.

THE BLACK MARKET IN CIGARETTES

Contraband Cigarettes in Facilities That Permit Smoking

As mentioned earlier, the six facilities that sold cigarettes all restricted inmate smoking in certain ways. Depending on the facility, these restrictions included the following: barring inmates from smoking anywhere inside the facility but allowing them to smoke on the prison grounds, prohibiting inmates from smoking in their individual cells but permitting smoking in the attached dayrooms, and prohibiting inmates from smoking in their cells if their cellmate objected. Violating the smoking policy led to further smoking restrictions, such as the loss of smoking privileges for certain periods of time.

In all the facilities that allowed inmates to smoke, smoking was prohibited in the isolation cells, known as the administrative segregation unit, which are reserved for egregious rule violators. However, when placed in the administrative segregation unit, inmates procured cigarettes in a secretive and costly manner, a practice that foreshadowed the emergence of black markets in facilities that banned tobacco.

For instance, a well-developed black market existed in the administrative segregation unit at one maximum security prison where smoking was permitted among the general population. According to several officers assigned to the unit, cigarettes entered the unit in a variety of ways. Inmates involved in the black market hid cigarettes in food trays or in bundles of laundry that were sent into the units. Cigarettes were also placed inside tennis balls, tossed into the outdoor recreational area, and then retrieved by inmates. Other inmates purposefully became involved in incidents requiring disciplinary action or requested protective custody in order to be temporarily placed in administrative segregation. Once in the unit, the new inmate provided smuggled cigarettes to other inmates at a substantial markup.

Because cells in the unit were frequently searched and monitored, inmates had to carefully smoke and hide their tobacco. One clever technique involved an inmate's placing tobacco and matches in a tightly sealed plastic toothbrush holder and then putting the holder in a toilet located in the inmate's cell. The inmate then flushed the holder, but the buoyant plastic became trapped in an air pocket located inside the toilet plumbing. When the inmate wished to smoke, he drained the toilet water into the sink. Removing the water caused the toothbrush holder to drop into the base of the toilet bowl. The tobacco and matches, still dry, were then removed from the holder. On lighting the cigarette, smoke was blown into the air-filled toilet plumbing. In this case, the toilet served the dual function of hiding the tobacco and concealing cigarette smoke.

Black Markets in Facilities That Banned Smoking

Among the 10 facilities that banned smoking, all prohibited administrative staff, correctional officers, and inmates from smoking tobacco anywhere inside of the facility, that is, both the administrative offices and the secured areas. However, certain policy variations existed that had implications for the development of a black market. For instance, one facility allowed inmates to smoke while they were off-site performing community service or while they were on work release. Most facilities allowed staff and officers to smoke on facility grounds in designated areas that were outside of the view of inmates. The most restrictive policy prohibited staff and officers from possessing or using tobacco while on facility property. In this case, staff and officers were pat-searched specifically to ferret out tobacco before entering the facility's secured area.

Ultimately, at all 10 facilities, the smoking bans produced subterranean, sometimes elaborate, practices for acquiring, exchanging, and smoking tobacco. In certain ways, these practices and exchanges are variations on other types of black market activity, such as illegal drugs, that emerge inside of correctional facilities. However, we describe how cigarette bans produce a unique black market because of the high demand by inmates for tobacco and the more pervasive involvement of correctional staff in the black market. In this section, we discuss three aspects of the cigarette black market: methods of acquiring and smuggling tobacco into a facility, dealing tobacco inside a facility, and smoking, lighting, and hiding practices.

Acquiring and Smuggling Tobacco The defining feature of a black market and its ability to thrive is the relationship between black marketers and individuals with access to cigarettes in the nonsecured sections of the facility as well as areas outside of the facility. The greater access inmates had to other inmates, visitors, staff, and officers, the more likely it was that a more organized black market arose. Interaction among inmates and others was typically influenced by the security level of the facility, facility architecture, and policing pragmatics, such as single-person cells versus two-person cells, cells versus dorm-housing units, indoor recreational areas versus outdoor recreational spaces, and security fences versus no fences. Essentially, greater interaction among inmates created more opportunities to exchange tobacco, resources, and information. Facilities with a higher security level, which meant greater restrictions among inmates, did have less black market activity.

An important dimension of security and interaction among inmates is whether a facility allowed certain inmates clearance, that is, permitted inmates to move into and out of the secure areas of the facility, including leaving the facility. Inmate trustees, who often work in the secured and nonsecured areas of a facility, represented one end of the clearance continuum and were referred to as having a low level of clearance. Typical trustee jobs included kitchen and janitorial work. Community service and work release inmates, who left the facility and returned to the community during scheduled times each day, denoted the other end of the continuum and were described as having a high level of clearance. Common jobs in the community included mowing fields along highways or painting city buildings and other properties. In facilities that had less black market collusion from staff and officers, inmates with a higher clearance status were the primary tobacco runners and suppliers. Overall, the great majority of jail and prison inmates had no clearance or low clearance and had to rely on the few inmates with higher levels of clearance or on officers to smuggle tobacco into the facility.

Inmates with a relatively low level of clearance at one jail, trustees who worked in the kitchen, had a successful smuggling operation for a period of time, until the scheme was uncovered by staff. The kitchen was staffed by inmate workers who lived together in one pod or section within the jail. These trustees were housed together due to their atypical schedule—they rose earlier than other inmates to prepare meals—and to minimize the possible flow of contraband between them and other inmates. Kitchen workers also wore white uniforms to distinguish them from other trustees and nontrustees. The kitchen was located behind the jail in an area that was infrequently patrolled and was fenced off from pedestrians. The kitchen's exterior wall consisted of vinyl siding that met directly with an outside, unsecured space. At some point, a hole about 1 inch in diameter was drilled or banged through the base of the exterior wall and into the kitchen. This small hole, which connected the interior of the kitchen directly to the outside world, became an artery for cigarettes and other contraband until it was discovered. Kitchen workers retrieved the cigarettes placed in the hole and either smoked them later or distributed them within the jail. Despite being housed together in one area, the kitchen staff had contact with other trustees during the day, which afforded them opportunities to route contraband around the jail. The civilian staff who managed the inmate kitchen workers represented an additional point of contact with the outside world and may have facilitated the smuggling operation. Hence, despite a jail's attempt to minimize the flow of contraband by segregating trustees from other inmates and civilians, this example highlighted a security breach that allowed a supply of cigarettes to enter the jail.

Community service workers and work release inmates represented a more reliable, steady supply of cigarettes. Such workers devised their own smuggling efforts, such as procuring cigarettes from civilian workers or having them drop off cigarettes in designated outdoor areas. Alternatively, inmates with no clearance reported arranging for civilian associates to leave bundles of cigarettes to be retrieved and later smuggled in by a "mule," such as an inmate working on a road crew.

These smuggling efforts were typically financed by a "send-in." Broadly, a send-in involved an inmate sending money out of the facility in exchange for a certain quantity of tobacco to be brought in, typically a carton or more. Send-ins were accomplished by one inmate sending money to an outside source who then bought the cigarettes and left them in a designated area for pick-up. Send-ins were risky investments because cigarettes could be lost, stolen, or confiscated before reaching their purchaser. However, send-ins were generally viewed as worthwhile risks because the street cost of a carton was relatively low compared with its black market price inside a jail or prison, which ranged from $200 to $500.

Work release inmates who smuggled in cigarettes faced certain risks. Depending on the attitudes projected by workers themselves and the number of officers staffing a post on particular times and days, returning workers might be strip-searched, pat-searched, or waved in without being explicitly searched. To evade detection during searches, inmates hid contraband in a variety of ways. For instance, the soles of shoes or sneakers were hollowed out, filled with loose tobacco or cigarettes, and then meticulously restored with glue to avoid suspicion. Likewise, linings of jackets and coats were sometimes cut open, filled with tobacco, and then resewn. Inmates who were permitted to take gear to a work site reported hiding tobacco inside tool belts or plastic mugs. A more invasive smuggling method involved wrapping cigarettes in plastic and then carrying them inside one's rectum.

Inmates who successfully smuggled in tobacco for other inmates generally received a portion of the tobacco as a form of payment. For instance, one inmate who bought tobacco via a send-in paid a mule 5 packs out of a 30-pack delivery, a 17% cost. Another inmate who bought five cans of tobacco paid his mule 9 oz of the 30 oz smuggled in, a 30% cost.

That such large amounts of tobacco, multiple cartons or cans, were often smuggled into certain facilities indicated a force beyond sheer cleverness or luck on the part of smugglers. Rather, correctional staff were complicit in some of these larger smuggling efforts. In fact, some mules developed relationships with the officers in charge of pat searches. For instance, certain mules paid officers a $20 "gate fee," which allowed reentry to the facility without any search.

Compared to other black market enterprises, such as illegal drugs, cigarettes represented a unique commodity because officers typically viewed them differently from other forms of contraband. Most officers interviewed did not view cigarettes as immoral or dangerous, as they might regard heroin, cocaine, or marijuana, because many were current or former smokers themselves. Rather, a cigarette's legal status in the civilian world placed it in a qualitatively different category than a sleeve of heroin or a vial of crack. Consequently, some correctional officers directly fueled the cigarette black market by smuggling or aiding the smuggling of tobacco into a facility.

An officer's participation in the black market consisted of developing explicit relationships with inmates focused on delivering certain quantities of tobacco. Some officers passed on a few cigarettes or a pack of cigarettes to an inmate in exchange for money or a job well done. More serious transactions involved officers working as suppliers of cigarettes into a facility or as couriers of inmate cigarette profits out of a facility. Inmates financed tobacco purchases indirectly through send-ins and more directly through accumulated cigarette profits. Regarding send-ins, inmates reported contacting civilian associates to deliver the appropriate money to an officer. On receipt of the money, the officer delivered the agreed on amount of tobacco. Inmates who generated large profits inside a facility, several hundred dollars at a time, reported paying officers directly inside the facility.

Significantly, officers collected large amounts of money supplying cigarettes. Inmates reported that officers charged between $20 and $50 for one pack of cigarettes, whereas cartons and cans of tobacco sold for between $50 and $100. That cigarettes are legal in the civilian world made procurement both easy and stigma-free. Ultimately, officers who earned between $7 and $10 as an hourly wage could earn an entire week's salary in one cigarette transaction. Consequently, officers who participated in the cigarette black market were motivated by multiple factors, some of which were easily rationalized.

Dealing Tobacco The tremendous markups enjoyed by officers who fueled the cigarette black market point to the great earning potential of dealing cigarettes. Apart from officers, two primary layers of inmate dealers existed in well-developed cigarette black markets. Inmates who had the resources to coordinate send-ins to officers or other civilian suppliers represented the primary dealers. These inmates purchased bulk amounts of tobacco, cartons and cans, and then sold packs and ounces to secondary dealers. Secondary dealers bought tobacco by trading commissary items or other possessions for tobacco. Alternatively, secondary dealers also did send-ins to primary dealers, which was accomplished by a secondary dealer sending money to a primary dealer's inmate account or to an outside location, such as a post office box or a civilian address. Tobacco was dispensed once the money "hit" the primary dealer's account or outside location.

Primary dealers reported amassing substantial amounts of money through black market participation. For instance, one dealer claimed that he sent $400 to $500 to his girlfriend each week, whereas another dealer reported saving $900 after dealing cigarettes for 3 months. Smuggling out such large amounts of cash often required the assistance of officers. One inmate said that he paid an officer $100 to deliver $400 to a civilian associate.

Compared to primary dealers, secondary dealers typically sold enough tobacco to pay for their own smoking habit, while earning a small profit on the side. For instance, a secondary dealer at one facility periodically spent $50 on a 6-oz can of tobacco and then recouped his investment by selling three 1-oz bags of tobacco for $20 per bag. Typically, $20 worth of commissary items, such as soap, snacks, and soups, were exchanged for the ounce or the ounce was purchased with "green money," U.S. currency. The remaining 3 oz were then smoked or periodically sold off for additional commissary items or other prison commodities. This example demonstrates that buying a $50 can of tobacco on the black market yields far greater returns, in terms of commissary purchasing power, than does adding $50 to an inmate account. Consequently, some inmates requested that family members undertake sendins for tobacco rather than adding money directly to their accounts.

In facilities with less developed black markets and where tobacco was less plentiful, packs of cigarettes (as compared to cartons) were the main quantities smuggled into facilities. For instance, primary dealers at one facility bought packs from officers for $20 in U.S. currency and then sold individual cigarettes for $5 a piece. Secondary dealers then broke the cigarettes down into "rollies," smaller cigarettes constructed out of tobacco and rolling papers, that sold for $2 or $3 a piece.

Like smuggling, dealing cigarettes carried certain risks. The penalties for possessing or selling tobacco varied from facility to facility, but the offense typically fell under the broader category of possessing or distributing contraband. In some institutions, dealing tobacco was regarded as seriously as dealing a controlled substance, such as marijuana or cocaine. In other facilities, tobacco was viewed more benignly, similar to possessing unauthorized clothing or books. Across facilities, sanctions ran the gamut from loss of certain privileges, such as commissary or visitors, to being moved to a higher security facility or increasing the length of one's sentence. Hence, established dealers were careful about handling tobacco.

In fact, some more experienced dealers, both primary and secondary, did not handle tobacco at all. Rather, the risks of possessing tobacco were absorbed by lower profile inmates who were not likely to have been "ticketed" for tobacco possession. In some cases, dealers chose nonsmokers to hold and deal tobacco for them. Other dealers hired two inmates: one to deal their tobacco and another to hold their tobacco for personal use. In turn, these subdealers and handlers were often paid in commissary items and/or tobacco for their work. For instance, one dealer paid an inmate $5 in commissary and 10 rollies to hold 6 oz of tobacco, which had a yard value between $50 and $60.

Hiding tobacco in personal space, such as lockers, cells, and beds, was difficult because these were the places that correctional officers searched during inmate shakedowns. Consequently, tobacco was hidden throughout some facilities in library books, behind lighting fixtures, underground, inside walls, and outside in recreation areas. In addition to hiring subdealers to hide tobacco, established dealers distributed free cigarettes, essentially hush money, to those inmates who threatened the secrecy of their operation.

Smoking, Lighting, and Hiding Practices Jail and prison inmates spent most of their waking and nonwaking hours in their housing units, that is, cells, day rooms, and dormitories, which were also the primary places where inmates exchanged and smoked cigarettes. Depending on the facility's architecture, inmates were either directly supervised by officers while in their housing units or indirectly monitored from remote locations. Under either approach, burning tobacco was readily discernible in spaces that were supposed to be smoke-free. Before charging an inmate with violating the smoking policy, an officer typically needed concrete evidence that an inmate had been smoking, such as a cigarette butt. To avoid detection, inmates craftily hid cigarettes, masked the smell of smoke with electric fans or cologne, and flushed cigarette butts down toilets. These evasion techniques frustrated many officers from actively pursuing cigarette smokers, whereas other officers simply looked the other way when detecting smoke. Some officers only pursued flagrant rule violators, such as inmates who openly smoked without any respect for the officer's authority.

Officers generally caught inmates with tobacco in one of three ways: while, smoking a cigarette in a cell, dayroom, or bathroom; during a cell or bed area shakedown; or while attempting to smuggle tobacco into the facility. Among these three scenarios, smoking a cigarette was a frequent way of getting caught because a burning cigarette emitted both visual and olfactory evidence, despite an inmate's best efforts to hide it. Also, the act of smoking caused some smokers to cough, which would attract an officer's attention. In addition, lighting a cigarette required a flame or spark that also transmitted visual, olfactory, and auditory clues of a smoking violation. Because matches and lighters were frequently more scarce than cigarettes, inmates devised a host of techniques to create fire, some of which occasionally led to their being caught.

A common lighting method was to place two pencil leads in an electrical outlet and set a third lead wrapped in toilet paper across the first two. Generally, the toilet paper caught fire, the cigarette was lit, and the lighting kit was discarded. Occasionally, the lighting process went awry and caused an outlet to short out, which then drew an officer's attention to the particular cell or section of the day room.

Overall, inmates reported adeptness at masking the smell of smoke, lighting cigarettes without detection, and discarding cigarette butts before they could be confiscated by officers as evidence. Rather, both inmates and officers reported that most tobacco violators were caught during shakedowns. Shakedowns were typically conducted for one of three reasons: periodic facility-wide shakedowns, random housing-unit shakedowns, and cell shakedowns following suspicious inmate activities or tips from other inmates. During periodic shakedowns, the entire facility—offices, classrooms, work sites housing units, and recreational areas—were inspected to ferret out contraband and uncover hiding places. During cell shakedowns, inmate cells were examined for extraneous possessions, such as clothing, plus contraband items, such as lighters, cigarettes, and illicit drugs.

Despite the policing mechanisms aimed at enforcing a smoking ban, inmates regularly violated the smoking policy. In the four prisons that banned smoking, at least half of the inmates interviewed in each facility smoked on a weekly basis. The amount and frequency of smoking varied from a few cigarettes per week at one facility to nearly half a pack of cigarettes everyday at another. Typically, inmates smoked less in higher security facilities. Inmates were more likely to be caught smoking or possessing tobacco in facilities where inmates detailed a more pervasive black market. Regardless of the facility, however, the number of violators who reported ever being caught and the rate of smoking violations per month was very low compared to the amount of smoking that occurred on a regular basis.

The amount of regular smoking occurring in certain facilities was influenced by officer ambivalence toward vigorously pursuing policy violators, as demonstrated by officers who looked the other way when smelling smoke or spotting tobacco. One particularly reluctant officer went so far as to proclaim, "smoke 'em if you got 'em," on entering a dormitory at the beginning of his shift, thereby signaling to inmates that smoking would be tolerated. In general, part of this ambivalence may have stemmed from the fact that many officers smoked cigarettes themselves and empathized with an inmate's desire to smoke. In addition, some officers who smoked cigarettes were embittered by the facility's smoking ban because it curbed their own smoking habit. Also, prior to smoking bans, cigarettes were a primary way for officers to motivate inmates, particularly poorer inmates, to accomplish certain tasks. Consequently, some officers reported that enforcing the smoking ban was counterproductive to carrying out their job, particularly more senior officers who had worked at a facility prior to the enactment of a smoking ban.

DISCUSSION

The preceding description of the structural components of the cigarette black market points to several factors that appear to influence the development of cigarette black markets. First, the design and age of a facility affected cigarette smuggling and smoking prospects among inmates. Black market activity seemed greater in older facilities that were less secure and that had less direct supervision of inmates by officers. Second, the security level of the institution, that is, the movement within and outside of the institution, affected smuggling activity. Higher level security facilities, which restricted movement within the institution and which prohibited inmates from leaving the institution, appeared to have less organized black markets. Third, officer attitudes toward the smoking policy affected the development of cigarette black markets in two ways. Officers who did not enforce the policy, that is, those who overlooked smoking violations, indirectly stimulated inmate demand for cigarettes by allowing inmates to develop or maintain a smoking habit. More serious, officers who smuggled cigarettes or aided smugglers fueled both a supply and a demand for cigarettes among inmates.

Other factors leading to a more developed black market were greater organization, communication, and black market skills among inmates. The structure of the cigarette black market as outlined here, with its kingpins, smugglers, middlemen, and dealers, is not too different from illegal street-level drug markets. In fact, inmates involved in the cigarette black markets were frequently individuals who had been incarcerated for drug crimes. These inmates were already skilled at financing and obtaining illegal substances; managing lieutenants, adversaries, and turf; and eluding social control agents. Consequently, banning an addictive substance in a setting filled with sophisticated inmates created an environment ripe for the development of a black market. As one inmate, who was serving a 90-year sentence in a maximum security prison for drug trafficking, lamented, "I would've never messed with coke on the street if I knew how much money I could've made selling cigarettes here in the joint."

Interestingly, prison wardens and jail administrators often reported a decline in illegal drugs entering their facilities since banning cigarettes and attributed the decline to a greater demand for cigarettes among inmates. Inmates suggested that demand is, in fact, greater for tobacco than other drugs. For instance, several inmates claimed that kicking nicotine had been more difficult than quitting heroin, and others said that they would much prefer a cigarette to a line of cocaine. However, in addition to demand for tobacco, an equally significant factor dampening the drug economy was that tobacco was a more profitable substance to sell than other drugs. Whereas illicit drugs, such as marijuana, heroin, or cocaine, may yield greater profits per sale, the volume of tobacco sold and its high profit margin made it a more lucrative commodity to sell.

CONCLUSION

Jails and prisons ban cigarettes for a variety of reasons, including tobacco control laws and ordinances that legislate bans throughout state and county buildings, inmate lawsuits and grievances that sue for smoke-free environments, jail and prison overcrowding that increases the amount of cigarette smoke within facilities, and new institutional architecture and technology that are harmed by tobacco smoke (Lankenau, Falkin, & Strauss, 1999). The elimination or reduction of the amount of potentially harmful cigarette smoke contacting staff, inmates, or facility infrastructure has been a primary objective of bans. Despite this seemingly positive intention, the cigarette black markets that emerged in response to cigarette bans typically had a negative impact on inmates in the facilities we visited. We conclude by describing several of the effects of the cigarette black market on inmates.

First, since smoking cessation aids, such as smoking cessation classes or nicotine replacement therapies, were virtually nonexistent in the facilities where bans were enforced, the inmates interviewed were compelled to quit cold turkey or contend with the vagaries of the black market. Most inmates interviewed chose to participate in the black market because their tobacco use rarely abated on entering a facility that banned cigarettes.

Second, the majority of inmates were compelled to pay considerably higher prices to continue their cigarette habits. For instance, prior to a ban at a maximum security prison, one inmate said he spent about $5 per week on a can or about $15 per week on a carton. Following the ban, he smoked about three cigarettes per day at a cost of $60 to $70 per week. Consequently, the high cost of cigarettes prompted many inmates to undertake various hustles or to become low-level dealers because paying for only a few cigarettes could cost a third of an inmate's monthly institutional pay. For instance, one 60-year-old inmate used his pension money to pay for black market cigarettes. He said he had been robbed six times and manhandled twice over cigarettes. Prior to the ban, he said he was never robbed or assaulted. Other inmates increasingly relied on family members to add money to commissary accounts or to finance send-ins, whereas the poorest inmates reported trading hygiene items, such as soap and toothpaste, or sexual favors for cigarettes.

Third, just as the criminalization of cocaine and heroin gives rise to impure drugs and a scarcity of sterile drug paraphernalia, cigarettes sold on the black market are often more harmful than those sold legally and are combined with less healthy smoking practices. For instance, because rolling papers were scarce, some inmates resorted to rolling tobacco with toilet paper wrappers or with pages from a Bible. Both contain ink or dyes that are harmful when burned. Also, inmates reported removing the filters on manufactured cigarettes to increase the potency of each drag of tobacco, Furthermore, inmates who might otherwise have smoked a lower tar cigarette had little choice but to smoke higher tar cigarettes.

Fourth, the great majority of inmates who smoked or dealt cigarettes eluded detection, but the consequences for cigarette violations caused certain hardships. Whereas violations in some facilities were handled informally by correctional officers, such as merely confiscating the cigarettes, more formal punishments included losing privileges, such as commissary and visitations; being confined to administrative segregation; being transferred to a higher security facility; and having the length of a sentence extended. Also, many inmates complained of tensions between themselves and officers over the policing of cigarette contraband and tensions among inmates, stemming from a fear of being ratted out by snitches.

Finally, despite the fact that an appreciable amount of cigarette smoking occurred in facilities where tobacco was banned, most inmates smoked considerably less than they did prior to entering the criminal justice system. For instance, inmates at one prison smoked approximately 30 fewer cigarettes per day under the cigarette ban compared to their daily smoking habits outside of prison. However, despite this large reduction, most of these inmates did not report many noticeable health improvements, such as improved breathing, lessened fatigue, or a heightened sense of taste or smell. Perhaps, this was the case because these inmates continued a habit of 5 to 10 cigarettes per day.

REFERENCES

Demelco, M. (1993). The convict body: Tattooing among male American prisoners. *Anthropology Today, 9*(6), 10–13.

Falkin, G., Strauss, S., & Lankenau, S. (1998). Cigarette smoking policies in American jails. *American Jails, 8*(3), 9–14.

Falkin, G., Strauss, S., & Lankenau, S. (1999). *Cigarette smoking policies in state prisons.* Unpublished manuscript. National Development and Research Institutes, Inc., New York.

Foster, T. (1982). "Mushfaking": A compensatory behavior of prisoners. *Journal of Social Psychology, 177,* 115–124.

Gleason, S. (1978). Hustling: The "inside" economy of prison. *Federal Probation, 42,* 32–40.

Guenther, A. (1978). Compensation in a total institution: The forms and functions of contraband. *Crime and Delinquency, 21,* 243–254.

Hunt, G., Riegel, S., Morales, T., & Waldorf, D. (1993). Changes in prison culture: Prison gangs and the case of the "Pepsi Generation." *Social Problems, 40*(3), 398–409.

Jackson, P., & Stearns, C. (1995). Gender issues in the new generation jail. *The Prison Journal, 75*(2), 203–221.

Kalinich, D. (1986). *Power, stability, and contraband: The inmate economy.* Prospect Heights, IL: Waveland.

Lankenau, S., Falkin, G., & Strauss, S. (1999). *Social forces shaping and resisting the trend toward banning cigarettes in U.S. jails and prisons.* Unpublished manuscript, National Development and Research Institutes, Inc., New York.

Radford, R. (1945). The economic organization of a P.O.W. camp. *Economica, 35,* 189–201.

Romero, C., & Connell, F. (1988). A survey of prison policies regarding smoking and tobacco. *Journal of Prison & Jail Health, 7*(1), 27–36.

Saum, C., Surratt, H., Inciardi, J., & Bennett, R. (1995). Sex in prison: Exploring the myths and realities. *The Prison Journal, 75*(4), 413–430.

Vaughn, M., & del Carmen, R. (1992). Research note: Smoking in prisons—A national survey of correctional administrators in the United States. *Crime and Delinquency, 39*(2), 225–239.

Williams, V., & Fish, M. (1974). *Convicts, codes, and contraband: The prison life of men and women.* Cambridge, MA: Ballinger.

REVIEW QUESTIONS

1. How does a prison policy change in which cigarettes become contraband affect the value and trading of cigarettes among inmates?
2. In what ways does a black market in cigarettes differ from other forms of prison contraband?
3. How do inmates change their daily routines to continue to smoke in a prison where smoking and cigarettes are considered illegal?

V

MANAGING AND RESPONDING TO MISCONDUCT

READING 11

Prison Crime in New York State

David R. Eichenthal

Laurel Blatchford

The authors set out to document the number of crimes that occur within New York State's prison system. They identify numerous factors that impede one's ability to assess the levels of crime and criminal justice response occurring in state prisons, and they provide rough estimates for various types of offenses. Records suggest that referrals for prosecution and actual prosecution for crimes committed behind bars are rare. The discussion on practical realities that hinder prosecution efforts and how prison focuses administrators often choose in-house administrative sanctions as an alternative set of consequences. The article concludes with the authors presenting a model prosecution program from the State of Texas and reviewing several other alternatives that prison administrators can pursue in response to criminal conduct among inmates.

PROBLEMS WITH UNDERENFORCEMENT OF PRISON CRIME

Some of the most violent criminals in New York State commit crimes without being punished under the criminal law. They reside in a jurisdiction with a population that would make it the state's seventh-largest city. In many cases, they assault individuals charged with the responsibility of policing their jurisdiction, yet they never get arrested. Even when criminals in this jurisdiction are arrested for their crimes, prosecutors often fail to prosecute criminal cases against them. In parts of the jurisdiction, prosecutors decline to prosecute as much as 75% of all cases referred to them. Prosecutors have also "decriminalized" virtually all misdemeanors. These crimes are committed by and among the population of New York's 63rd county—the 69,000-plus residents of the New York State corrections system.

The lack of attention devoted to crimes committed in prisons is striking given the important implications of the problem both for prison management and for public safety. Although research has yet to document a clear link between institutional offending and recidivism after release, it is intuitively plausible that inmates who commit crimes in prison may be more likely to continue their criminal activity once they return to their communities. . . .

To explore the extent of this problem in New York's prisons, this study was initiated by New York City Public Advocate, Mark Green. The findings and discussion that follow are based on interviews with corrections officials, review of state corrections department data, and surveys of prosecutors in more than one dozen counties where state prisons are located.

PROBLEMS IN MEASURING CRIME INCIDENCE AND PROSECUTION RATES IN NEW YORK STATE PRISONS

Although more than 69,000 New Yorkers currently reside in one of the 69 correctional facilities operated by the New York State Department of Correctional Services (DOCS), little information is kept regarding crimes committed in prison. If the current inmate population were concentrated in a single city, that city would be the seventh largest in New York State—more New Yorkers live in state prisons than in Binghamton, Mount Vernon, Schenectady, Elmira, or Plattsburgh (New York State Statistical Yearbook, 1995, p. 11). In each of those cities, crime is undoubtedly an important issue. But, except for inmates and correctional staff who may have been victimized, very few people seem to have been concerned about the amount of crime committed in state prisons.

There are three significant ways in which the amount of crime committed in the general population—outside of prisons—is counted: complaints (e.g., calls to the police department and other law enforcement agencies), victimization surveys (where individuals are surveyed to determine if they have been a crime victim in a given period), and arrest data. None of these data are precise because (a) not every crime victim files a complaint with law enforcement, (b) victimization results extrapolated from limited samples may contain flaws due to sampling error, and (c) arrest data may be a reflection of police productivity as much as actual criminal activity.

Strikingly, none of these data are available for crimes committed in state prison facilities. DOCS does not maintain a central database of criminal complaints or even of cases of criminal complaints resulting in referrals for criminal prosecution. To the extent that data exist, they are piecemeal and located at individual correctional facilities, prosecutors' offices, and with state police troops. In addition, DOCS maintains a record of all unusual incidents at state prisons. But, unusual incidents include both criminal conduct—assaults and possession of contraband—and noncriminal conduct—employee misconduct and disruptive behavior.

Data are even less available about what happens to prison crimes that are actually referred for criminal prosecution. Although a number of jurisdictions compiled such data at our request, even the most sophisticated prosecutorial offices in the state do not routinely maintain information on crimes committed in prisons.

- In New York County (Manhattan), where more than 2,500 inmates are housed in state correctional facilities, the Manhattan district attorney's office indicated that it "does not maintain a record of the number of referrals or declinations to prosecute in this type of case."[1]
- In Erie County, where more than 2,000 state inmates are in state correctional facilities, the district attorney's office indicated that "It is impossible in our computer system to distinguish inmate cases from the civilian population."[2]
- In Richmond County, where almost 1,000 state inmates are housed in Arthur Kill, District Attorney William Murphy responded that "Inasmuch as the current funding for my office precludes me from procuring the technology, and corresponding personnel, to maintain statistics such as those requested by you,

I am unable to provide you with an analysis of this office's prosecution of internal prison crime."[3]

ROUGH ESTIMATES

Although data are limited, what we know about prisons in general and the limited information about prison crime in New York suggests that there may be an extraordinary amount of crime committed in state prisons annually. Years of criminal justice research document the intuitive—that prisons are violent environments. Thus, although many advocate incarceration as a means of incapacitating criminals, it is likely that incarceration in many cases merely shifts the locus of criminal activity away from neighborhoods to correctional facilities (Eichenthal & Jacobs, 1991, p. 303).

In 1995, DOCS reports that there were 8,304 unusual incidents in state prison facilities. There were 1,738 reported cases of inmate-on-inmate assaults, 962 cases of inmate assaults on staff, and 3,550 incidents involving possession of prison contraband (Unusual Incident Report, 1996 p. 4). If all of these had been reported crimes, there would have been more than 6,000 crimes committed in state prisons in that 1 year. One type of crime where fairly good data exist—both for crimes committed inside prisons and in the general population—is murder. In 1995, there were 1,551 murders reported in New York State: a murder rate of 8.6 per 100,000 New Yorkers.[4] In that same year, according to DOCS, there were 6 homicides at DOCS facilities: a murder rate of 8.7 per 100,000 state prisoners.

Criminal activity in New York's prisons may also take the form of multi-inmate incidents—riots or near riots. "Since 1994, DOCS has experienced 23 disturbances involving large numbers of inmates. . . . Six times in the past three years, DOCS has employed its Correction Emergency Response Teams to quell incidents." (Capacity Options Plan, 1997, p. 5). Yet, another serious form of inmate criminal activity is the use of illegal substances. Within the last 4 years, seizures of illegal drugs in New York State prison facilities have more than doubled (Purdy, 1995, p. 54).

Not every crime that is committed in prison—or in any setting—is automatically referred to a prosecutor for prosecution. If there may have been as many as 6,000 prison crimes committed in 1995, how many were referred for criminal prosecution? It is possible to develop an estimate of the number of referrals of crimes to local prosecutors based on referral data from those few jurisdictions that were able to report it.

One estimate—merely apportioning referrals on the basis of inmate population—suggests there were an estimated 1,000 internal prison crime referrals for prosecution in 1995. Another estimate can be derived from a comparison between referrals and unusual incidents. District attorneys in four counties—Chautauqua, Franklin, Oneida, and Washington—provided information on prison case referrals for prosecution. In 1995, the four district attorneys considered a total of 167 prison crime cases. In the same year, according to DOCS, there were 528 inmate assaults on staff or other inmates in the state prison facilities in those four counties. In other words, even assuming there were no other types of cases, fewer than 1 in 3 cases were referred for prosecution. If there were approximately 6,000 cases, that suggests that there may have been as many as 2,000 referrals for prosecution. This higher estimate has a historical basis; in 1985, when the state's prison population was approximately half the 1995 population, there were an estimated 1,018 referrals.[5] Anecdotal evidence suggests the number of referrals may be much higher still. In Cayuga County, where close to 3,000 inmates are housed in two state prisons, the local district attorney reported that he receives "approximately 600 referrals each year from the two facilities."[6]

Crimes committed in prisons are prosecuted by the district attorney of the county in which the prison facility is located. Because many of the state's prisons are located in small, rural counties, many of these local prosecutors lack the resources to prosecute a high volume of cases coming from state prisons. For example, the present public advocate survey elicited detailed responses from district attorneys in Cayuga, Chatauqua, Chemung, Clinton, Franklin, Oneida, St. Lawrence, Saratoga, Washington, and Wayne counties. State correctional facilities in these 10 counties hold more than 22,000 state inmates, or approximately one-third the total state prison population. In those 8 counties, the average number of full-time assistant district attorneys was less than 4. Excluding Oneida County, on average, the remaining counties have just two full-time assistant district attorneys.[7] The result is that when prison crime cases are referred for prosecution, prosecutors frequently decline to handle the matter criminally. Prosecutors in 4 reporting counties declined 56.9% of felony prosecutions. By contrast, for all felony arrests, prosecutors statewide declined only 5.2%, with another 27.7% of felony arrests ultimately resulting in dismissals.

In Cayuga County, the local district attorney reported that he prosecutes only 5% of the hundreds of referrals he receives each year.[8] In Franklin County, where there are more than 1,800 inmates housed in two state prisons, the local district attorney declined to prosecute 75 out of 94 criminal cases referred by prison officials in 1995. In Clinton County, where approximately 4,000 inmates are housed in three prison facilities, the district attorney has adopted a policy to decline prosecutions involving assaults by inmates against other inmates unless there is a corrections officer witness. In addition, the district attorney will not prosecute most weapon possession cases unless there is evidence that the weapon was used or attempted to be used.[9]

Prosecutors in four counties—Cayuga, Chemung, Ulster, and St. Lawrence—where one dozen prisons house more than 10,000 inmates, report that they do not prosecute misdemeanors. Again, by contrast, prosecutors declined to prosecute only 3% of misdemeanor arrests and 29.1% were dismissed when the offenses took place in the general population. Prosecutors may be reluctant to prosecute inmates for misdemeanors because, if convicted to a consecutive sentence, the inmate would ultimately have to be housed in a local jail for punishment.

SPECIAL PROBLEMS IN PROSECUTING PRISON CRIME

Although a lack of resources may be one issue prompting prosecutors to decline high numbers of prison crime cases, prosecutors also identified a series of other problems. In inmate-on-inmate assault cases, prosecutors believe it is difficult to go forward without a noninmate witness. The lack of a credible witness was raised as a problem by six prosecutors, from Oneida, Wayne, Chautauqua, Chemung, Washington, and Franklin counties.

> We find it almost impossible to prosecute these crimes unless there are correction officers or prison employees as witnesses. (Washington County district attorney)
>
> The burden of proof cannot be sustained without forensic evidence corroborating the charges or correction officer's eyewitness testimony. (Franklin County district attorney)

In many cases, the problem is not even the credibility of a witness's testimony, it is the unwillingness to testify at all. District attorneys in three counties—Chemung, Oneida, and Ulster—indicated that this was a major problem in prosecuting inmate-against-inmate assaults.

Prosecutors in three counties—Chautauqua, St. Lawrence, and Oneida—also indicated that inmates involved in inmate-on-inmate assaults are frequently relocated to other state prisons, again creating an obstacle to successful investigation and prosecution. Two prosecutors—in Oneida and Franklin counties—indicated that prison crime prosecutions were limited by problems with the investigations conducted by DOCS personnel.

> Inadequate investigations clear defendants prior to our prosecution. (Oneida County district attorney)
>
> Inadequate criminal investigative training of DOCS personnel; failure by DOCS personnel to Mirandize inmates prior to questioning; failure to question inmates properly. (Franklin County district attorney)

Finally, two prosecutors—from Clinton and Ulster counties—expressed frustration with the existing Penal Law definition of physical injury for the purpose of prosecuting felony assault cases. Under Penal Law section 120.05(7), a person is guilty of Assault 2nd Degree when

> Having been charged with or convicted of a crime and while confined in a correctional facility, as defined in subdivision three of section forty of the correction law, pursuant to such charge or conviction, with intent to cause physical injury to another person, he causes such injury to such person or to a third person.

Under Penal Law 10.00(9), physical injury means "impairment of physical condition or substantial pain." The Clinton County district attorney has advised DOCS officials that "petty slaps, shoves, kicks and the like are not enough to meet this standard."[10] As a result, many simple inmate assaults are only prosecutable as a misdemeanor and, given the reluctance of county prosecutors to prosecute misdemeanors by inmates, are therefore not prosecuted.

INMATE CONSEQUENCES FOR CRIME IN PRISON

If inmates who continue to commit crimes while incarcerated are not punished under the criminal law, what happens to them? Many inmates who violate the criminal law are sanctioned internally through an administrative disciplinary process. These sanctions can include a loss of privileges, a change in conditions of confinement (e.g., solitary), and a loss of good time credit resulting in a longer period of incarceration. But, as the New York State Court of Appeals recently ruled, there is nothing that precludes imposing both administrative sanctions and criminal punishment on inmates who violate the law while in prison. In *Cordero v. Lalor* (89 NY 2d 521) and *People v. Vasquez* (655 NYS 2d 870, 1997), the court held that under double jeopardy, a prior prison sanction does not create a bar to a criminal prosecution.

> Prison disciplinary action is not designed to "vindicate public justice," but rather to further the separate and important public interest in maintaining prison order and safety. . . . Prisoners, by virtue of their status (resulting from a prior violation of the Penal Law) are subject not only to criminal laws, aimed at vindicating societal interests, but also to a whole array of internal prison rules and regulations, which serve the separate, legitimate and important institutional purposes of preserving prison order and safety. A prisoner who commits a crime in prison breaks both sets of rules, and may thus be sanctioned both internally to carry out the goals of the penal institution, and through criminal prosecution to vindicate public justice. (New York Law Journal, 1997, pp. 27–28)

The reality, however, is that the vast majority of inmates who commit a criminal offense are never tried through a criminal prosecution "to vindicate public justice."

LEARNING LESSONS FROM SUCCESS: THE TEXAS MODEL

In a prior study of prison crime prosecutions, the authors concluded that "the special prosecutor model is well suited to the prosecution of prison crimes. . . . Their mandate is to prosecute all prison crimes where sufficient evidence exists. Furthermore, a special prosecutor could develop long-term relations with the department of corrections and a close familiarity with prison operations and the prisoner subculture" (Eichenthal & Jacobs, 1991, p. 300).

For the past 12 years, prison crimes in the state of Texas have been prosecuted by the statewide Special Prison Prosecutions Unit (SPPU). In that time, SPPU has developed an effective partnership with the Texas Department of Corrections (TDC) and local law enforcement officials in counties containing state prisons. SPPU investigators claim that they have developed experience and expertise in obtaining the cooperation of witnesses and victims and developing special techniques for the investigation of prison crime (Eichenthal & Jacobs, 1991, p. 301).

More than 6 years ago, in testimony before the New York State Assembly Correction Committee, the then chief prosecutor of SPPU, David Weeks, described how his office had succeeded in reducing the number of murders, aggravated assaults on inmates, and—working with TDC—had helped to control gang violence in prisons. According to Weeks,

> The biggest problem . . . dealing with crimes inside the penitentiary is the code of silence that always exists. . . . But as we built our credibility, as inmates learned that they could talk to us and trust us . . . we've been able to gain more and more information. . . . Unless you understand the dynamics of the prison system, you can't prosecute crimes there.

Weeks also addressed the investigative problems specific to prison crime.

> We've taught them about taking photographs, keeping the crime scene as complete a picture as possible, maintaining what inmates were there, writing down if they talked to the inmate, what did the inmate say (Transcript of Public Hearing on Managing Rikers Island in the 1990s, Assembly Committee on Correction, 1990, November 8).

RECOMMENDATIONS

The findings of the public advocate's study mirror those of a 10-year-old study of prison crime nationally (Eichenthal & Jacobs, 1991). That study found a pattern of underreporting of prison crime, underenforcement of the criminal law, and many of the same obstacles identified by prosecutors in 1996. DOCS has recognized the problem and, in September of 1995, initiated a task force on prison crime. DOCS now regularly reaches out to prosecutors in prison counties to encourage prosecution and encourage prosecutors to seek reimbursement for the costs of prosecution under section 606 of the Correction Law.

But, more needs to be done to address this serious problem. The public advocate for the city of New York urges DOCS and the legislature to endorse a 5-point program to curb prison crime.

Create an Office of Special Prosecutor for Prison Crime. The state legislature should create an Office of Special Prosecutor for Prison Crime. The special prosecutor would have jurisdiction over all crimes committed in state correctional facilities.[11] For more than a decade, all crimes in Texas's state corrections system have been prosecuted by a special prosecutor, making it a national model.

Establish a joint state police or department of correctional services investigative team to centralize all prison crime investigations. Prisons are a unique and difficult setting in which to conduct criminal investigations. Prison crime investigators require special training in criminal investigations, which correction officers often lack, and a familiarity with the prison setting, which state police troopers often lack. To more effectively investigate and prosecute prison crime, the state police and DOCS should set up joint investigative teams specializing in prison crime investigations.

Create a single, centralized database to track all referrals of prison crimes for prosecution. DOCS should move immediately to establish a centralized reporting and tracking system for all crimes committed in state correctional facilities. All facilities should report on all referrals for prosecution and outcomes.

Amend the Correction Law to allow inmates convicted of misdemeanors committed in state prisons to be detained and serve out the misdemeanor sentence in state prison. It is unacceptable to decriminalize misdemeanors committed in state prisons. But local district attorneys are reasonably exercising their prosecutorial discretion because they are concerned that the burden of inmates serving consecutive sentences would shift to local jail facilities where misdemeanants are punished.

The legislature should change the Correction Law to require state correctional facilities to hold misdemeanants who are convicted of offenses committed while serving in that facility.

Require DOCS to provide an annual report on prison crime to the state legislature. If measures such as these are taken, significant progress will have been made in addressing many of the problems identified above.

NOTES

1. Letter from Steven M. Fishner, executive assistant district attorney to Laurel Blatchford, Office of the Public Advocate, March 21, 1997.
2. Letter from Yvonne Vertlieb, executive assistant district attorney to Mark Green, February 25, 1997.
3. Letter from District Attorney William Murphy to Mark Green, February 26, 1997.
4. Data provided by New York State Division of Criminal Justice Services.
5. Eichenthal and Jacobs (1991, p. 286). Both 1985 and 1995 data are affected by the underprosecution of prison crime. In 1985, two thirds of all referrals came from two counties where there were an inordinately high number of referrals, but virtually no prosecution. Presumably, in other counties, underprosecution deterred prison and police officials from making criminal referrals—resulting in an undercount of the number of crimes that would have been referred for prosecution had they been committed in a nonprison environment. The 1995 data are based on extrapolation from statistics in four counties where district attorneys were actually able to provide data on referrals. Out of 167 referrals, 94 were from one county—Franklin County. There, prosecutors decline to prosecute cases more than 75% of the time.
6. Letter to Mark Green, public advocate for the city of New York, from James B. Vargason, district attorney of Cayuga County, April 9, 1997.
7. Given limited resources, prosecutors may be naturally reluctant to divert any resources to the prosecution of prison crime. Particularly where both offender and victim are inmates, there is no local political interest in the prosecution of prison crime. See Eichenthal and Jacobs (1991. p. 294): (As one prosecutor noted, "[Prison crime cases are] not politically attractive. . . . Most people in society think if it's one inmate assaulting another, well who cares?").
8. Letter to Mark Green from James B. Vargason, district attorney of Cayuga County, April 9, 1997.
9. Letter from Penelope D. Clute, Clinton County district attorney to Daniel Senkowski, superintendent of Clinton Correctional Facility, February 17,1989: "ASSAULT ON ANOTHER INMATE . . . unless there is an employee witness, or the attacker admits the assault, a successful prosecution will be very difficult." Letter from Penelope Clute to Steve Pendergast, New York state police, January 3,1991: "Until further notice, we will not prosecute charges of weapon possession for general population inmates where there is no evidence that the weapon was used or attempted to be used."

10. Letter from Penelope Clute to Steve Pendergrast, New York state police, January 3, 1991.

11. Legislation to create a special prosecutor has been proposed in both houses of the state legislature. A.6693 was introduced in the Assembly by Assembly member Daniel Feldman, Chair of the Correction Committee. S. 4784 was introduced in the Senate by Senator James Lack.

REFERENCES

Capacity Options Plan (1997, January). Office of the Director of Criminal Justice, State of New York.

Eichenthal, D., and Jacobs, J. (1991) Enforcing the criminal law in state prisons. *Justice Quarterly, 8*(3), 283–303.

New York State Statistical Yearbook (1995). Nelson A. Rockefeller Institute of Government, State University of New York.

Parole and Absconder Status of New York City Arrestees. (1996, November). New York Police Department.

Purdy, M. (1995, December 17). Officials ponder expansion of drug searches in prison. *The New York Times*, p. 54.

Unusual Incident Report: January-December 1995. (1996, April). State of New York, Department of Correctional Services.

REVIEW QUESTIONS

1. What changes could be made that would facilitate the collection of accurate crime data for our nation's prisons?

2. What are the political and practical reasons that impede the prosecution of inmates who commit crimes behind bars?

3. What are the strengths and weaknesses of the Special Prison Prosecutions Unit of the Texas Department of Corrections?

READING 12

Gangs Behind Bars

Prevalence, Conduct, and Response

Mark Fleisher

Scott H. Decker

This article identifies a number of problems that plague researchers who study gangs in correctional settings, including gaining access to data, working with common definitions of what constitutes a gang, gaining the trust of correctional officials to be allowed to do research, and generalizing results from one study to other correctional facilities. The history of correctional gang research is reviewed, showing that gangs have been around for a long time, come in a variety of forms, and often have connections to street gangs. The authors note that prison gangs have unique structures, although their make up, form of organization, and major means of carrying out activities are likely to vary. The article concludes with a discussion of ways in which correctional systems and facilities seek to combat the "gang problem."

Decades of research show that affiliation with correctional gangs—those in jails and prisons, increases the probability of violent and non-violent misconduct. This chapter deals with prison gangs and violence. We do three things. First, we review the literature on prison gangs and their effect on inmate misconduct. Second, we present selected findings of a national study on special-needs inmates in jails with a focus on gang affiliates. Third, we present jail administrators' approaches to managing gang affiliates and an overview of prison gang management initiatives.

DIFFICULTY IN ENGAGING IN CORRECTIONAL GANG RESEARCH

There are no field studies on prison gangs. Data on prison gang activity must be obtained from interviews with inmates or prison staff or prison records. Since prisons are law enforcement organizations, like agencies in the community, they secure information to protect offender confidentiality and ensure secrecy of crime intelligence. Even if researchers have access to prison records, data validity depends on (changes in) prison discipline policy and its enforcement, disciplinary hearing outcomes, and on institution definitions of offenses for assault and weapons, among other complications.

The available data has a strong influence on the nature of analysis. An analysis that uses disciplinary infraction codes, without considering infraction details, may confound a prison gang member assaulting a staffer with urine or a knife. Finally, standard prison records data omits variables necessary for a detailed analysis of the impact of gang membership on violence. Incident reports, for instance, do not cite inmates' length of time as a gang member or embeddedness within a gang group as a core or peripheral member, or associate.

A difficult administrative challenge faced researchers decades ago (Fong & Buentello, 1991). These challenges still affect the quality of prison gang research. Correctional agencies screen research proposals and may consider appropriate only those projects with relevance to programs and operations of correctional institutions. Researchers must also receive approval from university and correctional agencies' Human Subjects committee. Months or years may pass before a researcher gains access to prison records or receives permission to interview inmates or prison staffers, if such permission is granted. Once permission is granted, researchers are not granted open access to prison records, such as disciplinary reports. Rather, researchers may be forced to rely on public-access agency reports. These reports are not likely to provide those data researchers need to study prison gang violence.

Finally, prison officials who may know the most about prison gangs are most likely to be restricted by correctional policy from participating in researchers' surveys and face-to-face interviews. These issues affect the data validity. As a result, research findings should be read with an informed understanding of the data on which an analysis was predicated.

Prison gangs' effects on correctional institutions are not uniform across correctional institutions within the same or different states and regions. What's more, prison gangs' specific disruptive influences, such as drug smuggling vs. extortion vs. power struggles, aren't necessarily uniform, either. That leads to a cautionary statement: generalizing prison gangs' adverse effects cannot be generalized with a high degree of certainty from either a spatial or temporal provenience. Prison gangs' adverse effects may differ from prison to prison and from month to month, year to year, or even week to week. In a single prison over time, the effects of prison gangs shift with management practices, gang intervention and prevention initiatives, prison gang composition, correctional classification, and highly influential court decisions such as Ruiz v. Estelle.

Gang violence outside the institution may not reflect gang violence in modern institutions. For example, the California Department of Corrections has been noted for its gang violence for quite some time (Fong et al., 1992). However, Irwin's (2005) recent study of California prisons showed gangs are not a source of systematic violence. This suggests that the activities of gangs on the street and gangs in prison may not be parallel in important respects.

Gaes et al. (2001) reported several significant findings on prison gangs and misconduct. First, core vs. other embedded position (p. 25) and younger members (p. 21) commit the most violent offenses. Second, "[i]rrespective of whether one was a member, suspect, or associate, the longer one was in a gang, the less likely he committed violent misconduct" (p. 21) and more likely has taken on a leadership role (p. 26). Third, prison gangs have differential probabilities for not only violence but also for different types of misconduct. Analyzing federal inmate data, they found:

> Border Brothers had a quite high discrete change in the probability of violent misconduct, relative to affiliation with the Texas Syndicate. Affiliation in the Mexican Mafia lowered the probability of drug misconduct. Affiliates of the Texas Syndicate were less likely than the Border Brothers to commit violent misconduct but more likely to commit drug misconduct (p. 24).

GANG DEFINITIONS

Correctional gangs are social groups in jails and prisons classified by correctional authorities as gangs. Lyman (1989, p. 48) defines a prison gang as "an organization which operates within the prison system as a self-perpetuating criminally oriented entity, consisting of a select group of inmates who have established an organized chain of command and are governed by an established code of conduct. The prison gang will usually operate in secrecy and has as its goal to conduct gang activities by controlling their prison environment through intimidation and violence directed toward non-members." Most prison systems, including the Federal Bureau of Prisons, use the term "Security Threat Groups" to include gangs. This term is used to better capture the diversity of criminal organizations within the prison, particularly hate groups based on race or ethnicity.

HISTORY OF RESEARCH ON CORRECTIONAL GANGS

The first known American prison gang was the Gypsy Jokers (Stastny and Tyrnauer, 1983). They formed in the 1950s in Washington state prisons (Orlando-Morningstar, 1997). In 1957 the Mexican Mafia (*Eme*) appeared in the California Department of Corrections. *Eme* was the first prison gang with nationwide ties.

Camp and Camp (1985) identified approximately 114 gangs with a membership of approximately 13,000 inmates. Of the 49 agencies surveyed, 33 indicated that they had gangs in their system: Pennsylvania reported 15 gangs, Illinois, 14. Illinois had 5,300 gang members; Pennsylvania had 2,400, and California 2,050. In Texas, there were 9 prison gangs with over 50 members each, totaling 2,407 (Ralph & Marquart, 1991). Fong (1990) reported 8 Texas gangs with 1,174 members. Illinois corrections reported that 34.3 percent of inmates belonged to a prison gang. At that time this was the highest percent of prison gang-affiliated inmates in the nation (Camp and Camp, 1985).

Lane (1989) said that the Illinois Department of Corrections (IDOC) estimated the inmate gang population to be nearly 90 percent of the entire population, attributing that number to the importation of gangs from Chicago's streets, which is supported by research (Jacobs 1974). Rees (1996) shows that Chicago police estimate over 19,000 gang members in that city, and a high percent of IDOC inmates were arrested in Cook County. Other correctional agencies, however, report their gang troubles started within rather than outside prison walls. Camp and Camp (1985) cite that of the 33 agencies surveyed, 26 report street counterparts to prison gangs.

Subsequent to Camp and Camp (1985), the American Correctional Association found that prison gang membership had doubled between 1985 and 1992, from 12,624 to 46,190 (Baugh, 1993), with relatively few gang members in minimum-security units. Montgomery and Crews (1998) argue that Knox and Tromanhauser overestimated the prison gang population and cite the American Correctional Association's 1993 study that reports some 50,000 inmate gang members.

Obtaining data on the number of prison gangs and gang membership has been difficult. Most estimates are now ten to twenty years old. These issues illustrate the general problems in researching prison gangs. Fong and Buentello (1991) suggest three major reasons for the paucity of prison gang research. First, official documentation on prison gangs is weak. What documentation exists is generally only for internal use for management purposes. Second, prison managers are reluctant to allow outside researchers into facilities to conduct prison gang research. Fear over security and vague suggestions that research might hamper the welfare of the prison are the often-cited reasons for excluding prison researchers. Third, prison gang members themselves are secretive and would not likely disclose sensitive information about prison gang activities to outside researchers.

PRISON GANGS STRUCTURE AND ORGANIZATION

Prison gang research has not established a consensus on the structural and organizational traits of prison gangs. Prison gangs are described as hierarchical with a single designated leader who oversees a council of members that determines gang activities. The United States Department of Justice (DOJ) (1992) suggests that leaders and hard-core members are 15 to 20 percent of a gang's membership. It is important to note, however, that DOJ reported that a majority of members do not have a vested interest in the organization's leadership. Fleisher and Krienert's 2006 study corroborates DOJ findings. However, Marquart & Sorenson (1997) and Fong & Buentello (1991) report that gangs have a creed or motto, unique symbols of membership, and a constitution that prescribes group behavior, such as absolute loyalty and secrecy. Violence can be used to move a member upward in the prison hierarchy.

Prison gangs focus on the business of crime, generally through drug trafficking. They have an interest in protecting the size and composition of their membership (Montgomery & Crews, 1998). Gang members are the essential capital in crime-oriented social groups. When members want to leave the group, such out-group movement jeopardizes group security instigating the so-called 'blood in, blood out' credo (Fong, Vogel, & Buentello 1995).

Despite a threat of death, inmates do leave prison gangs. Fong, Vogel, and Buentello (1995) surveyed 48 former prison gang members who defected and found the number of gang defectors was proportional to a prison gang's size. Reasons for defecting include: (1) most commonly, former members lost interest in gang activities. (2) The next most common reason was a refusal to carry out a hit on a non-gang member. (3) The least common reason for leaving was a disagreement with the direction of the gang's leadership. These reasons suggest that the internal social dynamics and the strength of prison gangs may be relatively weak and insufficient to maintain cohesion of highly structured group with a blood in, blood out credo.

Research suggests there are at least five major prison gangs, each with its own structure and purpose. The Mexican Mafia (*La Eme*) started at the Deuel Vocational Center in Tracy, California, in the 1950s, and is California's first prison gang (Hunt et al., 1993) composed of primarily *Chicanos,* or Mexican Americans.

Entrance into *La Eme* requires sponsorship by a member; the recruit undergoes a blood oath to prove his loyalty. The Mexican Mafia is not averse to killing its members who do not follow instructions. Criminal activities include drug trafficking, and conflict with other prison gangs, such as the Texas Syndicate, Mexikanemi, and Aryan Brotherhood, is common (Orlando-Morningstar, 1997).

The Aryan Brotherhood (AB), a white supremacist group, was started in 1967 in California's San Quentin prison by white inmates to oppose the racial threat of black and Hispanic inmates (Orlando-Morningstar, 1997). Pelz, Marquart, and Pelz (1991) suggest that the AB held distorted perceptions of blacks, and that many Aryans felt that black inmates were taking advantage of white inmates, especially sexually, thus the need to form and/or join the Brotherhood. Joining the AB requires a six-month probationary period (Marquart and Sorenson, 1997). Initiation, or "making one's bones," required killing someone. The AB trafficked in drugs and had a blood in, blood out rule; natural death was the only non-violent way out. Pelz, Marquart, and Pelz (1991) report that the Aryan Brotherhood committed eight homicides in 1984, 32 percent of all inmate homicides in the Texas correctional system. The ABs later became known as the "mad dog" of the Texas corrections.

Within the federal prison system the Aryan Brotherhood structure used a three-member council of high-ranking members. Until recently, the federal branch of the Aryan Brotherhood was aligned with the California Aryan Brotherhood, but differences in opinion caused them to split into separate branches. The federal branch no longer cooperates with the Mexican Mafia in such areas as drugs and contract killing, but as of October 1997, the California branch still continued to associate with the Mexican Mafia. Rees (1996) suggested that the Aryan Brotherhood might align with other supremacist organizations to strengthen their hold in prisons. The Aryan Brotherhood also has strong chapters on the streets (Valentine, 1995), which allows criminal conduct inside and outside prisons to support each other.

Black Panther George Jackson united black groups such as the Black Liberation Army, Symbionese Liberation Army, and the Weatherman Underground Organization to form one large organization, the Black Guerilla Family, which emerged in San Quentin in 1966. Founded on a Marxist and Leninist philosophy, the Black Guerilla Family was considered one of the more politically charged revolutionary gangs, which scared prison management and the public (Hunt, Riegel, Morales, & Waldorf, 1993). Recently, offshoots within the Black Guerilla Family have been appearing. California has reported the appearance of a related group known as the Black Mafia (Orlando-Morningstar, 1997).

La Nuestra Familia ("Our Family") was established in the 1960s in California's Soledad prison, although some argue it began in the Deuel Vocational Center (Landre, Miller, & Porter, 1997). The original members were Hispanics from Northern California's agricultural Central Valley who aligned to protect themselves from the Los Angeles-based Mexican Mafia. *La Nuestra Familia* has a formal structure and rules and a governing body known as *La Mesa,* or a board of directors.

The Texas Syndicate emerged in 1958 at Deuel Vocational Institute in California. It appeared at California's Folsom Prison in the early 1970s and at San Quentin in 1976, because other gangs were harassing native Texans. Inmate members are generally Texas Mexican-Americans, but now the Texas Syndicate offers membership to Latin Americans and perhaps Guamese as well. The Texas Syndicate opposes other Mexican-American gangs, especially those from Los Angeles (Hunt et al., 1993). Dominating the crime agenda is drug trafficking inside and outside prison, and selling protection to inmates (Landre et al., 1997).

Like other prison gangs, the Texas Syndicate has a hierarchical structure with a president and vice president in each local area, either a prison or in the community, and someone is appointed the gang's chairman (Orlando-Morningstar, 1997). The chairman watches over that area's vice chairman, captain, lieutenant, sergeant at arms, and soldiers. Lower-ranking members perform the gang's criminal activity. The gang's officials, except for the president and vice president, become soldiers again if they are moved to a different prison, thus avoiding local-level group conflict. Proposals within the gang are voted on, with each member having one vote; the majority decision determines group behavior.

The *Mexikanemi* (known also as the Texas Mexican Mafia) was established in 1984 and is an emerging threat. Its name and symbols cause confusion with the Mexican Mafia. As the largest gang in the Texas prison system, it is emerging in the federal system as well and has been known to kill outside as well as inside prison. The *Mexikanemi* spars with the Mexican Mafia and the Texas Syndicate, although it has been said that the *Mexikanemi* and the Texas Syndicate are aligning themselves against the Mexican Mafia (Orlando-Morningstar, 1997). The *Mexikanemi* has a president, vice president, regional generals, lieutenants, sergeants, and soldiers. The ranking positions are elected by the group, based on leadership skills. Members keep their positions unless they are reassigned to a new prison. The *Mexikanemi* has a 12-part constitution. For example, part five says that the sponsoring member is responsible for the person he sponsors; if necessary, a new person may be eliminated by his sponsor (Orlando-Morningstar, 1997).

Hunt et al. (1993) suggest that the *Nortenos* and the *Surenos* are new Chicano gangs in California. The New Structure and the Border Brothers also have been noted as new California prison gangs. The origins and alliances of these groups are unclear; however, the Border Brothers are composed of Spanish-speaking Mexicans and tend to remain solitary. The Border Brothers do seem to be gaining membership and control as more Mexicans are convicted and imprisoned.

The Crips and Bloods, traditional Los Angeles street gangs, are gaining strength in the prisons as well, as are the 415s, a group from the San Francisco area (415 is the San Francisco area code). The Federal Bureau of Prisons cites fourteen other disruptive groups within the federal system, which have been documented as of 1995, including the Texas Mafia, the Bull Dogs, and the Dirty White Boys (Landre et al., 1997). Knox's (2005) most recent survey of prison administrators identifies the following as the ten most frequently found prison gangs:

1. Crips
2. Gangster Disciples
3. Bloods
4. Latin Kings
5. Vice Lords

TABLE 1 A Comparison of Prison and Street Gangs

	Prison Gangs	Street Gangs
Race	Single race or ethnicity	Single race or ethnicity
Age	Concentrated in mid-twenties	Average age in upper teens
Structure	Hierarchical	Episodic/Hierarchical
Violence	Core activity	Core activity
Offending style	Entrepreneurial	Cafeteria Style
Visibility	Covert	Highly visible
Drug Trafficking	Key activity	Key activity
Loyalty	Absolute in prison	Weak bonds
Key to membership	Loyalty	Friendship groups
Key Psychological attribute	Oppositional	Oppositional

6. Aryan Brotherhood
7. Folks
8. White Supremacists
9. Surenos
10. Five Percenters

Seven of these names are drawn from street gangs, reflecting the fact that there may be more in common between prison and street gangs than previously was thought. In addition, there is an ongoing pattern of exchange between prison and street gangs, as street members cycle through prison and back to the street, or non-gang individuals (the majority of inmates at intake) join prison gangs and cycle back to the street. We created Table 1, above, to illustrate many of the similarities and differences between prison and street gangs. Indeed, Knox (2005) found that 88% of correctional administrators in a nationwide survey indicated that their most dangerous prison gang was also a street gang. Interestingly, further evidence for the relationship between the prison and the street with regard to gangs comes from the Arizona Department of Corrections that notes that there are more prison gang members on the streets in that state than in its prisons (Schriro, 2007).

CORRECTIONAL GANGS IN PRISON

Over several decades, correctional research provided a data set of the effects of prison gangs on inmate violent and non-violent misconduct. Far less is known about gangs in jail. Below we review research on prison gangs, and then move into an overview of jail gangs.

Ingraham and Wellford (1987) and others (Cox, 1996) argued that prison gangs are responsible for most prison violence. Camp and Camp (1985) reported that prison gang members were on aggregate 3 percent of the prison population but caused 50 percent or more of the prison violence. The interaction of prisons' physical space and relatively stable general population creates a pretext for violence as gangs compete to make available gambling and illegal drugs, among other illegal services (Fleisher, 1989; Gaston, 1996).

Offender-level characteristics contribute to prison-situated gang violence. Interviews with 704 inmate admissions in the Nebraska prison system showed that self-reported gang-affiliated inmates have longer criminal involvement, often with a greater severity of criminal conduct, as well as more individual-level risk factors, such as poor education, low job experience, and substance abuse (Krienert & Fleisher, 2001). Assaults committed by gang vs. non-gang members prior to incarceration illustrate the potential violence of gang affiliates: 13.7 percent of non-gang vs. 50 percent of gang members reported the commission of an assault (p. 52).

The adverse effect of gangs on prison life cannot be generalized with a high degree of certainty from either a spatial or temporal perspective. This is due in part to the paucity of studies linking gang affiliation to misconduct. Negative effects may differ from prison to prison and from month to month, year to year, or even week to week. Gang violence in the 1980s may not be indicative of gang violence in modern institutions. For example, the California Department of Corrections has been noted for its gang violence (Fong et al., 1992). Fong et al. (1992, p. 68) reported that in 1972, the Mexican Mafia incited 30 of 36 murders in the California prison system. Irwin's (2005) recent study of California prisons found that improved physical design, correctional management and supervision, and enhanced misconduct policies suppressed gang-linked violence (p. xi, 95). . . .

Prison gangs are often linked to wide ranging misconduct (Fleisher, 1989; Griffin and Hepburn, 2006), including prostitution and sexual violence. Fleisher and Krienert's (2006) study of sexual violence in 10 states and 30 prisons found that prison gangs do not have a specific role in gang-motivated sex-related violence, sexual slavery, or prostitution. "Most gangs forbid [gang-group rape]. If you are found out they would banish you or kick the shit out of you" (p. 203). To the contrary, they found that gangs protect homosexuals as they might other well-liked inmates: "[f]inding safety under a gang's umbrella depends on how well other members like an inmate, how he 'carries himself,' and his fighting ability" (p. 202). Prison gangs strongly oppose rape (p. 203). Griffin and Hepburn (2006) found that gang affiliation had an independent effect on violent inmate misconduct, controlling for relevant individual risk factors known to predict violence. Similarly, Huebner, Varano and Bynum (2007) found that gang membership was strongly correlated with recidivism. These studies indicate the difficulties in adjustment, both in the community and the institution faced by gang members.

It is difficult to overestimate the influence of gangs on prison activity. However, in a single prison over time, the influence of prison gangs shifts with management practices, gang intervention and prevention initiatives, prison gang composition, correctional classification, and highly influential court decisions such as *Ruiz*.

GANGS IN JAIL

The mission of America's some 3,300 jails focuses on the detention of offenders awaiting trial or serving sentences of less than 12 months. Just over 700,000 inmates reside in American jails (Harrison and Beck, 2005), and tens of thousands of offenders pass through booking in major urban centers. In the third quarter of 2005 the Los Angeles County jail system housed an average of 18,629 inmates (Ruddell, Decker, & Egley, 2006, p. 2). . . . Demographic data indicate that a substantial number of jail inmates and detainees are gang affiliated. On a national level, jail administrators report that 13.2 percent of jail inmates are gang affiliated (Ruddell, Decker, & Egley, 2006, p. 1). Jail gang membership was associated with larger jails and larger daily jail populations, though interestingly not with regions of the country. Gang members in jail engage in violent and non-violent misconduct. Other than individuals with mental health diagnoses, gang members were regarded as the most difficult group of jail inmates to deal with and were seen as the most violent group within jails. The jail administrators regarded intelligence gathering and segregation as the most effective strategies in dealing with this group.

INSTITUTIONAL GANG INTERVENTION STRATEGIES

In this section we summarize prison and jail gang intervention strategies. Note that the interventions we discuss have not been evaluated for their effectiveness in the prevention and intervention of gang activity.

Correctional agencies have developed policies guiding initiatives that control gang-affiliated inmates' misconduct. Carlson and Jarrett's 2006 collection of essays illustrates the diverse approaches major correctional agencies have implemented to manage with prison gangs.

Since the publication of Clemmer's (1958) *Prison Community,* prison scholars have debated the effects of prison administration and management on the formation of inmate groups and on individual behavior. We can ask: do prison policies and procedures intended to create safe prisons have iatrogenic effects on inmates, which then result in the formation of disruptive groups? In spite of prison managers' best efforts to create a positive environment will inmates form disruptive groups as a prison extension of their street behavior (Jacobs (1977; Hunt et al., 1993)?

Researchers argued that social affiliation through prison gangs meets a fundamental human need. Fong & Buentello (1991) argue that inmates' need for social identity and group membership contribute to the formation of inmate groups. Such groups also have the potential to protect inmates. Fleisher and Krienert (2006) identified inmate 'safe zones.' These are social affiliations, including religious groups, which also afford members physical protection.

Gaes et al. (2005) examined the influence of prison environments on inmate misconduct. They found that "compositional and contextual effects of staff, inmate, and ecological variables impact the probability of many forms of misconduct in addition to, and separate from, individual-level characteristics of inmates" (p. 30).

Earlier research had similar findings. Court decisions compel correctional agencies to adjust prison environments, Jacobs (1977, pp. 138–174) argues that the courts weakened the authority of correctional officers to control gangs' influences. Since the earliest cases on inmates' rights, prison administrators' flexibility in controlling violent groups has been curtailed by the limits of case law. In institutions where prison management controls are often weak and where prisons violate inmates' civil rights, there is often an increase in gang activity. This illustrates the oppositional character of prison gangs, a characteristic they share in common with street gangs (Fong, Vogel, & Buentello, 1995; DiIulio 1987; Ralph & Marquart, 1993).

Prison suppression and intervention strategies have different effects on gang-affiliated vs. non-gang inmates Shelden (1991) compared 60 gang members (45 black, 15 Hispanic) to 60 non-gang members and found similarities; they shared similar socioeconomic backgrounds, education levels, and marital status; both groups had substance abuse problems. Gang members, however, were more likely to have never been employed, more likely to have a juvenile crime record (30 percent of them had juvenile court records compared to eight percent on non-gang inmates); 32 percent of the gang members had 15 or more arrests compared to seven percent of non-members; and gang members were also more likely to have used a weapon than non-members. Sheldon also shows that while imprisoned, gang members were twice as likely to have more than five rule violations, were more likely to violate drug use sanctions, were more likely to fight, and less likely to be involved in treatment programs. Without in-prison treatment, education, and vocational training, the likelihood that gang-affiliated inmates would be prepared for a lawful lifestyle outside prison is low.

How have prison officials responded to prison gangs? Prisons have tried a variety of overt and covert strategies, including the use of inmate informants, the use of segregation units for prison gang members, the isolation of prison gang leaders, the lockdown of entire institutions, the vigorous prosecution of criminal acts committed by prison gang members, the interruption of prison gang members' internal and external communications, and the case-by-case examination of prison gang offenses. There are, however, no published research evaluations testing the efficacy of these suppression strategies on curbing prison gang violence and/or other criminal conduct inside correctional institutions. Below is brief summary of some of the anti-prison-gang initiatives.

The Texas state legislature passed a bill in September 1985 which made it a "felony for any inmate to possess a weapon" (Ralph & Marquart 1991, p. 45). The bill also limited the discretionary authority of sentencing judges: inmates convicted of weapon possession must serve that sentence subsequent to other sentences. Officials believe that laws like this one might help to keep inmates, especially those in prison gangs, under control (Ralph & Marquart, 1991).

A popular control procedure is segregation. Inmates are kept by themselves in a cell, twenty-three hours a day, with one hour assigned to recreation and/or other activities. Texas used administrative segregation and put all known prison gang members into segregation in 1985, in the hope of limiting their influence on mainline inmate populations. Violence in the general population decreased, with nine prison gang-motivated homicides from 1985 to 1990; fewer armed assaults were reported as well. By 1991, segregation housed more than 1,500 gang members (Ralph & Marquart, 1991).

Knox (2000) reports that over half of the 133 prison officials interviewed in a national survey on prison gangs believe a segregation policy is not effective, inasmuch as gang activity still occurs. Isolating gang leaders has become a popular control strategy. With prison gang leaders locked down, vertical communication within the gang would hypothetically decline, weakening it and eroding solidarity. One isolation strategy to control prison gang leaders transfers them among institutions or keeps them circulating between prisons (United States Department of Justice, 1992).

Another strategy to reduce gang membership requires "jacketing," or inserting an official notice of suspected gang activity in an inmate's file. This note follows an inmate and allows authorities to transfer him to a high-security facility.

Hunt et al. (1993) describe a "debriefing" technique. This requires prison gang inmates to relinquish information about their gangs as a precondition to being released from a high-security facility. Staff might also pressure inmates by threatening them with a transfer to such institutions unless they offer information. The legality of such techniques is questionable and may likely threaten the life of a debriefed inmate or those whom prison gang members believe have been debriefed. Orlando-Morningstar (1997) cites the need for better information gathering and sharing, particularly between law enforcement and corrections. A key to preventing gang violence and retaliation is knowledge of enemies and past behavior. Law enforcement can provide that to corrections for inmates entering facilities, while corrections can provide similar information for offenders returning to the community.

Correctional agencies now use databases to track prison gang members and gang activities. This allows for more effective communication between a correctional and a state police agency, and improves data accuracy because data can be entered as soon as they are gathered (Gaston, 1996). The New York City Department of Correction uses a system that allows for digitized photos, which document gang members' marks and/or tattoos. Database searches can be done by a tattoo or scars or other identifying marks. The speed and capacity to update intelligence information makes the use of a shared database an effective tool in prison gang management.

Providing alternative programming could become part of prison gang management strategies; however, prison gang members have not embraced such programming. The Hampden County Correctional Center in Ludlow, Massachusetts developed a graduated program for prison gang members wishing to leave segregation. The program uses movies, discussion sessions, and homework. At the program's end, participants must write a statement certifying they will no longer participate in gang activities. Two years into the program, 190 inmates were enrolled and 17 had been returned to segregation for gang activities (Toller & Tsagaris, 1996). Details of the program's evaluation were not available.

Another control strategy is the use of out-of-state transfers, which send key prison gang members out of state, in the hope of stopping or slowing a prison gang's activities. If a gang has already been established, it is hoped that such a transfer would disrupt a gang to the point of its demise; however, there are no data showing the effectiveness of this type of control strategy. In fact, transferring a high-ranking prison gang member could be the impetus to transfer his prison gang to yet another institution (United States Department of Justice, 1992).

Correctional agencies have tried to weaken prison gangs by assigning members of different prison gangs to the same work assignment and living quarters, in anticipation of limiting the number, thus the power of one prison gang over another at a specific place. The Texas Department of Corrections, for instance, assigned prison gang members to two or three high-security, lockdown institutions. Illinois tried this approach to no avail, because the inmate prison gang population was too large to control effectively within a few locations (United States Department of Justice, 1992).

Camp and Camp (1985) surveyed facilities and asked officials which strategies they were most likely to employ against prison gangs. Transfer was cited by 27 of the 33 agencies; the use of informers was cited 21 times; prison gang member segregation was cited 20 times; prison gang leader segregation was cited 20 times; facility lockdown down was cited 18 times; and vigorous prosecution and interception of prison gang members' communications was cited 16 times.

Some prison officials tried to quell prison gang disruptions by discussing those disruptions with gang leaders. And 5.5 percent of the wardens said they ignored prison gangs. These researchers show that fewer than half of the prisons surveyed provided any type of prison gang training; but recently, Knox (2000) showed that correctional officers training has improved, with a finding that over two-thirds of the 133 facilities surveyed provided some gang training in 1999. Despite this, only 20% of prison administrators surveyed by Knox (2005) indicated that they had programming for gang members who wanted to leave the gang.

Gangs have grown in importance as increasing concern has been expressed about prisoner re-entry. Huebner and her colleagues (2007) found that gang members had higher rates of recidivism, net of other characteristics. This finding was echoed by Petersilia (2000), who noted that prison gangs had an influence on communities and disrupted patterns of socialization and integration, making it more difficult for reintegration into the community. Correctional administrators surveyed by Knox (2005) identified six potential solutions to make their institutions safer, including: 1) increased sanctions against gang members, 2) special housing for gang members, 3) new restrictions on benefits for prison misconduct, 4) new services for prison gang members, 5) new policies to deal with prison gang members, and 6) increased staffing and resources.

A NEED FOR MORE COLLABORATION

We have little hard data on the demographics of today's prison gangs and the nature and levels of prison gang-related disorder in American prisons. Camp and Camp's (1985) inventory of prison gangs comes out of an earlier era in American corrections. Collaborative research between correctional officials and experienced gang and prison researchers can yield the data we need to develop effective prison gang intervention and suppression strategies and the data needed to test the efficacy of current strategies. Collaboration between correctional agencies and university researchers is the key to creating strong solutions to the difficult, persistent problems posed by prison gangs, and such collaboration is also the key to improving the likelihood that prison gang members will remain crime free upon release.

Imagine how strange today's job market must be for inmates who were imprisoned as recently as ten years ago. To be sure, the challenge of beginning a career, even for a college graduate, can be daunting. For a former inmate and a prison gang member, searching to find a lawful path will be difficult and alien, but it may feel impossible. Research has shown consistently that most inmates are poorly educated and ill-prepared to hold meaningful employment in today's high-tech society. Gang members are even less well prepared for job markets. Prisons and jails are our last chance to help lawbreakers learn to live lawfully in communities.

REFERENCES

Baugh, D.G. (1993). *Gangs in correctional facilities: A national assessment.* Laurel, MD: American Correctional Association.

Camp, G.M., & Camp, C.G. (1985). *Prison gangs: Their extent, nature, and impact on prisons.* Washington, D.C.: U.S. Government Printing Office.

Carlson, P., & Garrett, J.S. (Eds.), (2006). *Prison and Jail Administration: Practice and Theory (2nd Ed.).* Gaithersburg, MD: Aspen Publishing.

Clemmer, D. (1958). *The prison community.* New York: Holt, Rinehart, and Winston.

DiIulio, J.J. (1987). *Governing prisons: A comparative study of correctional management.* New York: Free Press.

Fleisher, M.S. (1989). *Warehousing violence.* Newbury Park, CA: Sage Publications.

Fleisher, M.S. (2006). Gang management in corrections. In P. Carlson and J.S. Garrett (Eds.), *Prison and Jail Administration: Practice and Theory (2nd Ed.).* Gaithersburg, MD: Aspen Publishing.

Fleisher, M.S., & Krienert, J.L. (2001). Gang membership as a proxy for social deficiencies: A study of Nebraska inmates. *Corrections Management Quarterly: Responding to the Threat of Gangs: Leadership and Management Strategies, 3,* 1, 47–58.

Fleisher, M.S., & Krienert, J.L. (2006). The Culture of Prison Sexual Violence. Washington, D.C.: National Institute of Justice. Final Report of Grant No. 2003-RP-BX-1001. www.NCJRS.gov.

Fong, R.S. (1990). The organizational structure of prison gangs: a Texas case study. *Federal Probation 59,* 36–43.

Fong, R.S., & Buentello, S. (1991). The detection of prison gang development: An empirical assessment. *Federal Probation, 55,* 66–69.

Fong, R.S., Vogel, R.E., & Buentello, S. (1992). Prison gang dynamics: A look inside the Texas Department of Corrections. In Benekos, P.J., & Merlo, A.V.

(Eds.). *Corrections: Dilemmas and directions.* Cincinnati: Anderson Publishing Company.

Fong, R.S., Vogel, R.E., & Buentello, S. (1995). Book in, blood out: The rationale behind defecting from prison gangs. *Journal of Gang Research, 2,* 45–51.

Gaston, A. (1996). Controlling gangs through teamwork and technology. *Large Jail Network Bulletin,* Annual Issue 1996, 7–10.

Gerald G. Gaes, Susan Wallace, Evan Gilman, Jody Klein-Saffran, and Sharon Suppa. The influence of prison gang affiliation on violence and other prison misconduct. http://www.bop.gov//news/research_projects/published_reports/cond_envir/oreprcrim_2br.pdf. Retrieved July 2, 2007.

The Influence of Prisons on Inmate Misconduct: A Multilevel Investigation. Scott D. Camp, Gerald G. Gaes, Neal P. Langan, William G. Saylor. http://www.bop.gov//news/research_projects/published_reports/prison_mgmt/oreprcamp_mis.pdf.

Griffin, Marie L. and John R. Hepburn. (2006). The Effect of Gang Affiliation on Violent Misconduct Among Inmates During the Early Years of Confinement. *Criminal Justice Review, 33,* 419–448.

Huebner, Beth M., Sean Varano, and Tim S. Bynum. 2007. Gangs, Guns and Drugs: Recidivism Among Serious, Young Offenders. *Criminology and Public Policy, 6,* 2, 183–222.

Hunt, G., Riegel, S., Morales, T., & Waldorf, D. (1993). Changes in prison culture: Prison gangs and the case of the "Pepsi generation." *Social Problems, 40,* 398–409.

Ingraham, B.L., & Wellford, C.F. (1987). The totality of conditions test in eighth-amendment litigation. In Gottfredson, S.D., & McConville, S. (Eds.). *America's correctional crisis: Prisons populations and public policy.* New York: Greenwood Press.

Jacobs, J.B. (1974). Street gangs behind bars. *Social Problems 21,* 395–409.

Jacobs, J.B. (1977). *Stateville: The penitentiary in mass society.* Chicago: University of Chicago Press.

Knox, G.W. (2000). A national assessment of gangs and security threat groups (STGs) in adult correctional institutions: Results of the 1999 Adult Corrections Survey. *Journal of Gang Research, 7,* 1–45.

Knox, George W. (2005). The Problem of Gangs and Security Threat Groups (STGs) in American Prisons Today: Recent Research Findings from the 2004 Prison Gang Survey. National Gang Research Center. http://www.ngcrc.com/corr2006.html

Landre, R., Miller, M., & Porter, D. (1997). *Gangs: A handbook for community awareness.* New York: Facts On File, Inc.

Lane, M.P. (1989, July). Inmate gangs. *Corrections Today, 51,* 98–99.

Lyman, M.D. (1989). *Gangland.* Springfield, IL: Charles C. Thomas.

Montgomery R.H., Jr., & Crews, G.A. (1998). *A history of correctional violence: An examination of reported causes of riots and disturbances.* Lanham, MD: American Correctional Association.

Orlando-Morningstar, D. (1997). Prison gangs. *Special Needs Offender Bulletin, 2,* 1–13.

Petersilia, Joan. (2000). When Prisoners Return to the Community: Political, Economic and Social Consequences. Research in Brief. *Sentencing and Corrections Issues for the 21st Century.* Washington, D.C.: National Institute of Justice.

Pelz, M.E., Marquart, J.W., & Pelz, C.T. (1991). Right-wing extremism in the Texas prisons: the rise and fall of the Aryan Brotherhood of Texas. *The Prison Journal, 71,* 23–37.

Ralph, P.H., & Marquart, J.W. (1991). Gang violence in Texas prisons. *The Prison Journal, 77,* 38–49.

Rees, T.A., Jr. (1996, Fall). Joining the gang: A look at youth gang recruitment. *Journal of Gang Research, 4,* 19–25.

Ruddell, Rick, Scott H. Decker, and Arlen Egley, Jr. (2006). Gang Interventions in Jails: A National Analysis. *Criminal Justice Review, 31:*1–14.

Shelden, R.G. (1991). A comparison of gang members and non-gang members in a prison setting. *The Prison Journal, 71,* 50–60.

Stastny C. and G. Tyrnauer. 1983. *Who rules the joint? The changing political culture of maximum-security prisons in America.* Lexington Books.

Toller, W., & Tsagaris, B. (1996). Managing institutional gangs: A practical approach combining security and human services. *Corrections Today, 58,* 100–111.

United States Department of Justice. (1992). *Management strategies in disturbances and with gangs/disruptive groups.* Washington, D.C.: U.S. Government Printing Office.

Valentine, B. (1995). *Gang intelligence manual.* Boulder, CO: Paladin Press.

REVIEW QUESTIONS

1. Why do the authors say it is difficult to do research on gangs in correctional settings? Which of these difficulties seem to be the most difficult to overcome and why?
2. Are prison gangs similar to street gangs? If yes, how so? If no, why not?
3. In what ways do race and ethnicity coincide with differing structures and goals of prison gangs?

READING 13

Prison Guards and the Use of Physical Coercion as a Mechanism of Prisoner Control

James W. Marquart

Drawing upon 19 months of participant observation as a prison guard, the author describes the formal and informal means through which the correctional staff seeks to control and sanction inmates. Data show that official control structures are supplemented by unofficial acts of verbal intimidation and physical coercion. Acts of unofficial physical force are broken down into several categories. The author details the normative and socially structured aspects of guards' use of physical coercion. It is observed that these unsanctioned acts of force are intended to maintain control over inmates, reinforce the status hierarchy between guards and inmates, curry favor and promotion from like-minded supervisors, and build solidarity among guards. The article concludes with the author contextualizing the acts of verbal and physical coercion within the larger organizational structure of the prison system.

In the past 40 years, the study of social control in prisons has generated a considerable body of research. Most of these studies have primarily focused on the formal prisoner control structure wherein internal order is achieved through such mechanisms as official rules and regulations (Clemmer, 1940; McCleery, 1960; Goffman, 1961; Cressey, 1968); formal disciplinary procedures involving "write-ups" and adjudication before disciplinary courts (Carroll, 1974; Gobert and Cohen, 1981); and the prison staff's use of such punishments as loss of privileges or solitary confinement (Cloward, 1960; Wright, 1973; Hawkins, 1976; Berkman; 1979). In addition, other researchers have examined the staff's official use of inmate elites as convict guards to maintain order (Mouledous, 1962; Marquart and Crouch, 1984).

Although most prisoner control research centers on formal measures, several studies have been conducted on the informal system. This line of inquiry typically shows that order is based on "trade-offs"; illegitimate rewards; guard accommodations with inmate elites (Cloward 1960; Carroll, 1974; Davidson, 1974; Jacobs, 1977); or concessions in which the staff overlook minor inmate rule violations (Sykes, 1958; Thomas, 1984). No research, to date, however, has examined the internal institutional order that is based on the guards' use of physical coercion.

In theory, the threat of force by guards is always present, but the literature lacks any systematic analysis of violence as a mechanism of social control in this setting. This neglect leaves an unbalanced picture of the structure and process of prisoner control. The present research documents with participant observation data how and why guards in one Texas penitentiary utilized unofficial physical force as a routine mechanism of informal social control. The research shows that the guards' use of coercion does not result from personality defects or the brutalizing nature of the institutional environment (Zimbardo, 1972). Neither did their use of coercive power precipitate any mass disorder or widespread retaliation from the prisoners (Sykes, 1958; Hepburn, 1985). Instead, this paper demonstrates that the guards' use of force was a socially structured tactic of prisoner control that was well entrenched in the guard culture.

RESEARCH STRATEGY

Data for this paper were collected at the Johnson Unit (a pseudonym), a large maximum security facility within the Texas Department of Corrections. The author entered the penitentiary, with the warden's permission, as a guard to collect data on social control and order for 19 months (June 1981 through January 1983), worked throughout the institution (for example, cell blocks, shops, dormitories), and observed how the guards meted out official and unofficial punishments, coopted inmate elites to act as "convict guards," cultivated snitches, and other guard work activities. Formal and informal interviews, documents and records, and direct observations were used (Lofland, 1971; Wax, 1971). In addition, over 20 key informants were cultivated among the guards and inmate elites or leaders who assisted in analyzing control and order as daily phenomena. Close relationships were developed with these informants, and their "expert" knowledge about prison life and prisoner control was essential throughout the fieldwork (Jacobs, 1974; Marquart, 1986). Most importantly, the daily routine of prison events (work, school, counts, cell and body searches, the administration of punishment) as well as various unexpected events (fights, stabbings, suicide attempts, escapes) were observed and noted.

After a time, the author became privy to guard violence and observed and simply noted 30 incidents wherein the guards physically punished inmates for various rule violations. Key guard informants also described an additional 20 force situations. These 50 cases occurred between December 1981 and November 1982. At this point, a general description of the incidents was written up and the altercations were discussed at great length with 7 guard and 15 inmate key informants. . . . Essentially, these 50 cases served as a base to further develop a systematic method of data collection and analysis. Then, after reviewing the literature on social control in prison and social control theory in general (as well as the police use of force), the author developed a systematic strategy to catalogue and code four functions of the guards' use of unofficial force. This analytic strategy was then applied to 30 cases of observed and informant-reported guard violence that occurred between December 4, 1982, and January 28, 1983. These latter 30 cases serve as the data base and will be examined at length throughout this paper.

THE RESEARCH SETTING

. . . . The staff at the prison numbered around 235 officers (85% white, 10% black, 5% Hispanic). This all-male security force was divided into two forces—building and field. The interest in this investigation lies with the building force that numbered nearly 145 officers. They were distributed between the three shifts. The apex of the organizational structure was the warden, and beneath him were two assistant wardens. Although the wardens were the prison's chief security officers, they served primarily as administrators. The actual management and supervision of the daily security measures and convict "business" was the responsibility of the Building Major. The Major supervised two captains who in turn supervised four lieutenants. Last, there were eight sergeants who helped the lieutenants manage the shifts.

Between the ranking staff and the line prison guards was a group of nearly 25 guards called hall officers. At Johnson, all officers began their careers working in the cell blocks or tanks. Officers who demonstrated they could "work a tank" were defined as "good officers" and were selected by their supervisors (lieutenants and sergeants) to become hall officers. Properly "working a tank" involved keeping correct inmate counts, breaking up fights, the maintenance of discipline in a "cool manner" without yelling and arguing with inmates or constantly writing disciplinary reports. Although counting ability and "common sense" (the ability to manage inmates in ordinary situations) were musts, the willingness and initiative to break up fights with inmates, not backing down in confrontations with inmates, and the inclination to actually fight inmates were the critical factors leading to selection for a hall "boss" slot. As one supervisor stated, "I don't want him (as a hall officer) if he doesn't have nuts." These officers were regarded as the best of the line prison officers, and selection for this position was regarded as a promotion, a status symbol, and a sign of a promising future within this prison system. The remaining officers staffed the cell blocks, dormitories, gun towers, dining halls, and other security-related jobs and were rarely promoted. This latter group supplied the rapid turnover cadre that characterizes all prisons.

INTIMIDATION AND PHYSICAL COERCION

To control the inmates at Johnson, the guard staff employed both rewards and punishments. In the official control structure, the guards used a privilege system (for example, good time, furloughs, improved job and living quarters) that provided the majority of prisoners with enough incentive to follow the rules most of the time. Failure to comply typically resulted in the loss of privileges and usually solitary confinement. Because Johnson was so highly regimented, the fear of getting caught and losing privileges deterred most inmates from serious rule infractions. However, those who frequently broke the rules or engaged in serious violations (for example, assaulted staff, fomented rebellion, or stabbed other inmates) were unofficially controlled by the guards through verbal intimidation and various degrees of physical punitive force.

Verbal Intimidation

Inmates who challenged an officer's authority (for example, by insubordination, cursing at him, or "giving him a hard time") usually received verbal assaults from ranking officers or supervisors (sergeants, lieutenants, and captains). Verbal assaults, though physically harmless, induced humiliation and were used to cripple or demean the erring inmate's self concept. In addition, this control tactic intimidated, ridiculed, or destroyed the "face" of the offending inmate and often involved racial epithets, name calling, derogation, threats, and scare tactics. The following verbal assault by one ranking officer upon an inmate illustrates a typical humiliation ceremony. "You stupid nigger, if you ever lie to me or any other officer about what you're doing, I'll knock your teeth in." On another occasion the researcher observed a supervisor make this frequently heard threat: "Say, big boy, you're some kind of mother fucker, aren't you? I ought just go ahead and whip your ass here and now. If you think you're man enough let's do it."

Verbal assaults such as these were daily occurrences. In some cases, inmates were threatened with extreme physical injury ("you'll leave here [the prison] in an ambulance") or even death ("nobody cares if a convict dies in here, we'll beat you to death"). Essentially, verbal assaults alluding to physical force were scare tactics meant to deter inmates from future transgressions. Those who failed to "internalize" the message and repeatedly violated the rules were roughed up as a matter of course.

Types of Coercion

The first type of unofficial physical coercion was called (by inmates and officers alike) a "tune up," "attitude adjustment," or "counselling." These force displays were used for minor officer-inmate offenses (for example, refusing to obey an order, swearing at or arguing with an officer, belligerence, and the expression of a flippant and negative attitude) and rarely involved serious physical injury. "Tune ups" consisted of verbal humiliation, shoves, kicks, and head and body slaps.

This type of coercion functioned as an "attention getter" and was meant to scare and intimidate the inmate-victim. The following account, related to the researcher by an officer eyewitness, illustrates the circumstances that led to most "tune ups."

> I [hall officer] had a hard time in the North Dining Hall with an inmate who budged in line to eat with his friend. Man, we had a huge argument right there in the food line after I told him to "Get to the back of the line." I finally got him out [of the dining hall] and put him on the wall. I told my supervisor about the guy right away. Then the inmate yelled "Yea, you can go ahead and lock me up [solitary] or beat me if that's how you get your kicks." Me and the supervisor brought the guy into the Major's office. Once in the office, this idiot [inmate] threw his chewing gum in a garbage can and tried to look tough. One officer jumped up and slapped him across the face and I tackled him. A third officer joined us and we punched and kicked the shit out of him. I picked him up and pulled his head back by the hair while one officer pulled out his knife and said "You know, I ought to just go ahead and cut your lousy head off."

Besides being roughed up, this inmate was indeed scared. He had actually believed that the officers would not hit him. I saw this inmate, who had several lumps and bruises on his face, standing "on the wall" by the Major's office and asked him what happened. He said "Man, I didn't think you got fucked up for smarting off." Although this inmate had been at Johnson for six months, he stated to the author that he knew the guards would use force, but he also believed they would not hit him for such a "petty ass" violation.

Many "tune ups" also took place after disciplinary court. One reliable officer informant told the researcher about two "tune ups" following the court procedure.

> The first inmate was tried for refusing to work. The tape recorder was shut off and a supervisor said, "You're going to work from now on, you understand?" After this, the supervisor slapped him on the head, kicked him in the ass, and literally threw him out the door. The next inmate came in and was tried and found guilty of self-mutilation. He ingested numerous razor blades. One supervisor yelled at him, "It's hard enough for me to keep the rest of these inmates in razor blades to shave with around here, let alone having you eat them all the time." The inmate stuttered and a supervisor slapped him twice across the face.

Inmates "tuned up" after court were the victims of multiple punishments. That is, they received both official (loss of privileges or solitary confinement) and unofficial forms of punishment.

The second form of physical coercion was dubbed "ass whippings" and befell inmates who broke more serious rules such as challenging an officers's authority, threatening an officer, totally defying an officer's authority, or fighting back during a "tune up." Further, these were force situations where the officers employed various types of weapons, such as blackjacks, riot batons, fist loads, or aluminum-cased flashlights. Although weapons were employed, the inmate-victims were not brutalized enough to require hospitalization or other extensive medical treatment. A noteworthy example occurred when a newly arrived inmate, who was in the Major's office for an initial interview retorted, "I can see I'm going to have trouble making it on this farm [prison]." Several officers immediately attacked the inmate and threw him to the floor. While one officer literally stood on the inmate's head (called a "tap dance"), another hit him on the buttocks and thighs with a riot baton, and several others kicked him. During this event, a supervisor was heard yelling, "Hurt him, hurt him" and even encouraged the other officers by saying "Go on, get you some of that ass."

The third type of force used at Johnson was the severe beating. Such beatings occurred infrequently and were reserved for inmates who violated certain "sacred" rules through such actions as attacking staff members, inciting work strikes or mob action, or escaping. The purpose of a beating was intentional physical injury and in some cases hospitalization. For example, while making a routine check of the inmates in a solitary confinement area, the author observed an inmate who had struck an officer earlier in the day; he was beaten so severely that he could not stand up. In this particular case, the inmate was forcibly dragged from the hall into the Major's office and beaten, and then beaten again while being locked in a solitary cell.

Beatings, like the latter two types of coercion, were primarily backstage events and conducted in closed settings to avoid witnesses. However, "public" beatings were occasionally staged to set an example. A good illustration of a "front-stage" beating occurred in the hall near a spot adjacent to the Major's office and was reported by an officer eyewitness.

> I was sitting at the Searcher's desk and Rick [convict] and I were talking and here comes Joe [convict] from 8-block. Joe thinks he knows kung fu, hell he got his ass beat about four months ago. He comes down the hall and he had on a

> tank top, his pants were tied up with a shoe lace, gym shoes on, and he had all his property in a large sack. As he neared us, Rick said, "Well, Joe's fixing to go crazy again today." He came up to us and Rick asked him what was going on and Joe said they [staff] were fucking with him by not letting him have a recreation card. I told him, "Well, take your stuff and go over there to the Major's office" and there he went. Officer A went over and stood in front of Joe, so did Officer B who was beside Joe, Officer C was in back of Officer A, and two convicts stood next to Officer A. Inmate James, an inmate who we tuned up in the hospital several days before, stood about ten feet away. All of a sudden Joe took a swing at Officer A. Officers A and B tackled Joe. I ran over there and grabbed Joe's left leg while a convict had his right leg and we began kicking his legs and genitals. Hell, I tried to break his leg. At the same time Officer B was using his security keys, four large bronze keys, like a knife. The security keys have these points on their ends where they fit into the locks. Well, Officer B was jamming those keys into Joe's head. Joe was bleeding all over the place. Then all of a sudden another brawl broke out right next to us. Inmate James threw a punch at Officer D as he came out of the Major's office to see what was going on. James saw Joe getting beat and he decided to help Joe out. I left Joe to help Officer D. By the time I got there (about two seconds), Officer D and about six convicts were beating the shit out of James. Officer D was beating James with a blackjack. Man, you could hear that crunch noise every time he hit him. At the same time a convict was hitting him in the stomach and chest and face. These other inmates were kicking him and stomping him at the same time. It was a wild melee, just like being in a war. I got in there and grabbed James by the hair and Officer D began hitting him on the head and face with a blackjack. I mean he was hitting him, no love taps. He was trying to beat his brains out and yelling, "You mother fucker, you think you're bad, you ain't bad, you mother fucker, son of a bitch, you hit me and I'll bust your fucking skull." I think we beat on him alone for ten minutes. I punched him in the face and head. Then Officer D yelled, "Take him [James] to the hospital." Officer C and me had to literally drag him all the way to the hospital. Plus we punched and stomped him at the same time. At the hospital, Officer D began punching James in the face. I held his head up so Officer D could hit him. Then Officer D worked James over again with a blackjack. We then stripped James and threw him on a bed. Officer D yelled at James, "I'm going to kill you by the time you get off this unit." Then Officer D began hitting him in the shins and genitals with a night stick. Finally, we stopped and let the medics take over. James had to leave via the ambulance. Joe required some stitches and was subsequently put in solitary.

This gruesome event occurred in the full view of many inmates in the hall and hospital. In addition, the screams of the inmate-victims were heard throughout the building and for several days after this event, the entire prison operated smoothly with few officer-inmate confrontations. This beating was the talk of the prison and many officers used the incident as a scare tactic. In others words, "If you don't do what I say you'll get what Joe and James got and worse."

Beatings such as these were not restricted specifically to serious altercations between officers and inmates. In early August 1982, during breakfast in the South Dining Hall, three inmates fatally stabbed another inmate. Seven officers armed with riot batons and baseball bats led the aggressors, weapons in hand, out of the dining hall to a spot near the Major's office. A supervisor ordered the inmates to throw down their weapons, but they refused. The supervisor made his plea one more time and the inmates still refused. At this point, two hall officers attacked the inmates with aluminum baseball bats. The inmates immediately dropped their weapons and were stripped, escorted to the Major's officer, and beaten severely. The staff was outraged at this homicide and made examples of the culprits.

The Legitimation of Violence

These latter examples of guard violence were obviously illegal and violated written departmental policy as well as civil and criminal law. The informal norms of the guard staff justified violence that violated legal and administrative policy in certain instances. The use of unofficial force was so common in the institution under study that the guards viewed it as an everyday operating procedure and legitimized its use. Further, Johnson was not an anomaly with regard to punitive force. Although this researcher did not observe the use of force in other Texas prisons, the trial proceedings from a prison reform case documented numerous (and quite similar) incidences of guard coercion in seven other state prisons. The Court found that the guards' use of punitive force was not an isolated phenomenon but constituted a routine (and rampant) guard activity (Ninth Monitor's Report to the Special Master, 1983).

In almost every situation where a staff member struck an inmate at Johnson, post facto explanations were manufactured (Van Maanen, 1978). Due to the intervention in recent years of the Federal courts into prisoner discipline, inmates frequently sued officers for various types of civil rights violations, particularly for brutality. In light of this fact, the staff involved in such force situations got together after the fact and wrote statements to the effect that the inmate-victim assaulted a staff member and force was needed to subdue the inmate (similar to "throw downs"). The more force used against an inmate, the more the inmate was said to have "fought back." The officers involved generally used a "covering charge" of striking an officer to justify physical coercion (Manning, 1977). For most "tune ups," statements were not made. However, "ass whippings" and beatings were quickly followed up with statement and disciplinary report writing sessions. Many times inmates filed civil suits concerning excessive force and brutality against the officers. These civil suits were routinely investigated by the Federal Bureau of Investigation but were quashed due to the weight of the staffs' evidence. In short, no medical reports were made to verify physical damage and, in the end, it was the word of one inmate against two, three, or more officers and sometimes several prostaff inmate witnesses as well.

FINDINGS AND ANALYSIS

The use of punitive force by the guards was not a random activity or directed against any particular prisoner for any particular reason. Instead, coercion was a socially structured and highly organized form of guard behavior. To understand why the guards relied on force, it is necessary to first describe the setting for this behavior.

Then four reasons for the use of coercion are analyzed. These are: (1) coercion maintains control and order; (2) coercion maintains status and deference; (3) coercion facilitates promotions; and (4) coercion builds guard solidarity.

The Setting for Coercion

Twenty-eight of the force situations occurred in the Major's office and two in a solitary confinement area. These areas were private settings free from the eyes of other inmates. Physically coercing or "adjusting an inmate's attitude" in private reduced the chances of the inmate-victim securing witnesses for a civil action. In this way, the victim's ability to win a brutality case was virtually impossible. The "hidden" force situation was difficult for the FBI or Department of Justice to investigate. If a suit was filed and investigated (and several were), the guards implicated simply denied knowledge of the event or else read a manufactured report that claimed self-defense, which in turn led to a dismissal of the inmate's claim of brutality.

The application of force was always done in the presence of more than one officer. Hall officers and ranking guards always carried out the physical punishment of inmates. In all 30 incidents, between 2 and 6 of these guards were present. Further, it was an unwritten rule that at least 2 staff members must be present, for safety and evidentiary reasons, whenever an inmate was physically punished. Most coercive situations were initiated by a ranking guard and then the other officers moved in and finished the episode. It was not uncommon for 4, 5, or even 6 officers to be involved in a "tune up" or other force situations.

Coercion Maintains Control and Order

The guards regarded force as an important means to achieve tight disciplinary control and punish recalcitrant inmates. Of the observed force situations, the majority (n = 21) involved inmates who challenged the guards' authority or disrupted the well-defined prison order (for example, refusing to obey an order, swearing at or threatening officers). On one occasion, for example, a guard ordered an inmate to quit talking while standing in line to receive some medicine. The inmate then stated, "I can talk to anybody I please and I sure as hell can talk as loud as I want." This inmate was immediately escorted to the Major's office where the officer made his report about the incident. The inmate was allowed to make a statement and then was slapped across the face and kicked in the buttocks by several ranking officers. Although these episodes were not serious, they were defined by the guards as mutinous and not to be tolerated.

The guards argued that these latter offenses undermined prison discipline and control and inmate violators had to be retaliated against. As guards, they also maintained that the prison was their domain and internal order was their paramount goal. These beliefs therefore justified their use of force, at least to themselves. They firmly believed that coercion was a legitimate mechanism of social control. Further, new officers at Johnson were constantly reminded, as well as placated, by ranking guards with the maxim, "We don't tolerate officers getting jumped on or talked crazy to around here, they'll [inmates] ride the ambulance if they try it."

Punitive force was not always directed against inmates who openly challenged the guards' authority. In some cases, inmates were "tuned up" for inmate-on-inmate offenses. For the most part, the guards did not consider minor inmate-on-inmate incidents (such as gambling, tattooing, stealing) as malicious or as undermining their authority or as serious breaches of prison order. However, for serious inmate-inmate rule infractions such as fighting with weapons, sexual attacks, or threatening other inmates, the guards generally took action. Nine of the 30 cases of force involved these latter offenses. Of these 9 cases, 3 were for homosexual threats, 4 for physical threats, and 2 for continuous fighting (these 2 inmates had several fights at work and in their cell). For example, a small black inmate told the staff that a larger, "stronger" black inmate was "talking sex stuff" to him and making other threatening advances. The aggressive inmate was called to the Major's office and confronted with the complainant's accusation. Although the aggressor denied the threats, he was slapped across the face several times and pushed around by one guard. During this episode, 6 other staff members repeatedly derogated and threatened the aggressor with severe bodily harm if he continued to make homosexual or any other kind of threats against other inmates.

Coercion Maintains Status and Deference

The data indicate that inmate deportment and race were critical elements in the guards' decision to use or not use force. After being confronted with a rule violation, those inmates who responded in an antagonistic or nondeferential attitude towards the staff typically provoked a physical response from the guards. Of the 30 force situations, 23 were directed against inmates who offered increased resistance, lied to, antagonized, or exhibited disrespect toward an officer either at the time of apprehension for a violation or at a later stage during interrogation. For example, on December 4, 1982, inmate Sims lied to an officer about the loss of his work boots. Sims concocted a story to obtain a new pair of boots by saying his old pair were stolen while he was bathing. The officer issued Sims a permit to procure new boots. One hour later, an inmate informer told the officer that Sims merely threw his old boots away in the cell block's trash can. The shoes were retrieved and Sims was "tuned up" for lying to the officer. On another occasion, an officer instructed several prisoners in a cell block dayroom (television room) to "Hold the noise down" whereupon inmate Warren retorted, "Shut up yourself and stay the hell out of the dayroom." Warren was ordered out of the dayroom, escorted to the Major's office where he was punched, kicked, and blackjacked by several officers.

These inmate-victims were physically coerced solely for not showing the officers proper deference and demeanor—passivity, civility, and politeness (Goffman, 1956; Manning, 1977). This finding parallels Reiss's (1971), Sykes and Clark's (1975), and Friedrich's (1983) research on police use of force against "disrespective" citizens. The finding is also similar to the research by Piliavin and Briar (1964), who argued that a juvenile's demeanor was an important determinant in the disposition of the case. Essentially, prisoners who failed to embrace their role or identity as subordinates were more likely to be coerced than "properly" behaved inmates. In sum, the guards used coercion to protect their superior status and the lack of deference or respect for an officer greatly affected the outcome of guard-inmate encounters.

Racial Factors The inmate's race also played an important role in the guards' willingness to use coercion to maintain social status. The inmates at Johnson were mostly urban blacks while the guards were primarily rural whites who viewed the black inmates as basically antiauthority, inferior, disrespectful, aggressive, and, most of all, nondeferential. Twenty-four of the force situations involved black prisoners. Only one Hispanic and five white inmates were physically punished. For the white guards, black prisoners represented troublesome, hostile, and rebellious prisoners who occasionally "needed" physical coercion to "keep them in their place." Racial prejudice was common, and this factor helped facilitate the belief on the part of the guards that black inmates were impolite and troublesome.

Coercion as a Route of Upward Mobility

All new officers began their careers in the cell blocks, which familiarized them with the prison routine and served as a type of character test. Cell block duty was often mentally taxing due to the constant interaction with the inmates, counting, and relaying messages. Those officers who "ran a good tank" and had "snap" were sometimes selected as hall officers. Working in the hall was regarded as a reward because it freed the officer from cell block duty, and it also put him in greater proximity to the ranking guards. Contact with supervisors was a plus and often paved the way for promotions. In fact, it was quite common for shift supervisors to personally groom three or four promising hall officers.

This process was actually a form of tutelage wherein the supervisor played the role of mentor and taught the "pupil" about, among other things, writing disciplinary reports, developing inmate snitches, and searching cells for contraband. More importantly, these "teachers" taught their officers about when, where, and how to use physical force. If an officer used "inappropriate" force (for example, "tuning up" an inmate in the hall, using too much force, beating up older inmates), then the supervisor warned the officer about unwanted investigations. On one occasion, a hall officer slapped an inmate in the inmate dining hall. He lost his hall officer position and was reassigned to an inmate housing unit. In another instance, a hall officer "tuned up" an inmate with a history of heart trouble as well as without other guard witnesses. He was reprimanded for his behavior and forbidden from using coercion. In short, coercion was subject to rules and those who used it in deviant ways were sanctioned.

It was at the level of hall officer that the guards began to learn about the use of force. For example, a new hall officer may be called upon to take part in a Disciplinary Court hearing and might observe a "tune up" or a new hall officer might see a "tune up" while helping to escort an inmate to a solitary confinement cell. In these situations the hall officer was expected to participate in the force display. If the neophyte participated, he also learned how to construct covering charges and post-facto explanations of the event. Fifteen guards were involved in the 30 incidents and 7 were hall officers, 4 were sergeants, 3 were lieutenants, and 1 was a captain. Line prison officers, or those working in cell blocks and other security areas, were not involved in a single case of unofficial coercion.

Becoming a hall officer did facilitate upward mobility, but the willingness of an officer to fight inmates was the primary variable affecting his acceptance by other hall officers and ranking guards. In the guard culture at Johnson, fighting an inmate ("getting on one" or "frapping his ass") was a measure of an officer's manhood or "nuts." Excessive or compulsive masculinity more commonly referred to as machismo was a highly valued personality trait (Toby, 1966). A cult of male honor prevailed in which personal violence was obligatory to establish the officer's reputation and status within the guard subculture (Reider, 1984). As one ranking guard stated, "You have to make a convict fear you or respect you or you won't make it here." Another ranking guard said, "Hell, some of these officers are crazier and meaner than the convicts." Those who embraced these subcultural tenets were labeled as good officers and were confirmed as members in the ruling clique of officers—hall officers and all ranking guards. Fighting an inmate was the equivalent of a rite of passage because this event solidified the perception of an officer as a person who could be trusted.

Personal toughness and "acting like a man" were the critical factors ranking guards employed to evaluate all employees. Specifically, officers who exhibited the "proper" traits were usually rewarded in the form of better duty assignments or promotions. The ranking officers viewed force as a legitimate control tactic and tacitly approved of this behavior. Hall officers were expected to use force when the situation arose, and those who could not or would not were quickly discovered, labeled weak or unloyal, and in some cases reassigned back to cell block duty. Earning a reputation as weak or cowardly was a personal disaster for the officer and parallels the spoiled identity concept commonly found in the deviance literature. In addition, exceptional hall officers were often promoted due to their past performances, thus enhancing their organizational careers. Excluding the 3 wardens, all 18 ranking officers of the building force were hall officers either at Johnson or at another of Texas's many correctional institutions. Promotion of hall officers ensured that this important subcultural value would be passed on to other officers.

Age Factors It should also be noted that the officers who were most likely to use force were young and had relatively few years of guard experience. Six of the 15 guards involved were between the ages of 18 and 24, while 7 were between 25 and 29. The remainder were over the age of 33. In addition, 5 of the officers had less than 1 year of experience, 5 had between 1 and 3 years, 4 had between 4 and 9 years, and only 1 had more than 10 years of prison experience. These data underscore the point that those guards most likely to employ force were young hall officers with little experience. These young men were also quite eager to make guardwork a career. It was precisely this group of officers who were being tailored or groomed for promotion by ranking guards. The primary reason older ranking guards were less likely to be involved was that they had already established themselves and did not have to continuously reaffirm their reputation. It was the younger officers who were under pressure to "perform," and their close proximity to ranking officers provided the push to employ force (Milgram 1965).

Indeed, upward mobility within the organization hinged on the acceptance and performance of physical coercion as a mechanism of control. This system or structure of unofficial prisoner control determined the content of guard socialization.

Racial Factors The race of the officer was also an important factor in the use of force. White guards, like their police counterparts (Friedrich, 1983), were more likely to use force than black or Hispanic guards. Twelve of the guards involved were white, 2 were black, and 1 was Hispanic. Minority officers were not trusted by the predominantly white ruling (administrative) elite, and they were rarely promoted and frequently terminated for "collaborating with the enemy" (Jacobs and Grear, 1977). Minority officers were generally concentrated in cell block duty far away from the settings where inmates were unofficially disciplined.

Of the 15 officers involved, 12 were white and 10 of these were born and raised near the institution, which was located in a rural area of the state. It is also important to note that almost half (47%) of the inmates in the prison were black. In addition, 68% of the inmates in this particular department of corrections were from urban areas. These data underscore the conclusion that rural white guards were using physical coercion against urban black inmates. The white guards at the prison under study openly expressed racial prejudice and tendencies toward discrimination. For example, one day the author of this paper entered the Major's office and found a hall officer punching a black inmate in the kidneys. As the inmate writhed and moaned on the floor, the officer stated nonchalantly, "I told the captain I was going to whip a nigger today."

Coercion Builds Solidarity

The use of coercion by the hall officers and ranking guards induced solidarity among this group. Only this group of officers participated in physical punishment, and those officers who were accepted by this group were deemed "successful." That is, they internalized and justified the use of coercion. These officers formed the "hard core" of the guard culture. Indeed, they were members of a primary group and social circle that had daily face-to-face interaction. These officers also associated with each other off the job. In addition, there was low turnover and high morale among this group. Ironically, this system created high turnover and low morale among the other line guards who refused, could not, or did not accept force as a tactic of control. The ruling elite viewed the nonforce group as "bodies," people needed to open and close doors. These "unsuccessful" guards either quit or eventually transferred to other Texas correctional institutions.

Secrecy was another factor enhancing solidarity. As a new hall officer became privy to force incidents, he also learned about the code of secrecy. A similar norm exists among police (Westley, 1970). There was an unwritten rule that hall and ranking officers refrain from talking about force displays with the lower-ranking guards. Being privy to this information as well as keeping "one's mouth shut" was an important norm that facilitated acceptance by the ruling clique of guards. It was not uncommon for low-ranking guards to ask hall officers about force situations. However, their queries were closed off with the standard answers, "I don't know what you're talking about" or "I wasn't here that day." These standard responses were also employed during FBI investigations into illegal use of force. In short, the ruling clique of guards represented a primary group that sustained a high degree of camaraderie (on and off the job) which in turn produced group loyalties and fostered group cohesion (Shils and Janowitz, 1948).

GUARD COERCION AND ORGANIZATIONAL STRUCTURE

Any inquiry into the dynamics of force within an institutional setting must concern itself with organizational structure. Police departments, for example, are highly centralized with numerous formalized policies that govern police-citizen encounters. Police organizations emphasize training and professionalism in which widespread abuse of citizens is not tolerated. Furthermore, these agencies frequently have an internal affairs division to investigate citizen claims about police misuse of force. This latter factor alone has without doubt severely curtailed the arbitrary use of force (and discretion) by police officers.

Although there appear to be no studies on the relationship between guard coercion and the prison's organizational structure, the research under discussion found that organizational structure affects guard aggression. The prison under study was part of a large bureaucracy. Rules, records, various departments, and accountability were present, but rarely did these bureaucratic elements affect the daily operation of Johnson. This prison, like the other Texas prisons, enjoyed a great deal of autonomy from the central administration. Moreover, there was a low level of interdependence between the various institutions. Specifically, the security staff at Johnson was permitted to carry out control activities with little or no interference from the main administration. Therefore, the guards possessed enormous discretion to control their charges as they saw fit. As a mechanism of social control, physical force became the cornerstone for inmate control. The use of coercion not only maintained order, but it also functioned as a means of cohesion and was an important element within the guard culture. This pattern emerged because of the lack of strong organizational controls unlike, for example, police departments.

On the one hand, it may be argued that in prison organizations characterized by decentralization and unit autonomy, the specter of coercion will always be present. Furthermore, the statuses and roles of the keepers and kept will be institutionalized, like a caste system, as superiors and inferiors. Inmates will be treated as social inferiors or as objects who enjoy few civil or due process rights. Physical coercion in these organizations will be employed as a control device (an instrumental need) as well as to maintain status, build cohesion, and facilitate upward mobility.

On the other hand, those prison organizations based on centralization and formalization (with little autonomy and discretion), such as the California system or the Federal Bureau of Prisons, will not support an inmate control system predicated on coercion and fear. Most of these latter systems have formalized inmate grievance procedures and some (such as the Virginia Department of Corrections) have a department of internal affairs to investigate inmate claims of guard brutality. Physical coercion in these latter organizations serves neither instrumental nor symbolic purposes but is the idiosyncratic and unstructured behavior of a "bad guard"—paralleling the "bad cop" in police organizations. In sum, guard violence is an open area of research, and future inquiries should look at force and its relation to organizational structure in order to better understand prisoner control structures.

CONCLUSION

This paper has demonstrated that guard violence was not idiosyncratic nor a form of "self-defense" and was relatively unprovoked. Instead, force was used against inmates as a means of physical punishment by a small but significant percentage of the guards. These officers were primarily hall officers and sergeants with relatively low-ranking positions in the guard hierarchy. It also demonstrated that force served not only as a control mechanism, but it also induced group cohesion, maintained status and deference, and facilitated promotions. Like Mischel (1968) and Milgram (1965), it was found that guard violence was not the sole result of sadistic or power-hungry motives, but was shaped by powerful social and situational forces. Officers learned violence from their peers and were rewarded by their superiors for their behavior. They also did not physically coerce inmates at random or for no reason. Punitive force was directed against inmates, particularly blacks, who refused (or appeared to refuse) the guards' definition of the situation. Indeed, any challenges to their authority were met with quick, calculated physical responses. The guards managed the penitentiary with an iron hand and inmates who upset the regimen were literally beaten into submission.

The correspondence of these findings with other state maximum security institutions is unknown. As a consequence, numerous research questions exist and future studies should address violence as a mechanism of social control in prison and extraprison settings. One line of research might examine the effects of the organizational culture and its impact on guard socialization processes and outcomes, values, and resultant guard personality traits. Research, particularly comparative research between northern and southern prison systems, would provide data and make an important contribution to the areas of social control theory, the sociology of violence, and the study of prison organizations.

REFERENCES

Berkman, Ronald. 1979. *Opening the Gates: The Rise of the Prisoners' Rights Movement.* Lexington, MA: Lexington.

Carroll, Leo. 1974. *Hacks, Blacks, and Cons: Race Relations in a Maximum Security Prison.* Lexington, MA: Lexington.

Clemmer, Donald. 1940. *The Prison Community.* New York: Holt, Rinehart and Winston.

Cloward, Richard A. 1960. Social control in the prison. In Donald Cressey (ed.), *Theoretical Studies in Social Organization of the Prison.* New York: Social Science Research Council.

Cressey, Donald. 1968. Contradictory directives in complex organizations: The case of the prison. In Lawrence Hazelrigg (ed.), *Prison within Society.* Garden City, NY: Anchor.

Davidson, Theodore. 1974. *Chicano Prisons: The Key to San Quentin.* New York: Holt, Rinehart and Winston.

Friedrich, Robert. 1983. Police use of force: Individuals, situations, and organizations. In Carl B. Klockars (ed.), *Thinking About Police.* New York: McGraw-Hill.

Gobert, James J. and Neil P. Cohen. 1981. *Rights of Prisoners.* Colorado Springs, CO: Shephard's/McGraw-Hill.

Goffman, Erving. 1956. The nature of the deference and demeanor. *American Anthropologist* 58: 473–501.

1961. *Asylums.* Chicago: Aldine.

Hawkins, Gordon. 1976. *The Prison, Policy and Practice.* Chicago: University of Chicago Press.

Hepburn, John. 1985. The exercise of power in coercive organizations: A study of prison guards. *Criminology* 23: 145–164.

Jacobs, James. 1974. Participant observation in prison. *Urban Life and Culture* 3: 221–240.

1977. *Stateville: The Penitentiary, in Mass Society.* Chicago: University of Chicago Press.

Jacobs, James and Mary Grear. 1977. Drop-outs and rejects: An analysis of the prison guard's revolving door. *Criminal Justice Review* 2: 57–77.

Lofland, John. 1971. *Analyzing Social Settings.* Belmont, CA: Wadsworth.

Manning, Peter K. 1977. Police Work: The Social Organization of Policing. Cambridge, MA: MIT Press.

Marquart, James W. 1983. Cooptation of the kept: Maintaining control in a southern penitentiary. Unpublished doctoral dissertation. College Station: Texas A & M University.

1986. Outsiders as insiders: Participant observation in the role of a prison guard. *Justice Quarterly* 3: 15–32.

Marquart, James W. and Ben M. Crouch. 1984. Coopting the kept: Using inmates for social control in a southern prison. *Justice Quarterly* 1: 491–509.

McCleery, Richard. 1960. Communication patterns as a basis of systems of authority. In *Theoretical Studies in Social Organization of the Prison.* New York: Social Science Research Council.

Milgram, Stanley. 1965. Some conditions of obedience and disobedience to authority. *Human Relations* 18: 57.

Mischel, Walter. 1968. *Personality and Assessment.* New York: Wiley.

Mouledous, Joseph C. 1962. Sociological perspectives on a prison social system. Unpublished master's thesis. Baton Rouge: Louisiana State University.

Ninth Monitor's Report of Factual Observations to the Special Master 1983.

Piliavin, Irving and Scott Briar. 1964. Police encounters with juveniles. *American Journal of Sociology* 37: 73–82.

Reider, Jonathan. 1984. The social organization of vengeance. In Donald Black (ed.), *Toward a General Theory of Social Control II: Fundamentals.* New York: Academic Press.

Reiss, Albert. 1971. *The Police and the Public.* New Haven, CT: Yale University Press.

Shils, Edward and Morris Janowitz. 1948. Cohesion and disintegration of the Wehrmacht in WW II. *Public Opinion and Quarterly* 12: 280–315.

Sykes, Gresham. 1958. *The Society of Captives.* Princeton, NJ: Princeton University Press.

Sykes, Richard E. and John P. Clark. 1975. A theory of deference exchange in police-civilian encounters. *American Journal of Sociology* 81: 584–600.

Thomas, James. 1984. Some aspects of negotiated order, loose coupling and meso-structure in maximum security prisons. *Symbolic Interaction* 4: 213–231.

Toby, Jackson. 1966. Violence and the masculine ideal: Some qualitative data. *The Annals* 364: 19–27.

1982. Fieldwork on the beat. In John Van Maanen (ed.), *Varieties of Qualitative Research.* Beverly Hills: Sage.

Van Maanen, John. 1978. The asshole. In Peter K. Manning and John Van Maanen (eds.), *Policing: A View from the Street.* Santa Monica, CA: Goodyear.

Wax, Rosalie H. 1971. *Doing Fieldwork: Warnings and Advice.* Chicago: University of Chicago Press.

Westley, William. 1970. *Violence and the Police.* Cambridge, MA: MIT Press.

REVIEW QUESTIONS

1. The author identified four underlying causes that were forwarded by guards to justify their unsanctioned use of coercion on inmates. Can you identify at least one legitimate security/disciplinary option that guards could turn to in order to achieve each of these four desired outcomes?
2. What factors might account for the fact that underlying racial factors were not associated with the status/deference and solidarity reasons for guard coercion?
3. What sorts of policies and procedures might prison administrators implement to curb the incidence of the verbal and physical coercion described in this article?
4. Are there negative consequences that would follow from a strict systemwide ban against verbal and physical coercion among guards?

VI

CORRECTIONAL STAFF

READING 14

A Typology of Correctional Officers

Mary Ann Farkas

Understanding the staff who work in correctional facilities is critical to understanding the daily activities, culture, and relationships that exist in such facilities. As the most common type of staff position, and those with most frequent and often most intense forms of interactions with inmates, correctional officers are critical to the operations of prisons and jails. In this reading, Farkas reviews the existing research literature about different varieties of correctional officers and reports on an original study designed to differentiate between orientations of correctional officers. Each of five main and three residual varieties is discussed, with an emphasis on how they fit into the structure of the prison and the occupational culture of the variety of officer.

Although there is abundant research identifying types of correctional officers (Kauffman, 1988; Klofas & Toch, 1982), there has been little scholarly attempt to systematically examine the multidimensional aspects of these types and the relationship to the formal and informal structures of the organization. This is important in understanding officers' approaches to their work and what variables affect these styles. Correctional officers play an influential role in the lives of many inmates because of their direct and prolonged interaction. Hepburn and Knepper (1993) contended that officers are responsible for creating and maintaining a humane environment in prison. Thus, differentiation of work styles is central to understanding the dynamics that occur between staff and inmates within the correctional organization. A typology of officers is also useful for correctional management. It allows administrators to identify and understand the various styles of officers, the cultural norms and values associated with each type, and whether these norms and values are in line with their organizational mission and objectives.

This study developed a classification of correctional officers and explored their underlying dimensions. It located the typology within the theoretical framework of an organization conceptualized by Allaire and Firsirotu (1984) that emphasized the interrelationship between the individual actors, the sociostructural or formal component, and the cultural or informal system. This study has four basic propositions:

Proposition 1: Underlying dimensions relating to authority, power, obligations to coworkers, and attitudes toward inmates distinguish each officer type.

Proposition 2: There are distinct types of correctional officers that are shaped by the interplay between the sociostructural system, the cultural system, and the individual actors.

Proposition 3: Officer types are actually modes of accommodation or adaptations to the unique structural and organizational aspects of their work situations.

Proposition 4: Officer types may be further differentiated by certain individual and work variables.

REVIEW OF THE LITERATURE

Correctional officers have been characterized in relation to their approach to the job and their attitudes and interactions with inmates and, to a lesser extent, coworkers. Some researchers have also described officer types in terms of career stages or processes (Owen, 1988). Several predominant types emerged from the literature. They generally fell under the categories of custodial or punishment oriented and human service or rehabilitative oriented. Johnson (1996) referred to the custodial type as the "public agenda" of officers and the human service type as their "private agenda." The tough facade of custodial officers was necessary to be accepted by their peers. Custodial types included *black and whiters* (Carter, 1994) and *by the book* (Owen, 1988). These officers followed rules and regulations to the letter in their everyday negotiations with inmates. They strongly relied on rule enforcement to maintain order and control and limited individualized relations with inmates. *Subcultural custodians* (Klofas & Toch, 1982) and *hard asses* (Kauffman, 1988) were also custodial types but with an important difference. These officers projected a personal physical dominance over inmates and tended to treat inmates in a more callous manner. They viewed themselves as a "special breed" and derived great satisfaction from their ability to control inmates by any means (Kauffman, 1988, p. 253). The custodial types were more likely to be newer officers still negotiating their role in the prison who had not yet found a comfortable way of working with inmates. As they became accustomed to working with inmates, they mellowed from their strict, by-the-book approach to a more flexible style.

The *supported majority* (Klofas & Toch, 1982), *human service officers* (Johnson, 1996; Lombardo, 1989), *white hats* or *pollyannas* (Kauffman, 1988), and *weathermen* (Carter, 1994) were types of human service officers. These officers were typically more experienced correctional officers. They developed a more relaxed, individualized approach, interpreting minor violations with a sense of fairness (Carter, 1994). They found enormous satisfaction and challenge in the human service aspects of the job, advising and referring inmates with institutional problems. Their desire to work closely with inmates and develop personalized relations was inhibited by their fear of rejection from other coworkers with anti-inmate sentiments.

Among residual types of officers were *functionaries* (Kauffman, 1988), *lazy-laid back officers* (Owen, 1988), *easy lifers* (Carter, 1994), and *burnouts* (Kauffman, 1988). Functionaries, lazy-laid back officers, and easy lifers were correctional officer types who were disinterested in the job. They were at best ambivalent, at worst indifferent, to the prison world around them and everyone in it (Kauffman, 1988). They were simply going through the motions of the job, getting through the day with the least amount of trouble. These officers avoided confrontation by allowing inmates to get away with things or by completely ignoring them (Carter, 1994). Burnouts were emotionally fatigued from the reality of working in prison and were unable to find solace in relations with coworkers or inmates (Kauffman, 1988). They were either less experienced officers who "got burned" by inmates or became disenchanted with the idea of corrections as a career or veteran officers who grew weary of the day-to-day realities of working in prison.

Although women were included in some of the aforementioned types, Zimmer (1986) identified three patterns of adaptation unique to women working as correctional officers. The *institutional* role was a type of officer who tried to perform the job on an equal basis with her male counterparts. She enforced rules strictly and followed procedures closely because of intense scrutiny by peers and supervisors. The *modified* role relied on the assistance and protection of her male colleagues to do the job because of a lack of confidence in her abilities. Women in the *inventive* role used their interpersonal skills and common sense to gain and maintain inmate compliance.

Although these typologies provided a very good description, they did not systematically relate these correctional officer types to the sociostructural and informal components of the organization. This study explored the impact of the correctional organization on the formation and perpetuation of types. Finally, the reality of the officer's experience was considered in developing the present typology. Correctional officers were asked to identify and describe what types of officers they saw working at the correctional institutions. In this regard, officers were asked for demographic information, predominant types of officers, and specific approaches or styles associated with the types. The officer typology was then cross-validated with the study's findings.

METHODOLOGY

Research Sites

The study was conducted at two correctional institutions in two medium-sized cities in a Midwestern state. One institution was located in a primarily urban area in the southeastern region of the state, and the other facility was located in a rural area in the northern part. Both sites were large, fairly new, medium-security correctional institutions for adult men. At each correctional institution, the average daily population of inmates was approximately 500, and the correctional officer staffing was approximately 200 officers. The majority of inmates were White (60%), with an average age of 34 at the rural institution. At the urban facility, the typical inmate profile was a White, 31-year-old man. The only difference was that inmates at the urban correctional institution were more likely to have a substance abuse problem because of a special program in place. Both facilities were organized structurally into pod units with direct inmate management.

Research Methods

The primary data-gathering technique consisted of interviews with 79 correctional officers. . . . These interviews were used to explore the major themes in the occupational culture of correctional work. Follow-up interviews with officers who expressed the desire to tell me more about their job were also conducted. . . .

Sample

Seventy-nine officers (approximately 23% of the entire population of correctional officers) were interviewed for this study. . . . Attempts were made to ensure that the sample was representative of the employee population by comparing the percentages of respondents along such dimensions as race, gender, and age to official personnel date. Percentages of officers and their ranking, shift, and work assignment were also cross-checked with official data and staffing patterns. . . .

RESULTS

. . . Correctional officers were categorized into five types—*rule enforcer, hard liner, people worker, synthetic officer,* and *loner*—based on their orientation toward rule enforcement, extent of mutual obligations toward colleagues, orientation toward negotiation or exchange with inmates, and their desire to incorporate human service activities into their approach. Three additional types were described by respondents: *officer friendly, lax officer,* and *wishy-washy.*

. . . Rule enforcers were the most common classification among officers in the sample. Forty-three percent (43%) of respondents were characterized as rule enforcers. People workers was the next most common type. Approximately 22% of the combined sample constituted people workers. Of all respondents, 14% were categorized as synthetic officers. The category of loners actually had the smallest number of respondents. Few correctional officers (8% of the combined sample) were classified as such. The following sections provide a description of each type in relation to the four dimensions and to the correctional organization.

RULE ENFORCER

Rule enforcers may be characterized as rule bound, inflexible in discipline, and as having an esprit de corps with others sharing their enforcement philosophy. This officer type was equivalent to the black and whiter (Carter, 1994) and by the book (Owen, 1988).

The rule enforcers constituted the largest percentage of respondents in the sample (43%). They were more likely to be a younger than age 25, with a baccalaureate degree. They tended to have less work experience and to work the later shifts, second and third shifts. They typically worked on posts involving direct inmate contact such as the regular housing units and the maximum-security, special management, or segregation units. These officers were likely to have entered corrections for extrinsic reasons including job security, benefits, and job availability.

The Sociostructural Component and Rule Enforcers

Rule enforcers embraced the formal goals and values of the sociostructural system and conformed closely to the official policies and procedures and rules and regulations. Distinctions of rank, chain of command, and rigid adherence to authority characterized their relations with one another. They adopted a militaristic approach toward inmates, expecting deference to their authority and obedience to their orders. They interpreted their official mandate to be custody and control and "maintaining order and proper conduct."

The Occupational Culture of Rule Enforcers

Keeping inmates from doing things such as "loitering, passing property or food, gathering in groups more than six, and seeing inmates obey rules" were duties described by rule enforcers. Invoking the rules was tantamount to maintaining order in the unit and teaching inmates discipline. As one officer explained,

> Watching them [inmates] is what makes them change. If they violate a rule, you must keep tabs on them. They may think you can't remember who did what with so many inmates. Notebook helps a lot. I carry a memo book to write down violations with inmates' names. They know I'm watching.

Advice to a new officer was to learn the rules fast and know them inside and out. Ignorance of the rules allowed inmates to manipulate an officer into letting inmates "get away with something."

Rule enforcers were not willing to negotiate or use exchange as a strategy to gain inmate compliance. A rule violation was considered a direct challenge to an officer's authority. Negotiating with inmates disrupted order by relinquishing control to inmates: "You've got to know the rules and not be afraid to enforce them. Inmates will test you, and if you fail, you will lose face with them. Once that happens, you will have problems getting them to obey you."

Norms of mutual obligation were particularly strong and well defined among the rule enforcer type, such as always supporting an officer's decision/action and never contradicting a coworker in the presence of inmates, other coworkers, or management (see Farkas, 1997, for an in-depth discussion of the normative code among correctional officers).

Rule enforcers believed that a human service role was inappropriate and potentially compromising. Advice to new officers included, "Don't ever trust an inmate" and "Watch out for the con." In fact, the majority of officers in this classification expressed a preference to work on job assignments with less inmate contact such as the tower or perimeter patrol. One correctional officer elaborated, "I don't like to get too close to inmates. I don't want to hear their problems. They want to get your sympathy or catch you with your guard down. They're always trying to get something over on you."

HARD LINER

The hard liner was essentially a subtype or, rather, an extreme paradigm of the rule enforcer. Respondents described this officer as hard, aggressive, power hungry, inflexible with rules, and possessing little interpersonal skill. This type was analogous to the hard ass (Kauffman, 1988) and subcultural custodian (Klofas & Toch, 1982). A small percentage of respondents (14%) were typed as hard liners. These officers were most likely to be male, with a high school education or general equivalency diploma (GED), and between the ages of 26 and 36. Respondents who worked the later shifts were also more likely to be designated as hard liners. They tended to work on maximum-security, special management, or segregation units.

Sociostructural Component and the Hard Liner

The hard liner type strongly supported the formal goals and values of the organization. Similar to rule enforcers, they endorsed the militaristic values of the formal organization: distinction and deference to rank, chain of command, and authority vested in the position. At times, however, they became abusive and aggressive toward inmates. Hard liners perceived acting tough or hard as the way that a correctional officer was supposed to act in accordance with official mandates to maintain order and control. However, they actually disavowed official goals and values when they abused their authority.

The Occupational Culture of Hard Liners

Hard liners strictly enforced rules to punish and to show authority. Rules were also used to play games with inmates and to aggravate them. This differed from the rule enforcer who imposed rules primarily to maintain order and teach discipline. Hard liners were not willing to negotiate for inmate compliance with rules because this was a sign of weakness. As one hard liner explained, "If you want the inmates to respect you, you've got to be tough. You can't be afraid of them. I don't let them get away with any shit. They do what I say."

An extremely negative attitude toward inmates was also characteristic of this type. Inmates were perceived as "always trying to get away with something" and were referred to by various pejorative terms such as the *criminal element* or *scumbags*. As several respondents complained, "These guys [inmates] are nothing but scumbags; they'll sucker you in. Don't trust an inmate" and "We deal with some real nasty individuals. These are inmate 'recycles' who have caused problems at other institutions, and now we've got them."

Hard liners identified strongly with the officers on their unit and particularly with officers who shared their negative orientation toward inmates. They often complained that inmates had it "too easy" in prison and that they had far too many privileges. This type deeply resented having to provide services to inmates. They preferred to work on posts with limited or no inmate contact. Segregation was their choice if they had to choose a post with inmate interaction.

PEOPLE WORKER

People workers were characterized by respondents as "professionals trying to be social, responsible, and trying their very best." This type was comparable to the supported majority (Klofas & Toch, 1982), human service workers (Johnson, 1996), weathermen (Carter, 1994), and the white hats (Kauffman, 1988). Approximately 22% of respondents were classified in this type. People workers were generally White, older, and more experienced correctional officers. They were also more likely to work the first shift and less likely to work the third shift. They also were inclined to work on regular units and less likely to work on maximum-security or "seg" units. Finally, the reason for becoming a correctional officer was likely to be due to intrinsic reasons, the challenging or interesting work.

Sociostructural Component and People Workers

People workers modified the formal goals and militaristic values of the official culture of correctional work. They developed a more workable, comfortable style of working with inmates. They were more flexible in rule enforcement and disciplinary measures with their own informal reward and punishment system. According to people workers, the way to gain inmate compliance was through interpersonal communication and personalized relations.

The Occupational Culture of People Workers

People workers regarded an overreliance on conduct reports as an indication of an officer's inability to resolve difficult situations. They were concerned with why an inmate committed the rule violation. Their action or inaction depended on the circumstances and the inmate's attitude. One people worker responded, "When an inmate 'goes off,' it usually means that they have a problem. If you figure out what's wrong, it is easier to settle things." Generally, they tried to resolve minor infractions through communication and reason.

People workers also stressed handling problems on an individual basis with an inmate. They discussed an issue privately with an inmate instead of fronting him (embarrassing him in front of peers). Verbally deescalating a situation with the least amount of trouble was another tactic of this type. Although some of these officers employed more creative methods of teaching inmates the rules:

> Rather than clog up the disciplinary process with minor violations, you have an inmate take care of a need for a unit, such as cleaning the back dock instead of writing a ticket. It's the time, effort, and embarrassment factors.

Norms of mutual obligation toward coworkers were not as pronounced as in the previous types. People workers would intervene in an altercation between an inmate and a coworker for the sole purpose of resolving it. They were more concerned with conflict resolution than with hurting a colleague's pride or undermining their authority. A correctional officer stated,

> I'd find a way to intervene. Distract his [inmate] attention to me and try to get an understanding of what the circumstances are. When everything's under control, I'd have a discussion with the other CO about rights and wrongs to see whether he handled it right.

According to these officers, an effective correctional officer relied on verbal skills and common sense in handling inmates and defusing situations. They felt that an officer should not become dependent on the emergency response team (Team 1) to resolve a situation: "I have learned to rely on my communication skills and not just on a Team 1 Response" and "Your personality is what starts it—how you display yourself—communication skills, this is what defuses a situation."

People workers enjoyed the challenge of working with inmates and actually preferred posts with more inmate contact. Most officers in this type planned to have a career in corrections simply because they liked the opportunity to help an inmate or make a difference in his life.

SYNTHETIC OFFICER

The synthetic officer was essentially a synthesis of the rule enforcer and the people worker types. There was no analogous type in the literature on correctional officers. The closest approximation was a probation officer type described by Klockars (1997). Fourteen percent of the sample was classified as synthetic officers. They were inclined to be an older correctional officer. Of those officers ages 37 or older, 28% were in this category. They were also typically more experienced officers who worked on the regular inmate housing units on the first shift. No officers from maximum-security, special management, or segregation units fit this category.

Sociostructural Component and Synthetic Officers

The synthetic officer tried to modify the formalized policies and procedures to emphasize organizational directives and interpersonal skills. They followed rules and regulations closely, yet they tried to consider the circumstances. They were careful not to deviate too far from procedure in the interest of "covering [their] ass." They differed from the people workers in their close identification with official goals and values and in their caution and mistrust in working with inmates.

The Occupational Culture of Synthetic Officers

Strict enforcement of rules and flexibility in enforcement were juggled in their interactions with inmates. Their strategy in handling inmates appeared to be highly situational, with action dependent on the circumstances. As several synthetic officers explained,

> Rule violation—it would depend on the inmate. If he seemed to be doing it seriously, I would notify a supervisor. If he didn't seem to be serious, I would talk to him and convince him to move along.

"An 'effective' correctional officer is someone who treats inmates fairly and with respect but enforces all the rules and doesn't take all the crap inmates try to give you." Norms of mutual obligations were evident as officers reported the difficulty of seeing a staff member in trouble with inmates or management. Many stated that they would be there to support or back the officer.

THE LONER

The loner was a correctional officer type with no counterpart in the literature. Similar to the rule enforcer, this type was characterized as rule bound but differed in the motivation behind their policy of strict enforcement. Loners closely followed rules and regulations because they feared criticism of their performance as an officer. Female and Black officers were more likely to be represented in the type. They were more likely to be between the ages of 26 and 36 and to be less experienced officers. They tended to work on solitary posts. No officers from maximum-security, special management, or segregation units were represented in this classification.

The Sociostructural Component and Loners

Loners accepted and identified with the formal goals and values of the organization, although they had difficulty identifying or feeling loyalty to coworkers. They conformed strictly to policies, procedures, rules, and regulations for two reasons: (a) to provide validation of their authority to inmates and coworkers and (b) to avoid making a mistake.

The Occupational Culture of Loners

Loners felt their job performance was more closely watched because of their female and/or minority status. This type also stated that they felt the need to continually "prove" themselves to coworkers and management:

> Because I am female, I am tested by both inmates and the officers I work with. Inmates try to manipulate me. I also feel that I am watched closely for mistakes. That's why I try to stay away from everyone; I don't have to prove myself to anyone.

They were unwilling to negotiate for inmate compliance, essentially because of their fear of being seen as "soft" or "unable to handle oneself." They felt that exchange or negotiation with inmates provided opportunities for manipulation and treachery by inmates.

This officer type did not feel accepted by other officers, and neither did they identify with them. Loners felt alienated from coworkers and hence did not endorse norms of mutual obligations.

A few loners expressed this feeling of alienation: "Officer respect—I don't care if they respect me. I feel no allegiance to them; all they do is gossip about everybody" and "The difficult aspect of correctional work—interacting with other officers. There are times when I work with male officers who don't talk directly to me the entire shift."

They were also wary of inmates. There was a basic mistrust, even fear of working with them. They believed inmates were always trying to set officers up or take advantage of them. They preferred to work on posts with social distance from inmates and coworkers such as the towers or perimeter patrol.

RESIDUAL TYPES

There were also three additional types that were identified by the correctional officers in the sample. The lax officer, officer friendly, and the wishy-washy officer were described by respondents in the interviews; however, these types were not found in the data analysis. These three types were officers who rejected the official values and goals of the formal organization. Their rule enforcement was erratic, inconsistent, or nonexistent. They compromised their authority by their inaction or by allowing themselves to be manipulated by inmates.

Lax Officer

Lax officers were officers described as passive, apathetic, or timid. This type was similar to the functionary characterized by Kauffman (1988). Officers stated that lax officers were generally veteran male correctional officers who were weary of arguments with inmates and writing conduct reports (CRs) to no avail. One officer gave this description of the type:

> This officer, he asked me why I write so many CRs. He said I was nuts; it was too much paperwork. He said he was an "eager beaver" like me when he was younger. He said he paid his dues and was waiting to retire.

Lax officers were just "doing their time," similar to the inmates, until their release or retirement. They simply wanted to get through the day with a minimum of effort. They felt no collective responsibility to their coworkers, and their colleagues did not like or respect them either. Their biggest complaint about lax officers was that they did not do their job: "For the rest of us, they make our jobs hell. We have to try to bring back discipline. If the unit is loud and unruly, I have to come in and straighten things out."

Officer Friendly

Officer friendly types were subtypes of people workers. They wanted to be liked by all inmates and were easily manipulated by inmates to give lots of "second chances." Officer friendly types negotiated with inmates to maintain order and gained compliance by overlooking minor violations or doing favors. Norms of mutual obligation were weak. They typically had little loyalty or affinity to other officers. One respondent described the type:

> The "soft type"—they're always trying to help inmates or make things easier for them by bending rules. They feel sorry for inmates. They think that inmates will help them if there's a problem and that inmates will obey you if you're nice.

Wishy-Washy Types

This type was portrayed as unpredictable, moody, running hot and cold, and inconsistent. It was equivalent to the wishy-washy type described by Kauffman (1988). Rule enforcement was inconsistent and uncertain. As one officer stated, "One day it's OK for an inmate to do something, the next day it's not. They enforce some of the rules some of time and all of the rules some of the time."

Wishy-washy officers communicated and helped inmates at one time and then were distant and rule oriented at another. They were likely to be accused of favoritism and mistrusted by inmates because they did not follow through on promises. Norms of mutual obligations were just as uncertain and unclear among these types of officers.

As aforementioned, these three types were not identified from officer interviews. The reason may be that officers were asked about their attitudes and course of action in work situations with inmates and colleagues. These residual types were distinguished by their inaction or indifference and were unlikely to exhibit or admit to these negative characteristics in interviews.

DISCUSSION

This study presented a systematic examination of types of correctional officers in relation to the three major components of an organization. There has been a tendency in past research to overlook the importance of the organizational features and to regard them as independent of officer types. The official system plays an influential role in associating the officer with the formal organization by defining the mission, approved values, and approved modes of conduct. Informal norms and values, alternative interpretations, and other approaches to the work are found in the occupational culture. The individual officers are meaningful in the analysis because it is through their interpretations, values, beliefs, and interests that approaches to the job are formulated.

Findings indicated that there were distinct and diverse styles of working with inmates among officers in the correctional institutions. Rule enforcers, hard liners, and loners reproduced the perceived official organizational goals of custody and control and conformed closely to rules and regulations in their patterns of interaction with inmates and other members. People workers and synthetic officers developed their own values, beliefs, interpretations, and patterns of interaction despite the formal organization's definitions and imperatives. Lax officers, officer friendly types, and wishy-washy types rejected or ignored the mission or objectives of the organization.

Types of officers were actually modes of accommodation or adaptation to the structural and organizational factors of the correctional institutions, including overcrowded conditions, more troublesome inmates, and a more litigious environment. Rule enforcers adopted their authoritarian distant approach because of their view of inmates as manipulative and untrustworthy and even dangerous. They also stuck by the book to "cover [their] ass" in the event of a grievance or lawsuit. Hard liners tended to work on maximum-security or segregation units with more troublesome inmates. They indicated that a tough approach was necessary to handle the more difficult inmates. Thus, identifying strongly with the formal organization's militaristic and custodial objectives provided rule enforcers and hard liners with a mode of accommodation to a tense, unpredictable situation with large numbers of more difficult inmates.

Loners also fully supported the formal goals and policies of the organization and strictly followed procedures, rules, and regulations. This category was more strongly represented by women and minorities. They followed the rules to avoid making a mistake. "Going by the book" and "keeping a distance" provided protection from criticism and allowed them to minimize interaction with coworkers and inmates. The loner type was a mode of accommodation to a situation in which these officers felt alienated and watched closely for mistakes.

People workers and synthetic officers developed their own interpretations, values, and approaches to the job. People workers mediated the formal rules, policies, and procedures to find a more workable way to supervise inmates with the least amount of trouble or confrontation. They valued common sense, good judgment, and interpersonal skills rather than inflexible rule enforcement and an authoritarian approach. Synthetic officers tried to blend strong rule enforcement with communication skills but were cautious and mistrustful in their relations with inmates. Similar to rule enforcers, they were concerned about covering their ass and not deviating too far from the rulebook.

This study also provided an examination of the influence of individual and organizational variables on correctional officers type. For instance, gender and race distinguished the loner. This type felt alienated from inmates and coworkers, which is consistent with previous research reporting a heightened level of stress among female officers working in traditionally male occupations. Minority officers also reported difficulties working with predominantly White supervisors. An interesting issue to consider is whether women and/or minorities were opting to work on solitary assignments as modes of accommodation to negative relations with inmates and coworkers or whether they were assigned to these positions for administrative purposes such as to protect the women from the more difficult assignments on the maximum-security or special management units. The small numbers of women and minorities in the sample signals for more research in this area.

Age and seniority was associated with officer types in the study. Rule enforcers and hard liners tended to be younger, less experienced correctional officers, whereas older, more experienced officers belonged to the people worker or synthetic officer categories. Findings were consistent with the theory that as officers mature, they become more interested in human service delivery (Klofas & Toch, 1982).

Education was a variable that produced some rather interesting results. Training of officers stresses professionalizing correctional work. Upgrading educational requirements is one strategy, with the assumption that more educated officers are inclined toward rehabilitation and less punitive or aggressive toward inmates. In this study, rule enforcers were more likely to have a baccalaureate or master's degree than officers in the other types. This suggests that education may not be as important as an indicator of human service attitudes.

Shift was another organizational variable that was examined. Previous research found that officers on the day shift were more human service oriented (Klofas & Toch, 1982). The rationale was that day-shift officers had more of an opportunity to work with inmates and to mingle with treatment staff. The more custodial types of officers worked the later shifts because they were newer officers. This study corroborated that human service types, people workers, worked the first shift, whereas many hard liners worked the later shifts.

Work assignment was included because it was overlooked in prior research. Hard liners were more likely to work on units with more difficult inmates such as maximum-security units, segregation, or special management units for inmates with behavior problems. This raises the question of whether these types chose to work on the more difficult units or whether the types were really modes of accommodation to their assignment. The rule enforcer and hard liner types may have adopted their no-nonsense or tough approach to supervise the more troublesome inmates. Loners tended to work on posts with limited contact with inmates or other staff such as perimeter patrol, tower, and gatehouse. People workers worked in housing units or on relief positions with the most inmate contact. Again, the issue of choice of post or mode of accommodation to an assigned position is raised.

Finally, reason for becoming a correctional officer was explored. Jurik (1985) found that officers who were interested in the job for intrinsic reasons such as the interest or challenge of the work held more favorable attitudes toward inmates. This study found that reason for becoming an officer was related to officer type. People workers were attracted to intrinsic factors of correctional work: its interesting and challenging aspects. Rule enforcers and hard liners became officers for extrinsic reasons: the job security and benefits of state employment, followed by the availability of the job.

In summary, the major purpose of the study was to identify and describe correctional officer types and their relation to the three major components of an organization. The conclusions are threefold. First, officer types may indeed be shaped by the interplay between the individual actors, the sociostructural system, and the cultural system. As proposed, this organizational analysis was important in showing how officer types appear to be modes of accommodation to the structural and organizational aspects of the correctional institution. Results indicated that a large percentage of officers were classified as rule enforcers. Management may need to reevaluate their goals to ensure that custodial types are in line with their objectives and organizational mission.

Second, findings suggested that certain individual and work variables may further define and differentiate types. Findings on age revealed that older officers were more interested in human service work. It may be that the officers who were more interested in extrinsic factors drop out or transfer to other areas in state employment, leaving behind human service officers. The human service officers, who enjoy the interest and challenge of the work, are those who intend on staying in corrections. Conversely, the maturity and life experience of the individual may be what really differentiate types.

The importance of work assignment and its impact on officer types cannot be overstated. The hard liner tended to work on posts that involved dealing with more troublesome inmates. These officers may need to be rotated periodically. Rotation might counterbalance the effects or "the rubbing off" (as one officer called it) of working on these units. Furthermore, hard liners may not be the best choice for working with disturbed, disruptive inmates.

Reason for becoming an officer was a salient factor in distinguishing officer types, The more custodial officers found the job security and benefits appealing, whereas the more human-service-oriented officers were attracted to intrinsic aspects such as the interesting and challenging work. Recruitment should consider the importance of why someone wants to become a correctional officer.

Future research is needed in correctional institutions of varying security levels to further examine the impact of the organizational context on styles of working with inmates. Research on officer types should also use larger samples and include an observational methodology to validate whether responses from interviews or surveys coincide with the actual behavior of subjects. Another suggestion would be to administer a large number of questions to a larger sample from several correctional institutions and then conduct a factor analysis to determine types of officers.

REFERENCES

Allaire, Y., & Firsirotu, M. E. (1984). Theories of organizational culture. *Organization Studies, 5*, 193–226.

Carter, K. (1994). Prison officers and their survival strategies. In A. Coffey & P. Atkinson (Eds.), *Occupational socialization and working lives* (pp. 41–57). Brookfield, VT: Ashgate.

Emerson, R. (1988). *Contemporary field research.* Prospect Heights, IL: Waveland Press.

Farkas, M. A. (1997). The normative code among correctional officers: An exploration of components and functions. *Journal of Crime and Justice, 20,* 23–36.

Goffman, E. (1959). *Presentation of self in everyday life.* Garden City, NY: Doubleday.

Hepburn, J., & Knepper, P. (1993). Correctional officers as human service workers: The effect on job satisfaction. *Justice Quarterly, 10,* 313–335.

Johnson, R. (1996). *Hard time: Understanding and reforming the prison.* Belmont, CA: Wadsworth.

Jurik, N. (1985). Individual and organizational determinants of correctional officer attitudes toward inmates. *Criminology, 23,* 523–539.

Kauffman, K. (1988). *Prison officers and their world.* Cambridge, MA: Harvard University Press.

Klockars, C. (1997). A theory of probation supervision. In J. W. Marquart & J. R. Sorenson (Eds.), *Correctional contexts* (pp. 343–357). Los Angeles: Roxbury.

Klofas, J., & Toch, H. (1982). The guard subculture. *Journal of Research in Crime and Delinquency, 19,* 238–254.

Lombardo, L. (1989). *Guards imprisoned.* Cincinnati, OH: Anderson.

Owen, B. A. (1988). *The reproduction of social control: A study of prison workers at San Quentin.* New York: Praeger.

Zimmer, L. (1986). *Women guarding men.* Chicago: University of Chicago Press.

REVIEW QUESTIONS

1. How do the five main varieties of officers differ in their orientation toward interactions with inmates?
2. Which of the eight varieties of officers identified is likely to be the most well liked by correctional administrators? Why?
3. Which of the types of officers identified is least likely to have a long and successful career in institutional corrections? Why?

READING 15

Correctional Officer Stress

A Cause for Concern and Additional Help

Peter Finn

Correctional officers are the front line staff, who most often interact with inmates of correctional institutions in the United States. This reading reviews the literature to establish the stressful nature of the job. A number of sources of stress are present for correctional officers, including inmates, co-workers, the organizational structure and culture of prisons, and external sources. The effects of stress are discussed and shown to have significant effects on many aspects of individual correctional officer's lives. Although some resources are available for attempting to mitigate or alleviate such sources of stress, these are not universal, and they are far from available to all who need it.

INTRODUCTION

Stress among correctional officers is an important concern. While the pervasiveness and severity of correctional officer stress are open to question, many officers clearly experience considerable work-related stress. Furthermore, some of the sources of stress for correctional officers appear to be getting worse. In addition to the personal suffering it causes, correctional officer stress can compromise safety at prisons and jails, create turnover that may force departments to hire less-qualified applicants than they would like, and require extra taxpayers dollars to pay overtime to officers covering for sick and disabled coworkers. . . .

This article begins by examining the evidence regarding the pervasiveness and severity of correctional officer stress. It then summarizes research about what causes this stress and what effects stress has on officers and correctional institutions. A review of selected efforts to help prevent and treat correctional officer stress follows.

The article is based on a review of the pertinent literature identified primarily through database searches conducted by the National Clearinghouse for Criminal Justice Information and the National Institute of Corrections. The article also is based on telephone interviews with nine line correctional officers, four mid-level administrators (lieutenants and captains) and two superintendents, nine providers of stress prevention and reduction services, and nine other knowledgeable individuals. Officers and administrators included individuals from public and private prisons and from federal, state, and local prisons and jails. . . .

CORRECTIONAL OFFICER STRESS: HOW BAD IS IT?

Most research on correctional officer stress has sought to identify the *sources* of stress among officers, not *how much* stress officers experience. Among the studies that have examined stress levels, no consistent evidence establishes the proportion of correctional officers who suffer stress or how severely they experience it (Huckabee, 1992). Nevertheless, the available empirical evidence suggests that stress is widespread and in many cases severe. For example, a 1984 study found that 39 percent of 241 line officers who returned a mailed questionnaire reported that their job was "very" or "more than moderately" stressful. A 1985 study found that 62 percent of 120 prison staff in daily contact with inmates reported that working with the institution bureaucracy was very or extremely stressful; at least 30 percent reported that dealing with coworkers, responding to supervisors, and the danger of the job were very or extremely stressful. Furthermore, as reviewed below, the widespread use of excessive sick time and the high turnover among correctional officers suggests that many of them are experiencing considerable stress. Anecdotal evidence from the literature (e.g., Kauffman, 1988) and the individuals interviewed for this article largely confirm this conclusion.

Several circumstances may have created increased stress for correctional officers in recent years:

- Inmate crowding has increased in state correctional facilities (BJS, 1997; Stephan, 1997).
- There has been an increase in the number of inmate assaults against staff. The number of attacks in state and federal prisons jumped by nearly one-third between 1990 and 1995 from 10,731 to 14,165 (Stephan, 1997).
- Because offenders are serving longer sentences, more prisoners do not fear any punishment or the authority of the correctional officers (Martinez, 1997). According to a superintendent, "Inmates today aren't afraid to assault staff; they don't care if they get put in segregation."
- There are more gangs—and more dangerous gangs—in prison (Martinez, 1997).

WHAT CAUSES STRESS FOR CORRECTIONAL OFFICERS?

A fundamental feature of working in prisons and jails that causes stress is that people do not like being held against their will and being closely supervised (Cornelius, 1994). According to a researcher, "Any organization or social structure which consists of one group of people kept inside who do not want to be there and the other group who are there to make sure they stay in will be an organization under stress" (Brodsky, 1982).

Studies (e.g., O'Brien & Gustafson, 1985; Harris, 1980) and several interviewees also reported that, as officers observe so many released inmates returning again and again, the officers come to feel they are wasting their time because the penal system does not result in rehabilitation. "There is no positive feedback for correctional officers," a stress prevention trainer observed.

Beyond these two general sources of stress, the interviews conducted for this article and the literature reviewed confirmed the observation that "researchers have yet to sufficiently identify the factors that contribute to the stress correctional officers experience" (Grossi, 1990). To provide a framework for discussing the disparate stresses, the discussion below distinguishes among stresses caused by the organization, those created by correctional work itself, and those brought on by factors external to the institution.

Organizational Sources of Stress

Much of the literature (e.g., Lindquist & Whitehead, 1986; Whitehead & Lindquist, 1986; Cheek & Miller, 1981) and many individuals interviewed for this article suggest that the "organization" is a major source of stress for many officers. The four work conditions officers identified most consistently as causing stress are understaffing, overtime, shift work, and supervisor demands.

Understaffing Understaffing in a correctional context is a chronic condition in which there are not enough officers available to staff authorized posts. Most interviewees reported that chronic and sometimes severe understaffing are prevalent in many prisons and jails as a result of unattractive salaries, high turnover, and excessive use of sick time and disability leave (see also, Thompson, 1994; Rosefield, 1988; Delmore, 1982; Brodsky, 1982; Harris, 1980; NIC, n.d-b). Understaffing can create different kinds of stress: lack of time to complete required tasks at all or in a conscientious manner, such as head counts, searches, and paperwork; working at breakneck speed every day to complete the required work; concern that there are too few officers on line or available as back-up should inmate violence occur; and inability to get time off for special occasions or family crises.

Overtime Staff shortages create the need for extensive and stress-producing overtime among remaining staff. As a result, some officers resort to subterfuge to avoid the extra work. According to an intake administer for a state department of corrections, "At least 100 officers have told me they don't answer their telephones because it might be the institution calling for overtime." Some officers get a second and unlisted telephone number that they keep secret from the department. In many cases, overtime is unavoidable, as when officers are told at the end of their shift that they have to remain to work the following shift to cover vacant posts (Kauffman, 1988). In one facility, officers are allowed to refuse overtime assignment only once a year; the second refusal results in a warning, the third results in a 1-day suspension, and the fourth may result in termination.

Several interviewees reported that they or some of their coworkers welcome overtime because of the extra money they can earn. However, supervisors and providers made clear that, even when officers volunteer to work overtime, the long hours result in sloppy work and, in some cases, burnout. One officer herself admitted, "Overtime is great—I worked three OTs a week for 18 months. But I got burned out, and my supervisors didn't even acknowledge my contribution." As a stress counselor observed, "Doing a double means spending 16 hours in a row with people who are not nice." Of course, if overtime causes burnout, both sick leave and turnover increase, resulting in still greater demands for overtime.

Shift Work Interviewees consistently reported that rotating shifts, still commonplace in many prisons and jails, create havoc with officers' family lives and reduce their ability to perform their responsibilities conscientiously because of fatigue and irritability (Cornelius, 1994; Kauffman, 1988). "You can tell when shift work is getting to officers," a lieutenant said. "Their work gets sloppy, their searches become careless, their units are filthy, and they stop following the rules." An officer doing rotating shifts reported, "One day I pulled over to the side of the road because I couldn't remember whether I was going to work or going home."

Supervisor Demands Several interviewees reported that supervisors are a source of stress because, as one officer said,

> They are always on you to do the job right, but you can't do it right [because of staff shortages]. There is supposed to be one officer per tier here, but now they've collapsed the posts and there is one officer for every two tiers. So there just isn't enough time for me to get inmates awakened, showered, and fed, keep my log books up to date, do my checks, and make sure the catwalks have all been cleaned and disinfected.

Of course, as another officer observed about a deputy warden who nitpicked him, "But that's his job."

The literature consistently has highlighted two other sources of organizational stress that interviewees did not identify as stressful: role conflict and role ambiguity.

Role Conflict Many surveys and literature reviews identify "role conflict" as a serious source of stress among correctional officers (e.g., Grossi, Keil, & Vito, 1996; Woodruff, 1993; Philliber, 1987; Lindquist & Whitehead, 1986; Crouch, 1986; Ratner, 1985; Dahl, 1979; Dahl & Steinberg, 1979). According to one researcher, "Role conflict appears in the literature to be the predominant sources of both stress and job dissatisfaction among correctional officers" (Grossi, 1990). Researchers define role conflict as the struggle officers engage in to reconcile custodial responsibilities (maintaining security such as preventing escapes and preventing inmate fights) with their treatment functions (helping inmates to rehabilitate themselves).

However, none of the correctional officers and supervisors interviewed for this article identified role conflict as a source of stress. Furthermore, there is evidence that some officers in facilities that have introduced education and treatment programs that involve the active participation of officers find the addition of a rehabilitation mission to their custodial function reinvigorating (Finn, 1997; Parent, 1990).

Role Ambiguity A second repeatedly mentioned source of organizational stress in the literature that interviewees did not single out is role ambiguity (Woodruff, 1993; Gerstein, Topp, & Correll, 1987; Crouch, 1986; Cullen et al., 1985; Rosefield, 1981, 1983; Brodsky, 1982; Harris, 1980; Dahl, 1979; Dahl & Steinberg, 1979; NIC, n.d.-a). Role ambiguity is the uncertainty created by supervisors who expect officers to "go by the book" and follow all rules to the letter when supervisors and line officers alike know that officers must be flexible and use judgment in their interactions with inmates. According to one survey,

> While officers work in a paramilitary organization marked by explicit lines of authority and a host of formal regulations, their task of managing inmates demands flexibility, the judicious application of discretionary justice, and the ability to secure inmate compliance through informal exchanges which deviate from written rules. Ambiguous and conflicting expectations are a likely result and a potential source of stress. (Cullen et al., 1985)

It is unclear why the literature consistently identifies role conflict and role ambiguity as significant sources of stress while the interviewees failed to mention them. However, it is important to note that excessive failure to follow institutional procedures puts daily facility administration on an ad hoc, unpredictable basis, resulting in reduced inmate control. There is clearly a need to find a workable middle ground between officer rigidity and complete discretion in following procedures.

Work-Related Sources of Stress

There is a consensus in the literature and among the interviewees regarding four aspects of correctional work that are stressful: the threat of inmate violence, actual inmate violence, inmate demands and attempts at manipulation, and problems with coworkers.

Threat of Inmate Violence Several published surveys of officers have identified the ever-present potential for inmate violence against officers as a significant source of stress. For example, Cullen et al. (1985) found the threat to be the second highest source of stress (see also, Kauffman, 1988; Crouch, 1986; Breen, 1986; Rosefield, 1983; Delmore, 1982; Lombardo, 1981; Dahl, 1979). More interviewees identified the threat of inmate violence as a source of stress than any other single feature of their occupation.

Inmate Violence Actual violence—including assaults, hostage taking, riots, inmates killing each other, and inmate suicides—can be a major source of stress for many officers not only during the episodes but afterwards (Freeman, 1997; Washington State Department of Corrections, 1992). According to one researcher, "Staff anxiety is intensified [after critical incidents] by the aftermath of recriminations, scapegoating, blaming, and job insecurity" (Freeman, 1997). Not all officers find these events stressful, at least once they are over. A survey of 182 officers in an institution in which 13 officers were taken hostage found that three-quarters of the staff claimed they experienced no problems in the aftermath (Montgomery, 1987).

Inmate Demands and Manipulation Many officers find the constant demands and attempts at manipulation by some inmates to be stressful (Cornelius, 1994; Woodruff, 1993; Marston, 1993). According to one correctional officer, "When officers are manipulated [successfully] by inmates . . . they may experience extreme stress" (Cornelius, 1992). A few interviewees reported that managing inmates is made still more stressful when there are cultural differences between inmates and officers or when staff members have not been trained in cultural differences and how to deal with them.

Problems with Coworkers Many officers experience stress working with other officers. One survey found that 22 percent of staff viewed "other staff" as creating more stress than any other single factor except for dealing with hostile, demanding inmates (Marston, 1993). Several interviewees expressed the same opinion. The following conditions can precipitate stress among coworkers:

- Burned out coworkers venting their frustrations to their colleagues (Cornelius, 1994);
- Officers competing for limited, choice assignments (Brodksy, 1982; Dahl, 1979);
- Apprehension that coworkers will refuse to back them up or protect them in a confrontation with inmates (Brodsky, 1982; Dahl, 1979), are too inexperienced (e.g., due to high turnover) to know how to help out (Brodsky, 1982; NIC, n.d.-a), or do not have the physical or emotional strength to be effective; and
- Inappropriate officer behavior toward inmates—bringing in contraband, getting too friendly, using unnecessary force, taking questionable disciplinary action, and failing to do their work conscientiously (ACA, 1996; Crouch, 1986; Brodsky, 1982; NIC, n.d.-a).

Stress from Outside the System

There appear to be two significant sources of stress for officers that originate outside the prison or jail: poor public image and low pay.

Low Public Recognition/Image According to one researcher, "Many [officers] feel they are perceived, and come to perceive themselves, as occupying the lowest rung of the law enforcement pecking order" (Brodksy, 1982; see also, Kantrowitz, 1996; Hill, 1994; Smith, 1994; Philliber, 1987; Stalgaitis, Meyers, & Krisak, 1982). Another researcher reported that "a negative image of corrections is regularly portrayed in the media . . . [with officers depicted] as stupid, animalistic, and senseless abusers of socially wronged individuals" (Van Fleet, 1992). As one officer said, "The public hasn't a clue as to what correctional officers do. Someone asked me just the other day if I beat inmates all the time."

As a result, "over the years, many husbands and wives of correctional officers have complained to me that they lie when asked what their spouses do for a living—not because they are ashamed of their spouses' work but because their spouses are ashamed of working in corrections" (Van Fleet, 1992). The end result is that some officers come to feel isolated and estranged from friends and family (Maghan & McLeish-Blackwell, 1991; Kauffman, 1988; Harris, 1980). A female officer said she routinely tells other people "I work for the State," refusing to specify her precise job.

Poor Pay Studies have reported that many officers cite low pay as a source of stress (Stohr et al., 1994; Stalgaitis, Meyers, & Krisak, 1982; Delmore, 1982; Brodsky, 1982; Cheek & Miller, 1981; Rosefield, 1981; NIC, n.d.-a). . . .

WHAT ARE THE EFFECTS OF STRESS?

Stress creates several problems for officers and for institutions:

Impaired Health In addition to causing unhappiness and suffering among those experiencing excessive stress, stress may result in physical illnesses ranging from heart disease to eating disorders. It also can precipitate substance abuse among susceptible individuals (Woodruff, 1993; Cheek & Miller, 1983).

Excessive Sick Time For many years, reports in the literature have suggested that correctional officers take excessive sick leave as a means of coping with stress on the job (e.g., Cornelius, 1994; Ratner, 1985; O'Brien & Gustafson, 1985; Brodsky, 1982; Cheek, 1982; Dahl & Steinberg, 1979). Studies in New York State and California found that correctional personnel used more sick leave than did other state workers (Cheek, cited in Cornelius, 1994). Most interviewees reported that officer stress still results in extensive overuse of sick time and disability leave—at a time when unscheduled absenteeism in industry as a whole is at its lowest rate this. decade (Maxwell, Perera, & Ballagh, 1997). One lieutenant guessed that 20 percent of officers who call in sick are just burned out. A captain estimated that 90 percent of officers abuse their sick time in this manner.

Excessive sick time increases the overtime required of other officers—and therefore exacerbates *their* stress and impairs *their* work performance. Thus, taking "mental health days" is a response to stress but also a cause of further stress. . . .

Burnout Numerous reports, confirmed by several interviewees, have indicated that stress can lead to burnout among officers (Cornelius, 1994; Woodruff, 1993; O'Brien & Gustafson, 1985; Cheek & Miller, 1981; Dahl & Steinberg, 1979).

High Staff Turnover Many studies (e.g., Slate, 1992; O'Brien & Gustafson, 1985; Brodsky, 1982) and interviewees reported that staff turnover is very high in many facilities. The average turnover in prisons nationwide in 1986 was nearly 12 percent (ACA, 1997), but in some states, such as Arizona, South Carolina, and South Dakota, the rate was over 25 percent. The high turnover is likely to be at least in part a result of stressful work conditions including low pay and burnout. Some rookies quit when they discover that the job is not what they expected.

The high rate of turnover is one explanation for understaffing—departing staff cannot be replaced quickly enough. However, turnover among experienced staff also forces remaining staff to work with a large number of rookies who are not as trustworthy or experienced coming to their aid in a crisis. "One day last month, my entire second shift were rookies," an anxious 3-year veteran officer reported. This problem is compounded when assignments are passed out on the basis of seniority, resulting in the least experienced officers staffing the least desirable—and typically the most dangerous and demanding—posts. Because these inexperienced officers are the ones who are least equipped to do thir jobs, performance may be impaired, leading to increased risk of conflict with inmates and other officers including supervisors. Finally, if constant turnover results in inmate exposure to officers who have not yet learned the institution's procedural rules and how to enforce them consistently, inmates may either increase their attempts to manipulate staff in an effort to test or exploit the officers' inexperience or be genuinely confused about what behavior is and is not allowed. Either result could increase officer stress.

Reduced Safety Several interviewees reported that stress often results in impaired work performance such as sloppy searches and careless counts. By making officers less patient, stress may reduce their ability to resolve confrontations peaceably, resulting in increased use force to get inmates to obey.

Prematurely Early Retirement Stress has been implicated in excessive disability retirements (Slate, 1992). Even when physical ailments are the reason for the disability, the illnesses may have been brought on by stress. . . .

Impaired Family Life The literature (e.g., Breen, 1986; Black, 1982) and interviewees agree that correctional officers experiencing excessive stress damage their family relationships by displacing their frustration onto spouses and children, ordering family members around just as they issue commands to inmates, and becoming distant by withholding information about their work that they feel family members will not understand. Shift work and overtime can create stress by making it difficult for officers to attend important family functions.

RESOURCES TO HELP OFFICERS ARE LIMITED

It appears that there are not many recognized resources correctional officers can access for help in coping with stress. In addition, many officers who do have access to assistance fail to take advantage of it. This review identified several programs designed to help prevent and treat stress among correctional officers. The types of available stress services fall into four categories:

- academy training;
- in-service training;
- critical incident stress management; and
- individual counseling.

Academy Training

Many correctional officer academies provide up to several hours of class time devoted to warning recruits about potential sources of stress, symptoms of stress, and coping mechanisms. However, most academy training appears to be generic rather than focused specifically on correctional work. Discussions focus on the nature of burnout rather than on features of the correctional environment that can cause stress. Coping mechanisms include meditation and exercise but exclude on-the-job strategies that might reduce the stresses of being a correctional officer. Perhaps for these reasons, one officer reported that what he learned about stress at the academy "went in one ear and out the other." Another said, "The problem with academy training is you forget it when you're on the job," adding that "the older staff tell you to forget everything you learned there anyway." . . .

In-Service Training

As far back as 1982, a researcher could write that "administrative departments in the United States are adding stress training segments to their curricula for new recruits to correctional services, in the hope that this will aid officers in doing their jobs effectively" (In-wald, 1982). A researcher recently reported that "it appears common practice for many correctional and detention managers to offer stress management training as a part of initial orientation and training or through scheduled in-service training sessions" (Marston, 1993). A recent *Corrections Compendium* survey of state departments of corrections confirms this observation (Hill, 1997). Among the 41 responding states, 13 reported devoting 1 to 2 hours of annual in-service training to stress programming, 12 reported 3 to 5 hours, and 4 reported 6 to 8 hours. Only 11 states reported devoting no time to stress programming.

Examination of several curricula used in these classes suggests that, as with academy classes, the presentations are generic in nature. Two psychologists with the New York City Department of Correction, while noting that "behavioral interventions such as stress management . . . have become common components of correctional training curricula," added that the courses

> may not be appropriately utilized, particularly if the skills have not been fully mastered. Moreover, these interventions may be too geoeric to effectively address the concomitants of a given individ-ual's exposure to prison violence. The very existence of such training may lull administrators and officers into a false sense of security with regard to its effectiveness in ameliorating the negative emotional effects of occupational violence. (Safran & Tartaglini, 1995). . . .

Individual Counseling

A few large prisons and sheriff's departments have in-house units (distinct from Employee Assistance Programs) devoted exclusively to treating officer stress. . . .

Some departments make use of private counseling organizations to provide stress counseling services. These organizations typically offer the entire spectrum of stress services including not only individual counseling but also academy and in-service training and critical incident debriefing. . . .

It appears that most prisons and jails throughout the country do not have access to these kinds of specialized, confidential services. According to Gary Dennis, Director of Mental Health for the Kentucky Department of Corrections, his nationwide training activities have led him to conclude that most officers only have Employee Assistance Programs (EAPs) to turn to for help. According to Gary Cornelius (1994), "EAPs, when properly staffed and used, can help correctional staff effectively deal with their stress." However, most interviewees reported that most officers feel EAPs will not maintain confidentiality and are unfamiliar with the nature of correctional officer stress. . . .

CONCLUSION

This review has confirmed that there is little reliable empirical evidence that identifies the severity and sources of stress for correctional officers, in large measure because existing research has relied almost entirely on self-reports and was conducted when several conditions presumed to be related to stress (e.g., crowding, increased violence, gangs) were less problematic than they are today. More reliable indicators of stress would make it possible for interventions to target more accurately the precise causes of officer stress. What is needed is a study that examined a range of surrogate, but objective, indicators of stress such as:

- staff turnover rate
- sick leave use
- absenteeism and tardiness
- inmate grievances or complaints
- disciplinary actions against officers
- disability claims
- premature retirements or disability pensions

Data permitting, the study should examine institutional conditions over time to determine whether they are associated with the proxy measures of stress identified above—for example, whether increased crowding is associated over time with increased absenteeism. Other institutional conditions that might be examined for any association with stress include:

- condition of the physical plant
- staff training levels
- inmate-officer ratios
- staffing levels
- numbers of assaults against officers and among inmates
- increases and decreases in programming levels
- increased cell time
- removal of amenities

The Federal Bureau of Prisons' Key Indicators Strategic Support System—KISSS—has collected time series indicator data on such variables as turnover and sick leave that could be used to study the relationship between stress (through the proxy measures) to the institutional conditions identified above. Studies in state and local or private facilities would require data extraction from existing administrative records.

REFERENCES

American Correctional Association. (1997, October 8). Unpublished data provided by Research Department.

American Correctional Association. (1996). *Corrections perspectives: The staff's view* [Videotape]. Laurel, MD: Author.

Black, R. (1982). Stress and the correctional officer. *Police Stress, 5*(1), 10–16.

Breen, L. (1986, February). *The forgotten keepers: Stress and the correctional employee.* Ottawa, Canada: Solicitor General.

Brodsky, C.M. (1982). Work stress in correctional institutions. *Journal of Prison & Jail Health,* 2(2), 74–102.

Bureau of Justice Statistics. (1997, May). *Correctional populations in the United States, 1995.* Washington, DC: U.S. Department of Justice.

Cheek, F.E. (1982). Reducing staff and inmate stress. *Corrections Today, 44*(5), 72–76, 78.

Cheek, F.E., & Miller, M.D. (1981). *Prisoners of Life: A study of occupational stress among state corrections officers.* Washington, DC: American Federation of State, County, and Municipal Employees.

Cornelius, G.F. (1992). Keys to effective inmate management: Avoiding manipulation. In American Correctional Association (Ed.), *The effective correctional officer* (pp. 75–82). Laurel, MD: Author.

Corneius, G.F. (1994). *Stressed out: Strategies for living and working with stress in corrections.* Laurel, MD: American Correctional Association.

Cross, T.M. (1988). *A report on the nature and extent of stress and stress-related problems among corrections officers in the State of Michigan.* West Bloomfield, ML: Author.

Crouch, B.M. (1986). Prison guards on the line. In K.C. Hass & G.P. Alpert (Eds.), *Dilemmas of punishment.* Prospect Heights, IL: Waveland Press.

Cullen, F.T., Link, B.G., Wolfe, N.T., & Frank, J. (1985). The social dimension of correctional officer stress. *Justice Quarterly, 2*(4), 505–533.

Dahl, J.J. (1979). *Management of stress in corrections: Participant's handbook.* Washington, DC: University Research Corporation.

Dahl, J.J., & Steinberg, S.S. (1979). *Management of stress in corrections: Participant's handbook.* Washington, DC: University Research Corporation.

Delmore, R.J. (1982, May). *Stress survey: A study of corrections employees' perceptions of potential stress-producing factors in the work environment.* Washington, DC: Department of Corrections, Office of Planning & Program Analysis.

Finn, P. (1997). *The Orange County, Florida, jail educational and vocational programs.* Washington, DC: U.S. Department of Justice, National Institute of Justice.

Freeman, R.M. (1997). Remembering the Camp Hill riot. *Corrections Today, 59*(1), 56, 58–59.

Gerstein, L.H., Topp, C.G., & Correll, C. (1987). Role of the environment and person when predicting burnout among correctional personnel. *Criminal Justice and Behavior, 14*(3), 352–369.

Grossi, E.L. (1990, March). *Stress and job dissatisfaction among correctional officers.* Paper presented at the annual meeting of the Academy of Criminal Justice Sciences, Denver, CO.

Grossi, E.L., Ksil, T.J., & Vito, G.F. (1996). Surviving "the joint": Mitigating factors of correctional officer stress. *Journal of Crime and Justice, 19*(2), 103–120.

Harris, G.A. (1980). *Stress in corrections.* Topeka, KS: Washburn University.

Hill, G. (1997). Correctional officer traits and skills. *Corrections Compendium, 22*(8), 1–12.

Hill, G. (1994). Improving the image of the professional corrections officer. *The Keeper's Voice, 15*(2), 8–10.

Huckabee, R.G. (1992). Stress in corrections: An overview of the issues. *Journal of Criminal Justice, 20*(5), 479–486.

Inwald, R.E. (1982). Research problems in assessing stress factors in correctional institutions. *International Journal of Offender Therapy and Comparative Criminology, 26*(3), 250–254.

Kantrowitz, N. (1996). Hollywood movies demean correctional officers. *The Keeper's Voice, 17*(4), 12.

Kauffman, K. (1988). *Prison officers and their world.* Cambridge, MA: Harvard University Press.

Lindquist, C.A., & Whitehead, J.T. (1986). Burnout, job stress and job satisfaction among southern correctional officers—Perceptions and causal factors. *Journal of Offender Counseling, Services and Rehabilitation, 10*(4), 5–26.

Lombardo, L.X. (1981). Occupational stress in corrections officers: Sources, coping strategies, and implications. *Corrections at the crossroads: Designing policy,* 129–149.

Maghan, J., & McLeish-Blackwell, L. (1991). Black women in correctional employment. In J.B. Morton (Ed.), *Change, challenges, and choices: Women's role in modern corrections* (pp. 82–99). Laurel, MD: American Correctional Association.

Marston, J.L. (1993). Stress and stressors: Inmate and staff perceptions. *American Jails, 7*(4), 21–30.

Martinez, A.R. (1997). Corrections officer: The "other" prisoner. *The Keeper's Voice, 18*(1), 8–11.

Maxwell, G., Perera, K., & Ballagh, J. (1997). *Absenteeism in the workplace.* Riverwoods, IL: Commerce Clearinghouse.

Montgomery, R.H. (1987). Kirkland correctional officer survey: An analysis of aftereffects from the April 1, 1986, riot. Washington, DC: National Criminal Justice Reference Service.

National Institute of Corrections. (n.d.-a). *Chronic and traumatic stress in the correctional environment.* Washington, DC: U.S. Department of Justice.

National Institute of Corrections. (n.d.-b). *Chronic and traumatic stress in the correctional environment: Lesson plans.* Washington, DC: U.S. Department of Justice.

O'Brien, B., & Gustafson. (1985, July). *Stress in corrections officers: Iowa Department of Corrections study.* Washington, DC: National Institute of Corrections.

Parent, D. (1990). *Shock incarceration: An overview of existing programs.* Washington, DC: U.S. Department of Justice, National Institute of Justice.

Philliber, S. (1987). Thy brother's keeper: A review of the literature on correctional officers. *Justice Quarterly, 4*(1), 9–35.

Ratner, A.M. (1985). *Administrative sources of occupational stress in a correctional setting.* Sacramento, CA: AIDE Behavioral Sciences.

Rosefield, H.A. (1983). What's killing our officers. In J.N. Tucker (Ed.), *Correctional officers—Power, pressure and responsibility.* Laurel, MD: American Correctional Association.

Rosefield, H.A. (1981). *Self-identified stressors among correctional officers* (Doctoral dissertation). Ann Arbor, MI: University Microfilms.

Safran, D.A., & Tartaglini, A.J. (1995). Barriers to the development of effective coping strategies for the psychological consequences of occupational violence. *The Keeper's Voice, 16*(3), 13.

Slate, R.N. (1992, November). *Stress levels and thoughts of quitting of correctional personnel: Do perceptions of participatory management make a difference?* Paper presented at the American Society of Criminology, New Orleans, LA.

Slate, R.N. (1993). *Stress levels of correctional personnel: Is there a difference between the sexes?* Washington, DC: U.S. Department of Justice, National Institute of Justice.

Smith, M.R. (1994). The public's distorted perception: Can it be changed? *The Keeper's Voice.*

Stalgaitis, S.J., Meyers, A.W., & Krisak, J. (1982). Social learning theory model for reduction of correctional officer stress. *Federal Probation, 46*(3), 33–40.

Stephan, J.J. (1997). *Census of state and federal correctional facilities, 1995.* Washington, DC: U.S. Department of Justice, Bureau of Justice Statistics.

Stohr, M.K., Lovrich, N.P., & Wilson, G.L. (1994). Staff stress in contemporary jails: Assessing problem severity and the payoff of progressive personnel practices. *Journal of Criminal Justice, 22*(4), 313–327.

Thompson, T. (1994). Holistic health comes to prison. *Federal Prisons Journal, 3*(3), 55–59.

Van Fleet, F. (1992). Correctional officers and their families: Dealing with stress. In American Correctional Association, *The effective correctional officer* (pp. 37–44). Laurel, MD: Author.

Washington State Department of Corrections. (1992). *Post trauma response and peer support.* Olympia, WA: Author.

Whitehead, J.T., & Lindquist, C.A. (1986). Correctional officer job burnout—A path model. *Journal of Research in Crime and Delinquency, 23*(1), 23–42.

Woodruff, L. (1993). Occupational stress for correctional personnel: Part one. *American Jails, 7*(4), 15–20.

Wynne, J.M. (1978). Prison employee unionism: The impact on correctional administration and programs. Washington, DC: U.S. Department of Justice, National Institute of Law Enforcement and Criminal Justice.

REVIEW QUESTIONS

1. What are the major sources of stress for correctional officers? Which are the most influential on the experience of stress?
2. How does high stress experienced by correctional officers negatively impact the work environment?
3. What aspects of an individual's life are negatively impacted by the experience of stress for correctional officers?

READING 16

The Correctional Orientation of Prison Wardens

Is the Rehabilitative Ideal Supported?

Francis T. Cullen

Edward J. Latessa

Velmer S. Burton, Jr.

Lucien X. Lombardo

As the policy-making and ultimate authority in an individual prison, the warden is the individual who both sets the agenda and goals for the prison and is ultimately held responsible for whether a facility does or does not meet those goals. However, wardens are only infrequently the focus of scholarly research. This reading reports on the results of a survey of prison wardens. The data show that prison wardens are generally oriented to the ideal of rehabilitating inmates, although maintaining custody and institutional order are high priorities in the day-to-day operations of institutions. Additionally, the influence of personal and institutional variables are assessed and shown to be only moderately influential on support for rehabilitation.

Academic studies of prison life have done much to illuminate the nature and dynamics of the "society of captives," but only in the past decade or so have a substantial number of researchers broadened their investigations to include the keepers as well as the kept. This research has revised prevailing caricatures of the guardians of the prison order and deepened our understanding of the complexities of correctional work (Philliber, 1987). At the same time, most researchers have kept their sights fixed on the cell block, examining correctional officers but not those further up the administrative hierarchy. . . .

DiIulio (1987, 1991) argues that the neglect of wardens and other prison administrators has resulted in fundamentally flawed conclusions about prisons. While traditional sociological studies emphasized the power of inmate social organization to shape the quality and stability of institutional life (Irwin, 1980; Sykes, 1958), DiIulio proposes that wardens' managerial style is the most salient determinant of whether prisons are safe, orderly, clean, and capable of providing inmates amenities. DiIulio's thesis has generated controversy and awaits further empirical verification, but his central point is well taken: Wardens are important actors in the correctional arena, and they warrant far more study than they have received to date. . . .

WARDENS IN CONTEXT

Ideological Crisis in Corrections

As Rothman (1980) observes, the rehabilitative ideal, with its policies of indeterminate sentencing, discretionary decisionmaking, and parole, was infused into the corrections system in the beginning decades of the 1900s (see also Platt, 1969). The reformers of the Progressive era, often with a faith in the power of newly founded social sciences to furnish the key to unlocking the mystery of crime's origins, were optimistic that individualized treatment could transform lawbreakers into the law abiding. This broad ideological framework, Rothman (1980:12) further notes, dominated correctional thinking well into the 1960s. At that time, in fact, it still was commonplace to decry the "crime of punishment" (Menninger, 1968) and to assert that "rehabilitation must be the goal of modern corrections" (Clark, 1970:200).

In the absence of systematic research, it is difficult to gauge whether Progressive wardens embraced their role as people changers rather than custodians. Rothman (1980:144–145) stops short of accusing these wardens of hypocrisy, but he does suggest that their support for rehabilitation was easily corrupted by custodial concerns and was rooted mainly in the discretionary powers they gained under indeterminate sentencing. Few critics of the day, moreover, spoke highly of wardens' commitment to reforming offenders (Barnes, 1970[1930]:182; Tannenbaum, 1922).

Irwin (1980:37–62) indicates that following World War II, many American prisons changed qualitatively—the "Big House" was replaced by the "correctional institution." Inmate classification systems and rehabilitation programs spread, and treatment personnel were hired—although others have contended that the changes were more cosmetic than fundamental (Hawkins, 1976:48–51; Johnson, 1987:43–44). In either case, it seems that at least on an ideological level, rehabilitation achieved renewed legitimacy as the professional orientation of many wardens (Jacobs, 1977:73–86; McCleery, 1968:124). Supportive of this view, a 1968 poll of administrators in adult correctional institutions on the "correctional goal most emphasized now" in their work setting revealed that "rehabilitation" was cited most often (39%), followed by "protect society" (37%) and "punishment" (22%). Nearly all respondents believed that rehabilitation should be either a "primary or secondary" goal of corrections (Harris and Associates, 1968:14–16).

In the 1970s, however, the general ideological hegemony of rehabilitation was shattered (Allen, 1981; Cullen and Gilbert, 1982). The Progressive design of individualized treatment was subjected to strong attack, points out Rothman (1980:12), and corrections became "anti-Progressive." Fearful that corrections officials would abuse their discretion to control insurgent inmates, liberals abandoned rehabilitation as good intentions gone bad and endorsed the rights-oriented "justice model" (Fogel, 1979; von Hirsch, 1976). In contrast, believing that treatment made corrections soft-hearted and decreased the costs of crime, conservatives proposed to reassert law and order by punishing the deserving, scaring straight the impressionable, and caging the chronically dangerous (van den Haag, 1975; Wilson, 1975).

In the ensuing years, the conservative agenda has dominated corrections (Cullen and Gilbert, 1982; Gordon, 1990). Public attitudes shifted in a punitive direction (Cullen et al., 1988; Flanagan and Caulfield, 1984; Rankin, 1979). Both leading and capitalizing on this shift (Scheingold, 1984), politicians jumped on the "get tough" bandwagon and initiated a wave of stringent policies—from mandatory and determinate sentences, to intensive and electronic supervision in the community, to prisons transformed into boot camps.

But conservative ideology and the more general critique of treatment have not enjoyed complete acceptance. Although citizens became more punitive, they were reluctant to reject rehabilitation as an important goal of correctional intervention (Cullen et al., 1989b; Warr and Stafford, 1984). Academic (Currie, 1985) and popular (Wicker, 1991) writers sought to illuminate the limits and costs of a "punitive state." And a revisionist movement emerged, in which it was argued that rehabilitation should be reaffirmed. "Between 1985 and 1990," observes DiIulio (1991:106–107), "the inevitable intellectual counteroffensive against the idea that 'nothing works' picked up speed. . . . Fifteen years ago, the academic chic was to deep-six rehabilitation; today, the academic chic is to jump-start it."

Corrections, then, has experienced an ideological crisis. The rehabilitative ideal was tarnished, if not discredited, in many quarters, but after two decades of a large experiment with punishment, the wisdom of abandoning the treatment model is less obvious (Cullea and Gendreau, 1989; Currie, 1989). Wardens have been enmeshed in and potentially affected by this context. It remains to be seen whether their correctional orientation has turned anti-Progressive or retains the Progressive prescription for wardens to be more than custodians (cf. Harris et al., 1989; Sluder and Reddington, in press; Whitehead and Lindquist, 1992).

Occupational Concerns

The correctional orientation of wardens undoubtedly is shaped by more than broad ideological changes. It seems likely, for example, that factors which impinge more directly on the occupational interests of wardens also would affect their thinking. Although the literature has not explored this issue systematically, we can identify several circumstances that may influence wardens' support for or opposition to rehabilitation.

We can propose four developments that may have strained wardens' belief in prison treatment First, as prisons and prison systems have grown in size and budget, and as they have been subjected to legal intervention and constraints, they have been transformed into "rational-legal bureaucracies" with a corresponding "rationalization" of correctional administration (Jacobs, 1977; cf. Spitzer, 1983). The tendency is for a "corporate" style of administration, which "stresses efficient and emotionally detached management" (Jacobs, 1977:104). The moral content of corrections, so prominent in rehabilitation, is displaced, if not out of place. Insofar as these pressures for rationalized management have taken hold, one can expect support for treatment as an occupational goal to be diminished.

Second, the forces of rationalization, in combination with the increased permeability of prison walls to external scrutiny, also have shrunk the managerial autonomy of wardens. Centralized authority in the state corrections department, legal restraints, and the threat of exposés by news reporters and citizen reform groups have "reduced the warden's role from a prison czar to a well-constrained manager" (Hawkins and Alpert, 1989:357). . . .

Third, a number of commentators have discussed the forces that have served to destabilize institutional order and create today's "violent prison" (Carroll, 1988; Colvin, 1992; Jacobs, 1977; Johnson, 1987; Irwin, 1980). Facing pressing concerns for order, it seems likely that, more than is usually the case, custodial interests would become increasingly salient and treatment commensurately less important Relatedly, in a context of declining control, correctional officers are likely to be suspicious of wardens who appear too "pro-inmate" (Jacobs, 1977) and offend the guards' custodial "public culture," which is disdainful of offender concerns (Johnson, 1987). The need to sustain viable staff relationships thus may constrain zeal for offender reform.

Finally, the impact on correctional ideology of crowding, identified by wardens as the most serious "criminal justice problem" (Grieser, 1988), remains to be determined. Yet insofar as crowding is viewed as a source of disorder and outstrips treatment resources, it may cause wardens to see rehabilitation as a luxury that is futile to pursue.

The forces arrayed against rehabilitation may seem formidable, but other considerations suggest that treatment may remain an important dimension of wardens' correctional orientation. First, empirical research on correctional officers reveals surprisingly strong support for treatment and for their conceptualizing their work as human services and not merely as custodial (Cullen et al., 1989a; Toch and Klofas, 1982; see also Johnson, 1987:137–155). It seems unlikely that wardens, ostensibly more professionalized and educated than correctional officers, would be less supportive of treatment.

Second, and relatedly, it is not clear if the professional influences on wardens have been decidedly antitreatment For example, *Corrections Today,* the official publication of the American Correctional Association, has not been overly antagonistic to treatment in its publications (see also *Federal Probation*). While the journal contains numerous advertisements for technology to facilitate custodial goals and has tracked punitive trends (e.g., boot camps, electronic monitoring), it also regularly includes articles describing, if not favorable to, offender treatment.

Third, while criminologists readily, embraced Martinson's dictum that "nothing works" in corrections (Cullen arid Gendreau, 1989; Walker, 1989), the everyday experiences of wardens may have contradicted this message. "Corrections practitioners," observes DiIulio (1991:107), are open to the movement to reaffirm rehabilitation. Why? DiIulio answers as follows:

> Their common sense tells them that exposing offenders to life-enhancing, skills-imparting programs is likely to keep at least some of them on the straight and narrow. And their experiences confirm that, under certain conditions, some types of programs do improve the post-release life prospects of some of the offenders who participate in them (p. 107).

Fourth, wardens' support for rehabilitation may also be rooted in its functionality. If Rothman (1980) and similar commentators are correct, wardens would see the decline of the rehabilitative ideal as eroding their discretionary powers. Similarly, based on qualitative data, DiIulio (1991:114–123) concludes that correctional administrators see rehabilitation programs as essential for "Institutional management." These programs lessen inmate idleness and discontent, enhance prison adjustment, provide an incentive administrators can use to reward good behavior, and create opportunities for staff-prisoner communication. Even in states that adopted determinate sentencing and embraced punishment as the purpose of their corrections systems, DiIulio (1991:115) points out, he could find no evidence that rehabilitation programs were cut back between 1975 and 1985 (see also Goodstein and Hepburn, 1985).

This discussion suggests that wardens have been at the nexus of competing forces that have had the potential to weaken or sustain their belief in correctional rehabilitation. One scenario, from the above discussion, would see wardens as working in a punitive context that devalues the delivery of human services to inmates and as facing increased custodial problems with fewer administrative powers; the result would be diminished concern with offender rehabilitation. A second scenario would portray wardens as having a professional commitment to human services, a commitment buoyed by their everyday experiences of seeing inmates change and by the functionality of treatment programs for institutional order; the result would be continued support for the rehabilitative ideal. The data presented below attempt to shed light on these competing views.

Variations in Correctional Orientation

Beyond the overall orientation of wardens, we investigated why some wardens more than others endorse correctional treatment. The literature on reactions to correctional work—whether job satisfaction, stress, or attitudes toward inmates—distinguishes two models. The *individual experiences-importation* model suggests that reactions to work are the result of the different types of experiences brought to the job by people drawn from different social statuses (e.g., race, education). In contrast, the *work role-prisonization* model hypothesizes that reactions are shaped predominantly by the organizational conditions of prisons and the nature of the work role and are similar regardless of individuals' status characteristics (Cullen et al., 1989a; Jurik, 1985; Jurik and Halemba, 1984; Van Voorhis et al., 1991; Whitehead and Lindquist, 1989).

We assess the relative merits of these two models in explaining wardens' correctional orientation. Previous research on correctional employees suggests support for both perspectives, although the ability of either model to explain variance in orientations has been modest to weak (Cullen et al., 1989a; Jurik, 1985; Whitehead and Lindquist, 1989, 1992). Further, the research is still too limited and conflicting to develop clear hypotheses about the effects of specific variables (Cullen et al., 1989a:35; Philliber, 1987; Whitehead and Lindquist, 1989:70–76); at best, we can draw expected relations. . . .

METHODS

Sample

Our study is based on a 1989 national survey of wardens of all 512 state and federal prisons. A modified version of Dillman's (1978) Total Design Method for mail surveys was employed; 375 wardens, 73.2% of the sample, returned usable questionnaires. . . .

RESULTS

Overall Correctional Orientation

Tables 1, 2, and 3 report data assessing the correctional orientation of wardens across the sample. Variations in orientation are considered in the multivariate analysis presented later in this section.

In general, the data suggest that wardens place a priority on custodial/prison order concerns but see rehabilitation as an important, if secondary, function of imprisonment and more specifically of their institution. Table 2 shows, for example, that the wardens sampled ranked incapacitation as the preferred goal of imprisonment. Rehabilitation (along with deterrence), however, was ranked second, and retribution lagged as the least supported correctional goal.

The wardens estimated that only a fourth of the inmates in their prison would be rehabilitated. Even so, they rejected the idea that conditions at their prison "should be harsher," tended to favor the delivery of human services, and gave the strongest agreement to the view that "rehabilitation programs have an important place in my institution." (See "general views" in Table 1.)

In responding to the question on the day-to-day operation of the "ideal prison" (Table 1), wardens once again placed preventing escapes and maintaining order as the most important goals/activities (26.8 and 29.0 points, respectively). Rehabilitation, however, was not dismissed as an important daily concern; it received almost 18 of the 100 points to be allotted. Similar results are found in Table 2, which reports the emphasis currently given by the wardens to various activities in administering their facility. Custodial/order concerns clearly ranked highest; even among the human services activities, the one with the greatest custodial value—"keeping inmates busy"—was rated highest. These results, however, do not mean that treatment was dismissed as unimportant. Although "providing programs to help inmates learn new skills" was the lowest rated activity, its mean of 7.0 indicates that it was accorded a degree of emphasis by wardens within their institutions.

Support for treatment is even clearer in Table 3. The data reveal that the wardens favored the expansion of educational, vocational, and counseling programs; conjugal visits were not supported. They also rejected eliminating good time, parole, and indeterminate sentencing—traditional elements of the rehabilitative ideal, which also have custodial uses. Finally, the wardens saw merit in making inmates do hard labor (although it is not clear whether they endorsed this policy due to a wish to punish or to keep offenders occupied) and in mandatory life sentences for habitual offenders.

Variations in Correctional Orientation

. . . For the individual-level variables, race had two significant but contradictory effects—nonwhite wardens placed more of an emphasis on rehabilitation and custody. Education's effects were negligible, with the exception that educated wardens were more likely to believe that inmates are amenable to treatment.

TABLE 1 Support for Rehabilitation, by Goals, Amenability to Treatment, General Views, and Ideal Activities

Should Be Goal of Imprisonment (rank order with 4 = first choice)	Mean
Rehabilitation	2.51
Incapacitation	3.35
Deterrence	2.50
Retribution	1.66
Amenability to Treatment (up to 100 percent)	
Percent of inmates in institution that warden believes will be rehabilitated (will not return to crime) because of their participation in prison treatment programs (e.g., counseling, work training, education)	25.70
General Views (1 to 7, with 7 = very strongly agree)	
I want correctional officers at my institution to be more sensitive to providing for inmates' daily needs than they now are	4.82
Rehabilitation programs have an important place in my institution	5.50
We need to provide more activities to occupy the inmates' time	4.84
Conditions at my institution are such that when inmates leave, they do so with a positive outlook toward their lives	4.32
Conditions at my institution should be harsher to deter inmates from future crime	2.84
Importance of Activity in Ideal Prison (assign points to total 100)	
Involving inmates in rehabilitation programs (e.g., counseling, educational programs, vocational training)	17.98
Keeping inmates busy by having them work	15.84
Preventing escapes	26.81
Maintaining security or order within the prison	29.01
Operating efficient and profitable industrial/agricultural production	8.63
Other	2.39

As for career variables, years in corrections and time at current, institution appear to heighten support for treatment and custody. Past occupational positions, however, exerted a minimal influence on orientations. Having been in the military was unrelated to all dependent variables. And only two significant effects were found for previous jobs held within corrections: having been a correctional officer led wardens to place more emphasis on rehabilitation, while having worked in correctional treatment led them to place less emphasis on custody.

TABLE 2 Emphasis Given to Activities in Day-to-Day Operation of Warden's Own Institution

Rehabilitation/Human Services	Mean
Providing programs to help inmates learn new skills	7.00
Providing activities to keep inmates busy	8.05
Providing adequate space and other needed services to inmates	7.60
Custody/Institutional Order	
Creating conditions that prevent escapes	8.74
Ensuring that institutional rules are followed by inmates	8.10
Ensuring that institutional procedures and regulations are followed by staff	8.60
Preventing the flow of contraband into prison	8.21
Preventing the flow or exchange of contraband goods/materials within the prison	7.69
Creating conditions which protect inmates from one another	8.04

Note: 1 = no emphasis; 10 = great emphasis.

Among organizational variables, the prison's age and maximum security classification exerted no effect on correctional orientation. As expected, however, support for rehabilitation was lessened by the number of inmates housed in the warden's facility and by administering a male prison. Compared with their counterparts in the federal system, wardens managing a state prison were more favorable toward rehabilitation and less supportive of custody.

TABLE 3 Support for Policies Favoring Rehabilitation/Human Services and Punishment

Rehabilitation/Human Services	Mean
Expanding educational and vocational training programs	3.48
Expanding psychological counseling programs	3.33
Conjugal visits for married inmates	1.95
Punishment	
Making inmates do "hard labor"	2.57
Eliminating good-time credit	1.48
Eliminating parole and the indeterminate sentence	1.73
Mandatory life sentences for "habitual" offenders	2.62

Note: 1 = oppose a great deal; 4 = favor a great deal.

Finally, as anticipated, the contextual effect of being a warden of a prison located in the South was in the direction of diminishing a treatment orientation.

DISCUSSION

The results of the survey are clear in showing that maintaining custody and institutional order are the dominant concerns of wardens. In their daily activities, as well as in their version of the "ideal" prison, preventing escapes and effecting a peaceful prison order are their priorities. These goals are not hidden behind the mask of the rehabilitative ideal, as some commentators suggest occurred in the past (Rothman, 1980), but are forthrightly expressed.

Although the lack of comparable longitudinal data makes it difficult to assess whether wardens' correctional orientation has shifted, the trends are at least suggestive. Recall the 1968 Harris poll of correctional administrators, cited above, which found strong support for treatment as the goal of prisons. In contrast, in our 1989 wardens' survey, incapacitation was named most often as the purpose of incarceration. These results lend credence to the proposition that larger changes in the broader ideological context and perhaps the increased challenge of keeping order in today's prisons, have heightened custodial concerns.

The "rationalization" thesis discussed previously also may derive a measure of support. It is instructive that wardens, despite some punitive sentiments (e.g., the merits of hard labor, mandatory life sentences), were highly utilitarian in their perspective on the prison's goals, ranking retribution as the least important of imprisonment's purposes. It seems that wardens do not see the prison as a setting in which to conduct a morality play, as might a commentator like Newman (1983), but rather as a pragmatic societal instrument to achieve crime control.

However, the wardens' support for rehabilitation as a secondary but fundamental goal of corrections is equally clear. To be sure, this support is not naively optimistic; recall that the wardens saw only a quarter of the inmates as good candidates for treatment. And there appears to be a strong dose of functionalism in their endorsements of the rehabilitative ideal: thus their desire to use programs to keep inmates busy and their opposition to eliminating good time, parole, and indeterminate sentencing. Even so, there is no evidence to indicate that they are disingenuous in stating that rehabilitation programs have an "important place" in their prisons or in expressing their desire to expand treatment opportunities.

As suggested earlier, the ongoing endorsement of treatment as *a* goal of prisons may reflect the prevailing correctional orientation among the public, which embraces punishment but does not reject rehabilitation (Cullen et al., 1988; DiIulio, 1991:124). If so, this means that wardens' views are "imported" into the prison. The other (and perhaps complementary) possibility is that the nature of guarding inmates—whether as a correctional officer or as a warden—prompts desires to assist (see also Clear, 1991:408). As DiIulio (1991:107) suggests, this may be due to the realities of seeing inmates change and benefit from programming. But a more general process may also be at work, one in which contact with "deviants" diminishes social distance and has a humanizing influence that softens punitive sentiments (see Bynum et al., 1986; Link and Cullen, 1986).

The continuing place of rehabilitation as a core element of the orientation of America's correctional elite is of potential consequence. Future research might profit from exploring whether, and if so to what extent, this support for rehabilitation shapes the prison's organizational culture and the wardens' openness to innovations in treatment (see, e.g., Andrews et al., 1991; DiIulio, 1991). Further, criminologists might revisit the widely accepted view that treatment is inevitably corrupted by custodial concerns (Rothman, 1980). According to DiIulio (1987:40–43), for example, a managerial approach that first achieves order is essential if prisons are to be an environment conducive to delivering treatment services (see also Jacobs, 1977). "Custody," observes DiIulio (1987:41), "may be a necessary condition for effective treatment." In this light, the wardens' strong custodial orientation may not be antithetical to rehabilitation but, if prudently acted upon, may facilitate the creation and efficacy of prison programming.

Finally, the ability of competing explanatory models (i.e., individual, career, organizational, contextual) to account for variation in wardens' correctional orientation met with only limited success, although the analysis revealed several interesting possibilities that might warrant further exploration. First, when race effects were present, members of minorities appeared to be more favorable toward both treatment and custody. This raises the prospect that minority members might bring a distinctive style to prison management, perhaps a "tough love" approach that emphasizes social support within the context of discipline—or what Braithwaite (1989) has called "reintegrative shaming."

Second, and relatedly, correctional experience also seems to breed a mix of reformism and control. Again, this might reflect a distinctive managerial orientation. Another possibility is that experienced wardens develop a flexible philosophy, one that is capable of reacting to "good inmates" through human services and to "bad inmates" through control.

Third, two organizational variables produced consistent results. The protreatment orientations of wardens of female and coed prisons may represent a belief that women are better candidates for reform. If so, it is ironic that compared with male prisons, female institutions historically have provided inferior, sex-stereotyped programming (Rafter, 1989). Wardens of state prisons also were more likely to endorse rehabilitation, thus lending credence to Wright and Saylor's (1992:70) observation that "the work environment of the federal prison system may be qualitatively different from that of state prison systems." Insofar as the Federal Bureau of Prisons is a more rationalized organization, this finding that their wardens are less treatment oriented and more custodial oriented would add support to the thesis that the trend toward rational-legal bureaucracy erodes a reformist orientation.

Fourth, the social context in which a warden is enmeshed seems important to consider. As hypothesized, wardens of southern prisons were less likely to endorse rehabilitation. It remains to be determined if their orientation reflects conscious organizational socialization and/or regional differences in attitudes toward crime and justice.

These various effects must be interpreted with caution, however, since the explanatory models, taken alone or in combination, accounted for a modest amount of variance in measures of correctional orientation. It is possible that more adequate measures might produce stronger results (Whitehead and Lindquist, 1989). Further, some research is suggestive that more variance might be explained in correctional ideology if the study had incorporated measures of organizational climate, such as an institution's racial composition, or measures of personality traits, such as the willingness to accept authority (Stowe, 1992; Wright and Saylor, 1992).

Even so, it might be recalled that previous research on the determinants of the orientations of correctional officers and staff have accounted for amounts of variance similar to that reported here (Cullen et al., 1989a; Jurik, 1985; Whitehead and Lindquist, 1989; Wright and Saylor, 1992). Assuming the absence of methodological artifacts in the data, the substantive meaning of the failure to uncover strong correlates of orientation may be that there is a large degree of normative consensus in work/inmate-related beliefs among correctional workers (see Rossi et al., 1974). Again, this consensus might reflect either the existence of a similar consensus on the purposes of prison among the general public from which corrections workers are drawn and/or a prisonization effect that reduces individual attitudinal differences by teaching prison workers the need to keep order *and* the rewards of helping inmates change.

REFERENCES

Allen, Francis A. 1981. *The Decline of the Rehabilitative Ideal: Penal Policy and Social Purpose.* New Haven: Yale University Press.

Allen, Harry E. and Clifford E. Simonson. 1992. *Corrections in America: An Introduction.* 6th ed. New York: Macmillan.

American Correctional Association. 1989. *ACA Directory—1988: Juvenile and Adult Correctional Departments, Institutions, Agencies, and Paroling Authorities.* College Park, Md.: American Correctional Association.

Andrews, D.A., Ivan Zinger, R.D. Hoge, James Bonta, Paul Gendreau, and Francis T. Cullen. 1991. Does correctional treatment work? A clinically relevant and psychologically-informed meta-analysis. *Criminology* 28:369–404.

Barnes, Harry Elmer. 1970. *The Story of Punishment: A Record of Man's Inhumanity to Man.* 1930. 2nd ed. Montolair, N.J.: Patterson Smith.

Braithwaite, John. 1989. *Crime, Shame and Reintegration.* New York: Cambridge University Press.

Burton, Velmer S., Jr., Francis T. Cullen, and Lawrence F. Travis III. 1987. The collateral consequences of a felony conviction: A national study of state statutes. *Federal Probation* 51:52–60.

Burton, Velmer S., Jr., R. Gregory Dunaway, and Reneé Kopache. In press. To punish or rehabilitate? A research note assessing the purposes of state correctional departments as defined by state legal codes. *Journal of Crime and Justice.*

Burton, Velmer S., Jr., Lawrence F. Travis III, and Francis T. Cullen. 1988. Reducing the legal consequences of a felony conviction: A national survey of state statutes. *International Journal of Comparative and Applied Criminal Justice* 12:101–109.

Bynum, Timothy S., Jack R. Greene, and Francis T. Cullen. 1986. Correlates of legislative crime control ideology. *Criminal Justice Policy Review* 1:253–267.

Carroll, Leo. 1988. *Hacks, Blacks, and Cons: Race Relations in a Maximum Security Prison.* 1974. Reprint ed. Prospect Heights, Ill.: Waveland.

Clark, Ramsey. 1970. *Crime in America.* New York: Pocket Books.

Clear, Todd R. 1991. Correction beyond prison walls. In Joseph F. Sheley (ed.), *Criminology: A Contemporary Handbook.* Belmont, Calif.: Wadsworth.

Clear, Todd R. and George F. Cole. 1990. *American Corrections.* 2nd ed. Pacific Grove, Calif.: Brooks/Cole.

Cohen, Jacob and Patricia Cohen. 1983. *Applied Multiple Regression/Correlation Analysis for the Behavioral Sciences.* 2nd ed. Hillsdale, N.J.: Lawrence Eribaum Associates.

Colvin, Mark. 1992. *The Penitentiary in Crisis: From Accommodation to Riot in New Mexico.* Albany: State University of New York Press.

Cullen, Francis T., John B. Cullen, and John F. Wozniak. 1988. Is rehabilitation dead? The myth of the punitive public. *Journal of Criminal Justice* 16:303–317.

Cullen, Francis T. and Paul Gendreau. 1989. The effectiveness of correctional rehabilitation: Reconsidering the "nothing works" debate. In Lynne Goodstein and Doris Layton MacKenzie (eds.), *The American Prison: Issues in Research and Policy.* New York: Plenum.

Cullen, Francis T. and Karen E. Gilbert. 1982. *Reaffirming Rehabilitation.* Cincinnati. Ohio: Anderson.

Cullen, Francis T., Faith Luize, Bruce G. Link, and Nancy Travis Wolfe. 1989a. The correctional orientation of prison guards: Do officers support rehabilitation? *Federal Probation* 53:33–42.

Cullen, Francis T., Sandra Evans Skovron, Joseph E. Scott, and Velmer S. Burton, Jr. 1989b. Public support for correctional treatment: The tenacity of rehabilitative ideology. *Criminal Justice and Behavior* 17:6–18.

Currie, Elliott. 1985. Confronting Crime: An American Challenge. New York: Pantheon.

1989. Confronting crime: Looking toward the twenty-first century. *Justice Quarterly* 6:5–25.

DiIulio, John J., Jr. 1987. *Governing Prisons: A Comparative Study of Correctional Management.* New York: Free Press.

1991. *No Escape: The Future of American Corrections.* New York: Basic Books.

Dillman, Don A. 1978. *Mail and Telephone Surveys: The Total Design Method.* New York: John Wiley & Sons.

Flanagan, Timothy J. and Susan L. Caulfield. 1984. Public opinion and prison policy: A review. *The Prison Journal* 64:31–46.

Fogel, David. 1979. *"We Are the Living Proof": The Justice Model for Corrections.* 2nd ed. Cincinnati, Ohio: Anderson.

Goodstein, Lynne and John Hepburn. 1985. *Determinate Sentencing and Imprisonment: A Failure of Reform.* Cincinnati, Ohio: Anderson.

Goodstein, Lynne and Doris Layton MacKenzie (eds.). 1989. *The American Prison: Issues in Research and Policy.* New York: Plenum.

Gordon, Diana R. 1990. *The Justice Juggernaut: Fighting Street Crime, Controlling Citizens.* New Brunswick, N.J.: Rutgers University Press.

Grieser, Robert C. 1988. *Wardens and State Corrections Commissioners Offer Their Views in National Assessment.* Washington, D.C.: National Institute of Justice.

Guynes, Randall. 1988. *Nation's Jail Managers Assess Their Problems.* Washington, D.C: National Institute of Justice.

Harris, Louis and Associates. 1968. *Corrections 1968: A Climate for Change.* Washington, D.C.: Joint Commission on Correctional Manpower and Training.

Harris, Patricia M., Todd R. Clear, and S. Christopher Baird. 1989. Have community supervision officers changed their attitudes toward their work? *Justice Quarterly* 6:233–246.

Hawkins, Gordon. 1976. *The Prison: Policy and Practice.* Chicago: University of Chicago Press.

Hawkins, Richard and Geoffrey P. Alpert. 1989. *American Prison Systems: Punishment and Justice.* Englewood Cliffs, N.J.: Prentice-Hall.

Irwin, John. 1980. *Prisons in Turmoil.* Boston: Little, Brown.

Jacobs, James B. 1977. *Stateville: The Penitentiary in Mass Society.* Chicago: University of Chicago Press.

Johnson, Robert. 1987. *Hard Time: Understanding and Reforming the Prison.* Monterey, Calif.: Brooks/Cole.

Jurik, Nancy C. 1985. Individual and organizational determinants of correctional officer attitudes toward inmates. *Criminology* 23:523–539.

Jurik, Nancy C. and Gregory J. Halemba. 1984. Gender, work conditions and the job satisfaction of women in a nontraditional occupation: Female correctional officers in men's prisons. *Sociological Quarterly* 25:551–566.

Lawes, Warden Lewis E. 1932. *Twenty Thousand Years in Sing Sing.* Philadelphia: Blakiston.

Link, Bruce G. and Francis T. Cullen. 1986. Contact with the mentally ill and perceptions of how dangerous they are. *Journal of Health and Social Behavior* 27:289–303.

Mattick, Hans W. 1976. Reflections of a former prison warden. In James F. Short, Jr. (ed.), *Delinquency, Crime, and Society.* Chicago: University of Chicago Press.

McCleery, Richard. 1968. Correctional administration and political change. In Lawrence Hazelrigg (ed.), *Prison Within Society.* Garden City, N.Y.: Anchor Books.

McGee, Richard. 1981. *Prisons and Politics.* Lexington, Mass.: Lexington Books.

Menninger, Karl. 1968. *The Crime of Punishment.* New York: Penguin.

Miller, Martin B. 1989. The prison warden study. Paper presented at the annual meeting of the Academy of Criminal Justice Sciences, Washington, D.C.

Murton, Thomas O. 1976. *The Dilemma of Prison Reform.* New York: Praeger.

Newman, Graeme. 1983. *Just and Painful: A Case for Corporal Punishment.* New York: Macmillan.

Philliber, Susan. 1987. Thy brother's keeper: A review of the literature on correctional officers. *Justice Quarterly* 4:9–37.

Platt, Anthony A. 1969. *The Child Savers: The Invention of Delinquency.* Chicago: University of Chicago Press.

Rafter, Nicole Hahn. 1989. Gender and justice: The equal protection issue. In Lynne Goodstein and Doris Layton MacKenzie (eds.), *The American Prison: Issues In Research and Policy.* New York: Plenum.

Rankin, Joseph H. 1979. Changing attitudes toward capital punishment. *Social Forces* 58:194–211.

Rossi, Peter H., Emily Waite, Christine E. Bose, and Richard E. Berk. 1974. The seriousness of crime: Normative structure and individual differences. *American Sociological Review* 39:224–237.

Rothman, David J. 1980. *Conscience and Convenience: The Asylum and Its Alternatives in Progressive America.* Boston: Little Brown.

Scheingold, Stuart A. 1984. *The Politics of Law and Order: Street Crime and Public Policy.* New York: Longman.

Shannon, Douglas. 1988. The educational background of correctional executives. Paper presented at the annual meeting of the Academy of Criminal Justice Sciences, San Francisco.

Shover, Neal and Werner J. Einstadter. 1988. *Analyzing American Corrections.* Belmont, Calif.: Wadsworth.

Sluder, Richard D. and Frances P. Reddington. In press. An empirical examination of the work ideologies of juvenile and adult probation officers. *Journal of Offender Rehabilitation.*

Spitzer, Steven. 1983. The rationalization of crime control in capitalist society. In Stanley Cohen and Andrew Scull (eds.), *Social Control and the State: Historical and Comparative Essays.* Oxford, England: Basil Blackwell.

Stojkovic, Stan and Rick Lovell. 1992. *Collections: An Introduction.* Cincinnati, Ohio: Anderson.

Stowe, Michael. 1992. Professional orientation of probation officers: Ideology and personality. Paper presented at the annual meeting of the Academy of Criminal Justice Sciences, Pittsburgh.

Sykes, Gresham M. 1958. *Society of Captives: A Study of a Maximum Security Prison.* Princeton, N.J.: Princeton University Press.

Tannenbaum, Frank. 1922. *Wall Shadows: A Study in American Prisons.* New York: G.P. Putnam's Sons.

Toch, Hans and John Klofas. 1982. Alienation and desire for job enrichment among correction officers. *Federal Probation* 46:35–44.

van den Haag, Ernest. 1975. *Punishing Criminals: Concerning a Very Old and Painful Question.* New York: Basic Books.

Van Voorhis, Patricia, Francis T. Cullen, Bruce G. Link, and Nancy Travis Wolfe. 1991. The impact of race and gender on correctional officers' orientation to the integrated environment. *Journal of Research on Crime and Delinquency* 28:472–500.

von Hirsch, Andrew. 1976. *Doing Justice: The Choice of Punishments.* New York: Hill and Wang.

Walker, Samuel. 1989. *Sense and Nonsense About Crime: A Policy Guide.* 2nd ed. Pacific Grove, Calif.: Brooks/Cole.

Warr, Mark and Mark Stafford. 1984. Public goals of punishment and support for the death penalty. *Journal of Research in Crime and Delinquency* 21:95–111.

Whitehead, John T. and Charles A. Lindquist. 1989. Determinants of correctional officers' professional orientation. *Justice Quarterly* 6:69–87.

1992. Determinants of probation and parole officer professional orientation. *Journal of Criminal Justice* 20:13–24.

Wicker, Tom. 1991. The heavy price of being a punitive society. *New York Times* (January 12):25.

Wilson, James Q. 1975. *Thinking About Crime.* New York: Random House.

Wolford, Bruce I. 1988. Wardens and superintendents: A diverse group. *Corrections Compendium* 13 (August):1, 6–7.

Wright, Kevin N. and William G. Saylor. 1992. A comparison of perceptions of the work environment between minority and non-minority employees of the federal prison system. *Journal of Criminal Justice* 20:63–71.

REVIEW QUESTIONS

1. How are prison wardens influential over the day-to-day operations of their facilities? In what ways can and do they shape the direction and operations of the prison?
2. What are the primary concerns of prison wardens in carrying out their duties? What are the most common goals of wardens?
3. What types of sources/variables appear to be most influential over wardens' views of rehabilitation? What are the issues that appear to be critical in shaping their views?

READING 17

Reasons for Professors to Teach in Prison

Richard Tewksbury

Based on interviews and direct observations, Tewksbury looks at the reasons why college professors choose to teach in prison-based programs. Motives include career advancement, expanding the reach of academic programs, pursuit of broad correctional goals, and attempts to improve society. These motivations encompass both personal, intrinsic reasons as well as altruistic, socially focused reasons. Through an expanded understanding of why correctional staff work in prisons and jails, it is possible to better understand how programs operate, where programs can be best emphasized so as to achieve maximum productivity and to better understand how various correctional staff positions both share and diverge on values, goals, and approaches to their work.

Correctional education, especially at the postsecondary level, is an important but frequently overlooked component of institutional corrections. Although the need for providing basic education to incarcerated persons is widely recognized, the value and appropriateness of advanced educational programs are not so widely accepted. . . .

. . . An analysis of the motivations of prison-based college faculty members supplements what is known currently about the impacts of programs on recidivism, about structures, and about impacts on individual inmate-students. An examination of the experiences of those who staff and administer these programs allows a deeper understanding of programs; it also provides materials with which policies and structures of programs may be revised efficiently and effectively. . . .

METHOD

This analysis is based on data obtained from two sources: in-depth interviews with postsecondary correctional educators and participant observation. I conducted semistructured, in-depth interviews with 40 postsecondary correctional educators, all of whom are employed by Wilmington (Ohio) College. All 40 educators teach in at least one of the three prisons where the college administers bachelor's degree-granting programs. . . .

The semistructured interview format encouraged respondents to identify issues central to their experiences as well as core issues concerning personal and professional histories, descriptions and assessments of personal teaching styles, perceptions of programmatic and institutional relationships, and social demographics. Interviews were 45 minutes to 3½ hours long; all interviews were transcribed in full. . . .

Supplemental data also are drawn from six months' participant observation in the college classrooms, offices, and common areas at the three prisons. Informal interviews, classroom observations, official (college and institutional) announcements, personal asides, and unsolicited observations from faculty members, students, administrators, and correctional employees contribute to an understanding of actions, interactions, and personal perspectives. . . .

RESULTS

Analysis of educators' accounts reveals five distinct, yet overlapping, dominant motivations for teaching in a postsecondary correctional education program: 1) alternative career paths, 2) academic idealism, 3) institutional objectives, 4) educational expansion, and 5) social reform. Three of these motivations, which account for 55 percent of the educators, are egocentric—alternative career paths, academic idealism, and institutional objectives; these focus primarily on individual goals and concerns. Motivations related to alternative career paths (dominant in 37.5% of the sample) center on perceptions of correctional education as an easily accessible alternative point of entry to an academic career. Academically idealistic motivations are reported by 10 percent of the educators, who believe that traditional institutions of higher education represent intellectual oppression and exploitation; among these respondents, prison teaching is motivated by a pursuit of "pure" intellectual goals, not those required by traditional educational institutions. Pursuit of institutional objectives dominates the accounts of 7.5 percent of the instructors. These are adjunct faculty members whose full-time occupation is in corrections. These men teach college courses both to earn extra income and to facilitate rapport and relationships with inmates.

The two remaining motivations are altruistic. Motivations related to educational expansion (25% of the sample) and to social reform (20% of the sample) are guided by individuals' desires, and their perceptions of opportunities, for inducing change in social structures and individuals. Motivations pertaining to educational expansion focus on altering social structures and systems. If educational opportunities are expanded to include populations traditionally excluded from higher education (for cultural and economic reasons), the structure of both educational and community institutions necessarily will be altered. Concerns about social reform focus largely on individuals and on "changing" or "improving" individual students. Instead of modifying institutions (and institutionalized patterns of behaviors), educators motivated in this way strive for social change, starting with individual change.

The following discussion elaborates on these five motivations and on how each one affects postsecondary correctional educators' social construction of experience. I discuss each motivation separately, although in practice they are found in combinations. Although each motivation entails a distinct set of goals, concerns, and foci, secondary motivations also influence most educators. In order to understand the unity among, and the distinctions between, motivations, it is important to examine them through the accounts of individual educators.

Alternative Career Paths

More than one-third of the postsecondary correctional educators, including full-time and especially adjunct faculty members, provide accounts that suggest that their work in the prison is motivated primarily by a desire to initiate an academic career. This is not to say that prison faculty members always plan for a career in academia; some find academic careers "accidentally," or more easily, by entry through the prison program. For some instructors, prison college programs offer a way to reestablish an academic career after work in applied or industrial settings. For some graduate students, such offer opportunities to gain valuable teaching experience.

Most of the educators motivated in this way report feeling that they are not prepared or that they lack proper credentials for traditional academic positions. Many prison instructors are in their first college-level teaching job; they define as their goals gaining experience and building marketable skills for a later move into a traditional academic institution. . . .

Similarly, for a variety of reasons, faculty members (especially adjunct professors), who derive their primary satisfaction from classroom interactions may not wish to pursue a full-time career in academia. Prison-based college programs offer an attractive alternative: a continuing, part-time, adjunct teaching position. Others view prison teaching as a professional alternative that is more enjoyable than one's established occupation. . . . For most faculty members in this group, however, teaching in prison simply provides an enjoyable, financially and experientially beneficial alternative point of entry to the academic realm.

Academic Idealism

Some postsecondary correctional educators are motivated primarily by the egocentric goal of working in an environment that facilitates "real" or "ideal" education. Many such educators perceive prison college programs as a potential academic utopia, where knowledge is pursued for its own sake and where students work for personal enrichment, not for mere credentials. Such perceptions motivate 10 percent of the present sample. The combination of a relatively small student population, . . . the unique interests of the students, and the mission of the college facilitate the teaching of substantive materials and the use of instructional techniques that are uncommon or innovative when employed in traditional postsecondary institutions. Consequently some educators define the prison as a potentially "ideal" or "idealistic" academic environment

In further support of the "ideal" nature of prison academics, the course offerings reflect the instructors' specific—sometimes narrowly defined—intellectual interests. During the period of this research, the offerings included such highly specialized courses as Music in Foreign Cultures, Seminar in Social Justice, Socrates and Plato, International Economic Theory, and Modern European Drama. Although these may not seem unusual for a traditional college curriculum, they are offered in the prisons for semester-long terms, with an average of only 63 courses spread across 20 disciplines.

Instructors with idealistic academic motivations value postsecondary correctional education because in prison classrooms students are encouraged to critically analyze ideas and values, and do so. Opportunities to work with students and to influence them personally are important to instructors motivated by academic idealism. Thus, despite structural differences in facilities and programs, it is the intangibles that present educators with their most highly valued challenges and opportunities. . . .

Institutional Objectives

A small proportion (7.5%) of postsecondary correctional educators are motivated mainly by the pursuit of penological goals. These instructors are full-time employees of correctional institutions who teach college courses because they believe that such interactions will increase the likelihood of achieving their correctional goals. This perspective is acknowledged in the orientations and characteristics of the correctional educators whom Gehring (1981) calls "good old boys." Such educators are highly valued by correctional authorities because they are "safe"; when educators motivated in this way are influential or predominate on a faculty, "learning becomes an incidental benefit instead of a primary goal" (Gehring 1981:21).

This is not to say that instructors whose work is guided by institutional objectives are not also devoted at least minimally to the processes and values of education. Typically these persons believe that their full-time positions inhibit direct contact with inmates; to overcome such obstacles and to attempt to establish extended contact with inmates, these men have elected to teach college courses part-time. . . .

The presence of persons who focus mainly on institutional objectives disturbs many instructors with other primary motivations. According to some of the more vocal faculty members, especially full-time faculty members with social reform and academic ideal motivations, correctionally oriented professionals are employed merely to placate correctional administrators. Some instructors believe the employment of such persons is similar to bribery; it is like a payment made in order to remain in the good graces of prison administrators. By including these persons on the faculty, some instructors believe that the program "purchases" acceptance, stability and security. . . .

Expansion of Education

A fourth guiding motivation, one of two altruistic motivations, is a desire to make higher education more available to an increasingly large and diverse population. Instructors who are motivated by this desire build on the belief that education is the primary mechanism for achieving a desirable quality of life. If education is made available, they believe that individual rehabilitation may be facilitated. If social structures are changed, they hope individuals may be changed.

Educators in this group believe that all members of society, regardless of status or alleged activities, are entitled to an education. In their view, being educated, and hence having the tools necessary to improve one's place in a stratified society, is the right of all persons, not something to be earned or a privilege reserved for "deserving" members of society. The fact that one is incarcerated does not mean that one forfeits the right to an education or that opportunities for improving one's quality of life are to be diminished. One instructor with strong concerns in this area speaks about this motivation as follows:

> I think that people are entitled to an education, wherever, and so certainly there is nothing else going on in corrections. . . . My attitude is I have a perspective on the world that I think is useful, I'm willing to share it with you, it's up to you do with it what you want.

Direct efforts to change students' beliefs and attitudes are couched in discussions about altering the scope and structure of the institution of education. The rationale for providing educational opportunities to traditionally underserved populations is based on the desire to enable students to improve their own lives:

> To me there's nothing more exciting than discussing with people ideas and the application of those ideas to life circumstances, looking at life and figuring out how we're going to live better. To me, knowledge isn't of use unless it's applied.

These educators acknowledge the idealism behind their goals, but believe they are succeeding to some degree; hence they find their work highly rewarding.

Social Reform

A second altruistic motivation, the last of the five primary motivations, is found among individuals who teach in a prison-based college program in an effort to reform individual inmates. Social reform motivations and the accomplishments that result from pursuing such goals may serve to attract educators to prison programs and/or to solidify individual educators' commitments once they become familiar with inmate-students. Accordingly, a number of educators believe that teaching in the prison college program is an efficient and productive mechanism for integrating professional activities with personal values. When instructors are motivated primarily by social reform concerns, work is not merely work; it is a politically and socially conscious attempt to improve society. In the words of one adjunct English instructor,

> I have a lot of political activist kind of stuff too. Part of me was drawn to the idea of teaching in prison for that reason, more of a maybe socially relevant thing to do than teaching 18-year-olds.

Teaching in prison is commonly only one of several efforts made in the pursuit of social reform. The social issues with which instructors are involved include minority civil rights, prison reform, abolition of the death penalty, the peace movement, urban community organizing, and foster parenting.

Like those who are motivated by expanding educational opportunities, educators with social reform motivations believe that education can and will enhance one's quality of life. These instructors, however, are distinguished by a nearly exclusive focus on the positive *consequences* of education. . . .

Educators motivated by social reform focus on the consequences of education for individual students. These instructors' motivations are primarily external; personal satisfaction and the drive to continue their work are elicited by the changes and enrichments they see in their students. Social reform motivations are associated most commonly with instructors who feel a sense of personal accomplishment in their work but who report this as secondary to altering individual students' values and behaviors.

DISCUSSION

I have discussed here the professional motivations that guide the work of postsecondary correctional educators. It is important, however, not to view these motivations as mutually exclusive, either as guiding forces or as categories of instructors. Although I discussed each motivation individually, they interact. Integrations of secondary motivations direct specific micro aspects of instructors' actions and interactions. Therefore, when integrated sets of motivations are combined with individuals' backgrounds, a range of socially constructed experiences is possible. . . .

The motivations that guide postsecondary correctional educators' experiential constructions can be identified as having an egocentric or an altruistic focus. Egocentric foci may be individually formulated sets of goals, as in the cases of alternative career paths and contributions to institutional objectives. Concerns about academic idealism are egocentric and are socially focused and formulated. Accounts by instructors with these concerns emphasize the benefits that they derive from their work. Pragmatic interactional considerations and curricular issues, however—from which satisfactions are derived—are determined largely by social and contextual forces. Motivations based on social reform and educational expansion are altruistic; they are directed respectively at individual and at social alterations. Social reform motivated instructors focus on changing ("reforming") individuals. In contrast, instructors motivated primarily by educational expansion are concerned mainly with inducing changes in social structure, thereby (they hope) facilitating individual changes.

By identifying and understanding educators' motivations and their subsequent interactions and purposeful behaviors, we gain a more complete understanding of the administration of correctional higher education programs. By learning why educators enter and remain in correctional education, administrators may be able to meet educators' self-identified psychosocial needs more effectively. By modifying program structures and maximizing particular opportunities (for both instructors and students), administrators may enhance job satisfaction. By providing instructors with an environment that complements (or at least does not interfere with) their goals, they may reduce job stresses. Also, if instructors are encouraged to pursue their special intellectual interests, the scope and quality of the educational experience may be enhanced. In such a context, inmate-students benefit from higher-quality instruction, a potentially more diverse faculty and curriculum, and a greater likelihood of a stable faculty. . . .

When correctional education programs become more organizationally stable and more consistent, they may be expected to demonstrate efficiency and productivity (i.e., to reduce recidivism). A program that takes into account the needs and motivations of faculty members as well as of students is likely to operate more efficiently and thereby to be accepted and valued as an important component of correctional programming. In this way correctional educators can and will make significant contributions to both the internal functioning of the program and the acceptance (and consequent assistance) received inside the correctional institution. . . .

REFERENCES

Allen, J.P. (1988) "Administering Quality Education in an Adult Correctional Facility." *Community Services Catalyst* 18(4):28–29.

Alston, J.G. (1981a) "Preparation for Life after Incarceration." Paper presented at the meetings of the American Association of Community and Junior Colleges, Washington, D.C.

——— (1981b) "The Role of the Community College in Instruction for the Incarcerated." *Community College Review* 9(2):10–14.

Arshad, C. (1975) "A Descriptive Analysis of Selected Personal, Social and Professional Needs of the Teaching Staff in the State of Ohio's Correctional Institutions." Unpublished doctoral dissertation, University of Cincinnati.

Blackburn, F.S. (1981) "The Relationship between Recidivism and Participation in a Community College Program for Incarcerated Offenders." *Journal of Correctional Education* 32(3):23–25.

Brown-Young, C. (1986) "Deconstructing Correctional Education: An Ethnographic Study of the Contexts of Prison Schools." Unpublished doctoral dissertation, The Ohio State University.

Cheatwood, A.D. (1988) "The Impact of the Prison Environment on the Incarcerated Learner." *Journal of Correctional Education* 39(4):184–86.

Cioffi, F. (1981) "Teaching College Humanities Courses in Prison." *Alternative Higher Education* 6(1):49–59.

Clendenen, R.J., J.R. Ellingston, and R.J. Severson (1979) "Project Newgate: The First Five Years." *Crime and Delinquency* 25(1):55–64.

Conrad, E., R. Bell, and T. Laffey (1978) "Correctional Education: A Summary of the National Evaluation Project." *Quarterly Journal of Corrections* 2(2):14–20.

Conrad, J.P. (1981) *Adult Offender Education Programs.* Washington, DC: National Institute of Justice.

DeGraw, D. (1987) "A Study of Correctional Educators in Adult Correctional Institutions." *Journal of Correctional Education* 38(1):18–20.

Fox, T. (1991) "Prison Educators' Practice of Adult Education in Prison Education Programmes: A Canadian Case Study." *International Journal of Lifelong Education* 10(1):35–44.

Gagnon, G.O. (1977) "Prison Education Network Impacts Total Program." *Community and Junior College Journal* 48(2):26–28.

Gehring, T. (1981) "The Correctional Education Professional Identity Issue." *Journal of Correctional Education* 33(1):9–10.

Gendron, D. and J.J. Cavan (1988) "Inmate Education: The Virginia Model." Paper presented at the meetings of the American Association of Community and Junior Colleges, Las Vegas.

——— (1990) "Managing a Successful Inmate-Education Program: Why and How?" *Community College Review* 18(1):31–38.

George, P.S., C. Ramsey, and G. Krist (1980) "The College Program in the Georgia State Prison." *Community College Frontiers* 8(2):21–25.

Haber, G.M. (1983) "The Realization of Potential by Lorton, D.C. Inmates with UDC College Education Compared to Those without UDC Education." *Journal of Offender Counseling, Services and Rehabilitation* 7(3–4):37–55.

Hawke, S.D. and J. Ritter (1988) "Teaching Biology behind Prison Walls." *Journal of College Science Teaching* 18(1):22–25.

Holloway, J. and P. Moke (1986) *Post Secondary Correctional Education: An Evaluation of Parolee Performance.* (ERIC Document Reproduction Service No. ED 269578)

Kiser, G.C. (1987) "Teaching College Courses to Inmates." *Journal of Correctional Education* 38(3):102–107.

Knepper, P. (1989) "Selective Participation, Effectiveness, and Prison College Programs." *Journal of Offender Counseling, Services and Rehabilitation* 14(2): 109–35.

Loeffler, C.A., T.C. Martin, D.L. Henderson, and R. McNeese (1986) "Anatomy of a Prison Educator: A Profile of Correctional Educators in the Windham School System, Huntsville, Texas." *Journal of Correctional Education* 37(1): 24–29.

Lombardi, J. (1984) "The Impact of Correctional Education on Length of Incarceration: Non-Support for New Paroling Policy Motivation." *Journal of Correctional Education* 35(1):54–57.

Mahoney, J.R. (1976) *Offender Assistance Through Community College Programs.* Washington, DC: American Association of Community and Junior Colleges.

McCracken, G. (1988) *The Long Interview.* Beverly Hills: Sage.

Michalek, W.F. (1985) "Correctional Education and Prison Adjustment: How Pre-Incarceration Characteristics, Prison Environments, and Incarceration Characteristics Influence Prison Adaptation." Unpublished doctoral dissertation, Cornell University.

O'Neil, M. (1990) "Correctional Higher Education: Reduced Recidivism?" *Journal of Correctional Education* 41(1):28–31.

Parker, E.A. (1990) "The Social-Psychological Impact of a College Education on the Prison Inmate." *Journal of Correctional Education* 41(3):140–46.

Peak, K. (1983) "Directors of Correctional Education Programs: A Demographic and Attitudinal Profile." *Journal of Correctional Education* 34(3):79–83.

Peak, K. (1984) "Postsecondary Correctional Education: Contemporary Program Nature and Delivery Systems in the U.S." *Journal of Correctional Education* 35(2):58–62.

Pittman, V. and E.M. Whipple (1982) "The Inmate as College Student." *Lifelong-Learning: The Adult Years* 5(7):4–5, 30.

Roundtree, G.A., D.W. Edwards, and S.H. Dawson (1982) "The Effects of Education on Self-Esteem of Male Prison Inmates." *Journal of Correctional Education* 32(4):12–18.

Russell, J.E. (1984) *An Analysis of Student Activity at Graham Correctional Center.* Springfield, IL: Lincoln Land Community College.

Schumacker, R.E., D.B. Anderson, and S.L. Anderson (1990) "Vocational and Academic Indicators of Parole Success." *Journal of Correctional Education* 41(1): 8–13.

Scott, J.E. (1976) "A Perceptual Model of a Correctional Educator's Education Program." Unpublished doctoral dissertation, The Ohio State University.

Smith, N.E. (1988) "Impression Management in the Prison." Unpublished doctoral dissertation, The Ohio State University.

Stein, M. (1989) "Teaching Deviance to Deviants: The Prison Classroom Experience." *Free Inquiry in Creative Sociology* 17(2):185–91.

Tewksbury, R.A. (1991) "The Social Construction of Experience and Identity Management among Postsecondary Correctional Educators." Unpublished doctoral dissertation, The Ohio State University.

Thorpe, T., D. MacDonald, and G. Bala (1984) "Follow-up Study of Offenders Who Earn College Degrees While Incarcerated in New York State." *Journal of Correctional Education* 35(3):86–88.

Toupin, L. (1988) "Practical Experience and Instructional Approach by Teachers in Quebec Federal Penitentiaries." *Journal of Correctional Education* 39(3): 108–13.

Trent, C. and J.F. Ragadale (1976) "Community College Programs for Prisoners." *Community College Review* 4(2):43–47.

Watson, R.J. (1975) *Letters from Jessup: Notes on a Prison College Program.* Jessup, MD: Essex Community College.

Weeks, E.S., Jr. and J.C. Coltharp (1985) "College Prison Education in Georgia: A Profile of Postsecondary Education Institutions." *Journal of Correctional Education* 36(3):94–97.

Williams, D.N. (1989) *Correctional Education and the Community College.* Washington, DC: Office of Educational Research and Improvement.

Wolf, J.G. and D. Sylves (1981) *The Impact of Higher Education Opportunity Programs. Post Prison Experience of Disadvantaged Students: A Preliminary Follow-up of HEOP Ex-offenders.* Albany, NY: New York State Education Department.

Wolford, B.I. and J.F. Littlefield (1985) "Correctional Postsecondary Education: The Expanding Role of Community Colleges." *Community/Junior College Quarterly of Research and Practice* 9(3):257–72.

Wolford, B.I. and R.W. Snarr (1987) "What Is the Goal of Correctional Education?" *Journal of Correctional Education* 38(2):60–64.

REVIEW QUESTIONS

1. What are the reasons that college professors choose to teach in prison programs?
2. What types of issues, intrinsic or extrinsic, are responsible for most prison-based college instructors?
3. In what ways do the motivations of social reform and academic idealism differ from one another?

VII

INSTITUTIONAL PROGRAMMING

READING 18

Insiders' Views of Prison Amenities

Beliefs and Perceptions of Correctional Staff Members

Richard Tewksbury

Elizabeth Ehrhardt Mustaine

In this reading, the authors discuss whether prison staff endorse or oppose the presence and use of a variety of "amenities" for prison inmates. As a result of a political movement to remove "extras" from prisons and to make them generally stark, barren, and devoid of recreational and programmatic opportunities, many systems and facilities have removed such items. In this study, the authors show that prison staff members hold different views than many policy makers do, and believe that the provision of recreational opportunities and entertainment media and programming is important and should be available to prison inmates. Additionally, when looking at correctional staff based on types of jobs held (administration, security, programming), length of time working in corrections and whether the individual holds a college degree, important differences in views exist.

As American correctional institutions continue to expand in number and population (Harrison & Beck, 2005), they increasingly become points of political and community attention (see No Frills Prison Act of 1996; Hensley, Miller, Tewksbury, & Koscheski, 2003). Much discourse in this arena focuses on issues of the consequences of incarceration (for society in general and offenders in particular) and what (if anything) should be done with, for, and to inmates. Should correctional administrators attempt to rehabilitate offenders, or should prisons simply warehouse offenders in stark and sparse conditions? Should inmates be provided with access to products, services, and opportunities that those at the bottom of society's economic structure are unable to access? Where is the line regarding what should and should not be available for prison inmates? These questions form the basis of the present study. What products, services, and programmatic opportunities do correctional staff persons believe are appropriate and inappropriate for incarcerated offenders? And how do variations in staff members' characteristics influence these beliefs?

Both the debate about and research assessing the beliefs of individuals (and categories of individuals) regarding the appropriateness of providing various amenities to inmates are fairly recent developments (e.g., No Frills Prison Act of 1996; Applegate, 2001; Hensley et al., 2003; Johnson, Bennett, & Flanagan, 1997; Lenz, 2002). Only during the past two decades has a discussion of whether inmates should have access to a variety of products, services, and programs been popularly debated. And research about attitudes and beliefs concerning inmates' access to amenities is a recently emerging and underdeveloped field (Applegate, 2001; Bryant & Morris, 1998; Hensley et al., 2003; Johnson et al., 1997; Lenz, 2002).

This study endeavors to add to this underdeveloped field by considering the views of correctional staff about a variety of prison amenities as well as assess any relationship between these views and correctional staff characteristics. . . .

REVIEW OF THE LITERATURE

The Public Debate Regarding Prison Amenities

At the core of the debate about what prison inmates should and should not be allowed to have or have access to is the concept of least eligibility. In short, the principle of least eligibility is the idea that "prisoners should not be given programs and services or live under conditions that are better than those of the lowest classes of the noncriminal population in society" (Champion, 2005, p. 200). According to this way of thinking, convicted and incarcerated offenders should not be provided with anything better than that provided or accessible to anyone in the general population. This is contrasted with those who take the position that by incarcerating an individual, the state assumes responsibility for providing for that individual's needs because the inmate is unable to do so oneself (the principle of *parens patriae*).

Since the mid-1990s, there has been a sharp shift toward limiting prison inmates' access to amenities and to removing extras and luxuries from inside prisons. The most important stimulus in this movement was the passage of the 1996 federal legislation known as the No Frills Prison Act. This law prohibits in-cell televisions (except for inmates in segregation); coffee pots; hot plates; movies rated R, X, or NC-17; boxing, wrestling, or any martial arts, bodybuilding, and weightlifting equipment; and possession of any personal electronics or musical instruments in federal prisons. This development also spurred state Departments of Corrections (DOCs) to pass similar state-level legislation or to remove many inmate amenities by administrative action (see Corrections Compendium, 2002).

Where access to amenities has been maintained, access has been restricted (or curtailed) through the imposition of fees for services. According to a survey of state DOCs in 2002, the legal developments of the mid- to late 1990s did create a "trend for decreased privileges . . . and will likely continue in the future" (Corrections Compendium, 2002, pp. 8–9). The restrictions on luxuries has led to the prohibition of smoking in 53% of American prisons, R-rated movies are not allowed in 58% of prisons, and many institutions and systems have strict restrictions on books and magazines (e.g., no magazines more than 3 months old, only one book to be in an inmate's possession at a time; Corrections Compendium, 2002).

The movement toward no-frills prisons appears to be in response to a perceived political belief that the public wants prisons to be austere environments. However, the veracity of this assumption has not been supported by the research literature (Applegate, 2001; Bryant & Morris, 1998; Hensley et al., 2003; Lenz, 2002). Correctional administrators largely believe that removing all amenities may pose safety risks and seriously restrict their abilities to manage inmate behavior through the availability of incentives and rewards (see below).

Research on Perceptions of Prison Amenities

Accompanying this shift in thinking and practice has been the initial development of a line of inquiry regarding what the general public and correctional policy makers believe about amenities for prison inmates. This line of inquiry has grown out of a long history of research about public perceptions of corrections and correctional practices (e.g., Applegate, Cullen, Turner, & Sundt, 1996; Cullen, Fisher, & Applegate, 2000; Keil & Vito, 1991; Whitehead & Blankenship, 2000); however, as summarized by Applegate (2001), "none of those who cite public opinion as the catalyst for increasing Spartan prison environments have provided any supporting empirical evidence" (p. 254). There have been few studies of the general public's views of prison amenities and only one study of correctional officials' attitudes. It is interesting that, to date, no research has been completed that addresses the views of frontline correctional staff.

The initial efforts regarding perceptions of the appropriateness of inmate amenities focused on public attitudes and beliefs, with all of the research to date on public attitudes coming from the state of Florida. The first of this line of inquiry, a telephone survey of 1,002 Floridians, revealed that the public was not well informed about what programs, services, and resources were available in prisons. Additionally, many amenities were not supported by the state's residents (Bureau of Economic and Business Research, 1997). Residents also significantly overestimated the true availability of numerous amenities, including things such as air conditioning.

Shortly thereafter, Bryant and Morris (1998) reported that two thirds of Floridians approved of air conditioning in the state's prisons and nearly one half supported inmates having access to television and weightlifting equipment. More recently, Applegate (2001) assessed the views of Orange County, Florida, residents regarding a variety of prison amenities. This study reported higher levels of support than anticipated (or suggested by political rhetoric) for 26 assessed items. In general, this sample was supportive of treatment-oriented programs (education, health care, mental health care, and legal assistance). Lower levels of support were expressed for programs, services, and resources defined as less central to the mission of maintaining an inmate's well-being; recreational and entertainment-oriented items were less likely to be seen as valuable and important to these community members.

Applegate (2001) reported that seven amenities (cigarettes and tobacco, cable television, pornography, boxing and martial arts, R-rated movies, tennis, and condoms) were advocated for removal by more than 50% of his sample. An additional six amenities (college education programs, legal assistance, basic television, arts and crafts programs, weightlifting equipment, and radios and tape players) were seen by at least one third of the sample as things that should be removed from prisons. In contrast, 13 amenities (psychological counseling, basic literacy programs, job training programs, GED courses, access to law books and materials, HIV/AIDS treatments, books, newspapers and magazines, basketball, supervised family visits, conjugal visits, telephone calls, and air conditioning) were supported and advocated for retention by more than two thirds of the sample. Applegate (2001) concludes that

> public views on prison amenities, like their views about a variety of other correctional issues, are not as harsh as many have assumed. . . . The public seems to recognize the need for prisons to be productive. They do not want luxurious prisons. Taxpayers want institutions which are humane and seek to improve inmates during their incarceration. Moreover, they are willing to provide the material resources necessary to reach these goals. (p. 266)

An additional Florida-based study (Lenz, 2002) assessed whether community residents' views on amenities were contingent on the sources that paid for the programs, services, or resources. Pinellas County residents were most supportive of amenities such as television, cable television, books, periodicals, radios, weights, special meals, and musical instruments when they believed inmates paid for such items; significantly lower levels of support were seen when respondents were led to believe that tax dollars were used to provide such items. Educationally oriented items were those most likely to be seen as important and as things that should be maintained in prison. One important exception appears in Lenz's (2002) results, however. Support for prisons having air conditioning was not contingent on the source of funds to pay for it. Keeping in mind that this was a Florida-based study, it appears that some items perceived in some circles (and locations) as luxuries may not be seen as such by all persons.

This raises the question of whether views such as those reported for Florida residents would be found in other geographic areas and among other types of samples. To date, only two sets of researchers (Hensley et al., 2003; Johnson et al., 1997) have examined this issue with specified populations. Johnson et al. (1997) focused on prison wardens and reported that among their sample of 641 wardens, the majority support the removal or restrictions on many luxury items and practices in prisons (including pornographic materials, conjugal visits, boxing, tobacco, personal clothing, and reception of disability benefits). Wardens strongly supported retaining some types of amenities, however; those most likely to receive their support were educational programs, medical services, and access to legal materials. Yet despite administrators' wishes to maintain many amenities, both the luxuries and the educational and treatment programs were curtailed and eliminated in many systems.

The second set of researchers to address a special population looked at future criminal justice staff—college students preparing for a career in criminal justice (Hensley et al., 2003). . . . Students' views do not differ significantly from those of general community residents, and it is interesting that there are no statistically significant differences between criminal justice majors and other students. This would suggest that individuals employed in the criminal justice system may hold very similar views to those of the general public. However, to date, no research has examined this assumption, and except for limited knowledge about wardens' views, there is nothing beyond anecdotal data available concerning the views of correctional staff on prison amenities. . . .

Method

Data for the present study were gathered via surveys administered to all staff working at 6 (of the 14) prisons in the Commonwealth of Kentucky during spring 2003. . . .

Findings: Staff Members' Views of Prison Amenities

. . . Table 1 reports the percentages of staff members who report that they believe each of the assessed amenities should be kept in prisons where they are available. The table also provides a rank ordering of the amenities, starting with the amenity that received the most support for retention and ending with the amenity that

TABLE 1 Percentage of Correctional Staff Members Believing Amenities Should Be Kept

Amenity	% Staff Advocating to Keep Amenity
Books	98.3
Psychological counseling	96.8
Basic literacy programs	96.4
Supervised family visits	96.2
GED classes	95.1
Basketball	94.8
Newspapers and magazines	93.9
Basic TV (no cable)	93.8
Telephone calls	92.2
Radios and tape players	92.0
Job training programs	91.4
Air conditioning	91.2
HIV/AIDS treatment	87.4
Arts and crafts	86.8
Legal assistance	81.3
Law books and legal library	77.7
Weightlifting equipment	64.6
College education programs	62.8
Cigarettes and other tobacco	62.3
Tennis	56.2
Cable TV	47.1
R-rated movies	35.5
Condoms	19.9
Pornography	17.6
Conjugal visiting	12.5
Boxing and martial arts	12.3

received the least support for retention (or the most support for elimination). This analysis of frequency can highlight the views of staff about particular amenities as well as give some information about the types of amenities that are seen as the most and least worthy.

To elaborate, as can be seen, there are 12 amenities that at least 90% of staff believe should be retained in prisons; these include items that represent such areas as basic prison conditions (psychological counseling, books, supervised visits with family, telephone calls, and air conditioning), educational programming (job training, GED classes, and basic literacy programs), and some forms of mild entertainment (radios and tape players, basic television, and newspapers and magazines). Additionally, there are six amenities (boxing and martial arts, conjugal visits, pornography, condoms, R-rated movies, and cable TV) that a majority of staff persons believe should be eliminated from prison.

The remaining amenities (HIV/AIDS treatment, arts and crafts, legal assistance, law books and legal libraries, weightlifting equipment, college education programs, cigarettes and tobacco, and tennis) are items believed by at least two thirds of staff members to be appropriate for prison. These items do not receive the same resounding support as the top amenities listed (all with more than 90% support for retention) but are still viewed as being valuable for a successful prison experience for inmates and/or successful maintenance of prison security and safety of those there (inmates and staff). . . .

This is similar to Applegate's (2001) findings that the Florida public was more supportive of prison amenities than perhaps previously assumed. Fully 19 of the 26 amenities assessed were supported by the majority of those persons interviewed. Additionally, as a point of interest, the amenities supported for retention as well as those supported for elimination are very similar for those reported as such by Applegate's Florida citizens and the correctional staff in the present study. (Amenities marked for elimination in Applegate's study were identical to those in the present study, with the exceptions that the majority of the Florida public felt that tennis and cigarettes and other tobacco should be eliminated and conjugal visits should be kept.)

Of course, correctional staff members' views on amenities may be influenced by their personal attributes. As such, we turn to the cross-tabulation analysis to assess any differences in views on prison amenities by several correctional staff member characteristics (type of job, job tenure, and educational attainment). . . .

Turning to Table 2, when examining differences across staff members based on type of job, some variation comes forth. As noted above, for this comparison, we use three broad categories of jobs (administration, security, and programs). Specifically, for 13 of the amenities, there is a significant relationship between the three types of correctional staff positions and their views on the particular amenity. First, for several of the amenities, it appears that it is security staff members who have a distinctive view from both administrators and program staff members. These seven amenities are GED classes, newspapers and magazines, job training programs, arts and crafts, legal assistance, law books and legal library, and college education programs. In all cases, security staff members have a lower level of support for retention of these amenities than do administrators and program

TABLE 2 Results of Cross-Tabulations on Attitudes About Keeping Prison Amenities by Correctional Staff Position

Amenity	% Administrators	% Security Staff	% Program Staff	Pearson χ^2
Books	98.8	98.0	99.2	0.784
Psychological counseling	97.6	96.1	98.3	1.618
Basic literacy programs	98.8	95.2	98.3	3.945
Supervised family visits	97.6	95.3	98.3	2.688
GED classes	98.8	91.8	100	15.211*
Basketball	97.6	93.7	95.7	2.176
Newspapers and magazines	97.6	91.7	98.3	8.897*
Basic TV (no cable)	95.2	93.9	95.0	0.294
Telephone calls	88.2	92.5	95.9	4.243
Radios and tape players	92.9	90.2	95.8	3.630
Job training programs	96.4	86.6	97.5	15.773*
Air conditioning	92.9	92.0	94.2	0.556
HIV/AIDS treatment	97.6	82.0	90.0	15.772*
Arts and crafts	91.7	82.8	91.7	7.807*
Legal assistance	90.6	78.6	89.3	10.511*
Law books and legal library	88.7	72.1	91.7	20.797*
Weightlifting equipment	66.7	58.7	74.2	8.694*
College education programs	75.0	53.5	74.8	22.035*
Cigarettes and other tobacco	61.2	59.7	65.3	1.089
Tennis	59.8	53.5	59.8	1.788
Cable TV	49.4	44.3	52.9	2.590
R-rated movies	31.0	32.0	45.4	7.173*
Condoms	16.5	12.7	41.4	40.439*
Pornography	7.1	20.6	16.8	8.087*
Conjugal visiting	11.8	11.1	14.5	0.845
Boxing and martial arts	12.2	10.0	20.0	7.209*

$*p \leq .05$.

staff members. For example, although 98.8% and 100% of administrators and program staff members are in support of the retention of GED classes for inmates in prisons, only 91.8% of security officers feel these classes should be retained. Certainly, it is the case that, overall, the vast majority of correctional staffers in general are supportive of this program. Nonetheless, a noticeably higher proportion of security officers do not support inmates taking classes to get their GEDs. Other examples are that fewer security staff members support job training programs, arts and crafts, college education programs, newspapers and magazines, law library and legal books, and legal assistance (even though they are, for the most part, supportive of these programs) than administrators and program staff.

For three of the amenities, where there is a significant relationship between the type of job held and views on prison amenities, it appears that it is program staffers who have the distinct view. In all cases, they are significantly more likely to favor retaining the amenity than are administrators and security staff members. To elaborate, 45.4%, 41.4%, and 20% of program staff members are in favor of retaining R-rated movies, condoms, and boxing and martial arts programs, respectively. Fewer administrators (31%, 16.5%, and 12.2%, respectively) and security staff (32%, 12.7%, and 10%, respectively) support retaining these amenities. . . .

Finally, three amenity views that are significantly related to type of job held seem to have distinct views across all job categories. To specify, administrators are the most likely to support the retention of HIV/AIDS treatment (97.6%), fewer program staffers favor HIV/AIDS treatment (90.9%), and still fewer security staff want to keep HIV/AIDS treatment (82%). In this case, it may be that administrators are the most in favor of this amenity because they know it is legally mandated (but we did not directly test this assertion). Weightlifting equipment seems to be another amenity that has distinctive views across all types of jobs. Specifically, security staff have the least amount of support for it (58.7%), administrators are next with 66.7% being in support of retaining it, and the highest proportion of program staff members support keeping weightlifting equipment (74.2%). Obviously, staff members' types of jobs in prison have significant influences over their views on the retention or elimination of various prison amenities.

An alternative relationship to consider is the association between correctional staff members' views on prison amenities and their tenure on the job, or the length of time staff members have been in corrections. . . . The first group, representing the least experienced staff, is the one with members who have worked in corrections for 4 years or less. The second group reports tenure of more than 4 years to 13 years, and the final group reports more than 13 years of experience in correctional work. An examination of Table 3 indicates that there is a relationship between tenure on the job and correctional staff members' views on the retention or elimination of particular prison amenities. However, this relationship is present for fewer amenities ($n = 5$) than the relationship between views on amenities and type of job ($n = 13$). . . .

Another important consideration in assessing the relationship between correctional staff members' personal characteristics and their views on inmates' amenities is the level of education completed by staff members. Table 4 illustrates the association between these two factors. Although a significant link does exist, there are only three particular amenities about which views on them are related to correctional staff members' level of educational attainment: law books and legal library, condoms, and boxing and martial arts. In all cases, a significantly higher proportion of correctional staff members with a college education or more support

TABLE 3 Results of Cross-Tabulations on Attitudes About Keeping Prison Amenities by Tenure on Job

Amenity	% Short Job Tenure (0 to 4 Years)	% Midlevel Job Tenure (4 to 13 years)	% Long Job Tenure (13 or More Years)	Pearson χ^2
Books	97.6	98.3	99.4	1.573
Psychological counseling	97.1	97.1	95.6	0.747
Basic literacy programs	95.8	97.7	95.6	1.269
Supervised family visits	95.9	97.1	96.2	0.401
GED classes	94.7	97.1	94.9	1.429
Basketball	97.0	94.7	92.9	2.786
Newspapers and magazines	95.3	93.0	95.6	1.308
Basic TV (no cable)	90.4	97.7	93.5	7.794*
Telephone calls	92.9	94.2	90.5	1.627
Radios and tape players	91.1	92.4	92.9	0.420
Job training programs	89.9	91.3	94.9	2.883
Air conditioning	89.9	94.7	88.5	4.384
HIV/AIDS treatment	83.1	86.5	93.0	7.453*
Arts and crafts	87.4	87.7	86.0	0.246
Legal assistance	79.2	84.3	82.2	1.523
Law books and legal library	75.4	76.0	84.2	4.547
Weightlifting equipment	68.9	59.0	69.9	5.436
College education programs	66.3	58.5	65.8	2.773
Cigarettes and other tobacco	67.5	59.5	58.6	3.347
Tennis	63.9	57.3	46.1	10.393*
Cable TV	43.5	43.4	58.3	9.560*
R-rated movies	34.9	31.7	41.2	3.183
Condoms	23.0	20.4	17.2	1.604
Pornography	22.0	11.6	17.4	6.551
Conjugal visiting	19.6	11.8	4.8	15.591*
Boxing and martial arts	13.6	12.9	11.1	0.482

*$p \leq .05$.

TABLE 4 Results of Cross-Tabulations on Attitudes About Keeping Prison Amenities by Education Level

Amenity	% Less Than College Degree	% College Degree or More	Pearson χ^2
Books	97.8	99.1	1.308
Psychological counseling	96.8	96.7	0.002
Basic literacy programs	95.8	97.2	0.721
Supervised family visits	95.2	97.7	2.148
GED classes	93.6	97.2	3.539
Basketball	95.5	93.8	0.742
Newspapers and magazines	93.6	94.4	0.153
Basic TV (no cable)	94.4	93.0	0.461
Telephone calls	92.0	92.6	0.071
Radios and tape players	91.3	93.0	0.461
Job training programs	91.0	92.1	0.220
Air conditioning	89.4	93.9	3.263
HIV/AIDS treatment	88.3	86.0	0.621
Arts and crafts	85.2	89.2	1.763
Legal assistance	79.4	84.2	1.952
Law books and legal library	74.0	83.2	6.226*
Weightlifting equipment	61.3	69.3	3.562
College education programs	59.5	67.6	3.567
Cigarettes and other tobacco	63.3	60.9	0.294
Tennis	54.7	58.4	0.698
Cable TV	44.9	50.5	1.595
R-rated movies	32.5	39.9	3.037
Condoms	14.3	28.2	14.748*
Pornography	19.6	14.6	2.236
Conjugal visiting	11.7	13.8	0.482
Boxing and martial arts	9.1	16.8	6.942*

$^*p \leq .05$.

retaining the amenity than those correctional staff with an educational attainment of less than a college degree. . . .

DISCUSSION AND CONCLUSION

The present study has endeavored to provide a first look at the views of correctional staff members regarding the retention or elimination of various prison amenities. Previous research has examined the attitudes of citizens as well as prison wardens, but we know very little about the views of other correctional staff members, especially those with frequent and intense inmate contact. Additionally, the present study has examined the relationship between these views and several correctional staff member characteristics.

The current study has illustrated that correctional staff members generally support the retention of most assessed amenities. There are only four amenities that received less than 20% support for retention (boxing and martial arts, conjugal visiting, pornography, and condoms), and only two additional amenities that received more than one third but less than one half support for retention (cable TV and R-rated movies). For the remaining amenities, at least a majority of the correctional staff members surveyed supported their retention in prison. Additionally, nearly half (12) of the amenities assessed received support for retention by at least 90% of the sample. This is an instructive finding. Those who actually work in the prison setting, as administrators, security staff members, or program staff members, are generally supportive of most of the prison services, programs, and activities that are currently offered (at least in some facilities) to inmates. Obviously, the belief is that there is at least some tangible benefit to having these amenities available to inmates.

Another contribution of the present research is the comparison of correctional staff views on prison amenities with those of community residents not intimately involved in corrections. We compare our data with that of Applegate's (2001) Florida citizens and find, in general, that correctional staff members are more or similarly tolerant toward all types of prison amenities as citizens. As such, contrary to assumptions, popular belief, or political rhetoric, correctional staff members are accepting of many prison amenities. Perhaps this is because they have direct experience with life in prison and are more familiar with the value that these items have for inmates and for maintaining a smooth running institution. . . .

This research has also shown that correctional staff views are contingent on several correctional staff member characteristics: type of job, tenure on the job, and level of education. Generally, we find that administrators and program staff are tolerant of many amenities, whereas fewer correctional officers are as tolerant in their views on these same amenities. Furthermore, length of time on the job is significantly related to several amenities (basic TV, HIV/AIDS treatment, tennis, cable TV, and conjugal visits), as is educational attainment (law books and legal libraries, condoms, and boxing and martial arts). Although the pattern of the relationship with length of time on the job is variable (e.g., the longer the job tenure, the more support for HIV/AIDS treatment; the longer the job tenure, the less support for tennis and conjugal visits), the relationship is present. This is certainly noteworthy (and perhaps intellectually confirmatory) because it highlights the fact that experience on the job changes one's views about what makes the prison experience successful and what the important elements are in prison life. . . .

It is interesting that the most unique characteristic of a prison employee that influences his or her views on prison amenities is being a correctional security officer. To elaborate, security officers appear to have more negative views on prison amenities than other members of the prison staff. Furthermore, their views on amenities are distinctive more of the time than that for any other characteristic assessed.

This research also has implications for political discourse. Many politicians imply that most people's views about prison amenities are harsh and intolerant, seeing a prison sentence as "easy and comfortable." These arguments are often used to persuade constituents and other lawmakers to support "no frills" approaches. However, as can be seen here, it may be that those who actually work in the system have different views than those represented by politicians and support programs, services, and resources to meet inmates' multitude of needs while also normalizing the environment. Evidence suggests that the views of correctional staff are much more tolerant than many politicians and the general public may think they are. . . .

REFERENCES

Applegate, B. (2001). Penal austerity: Perceived utility, desert, and public attitudes toward prison amenities. *American Journal of Criminal Justice, 25,* 253–268.

Applegate, B., Cullen, F. T., Turner, M. G., & Sundt, J. L. (1996). Assessing public support for three-strikes-and-you're-out laws: Global versus specific attitudes. *Crime & Delinquency, 42,* 517–534.

Bryant, P., & Morris, E. (1998). What does the public really think? A survey of the general public's perceptions of corrections yields some surprising results. *Corrections Today, 59,* 26–28, 79.

Bureau of Economic and Business Research. (1997). *Corrections in Florida: What the public, news media, and Department of Corrections staff think.* Available at www.dc.state.fl.us

Champion, D. J. (2005). *The American dictionary of criminal justice.* Los Angeles: Roxbury.

Corrections Compendium. (2002). Inmate privileges and fees for service. *Corrections Compendium, 27,* 8–26.

Cullen, F. T., Fisher, B. S., & Applegate, B. K. (2000). Public opinion about punishment and corrections. In M. Tonry (Ed.), *Crime and justice: A review of research. Vol. 27* (pp. 1–79). Chicago: University of Chicago Press.

Harrison, P., & Beck, A. (2005). *Prison and jail inmates at midyear 2004.* Washington, DC: Bureau of Justice Statistics.

Hensley, C., Miller, A., Tewksbury, R., & Koscheski, M. (2003). Student attitudes toward inmate privileges. *American Journal of Criminal Justice, 27*(2), 249–262.

Hopkins, W. G. (2000). A new view of statistics. *Internet Society for Sport Science*. Retrieved January 23, 2005, from http//www.sportsci.org/resource/stats/

Johnson, W., Bennett, K., & Flanagan, T. (1997). Getting tough on prisoners: Results from the national corrections executive survey, 1995. *Crime & Delinquency, 43,* 24–41.

Keil, T. J., & Vito, G. F. (1991). Fear of crime and attitudes toward capital punishment: A structural equations model. *Justice Quarterly, 8*(4), 447–464.

Lenz, N. (2002). "Luxuries" in prison: The relationship between amenity funding and public support. *Crime & Delinquency, 48,* 499–523.

Whitehead, J. T., & Blankenship, M. B. (2000). The gender gap in capital punishment attitudes: An analysis of support and opposition. *American Journal of Criminal Justice, 25,* 1–13.

REVIEW QUESTIONS

1. How does the principle of least eligibility frame the discussion about whether prison inmates should have access to a variety of goods, services, and programming opportunities?
2. How do the views of correctional staff compare with those of community residents regarding what amenities should and should not be available to prison inmates?
3. What is the most influential variable affecting prison staff members' views of amenities for inmates: type of job, length of time working in corrections or educational level? What would explain this being the most influential on this issue?

READING 19

Drug Abuse Treatment in Prisons and Jails

Carl G. Leukefeld

Frank R. Tims

Drug abuse treatment in correctional settings has a long history in the United States. However, the need for such far outdistances the number of programs and number of available slots/beds in such programs. Several approaches to the provision of drug abuse treatment are currently used in corrections, with no one model establishing itself as particularly better at achieving goals than the others. Evaluations of drug abuse treatment programs in correctional settings are not numerous, and when they are available their results need to be viewed with caution because of methodological challenges and weaknesses in the research. However, there are some universally agreed-upon directions that treatment programs and the larger correctional structures that house such programs should pursue, at least in the eyes of "experts" in drug abuse treatment.

INTRODUCTION

A large number of drug abusers come into contact with the criminal justice system through jails and lockups. The impressions of those who work in prison and jails are supported with data from the Drug Use Forecasting (DUF) system. DUF reports show that approximately 60% of arrestees in 22 major cities were using a drug, other than alcohol, at the time of their arrests (Wish, 1989). In fact, the criminal justice system is awash with drug users, and the need for expanding drug abuse treatment in prisons and jails has been identified.

Prison treatment for drug abuse has a varied history in the United States. Treatment for incarcerated federal offenders formally began with two United States Public Health Service Hospitals, which were opened at Lexington, Kentucky, in 1935 and Fort Worth, Texas, in 1938. It is interesting to note that the need for these federal treatment facilities was first recognized by the Director of the Federal Bureau of Prisons who urged the Congress to establish Narcotic Farms in these locations. These facilities evolved from farms to hospitals to clinical research centers, were transferred from the U.S. Public Health Service, and are now part of the Federal Bureau of Prisons.

Drug abuse treatment in prisons has been influenced by the Therapeutic Community movement, which incorporates former drug users who provide a structured therapeutic environment within a prison. However, prison drug abuse treatment is currently limited. This can be related to the atmosphere that resulted from the antirehabilitation research findings published in the late 1960s (Martinson, 1974). Treatment for drug abusers in jails is even more limited, which should be expected given the brief length of stay (Peters & May, 1992).

For those who are not aware of the limited, but currently expanding, drug abuse treatment programs in the nation's prisons; there is initial shock, followed by the question, "Why?" The response to this question is not simple. It is complicated by both policy and science. The science may be easier to describe than the related policy issues, but it is also complicated. As Lipton, Falkin, and Wexler (1992) suggest, the backlash of antirehabilitation, cited above, which is called the Martinson report (1974) concluded, after reviewing available research from correctional rehabilitation studies, that rehabilitation efforts did not work. Although this interpretation was subsequently reversed after additional study, the report's influence as well as the aftermath for drug abuse treatment in prisons and jails was enormous. New treatment programs were not opened, and existing treatment and rehabilitation programs were also terminated (Murray, 1992).

The current reemphasis on drug abuse treatment in prisons and jails appears to be anchored in the need to do something about the large numbers of drug abusers in prisons. This is complemented with recent research findings that drug abuse treatment is effective (Hubbard, Marsden, Rachael, Cavanaugh, & Ginzburg, 1989). The effectiveness of drug abuse treatment is specifically related to the length of time an individual remains in drug abuse treatment, regardless of the type of treatment. However, along with the recognition must come the realization that drug abuse is both chronic and relapsing once a person is addicted. The chronicity and relapsing aspects of drug abuse often make the effectiveness of drug abuse treatment difficult for many to understand. Viewed from a health perspective, treatment should be followed by "cure" and no drug abuse. Viewed from a correctional perspective, recidivism should be reduced coupled with no drug abuse. These goals are compatible but are frequently implemented differently, often causing tension without meaning to. There is also criticism about the limitations of drug abuse treatment in spite of the research, which has consistently supported the effectiveness of drug abuse treatment (Hubbard, Marsden, Rachael, Cavanaugh, & Ginzburg, 1989) and specifically when combined with criminal justice sanctions (Leukefeld & Tims, 1986).

Experiences related to treating drug abusers in prisons and jails is largely from the United States. Unfortunately, these experiences are closely related to the rapid expansion of drug use in our larger cities and the associated crime, most recently crack cocaine. These "epidemics" strain both correctional facilities and community treatment settings. The current recognition of the expanding drug abuse problem provides criminal justice practitioners with a window of opportunity to establish drug abuse treatment interventions that are documented with research data and supported by practice. In fact, criminal justice practitioners are recognizing the important control function that drug abuse treatment can have in an institution, a major purpose for some and a bonus for others. Whichever reason, this article seeks to add to our knowledge about drug abuse treatment in prisons and jails. . . .

CURRENT STATUS OF DRUG ABUSE TREATMENT IN PRISONS AND JAILS

Lipton, Falkin, and Wexler (1992) overview institutional drug abuse treatment and examine the chronicity of drug abuse. . . . Unfortunately, limited research evidence currently exists to support the effectiveness of drug abuse treatment in prisons, including the most traditional forms of drug abuse treatment such as drug education, self-help groups, individual counseling, group counseling, and milieu therapy. However, therapeutic community research has shown promise, with positive outcomes from the Stay'n Out Program (Wexler, Falkin, Lipton, & Rosenbaum, 1992) and the Cornerstone Program (Field, 1992).

Brown (1992) presents five program models that are available for incarcerated drug abusers in correctional settings: 1) no specialized services, which is most typical, 2) drug education and/or drug abuse counseling, 3) residential units dedicated to drug abuse treatment, 4) client-initiated and/or maintained services, and 5) specialized services for drug abusers not directly targeted at their drug abuse problems. He also discusses three service delivery models that serve as alternatives to incarceration: (a) probation, a mix of counseling, support, and surveillance—which is most typical; (b) surveillance, which includes house arrest and electronic monitoring; and (c) diversion, which is represented by TASC (treatment alternatives to street crime).

Our nation's jails provide a reservoir for drug abusers. A survey completed by the American Jail Association examined the scope of drug abuse treatment services in jails across the county (Peters & May, 1992). With 57% ($N = 1{,}737$) of the jails responding to a mailed questionnaire, only 28% of the responding jails indicated that they offered drug abuse treatment in their jails. Moreover, only 19% indicated that they funded drug treatment programs and only 12% of the drug treatment programs were isolated from the general jail population. In addition, the average jail drug treatment program focused on whites (66% of program participants), had an average size of 42, average age of 26, employed three staff, and over 80% had volunteer staff. Using data from the 1,687 jails that provided inmate census information, only 6.7% of the average inmate population were enrolled in drug treatment. A major conclusion reached by Peters and May is the need for jails to develop liaison with community drug abuse treatment programs, especially for smaller jails.

The AIDS virus is a major problem in the nation's prisons and jails. However, the number of HIV-1 positive individuals in prisons is not as large as initially projected. There is speculation that AIDS education may be more effective for this group than others. By October 1989, 5,411 cases of AIDS were reported from U.S. prisons and jails (Hammett, 1990). Seroprevalence rates also vary by region, with 7% in Maryland and 17.4% in New York. Vlahov (1992) identifies three responses to HIV-1 in correctional settings. One, educating inmates at risk in correctional settings about unlikely routes of transmission, with emphasis on intravenous drug use. Two, serological screening which focuses on inmate identification to start confidential chemotherapeutic protocols. Costs and benefits of such testing must be weighed. Three, treating drug abusers is important for intravenous drug abusers to decrease their needle use. Vlahov (1992) suggests that correctional settings serve as an opportune environment to begin the HIV treatment for these difficult-to-reach individuals.

DRUG ABUSE TREATMENT APPROACHES

Murray (1992) indicates that the Federal Bureau of Prisons (BOP), in order to intervene with the increasing number of drug abusers, is expanding drug abuse interventions. Murray reviews the Bureau's history of providing treatment to drug abusers and then quickly moves to contemporary issues. . . . After reviewing select studies, Murray adds that addiction is a multiplier of crime. With that background, he outlines the Bureau's comprehensive drug abuse treatment strategy, which includes a multitiered approach as well as a comprehensive evaluation, described by Pellissier and McCarthy (1992). The Bureau's layered approach includes one level of drug education, three treatment levels, and one level of transitional services: (a) drug education programs, which will be mandatory for inmates with a substance abuse history; (b) individual, group, and self-help drug abuse counseling services will be available on an outpatient basis to volunteers; (c) comprehensive residential drug treatment units, . . .

Brenna (1992) provides a different perspective of drug abuse treatment by focusing on substance abuse services for juvenile offenders. The State of Washington experience in treating juvenile offenders has developed within the goals of offender accountability, coupled with rehabilitation. Based on this explicit philosophy, the Washington model of integrated services evolved as a continuum of services based on client dysfunction. The integrated service model incorporates (a) inpatient chemical dependency cottages located on institutional campuses; (b) specially trained staff who coordinate and provide treatment services; (c) specifically designed drug education provided by the institutional school programs; (d) chemical dependency assessments by diagnostic staff; and (e) on-site drug detection.

The Florida Department of Corrections has established a four-tiered approach for their Comprehensive Statewide Abuse Program. Bell, Mitchell, Williams, Benvino, and Darabi (1992) indicate that more than 50% of Florida's inmates admit to a serious substance abuse problem. They go on to describe Florida's Tiers program, which commences with an assessment to determine the severity of substance abuse classification and to recommend a treatment level. The four tiers can be described as follows: Tier I is a 40-hour program focused on providing educational drug abuse information for those identified with a less-than-severe substance abuse history, deny having a problem, and have a short sentence; Tier II is an intensive 8-week residential modified therapeutic community program for those diagnosed with a serious drug problem; Tier III is residential therapeutic community treatment for 9 to 12 months in the community provided through contract services for 54 beds available to those who meet work release requirements; Tier IV is 10 weeks of community counseling focused on relapse prevention and supportive therapy for inmates assigned to Community Correctional Centers. These service providers contribute information and use information from the Substance Abusing Offender Treatment Information Network for treatment management. In addition, three types of evaluations are being carried out: (a) screening and assessment to determine, among other things, severity and treatment intervention; (b) process evaluation for program integrity; and (c) outcome evaluation to examine knowledge, attitudes, and behaviors.

Vigdal & Stadler (1992) emphasize the importance of providing a system-wide approach to treating drug-abusing offenders. Using the Wisconsin Department of Corrections as an example, they examine various strategies and programs that support continuity of care. Wisconsin's specialized substance abuse programming began in 1975 with an alcohol treatment unit, with demonstrated effectiveness (Vigdal, Stadler, Goodrick, & Sutton (1980)). Within that context, the current program evolved, which includes an Alternative to Revocation component with 10% of the treatment beds reserved for offenders who are being revoked and for whom no community treatment is available; special treatment programs, one for alcohol and two for drugs other than alcohol; a residential therapeutic community for 9 to 12 months; intensive supervision positions, combined with drug testing for five teams of two officers with a 40-person caseload for each team; and day treatment programs, as an intermediate sanction, for coordinated care with correctional treatment facilities. At the heart of this systems approach are the assessment procedures, which are used to match treatments and offenders along four dimensions: alcohol dependence, other drug involvement, psychiatric impairment, and psychopathic tendencies.

Field (1992) outlines the rich experience and evaluation findings Oregon has had with innovative drug treatment services. The Cornerstone Program, located on the grounds of the Oregon State Hospital, is a 32-bed therapeutic community that began in 1975. With Cornerstone as a model, the state currently funds three additional therapeutic communities, which also partially serve drug abuse offenders who are sex offenders, mentally ill, and mentally or socially retarded. Oregon also supports the following drug abuse interventions: two additional residential treatment programs, correctional institutional group counseling through contracts with community treatment professionals, several cooperative agreements for community treatment, a pilot program with subsidy funds for releases who are poor risks, a demonstration project to examine coordinated community services, the use of Alcoholics Anonymous and Narcotics Anonymous groups, alcohol and drug education classes for alcoholics and addicts, and institutional Information Centers to assist inmate recovery. In addition, all inmates are subject to random urine testing. Research results indicate that Cornerstone clients showed, as a function of the treatment program, enhanced self-esteem, reduced psychiatric symptomatology, increased knowledge in critical treatment areas, reduced criminal activity, and reduced criminal recidivism (Field, 1985). . . .

EVALUATIONS

Wexler, Falkin, Lipton, and Rossenbaum (1992) present data from a study which examines the Stay'n Out therapeutic community program in New York. Using a sample of 1,500 subjects from the program, which has operated in New York's correctional system for over 12 years, they report that prison-based therapeutic community treatment reduced recidivism rates for both males and females. A quasi-experimental design was used to compare the Stay'n Out intervention with inmates who volunteered for the program but never participated, participants in a counseling program, and participants in a milieu therapy program. Parole outcomes are compared for four groups of males and three groups of females. A female milieu treatment comparison group was not available. Three parole outcome variables are reported: the percent arrested, the mean time until first arrest for those arrested, and the percent positively discharged. Based on these analyses, the major finding is that the Stay'n Out therapeutic community was effective in reducing recidivism and that this effect increased as time in program increased, but reduced after 12 months. Positive parole completion, no arrest, and time until arrest increased with time in the therapeutic community but did not increase for the other interventions.

Implementing and evaluating a prison drug treatment program can be complicated by many things. Inciardi, Martin, Lockwood, Hooper, and Wald (1992) review obstacles and present their experiences in implementing Delaware's KEY therapeutic community program. Specific implementation issues cited include a budget that did not include adequate funds for program materials, support services, public relations, and special events; selecting an initial facility that was not conducive and not appropriate for a therapeutic community, which delayed implementation and resulted in selecting another facility; staff recruitment problems that rely on a professional model and prohibit hiring ex-felon addicts; nonspecification of client admission criteria; failure to develop close working relationships with the Delaware Classification Board and other programs; lack of program autonomy; and the lack of aftercare services. Although the program is therapeutically driven rather than research driven, a follow-up evaluation has started. An initial analysis reveals that KEY residents are typically black, older, have had prior treatment, and have used multiple drugs more than the general prison population.

Methadone treatment has not been used by the criminal justice system. Hubbard, Marsden, Rachael, Cavanaugh, and Ginzburg (1989) report that only 3% of persons in methadone treatment were referred by the criminal justice system, compared with about 30% for outpatient drug free and 30% for therapeutic community treatments. In spite of that low referral rate, Magura, Rosenbaum, and Joseph (1992) present research findings from a criminal justice methadone maintenance program called KEEP (Key Extended Entry Program). KEEP was established in 1987 to provide methadone maintenance to addicts charged with misdemeanors at Rikers Island in New York City and to provide referral to community methadone programs with dedicated treatment slots. Reporting on a long-term follow-up study that includes a cohort of 225 KEEP participants and controls, Magura et al. (1992) indicate that KEEP sociodemographic characteristics were similar to those of other Rikers Island prisoners. They were daily cocaine users, more than half (54%) of the injectors reported sharing needles or works in the previous 6 months, and property crimes were their most frequent arrest charge. There was also a high attrition rate, 60% for men and 67% for women, for those not in methadone treatment when released to community treatment.

SPECIAL ISSUES

Transition from institutional settings to the community is difficult for drug offenders. Gregrich (1992) explores issues related to managing the drug-abusing offender and suggests that institutional crowding, driven by the drug-abusing offender, will require community transition and placements. Case management will receive additional attention and could be held accountable for making the criminal justice system work—a responsibility to be avoided. Clearly, there is no unifying voice or group for case management but there are advocates for community services, especially now with planning for additional intermediate sanctions. In addition, Gregrich (1992) posits several principles related to drug abuse treatment: Treatment and coercion work together, drug abuse offenders are harder to treat than others, interventions must focus on the chronic and related deviant behaviors, offender and other drug treatment programs share certain characteristics, intensive surveillance produces results, and interventions must be organized and orthodox.

Continuing with the theme that drug abusers present special risks as they make the transition from the institution to the community, Weinman (1992) suggests that this transition should follow a specific course that monitors drug abuse and other behaviors. TASC, working together with parole, can successfully and systematically intervene with the drug-abusing offender. Case management, through TASC, incorporates the following elements: support, staff training, data collection, client identification based on eligibility criteria, assessment and referral, urinalysis, and monitoring. Weinman (1992) cites several studies that indicate that TASC is successful. She also explores the benefits of a TASC and parole partnership to help avoid prison crowding. She identifies four necessities for managing drug offenders: (a) early identification (b) thorough assessment, (c) substantial monitoring, and (d) unbroken contact; and concludes that these principles define the TASC/Parole partnership.

Fletcher & Tims (1992) explore methodological issues, with emphasis in four areas: treatment outcomes, treatment process, environmental/situational factors, and transitional factors. Treatment outcome studies should focus on specific questions for behavioral change and optional treatment. Treatment process studies should examine which treatment produces behavioral change as well as how treatment can be improved. Environmental and situational factors should incorporate the influence of prison contexts on treatment process and outcomes. Transitional factors should be taken into account, including treatment carry over from the institution to the community and how well institutional treatment prepares for community reentry. Finally, Fletcher and Tims (1992) remind us that research is frequently carried out in a hostile research environment. . . .

RECOMMENDATIONS

The following statements represent areas of agreement reached by the group of criminal justice practitioners and researchers with extensive experience in correctional drug abuse treatment who attended the National Institute on Drug Abuse meeting on Drug Abuse Treatment in Prisons and Jails. The most intense discussion focused around the type and extent of need for drug abuse treatment in correctional settings as well as the types of treatment interventions that should be available to drug abusers in prisons and jails. In addition, discussion related to staffing drug abuse treatment activities with former abusers or professionals was reviewed as a possible anchor point on a continuum, with a middle ground of combining staff as most viable. The specific points of agreement are as follows:

Treatment Interventions

- A continuum of treatment program options, balanced between institutional and community-based treatment interventions, should be available for drug-abusing offenders.
- The unique needs of special population groups, including women and minority offenders, should receive special attention.
- Successful correctional drug abuse treatment programs must have commitment from top administrators and others throughout the relevant organizations to sustain such efforts.
- If programmatic compromises, based on limited and competitive resources, are necessary, then evaluation data should be used to develop cost efficient and integrated service models.
- Program goals should be established that incorporate the primary objective of reducing criminal activity and drug abuse as well as reducing recidivism with secondary or interim objectives of reducing criminal activity and managing inmate behavior. Emphasis should be placed on joint custody within a framework of healing and punishing.
- Although assessment and diagnosis are key to good programming, assessments should be balanced with needed and available treatment services.
- New and innovative service models must be developed and evaluated.
- Drug testing should be part of correctional drug abuse treatment.
- It is suggested that a drug treatment program be physically isolated from the general prison or jail population and that treatment also be available to the general prison population.
- Correctional drug abuse treatment initiatives for juveniles, which are very different from adult drug abuse treatment, need to be developed and expanded.
- Modeling is an important component of drug abuse treatment, and recovering persons have been successful in correctional drug abuse treatment programs.
- Aftercare services should be more than self-help activities (i.e., AA, NA).
- Although therapeutic communities are widely used in prison and jails for the treatment of drug abusers therapeutic community treatment is not the only successful approach to be used in these settings and is not appropriate for all offenders.
- Educational and vocational services should be available.
- Transition from prison to community programs should receive emphasis, including relapse prevention approaches.

Research

- A historical review of past programmatic efforts using meta-analytic procedures should be initiated to add clarity about the impact of correctional drug abuse treatment programs.
- In order to facilitate planning, comprehensive epidemiological studies should be initiated with uniform measurement criteria to examine current patterns and project future patterns of drug abuse.
- A standardized correctional drug abuse treatment topology should be developed that incorporates uniform definitions of treatment and system components (i.e., assessment, education, intervention, treatment, and continuity of care).
- A series of studies might be initiated to develop consistent outcome measures across sites with an eye to developing operational program performance standards.
- A survey of correctional and community programs focused on drug abuse interventions would go a long way toward clarifying the existing universe of services as well as identifying new intervention approaches.
- Further studies of the economic impact of drug abuse on crime should be initiated.
- A series of studies should be carried out that examine the relationship of sequencing surveillance with drug abuse treatment, combined with either probation or parole.

Evaluation

- Program evaluation information and feedback must be given as quickly as possible to intervention staff, because evaluation information can help staff better understand their interventions and can provide guidance for program modifications.
- A large scale and multisite program evaluation should be initiated to examine the long-term efficacy of correctional drug abuse treatment efforts, including institutional and community interventions.
- Treatment comparison and control groups, randomized if possible, should be incorporated into evaluation designs.
- Study dropouts and those persons entering correctional drug abuse treatment programs should be taken into consideration when outcome data are analyzed.
- Quasi-experimental designs with "wait list" controls are a realistic possibility when evaluating correctional drug abuse treatment programs.
- Longitudinal and nested evaluation designs should be initiated to clarify the efficacy of interventions and to better understand drug abuse and criminal careers.
- Evaluation efforts within correctional environments should be planned to take into account such factors as the impact of wellness activities and religious beliefs.
- Studies should be initiated to better understand correctional system dropouts and failures as well as those who refuse treatment.
- Special studies should be initiated to examine the impact of prison drug abuse treatment on long-term inmates.

- Ethnographic studies should be incorporated into evaluations along with systematically reporting anecdotal information.

Demonstrations

- Replicable drug abuse treatment demonstration programs should be initiated in all phases of the criminal justice system.
- Demonstration programs should be initiated to examine the feasibility of establishing model drug abuse treatment initiatives. Such demonstration programs should combine staff training activities for prison facilities that are combined with community-based treatment programs.

Management Information

- A standardized management information system should be developed to provide uniform data for decision making and program evaluation. This information could also be used to garner support from policy makers and to provide uniform data points across all components.

Community Linkage

- Citizen advisory groups should be established to provide suggestions and policy input for correctional drug abuse treatment programs.
- Additional emphasis must be placed on presenting the positive aspects of correctional drug abuse treatment to both consumers and to the general public.
- Joint and interagency linkages, designed to enhance drug abuse interventions, should be developed at all levels.

Training

- As drug treatment is expanded in jails and prisons, additional personnel including former users, correctional officers and professionals must be cross-trained and jointly trained to provide drug abuse treatment.
- Training capacity and uniform training standards should be developed for correctional drug abuse treatment practitioners.
- Internships and research training should be available to encourage a new generation of researchers who are interested and committed to correctional research and evaluation in the area of drug abuse.

Technical Assistance

- A centralized and ongoing technical assistance effort should be established and standardized criteria developed pertaining to client variables, program variables, process variables, and outcome measures for correctional drug abuse settings.

Funding

- Adequate funding should be stable and consistent to provide institutional drug abuse treatment linked with community treatment.

REFERENCES

Bell, W.C., Mitchell, J.G., Williams, B.T., Benvino, J., & Darabi, A. (1992). Florida Department of Corrections substance abuse programs. In C.G. Leukefeld & F.M. Tims (eds.), *Drug abuse treatment in prisons and jails* (pp. 110–125). Washington, DC: U.S. Government Printing Office.

Brenna, D. (1992). Substance abuse services in juvenile justice: The Washington experience. In C.G. Leukefeld & F.M. Tims (Eds.), *Drug abuse treatment in prisons and jails* (pp. 99–109). Washington, DC: U.S. Government Printing Office.

Brown, B.S. (1992). Program models. In C.G. Leukefeld & F.M. Tims (Eds.), *Drug abuse treatment in prisons and jails* (pp. 31–37). Washington, DC: U.S. Government Printing Office.

Field, G. (1985). The cornerstone program: A client outcome study. *Federal Probation,* 49, 50–55.

Field, G. (1992). Oregon prison drug treatment programs. In C.G. Leukefeld & F.M. Tims (Eds.), *Drug abuse treatment in prisons and jails* (pp. 142–155). Washington, DC: U.S. Government Printing Office.

Fletcher, B., & Tims, F.M. (1992). Methodological issues in researching drug abuse treatment in prisons and jails. In C.G. Leukefeld & F.M. Tims (Eds.), *Drug abuse treatment in prisons and jails* (pp. 246–260). Washington, DC: U.S. Government Printing Office.

Gregrich, R.J. (1992). Management of the drug abusing offender. In C. G. Leukefeld & F.M. Tims (Eds.), *Drug abuse treatment in prisons and jails* (pp. 211–231). Washington, DC: U.S. Government Printing Office.

Hammett, T.M. (1990). *Update 1989: AIDS in correctional facilities.* Washington, DC: National Institute of Justice.

Hubbard, R.L., Marsden, M.E., Rachal, J.V., Cavanaugh, E.R., & Ginzburg, H.M. (1989). *Drug abuse treatment: A national study of effectiveness.* Chapel Hill, NC, and London: University of North Carolina Press.

Iniardi, J.A., Martin, S.S., Lockwood, D., Hooper. R.M., & Wald, B.M. (1992). Obstacles to the implementation and evaluation of drug treatment programs in corrections, settings: Reviewing the Delaware KEY Experience. In C.G. Leukefeld & F.M. Tims (Eds.), *Drug abuse treatment in prisons and jails* (pp. 176–191). Washington, DC: U.S. Government Printing Office.

Leukefeld, C.G., & Tims, F.M. (Eds.). (1988). *Cumpulsory treatment for drug abuse: Research and clinical practice* (NIDA Research Monograph #86). Washington, DC: U.S. Government Printing Office.

Lipton, D.S., Falkin, G.P., & Wexler, H.K. (1992). Correctional drug abuse treatment in the United States. In C.G. Leukefeld & F.M. Tims (Eds.), *Drug abuse treatment in prisons and jails* (pp. 8–30). Washington, DC: U.S. Government Printing Office.

Magura, S., Rosenbaum, A., & Joseph, H. (1992). Evaluation of in-jail methadone maintenance: Preliminary results. In C.G. Leukefeld & F.M. Tims (Eds.), *Drug abuse treatment in prisons and jails* (pp. 192–210). Washington, DC: U.S. Government Printing Office.

Martinson, R. (1974). What works? Questions and answers about prison reform. *The Public Interest,* 35, 22–54.

Murray, D.W. (1992). Drug abuse treatment programs in the Federal Bureau of Prisons: Initiatives for the 90's. In C.G. Leukefeld & F.M. Tims (Eds.), *Drug abuse treatment in prisons and jails* (pp. 62–83). Washington, DC: U.S. Government Printing Office.

Pellissier, B., & McCarthy, D. (1992). Evaluation of the Federal Bureau of Prison's drug treatment programs. In C.G. Leukefeld & F.M. Tims (Eds.), *Drug abuse treatment in prisons and jails* (pp. 261–278). Washington, DC: U.S. Government Printing Office.

Peters, R., & May, B. (1992). Drug treatment services in jails. In C.G. Leukefeld & F.M. Tims (Eds.), *Drug abuse treatment in prisons and jails* (pp. 38–50). Washington, DC: U.S. Government Printing Office.

Vigdal, G.L., & Stadler, D.W. (1992). Comprehensive system development in corrections for drug abusing offenders: The Wisconsin Department of Corrections. In C.G. Leukefeld & F.M. Tims (Eds.), *Drug abuse treatment in prisons and jails* (pp. 126–141). Washington, DC: U.S. Government Printing Office.

Vigdal, G.L., Stadler, D.W., Goodrick, D.D., & Sutton, D.J. (1980). Skills training in a program for problem-drinking offenders: A one year follow up evaluation. *Journal of Offender Counseling Rehabilitation,* 5: 61–73.

Vlahov, D. (1992). HIV-1 infection in the correctional setting. In C.G. Leukefeld & F.M. Tims (Eds.), *Drug abuse treatment in prisons and jails* (pp. 51–61). Washington, DC: U.S. Government Printing Office.

Weinman, B. (1992). A coordinated approach for drug abusing offenders: TASC and parole. In C.G. Leukefeld & F.M. Tims (Eds.), *Drug abuse treatment in prisons and jails* (pp. 232–245). Washington. DC: U.S. Government Printing Office.

Wexler, H.K., Falkin, G.P., Lipton, D., & Rosenbaum, A.B. (1992). Outcome evaluation of a prison therapeutic community for substance abuse treatment. In C.G. Leukefeld & F.M. Tims (Eds.), *Drug abuse treatment in prisons and jails* (pp. 156–175). Washington, DC: U.S. Government Printing Office.

Winett, D.L., Mullen, R., Lowe, L.L., & Missakian, E.A. (1992). Amity/Right turn: A State of California demonstration drug abuse treatment program for inmates and parolees. In C.G. Leukefeld & F.M. Tims (Eds.), *Drug abuse treatment in prisons and jails* (pp. 84–98). Washington, DC: U.S. Government Printing Office.

Wish, E.D., & O'Neil, J.A. (1989, September). *Drug use forecasting (DUF) research update, January to March, 1989.* Washington, DC: National Institute of Justice.

REVIEW QUESTIONS

1. How well does the availability of drug abuse treatment in prisons and jails meet the need for such services?
2. Based on the evaluation studies of correctional drug abuse treatment programs, how well do such programs work?
3. Based on the recommendations of experts in drug abuse treatment, what are the major issues/themes that run through the consensus recommendations that are presented in the reading?

VIII

HEALTH CARE ISSUES

READING 20

Health Condition and Prisoners

A Review of Research and Emerging Areas of Inquiry

James W. Marquart

Dorothy E. Merianos

Jaimie L. Hebert

Leo Carroll

In this article, the authors compare the health conditions of prison inmates to those of individuals in the poorest strata of society, noting numerous deficiencies that exist for the inmate group. The authors contend that various failures in public health systems in the community lead to a situation where inmates arrive at prison with myriad health problems, all of which require treatment. As a result, the costs of providing Constitutionally required health care adds millions of dollars to the costs of corrections. Discussion of the causes, consequences, and some possible responses to such a situation are provided.

Expansion of the prisoner population, which now numbers more than 1 million, has been relentless since the 1980s and shows no signs of diminishing. Much of the growth can be attributed to the public's increased fear of crime and resulting crime and drug wars initiated in the 1980s. In response to anticrime concerns, numerous states (e.g., Alaska, California, Connecticut, Georgia, Idaho, Mississippi, Missouri, Nebraska, New Jersey, Ohio, Pennsylvania, South Carolina, Virginia, Washington) have enacted legislation calling for lengthy determinate sentences, the elimination of good time, and "truth-in-sentencing" (Mendelsohn, 1995). Current criminal justice policy making will no doubt increase this nation's prisoner population.

Discussions about the growth of the prisoner population consistently dwell on the costs of prison construction and custody. In fiscal year 1995, the nation's 52 correctional agencies cost $21 billion to operate (e.g., staff, programs, equipment, training, food) (Camp & Camp, 1995). Correctional spending is now the fastest growing item in state government (Senna & Siegel, 1995), Prisoner health care and prison health care delivery systems, however, represent "hidden costs" that legislators, correctional managers, and the public at large have so far disregarded but will have to make some serious choices about in the not so distant future.

Moreover, correctional personnel in three state prison systems have claimed that there has been a major decline over the past decade in the overall health of inmates entering their prison systems (Belbot, Cuvelier, & Marquart, 1995), Although specific empirical data are not readily available to test this assertion, these officials' perceptions are indirectly supported by public health data that show "American men's and women's health has worsened since the late 1950s, especially since the 1970s" (Verbrugge, 1984). The implications of this general decline in the health status of Americans, especially among the urban poor, loom large for prison organizations.

The idea that health "matters" for prison organizations is clearly illustrated in the case of HIV. In 1992, the HIV incidence rate among the U.S. population was 18 cases per 100,000, whereas the rate among prisoners was estimated to be 362 per 100,000 (McDonald, 1995). This large differential can be traced to the recent "War on Drugs" in which large numbers of injection drug users were incarcerated (Blumberg, 1990). Further, in the New York, Florida, California, and Texas prison systems, AIDS is the leading cause of death among prisoners and an increasingly expensive focus of the prison health care delivery system (Hopper, 1995; Lyons, Griefinger, & Flanery, 1994; Weiner & Anno, 1992). . . . Death in prison today (especially in large prison systems) is far more likely to result from AIDS-related complications than from lethal assaults, work-related accidents, or executions. Costs associated with housing an increasing number of HIV-positive inmates are incurred through hospitalization of those who are gravely ill as well as through the use of antiretroviral drug therapy (McDonald, 1995).

The point here is that criminal justice policy making affects not only who goes to prison but also the level and type of health care that prison organizations must deliver to prisoners. Given the current climate in criminal justice policy making, it is time to take stock of what we know about the physical health status of inmates at admission, their utilization of health services while incarcerated, the consequences of incarceration on health condition, and the various options open to policy makers in the face of rising prisoner populations and accompanying health care costs.

This article extends previous work on health-related issues in prison organizations in three primary ways: (a) It presents a conceptual model by which to explore and explain the health condition of prisoners during incarceration (including morbidity/mortality); (b) it reviews relevant research on inmate health condition at admission, utilization of prison health services, health condition while in prison, and proposes a research agenda on prisoner health issues; and (c) it explores options open to policy makers. The article demonstrates that continued declines in the health status of the American population in general, and the poor specifically, coupled with punitive sentencing policies, will strain correctional health care delivery systems.

CONCEPTUAL FRAMEWORK

An important contribution of research on the criminal justice system is the identification of background characteristics of persons brought into the system and an examination of how the system affects their lives. To accomplish this goal as it relates to prisoners, researchers must come to understand health condition and ultimately morbidity/mortality within correctional populations as an outcome linked to personal attributes, acquired risks, biological risks, efforts at self-care, and the severity of injuries, diseases, and stressors of daily life on the streets—the pre-institutional dimension. In short, scholars must examine the health condition of prisoners prior to confinement and explore how prisoner health condition during confinement is affected by confinement.

To guide future thinking and inquiry on prisoner health issues in general, and morbidity/mortality specifically, we need a conceptual framework. We suggest a broad "public health" perspective to organize the relevance of past literature, identify key concepts and the multiple dimensions of health condition, and generate questions and hypotheses for research. Our conceptual model is based on Verbrugge's (1985) research on the relationship between gender and health.

In general, the model suggests that morbidity and mortality in prison is affected by numerous noninstitutional and institutional forces. To capture a series of health transitions, the model incorporates the life course perspective because it links health-related factors in the free world to health conditions in the prison and beyond (Elder, 1974). The life course perspective would specify an interaction effect between personal attributes, acquired risks in the free society, and the prevalence of disease and injury in prison. For instance, male offenders sentenced to prison for drug-related crimes may have higher rates of morbidity and utilize correctional health services more often than male prisoners sentenced to prison for embezzlement, credit card abuse, or income tax evasion. Drug offenders (especially injection drug users) represent high "health risks" inside due to risky lifestyles on the outside. . . .

Over the life course, an individual's lifestyle and health habits bear directly on his or her risk of disease, illness, and injury. Job-related injuries, household tasks, management and reaction to stress, and social bonds affect an individual's health condition. Men are more likely than women to engage in activities that pose health risks. Although tobacco use has declined in the general population, it has remained constant among persons with less than a high school education and for those employed in blue-collar jobs. Health risks and socioeconomic status are strongly related, with poverty being a predisposing factor in high blood pressure (and heart disease and stroke). Low-income persons are more likely to acquire and be exposed to health risks across their life course (House et al., 1990)

A prisoner's health condition is also affected by the prison context. Our prison health model suggests inmates are exposed to a whole new set of circumstances and experiences that influence and precipitate changes in health condition and morbidity. For example, inmates housed in areas of extreme confinement (e.g., administrative segregation, protective custody, death row) may experience higher levels of stress, risks, and hazards than inmates confined in general population or lower custody/security grades. Prisoners working in industrial areas or in plants utilizing fibers (e.g., cotton products, metal working operations) may be exposed to environmental risks (e.g., noise, pesticides, airborne pollutants) that may precipitate different patterns of morbidity than inmates working in nonindustrial areas. Prisoners also live and work with inmates carrying deadly diseases (e.g., HIV, TB), and this exposure represents a high risk for transmission within penal settings.

We model the process by which morbidity and mortality in prison are strongly influenced by a prisoner's personal attributes and other social structural components including gender, age, race/ethnicity, family background, and socioeconomic status. Research too must include the prison context. In short, the model underscores the complex relationship between population morbidity/mortality and the incidence and prevalence of disease and injury in the prisoner population in the past, present, and future. The model is incomplete and does not specify or account for all interactions. Scholars can add constructs and variables, or rearrange the ordering where appropriate. We view the model as a device to sensitize scholars about the complex nature of health condition and morbidity/mortality within penal settings—an area nearly devoid of systematic inquiry.

AN AGENDA FOR RESEARCH

Most inmates, because of their background, bring a constellation of health risks to the prison setting. The following sections review the extant literature on inmate health. Each section represents a specific area of inquiry in relation to the conceptual model.

The American Prisoner and Health at Admission to Prison

Over the last several decades, research has clearly established that most offenders admitted to prison are (a) male, (b) non-White, (c) poorly educated and of low socioeconomic status, (d) prior drug users, (e) unattached, (f) between the ages of 17 and 30, and (g) from metropolitan areas (Braith-waite, 1989; Duster, 1987; Good & Pirog-Good, 1987; Rieman, 1990). More state prisoners reside in southern prisons (Bureau of Justice Statistics, 1993; Perkins, 1994). Prisoners are disproportionately from "underclass" areas typified by limited job opportunities and social isolation in impoverished neighborhoods (Wilson, 1993). Coincidentally, most prisoners come from that segment of the American population that public health researchers have found to possess the poorest health condition.

Frank Rector (1929) conducted the first systematic prison health study when he surveyed the medical conditions in American penitentiaries. Since his research, scholars have examined health care standards in prisons (Dubler, 1986), the health care demands of women prisoners (McGaha, 1987), mortality among prisoners (King, & Whitman, 1981), elderly prisoners (Dugger, 1988), the health risks of imprisonment (Jones, 1976), and the management of infectious diseases in correctional settings (Blumberg, 1990). Despite the diversity of this inquiry, scholars have not systematically analyzed prisoner health characteristics at admission (Novick & Al-lbrahim, 1977). What we know comes primarily from studies of jail inmates.

Raba and Obis (1983) examined health conditions of male admissions (N = 987) at the Cook County Jail in Chicago. They collected data through physical exams on inmates' medical condition, psychiatric referrals, surgical history, blood pressure, genitourinary abnormalities, drug history, and tuberculin tests. After analyzing the data, they concluded that:

> The admissions were young and largely members of minority groups. In spite of the young overall age, over 17% were on chronic medication for asthma, hypertension, psychosis, diabetes mellitus, or seizure disorder. The group was found to have a high incidence of tobacco, alcohol, and drug use. Psychoses, venereal diseases, seizure disorders, asthma, hypertension, tuberculosis contacts, and post-trauma sequaelae were detected in higher incidence than found nationally. (p. 21)

Fitzgerald, D'Atri, Kasl, and Ostfeld (1984) examined the health condition of 366 male prisoners in a Massachusetts house of corrections. Data were collected from inmate self-reports on current and past medical complaints. They found that:

> Psychological problems, trauma, oral diseases, and the use of alcohol, tobacco, and illicit drugs were the most frequent health conditions observed or reported among these male prisoners at intake. . . . [The self report data] support the contention that these young male prisoners suffered disproportionately from poor health. . . . [Most] were predominantly of low socioeconomic status. . . . Lifestyle factors also are involved. The frequent use of alcohol and illicit drugs among these men, for instance, may explain their relatively high prevalences of hepatitis and seizure disorders, (p. 63)

Finally, the researchers concluded that the inmate subjects, compared to the noninstitutionalized U.S. population, had higher prevalence rates of TB, tobacco use, epilepsy, heroin use, diabetes, asthma, barbiturate use, high blood pressure, amphetamine use, ulcers, alcoholism, and arthritis (Fitzgerald, et al., 1984). Whalen and Lyons (1962), Jones (1976), King and Whitman (1981), Derro (1978), Litt and Cohen (1974), Baird (1977), Twaddle (1976), and Novick, Della Penna, Schwartz, Remmlinger, and Loewenstein (1977) have corroborated these findings. Fogel (1988) reported a similar pattern among women prisoners in a southern prison.

One overlooked aspect of the overall health condition of prisoners at admission concerns psychological impairments. This is particularly noteworthy in view of a 1980 Comptroller General report finding that "on any given day, some 20–60 percent of jail inmates have mental health problems" (Krefft & Brittain, 1983). Fitzgerald et al. (1984) found, in their study of health problems in a cohort of male prisoners, that 52% reported psychological problems at an intake medical history review. More recently, Olderman-Jones (1992) found that nearly 20% of a sample of jail inmates had, prior to confinement, contacts (for personal/legal reasons) with the public mental health system and/or state psychiatric hospitals. Most important, the jail inmates who had been mental health clients stayed in jail longer and had more prior arrests than inmates who had not been clients of the mental health system (Olderman-Jones, 1992).

These findings raise the issue of a critical latent consequence that resulted from the policies of deinstitutionalization in the 1960s and the 1970s. Many mentally disabled persons were (and are today) incarcerated because the jail was the only resource in the community for handling these offenders (Steadman, Monahan, Duffee, Harstone, & Robbins, 1984; Teplin, 1983). Some mentally disabled offenders eventually go to prison. Although researchers (Halleck, 1986) estimate that as many as 20% of state inmates need psychiatric treatment at some point during confinement, the exact number of disturbed offenders in prison is unknown. Adams (1992) suggests that our prisons contain prisoners who look like typical mental health clients rather than hardened criminals. The extent to which mentally disabled prisoners are admitted to prison and their physical health condition at admission are important issues in light of the explosion of the prisoner population. . . .

Utilization of Prison Health Services and Health Condition While in Prison

Prison health utilization studies, excluding dental visits, report usage rates ranging from 18.5 visits per inmate per year (Fitzgerald et al., 1984) to 17.8 (Twaddle, 1976) to 7.7 (Derro, 1978). Sheps, Schechter, and Prefontaine (1987) found that Canadian prisoners averaged 5.2 health encounters per prisoner over 12 months or "2.4 times higher than the mean annual physician visit rate for noninstitutionalized men in Canada" (p. 4). In these studies, the researchers did not control for age, sex, or institutional context Research has indicated that African American prisoners have the highest utilization rates, In spite of these problems with the data, it can be inferred that inmates utilize prison medical services at greater rates than the noninstitutionalized population (Suls, Gaes, & Philo, 1991). . . .

Research has shown that women prisoners, like their free-world counterparts, utilize health care services more often than do men ("National Commission Accredits," 1994). Compounding this is the finding that women are more likely than men to use addictive drugs (e.g., heroin and crack, cocaine). In a 1991 survey of state prison inmates, 21.8% of females, compared to 13.7% of males, responded they had used heroin frequently. Crack cocaine use showed similar use patterns. Of females. 22.6% admitted they had regularly used crack cocaine; 12.4% of the males reported regular use (Bureau of Justice Statistics, 1992). . . .

Consequences of Confinement

Ample support exists in the research literature for the stress/illness connection (Rabkin & Struening, 1976). life in prison affords a chronically stressful environment, with its coerced regimentation, loss of control, and daily potential for violence. In their 1982 study examining the relationship between inmates' life stressors and upper respiratory illness, McClelland, Alexander, and Marks (1982) found that those inmates who reported more "aggravations, worries and sources of stress" had more respiratory illness. This mirrors the findings of Suls et al. (1991) who observed a connection between negative life events and increased clinic use by inmates at the time of the life stressor and in the months following.

Another important institutional issue concerns an inmate's health status across the confinement period. What are the health-related consequences of incarceration? Wallace, Klein-Saffran, Gaes, and Moritsugu (1991) examined a sample of Federal Bureau of Prison inmates at admission and at release to assess changes in their overall health condition. They found that 9 out of 10 inmates experienced no change in their health status during incarceration, whereas 4% showed improvement and 6% worsened. Due to long histories of illicit drug use, Hispanic inmates were more likely to exhibit a decline in health status during confinement General population inmates classified in high-security statuses were more likely to experience a worsening in health status during confinement (Wallace et al., 1991).

To control rebellious and violent inmates, prison systems have traditionally relied on isolation and/or administrative segregation. The trend today, however, has been the construction of "super-max" units (e.g., Marion, Pelican Bay) that employ sophisticated technology, isolation, and architecture to control recalcitrant prisoners (Haney, 1993), These units isolate the inmate and also eliminate human contact. The concomitant sensory deprivation, isolation, and stress of this form of confinement may actually increase health problems and utilization. Preliminary evidence suggests that the Pelican Bay experiment for some inmates led to social withdrawal, an inability to initiate behavior, high levels of frustration, and the creation of alternative realities to cope and survive (Haney, 1993). The full impact of these conditions of confinement on the physical and mental health of prisoners has yet to be systematically examined by prison scholars.

One consequence of incarceration is simply the risk of living in prison. We know that prison is a stressful place and the potential for violence and victimization is high (Johnson, 1996). Another risk of living in prison is exposure to diseases, notably tuberculosis and HIV. We know that HIV is transmitted when virus particles or infected cells gain direct access to the bloodstream. This can occur from all forms of sexual intercourse as well as oral-genital contact with an infected partner and needle sharing, practices that although forbidden in prisons, do occur (Auerbach, Wypijewska, & Brodie, 1994). . . .

Implications of Prisoner Health Condition for Policy

An important policy area of concern will be the costs associated with prison medical care. We briefly examined public health expenditures and found that the per capita cost of correctional health care far exceeds similar figures in free world health care spending (U.S. Congress, Office of Technology Assessment, 1993). Per capita health expenditures for all prisons have been consistently higher than free world public funding (federal and state monies).

We also projected costs (crude estimates based on linear regression models) for the seven largest U.S. prison systems (California, Florida, Georgia, Illinois, New York, Ohio, and Texas). Whereas free world public spending and spending for all prison systems are increasing at comparable rates, health care spending is escalating more rapidly for these seven systems. Health costs for these systems began to rise in the late 1980s, around the same time HIV began to grow in epidemic proportions, particularly in the New York, Texas, and California systems (Brien & Harlow, 1995; Hammett, Harold, Gross, & Epstein, 1994). . . .

The rising cost of prison medical care will almost certainly force prison managers to seek alternatives or redistribute the cost burdens to other state agencies. For example, correctional policy makers may resort to enacting legislation to release large numbers of long-term prisoners. Alternatively, correctional policy analysts may also conduct research on the "health trajectories" of high-risk, high-cost prisoners such as those with HIV to determine the point at which an *individual's* health care costs exceed ordinary confinement costs and then seek to have "costly" prisoners released and cared for by community health services.

Another policy option available to contain prisoner medical costs is the copayment system. . . . Copayment plans have been found to reduce health costs (Brien & Harlow, 1995; Hammett et al., 1994). In Virginia, a copayment program was recently implemented and raised $32,000 in the first month of operation and "reduced inmate sick calls by about 35%" ("Thirteen Facilities Awarded," 1995; "VA Copayment Plan Yields," 1995).

The trend will certainly be toward copayment programs. However, a no-pay-no-care system would violate the deliberate indifference standard set forth in *Gamble* and might actually discourage inmates with legitimate problems from reporting them. Case law on this issue is sparse and represents a new area for judicial scrutiny. Other methods could be used to trim medical costs, including obtaining physicians' services at reduced costs, expanding the roles of paraprofessionals and RNs, enacting price controls, operating hospitals within prison systems instead of purchasing services from community hospitals, and negotiating aggressively better prices for pharmaceuticals and other services (McDonald, 1995).

Prison systems will also seek to cut costs through privatizing prisoner health services. Recently, the state of Texas created a managed health care system in which the prison system contracts with two public state medical schools to provide medical services to inmates, the University of Texas Medical Branch and the Texas Tech University Health Sciences Center (Caruso, 1995). Like health maintenance organizations in the public sector, the prison health providers will seek to contain costs. To this end, they have implemented telemedicine and other cost reduction measures as strategies to cut $100 million from the Texas Department of Criminal Justice budget over the next 2 years (Mooney & Mendelsohn, 1995). How and to what extent private vendors can balance the constitutional obligation to provide health care and at the same time contain costs while remaining profitable is a question that deserves serious attention.

In 1994, the National Commission on Correctional Health Care (NCCHC) reported that 280 correctional facilities had earned accreditation status; 13 more were accredited in 1995 (National Commision on Correctional Health Care, 1995). The American Correctional Association established standards for voluntary accreditation of prisons in 1978 and since then more than 1,500 correctional facilities (including 363 adult correctional institutions and programs) have been accredited (American Correctional Association, Commission for Accreditation for Corrections, 1995). Both organizations expect an increase in the number of institutions seeking accreditation in the near future.

Maintaining an accredited facility or prison system may well be too costly and force some agencies to relinquish accreditation. Increasing health care costs coupled with the costs of complying with standards may force some agencies to rethink the overall worth of accreditation. Ironically, accreditation may also be locking present prison managers into providing health services that surpass free world care and may be beyond current fiscal and programmatic realities.

Accreditation standards define what is acceptable from a medical point of view, not what is the best care. Legal standards, however, define the absolute minimum below which the lack of care would be considered to be cruel and unusual punishment. This was made clear in *Brown v. Beck* (1980), which held that the medical care provided to prisoners need not be "perfect, the best obtainable or even very good." All the courts require is that the medical care provided be reasonable. . . .

To date, there exists a considerable gap between what correctional and medical professional associations would like to see in prisons and what courts will allow. Moreover, there is further consideration of the legal standard employed to assess liability. Although *Estelle v. Gamble* created an obligation to provide for serious medical needs, it did so in the negative by prohibiting deliberate indifference to serious medical needs (1976). Most recently in *Farmer v. Brennan* (1994), the Supreme Court held that deliberate indifference occurred when officials knew of a substantial risk of harm and recklessly disregarded that risk; officials must consciously know that a condition or set of conditions pose a substantial risk to inmate health or safety and must be shown to have recklessly disregarded that risk.

This ruling seems to give prison officials considerable room to maneuver as the cost of health care increases. Suppose, for example, medical staffing is grossly inadequate because the legislature refuses to appropriate the funds needed to hire the necessary physicians and nurses despite requests from prison officials. Does that mean there is no deliberate indifference? In a recent case, a federal appeals court ruled in favor of prison medical personnel who had prescribed an ineffective antibiotic treatment for an inmate with severe asthma despite the fact that more appropriate and costly medication may have saved the inmate's life. The court held that the physicians may have been negligent but not deliberately indifferent (*Adams v. Poag,* 1995). . . .

CONCLUSION

. . . We have shown that there is considerable overlap between the health condition of individuals in poverty and those in the incarcerated population. Federal policies designed to improve the health conditions of the poor must include prisoners. Improvements in the health condition of prisoners during confinement will be felt in the urban society at large (Schilling et al., 1994).

Nearly two decades ago, James Jacobs (1977) suggested the prison was an institution affected by social trends and processes far beyond the walls. His notion of the prison in mass society is important for understanding the link between health inequalities in the "free world" and their parallels within the prison community. Scholars and policy makers can no longer ignore the relationship between fundamental social and health inequalities, health condition, and the administration of justice, because this relationship has powerful implications for the way we treat criminal offenders. We hope that future research on prisoner health issues can be used to answer perennial questions about the goals of incarceration and expand our knowledge about the consequences of confinement. An improved understanding of the health condition and behavior of offenders in the free world would be of assistance in the rational planning of crime control policies and preventive and corrective interventions.

REFERENCES

Adams v. Poag, 61 F.3d 1537 (11th Cir, 1995).

Adams, K. (1992). Who are the clients? *The Prison Journal, 72,* 120–141.

Aday, R. (1994). Golden years behind bars. *Federal Probation, 58,* 47–54.

American Correctional Association, Commision for Accreditation for Corrections, (1995). *Accredited facilities and programs.* Laurel, MD: Author.

Anno, B. (1990). The cost of correctional health care: Results of a national survey. *Journal of Jail and Prison Health, 9,* 105–127.

Auerbach, J., Wypijewsks, C., & Brodie, H. (1994). *AIDS and behavior: An integrated approach.* Washington, DC: National Academy Press.

Baird, J. (1977). Health care in correctional facilities. *Journal of Florida Medical Association, 64,* 813–818.

Belbot, B., Cuvelier, S., & Marquart, J. (1995). *Assessing current prisoner classification systems, legal environments, and technological developments. Final Report,* Unpublished manuscript, National Institute of Justice.

Belbot, B., & Del Carmen, R. (1991). AIDS in prison: Legal issues. *Crime and Delinquency, 37,* 134–153.

Blumberg, M. (1990). Issues and controversies with respect to the management of AIDS in corections. In M. Blumberg (Ed.), *AIDS: The impact of the criminal justice system.* Washington, DC: National Institute of Justice.

Braithwaite, J. (1989). *Crime, shame, and reintegration.* Cambridge: Cambridge University Press.

Brien, P., & Harlow, C. (1995). HIV in prisons and jails, 1993. *Bureau of Justice Statistics Bulletin.* Washington, DC: U.S. Department of Justice.

Brown v. Beck, 481 F. Supp 723 (S.D. GA 1980).

Bureau of Justice Statistics. (1992). *Drugs, crime, and the justice system.* Washington, DC: U.S. Government Printing Office.

Bureau of Justice Statistics. (1993). *Survey of state prison inmates, 1992.* Washington, DC: U.S. Department of Justice.

Camp, G., & Camp, C. (1995). *Corrections yearbook.* South Salem, NY: Criminal Justice Institute.

Camp, G., & Camp, C. (1986–1995). *Corrections yearbook.* South Salem, NY: Criminal Justice Institute.

Caruso, K. (1995). Correctional managed health care in the state of Texas. *CorrectCare, 9,* 6.

Centers for Disease Control and Prevention. (1995). HIV/AIDS surveillance report, 21. Atlanta, GA: Public Health Service, U.S. Department of Health and Human Services.

Department of Health and Human Services. (1990). *Healthy people 2000.* Washington, DC: U.S. Government Printing Office.

Derro, R. (1978). Admission health evaluation of inmates of a city-county workhouse. *Minnesota Medicine, 61,* 333–337.

Dubler, N. (1986). *Standards for health services in correctional institutions.* Washington, DC: American Public Health Association, Prisons and Jails Task Force.

Dugger, R. (1988, June). The graying of America's prisons. *Corrections Today,* pp. 26–34.

Duster, T. (1987). Crime, youth unemployment and the underclass. *Crime and Delinquency, 33,* 300–316.

Elder, G. (1974). *Children of the great depression.* Chicago, IL: University of Chicago Press.

Enter, J. (1995, June/July). Aging populations in a correctional facility. *Corrections Managers' Report,* pp. 11, 15.

Estelle v. Gamble, 429 U.S. 97 (1976).

Farmer v. Brennan, 112 U.S. 1970 (1994).

Fasano, C., & Anno, B. (1988, Spring). Health care accreditation—Is it worth it? *American Jails,* pp. 24–28.

Feinstein, J. (1993). The relationship between socioeconomic status and health: A review of the literature. *Milbank Quarterly, 71,* 279–322.

Fitzgerald, E., D'Atri, D., Kasl, S., & Ostfeld, A. (1984). Health problems in a cohort of male prisoners at intake and during incarceration. *Journal of Jail and Prison Health, 4,* 61–76.

Fogel, C. (1988). Expecting in prison: Preparing for birth under conditions of stress. *Journal of Obstetrics and Gynecology and Neonatal Nursing, 15,* 454–458.

Goetting, A. (1983). The elderly in prison: Issues and perspectives. *Journal of Research in Crime and Delinquency, 2,* 291–309.

Goffiman, E. (1961). *Asylums.* Garden City, NJ: Anchor.

Good, D., & Pirog-Good, M. (1987). A simultaneous probit model of crime and employment for Black and White teenage males. *The Review of Black Political Economy, 16,* 109–127.

Graves, E. (1995). 1993 Summary: National hospital discharge survey. *U.S. Department of Health and Human Services.* Advance Data 264. Hyattsville, MD: National Center for Health Statistics.

Halleck, S. (1986). The mentally disordered offender. Hyattsville, MD: National Institute of Mental Health.

Hammett, T., Harold, L., Gross, M., & Epstein, J. (1994). 1992 Update: HIV/AIDS in correctional facilities. Washington, DC: National Institute of Justice.

Haney, C. (1993). Infamous punishment. *National Prison Project, 8,* 3–7, 21.

Hopper, L. (1995, September 16). Biggest killer in Texas prisons: AIDS. *Austin American-Statesman,* p. 1.

House, J., Kessler, R., Herzog, A., Mero, R., Kinney, A., & Breslow, M. (1990). Age, socioeconomic status, and health. *The Milbank Quarterly, 68,* 383–411.

Inciardi, J. (1996). *Criminal justice.* Ft. Worth, TX: Harcourt Brace.

Jacobs, J. (1977). *Stateville.* Chicago, IL: University of Chicago Press.

Johnson, R. (1996). *Hard time.* Belmont. CA: Wadsworth.

Jones, D. (1976). *Health risks of imprisonment.* Lexington, MA: Lexington Books.

Kart, C. & Dunkle, R. (1989). Assessing capacity for self-care among the aged. *Journal of Aging and Health, 1*(4), 430–450.

King, L., & Whitman, S. (1981). Morbidity and mortality among prisoners: An epidemiologic review. *Journal of Prison Health, 1,* 7–29.

Krefft, K., & Brittain, T. (1983). A prisoner assessment survey: Screenings of a municipal prison population. *International Journal of Law and Psychiatry, 6,* 113–124.

Lilienfeld, A. (1976). *Foundations of epidemiology.* New York: Oxford University Press.

Litt, I., & cohen M. (1974). Prisons, adolescents, and the right to quality medical care. *American Journal of Public Health, 64,* 894–897.

Lyons, J., Griefinger, R., & Flanery, T. (1994). *Deaths of New York State inmates 1978–1992.* New York: New York State Department of Correctional Services.

Makuc, D., Feldman, J., Kleinman, J., & Piecre, M. (1990). Sociodemographic differentials in mortality. In J. Comoni-Huntley, R. Huntley, & J. Feldman (Eds.), *Health status and well-being of the elderly.* New York: Oxford University Press.

Manton, K., Patrick, C., & Johnson, K. (1987). Health differentials between Blacks and Whites: Recent trends in mortality and morbidity. *The Milbank Quarterly, 65,* 129–199.

McCarthy, M. (1983, February). The health status of elderly inmates. *Corrections Today.* pp. 64–65, 74.

McClelland, D., Alexander, C., & Marks, E. (1982). The need for power, stress immune function, and illness among male prisoners. *Journal of Abnormal Psychology, 91,* 61–70.

McDonald, D. (1995). *Managing health care and costs.* Washington, DC: U.S. Department of Justice. National Institute of Justice.

McGaha, G. (1987). Health care issues of incarcerated women. *Journal of Offender Counseling Services and Rehabilitation, 12,* 53–59.

Mendelsohn, B. (1995). States leaping on anti-crime bandwagon. *Corrections Alert, 2,* I.

Mooney, S., & Mendelsohn, B. (1995). TX conducts health care by head-count. *Corrections Alert, 2*(11), 4–5.

National Center for Health Statistics. (1992). *Health, United States, and Health People 2000 Review.* Hyattsville, MD: Public Health Service.

National Commission Accredits Forty Facilities. (1994). *CorrectCare, 8*(4), 4, 10.

National Commission on Correctional Health Care. (1994). *Women's health care in correctional settings.* Chicago: Author.

National Commission on Correctional Health Care. (1995). *Health services accreditation.* Chicago: Author.

Neisser, E. (1977). Is there a doctor in the joint? The search for constitutional standards for prison health care. *Virginia Law Review, 63,* 921–973.

Novick, L., & Al-Ibrahim, M. (1977). *Health problems in the prison setting.* Springfield. IL: Charles C. Thomas.

Novick, L., Della Peuna, R., Schwartz, M., Remmlinger, E., & Loewenstein, R. (1977). Health status of the New York City prison population. *Medical Care, 15,* 205–216.

Olderman-Jones, J. (1992). Jail inmates and mental health contact. *Systemstats, 8,* 1–5.

Perkins, C. (1994). *National corrections reporting program, 1992.* Washington, DC: U.S. Department of Justice. Bureau of Justice Statistics.

Raba, J., & Obis, C. (1983). The health status of incarcerated urban males: Results of admission screening. *Journal of Jail and Prison Health, 3,* 6–24.

Rabkin, J., & Streaming, E. (1976). Life events, stress and illness. *Science, 194,*1012–1020.

Rector, F. (1929). *Health and medical service in American prisons and reformatories.* New York: National Society of Penal Information.

Rice, D. (1989). Health and long-term care for the aged. *American Economic Review, 79,* 343–348.

Rice, D., & Feldman, J. (1983). Living longer in the United States: Demographic changes and health needs of the elderly. *Milbank Quarterly/Health and Society, 61,* 362–396.

Rieman, J. (1990). *The rich get richer and the poor get prison.* New York: Macmillan.

Ross, C., & Wu, C. (1995). The links between education and health. *American Sociological Review, 60,* 719–745.

Schilling, R., El-Bassel, N., Ivanoff, A., Gilbert, L., Hsien, K., & Safyer, S. (1994). Sexual risk behavior of incancerated, drug-using women, 1992. *Public Health Reports, 109,* 539–546.

Selik, R., Castro, K., Papaionnou, M., & Ruehler, J. (1989). Birthplace and the risk of AIDS among Hispanics in the United States. *American Journal of Public Health, 79*(7), 836–839.

Senna, J., & Siegel, L. (1995). *Essentials of criminal justice.* Minneapolis, MN: West.

Sharp, J. (1996, January). Health care behind bars. *Fiscal Notes,* (1), 8–12.

Shenson, D., Dubler, N., & Michaels, D. (1990). Jails and prisons: The new asylums? *American Journal of Public Health, 80,* 655–656.

Sheps, S., Schechter, M., & Prefontaine, R. (1987). Prison health services: A utilization study. *Journal of Community Health, 12,* 4–22.

Standards of Health Services in Prison. (1992). National Commission on Correctional Health Care. Chicago, IL.

Steadman, H., Monahan, J., Duffee, B., Hartstone, E., & Robbins, P. (1984). The impact of state hospital deinstitutionalization on United States prison populations. 1968–1979. *Journal of Criminal Law and Criminology, 75,* 474–490.

Stewart, R., & Reinert, P. (1996, August 18). Death sentence. *Houston Chronicle,* pp. D 1–2.

Suls, J., Gaes, G., & Philo, V. (1991). Stress and illness behavior in prison: Effects of life events, self-care attitudes, and race. *Journal of Prison and Jail Health, 10,* 117–132.

Sykes, G. (1958). *The society of captives.* Princeton, NJ: Princeton University Press.

Teplin, L. (1983). The criminalization of the mentally ill. *Psychological Bulletin, 94,* 54–67.

Thirteen Facilities Awarded Initial NCCHC Accreditation. (1995). *CorrectCare.* *9*(3), 3.

Twaddle, A. (1976). Utilization of medical services by a captive population. *Journal of Health and Social Behavior, 17,* 236–248.

U.S. Congress, Office of Technology Assessment. (1993). *International health statistics: What the numbers mean for the United States* (background paper). Washington, DC: U.S. Government Printing Office.

VA Copayment Plan Yields Impressive Results. (1995). *Corrections Alert, 2,* 3.

Verbrugge, L. (1984). Longer life but worsening health? Trends in health and mortality of middle-aged and older persons. *Milbank Quarterly, 62,* 475–519.

Verbrugge, L. (1985). Gender and health: An update on hypotheses and evidence. *Journal of Health and Social Behavior, 26,* 156–182.

Vito, G., & Wilson, D. (1985). Forgotten people: Elderly inmates. *Federal Probation, 49,* 18–24.

Waldron, I. (1983). Sex differences in human mortality: The role of genetic factors. *Social Science and Medicine, 17,* 321–333.

Wallace, S., Klein-Saffran, J., Gaes, G., & Moritsugu, K. (1991). Health status of federal inmates: A comparison of admission and release medical records. *Journal of Jail and Prison Health, 10,* 133–151.

Weiner, J., & Anno, B. (1992). The crisis in correctional health care: The impact of the national drug control strategy on correctional health services. *Annals of Internal Medicine, 117,* 71–77.

Whalen, R., & Lyons, J. (1962). Medical problems of 500 prisoners on admissions to a county jail. *Public Health Reports, 77,* 497–502.

Wilson, W. (1993). *The ghetto underclass.* Newbary Park. CA: Sage.

Wingard, D. (1982). The sex differential in mortality rates. *American Journal of Epidemiology, 115,* 205–216.

Wolinsky, F., Mosely, R., & Coe, R. (1986). A cohort analysis of the use of health services by elderly Americans. *Journal of Health and Social Behavior, 27,* 209–219.

REVIEW QUESTIONS

1. How does the health condition of prison inmates (on the whole) compare to that of average Americans?
2. How does being incarcerated affect inmates' health?
3. What are the consequences of inmates' poor health status for correctional institutions/systems and society?

READING 21

The Impact of HIV/AIDS on Corrections

Mark Blumberg

J. Dennis Laster

This article provides an overview of the challenges that HIV/AIDS poses for prison administrators. The authors present summary data on the prevalence and risk factors associated with HIV/AIDS in prison populations. The current policy landscape with respect to three controversial issues facing prison administrators (mandatory HIV testing of inmates, segregation of infected prisoners, and preventative condom distribution) is reviewed, as are the pro and con arguments underlying the competing positions on these issues. The authors also provide a comprehensive review of the treatment concerns raised by HIV/AIDS infected inmates and how the court system has ruled on a wide range of inmate lawsuits. The article concludes with a consideration of the risks that infected inmates pose to the correctional officials who must interact with them on a daily basis.

CORRECTIONAL INSTITUTIONS

HIV/AIDS is a serious concern for prisons and jails. The number of "high-risk" inmates has increased dramatically in recent years as a result of the "war on drugs." Harlow (1993:5) reports that approximately 25 percent of state prison inmates have a history of intravenous drug use. Many inmates engage in the types of "high-risk" behavior during incarceration that pose a significant danger of viral transmission. Although levels of activity vary among facilities, both illicit sex and drug injection do take place in correctional facilities (Mahon, 1996). Furthermore, tattooing is not uncommon in many facilities (Braithwaite, Hammett, and Mayberry, 1996), and there are reports in the medical literature of HIV infection among prisoners that resulted from this practice (Doll, 1988).

Correctional administrators must confront a variety of complex issues as they struggle to develop policies that are designed to prevent transmission of this virus within the institutional setting, Many of these are issues that the outside society has also faced: whether to conduct mandatory HIV testing, whether infected persons should be placed in segregation, the appropriate content of educational programs designed to reduce the level of "high-risk" behavior (i.e., whether to teach abstinence or "safer sex"), and the question of condom distribution. At the heart of the debate is the following question: Should prisons and jails adhere to the practices of the larger society or is the institutional environment so unique that deviations from these established policies are justified?

This article explores the policy ramifications of various options designed to minimize the impact of the HIV/AIDS epidemic on prisons and jails. After a brief examination of the empirical data regarding the prevalence and transmission of

Waveland Press-Hass-Alpert-*The Dilemmas of Corrections*

HIV within correctional institutions, the pros and cons of mandatory HIV testing, segregating inmates infected with HIV/AIDS, and condom distribution are explored. This is followed by a discussion of some of the challenges that prisons and jails face as they attempt to provide quality medical care to inmates with HIV/AIDS. Next, there is a review of some of the legal issues that correctional administrators have been forced to confront as a result of the HIV/AIDS crisis. Finally, the article examines the question of whether institutional staff should be concerned about job-related HIV transmission as a result of their employment.

Prevalence and Transmission of HIV Within Correctional Institutions

According to a Bureau of Justice Statistics report, 24,226 inmates (2.3 percent of the total) were infected with the AIDS virus in 1995. Approximately 20 percent of these individuals had progressed to "fullblown" AIDS (Maruschak, 1997:1). Nationally, the rate of AIDS cases among inmates is almost six times greater than that of the adult U.S. population (Hammett and Widom, 1996:268).

The percentage of seropositive[1] prisoners varies dramatically among jurisdictions. New York has the highest percentage of inmates (13.9) who are infected. In fact, more than one-third of all seropositive inmates in the nation are incarcerated in that state (Maruschak: 1). On the other hand, 27 states reported that fewer than 1.0 percent of their inmate population was HIV-positive, and 8 states held 10 or fewer HIV-positive inmates (Maruschak, 1997:3). In general, correctional systems in the Northeast have more AIDS cases because a higher proportion of intravenous drug users in that region are seropositive (Gaiter and Doll, 1996). In the United States, most institutional HIV/AIDS cases have been diagnosed among individuals with a history of intravenous drug use prior to incarceration (Vlahov, 1990).

Several studies have been conducted which seek to determine how frequently HIV is transmitted among prison populations. The most comprehensive study to date found that only 0.3 percent of a sample of Illinois male inmates who had initially been seronegative[2] tested positive after spending one year in prison (Hammett et al., 1994:28). Low rates of seroconversion[3] have also been reported in Maryland (Brewer et al., 1988) and Nevada (Horsburgh et al., 1990). However, even a rate of 0.3 percent per year translates into a 6 percent risk of HIV infection after 20 years of incarceration. Furthermore, young first-time offenders, a small proportion of the prison population, are probably at greatest risk. Therefore, inmates in this vulnerable group probably have good reason to be concerned. In addition, a study conducted in the Florida Department of Corrections found a disturbingly high rate of infection among inmates who had been continuously incarcerated since the beginning of the HIV/AIDS epidemic (Mutter, Grimes, and Labarthe, 1994). This research suggests that "inmates have a substantial risk of contracting HIV infection while incarcerated" (p. 795). However, the Florida study only tested a small proportion of long-term inmates and the sample may have been self-selected (Braithwaite, Hammett, and Mayberry, 1996).

Clearly, much more research is needed on this question. It is known that there are substantial differences between jurisdictions with regard to the rate of seroprevalence[4] among inmates (Hammett et al., 1994:22–23). It is quite likely that there are also differences between facilities with respect to the level of supervision and the frequency with which "high-risk" behaviors occur. At this point, it is clear that institutional transmission of HIV does take place. What remains unknown is how frequently.

Mandatory HIV Screening

In the United States, public health officials have attempted to control the spread of HIV through education, voluntary testing, and counseling of persons who may be at high risk of HIV. With the exception of immigrants, blood donors, and military recruits (Andrus et al., 1989), most testing has been conducted on a voluntary basis. From the beginning of the epidemic, one of the most strongly debated questions has been whether this policy should also be pursued in correctional institutions. Because prisons and jails contain numerous individuals who have demonstrated a capacity to engage in antisocial behavior and homosexual activity (Nacci and Kane, 1983; Wooden and Parker, 1982), there have been frequent calls by correctional officers for the mandatory testing of inmates (Mahaffey and Marcus, 1995).

Advantages Proponents argue that mass screening is the best way to Identify seropositive inmates. Such a policy provides correctional administrators with an opportunity to target education and prevention programs. In addition, infected inmates can be placed under special supervision to ensure that they do not transmit the virus to others. It is also suggested that mass screening will provide a more accurate projection regarding the number of future AIDS cases that will develop in a particular institution. This will enable correctional officials to plan more effectively and to seek an appropriate level of funding to meet future needs. Finally, supporters of mandatory testing assert that institutions must pursue this policy to insure that infected inmates receive appropriate medical treatment that can prolong their lives.

Disadvantages Critics of mandatory testing do not accept these rationales. They assert that education and prevention programs must be directed toward all inmates, and that all prisoners should be encouraged to refrain from "high-risk" behavior, not just those Identified as seropositive. Furthermore, opponents of mass screening decry the practice of segregating infected individuals from the inmate population. Because the current medical technology cannot identify all infectious individuals,[5] any policy that utilizes isolation runs the risk of inadvertently encouraging "high-risk" behavior by creating the false perception that all inmates who remain in the general prison population are uninfected.

The claim that correctional institutions must be able to accurately project the future number of AIDS cases is not disputed. However, anonymous epidemiological screening can satisfactorily achieve this goal. In fact, many correctional systems have utilized this procedure to ascertain the rate of seroprevalence in various institutions within their jurisdiction (Braithwaite, Hammett, and Mayberry, 1996). Blood samples are simply coded in a manner that ensures prison officials cannot learn the names of infected inmates.

Opponents of mandatory screening also agree that early identification of seropositives is important. Recent scientific advances have contributed to a significant reduction in the fatality rate among HIV/AIDS-infected individuals who receive these medications (Okie, 1997). However, opponents do not believe that mandatory testing is necessary to accomplish this goal because inmates with a history of "high-risk" behavior have a medical incentive to learn their antibody status in order to receive treatment. Their case is buttressed by two studies which found that the majority of infected inmates are reached by voluntary testing programs (Andrus et al., 1989; Hoxie et al., 1990).

There are other objections to mandatory testing. One concern is that mass screening will create a class of outcasts within the institution (Whitman, 1990). HIV-infected inmates could be subjected to harassment, discrimination, and perhaps even violence within the prison—and to difficulties in obtaining employment or housing upon release. Finally, it is argued that such a policy is not a wise expenditure of scarce correctional resources. Critics assert that these funds would be better spent if directed towards HIV/AIDS education or inmate medical care.

Current Policy During 1994, the Centers for Disease Control and the National Institute of Justice jointly sponsored the eighth annual survey to determine what policies state/federal prison systems and city/county jails are pursuing with respect to HIV (Braithwaite, Hammett, and Mayberry, 1996). It found that sixteen state prison systems and the Federal Bureau of Prisons require all inmates to be screened for HIV. No city/county jail system which responded to the survey followed this policy. The list of systems with mandatory mass screening has remained unchanged since 1990 (Braithwaite, Hammett and Mayberry, 1996; Hammett et al., 1994:49).

Segregation of Inmates with HIV/AIDS

Advantages Proponents of segregation assert that it is necessary to prevent transmission of HIV within the institution. In making the case for this policy, advocates note that various types of "high-risk" activities occur in correctional Institutions. They note that: 1) previous research indicates homosexual activity does take place in prison (Nacci and Kane, 1983; Wooden and Parker, 1982); 2) other sexually transmitted diseases (e.g., rectal gonorrhea) are sometimes transmitted in the correctional setting; 3) tattooing (although prohibited in most institutions) is a very common practice; 4) illicit drug use probably takes place as well in some facilities (Polonsky et al., 1994); and 5) there is a small proportion of inmates who are sexually assaulted during incarceration (Bowker, 1980).

Disadvantages Civil libertarians are opposed to the practice of segregation except for valid medical reasons or in cases involving protective custody. They argue that because HIV is not spread through casual contact, special housing is not necessary. It is asserted that segregation undermines the basic public health message that HIV is not transmitted except through certain "high-risk" behaviors.

Opponents of this practice also express concern because infected inmates are sometimes placed in substandard living quarters and denied an opportunity to participate in certain work assignments, rehabilitation, and recreation programs—or to be eligible for work release. Furthermore, because these prisoners are excluded from many institutional programs, they frequently also lose the opportunity to earn "good time" credit toward eventual release.

Segregation raises other problems as well. In those jurisdictions that have a large number of infected inmates, this policy would require the development of what is in fact a second corrections system. Officials may be required to duplicate many existing programs. As the number of cases continues to increase, this policy would put further pressure on correctional budgets that are already severely strained.

There is also concern that inmates will be less likely to come forward for voluntary HIV testing if they are placed in segregation as a consequence of a positive result (Hammett et al., 1994:62). Finally, as already noted, a policy of mass screening and segregation could actually be counterproductive by providing inmates in the general prison population with a false sense of security that all HIV/AIDS-infected persons had been placed in isolation.

Clearly, correctional administrators have a responsibility to pursue policies that minimize the transmission of HIV within the institution. However, it is questionable whether a blanket policy of segregation is the best way to accomplish this objective. As an alternative, prison and jail administrators could reduce the incidence of "high-risk" behavior through such steps as increasing supervision of inmates, hiring more correctional officers, implementing intensive educational programs, and imposing harsh penalties for sexual assault (Vald, 1987:238). In addition, the classification process can be used to identify inmates who are likely to engage in predatory behavior as well as those who are likely to be victimized.

Current Policy According to the various CDC/NIJ surveys of correctional policy, there is a strong trend toward mainstreaming inmates with HIV/AIDS into the general prison population. Between 1985 and 1994, the number of prison systems that segregated persons with AIDS declined from 38 to 4. For asymptomatic seropositives, the corresponding decline was from 8 to 2 (Braithwaite, Hammett, and Mayberry, 1996: Table 5.5). Many systems have been able to successfully reintegrate inmates without serious incident (Hammett et al., 1994:59). In fact, Alabama and Mississippi remain the only systems that continue to isolate all known HIV-infected inmates (Braithwaite, Hammett, and Mayberry, 1996).

Distribution of Condoms

Previous research indicates that sexual activity does take place in correctional institutions. For this reason, some have suggested that administrators have an obligation to make condoms available in order to protect inmates from infection. However, very few jurisdictions have chosen to follow this course of action. Most have taken the view that homosexual behavior is forbidden in prisons and jails and that distribution of condoms would imply tacit approval of this activity. In addition, concern has been expressed that inmates could use these devices to make weapons or hide contraband. Finally, there is the question of whether condoms actually provide significant protection during anal intercourse.

Although condoms are distributed to prison inmates in 18 nations (Mahon, 1996:1215), only six jurisdictions in the United States (Braithwaite, Hammett, and Mayberry, 1996:83–4) have chosen to do so (Mississippi, New York City, Philadelphia, San Francisco, Vermont, and Washington, D.C.). These correctional systems report few problems. Fears that inmates would use these devices to fashion weapons or smuggle contraband appear to be unwarranted. Nonetheless, the number of institutions providing condoms has changed little in recent years. Although many other jurisdictions have considered the possibility of implementing a distribution policy, none have chosen to do so at the current time (Hammett et al., 1994).

It should be noted that not all systems distribute condoms in the same manner (Hammett et al., 1994:46–47). New York City and Vermont limit inmates to one per medical visit. In Mississippi, an unlimited number may be purchased at the canteen. San Francisco makes them available as part of their AIDS educational program. Washington, D.C., has also chosen this policy as well as allowing inmates to obtain condoms at the infirmary. Finally, Philadelphia offers these items during counseling sessions associated with HIV antibody testing.

CORRECTIONAL HEALTH CARE

AIDS has become one of the leading causes of death in the United States. Fortunately, in recent years, a new class of drugs called "protease inhibitors" has been developed. This treatment has reduced the number of deaths from this disease and may change HIV/AIDS from a fatal to a chronic condition. However, it is important to recognize that these drugs are not a cure. Many questions remain unanswered, including whether the virus will eventually become resistant to this medication.

Protease inhibitors are rapidly becoming the standard of care for seropositive individuals in the community. However, prisons and jails face enormous difficulty in trying to provide this treatment. The annual retail cost of providing this medication to one individual is between $12,000 and $16,000 (Waldholz, 1996b:1). Correctional institutions with large numbers of HIV-infected inmates could easily have their entire health care budget consumed by this expense. In addition, persons receiving this treatment must take between 14 and 20 pills each day in accordance with a rigid dosing schedule and often have to adhere to strict dietary restrictions (Waldholz, 1996b). These requirements can pose serious logistical problems for correctional institutions.

Policies vary widely with respect to protease inhibitors. New York City expects to spend $5.4 million in 1998 to provide these drugs. On the other hand, Louisiana reserves this treatment for inmates who were already receiving this medication prior to incarceration (Purdy, 1997). Given the efficacy of these drugs, there is clearly an ethical obligation on the part of medical personnel to provide inmates with this treatment. Whether there is also a legal obligation is uncertain.

Although the U.S. Supreme Court has ruled that inmates have a constitutional right to adequate medical care (*Estelle v. Gamble,* 1976), this decision did not grant inmates "unqualified access to health care." Furthermore, lower courts have subsequently interpreted this standard to mean that inmates rarely have a right to the best medical care (Vaughn and Carroll, 1996).

There are other factors that complicate the treatment of seropositive inmates. To date, many of the important advances in the treatment of HIV/AIDS have come from experimental medications. However, many states forbid inmates from participating in experimental trials of new drugs. In those jurisdictions that do allow such trials, few inmates are actually participating (Collins, Baumgartner, and Henry, 1995). Although the rules which prevent prisoners from taking part in experimental research were initially designed to protect incarcerated individuals, it is clear that these policies are now preventing some inmates from receiving potentially beneficial treatments.

Finally, it should be noted that the treatment of HIV/AIDS has become quite complex. Outside the correctional setting, the management of this disease has increasingly become the responsibility of specialists (Purdy, 1997). Unfortunately, many prisons and jails are forced to rely on primary care doctors who may lack the necessary expertise to provide the most up-to-date care. For these reasons, it is not surprising that the level of care varies dramatically among jurisdictions and sometimes even varies between different facilities within the same correctional system. In fact, the best care is often provided by those institutions which are operating under a court order to improve medical care (Purdy, 1997).

LEGAL ISSUES

Several issues have been raised in a proliferation of litigation challenging the HIV/AIDS policies of correctional institutions. The many lawsuits have presented a variety of constitutional and statutory claims. Cases have been brought by infected inmates seeking relief from institutional policies and by uninfected inmates and correctional personnel seeking protection from transmission of the virus. Of particular importance to correctional administrators are those cases which seek to impose civil liability for a failure to prevent infection in the institution.

Lawsuits brought by infected and uninfected inmates based on constitutional challenges to prison policies and procedures have met with little success. Correctional officials have been effective in defending these cases primarily as a result of *Turner v. Safley,* decided by the U.S. Supreme Court in 1987. In *Turner,* the Court pronounced the standard to be applied in cases alleging constitutional claims brought by prisoners. The Court held that institutional policies and procedures are valid if they are "reasonably related to legitimate penological interests" (*Turner* at p. 89). This requirement of reasonableness, as opposed to more stringent standards of substantial or compelling interests, has made it considerably easier for correctional officials to implement policies which restrict prisoners' rights. In applying the *Turner* standard to HIV-related cases, lower courts have consistently upheld prison policies that restrict the rights of both infected and uninfected inmates.

Most of the suits brought by infected inmates allege differential treatment or the denial of privileges. In *Dunn v. White* (1989), mandatory screening of inmates for HIV infection was challenged on grounds that testing constituted an unreasonable search and seizure and was therefore prohibited under the Fourth Amendment. The court upheld the prison's screening policy and, applying the *Turner* standard, concluded that there was a logical connection between mandatory testing and the prison's goal of preventing the spread of AIDS. Mass screening for the purpose of segregating infected prisoners into HIV dormitories has also been upheld under the same rationale (*Harris v. Thigpen,* 1991). Courts have reached similar results in cases where individual inmates have been singled out for testing after an incident that posed a risk of transmission, as in cases of prison rape. A policy of not testing inmates after potential transmission occurrences has likewise been upheld (*Lile v. Tippecanoe County Jail,* 1992).

Prison policies regarding the segregation of HIV positive inmates has been fertile ground for litigation as well. Despite a consistent trend in favor of mainstreaming seropositive prisoners into the general prison population, the courts have taken a "hands-off" position on the issue and left housing policy decisions to prison officials. Whether the institution chooses segregation or mainstreaming, the policy has been upheld. Thus, infected inmates who bring suit to challenge mandatory segregation policies have not been successful. Courts have also upheld segregation policies against constitutional challenges based on the following claims: cruel and unusual punishment under the Eighth Amendment (*Cordero v. Coughlin,* 1984); equal protection under the Fourteenth Amendment (*Moore v. Mabus,* 1992); due process under the Fifth and Fourteenth Amendments (*Harris v. Thigpen,* 1991). The case of *Nolley v. County of Erie* (1991) represents a rare departure from those decisions upholding mandatory segregation of infected prisoners. Nolley, solely on the basis of her status as an HIV positive inmate, was forced into a segregation unit for prisoners who were suicidal or mentally disturbed. Evidence in the case made it clear that she was not placed in the unit to receive medical care or for her safety. The court found merit in Nolley's assertions that her due process and right of privacy protections were violated. *Nolley* is distinguishable from other cases, however, since the institution failed to follow its own policies regarding the placement of seropositive inmates.

Inmates have also brought suit alleging the unauthorized disclosure of their HIV status. This claim is based on the fact that individuals in the free world have a constitutional right to protect their medical records from unauthorized disclosure (Vaughn and Carroll, 1996). However, the courts have ruled that this principle does not apply to incarcerated individuals and that disclosing an inmate's HIV positive condition to correctional personnel and other inmates does not violate the constitutional right of privacy (*Anderson v. Romero,* 1995).

In other areas as well, courts have applied the *Turner* standard and given prison administrators wide discretion in making decisions that impact upon infected inmates. Courts have upheld prison policies against challenges by inmates asserting differential treatment or a denial of privilege in cases involving exclusion from a community work program (*Williams v. Sumner,* 1986) and prohibiting work in prison cafeterias and hospitals (*Farmer v. Moritsugu,* 1990).

Attempts to invoke the protections of federal statutes have also met with limited success. For example, in *Gates v. Rowland* (1994), infected inmates claimed that their exclusion from certain work assignments was in violation of Section 504 of the Rehabilitation Act of 1973. Courts have ruled that seropositive individuals fall under the protection of this act. Section 504 provides that handicapped persons are entitled to a reasonable accommodation of their employment needs and other activities if they are otherwise qualified to perform the work or participate in the activities. The question in *Gates* was how should the Rehabilitation Act be applied to correctional institutions. The court's decision applied the same test to this statutory claim that it has applied to constitutional claims, namely the *Turner* standard. The court found that the exclusion of infected inmates from prison programs, arguably in violation of the Rehabilitation Act, was permissible since the policy was reasonably related to the prison's goal of promoting the safety of inmates.

Some cases have been brought by uninfected inmates and correctional personnel seeking to require institutions to implement policies to reduce the risk of transmission in the prison environment. These cases have also met with little success. Courts have not recognized a constitutional right that would require correctional authorities to implement policies of mass screening or segregation (Haas, 1993). As previously noted, most prisons have not adopted policies mandating either of these practices.

The risk of institutional transmission is likely to be the source of an increasing number of cases seeking to hold correctional officials civilly liable for the payment of monetary damages. Prison administrators are charged with protecting the inmates in their custody. Although most studies find that HIV is transmitted infrequently in prisons and jails, the possibility that an inmate might be infected as a result of an attack has been described as "perhaps the most explosive legal and moral issue related to HIV/AIDS in correctional facilities" (Braithwaite, Hammett, and Mayberry, 1996). The case of *Billman v. Indiana Department of Corrections* (1995) is illustrative of the types of inmate claims that may prove worrisome to prison authorities. Billman brought suit under 42 U.S.C. Section 1983, the federal civil rights statute that provides monetary damages for violations of federally protected rights by state officials. The plaintiff alleged that he was the victim of cruel and unusual punishment inflicted upon him by prison authorities in violation of his Eighth Amendment rights. The complaint alleged that employees of the prison system placed a seropositive inmate in the same cell with Billman. Although prison staff were alleged to have knowledge of both the inmate's HIV status and his history of sexually assaulting cellmates, they did nothing to warn Billman of the danger. Billman further alleged that he was raped by the inmate and that prison employees did not act to prevent or interrupt the rape. The court assumed that Billman was not infected, but found that the fear of the rape itself and the additional fear of being infected could give rise to damages. While the court did not reach a decision on the merits of Billman's assertions and remanded the case for other reasons, it did identify the standards to be applied in such cases. The court found the applicable test in cruel and unusual punishment cases to be the "deliberate indifference" standard enunciated by the United States Supreme Court in *Farmer v. Brennan* (1994). Thus, inmates seeking to impose civil liability based on the infliction of cruel and unusual punishment must show that prison officials acted with deliberate indifference to a known substantial risk of physical harm. If Billman could prove the allegations of his complaint, there is little doubt that he would recover damages for the injury suffered. Still, inmate plaintiffs in other cases will find the deliberate indifference standard to be an obstacle that is difficult to overcome.

Historically, correctional authorities have been given broad leeway to develop and implement policy within their institutions. The judiciary has taken a passive role and left the day-to-day operations of the prison to its administrators. This reluctance to intervene is clearly evident from a review of HIV/AIDS-related cases.

HIV AND THE CORRECTIONS OFFICER

Repeated surveys by the National Institute of Justice reveal that not a single corrections officer in the United States has become infected with HIV as a result of his or her occupational duties (Hammett et al., 1994:13). Despite this fact, correctional personnel often express anxiety that their employment places them at increased risk of infection (Mahaffey and Marcus, 1995). In the earlier days of the epidemic, there were reports that certain staff members in some facilities refused to perform assigned tasks (e.g., transporting a seropositive inmate) because they feared infection (Hammett, 1989:106). Although this type of inappropriate response is now quite uncommon, some correctional officers continue to be concerned that the following types of incidents could place them in jeopardy: 1) being bitten or spat upon by an infected prisoner; 2) a needlestick injury (either received inadvertently during a search or as the result of an assault); and 3) coming into contact with infected blood in the course of attempting to terminate a fight among inmates. Examination of the dynamics of HIV transmission suggest that it is highly improbable that any correctional officer will become infected under these circumstances.

Lifson (1988) reports that follow-up investigations of persons bitten by HIV/AIDS-infected individuals revealed no cases in which the virus had been transmitted in this manner. Bites apparently present little risk because it is the assailant and not the victim who comes into contact with blood during the assault. As a consequence, transmission would be highly unlikely unless the perpetrator had blood in his or her mouth.

Spitting incidents pose little danger (Blumberg, 1990) for two reasons: 1) the virus does not pass through intact skin and 2) HIV is not present in sufficient quantity in saliva to transmit the virus. In fact, the Centers for Disease Control and Prevention (1988) no longer recommend that health care workers take universal precautions when contact with saliva is anticipated unless it contains visible blood.

Needlestick injuries do pose a slight risk of HIV transmission. Studies of health care workers who have accidentally pricked themselves with HIV-infected needles indicate that viral transmission occurs in approximately 0.5 percent of the cases (Centers for Disease Control, 1989:5). In other words, infection resulted in about 1 out of every 200 needlesticks where the victim had been exposed to contaminated blood.

Correctional institutions can take a number of steps to further reduce this risk. These should include: 1) implementing a comprehensive HIV/AIDS education and training program; 2) developing policies and procedures which teach officers how to conduct searches in a manner that minimizes their likelihood of injury; and 3) ensuring that correctional staff follow all prescribed infection control guidelines issued by the Centers for Disease Control (1989).

Finally, institutional personnel have expressed anxiety that the virus could be transmitted during actions taken to break up fights. Specifically, the concern is that one of the participants will be seropositive and that blood from this inmate will come in contact with an officer who has an open sore. Under these circumstances, there is a theoretical possibility that transmission could occur. However, more than one decade has passed since the beginning of the AIDS epidemic, and not a single case has been reported in which a person working in a prison or jail became infected in this manner. Clearly, the risk posed by such incidents, especially for those personnel who follow recommended Centers for Disease Control guidelines, is more theoretical than real. . . .

CASES

Anderson v. Romero, 72 F.3d 518 (7th Cir. 1995).
Billman v. Indiana Department of Corrections, 56 F.3d 785 (7th Cir. 1995).
Cordero v. Coughlin. 607 F. Supp. 9 (S.D.N.Y. 1984).
Dunn v. White, 880 F.2d 1188 (10th Cir. 1989), cert, denied, 110 S. Ct. 871 (1990).
Estelle v. Gamble, 429 U.S. 97 (1976).
Farmer v. Brennan, 511 U.S. 825 (1994).
Farmer v. Moritsugu, 742 F. Supp. 525 (W.D. Wis. 1990).
Gates v. Rowland, 39 F.3d 1439 (9th Cir. 1994).
Harris v. Thigpen, 941 F.2d. 1495 (11th Cir. 1991).
Lile v. Tippecanoe County Jail, 844 F. Supp. 1301 (N.D. Ind. 1992).
Moore v. Mabus, 976 F.2d 268 (5th 1992).
Nolley v. County of Erie, 776 F. Supp. 715 (W.D.N.Y. 1991).
Turner v. Safley, 428 U.S. 78 (1987).
Williams v. Sumner, 648 F. Supp. 510 (D. Nev. 1986).

NOTES

1. This term refers to individuals whose HIV antibody test indicates that they have become infected with the virus, regardless of whether they exhibit symptoms of illness.

2. This term refers to individuals whose HIV antibody test indicates that they are not infected with the AIDS virus.

3. Seroconversion refers to a positive HIV antibody test on the part of an individual who was previously not infected with the virus.
4. This term refers to the proportion of individuals in a specific group who are seropositive.
5. The HIV antibody test does not detect infection until at least 6 to 12 weeks after exposure to the virus.

REFERENCES

Altman, Dennis (1987). *Aids in the Mind of America: The Social, Political and Psychological Impact of a New Epidemic.* Garden City, NY: Anchor Books.

Andrus, Jon K., David W. Fling, Catherine Knox, Robert O. McAlister, Michael R. Skeels, Robert E. Conrad, John M. Horan, and Laurence R. Foster (1989). "HIV Testing in Prisoners: Is Mandatory Testing Mandatory?"*American Journal of Public Health.* Vol. 79, No. 7, pp. 840–842.

Blumberg, Mark (1990). "The Transmission of HIV: Exploring Some Misconceptions Related to Criminal Justice," *Criminal Justice Policy Review,* Vol. 4, No. 4, pp. 288–305.

Bowker, Lee H. (1980). *Prison Victimization.* New York: Elsevier.

Braithwaite, Ronald L., Theodore M. Hammett, and Robert M. Mayberry (1996). *Prisons and AIDS: A Public Health Challenge.* San Francisco: Jossey-Bass.

Brewer, T. Fordam, David Vlahov, Ellen Taylor, Drusilla Hall, Alvaro Munoz, and B. Frank Polk (1988). "Transmission of HIV Within a Statewide Prison System,"*AIDS.* Vol. 2, No. 5, pp. 363–366.

Centers for Disease Control and Prevention (1996). *HIV/AIDS Surveillance Report.* 8(2).

——— (1989). "Guidelines for Prevention of Transmission of Human Immunodeficiency Virus and Hepatitis B Virus to Health Care and Public Safety Workers,"*Morbidity and Mortality Weekly Report.* Vol. 38, No. S-6 (June 23).

——— (1988). "Update: Universal Precautions for Prevention of Transmission of HIV, Hepatitis B Virus, and Other Blood-Borne Pathogens in Health Care Settings,"*Morbidity and Mortality Weekly Report.* Vol. 37, No. 24 (June 24).

Collins, Abigail, Dana Baumgartner, and Keith Henry (1995). "U.S. Prisoners' Access to Experimental HIV Therapies," *Minnesota Medicine*. Vol. 78: 45–48.

Doll, Donald C. (1988). "Tattooing in Prison and HIV Infection," *The Lancet.* January 2/9: 66–67.

Friedland, Gerald H., and Robert S. Klein (1987). "Transmission of the Human Immunodeficiency Virus," *The New England Journal of Medicine.* Vol. 317, No. 18, pp. 1125–1135.

Gaiter, Juarlyn, and Lynda S. Doll (1996). "Editorial: Improving HIV/AIDS Prevention in Prisons Is Good Public Health Policy," *American Journal of Public Health.* Vol. 86, No. 9, pp. 1201–1203.

Haas, Kenneth C. (1993). "Constitutional Challenges to the Compulsory HIV Testing of Prisoners and the Mandatory Segregation of HIV-Positive Prisoners," *The Prison Journal.* Vol. 73 (September–December).

Hammett, Theodore M. (1989). *1988 Update: AIDS in Correctional Facilities.* National Institute of Justice, Washington, DC (June).

Hammett, Theodore M., Lynne Harold, Michael Gross, and Joel Epstein (1994). *1992 Update: HIV/AIDS in Correctional Facilities.* National Institute of Justice and Centers for Disease Control and Prevention, Washington, DC (January).

Hammett, Theodore M., and R. Widom (1996). "HIV/AIDS Education and Prevention Programs for Adults in Prisons and Jails and Juveniles in Confinement Facilities—United States, 1994," *MMWR.* Vol. 45, No. 13, pp. 268–271.

Harlow, Caroline Wolf (1993). *HIV in U.S. Prisons and Jails.* Bureau of Justice Statistics, Washington, DC (September).

Horsburgh, C. Robert, Joseph Q. Jarvis, Trudy McArthur, Terri Ignacio, and Patricia Stock (1990). "Seroconversion to Human Immunodeficiency Virus in Prison Inmates," *American Journal of Public Health.* Vol. 80, No. 2, pp. 209–210.

Hoxie, Neil J., James M. Vergeront, Holly R. Frisby, John R. Pfister, Rjurik Golubjatnikov, and Jeffrey P. Davis (1990). "HIV Seroprevalence and the Acceptance of Voluntary HIV Testing Among Newly Incarcerated Male Prison Inmates in Wisconsin," *American Journal of Public Health.* Vol. 80, No. 9, pp. 1129–1131.

Lifson, Alan R. (1988). "Do Alternative Modes for Transmission of the Human Immunodeficiency Virus Exist?", *Journal of the American Medical Association.* Vol. 259, No. 9, pp. 1353–1356.

Mahaffey, Katherine J., and David K. Marcus (1995). "Correctional Officers' Attitudes Toward AIDS,"*Criminal Justice and Behavior.* Vol. 22, No. 2, pp. 91–105.

Mahon, Nancy (1996). "New York Inmates' HIV Risk Behaviors: The Implications for Prevention Policy and Programs," *American Journal of Public Health.* Vol. 86, No. 9, pp. 1211–1115.

Maruschak, Laura (1997). "HIV in Prisons and Jails." Bureau of Justice Statistics, Washington, DC (August).

Mutter, Randal C., Richard M. Grimes, and Darwin Labarthe (1994). "Evidence of Intraprison Spread of HIV Infection," *Archives of Internal Medicine.* Vol. 154, pp. 793–795.

Nacci, Peter L., and Thomas R. Kane (1983). "The Incidence of Sex and Sexual Aggression in Federal Prisons," *Federal Probation.* Vol. 47, No. 4 (December), pp. 31–36.

Okie, Susan (1997). "The Downturn in AIDS Deaths," *Washington Post National Weekly Edition.* July 21 and 28, pp. 37.

Polonsky, Sara, Sandra Kerr, Benita Harris, Juarlyn Gaiter, Ronald P. Fichtner, and May G. Kennedy (1994). "HIV Prevention in Prisons and Jails: Obstacles and Opportunities," *Public Health Reports.* Vol. 109, No. 5, pp. 615–625.

Purdy, Matthew (1997). "As AIDS Increases Behind Bars, Costs Dim Promise of New Drugs." *New York Times.* May 26, p. 1.

Vald (1987). "Balanced Response Needed to AIDS in Prison," *National Prison Project Journal,* No. 7 (Spring), pp. 1–5.

Vaughn, Michael S., and Leo Carroll (1996). "Separate and Unequal: Prison versus Free-World Medical Care," paper presented at Annual Meeting of the American Society of Criminology in Chicago, Illinois.

Vlahov, David (1990). "HIV-1 Infection in the Correctional Setting,"*Criminal Justice Policy Review.* Vol. 4, No. 4, pp. 306–318.

Waldholz, Michael (1996a). "AIDS Conferees Debate How Early to Offer New Drugs," *Wall Street Journal.* July 12, p. B1.

——— (1996b). "New AIDS Treatment Raises Tough Question of Who Will Get It," *Wall Street Journal.* July 3, p. 1A.

Whitman, D. (1990). "Inside an AIDS Colony," *U.S. News and World Report.* January 29, pp. 20–26.

Wooden, Wayne S., and Jay Parker (1982). *Men Behind Bars: Sexual Exploitation in Prison.* New York: Plenum Press.

REVIEW QUESTIONS

1. Does your personal position and rationale on mandatory screening and condom distribution differ for inmates and free citizens? If so, how and why?
2. What is your assessment of the Court's decision in the Turner case and why?
3. What sorts of innovative policies and procedures might prison administrators implement to better protect correctional officers from the threat of HIV transmission?
4. Should inmates who infect a guard or inmate with the HIV virus during the course of a fight that they started be subject to criminal prosecution?

READING 22

Incompetent Jail and Prison Doctors

Dean A. Dabney

Michael S. Vaughn

This article considers the professional competence of medical professionals who deliver care to jail and prison inmates. The authors conduct a content analysis of prisoner lawsuits filed over a twenty-year period that allege poor medical care on the part of correctional authorities. Data drawn from these legal rulings are used to portray instances of alleged substandard care and/or misconduct and assess the ways in which correctional physicians responded to these allegations. Cases of alleged misconduct and negative health outcomes are organized into several substantive categories with detailed examples provided for each. The authors provide a conceptual understanding of the ways in which the physicians rationalized their behaviors to the court. Correctional physicians are shown to rarely accept responsibility for their actions. The names of the doctors identified in the lawsuits were cross-referenced with a federal database that documents disciplinary actions taken against licensed medical professionals. This exercise revealed that the vast majority of doctors named in lawsuits experienced no formal actions against their licenses to practice medicine. The article concludes with a discussion of the ethical implications and policy deficiencies related to the delivery of medical care in correctional facilities.

. . . Because contemporary penal policy defines prisoners as enemies and ascribes to them "attributes that make them initially less deserving of the most basic amenities and civilities, and ultimately less than human" (King, 1998, p. 617; Vaughn, 1999), correctional health care systems do not provide "attractive employment prospects for most" physicians (Friedman, 1992, p. 942). Indeed, previous research has questioned the medical skills, competence, and ethics of physicians who work in correctional institutions (Vaughn & Smith, 1999a, 1999b). The central question guiding this article is, Why would a physician voluntarily work in a health care setting where staff believe that all their patients manipulate providers and feign illness? Our hypothesis is that correctional physicians' employment opportunities are limited, because they experience higher rates of disciplinary action and sanction against their license to practice medicine than physicians at large. Grounded within the principle of less eligibility (Vaughn & Carroll, 1998), we posit that prisoners' low social status makes them less deserving of high-quality medical care, explaining why physicians with questionable medical qualifications practice disproportionately within correctional health care systems.

To explore these issues, we examine two mechanisms of formal social control employed against physicians in correctional facilities. First, we assess lawsuits filed by prisoners in state courts seeking monetary damages and injunctive relief for inadequate correctional medical care. Here, we analyze the content of court rulings to develop a descriptive profile of how inmates, doctors, and the courts are defining and responding to medical misconduct in U.S. correctional facilities. Second, we cross-reference physicians identified in our case law analysis with physicians who have had state or federal disciplinary action taken on their license to practice medicine. The article concludes by questioning the ethics of sentencing incompetent doctors to exclusively practice in correctional facilities, and by calling for more systematic research on correctional physicians who have had disciplinary action taken against their privilege to practice medicine.

LITERATURE REVIEW

Free World Physicians Rationalize Deviance

The Institute of Medicine within the National Academy of Sciences (Kohn, Corrigan, & Donaldson, 2000) estimates that 44,000 to 98,000 patients die annually in the United States due to medical errors or mistakes. News accounts (Pear, 1999; Stolberg, 1999) indicate that the public is both shocked and concerned about the fact that such large numbers of mistakes occur and, more important, that an organizational code of silence allows these actions to go largely unchecked. Rosenthal (1995) documented that free world physicians engage in a delicate mental and verbal exercise when confronted with negative health outcomes. His interviews with physicians revealed that they rarely admitted their mistakes and seldom accepted culpability when their patients experienced negative health outcomes. Instead, physicians' discussions of negative patient outcomes revolved around issues such as "permanent uncertainty," "necessary fallibility," "shared personal and professional responsibility," and the "exclusivity of professional judgment." Rosenthal concluded that these verbal and cognitive exercises on the part of doctors serve to reconstruct mistakes as accidents, and the doctors adeptly convince themselves and others that they were (a) not at fault and (b) should not be held directly responsible for their patients' negative health outcome.

Jesilow, Pontell, and Geis (1993) engaged in a similar exercise in which they reviewed a sample of disciplinary proceedings taken against California doctors accused of Medicare/Medicaid fraud. Categorizing physicians' written responses to charges using Sykes and Matza's (1957) techniques of neutralization, Jesilow et al. (1993) explored how physicians redefine their behaviors so as to avoid the displeasures that go with negative personal and public definitions of their improprieties.[1] As predicted by Sykes and Matza, Jesilow et al. reported that physicians use verbal and cognitive rationalization schemes to account for or justify their behaviors. That is, physicians' comments and thought processes downplayed the fault associated with their actions and, in doing so, drew on a finite set of explanations. Similar cognitive exercises also have been observed among free world nurses (Dabney, 1995) and pharmacists (Dabney & Hollinger, 1999).

Correctional Physicians' Competence

There is a widespread belief in the medical community that correctional physicians are inept and cannot find free world employment, necessitating their appointment in prisons and/or jails (Becker, 1999a; Skolnick, 1998b; Steptoe, 1986).

Indeed, journalistic, scholarly, and legal representations of the clinical qualifications and professional competence of correctional health personnel paint a disturbing portrait. Journalists report that "disciplined doctors who are not allowed to practice on the general public are permitted to do so behind bars—even if they have lost their Drug Enforcement Administration (DEA) license for prescribing controlled substances" (Allen & Bell, 1998, p. G2). Although the exact number is unknown, investigative reporters have estimated that somewhere between 15% to 78% of correctional physicians practice medicine with restrictions on their medical license (Allen & Bell, 1999). For example, 30% of the 129 doctors who work in Florida's prison system were "not fully licensed or have a blot on their record" (Becker, 1999b, p. 1B). According to Skolnick and Bell (1998, p. G9), 9 of 35 prison physicians working for Correctional Medical Services (CMS) in Missouri experienced disciplinary action on their license to practice medicine. This means that 26% of CMS physicians in Missouri and 30% of Florida's prison doctors (compared to 2.4% of physicians in the general population) have had sanction on their medical license for misconduct (Wolfe, Franklin, McCarthy, Bame, & Adler, 1998, p. 5).

With respect to civil litigation, numerous courts have ruled that prison health staff lack adequate training and credentials. A federal judge in 1994, for example, ordered the District of Columbia to "'replace its unlicensed' personnel . . . finding that 'many of the front line treatment staff were unlicensed, inadequately trained, and poorly supervised paraprofessionals'" (Vaughn & Carroll, 1998, p. 21; Lezin, 1996, p. 194). In another case, the U.S. Court of Appeals for the Eleventh Circuit commented that "it is difficult . . . to obtain [medical] experts . . . who are willing to accept full-time employment in a penal institution. . . . The lack of knowledge of certain primary care physicians . . . relating to some seemingly basic terminology about the diagnosis, prophylaxis, monitoring, and treatment of [serious health conditions] is disturbing" (*Harris v. Thigpen,* 1991, p. 1508). Likewise, correctional physicians have been implicated in denying and delaying medical care to prisoners, resulting in nontreatment of serious injuries and illnesses, denial of life-sustaining care, needless pain and suffering, and the alternation of free world physicians' diagnoses and care recommendations for nonmedical reasons (Vaughn, 1995, 1999). Civil courts also have ruled that correctional physicians mishandle adequate pain control regimens, render improper diagnoses and treatments, replace adequate care with inefficacious care for punitive reasons, engage in a disproportionate number of practices leading to medication errors, and perform contraindicated medical procedures on inmates (Vaughn, 1997, 1999).

The scholarly literature also provides evidence that health personnel who work in corrections are less qualified than their colleagues who work in the free world (Berkman, 1995; Blumberg & Mahaffey-Sapp, 1997). "Prison medical care sometimes is delivered by unlicensed physicians, doctors with substance abuse problems, doctors with criminal histories, and licensed and qualified doctors that treat ailments for which they lack training or experience" (Vaughn & Carroll, 1998, p. 20). At a prominent prison hospital, for example, the "consulting cancer specialist . . . never qualified to take the specialty boards and is not a member of either of the two medical societies for cancer specialists" (Berkman, 1991, p. 420). In too many facilities, correctional medical personnel with "no nationally recognized qualifications" administer a majority of the care (Loveday, 1993, p. 17). According to the Federal Bureau of Prisons, physician assistants (PAs) provide 75% to 80% of all primary care to inmates ("BOP and DOD," 1997); however, many PAs "do not meet the training and certification requirements of the medical community outside" of correctional facilities (U.S. General Accounting Office, 1994, p. 3). For example, "34 of the 66 physician assistants working in the Federal Bureau of Prisons at its seven medical referral centers have not . . . graduated from a program approved by the American Medical Association nor obtained certification from the National Commission on Certification of Physician Assistants" (U.S. General Accounting Office, 1994, p. 11). In sum, journalists, courts, and scholars paint a disturbing picture of the clinical qualifications and professional competence of correctional medical personnel. Framed within the principle of less eligibility, evidence suggests that prisoners are less entitled to the services of highly trained health care providers compared to citizens in the free world.

METHODOLOGY

From January 1, 1980 to November 4, 1999, we identified correctional physicians who were sued in state courts through the Westlaw online database.[2] In the "allstates" database, our search strategy identified the terms *prison* or *jail* within the same paragraph with the word *medical,* and linked those terms to the word *liability.* This produced 977 cases, including hundreds that either (a) did not pertain to a prison or jail medical care lawsuit or (b) did not identify by name a physician in the correctional setting. Moreover, we had many cases that pertained to correctional health care that were omitted from our analysis because the defendant was the institution, administrators, or medical care staff other than physicians. Thus, we selected only those cases ($n = 121$) where the correctional physician was identified by name.[3]

Given that prisoners were the plaintiffs in all of these cases, their input on the subject was gleaned from those sections of the court rulings that detailed the factual specificity and legal basis for their claims. Relevant cases were read individually, and the following descriptive information was recorded/summarized on a standardized data collection template: the names of the legal parties involved, the legal citation, the court in which the claim was made, the names of the physicians affiliated with the correctional facility in question, the factual basis of the plaintiffs' claim, the legal basis for the plaintiffs' claim, the physicians' response, and the courts' disposition of the case.[4] Aspects of these descriptive data were then used as the basis for a series of subsequent second-order coding passes. In the first of these coding passes, we identified the precipitating treatment actions/inactions that motivated the prisoners to seek civil remedies. Here, we referenced the section of the data template that contained a summary of the plaintiffs' allegations and categorized them using the following eight-part classification scheme: denial of care, delay of care, poor or improper delivery of care, faulty diagnosis, unauthorized/unwanted delivery of care, unqualified/unlicensed care, unethical/inhumane behavior, and an improper response to a hunger strike.

The next second-order coding pass sought to determine the nature of the alleged negative health outcomes that resulted from the physicians' actions/inactions. By specifying the negative physical and/or mental health outcomes that resulted from physicians' actions/inactions, we classified prisoners' claims according to whether they resulted in death, permanent disability, temporarily diminished quality of life (e.g., pain or discomfort), or permanently diminished quality of life (e.g., cosmetic scarring or chronic illness).

Building on the insights gained by Rosenthal (1995) and Jesilow et al. (1993), this article assesses the ways that the doctors responded to formal social control efforts (court actions) that alleged substandard care or instances of medical misconduct. As such, in our final second-order coding of the case summaries, we sought to determine the physicians' responses to the plaintiffs' claims. Here, details from the cases were used to classify the physicians' responses to charges within Sykes and Matza's (1957) neutralization framework. That is, we classified each physician's response as an example of one of the following: denial of responsibility, denial of injury, denial of victim, condemnation of condemners, and appeal to higher loyalties. Like Jesilow et al. (1993), we note that because we used the physicians' after-the-fact legal defenses, "we could not determine whether the doctors had fashioned their explanations before or after they committed the abuses" (p. 154).

Given the poor work conditions, low pay, and diminished prestige that goes with being a correctional physician, one would expect that this line of medical work would run the risk of attracting the least qualified and competent members of the medical profession. Namely, this will be evidenced, to some degree, via the above detailed analysis centered on prisoner-initiated judicial actions against correctional doctors. This line of inquiry allows us to determine the frequency with which prisoners turn to the state-level judicial system to seek remedies for the poor medical care that they allegedly received at the hands of correctional physicians. However, these data only speak to the patients', and subsequently, a court's appraisals of a correctional doctor's competency. They do not allow us to assess the medical profession's judgment of the physician's competence.

To tap this domain, our analysis also assessed a second form of social control directed toward allegations of medical misconduct by jail and prison physicians. Namely, we cross-referenced the names of correctional physicians sued with a sourcebook on formal social control by the medical profession to determine if those individuals have had disciplinary action on their license to practice medicine. Gray (1992) observes that there are a wealth of state and federal licensing and regulatory entities that indirectly speak to the issue of competency via the formal social control efforts that are placed on practicing physicians. Unfortunately, scholars have concluded that there exists little communication and data sharing between these various regulatory entities (Dodge, 1998; Skolnick, 1998a, 1998c).[5]

The Public Citizen Health Research Group was formed, in part, to remedy this situation. This nonprofit consumer advocacy organization seeks to provide citizens with up-to-date information on instances of medical misconduct. Since 1987, this organization has been collecting, analyzing, and distributing data on disciplinary actions taken against practicing physicians. The resulting database, entitled *16,638 Questionable Doctors Disciplined by State and Federal Governments*

(Wolfe et al., 1998), offers summary data on all disciplinary actions taken by the following four types of regulatory entities: (a) the State Medical Boards from all 50 states and the District of Columbia, (b) the DEA's disciplinary actions taken against doctors who violate mandate practices for the dispensing of controlled substances, (c) the Food and Drug Administration's (FDA's) disciplinary actions against doctors who violate the regulations and policies that govern clinical research on patients, and (d) the U.S. Department of Health and Human Sciences' disciplinary actions taken against doctors who violate the terms of the Federal Medicare program.

For each of the doctors named in the above-mentioned case law analysis, we referenced this four-volume set to determine if there had been any formal regulatory or licensure action taken against the individual from 1987 to 1998. Where the cross-referencing technique yielded a match, we recorded the following information: the doctor's name and license number, the regulatory or licensure entity that initiated the action, the date of the action, the nature of the offense in question, and the resulting disciplinary action. The authors of the four-volume set enlist a user-friendly set of codes to categorize both the nature of the offense and the disciplinary actions for each case. We used these codes to provide the reader with descriptive information on the past offense types and the resulting disciplinary actions taken against correctional physicians named in the court cases.

RESULTS

Judicial Social Control of Jail and Prison Physicians

Prisoners' Allegations of Physician Misconduct Overall, we found 189 physicians using the case law search detailed above. Some of these doctors were named in several actions; thus, the number of claims against doctors totaled 202.[6] Of this group, 139 of the physicians were identified by their full name or initials, and 50 physicians were identified in the court case only by their last name. As reported in Table 1, our coding of the court opinions revealed that allegations of poor or improper care were the primary impetus for the plaintiff's court action, accounting for half (50%, n = 100) of the 202 claims against jail and prison physicians. By way of example, these allegations included the failure to render proper care to an inmate with a spinal injury (*Luther v. Compton,* 1998), an inmate with a skin disorder (*Gunter v. State,* 1987), an inmate with an abscessed tooth (*Gordon v. Cannell,* 1996), an inmate with a lung condition (*Flamer v. Redman*, 1988), and an inmate with a broken leg (*Auger v. State,* 1999).

Table 1 shows that a charge of denial of care was issued against 40 doctors (20%). Examples of these charges included a doctor who ordered no tests and provided no treatment despite an inmate's 105° fever (*Ochoa v. Superior Court of Santa Clara County,* 1983), a doctor who refused to treat a diabetic inmate's foot injury (*Cantrell v. Thurman,* 1998), a doctor who refused to provide a diabetic-appropriate diet to a diabetic inmate (*Montanez v. Questcare,* 1996), and a

TABLE 1 Prisoners' Allegations of Physician Misconduct (N = 202)

Type of Allegation	*n*	Percentage
Poor or improper care	100	50
Denial of care	40	20
Faulty diagnosis	26	13
Delay of care	12	6
Unethical/inhumane care	9	4
Unqualified/unlicensed delivery of care	6	3
Unwanted/unauthorized care	5	3
Forcible response to a hunger strike	3	1

doctor who provided no remedial care to an inmate stroke victim (*Napier v. Warden,* 1990).

A faulty diagnosis was the impetus for 26 (13%) of the claims (see Table 1). This included the doctor who did not diagnose a prisoner with hepatitis (*Oliver v. Townsend,* 1988), the doctor who failed to diagnose an inmate's herniated lumbar disk (*Rewald v. San Pedro Peninsula Hospital,* 1994), the doctor who failed to diagnose an inmate's rectal cancer (*Ballengee v. Ohio Department of Rehabilitation and Correction,* 1996), and the doctor who failed to diagnose an inmate with a perforated ulcer (*Gillam v. Lloyd,* 1988). Data in Table 1 reveal that a perceived delay in care was charged against 12 (6%) of the physicians. For example, there was the doctor who admitted an inmate having a heart attack to the prison infirmary instead of sending him to the hospital for immediate treatment (*Pan v. California State Personnel Board,* 1986); the doctor who refused to authorize corrective surgery for an inmate, even though two other physicians recommended it (*Keenan v. Maass,* 1996); the doctor who refused to surgically remove a painful cyst, instead incising and draining it periodically (*Wilson v. Hun,* 1995); and the doctor who did not timely treat an inmate's ear infection, resulting in hearing loss (*Kagan v. State,* 1996).

Nine doctors (4%) were accused of unethical/inhumane care (see Table 1). These allegations included exposing an inmate to asbestos (*Hampton v. Lloren,* 1997), enrolling an inmate without his consent into a Hepatitis B Virus study (*McNeil v. Brewer,* 1999), failing to take precautions to protect noninfected inmates from inmates who had tuberculosis (*Bilbo v. Thigpen,* 1994; *McFadden v. State,* 1989), and laughing at a naked female inmate on suicide watch (*Rushing v. Wayne County,* 1990).

Referring again to Table 1, six (3%) jail and prison doctors were said to be unqualified or unlicensed to deliver the care in question. Most notable among this category was the pediatrician/director of the prison medical unit who denied an inmate orthopedic surgery recommended by a free world specialist without consulting the medical records or conducting an examination (*Kirsch v. Start,* 1994).

Table 1 also shows that five (3%) of the physicians were accused of providing unwanted or unauthorized care. There was the doctor who mistakenly removed an inmate's prostate (*Smith v. Ohio State University Hospital,* 1996), and the doctor who assisted the state in forcibly medicating an inmate (*California Department of Corrections v. Office of Administrative Hearings,* 1997). In another case (*Horton v. Collins,* 1996), the doctor prescribed penicillin to an inmate, even though his medical chart indicated an allergy. Yet another example involved the doctor who sought to compel an inmate to undergo unwanted kidney dialysis (*Polk County Sheriff v. Iowa District Court for Polk County,* 1999). Three physicians (1%) were challenged for the way that they forcibly responded to an inmate's hunger strike, including the doctor who testified that the inmate suffered from borderline personality disorder (*Department of Public Welfare v. Kallinger,* 1990) and the doctor who testified that a liquid diet was not medically indicated (*Stevenson v. Lanham,* 1999).

Prisoners' Negative Health Outcomes The court narratives revealed that actions or inactions on the part of the correctional physicians resulted in a variety of negative health outcomes for the prisoners in question. Table 2 indicates that the actions led to 19 (9.4%) prisoner deaths. For example, there was the doctor who did not treat a diabetic prisoner (*Howard v. City of Columbus,* 1995), the doctor who did not refer an inmate with a brain abscess to a specialist for 10 days (*LeFay v. Coopersmith,* 1990), the jail doctor who refused to transfer a detainee with a torn colon to a hospital after a car accident (*Hill v. City of Saginaw,* 1986), and the doctor who did not properly monitor an asthmatic inmate's use of medications (*Baltzer v. Ohio Department of Rehabilitation and Correction,* 1993).

Table 2 reveals that 48 prisoners (15.3%) claimed to suffer permanent physical disabilities (e.g., loss of limbs or vital senses) at the hands of jail and prison doctors. Included in this group was the inmate whose leg was amputated from gangrene after being returned to an unsanitary facility following surgery (*Kyriss v. State,* 1985); the inmate with a perforated ulcer who went undiagnosed for 22 hours (*Flores v. Natividad Medical Center,* 1987); the inmate who was forced to take a shower with a cast on his leg, resulting in gangrene and amputation of several toes (*Vega v. Morris,* 1995); the inmate who had an abscessed testicle surgically removed after 4 months of nontreatment (*Zuck v. State,* 1988); the inmate who was improperly treated, resulting in blindness (*Wright v. State,* 1985); and the inmate whose leg was amputated after the prison doctor refused to administer antibiotics for infections (*Gullette v. State Through Department of Corrections,* 1980).

TABLE 2 Prisoners' Negative Health Outcomes ($N = 202$)

Type of Negative Health Outcome	n	Percentage
Death	19	9.4
Permanent physical disability	48	15.3
Permanent loss in quality of life	34	16.8
Temporary loss in quality of life	118	58.4

Thirty-four (16.8%) prisoners (see Table 2) claimed to suffer some form of permanent loss in their quality of life (e.g., noticeable scarring or chronic illness). Some examples of these claims included the doctor who failed to remove bone fragments from an inmate's nasal passages after surgery, resulting in a deviated septum (*Jacques v. State,* 1984); the doctor who did not get an inmate emergency treatment for cardiac problems, which resulted in a heart attack (*Fiedler v. Spoelhof,* 1992); the doctor who did not timely treat an inmate's developing diabetes (*Nelson v. State,* 1982); and the doctor who did not perform surgery on an inmate's torn Achilles tendon, resulting in permanent range of motion restrictions (*Watson v. State,* 1993).

A total of 118 (58.4%) prisoners claimed to sustain some form of temporary loss in their quality of life (e.g., pain or discomfort) at the hands of the doctor in question (see Table 2). These claims included the inmate who suffered withdrawal when the doctor discontinued his pain medication (*Cooper v. Bowers,* 1986), the inmate who suffered through 7 months of untreated tuberculosis (*Haavisto v. Perpich,* 1994), the inmate who suffered from untreated back pain effectively treated previously by free world physicians (*Howard v. Jonah,* 1993), the inmate who experienced pain when a prison physician failed to remove sutures following hernia surgery (*Goad v. Pasipanodya,* 1997), and the paraplegic inmate who was locked in a room without a wheelchair for 9 days by the prison physician and was forced to void his bowels with his hands (*Brown v. State,* 1980).

Correctional Physicians' Rationalizations Our efforts to code the doctor's responses to the allegations within Sykes and Matza's (1957) techniques of neutralization yielded interesting results. According to Table 3, more than one third (36.6%, $n = 74$) of the doctors offered explanations that best fit under the heading of denial of responsibility. Most often, this meant that they skirted direct responsibility for the negative outcomes by blaming them on external entities such as other jail or prison staff members, free world doctors, or private companies who contracted with the government to provide medical services. In effect, correctional physicians attempted to shift responsibility away from themselves and onto those health care providers who either diagnosed the condition or performed the care in question. Such was the case in *Herbert v. District of Columbia* (1998), where medical staff at the District of Columbia jail worked for the Professional Developmental Corporation, a private firm who had contracted with the District to provide medical services to prisoners. When an inmate suffered from "nausea and abdominal cramping secondary to withdrawal from narcotic addiction," medical officials injected "dextrose or dextrose-and-sodium-chloride" into both of her thighs, causing "swelling, redness, blistering, and cellulitis." In response to the inmate's lawsuit, jail physicians argued they were not state actors because they worked for a private corporation. These physicians engaged in a textbook example of denial of responsibility, in which they blamed their malpractice on the private corporation providing the care, refusing to accept full blame for their acts.

In other cases, doctors denied responsibility by attributing the unwanted health outcome to an unanticipated or unforeseen mistake. In short, they claimed that nature's outcome was beyond their control as a doctor. For example, in *District of*

TABLE 3 Correctional Physicians' Rationalizations ($N = 202$)

Technique of Neutralization	n	Percentage
Denial of responsibility	74	36.6
Denial of injury	51	25
Condemnation of condemners	33	16.3
Apologia	19	9.4
Denial of victim	15	7.4
Appeal to higher loyalties	10	5

Columbia v. Anderson (1991), a diabetic inmate who suffered from vascular and circulatory problems was seen by the prison doctor. While attempting to trim the inmate's toenails, the doctor cut the little toe on the inmate's left foot. The doctor gave the inmate an antiseptic ointment, but provided no further follow-up care. In the days that followed, his condition worsened significantly as an infection developed. As a result, his left leg was amputated at the knee. The inmate sued, and the prison doctor claimed that the inmate's diabetes was the cause of the amputation, not medical malpractice. In this case, the prison physician denied responsibility, arguing that that the inmate's amputation resulted from the natural progression of the disease, not the incompetence of the doctor.

We concluded that one fourth of the doctors ($n = 51$) adhered to an explanation that could best be described as a denial of injury (see Table 3). Here, the doctor might simply contend that he or she provided ample or even exemplary care to the inmate in question. In *Sloan v. Ohio Department of Rehabilitation and Correction* (1997), a 300-pound inmate entered prison with a below-the-knee amputation. At the prison, he initially used a wheelchair and aluminum crutches. For security reasons, the prison physician took these items and gave the inmate wooden crutches. The inmate complained, saying the wooden crutches were unsafe, buckling, and slipping on the floor. When the prisoner's crutches snapped in two, he fell to the ground and broke his arm, which resulted in a permanent disability. The doctor argued that given the need to preserve institutional security and safety, the health care provided to the inmate was appropriate and within acceptable medical standards. Thus, the prison physician asserted that no injury could be attributed to him. By "citing the superordinate benefits of the act" (Jesilow et al., 1993, p. 161), the physician was attempting to justify removal of the metal crutches on the basis of institutional security and custody. Sykes and Matza (1957) argued that denial of injury occurs in situations of "gang fighting . . . [which are viewed] as a private quarrel, an agreed upon duel between two willing parties, and thus of no concern" (p. 667) to the physician. Under these conditions, there is a "question . . . whether or not anyone has clearly been hurt by the [physician's] deviance, and this matter is open to a variety of interpretations" (p. 667). In this case, the prison physician denied that his failure to timely diagnose and treat the inmate's medical problems was the cause of any injury.

Denial of victim was manifested in 15 (7.4%) doctors' claims when they argued that though their actions did lead to a negative health outcome, it was an acceptable or possible consequence in the occasion in question. Here, jail and prison physicians matter-of-factly asserted that health care complications result from the blameworthy behavior of inmates, not from inadequacies of the correctional medical staff. For example, doctors posited that they should not be held liable for health-related complications resulting from inmate-on-inmate assaults. Such was the case in *Sherrod v. State* (1997), where an inmate in the Nebraska prison system suffered a serious injury when he was beaten with a steel rod by his cellmate. Although the inmate received some health care, the prison doctor did not diagnose the seriousness of the injury, meaning that therapy and treatment was not as comprehensive as it could have been. A definitive diagnosis only occurred after the inmate was released from prison.

Referring to Table 3, we classified 33 (16.3%) of the doctor's responses under the heading of condemnation of condemners. Here, the principal modus operandi was to challenge inmates' allegations by emphasizing the legitimacy gap that exists between the doctor and the inmate. Doctors simply portrayed themselves as honorable, learned professionals, and prisoners as untrained lay persons; hence, physicians claimed that inmates were attempting to manipulate the correctional health care system by disagreeing with the physicians' professional medical judgment. This occurred in *Proffitt v. Prison Health Services* (PHS) (1996), in which an orthopedic specialist determined that a prisoner needed surgery to remove pins and screws in her knee for her femur bone to heal properly. The prison medical director gave the surgery a low priority, which had the effect of delaying the surgery for more than 6 months. As a result, the inmate was released before the surgery occurred. The central allegation raised by the inmate was that PHS delayed the surgery to save money. PHS argued that prison physicians assessed the treating physicians' recommendations and determined that the surgery was not an emergency and could be put on the nonemergency schedule. Indeed, the surgery had been scheduled, but the inmate was released before it was performed. By condemning the prisoner as an untrained lay person who dared to question the scheduling decision, PHS attempted to "shift the focus of attention from [their] own deviant acts to the motives and behavior of those who disapprove[d]" (Sykes & Matza, 1957, p. 668). This rationalization juxtaposes the prisoner's disagreement with the prison doctors' professional judgment, calling into question the prisoner's competence. "By attacking others, the wrongfulness of [the prison physician's] own behavior is more easily repressed or lost to view" (p. 668).

A small number of doctors (5%, n = 10) enlisted what Sykes and Matza (1957) would call an appeal to higher loyalties (see Table 3). Here, the individual would portray the negative outcome as a choice between the lesser of two evils. In effect, correctional physicians claimed that this outcome had to be accepted to protect some larger professional or societal commitment. Some of these cases involved the doctors attempting to uphold the moral authority of the state by forbidding the inmate to go on a hunger strike. For example, in *Thor v. Superior Court (Andrews)* (1993, p. 384), an inmate in the California Department of Corrections refused to be fed and went on a hunger strike. The prison physician sought a court order to force-feed the inmate, arguing that the state had a moral duty to preserve life. The Supreme Court of California ruled that there was "no countervailing state interest in the preservation of life sufficient to sustain a duty on the part of [the prison doctor] superseding the right [of the prisoner] to refuse unwanted medical treatment." Notice that the prison physician disavowed the rights of the prisoner while according more value to societal norms he obviously "held to be more pressing or involving a higher loyalty" (Sykes & Matza, 1957, p. 669).

In other situations, medical officials may appeal to higher loyalties by claiming that their course of action is directed toward achieving a higher societal purpose, such as the desire to reduce drug addiction. Indeed, medical officials who work in prisons are taught that custody and security are the most important variable (Fleisher & Rison, 1997, p. 328) and that they must suspect feigned illnesses because prisoners are "skilled in manipulation and deceit" (Vause, Beeler, & Miller-Blanks, 1997, p. 62). This issue arose in *Austin v. Warden* (1996), in which an inmate had been taking antiseizure medication for epilepsy for 20 years. Because the prison doctor never saw the inmate have a seizure, he testified that he believed the inmate was faking an illness; therefore, the prison doctor stopped the inmate's medication. The doctor removed the medication to appeal to the greater societal good of reducing drug addiction. According to the doctor, it is "not unusual for an inmate to feign bizarre behaviors in order to obtain prescriptive medications, or simply to draw attention to one's self" (p. 3). In these cases, correctional physicians apparently had no moral quandary denying prescription medication to prisoners, appealing to the moral superiority of the state to fight drug addiction.

Surprisingly, the data in Table 3 show that several of the doctors simply admitted blame (9.4%, $n = 19$). This course of action is what Scott and Lyman (1968) referred to as an apologia. These authors argued that some individuals, when confronted with evidence of their wrongdoing, will admit fault and accept responsibility. These physicians generally pursued a face-saving course of action that points to some positive lessons or repentance that has resulted from the situation. In the case of the doctors analyzed here, this manifested itself in ways such as in *Matter of Napoleon* (1997), where the prison doctor had his license to practice medicine revoked. Admitting some wrongdoing, the doctor sought indemnification from the state and from the Attorney General's office. A New Jersey court denied the doctor's request, saying that while practicing correctional health care, the doctor engaged in professional misconduct, gross malpractice, gross negligence, and gross incompetence, including acts that evidenced the intentional and deliberate infliction of unnecessary pain on inmates. In this case, the prison physician asked the government to provide a vigorous defense on his behalf, even though the doctor accepted some responsibility for his professional shortcomings.

Prisoners' Causes of Action Referring now to the legal basis for the plaintiffs' claims, we observed that 50 (26%) of the 189 doctors were held liable for at least one cause of action. Of these, 19 (38%) included medical malpractice actions, 12 (24%) were medical negligence lawsuits, 11 (22%) were lawsuits pursuant to 42 U.S.C. § 1983, 4 (8%) represented writ of habeas corpus actions, 2 (4%) revolved around writ of certiorari actions, and 2 (4%) were deemed other types of lawsuits.

Although there were 189 physicians sued, our sample contained only 121 court cases. This is a result of the fact that multiple physicians within a single case were often named as defendants. Table 4 shows that within the 121 cases, there were 244 causes of action pursued, including 93 (38%) medical malpractice actions, 79 (32%) lawsuits pursuant to 42 U.S.C. § 1983, 24 (10%) medical negligence lawsuits, 17 (7%) habeas corpus actions, 5 (2%) writ of certiorari actions, and 26 (11%) other types of lawsuits.

Data in Table 4 reveal that of the 244 causes of action, plaintiffs prevailed 36% of the time ($n = 88$).[7] Conversely, defendants prevailed 53% of the time ($n = 130$).[8] When plaintiffs prevailed, they did so most frequently in medical malpractice actions (38%, $n = 33$). In one such case, *Jacques v. State* (1984), rhinoplasty was performed on an inmate who was discharged to the general inmate population without antibiotics. A week later, the inmate developed a serious infection in the nasal/eye area. At that point, he received antibiotics, but he was hospitalized with complications and pus had to be surgically drained from the infected areas. As a result, the inmate suffered additional pain, underwent subsequent surgery, and was permanently scarred under his left eye. The inmate brought a medical malpractice action against the prison physician for failing to prescribe antibiotics immediately after surgery. The Court of Claims of New York held that "failure to use antibiotics post-surgery constituted medical malpractice" (p. 466).

Although it is difficult for prisoners to win inadequate medical care lawsuits filed under 42 U.S.C. § 1983 (Vaughn & Carroll, 1998), Table 4 reveals that plaintiffs prevailed in 31% ($n = 27$) of these claims. In *Santiago v. Leik* (1993), for example, an inmate with amyotrophic lateral sclerosis (ALS) was not properly fed or given assistance with his living arrangements. The Wisconsin Court of Appeals reversed the dismissal of the inmate's Section 1983 lawsuit, saying that the prison doctor did not take proper measures to feed the severely ill inmate who could not eat on his own. Likewise, in *Ennis v. Dasovick* (1993), an inmate who wore

TABLE 4 Prisoners' Causes of Action ($N = 244$)

	Overall		Plaintiffs Prevailed	
Type of Claim	n	Percentage	n	Percentage
Malpractice actions	93	38	33	38
42 U.S.C Section 1983	79	32	27	31
Medical negligence	24	10	21	24
Writ of habeas corpus actions	17	7	4	4
Writ of certiorari actions	5	2	3	3
Other	26	11	0	0
Total	244	100	88	36

glasses for 28 years was denied a new pair of eyeglasses by prison medical officials. The North Dakota Supreme Court reinstated the inmate's Section 1983 lawsuit, saying that the doctor may be liable for refusing to provide new eye glasses to the inmate at the state's expense.

When plaintiffs filed medical negligence lawsuits (see Table 4), they prevailed in slightly less than one fourth of their claims (24%, $n = 21$). Such was the case in *Tomcik v. Ohio Department of Rehabilitation and Correction* (1991), where a female inmate was given a "cursory" breast examination by a prison doctor—for 10 seconds, he pressed "lightly upon each breast" and found no lumps. The next day, when the inmate examined her own breasts, she found a lump the size of a pea. She submitted daily requests to be examined further by prison medical officials, but was not seen by a nurse until 3 weeks later. Three months later, the inmate was transferred to another correctional facility, where she was examined by medical personnel who found a golf ball–sized tumor in her breast. Shortly thereafter, she underwent a radical mastectomy, in which her right breast was removed.

The inmate filed a medical negligence claim against prison medical officials, alleging that "the cancer was allowed to progress to the stage where plaintiff was unable to utilize certain breast conserving procedures, but instead was required to have her entire right breast removed" (p. 902). An Ohio court said that the doctor rendered "substandard medical care" by "merely" pressing on the "plaintiff's breasts," and ruled that "such acts would not necessarily disclose lumps in breasts" (p. 903). Moreover, the court found that the tumor was present and "quite small" when the doctor initially examined the inmate, and that the "plaintiff preferred the breast conserving lumpectomy procedure;" that procedure, however, was "not feasible," because when the tumor was finally diagnosed, its size required more invasive surgery (p. 904). Awarding the inmate $85,000 in damages, the court concluded that the plaintiff suffered physical pain, emotional suffering, permanent damage, and disfigurement, and that her life expectancy was reduced by 15%.

When defendants prevailed, they were most successful in medical malpractice actions, winning 46% ($n = 60$) of these cases.[9] A typical case was *Steedley v. Correctional Medical Services* (1998), in which an inmate tested positive for tuberculosis. Evidence showed that the inmate's prison work assignment was to clean the infirmary where inmates with active tuberculosis were housed. The prison doctor testified that only a person with a compromised immune system would have contracted tuberculosis in the infirmary. A Delaware court dismissed the case because the inmate was unable to link his tuberculosis with unacceptable medical care performed by the prison physician.

As mentioned, previous research shows that it is difficult for plaintiffs to win inadequate medical care lawsuits litigated under 42 U.S.C. § 1983 (Vaughn & Carroll, 1998). The present analysis reveals that defendants won 40% ($n = 52$) of the state court cases litigated pursuant to Section 1983. An illustrative case was *Montanez v. Questcare* (1996), in which an inmate with diabetes in the Alabama prison system disagreed with the course of health care that was prescribed by the prison physician. The inmate's lawsuit was dismissed, even though the doctor refused to alter his course of medical treatment to meet with the inmate's satisfaction.

Defendants also won 13 cases (10%) litigated under a writ of habeas corpus. In recent years, the U.S. Congress and U.S. Supreme Court has made it more difficult for inmates to win cases pursuant to habeas corpus petitions (Clear & Cole, 2000). In *Roberson v. Warden* (1996), for example, a prisoner in Connecticut passed blood in his urine and experienced urinary tract discomfort. The prison physician conducted numerous diagnostic tests, but was unable to identify the cause of the inmate's ailment. The Connecticut Superior Court dismissed the inmate's petition for a writ of habeas corpus, saying that the "Department of Corrections is now and will continue to provide adequate medical care" to the inmate (p. 1).

Regulatory Social Control of Jail and Prison Physicians

Correctional physicians implicated in inmate litigation were cross-referenced to the *16,638 Questionable Doctors Disciplined by State and Federal Governments* (Wolfe et al., 1998) to determine if they have had any formal action taken against their medical license. Of the 189 prison doctors identified in the case law analysis above, we were able to definitively determine, using complete first and last names, that 14 had some form of formal action taken against their license in the years since 1987. In three additional cases, we were able to locate an instance of licensure action in the sourcebook that was taken against a doctor with the same last name and first initial as one of the doctors from the case law analysis. In each of these three cases, a process of cross-referencing the documented facts of the two or more hearings led us to conclude that the actions were most likely taken against the same person. This exercise leads us to conclude that roughly 9% ($n = 17$) of the 189 doctors named in the medical misconduct case law analysis also had some form of licensure action taken against them between 1987 and 1998. As such, our analysis reveals a higher degree of disciplinary sanction taken against prison physicians (9%) than physicians who practice in the free world (2.4%) (Wolfe et al., 1998, p. 5). Moreover, during this 11-year time period, these 17 doctors had a total of 30 actions taken against their licenses by one of the following regulatory entities: a state medical board, the DEA, the FDA, or the U.S. Department of Health and Human Services. For more than 75% ($n = 13$) of these doctors, we were able to determine that the licensure action resulted from behaviors unrelated to the court ruling in which we identified their names. Thus, the correctional medical lawsuit filed by prisoners had little bearing on physicians' licensure actions.

In 27 of the 30 (90%) actions, the sourcebook data revealed that the licensure sanctions were pursued by a state medical board. The remaining actions originated from the U.S. Department of Health and Human Service investigations into Medicare violations ($n = 2$) or from a DEA investigation into a prescription drug dispensing violation ($n = 1$).

We note that the above-mentioned 30 licensure actions resulted from a wide range of alleged offenses. In particular, when we applied the 18-category coding system provided in the sourcebook to the accompanying narratives, we were able to identify 48 different legal or ethical offenses that led to these 30 licensure actions. The most common reason for the licensure action was that the regulatory entity became aware that the doctor in question had been subject to a criminal conviction. This was the case for 9 of the 30 actions. Several of the doctors were convicted of serious, violent crimes. For example, there was the Ohio doctor who was convicted of aggravated murder and abuse of a human corpse. The year before the conviction, an Ohio court ruled that he was not liable in a medical malpractice claim. Specifically, the court in *Perotti v. Ohio Department of Rehabilitation and Correction* (1989) supported the doctor's decision to deviate from a free world physician's order that the inmate be prescribed narcotic-based analgesics to alleviate orthopedic pain in his foot. The Court of Appeals of Ohio ruled that the inmate had "suffered no ill effect" from the prison's failure to administer the exact pain medication prescribed (p. 177), and agreed that a desire to "maintain security within the institution and prevent drug addiction among inmates" (p. 176) superseded administering "habit-forming drugs" to the inmate.

In our cross-referencing, we also found a Tennessee doctor who was convicted of first-degree sexual abuse against a nonpatient, and a California doctor who was convicted of a drunk driving charge. Several doctors also were convicted on drug charges. For example, there was a California doctor who was convicted of drug offenses on two separate occasions—once for illegally dispensing prescription substances to an addict, and later on a possession charge. There was also a Georgia doctor who was first convicted in 1988 on a single charge of illegally dispensing controlled substances, and in 1994 was convicted of 15 counts of distributing and dispensing controlled substances for other than legitimate medical purposes and 40 counts of aiding and abetting the same. Ironically, a 1998 Georgia court ruling found him not liable in an action alleging that he refused to dispense treatment and medications to an inmate who was suffering from a painful foot injury. That case, *Cantrell v. Thurman* (1998), involved a jailed prisoner who injured his foot, and the sanctioned doctor diagnosed the injuries as two broken toes, concluding that "there was no treatment for plaintiff's condition" (p. 418). The jail doctor saw the prisoner five different times and administered 600 mg of ibuprofen; however, the physician performed no blood tests, no X rays, and did not prescribe antibiotics. The prisoner developed a fever of 107°, complained of severe foot pain, and saw his foot swell and turn red, blue, purple, and black. Because of his deteriorating condition, jail officials took the prisoner to the hospital, where he was diagnosed as a diabetic with gangrene. Several surgeries were performed to save the foot from amputation, but the prisoner suffered severe tissue damage, the amputation of several toes, and remained permanently disabled. In the prisoner's medical malpractice lawsuit, the Court of Appeals of Georgia affirmed the trial court's grant of summary judgment to the defendant, saying that he received treatment from the doctor and jail nurses on 13 occasions.

The most serious property offense conviction was handed down to a Pennsylvania doctor, who in 1996 was convicted of fraud when it was found that he was exploiting maternal and child health services block grants to defraud the Medicare system of large sums of money. This doctor was one of several defendants in *Simons v. State Correctional Institute* (1992). In that case, a prisoner developed

Hodgkin's disease while he was incarcerated, and claimed that the physicians who provided medical care did not appropriately diagnose and treat his cancer. Without commenting on the merits of the case, the Commonwealth Court of Pennsylvania transferred the prisoner's lawsuit to the proper jurisdiction.

In seven cases, the licensure action in question resulted from an act of information sharing, that is, one regulatory agency was notified of a disciplinary action of another state or agency and thus decided to implement their own sanctions. These actions included federal actions against doctors who were sanctioned by the U.S. Department of Health and Human Services for abusing the Medicare/Medicaid system. For example, there was the New York doctor—excluded from participating in the Medicare/Medicaid system—who was sued by an inmate for performing unnecessary surgery. In that case, *Rivers v. State* (1989), a prison physician diagnosed an inmate with a left inguinal hernia and recommended surgery. The inmate was transferred to a free world physician, who contracted his services to the Department of Correctional Services to perform surgeries. Although the inmate's medical records indicated a left inguinal hernia, the admitting records indicated that the diagnosis was a right inguinal hernia. The contractual physician testified that he never physically examined the patient, but once the inmate was unconscious, he noticed a "large left hernia bulge, which was obviously visible to the naked eye" (pp. 969–970). Nevertheless, according to the contractual physician, he was "forced to proceed . . . [and ignore the fact that the left was there] . . . with the right . . . inguinal repair because [those] records [were] available—he had signed the consent for the right inguinal hernia and the admission record stated right inguinal hernia" (p. 970). Evidence showed that the prison physician and contractual physician did not consult about the inmate's conditions at any time, nor were the inmate's prison medical records forwarded to the contractual physician for the operation.

A hearing committee of the New York State Board for Professional Medical Conduct found that the contractual physician "did not properly examine [the prisoner], that he did not obtain an adequate medical history, and that he did not properly evaluate [the prisoner's] medical condition prior to performing surgery. . . . [The doctor] failed to perform a left inguinal repair and subjected [the prisoner] to unnecessary surgery in the right inguinal area." As a result, the Board recommended that the doctor's "license to practice medicine in the State of New York be revoked for his actions in this and other cases" (*Rivers v. State,* 1989, p. 970).

In another case, an anesthesiologist had his license either restricted or revoked by three separate state medical boards after a series of charges that he repeatedly delivered substandard care. The doctor retained his baseline license to practice medicine, took a job in a Wisconsin prison, and was sued again for improperly prescribing medications. This particular case, *Munroe v. McCaughtry* (1997), involved an inmate who suffered atopic numular eczema, a skin disease that can be successfully treated with specific medications and Dove soap. The prison doctor refused to provide the inmate with Dove soap, prescribing instead medications that "gave [him] chemical burns and caused the loss of pubic hair" (p. 1). Evidence showed that the prison doctor was hired by the prison even though he had not passed his state medical board examination. Correctional physicians also refused to approve surgery for the inmate to remove a "mona (lipoma)" (p. 1). By denying this care, correctional medical personnel exacerbated the inmate's "skin disease, thereby causing his skin to breakout in large rashes and sores, causing him physical and emotional suffering" (p. 1).

The inmate sued, but the Court of Appeals of Wisconsin ruled that an expert witness was necessary to establish that medical officials breached their duty to adhere to the appropriate standard of care. The court concluded that "without an expert witness, [the inmate] would not be able to show that his eczema skin condition was worsened by the defendant's acts" (p. 2). This case also speaks to the principle of less eligibility, because courts rule an inmate must have an expert witness to show if a prison physician breached to appropriate standard of medical care. Yet prison systems are not required to appoint an expert medical official to an indigent inmate. This is significant because most inmates have no way of paying for medical expert witnesses and are far removed from the professional network of colleagues that would make the best medical experts available to them.

The sourcebook also contains a broad offense category termed "professional misconduct." Specifically, this category "includes a variety of offenses that are more serious than the violation of a professional rule but do not fit into any other [16 specific] categories" (Wolfe et al., 1998, p. 90). The licensure narratives from the 30 actions in question revealed five different instances of professional misconduct. These included cases of doctors performing unnecessary or inappropriate procedures, breaching doctor-patient confidentiality, selling drugs or devices for personal gain, and sexual abuse of a nonpatient.

In three of the cases, the licensure action involved the doctor's failure to comply with a professional rule (e.g., failure to report a disciplinary action of another state, failure to meet continuing medical education requirements, or failure to respond to a board order). We identified three cases in which the doctor was accused of "overprescribing or misprescribing drugs" and three cases alleging "substandard care, incompetence, or negligent care." Two doctors were accused of each of the following offenses: practicing without a valid license, or the offense of "insurance, Medicare, or Medicaid fraud." Finally, one doctor was implicated in each of the following offenses: failure to comply with a previous board order, overcharging, and substance abuse.

One Illinois physician, who was among those disciplined for practicing medicine without a valid license, was also a defendant in *Moss v. Miller* (1993). This case was brought forth by an inmate who was severely beaten by a group of inmates, causing his eyes to swell shut. The injured inmate was examined by two correctional physicians and an optometrist, who testified that they were aware of his serious injuries, including the possibility of an orbital fracture or blow-out fracture of the eye socket.[10] Prison physicians and the optometrist examined the inmate 10 times, and arranged for Xrays and an eye patch. Although the inmate reported that he experienced double vision and his eye deviated 20 diopters upward and outward, no referral was made to an ophthalmologist for more than 2 months.

The ophthalmologist diagnosed the inmate with a blow-out fracture, finding that he lost about 50% of his ability to look down and his eye was turned outward 25%; his double vision remains a permanent disability. In the inmate's lawsuit, evidence showed the injuries might have been less severe if he had been referred to an ophthalmologist and been treated within 14 days after the injury. A jury found that the optometrist violated a national standard of care, awarding the inmate $75,000. The jury did not find the jail physicians liable, in part because their attorneys argued that they were obligated to standards of care commonly used by prison doctors practicing in correctional facilities. On appeal, an Illinois court reversed and remanded a new trial on the claim against the two correctional physicians, saying that "reversible error took place because the [jury] instructions indicated a [local] standard of care was required" (p. 1052), instead of a national standard. Finding that the physicians engaged in gross negligence (p. 1054), the court concluded that "evidence established that [the inmate] suffered a severe injury which could cause him problems the rest of his life. There was testimony of double vision, disfigurement, and dizziness, all of which interfere with everyday activities" (p. 1055).

The narratives contained in the Public Citizen sourcebook suggest that the various regulatory/licensure entities generally took the above-mentioned allegations seriously. Nine of the doctors had their license to practice medicine revoked. Another three were forced to surrender their license, and two were denied renewal on an expired license. Lesser sanctions (often handed down together) included five license suspensions, one emergency suspension of a license, nine orders of probation, seven fines, two orders for the individual to be excluded from the Medicare program, one order to disclose a board-imposed order to their employer and patients, and one suspension of the authority to prescribe prescription substances. There were, however, some very precarious rulings handed down by the acting agencies. Most notably, after rendering a patient brain dead due to a failure to diagnose the individual of meningitis, the Texas Board of Medicine imposed a licensure restriction decreeing that the doctor "shall practice only in a facility of the Texas Department of Criminal Justice" (Wolfe et al., 1998, p. 46). One year later, this same doctor found his way into our case law analysis after an inmate brought a malpractice claim against him after an alleged failed diagnosis resulted in the need to surgically remove the inmate's right testicle. In that case, *Johnson v. Chaney* (1996), an inmate hurt his groin and testicles while working in the Texas prison system. The staff physician in question treated the inmate for his injuries for 10 days. The inmate claimed the doctor provided inadequate medical care because he refused to refer him to a specialist at a free world hospital. As a result of the inadequate treatment, the inmate's right testicle was surgically removed. The inmate sued the prison doctor for medical negligence. Affirming the district court's dismissal of the inmate's lawsuit, the Court of Appeals of Texas ruled that the inmate suffered no compensable injury due to the "treatment or lack of treatment he received from" the doctor (p. 4). This case also highlights the principle of less eligibility because the prison doctor was deemed not competent to practice in the free world, but suitable to work with inmates.

CONCLUSION

Anecdotal reports that originate from correctional administrators, prisoners' rights advocates, and the media have raised the suspicion that correctional physicians deliver substandard care, exhibit diminished levels of professional competence, and engage in a host of unethical behaviors. Moreover, the underclass status of the available patient pool, when coupled with the poor working environment, leads to the suspicion that there is not much competition within the medical profession to seek out and procure jobs as correctional physicians. Instead, it is safe to assume that these jobs are among the least desirable ones that a doctor could obtain. Using the principle of less eligibility, we hypothesized that this situation would result in low levels of professional competence among correctional physicians. We turned to judicial records as the first way to assess this hypothesis. In particular, we referenced civil actions filed by prisoners in state courts seeking monetary damages and/or injunctive relief for inadequate correctional health care as a proxy measure of the level and nature of judicial social control directed toward correctional physicians' professional competence. Our analysis of 121 court rulings, involving 189 doctors and 202 legal claims, provides considerable evidence of unethical behavior and professional incompetence among correctional physicians.

The case law analysis suggests that prisoners were subject to a wide variety of substandard health care practices. Half of the civil actions analyzed alleged poor or improper care. In 20% of the cases, inmates claimed that they were completely denied care by a correctional physician. Other reasons for pursuing civil litigation included faulty diagnoses (13%), delayed care (6%), exposure to unethical or inhumane care (4%), being treated by unqualified or unlicensed physicians (3%), being subject to unwanted or unauthorized forms of care (3%), and a doctor's forcible response to a prisoner's hunger strike (1%).

We found evidence that the above-mentioned actions/inactions on the part of correctional physicians resulted in a variety of negative health outcomes for prisoners. Most disturbingly, we documented 19 prisoner deaths. In 15.3% of the cases, prisoners suffered permanent physical disabilities as a consequence of the doctors' actions/inactions. Permanent loss in quality of life was the alleged negative health outcome in 17% of the cases, whereas in 58% of the cases, prisoners claimed to suffer some form of temporary loss in quality of life.

It is clear that correctional physicians rarely accept responsibility for the above-mentioned negative health outcomes. In fact, less than 10% of the doctors accepted full responsibility for their behaviors, and subsequently offered some form of apologia (Scott & Lyman, 1968). Instead, in the vast majority of the cases, we found that doctors attempted to justify or minimize their blameworthiness. Drawing on Sykes and Matza's (1957) techniques of neutralization, we concluded that the most common physician response was denial of responsibility (36.6%). Other responses were categorized as denial of injury (25%), condemnation of condemners (16.3%), denial of victim (7.4%), and appeal to higher loyalty (5%).

The content of the state court rulings leads us to conclude that incompetent doctors were being subject to only marginal levels of punitive judicial social control. Courts recognized a variety of legal claims, including malpractice actions

(38%), actions pursuant to 42 U.S.C. Section 1983 (32%), medical negligence (10%), writ of habeas corpus actions (7%), and writ of certiorari actions (2%). We observed that only 26% of the doctors were held liable for at least one legal claim, and plaintiffs prevailed in only 36% of cases. In fact, there was no one form of legal claim that resulted in legal victory for more than half of plaintiff litigants.

Turning to regulatory social control as a means of assessing the competence of correctional physicians, our analysis suggests that correctional physicians who are sued in state courts experience higher rates of disciplinary actions on their medical license than physicians at large. In particular, we found that 9% ($n = 17$) of 189 jail and prison doctors who were subject to judicial social control also experienced some form of state and/or federal regulatory social control. This represents almost four times the level of state and/or federal regulatory social control that is experienced by free world physicians (2.4%). These data support our hypothesis that correctional physicians possess limited employment opportunities because of questionable clinical qualifications and professional competence. Highlighting the principle of less eligibility, the data here show how substandard doctors practicing within correctional health care systems deliver poor quality medical care to prisoners (see also Vaughn, 1999; Vaughn & Smith, 1999a, 1999b). . . .

Looking ahead, more research needs to be conducted on physicians who work in correctional facilities. We must develop creative and more reliable ways to more accurately assess the quality of care and competency of physicians who practice in correctional settings. Despite spending billions on correctional health care, we know very little about the men and women who work in this field.[11] This article raises profound ethical questions about disproportionately staffing correctional health units with physicians who have been disciplined for misconduct. Equally scandalous is the medical community's complicity in placing sanctioned physicians in correctional health settings, and correctional personnel within federal, state, and local governments who refuse to document and/or recognize that a problem exists. Because health care must be constitutionally provided to prisoners (*Estelle v. Gamble,* 1976), the problem of questionable doctors practicing in correctional systems will only grow as correctional populations continue to expand and as medical inflation consumes a larger part of corrections' budgets.

NOTES

1. Sykes and Matza (1957) settled on a series of five generic "techniques of neutralization" that they said were likely to be enlisted by juvenile delinquents: denial of responsibility, denial of injury, denial of victim, condemnation of condemners, and appeal to higher loyalties.
2. Physicians who work in jails and prisons.
3. Although each case in our sample was pursued by a lone plaintiff (i.e., prisoner), any given case may name multiple defendants (i.e., doctors), be based on prisoner's assertions that he or she was subject to behaviors that constitute multiple legal claims (e.g., denial of care, poor or improper care, faulty diagnosis), and/or the court may recognize multiple causes of action (e.g., medical

malpractice, medical negligence, writs of habeas corpus). Each of these factors provide a potential unit of analysis within the context of this article. As such, we note that these 121 cases named 189 doctors. Of the 189 doctors, 6 had more than one legal claim (e.g., an inmate alleged that Doctor X was guilty of both a faulty diagnosis and subsequent poor care), thus yielding a total number of 202 legal claims. The court often decided that a single legal claim provided grounds for multiple causes of action. For example, the court could rule that a defendant doctor's failure to diagnose a cancerous condition represented grounds for both a medical malpractice and a Section 1983 action. Thus, there were a total of 244 causes of action heard within this sample of 121 cases. The reader is cautioned that sample sizes will change as we shift the forthcoming discussion from one unit of analysis to another. When discussing the aspects of prisoners' allegations or the doctors' responses, we will focus on legal claims as our unit of analysis ($N = 202$). Conversely, when we summarize the legal outcomes, we will enlist formal causes of action as the unit of analysis ($N = 244$).

4. For purposes of coding, plaintiffs prevailed if they won the specific legal issues being litigated; the same applied to defendants. Because many of these cases were interlocutory appeals, the party that won the legal issue may not have ultimately prevailed in the final disposition of the case.

5. Congress created the National Practitioner Databank to identify problem physicians, but access is strictly limited to law enforcement agencies, regulatory bodies, and prospective health care providers who seek to employee physicians. The general public and researchers are barred from using the database (Cagle, Martinez, & Richardson, 1999, p. 753).

6. Of the 189 physicians, 6 had 13 separate claims brought against them.

7. Plaintiffs also prevailed in four (4%) actions under a writ of habeas corpus and three (3%) actions pursuant to a writ of certiorari.

8. In 11% ($n = 26$) of the legal dispositions, neither the plaintiff nor defendant prevailed.

9. Defendants also prevailed in three (2%) medical negligence actions and two (2%) actions pursuant to a writ of certiorari.

10. "An orbital fracture, or blow-out fracture, occurs when blunt trauma to the eye causes the bony structure of the eye socket (orbit) to rupture" (*Moss v. Miller,* 1993, p. 1047).

11. The U.S. Department of Justice reported that "states spent nearly $2.5 billion on prisoner medical and dental care in FY 1996 or about 12% of total prison operating expenditures" (Stephan, 1999, p. 7). This figure does not include the cost of jail medical care.

REFERENCES

Allen, W., & Bell, K. (1998, September 27). Health care behind bars: Death, neglect, and the bottom line. *St. Louis Post Dispatch,* pp. G1–G12.

Allen, W., & Bell, K. (1999, February 10). Missouri revamps the way it monitors prison health care. *St. Louis Post Dispatch,* p. A1.

Auger v. State, 693 N.Y.S.2d 343 (N. Y. App. Div. 3 1999).

Austin v. Warden, WL 649328 (Conn. Super. 1996).

Ballengee v. Ohio Department of Rehabilitation and Correction, 670 N.E.2d 1383 (Ohio Ct. Cl. 1996).

Baltzer v. Ohio Department of Rehabilitation and Correction, 644 N.E.2d 737 (Ohio Ct. Cl. 1993).

Becker, J. (1999a, September 27). Many prison doctors have troubled past. *St. Petersburg Times,* p. 1A.

Becker, J. (1999b, October 2). Bush admits neglect in prisons. *St. Petersburg Times,* p. 1B.

Belbot, B. A., & del Carmen, R. V. (1991). AIDS in prison: Legal issues. *Crime & Delinquency, 37,* 148–153.

Bennett, K., & del Carmen, R. V. (1997). A review and analysis of prison litigation reform act court decisions: Solution or aggravation? *The Prison Journal, 77,* 405–455.

Berkman, A. (1991). Prisoner/patient struggles: A view from the inside. *Humanity and Society, 15,* 417–421.

Berkman, A. (1995). Prison health: The breaking point. *American Journal of Public Health, 85,* 1616–1618.

Bilbo v. Thigpen. 647 So.2d 678 (Miss. 1994).

Blumberg, M., & Mahaffey-Sapp, C. (1997). Health care issues in correctional institutions. In M. D. Schwartz & F. L. Travis (Eds.), *Corrections: An issues approach* (4th ed., pp. 333–344). Cincinnati, OH: Anderson.

BOP and DOD offer joint physician assistants training. (1997, June 30). *Monday Morning Highlights,* p. 4.

Brown v. State, 392 So.2d 113 (La. App. 1980).

Cagle, M. C., Martinez, J. M., & Richardson, W. D. (1999). Privatizing professional licensing boards: Self-governance or self-interest? *Administration and Society, 30,* 734–770.

California Department of Corrections v. Office of Administrative Hearings, 61 Cal. Rptr.2d 903 (App. 2 Dist. 1997).

Cantrell v. Thurman, 499 S.E.2d 416 (Ga. App. 1998).

Clear, T. R., & Cole, G. F (2000). *American corrections* (5th ed.). Belmont, CA: West/Wadsworth.

Cooper v. Bowers, 706 S.W.2d 542 (Mo. App. 1986).

Dabney, D. A. (1995). Neutralization and deviance in the workplace: Theft of supplies and medicines by hospital nurses. *Deviant Behavior, 16,* 313–331.

Dabney, D. A., & Hollinger, R. C. (1999). Illicit prescription drug use among pharmacists: Evidence of a paradox of familiarity. *Work and Occupations, 26,* 77–106.

Department of Public Welfare v. Kallinger, 580 A.2d 887 (Pa. Cmwlth. 1990).

District of Columbia v. Anderson, 597 A.2d 1295 (D.C. App. 1991).

Dodge, M. (1998, November). *Diagnosing doctors: Profiles of the California Physician Disclosure Law.* Paper presented at the meetings of the American Society of Criminology, Washington, DC.

Ennis v. Dasovick, 506 N.W.2d 386 (N.D. 1993).

Estelle v. Gamble, 429 U.S. 97 (1976).

Fiedler v. Spoelhof, 483 N.W.2d 486 (Minn. App. 1992).

Flamer v. Redman, WL 15322 (Del. Super. 1988).

Fleisher, M. S., & Rison, R. H (1997). Health care in the federal bureau of prisons. In J. W. Marquart & J. R. Sorensen (Eds.), *Correctional contexts: Contemporary and classical readings* (pp. 327–334). Los Angeles: Roxbury.

Flores v. Natividad Medical Center, 238 Cal. Rptr. 24 (Cal. App. 1 Dist. 1987).

Fradella, H. F. (1998). A typology of the frivolous: Varying meanings of frivolity in Section 1983 prisoner civil rights litigation. *The Prison Journal, 78,* 465–491.

Friedman, M. C. (1992). Cruel and unusual punishment in the provision of prison medical care: Challenging the deliberate indifference standard. *Vanderbilt Law Review, 45,* 921–949.

Gillam v. Lloyd. 432 N.W.2d 356 (Mich. App. 1988).

Goad v. Pasipanodya, WL 749462 (Tenn. App. 1997).

Gordon v. Cannell, 545 N.W.2d 722 (Neb. 1996).

Gray, J. (1992). Why bad doctors aren't kicked out of medicine. *Medical Economics, 69,* 126–149.

Gullette v. State Through Department of Corrections, 383 So.2d 1287 (La. App. 1980).

Gunter v. State, 736 P.2d 1198 (Ariz. App. 1987).

Haavisto v. Perpich, 520 N.W.2d 727 (Minn. 1994).

Hampton v. Lloren, WL 426951 (Wis. App. 1997).

Haney, C. (1998). Riding the punishment wave: On the origins of our devolving standards of decency. *Hastings Women's Law Journal, 9,* 27–78.

Harris v. Thigpen, 941 F.2d 1495 (11th Cir. 1991).

Herbert v. District of Columbia, 691 A.2d 1175 (D.C. App. 1997), rev'd, 716 A.2d 196 (D.C. App. 1998) (en banc).

Hill v. City of Saginaw, 399 N.W.2d 398 (Mich. App. 1986).

Horton v. Collins, WL 544427 (Tex. App. Houston 14 Dist. 1996).

Howard v. City of Columbus, 466 S.E.2d 51 (Ga. App. 1995).

Howard v. Jonah, 430 S.E.2d 833 (Ga. App. 1993).

Jacques v. State, 487 N.Y.S.2d 463 (Ct. Cl. 1984).

Jesilow, P., Pontell, H. N., & Geis, G. (1993). *Prescription for profit: How doctors defraud Medicaid.* Berkeley: University of California Press.

Johnson v. Chaney, WL 671248 (Tex. App. Houston 14 Dist. 1996).

Kagan v. State, 646 N.Y.S.2d 336 (A.D. 2 Dept. 1996).

Keenan v. Maass, 911 P.2d 331 (Or. App. 1996).

King, R. D. (1998). Prisons. In M. Tonry (Ed.), *Handbook of crime and punishment* (pp. 589–625). New York: Oxford University Press.

Kirsch v. Start, WL 53801 (Wis. App. 1994).

Kohn, L. T., Corrigan, J. M., & Donaldson, M. S. (2000). *To error is human: Building a safer health system.* Washington, DC: National Academy Press.

Kyriss v. State, 707 P.2d 5 (Mont. 1985).

LeFay v. Coopersmith, 576 A.2d 192 (Me. 1990).

Lezin, K. (1996). Life at Lorton: An examination of prisoners' rights at the District of Columbia correctional facilities. *Boston University Public Interest Law Journal, 5,* 165–211.

Loveday, B. (1993). The contemporary prison debate. *Reviewing Sociology, 8*(3), 10–18.

Luther v. Compton, WL 117296 (Tenn. Crim. App. 1998).

Maeve, M. K. (1997). Nursing practice with incarcerated women: Caring within mandated [sic] alienation. *Issues in Mental Health Nursing, 18,* 495–510.

Marquart, J. W., Brewer, V. E., Mullings, J. L., & Crouch, B. M. (1999). Health risk as an emerging field with the new penology. *Journal of Criminal Justice, 27,* 143–154.

Marquart, J. W., Merianos, D. E., Cuvelier, S. J., & Carroll, L. (1996). Thinking about the relationship between health dynamics in the free community and the prison. *Crime & Delinquency, 42,* 331–360.

Marquart, J. W., Merianos, D. E., Hebert, J. L., & Carroll, L. (1997). Health condition and prisoners: A review of research and emerging areas of inquiry. *The Prison Journal, 77,* 184–208.

Matter of Napoleon, 697 A.2d 574 (N.J. Super. A.D. 1997).

McFadden v. State, 542 So.2d 871 (Miss. 1989).

McNeil v. Brewer, 710 N.E.2d 1285 (Ill. App. 3 Dist. 1999).

Montanez v. Questcare, 675 So.2d 466 (Ala. Civ. App. 1996).

Moss v. Miller, 625 N.E.2d 1044 (Ill. App. 4 Dist. 1993).

Munroe v. McCaughtry, WL 378012 (Wis. App. 1997).

Napier v. Warden, WL 282620 (Conn. Super. 1990).

Nelson v. State, 188 Cal. Rptr. 479 (Cal. App. 4 Dist. 1982).

Ochoa v. Superior Court of Santa Clara County, 191 Cal. Rptr. 907 (Cal. App. 1 Dist. 1983).

Oliver v. Townsend, 534 So.2d 1038 (Ala. 1988).

Pan v. California State Personnel Board, 225 Cal. Rptr. 682 (Cal. App. 3 Dist. 1986).

Pear, R. (1999, December 7). A Clinton order seeks to reduce medical errors. *New York Times,* pp. A1, A17.

Perotti v. Ohio Department of Rehabilitation and Correction, 572 N.E.2d 172 (Ohio App. 1989).

Polk County Sheriff v. Iowa District Court for Polk County, 594 N.W.2d 421 (Iowa 1999).

Proffitt v. Prison Health Services, WL 426779 (Tenn. App. 1996).

Rivers v. State, 537 N.Y.S.2d 968 (Ct. Cl. 1989), rev.d, 552 N.Y.S.2d 189 (A.D. 3 Dept. 1990).

Rewald v. San Pedro Peninsula Hospital, 32 Cal. Rptr.2d 411 (Cal. App. 2 Dist. 1994).

Roberson v. Warden, WL 383388 (Conn. Super. 1996).

Rosenthal, M. M. (1995). *The incompetent doctor: Behind closed doors.* Buckingham, UK: Open University Press.

Ross, D. L. (1997). Emerging trends in correctional civil liability cases: A content analysis of federal court decisions of Title 42 United States Code Section 1983. *Journal of Criminal Justice, 25,* 501–514.

Rushing v. Wayne County, 462 N.W.2d 23 (Mich. 1990).

Santiago v. Leik, 508 N.W.2d 456 (Wis. App. 1993).

Schultz-Ross, R. A. (1993). The prisoner's prisoner: The theme of voluntary imprisonment in the staff of correctional facilities. *Bulletin of the American Academy of Psychiatry and the Law, 21,* 101–106.

Scott, M. B., & Lyman, S. M. (1968). Accounts. *American Sociological Review, 33,* 46–62.

Sherrod v. State, 557 N.W.2d 634 (Neb. 1997).

Simons v. State Correctional Institute, 615 A.2d 924 (Pa. Cmnlth. 1992).

Skolnick, A. A. (1998a). Critics denounce staffing jails and prisons with physicians convicted of misconduct. *Journal of the American Medical Association, 280,* 1391–1392.

Skolnick, A. A. (1998b, September 27). Physicians with troubled pasts have found work behind bars. *St. Louis Post Dispatch,* p. G9.

Skolnick, A. A. (1998c). Prison deaths spotlight how boards handle impaired, disciplined physicians. *Journal of the American Medical Association, 280,* 1387–1390.

Skolnick, A. A., & Bell, K. (1998, September 27). Prisoner, doctor who treated him, both had drug arrests. *St. Louis Post Dispatch,* p. G9.

Sloan v. Ohio Department of Rehabilitation and Correction, 695 N.W.2d 298 (Ohio App. 10 Dist. 1997).

Smith v. Ohio State University Hospital, 674 N.E.2d 721 (Ohio App. 10 Dist. 1996).

Steedley v. Correctional Medical Services, WL 962069 (Del. Super. 1998).

Stephan, J. J. (1999). *State prison expenditures,* 1996. Washington, DC: U.S. Department of Justice.

Steptoe, S. (1986, May 15). Careless treatment: Inmates claim prisons are failing to provide adequate medical care. *Wall Street Journal,* p. 1.

Stevenson v. Lanham, 736 A.2d 363 (Md. Ct. Spe. App. 1999).

Stohr, M. K., & Zupan, L. L. (1992). Street-level bureaucrats and service provision in jails: The failure of officers to identify the needs of inmates. *American Journal of Criminal Justice, 16*(2), 75–94.

Stolberg, S. G. (1999, December 5). Breaking down medicine's culture of silence. *New York Times,* Sec. 4, pp. 1, 18.

Sykes, G. M., & Matza, D. (1957). Techniques of neutralization: A theory of delinquency. *American Sociological Review, 22,* 664–670.

Thor v. Superior Court (Andrews), 855 P.2d 375 (Cal. 1993) (en banc).

Tomcik v. Ohio Department of Rehabilitation and Correction, 598 N.E.2d 900 (Ohio Ct. Cl. 1991).

U.S. General Accounting Office. (1994). *Bureau of prisons health care.* Washington, DC: U.S. Government Printing Office.

Vaughn, M. S. (1995). Section 1983 civil liability of prison officials for denying and delaying medication and drugs to prison inmates. *Issues in Law and Medicine, 11,* 47–76.

Vaughn, M. S. (1997). Civil liability against prison officials for prescribing and dispensing medications and drugs to prison inmates. *Journal of Legal Medicine, 18,* 315–344.

Vaughn, M. S. (1999). Penal harm medicine: State tort remedies for delaying and denying health care to prisoners. *Crime, Law, and Social Change, 31,* 273–302.

Vaughn, M. S., & Carroll, L. (1998). Separate and unequal: Prison versus free-world medical care. *Justice Quarterly, 15,* 3–40.

Vaughn, M. S., & Smith, L. G. (1999a). Practicing penal harm medicine in the United States: Prisoners' voices from jail. *Justice Quarterly, 16,* 175–231.

Vaughn, M. S., & Smith, L. G. (1999b). Questioning authorized truth: Resisting the pull of the policy audience and fostering critical scholarship in correctional medical research—a reply to Kerle et al. *Justice Quarterly, 16,* 907–918.

Vause, R. C., Beeler, A., & Miller-Blanks, M. (1997). Seeking a practice challenge? PAs in federal prisons. *JAAPA/Official Journal of the American Academy of Physician Assistants, 10*(2), 59–67.

Vega v. Morris, 905 P.2d 535 (Ariz. App. Div. 1 1995).

Watson v. State, 26 Cal. Rptr.2d 262 (Cal. App. 2 Dist. 1993).

Wilson v. Hun, 457 S.E.2d 662 (W. Va. 1995).

Wolfe, S., Franklin, K. M., McCarthy, P., Bame, A., & Adler, B. M. (1998). *16,638 questionable doctors disciplined by state and federal governments.* Washington, DC: Public Citizen Health Research Group.

Wright v. State, 488 N.Y.S.2d 917 (A.D. 4 Dept. 1985).

Zuck v. State, 764 P.2d 772 (Ariz. App. 1988).

REVIEW QUESTIONS

1. What factors account for the fact that most correctional doctors named in misconduct/malpractice lawsuits experience no corresponding licensure actions?
2. What dimensions of the medical subculture serve to influence the six techniques of neutralization outlined in this article?
3. What sort of effort could be undertaken to enhance the quality of doctors delivering care in correctional facilities?
4. What are some of the tensions that exist between the goals of practicing medicine and providing custody functions within a correctional institution?

IX

INMATE FAMILIES

READING 23

Families and Children

Jeremy Travis

This reading outlines the social consequences of incarceration of family members of inmates, effects of a parent's incarceration on children, negative consequences for the formation of families as a result of community incarceration rates, and how family members play a role in the experience of inmates returning to the community after incarceration. It is noted that the incarceration of large numbers of men reduces the number of available men for marriage and family construction in communities, thus leading to increasing numbers of female-headed households, poverty, and unsupervised children. A parent being incarcerated introduces psychological, emotional, financial, and social stresses on children. When inmates return to the community from incarceration, there are also likely to be stressful adjustments that must be made, by both the offender and the family to which the offender returns. When offenders return from incarceration, a number of challenges and stresses also are experienced by families and offenders.

As the nation debates the wisdom of a fourfold increase in our incarceration rate over the past generation, one fact is clear: Prisons separate prisoners from their families. Every individual sent to prison leaves behind a network of family relationships. Prisoners are the children, parents, siblings, and kin to untold numbers of relatives who are each affected differently by a family member's arrest, incarceration, and ultimate homecoming.

Little is known about imprisonment's impact on these family networks. Descriptive data about the children of incarcerated parents only begin to tell the story. During the 1990s, as the nation's prison population increased by half, the number of children who had a parent in prison also increased by half—from 1 million to 1.5 million. By the end of 2002, 1 in 45 minor children had a parent in prison (Mumola 2004).[1] These children represent 2 percent of all minor children in America, and a sobering 7 percent of all African-American children (Mumola 2000). With little if any public debate, we have extended prison's reach to include hundreds of thousands of young people who were not the prime target of the criminal justice policies that put their parents behind bars.

In the simplest human terms, prison places an indescribable burden on the relationships between these parents and their children. Incarcerated fathers and mothers must learn to cope with the loss of normal contact with their children, infrequent visits in inhospitable surroundings, and lost opportunities to contribute to their children's development. Their children must come to terms with the reality of an absent parent, the stigma of parental imprisonment, and an altered support system that may include grandparents, foster care, or a new adult in the home. In addition, in those communities where incarceration rates are high, the experience of having a mother or father in prison is now quite commonplace, with untold consequences for foster care systems, multigenerational households, social services delivery, community norms, childhood development, and parenting patterns.

Imprisonment profoundly affects families in another, less tangible way. When young men and women are sent to prison, they are removed from the traditional rhythms of dating, courtship, marriage, and family formation. Because far more men than women are sent to prison each year, our criminal justice policies have created a "gender imbalance" (Braman 2002), a disparity in the number of available single men and women in many communities. In neighborhoods where incarceration and reentry have hit hardest, the gender imbalance is particularly striking. Young women complain about the shortage of men who are suitable marriage prospects because so many of the young men cycle in and out of the criminal justice system. The results are an increase in female-headed households and narrowed roles for fathers in the lives of their children and men in the lives of women and families in general. As more young men grow up with fewer stable attachments to girlfriends, spouses, and intimate partners, the masculine identity is redefined.

The family is often depicted as the bedrock of American society. Over the years, we have witnessed wave after wave of social policy initiatives designed to strengthen, reunite, or simply create families. Liberals and conservatives have accused each other of espousing policies that undermine "family values." In recent years, policymakers, foundation officers, and opinion leaders have also decried the absence of fathers from the lives of their children. These concerns have translated into a variety of programs, governmental initiatives, and foundation strategies that constitute a "fatherhood movement." Given the iconic stature of the family in our vision of American life and the widespread consensus that the absence of father figures harms future generations, our national experiment with mass incarceration seems, at the very least, incongruent with the rhetoric behind prevailing social policies. At worst, the imprisonment of millions of individuals and the disruption of their family relationships has significantly undermined the role that families could play in promoting our social well-being.

The institution of family plays a particularly important role in the crime policy arena. Families are an integral part of the mechanisms of informal social control that constrain antisocial behavior. The quality of family life (e.g., the presence of supportive parent-child relationships) is significant in predicting criminal delinquency (Loeber and Farrington 1998, 2001). Thus, if families suffer adverse effects from our incarceration policies, we would expect these harmful effects to be felt in the next generation, as children grow up at greater risk of engaging in delinquent and criminal behavior. The institution of marriage is another important link in the mechanism of informal social control. Marriage reduces the likelihood that ex-offenders will associate with peers involved in crime, and generally inhibits a return to crime (Laub, Nagin, and Sampson 1998). In fact, marriage is a stronger predictor of desistance from criminal activity than simple cohabitation, and a "quality" marriage—one based on a strong mutual commitment—is an even stronger predictor (Horney, Osgood, and Marshall 1995). Thus, criminal justice policies that weaken marriage and inhibit spousal commitments are likely to undermine the natural processes of desistance, thereby causing more crime. In short, in developing crime policies, families matter. If our crime policies have harmful consequences for families, we risk undermining the role families can play in controlling criminal behavior.

This chapter examines the impact of incarceration and reentry on families. We begin by viewing the antecedents to the creation of families—the relationships between young men and young women—in communities where the rates of arrest, removal, incarceration, and reentry are particularly high. Then we discuss imprisonment's impact on relationships between an incarcerated parent and his or her children. Next we examine the effects of parental incarceration on the early childhood and adolescent development of children left behind. We then observe the family's role in reentry. We close with reflections on the impact of imprisonment on prisoners' family life, ways to mitigate incarceration's harmful effects, and ways to promote constructive connections between prisoners and their families.

THE "GENDER IMBALANCE"

To understand the magnitude of the criminal justice system's impact on the establishment of intimate partner relationships, we draw upon the work of Donald Braman (2002, 2004), an anthropologist who conducted a three-year ethnographic study of incarceration's impact on communities in Washington, D.C. In the District of Columbia, 7 percent of the adult African-American male population returns to the community from jail or prison each year. According to Braman's estimates, more than 75 percent of African-American men in the District of Columbia can expect to be incarcerated at some point during their lifetime. One consequence of these high rates of incarceration is what Braman calls a "gender imbalance," meaning simply that there are fewer men than women in the hardest hit communities. Half of the women in the nation's capital live in communities with low incarceration rates. In these communities, there are about 94 men for every 100 women. For the rest of the women in D.C.—whose neighborhoods have higher incarceration rates—the ratio is about 80 men for every 100 women. Furthermore, 10 percent of the District's women live in neighborhoods with the highest incarceration rates, where more than 12 percent of men are behind bars. In these neighborhoods, there are fewer than 62 men for every 100 women.

This gender imbalance translates into large numbers of fatherless families in communities with high rates of incarceration. In neighborhoods with a 2 percent male incarceration rate, Braman (2002) found that fathers were absent from more than one-half of the families. But in the communities with the highest male incarceration rates—about 12 percent—more than three-quarters of the families had a father absent. This phenomenon is not unique to Washington, D.C., however. In a national study, Sabol and Lynch (1998) also found larger numbers of female-headed families in counties receiving large numbers of returning prisoners.

Clearly, mass incarceration results in the substantial depletion in the sheer numbers of men in communities with high rates of imprisonment. For those men who are arrested, removed, and sent to prison, life in prison has profound and long-lasting consequences for their roles as intimate partners, spouses, and fathers. In the following sections, we will document those effects. Viewing this issue from a community perspective, however, reminds us that incarceration also alters the relationships between the men and women who are not incarcerated. In her research on the marriage patterns of low-income mothers, Edin (2000) found that the decision to marry (or remarry) depends, in part, on the economic prospects, social respectability, and reliability of potential husbands—attributes that are adversely affected by imprisonment. Low marriage rates, in turn, affect the life courses of men who have been imprisoned, reducing their likelihood of desistance from criminal activity. Thus, the communities with the highest rates of incarceration are caught in what Western, Lopoo, and McLanahan (2004, 21) call the "high-crime/low-marriage equilibrium." In these communities, women "will be understandably averse to marriage because their potential partners bring few social or economic benefits to the table. Men, who remain unmarried or unattached to stable households, are likely to continue their criminal involvement."

Braman quotes two of his community informants to illustrate these ripple effects of the gender imbalance. "David" described how the shortage of men affected dating patterns:

> Oh, yeah, everybody is aware of [the male shortage]. . . . And the fact that [men] know the ratio, and they feel that the ratio allows them to take advantage of just that statistic. 'Well, this woman I don't want to deal with, really because there are six to seven women to every man.' (2002, 166)

The former wife of a prisoner commented that women were less discerning in their choices of partners because there were so few men:

> Women will settle for whatever it is that their man [wants], even though you know that man probably has about two or three women. Just to be wanted, or just to be held, or just to go out and have a date makes her feel good, so she's willing to accept. I think now women accept a lot of things—the fact that he might have another woman or the fact that they can't clearly get as much time as they want to. The person doesn't spend as much time as you would [like] him to spend. The little bit of time that you get you cherish. (2002, 167)

The reach of our incarceration policies thus extends deep into community life. Even those men and women who are never arrested pay a price. As they are looking for potential partners in marriage and parenting, they find that the simple rituals of dating are darkened by the long shadow of imprisonment.

THE IMPACT OF INCARCERATION ON PARENT-CHILD RELATIONSHIPS

The Family Profile of the Prisoner Population

Before turning to a closer examination of the effects of imprisonment on the relationships between incarcerated parents and their children, we should first describe the family circumstances of the nation's prisoners. In 1997, about half (47 percent) of state prisoners reported they had never been married. Only 23 percent reported they were married at the time of their incarceration, while 28 percent said they were divorced or separated. . . . Yet most prisoners are parents. More than half (55 percent) of all state prisoners reported having at least one minor child. Because the overwhelming majority of state prisoners are men, incarcerated parents are predominantly male (93 percent). The number of incarcerated mothers, however, has grown dramatically in the past decade. Between 1991 and 2000, the number of incarcerated mothers increased by 87 percent, compared with a 60 percent increase in the number of incarcerated fathers. Of the men in state prison, 55 percent have children—a total of about 1.2 million—under the age of 18. About 65 percent of women in state prison are mothers to children younger than 18; their children number about 115,500 (Mumola 2000).

A mother's incarceration has a different impact on living arrangements than does that of a father. Close to two-thirds (64 percent) of mothers reported living with their children before incarceration, compared with slightly less than half (44 percent) of fathers in 1997. Therefore, as the percentage of women in prison increases, more children experience a more substantial disruption. We should not conclude, however, that the imprisonment of a nonresident father has little impact on his children. Research has shown that nonresident fathers can make considerable contributions to the development and well-being of their children (Amato and Rivera 1999; Furstenberg 1993). They contribute to their children's financial support, care, and social support even when they are not living in the children's home (Edin and Lein 1997; Hairston 1998; Western and McLanahan 2000). Therefore, a depiction of families' living arrangements only begins to describe the nature of the parenting roles played by fathers before they were sent to prison. . . .

We know little about the nature of these parent-child relationships. As was noted above, even absent fathers can provide emotional and financial support prior to their incarceration. However, the profiles of incarcerated parents also point to indicia of stress and dysfunction within these families. More than three-quarters of parents in state prison reported a prior conviction and, of those, more than half had been previously incarcerated. During the time leading up to their most current arrest and incarceration, nearly half were out of prison on some type of conditional release, such as probation or parole, in 1997. Nearly half (46 percent) of incarcerated fathers were imprisoned for a violent crime, as were one-quarter (26 percent) of the mothers. Mothers in prison were much more likely than fathers to be serving time for drug offenses (35 percent versus 23 percent). Nearly one-third of the mothers reported committing their crime to get either drugs or money for drugs, compared with 19 percent of fathers. More than half of all parents in prison reported using drugs in the month before they were arrested, and more than a third were under the influence of alcohol when they committed the crime. Nearly a quarter of incarcerated mothers (23 percent) and about a tenth (13 percent) of incarcerated fathers reported a history of mental illness (Mumola 2000). Clearly, these individuals were struggling with multiple stressors that, at a minimum, complicated their role as parents. . . .

The Strain of Incarceration on Families

We turn next to a discussion of the impact of parental incarceration on the families left behind. One obvious consequence is that the families have fewer financial resources. According to the Bureau of Justice Statistics, in 1997 most parents in state prison (71 percent) reported either full-time or part-time employment in the month preceding their current arrest (Mumola 2002). Wages or salary was the most common source of income among incarcerated fathers before imprisonment,

60 percent of whom reported having a full-time job. Mothers, on the other hand, were less likely to have a full-time job (39 percent), For them, the most common sources of income were wages (44 percent) or public assistance (42 percent). Very few mothers reported receiving formal child support payments (6 percent) (Mumola 2000). During incarceration, the flow of financial support from the incarcerated parent's job stops, leaving the family to either make do with less or make up the difference, thereby placing added strains on the new caregivers. Eligibility for welfare payments under the TANF (Temporary Assistance for Needy Families) program ceases as soon as an individual is no longer a custodial parent—i.e., upon incarceration. In some cases, a caregiver may continue to receive TANF payments when the incarcerated parent loses eligibility, but because these benefits are now "child-only," they are lower than full TANF benefits. Food stamps are also unavailable to incarcerated individuals.

New caregivers often struggle to make ends meet during the period of parental incarceration. Bloom and Steinhart (1993) found that in 1992 nearly half (44 percent) of families caring for the children of an incarcerated parent were receiving welfare payments under TANF's predecessor program, AFDC (Aid to Families with Dependent Children). Under the recent welfare reform laws, however, TANF support is more limited than in the past, as lifetime eligibility has been capped at 60 months, work requirements have been implemented, and restrictions have been placed on TANF funds for those who have violated probation or parole, or have been convicted of certain drug crimes (Phillips and Bloom 1998). Even under the old AFDC program, most caregivers reported that they did not have sufficient resources to meet basic needs (Bloom and Steinhart 1993). Moreover, these economic strains affect more than the family's budget. According to several studies, financial stress can produce negative consequences for caretakers' behavior, including harsh and inconsistent parenting patterns, which, in turn, cause emotional and behavioral problems for the children (McLoyd 1998).

Other adjustments are required as well, Because most prisoners are men, and 55 percent of them are fathers, the first wave of impact is felt by the mothers of their children. Some mothers struggle to maintain contact with the absent father, on behalf of their children as well as themselves. Others decide that the incarceration of their children's father is a turning point, enabling them to start a new life and cut off ties with the father. More fundamentally, Furstenberg (1995) found that a partner left behind often becomes more independent and self-sufficient during the period of incarceration, changes that may ultimately benefit the family unit or lead to the dissolution of the relationship. At a minimum, however, these changes augur a significant adjustment in roles when the incarcerated partner eventually returns home.

In some cases, the incarceration period can have another, longer-lasting effect on the legal relationships between parents and children. In 1997, Congress enacted the Adoption and Safe Families Act (ASFA) to improve the safety and well-being of children in the foster care system as well as to remove barriers to the permanent placement, particularly adoption, of these children.[2] The ASFA stipulates that "permanency" decisions (determinations about a child's ultimate placement) should BJS, among inmates who were in prison for a sex crime against a child, the child was the prisoner's own child or stepchild in a third of the cases (Langan, Schmitt, and Durose 2003). Yet there has been very little research on the nexus between this form of family violence, incarceration, and reentry. . . .

Even without a deeper understanding of the parenting roles played by America's prisoners, we still must face several incontrovertible, troubling facts. First, expanding the use of prison to respond to crime has put more parents in prison. Between 1991 and 1999, a short eight-year period, the number of parents in state and federal prisons increased by 60 percent, from 452,500 to 721,500 (Mumola 2000). By the end of 2002, 3.7 million parents were under some form of correctional supervision (Mumola 2004). Second, many children are left behind when parents are incarcerated. By 1999, 2 percent of all minor children in the United States—about 1.5 million—had a parent in state or federal prison. (If we include parents who are in jail, on probation or parole, or recently released from prison, the estimate of children with a parent involved in the criminal justice system reaches 7 million, or nearly 10 percent of all minor children in America [Mumola 2000].) Third, the racial disparities in America's prison population translate into substantial, disturbing racial inequities in the population of children affected by our current levels of imprisonment. About 7 percent of all African-American minor children and nearly 3 percent of all Hispanic minor children in America have a parent in prison. In comparison, barely 1 percent of all Caucasian minor children have a parent in prison (Mumola 2000). Finally, most of the children left behind are quite young. Sixty percent are under age 10, while the average child left behind is 8 years old.

In this era of mass incarceration, our criminal justice system casts a wide net that has altered the lives of millions of children, disrupting their relationships with their parents, altering the networks of familial support, and placing new burdens on such governmental services as schools, foster care, adoption agencies, and youth-serving organizations. As Phillips and Bloom succinctly concluded, "by getting tough on crime, the United States has gotten tough on children" (1998, 539). These costs are rarely included in our calculations of the costs of justice.

Parent-Child Relationships During Imprisonment

When a parent is arrested and later incarcerated, the child's world undergoes significant, sometimes traumatic, disruption. Most children are not present at the time of their parent's arrest, and arrested parents typically do not tell the police that they have minor children (ABA 1993). Family members are often reluctant to tell the children that their parent has been incarcerated because of social stigma (Braman 2003). Therefore, the immediate impact of an arrest can be quite traumatizing—a child is abruptly separated from his or her parent, with little information about what happened, why it happened, or what to expect.

The arrest and subsequent imprisonment of a parent frequently results in a significant realignment of the family's arrangements for caring for the child. Not surprisingly, the nature of the new living arrangements depends heavily on which parent is sent to prison. Recall that about two-thirds of incarcerated mothers in state prison lived with their children before they were imprisoned. Following the mother's incarceration, about a quarter (28 percent) of their children remain with their fathers. Most children of incarcerated mothers, however, are cared for by an extended family that is suddenly responsible for another mouth to feed and child to raise. More than half of these children (53 percent) will live with a grandparent, adding burdens to a generation that supposedly has already completed its child-rearing responsibilities. Another quarter of these children (26 percent) will live with another relative, placing new duties on the extended family. Some children have no familial safety net: almost 10 percent of incarcerated mothers reported that their child was placed in foster care (Mumola 2000).[3]

The story for incarcerated fathers is quite different. Less than half (44 percent) lived with their children before prison; once they are sent to prison, most of their children (85 percent) will live with the children's mother. Grandparents (16 percent) and other relatives (6 percent) play a much smaller role in assuming child care responsibilities when a father in incarcerated. Only 2 percent of the children of incarcerated men enter the foster care system. In sum, a child whose father is sent to prison is significantly less likely to experience a life disruption, such as moving in with another family member or placement in a foster home.

The nation's foster care system has become a child care system of last resort for many children with parents in prison. Research by the Center for Children of Incarcerated Parents (Johnston 1999) found that, at any given time, 10 percent of children in foster care currently have a mother—and 33 percent have a father—behind bars. Even more striking, 70 percent of foster children have had a parent incarcerated at one time or another during their time in foster care.

When a parent goes to prison, the separation between parent and child is experienced at many levels. First, there is the simple fact of distance. The majority of state prisoners (62 percent) are held in facilities located more than 100 miles from their homes. (Mumola 2000). Because prison facilities for women are scarce, mothers are incarcerated an average of 160 miles away from their children (Hagan and Coleman 2001). . . .

Geographic distance inhibits families from making visits and, for those who make the effort, imposes an additional financial burden on already strained family budgets. . . .

. . . Mothers in prison stay in closer contact with their children than do fathers. According to BJS, nearly 80 percent of mothers have monthly contact and 60 percent have at least weekly contact. Roughly 60 percent of fathers, by contrast, have monthly contact, and 40 percent have weekly contact with their children (Mumola 2000). These contacts take the form of letters, phone calls, and prison visits. Yet, a large percentage of prisoners serve their entire prison sentence without ever seeing their children. More than half of all mothers, and 57 percent of all fathers, never receive a personal visit from their children while in prison.

Particularly disturbing is Lynch and Sabol's finding (2001) that the frequency of contact decreases as prison terms get longer. Between 1991 and 1997, as the length of prison sentences increased, the level of contact of all kinds—calls, letters, and visits—decreased. . . . This is especially troubling in light of research showing that the average length of prison sentences is increasing in America, reflecting more stringent sentencing policies. Thus, prisoners coming home in the future are likely to have had fewer interactions with their children, a situation that further weakens family ties and makes family reunification even more difficult.

In addition to the significant burden imposed by the great distances between prisoners and their families, corrections policies often hamper efforts to maintain family ties across the prison walls. The Women's Prison Association (1996) has identified several obstacles to constructive family contacts, some of which could easily be solved. The association found that it is difficult to get simple information on visiting procedures, and correctional administrators provide little help in making visiting arrangements. The visiting procedures themselves are often uncomfortable or humiliating. Furthermore, little attention is paid to mitigating the impact on the children of visiting a parent in prison. . . .

Family Contact During Imprisonment: Obstacles and Opportunities

For a number of reasons, it is difficult to maintain parent-child contact during a period of incarceration. For one thing, many prisons narrowly define the family members who are granted visiting privileges. The State of Michigan's corrections department, for example, promulgated regulations in 1995 restricting the categories of individuals who are allowed to visit a prisoner. The approved visiting list may include minor children under the age of 18, but only if they are the prisoner's children, stepchildren, grandchildren, or siblings. Prisoners who are neither the biological parents nor legal stepparents of the children they were raising do not have this privilege. Finally, a child authorized to visit must be accompanied by either an adult who is an immediate family member of the child or of the inmate, or who is the child's legal guardian.[5] Many prisoners' extended family networks, including girlfriends and boyfriends who are raising prisoners' children, are not recognized in these narrow definitions of "family."[6] Limitations on visiting privileges are commonly justified on security or management grounds, but fail to recognize the complexity of the prisoner's familial networks. Rather than allowing the prisoner to define the "family" relationships that matter most, the arbitrary distinctions of biology or legal status are superimposed on the reality of familial networks, limiting meaningful contact that could make a difference to both prisoner and child.

Telephone contact is also burdened by prison regulations and by controversial relationships between phone companies and corrections departments. Prisoners are typically limited in the number of calls they can make. Their calls can also be monitored. The California Department of Corrections interrupts each call every 20 seconds with a recorded message: "This is a call from a California prison inmate." Most prisons allow prisoners to make only collect calls, and those calls typically cost between $1 and $3 per minute, even though most phone companies now charge less than 10 cents per minute for phone calls in the free society (Petersilia 2003). Telephone companies also charge between $1.50 and $4 just to place the collect call, while a fee is not charged for collect calls outside of prison.

The high price of collect calls reflects sweetheart arrangements between the phone companies and corrections agencies, under which the prisons receive kickbacks for every collect call, about 40 to 60 cents of every dollar. This arrangement translates into a substantial revenue source for corrections budgets. In 2001, for example, California garnered $35 million, based on $85 million of total revenue generated from prison calls. Some states require, by statute or policy, that these revenues pay for programs for inmates. Most states simply deposit this money into the general budget for their department of corrections.

Yet who bears these additional costs for maintaining phone contact with prisoners? The families of prisoners do, of course. . . .

This monopolistic arrangement between phone companies and prisons makes families the unwitting funders of the prisons holding their loved ones. In essence, the states have off-loaded upwards of hundreds of millions of dollars of prison costs on to prisoners' families. Subsequently, families are placed in the unacceptable position of either agreeing to accept the calls, thereby making contributions to prison budgets, or ceasing phone contact with their loved ones. Of course, there are other, deeper costs attached to this practice. If a family chooses to limit (or stop) these phone calls, then familial ties are weakened and the support system that could sustain the prisoner's reintegration is damaged. If the family chooses to pay the phone charges, then those financial resources are not available for other purposes, thereby adding to the strain the household experiences. In recent years, efforts to reform prison telephone policies have been successful in several states.[7] Yet, while these reform efforts are under way, tens of thousands of families are setting aside large portions of their budgets to pay inflated phone bills to stay in touch with their imprisoned family members. . . .

IMPACT OF PARENTAL INCARCERATION ON CHILDHOOD DEVELOPMENT

Limits of Existing Research

Having examined the impact of incarceration on the institution of family and the relationships of incarcerated parents with their children, we turn next to an assessment of incarceration's impact on the children involved. Given the current state of research, it is very difficult to measure the consequences for children when a mother or father is arrested, convicted, sent to prison, and returned home. Very few studies have been conducted that directly examine the lives of the children of incarcerated parents. . . .

The extant sparse research literature only underscores the importance of more research in this area. These studies suggest that children of incarcerated parents are more likely to exhibit low self-esteem, depression, emotional withdrawal from friends and family, and inappropriate or disruptive behavior at home and in school. Two studies, each with a very small sample size, suggested that children of incarcerated parents may be more likely than their counterparts to enter the criminal justice system (Johnston 1991, 1993).[8] . . .

Understanding Parental Loss

We can also draw upon the general literature exploring how parental loss affects child development to create some hypotheses about the impact of parental incarceration.

According to this literature, children always experience the loss of a parent as a traumatic event. Whether the loss is due to death, divorce, moving away, or incarceration, this event has negative consequences, including attachment difficulties, anger, depression, regression, and other antisocial behaviors. Similarly, a traumatic event in a child's life diverts energy from the developmental work that child is normally performing. When life becomes overwhelming for a child, emotional survival may take precedence over developmental tasks, resulting in delayed development, regression, or other maladaptive coping strategies (Wright and Seymour 2000). Given these general principles of child development, parental incarceration should be viewed as a traumatic event, limiting the child's emotional growth, producing stress and anger, and isolating the child from needed social supports.

It is also well documented in the child development literature that children have difficulty coping with uncertainty. The criminal justice process is filled with uncertainty. A child might have to live with such questions as, "Will Mom be arrested again?" "Will Dad be convicted and, if so, sent to prison? If so, how long will he be there?" "Will Mom get released on parole? If so, will she be sent back to prison if she uses drugs again, or if she is in the wrong place at the wrong time?" This uncertainty, which is inherent in the workings of our criminal justice system, is often compounded by the family's reluctance to tell children exactly what is happening to their parents. In his ethnographic study in Washington, D.C., Braman (2002) found that most family members rarely discuss their relative's incarceration at all outside the immediate family, even in neighborhoods where incarceration rates are high. Most family members explained that their silence stemmed from concerns about the stigma associated with incarceration, Although well-intentioned as a protective response, withholding basic information about a parent's status may only heighten children's feelings of stress and uncertainty.

Finally, the children themselves must deal with the issue of stigma. When a mother or father is imprisoned, a child may experience the disapproval of his or her peers, teachers, or other family members, resulting in feelings of shame and low self-esteem. Perhaps in neighborhoods of a high concentration of incarceration among the adults, losing one's parent to prison is so common that the social stigma is diminished, but the experience still requires the child to work through a complex set of feelings about the actions of the parent in prison. In addition, even those children who are coping well with parental incarceration may have the added challenge of overcoming the stereotype that they are destined for a life of behavioral problems and failure.

Impact by Children's Age Group

The child development literature also provides a framework for assessing the differential impact of parental incarceration on children of various ages. The chart developed by Gabel and Johnston (1995) clarifies the intersection between developmental markers and the removal of a parent to prison (table 6.1). For example, among infants (0–2 years), parental incarceration's major effect is likely a disruption of parental bonding, with the potential for later attachment difficulties. Research on this age group also shows, however, that infants can recover quickly from the loss of a parent if they experience a new, nurturing, caregiving relationship

TABLE 6.1 Possible Effects of Parental Arrest and Incarceration on Young Children's Development

Developmental State	Developmental Characteristics	Developmental Tasks	Influencing Factors	Effects of Separation
Infancy (0–2 years)	Limited perception, mobility Total dependency	Development of trust and attachment	Parent-child separation	Impaired parent-child bonding
Early childhood (2–6 years)	Increased perception, mobility, and improved memory Greater exposure to environment. Ability to imagine	Development of sense of autonomy, independence, and initiative	Parent-child separation Trauma	Inappropriate separation anxiety Impaired socioemotional development Acute traumatic stress reactions and survivor guilt
Middle childhood (7–10 years)	Increased independence from caregivers and ability to reason Peers become important	Sense of industry Ability to work productively	Parent-child separation Trauma	Developmental regressions Poor self-concept Acute traumatic stress reactions Impaired ability to overcome future trauma
Early adolescence (11–14 years)	Organization of behavior in pursuit of goals Increased abstract thinking Puberty Increased aggression	Ability to work productively with others Controlled expression of emotions	Parent-child separation Enduring Trauma	Rejection of limits on behavior Trauma-reactive behaviors
Late adolescence (15–18 years)	Emotional crisis and confusion Adult sexual development and sexuality Formal abstract thinking Increased independence	Development of cohesive identity Resolution of conflicts with family and society Ability to engage in adult work and relationships	Parent-child separation Enduring trauma	Premature termination of dependency relationship with parent Intergenerational crime and incarceration

Source: Gabel and Johnston (1995). Reprinted with permission.

(Shonkoff and Phillips 2000). During the early childhood years (2–6 years), children have a greater ability to perceive events around them, but have not yet developed the skills to process traumatic occurrences. Children at this age have not yet completely separated themselves from their parents, so they tend to perceive threats or harm to their parents or caregivers as directed at themselves. Several studies suggest that traumatic stress at this age may have profound long-term effects, particularly if there is no intervention to help the child sort through those experiences (Furman 1983).

In the middle childhood years (7–10 years), when children are developing their social skills and a sense of independence, separation from a parent creates a sense of loss because a role model is taken away. If a child has poor coping skills to begin with, and particularly if he or she moves from home to home following the parent's departure, such disruptions may accelerate a spiral of strain in the child's life. Johnston and Carlin (1996) use the term "enduring trauma" to describe a situation where a child experiences several traumatic events with no time to recover and where the cumulative effect may overwhelm the child's ability to cope. A child experiencing this level of trauma may display aggression, hypervigilance, anxiety, concentration problems, and withdrawal.

The impact of incarceration on adolescents (11 to 18 years) is likely quite different. Adolescence is a time when young people test boundaries, begin to navigate the world of romantic relationships, exercise more independence, explore the adult world of work, and develop a sense of self. The arrest and incarceration of an adolescent's parent can derail those transitions to adulthood. These children may question the authority of the incarcerated parent and doubt the parent's concern for them. They may take on new roles as parent figures to fill the void left by the incarcerated parent. Some studies have shown an increase in dependence and developmental regression among adolescents of incarcerated parents (Johnston 1992).

About 1.5 million minor children have a parent in prison, most frequently a father. In many ways, these children are no different from others of their age group, but they are experiencing a distinctive disruption in their lives. They have the same emotional needs to bond with a parent or other caregiver, to establish themselves as unique individuals in a social context, and to test their independence from the adults in their lives. All these development processes are made more complicated by the loss of a parent to prison, and more complicated still if the parent was arrested for behavior involving harm to the family or child.

RECONNECTING WITH FAMILY AT THE TIME OF REENTRY

In this section, we shift our focus from an inquiry into the impact of incarceration on parent-child relationships and child development to ask what role prisoners expect their families to play in the reentry process, what role families actually play, and what consequences befall families during this critical period.

When prisoners return home, they face multiple hurdles, many of which relate directly to the functioning of their families. They need to find housing, which may be with their relatives or immediate families. They need to find employment, which could add income to family budgets. Some have health concerns and may need to receive care for an HIV infection, secure medication for mental illness, or find substance abuse treatment to reduce the risk of relapse, all of which, if successful, would avert additional burdens and risks for their families. Many will owe the state child support payments, which, according to an extensive analysis in Colorado and Massachusetts, averaged more than $16,000 (Thoennes 2003).[10] Most prisoners will be under legal supervision, bringing a state parole agency into their homes and lives. . . .

LOOKING FORWARD

Imprisonment causes ripple effects that are felt throughout a prisoner's family network. The policies that have resulted in the imprisonment of well over a million people have magnified those effects in a strong undercurrent that is eroding the familial infrastructure of America's poorest communities, Virtually every social institution that deals with children—including families, schools, child welfare agencies, foster care, and kinship care systems—is touched by the high rates of parental imprisonment. At the center of these community institutions are children—1.5 million of them—who are buffeted about between prison visits, time with foster parents, and life with grandparents and other new adults in their lives. These children are likely to grow up in families that have been weakened, increasing the challenges they face in staying out of the criminal justice system and leading productive lives. As they reach early adulthood, they will find that their choices of life partners are more limited than a generation ago, and their family structures will be quite different.

In view of the negative effects stemming from current imprisonment policies, we must ask whether society has an obligation to mitigate these harms. The research literature provides some limited guidance as we consider the efficacy of policies that would reflect such a social commitment. Keeping families strong would reduce future criminality, enhance child development, reduce child and family trauma and stress, and increase the likelihood that the children left behind would lead productive lives. Beyond these calculations of preventable harm, the next question pertains to who would be responsible for carrying out policies that would produce these results. Certainly there is much more that corrections agencies could do, but they would first have to see family strengthening as part of their mission. This, in turn, would require governors and state legislatures to lead efforts to expand both the mission statements and the financial support of state departments of corrections. With this support, corrections agencies could improve their visitation policies, encourage rather than discourage phone calls, provide video links between prisons and community centers, find secure means for Internet communications between prisoners and families, bring families to their prisons, create family advocate positions within their organizations, eliminate the imposition of child support payments during the incarceration period, offer classes in parenting skills, and assist prisoners in asserting their rights in custody proceedings. We have no shortage of ideas, just a lack of mandate and the needed resources to carry out the new mandate. . . .

NOTES

1. This is a single-day prevalence and does not take into account minor children whose parents were previously incarcerated; it accounts only for those who are currently incarcerated in state and federal prisons in 2002.
2. Public Law 105-89.
3. Figures do not total 100 percent because some prisoners had children living with multiple caregivers.
4. The Michigan restrictions were challenged in court as unconstitutional because they violated the Fourteenth Amendment's guarantee of due process, the First Amendment's guarantee of free association, and the Eighth Amendment's prohibition against cruel and unusual punishment. The Supreme Court upheld the regulations, finding that the restrictions "bear a rational relation to the [department of correction's] valid interests in maintaining internal security and protecting child visitors from exposure to sexual or other misconduct or from accidental injury. . . . To reduce the number of child visitors, a line must be drawn, and the categories set out by these regulations are reasonable" (*Overton v. Bazzetta,* 539 U.S. 94 [2003]).
5. The definition of who can visit or take children to visit is an even bigger problem in light of cultural traditions, i.e., the extended family network and fictive kin arrangements that exist in many African-American families. Family duties and responsibilities are shared among a group of individuals; e.g., a young uncle may be expected to take on the father's role and do things such as take the child to a game or on a prison visit while the grandmother provides day-to-day care and an aunt with a "good" job provides financial subsidies. Apparently this perspective was either not presented or ignored as unimportant in the Michigan case (Personal communication with Creasie Finney Hairston, January 6, 2004).
6. Missouri has announced that its next contract with prison telephone systems will not include a commission for the state. The Ohio prison system entered into a contract that will reduce the cost of prison phone calls by 15 percent. California will reduce most prisoner phone calls by 25 percent. In 2001, the Georgia Public Service Commission ordered telephone providers to reduce the rates for prisoner calls from a $3.95 connection fee and a rate of $0.69 per minute to a $2,20 connection fee and a rate of $0.35 per minute. The new telephone contract for the Pennsylvania Department of Corrections will reduce the average cost of a 15-minute telephone call by 30 percent. And litigation has been initiated in a number of states—including Illinois, Indiana, Kentucky, Ohio, New Hampshire, New Mexico, New York, South Dakota, Washington, Wisconsin, and the District of Columbia—to reduce the cost of prison phone calls and kickbacks to the state (eTc Campaign 2003).
7. The Children of Offenders study and the Jailed Mothers study both had small sample sizes and were not randomized, making it difficult to conclude a causal link between parental incarceration and children's involvement in the criminal justice system. In the Children of Offenders study (Johnston 1992, 1993), the sample (N = 56, N = 202) targeted children of offenders who already demonstrated disciplinary problems in school or delinquent behaviors, presenting

the highest likelihood of second-generation incarceration (Johnston 1995). In the Jailed Mothers study, Johnston (1991) relied on self-reported data from the surveys of 100 jailed mothers on their children's living arrangements, risk factors, and problem behaviors.

8. This figure represents both pre-prison and during-prison nonpayment. Depending on the law of the state, prisoners may continue to accrue child supports arrears while incarcerated. According to Thoennes (2003), Massachusetts prisoners accrued on average $5,000 in arrears while behind bars.

REVIEW QUESTIONS

1. How do incarceration rates in communities impact the construction and maintenance of family units in the community?

2. What effects does a parent's incarceration have on the parent's children?

3. What are the stresses and challenges that families encounter when a family member returns from incarceration?

READING 24

In the Tube at San Quentin

The "Secondary Prisonization" of Women Visiting Inmates

Megan L. Comfort

This reading provides a description of the processes that individuals coming to prison to visit loved ones go through to gain entry to one prison. As the author explains, there are myriad rules and regulations, which change often, may be enforced irregularly, and often seem to defy logic or justification. Because the vast majority of prison visitors are women, the rules that are enforced frequently appear to take on a gendered existence and are argued in this reading to reinforce gender hierarchies and stereotypes. The unpredictable and sometimes humiliating treatment that is described is presented by the author as a form of prisonization and punishment of the loved ones of prison inmates.

. . . The "collateral damage" caused by imprisonment—and particularly the American model of "mass incarceration" (see Garland 2001)—must be assessed to understand how prisons contribute to social and family instability (Hagan and Dinovitzer 1999). As the United States continues to champion "zero-tolerance" policing and severe sentencing and imprison large numbers of poor people and people of color (Tonry 1995), women whose loved ones and close acquaintances are caught in the revolving door of "corrections" experience restricted rights, diminished resources, social marginalization, and other consequences of penal confinement, even though they are legally innocent and reside outside of the prison's boundaries. This punishment of women reverberates through their interactions with community members, employers, children, and other kin and can result in poverty, homelessness, physical and mental health problems, family disruption, or stigmatization. The current national penal policy debate considers none of these deleterious effects of incarceration, concerning itself instead with the hypertrophic expansion of the carceral population and ignoring those condemned to live in the "long shadow" of the prison.

In this article I concentrate on one facet of the regulation and distortion of women's lives that occurs due to the imprisonment of family members, lovers, and friends: the experience of visiting an inmate in a correctional facility. People who temporarily enter prisons to visit their spouses, romantic partners, kin, and kith detained therein constitute a peculiar category of "prisoner." Not convicted felons, but not beyond the suspicion of authorities or the taint of "courtesy stigma" (Goffman 1963), their penetration of a guarded, secure space catalyzes a tug-of-war between contradictory processes of identification and attributed group membership. Correctional officers, charged with the maintenance of order through the reduction of incarcerated bodies to depersonalized, manageable units (Conover 2000; Kauffman 1988), attempt to denude prison visitors and transform them into an obedient corps of unindividuated, nonthreatening entities who can be organized according to the prison's rules. Heaving on the other side of the rope, visitors—cognizant of their status as legally "free" people—resist this imposed prisoner label, clamor for respectful, nonpunitive treatment, and fiercely struggle to import the "outside world" into the facility via their personally stylized appearance and comportment. The ongoing clash between forcibly assigned, quasi-penal properties and defended civil attributes unfolds in the border region of the prison where outsiders first enter the institution and come under its gaze. The space surrounding this battleground therefore becomes the site of contested personhood, an intermediary zone where visitors continually define and defend their social and physical integrity against the degradation of self (Garfinkel 1968) required by the prison as a routine condition for visiting.

This article draws on direct examination of one such area—a desolate, drab hallway at California's San Quentin State Prison known as "the Tube"—to analyze officials' management and mortification of prison visitors through the systematic devaluation of their time and the rigorous curtailing of their bodily comfort and presentation under the guise of an institutional rhetoric of "security." San Quentin, the state's oldest prison, currently houses upwards of six thousand men and occupies 432 acres of prime real estate property in Marin County, an affluent area north of the San Francisco Bay. From April to December 2000, I conducted intensive fieldwork documenting how the incarceration of a partner infiltrates and systematically distorts women's personal, domestic, and social worlds. In addition to interviewing fifty women whose husbands, fiances, or boyfriends were in prison, I spent nearly three hundred hours in "the Tube," the designated zone in which people must wait before they are permitted entry to San Quentin during the seven hours of visiting scheduled each Thursday, Friday, Saturday, and Sunday. I carried out a methodical observation of this area, arriving early in the morning and camping out in the hallway for six- or seven-hour stretches to watch the dynamics among the visitors and their interactions with the authorities as they waited to be "processed" into the prison.

Early on in my fieldwork, I realized that the Tube is a distinctly *female* space: based on my observations and information provided by correctional officers, I calculate that approximately 95 percent of the several hundred daily adult visitors at the facility are women. . . .

A close analysis of the strictures applied to visitors in the Tube as they attempt to enter the prison grounds illuminates the peculiar ways in which the correctional facility extends its penal reach to women through the regulation of their time and bodies. In the following, I dissect the Tube as a zone of friction in which women prepare for, submit to, and chafe against the control San Quentin officials attempt to exert over their behaviors and physical expression as a requisite for admittance to the facility. I begin with an examination of the architecture and design of this fraught corridor, considering the psychological and corporeal consequences of spending substantial amounts of time hemmed therein. I then explore the practices of erratic scheduling and prolonged queuing for entry to the prison, which channel hours of women's lives into forced idleness. The third section probes the management of women's bodies and sexual expression through the implementation of a stringent and shifting dress code. Finally, I conclude by extending Sykes's (1958) classic analysis of the "pains of imprisonment" to the experiences of prison visitors, proposing that women undergo a form of *secondary prisonization* through their sustained contact with the correctional institution.

"IT REMINDS ME OF A SLAVE-HOLDING TANK": ARCHITECTURE AND DESIGN OF THE TUBE

. . . No one could tell me when the moniker "the Tube" came into use, but correctional staff and visitors alike use it to refer to the eighty-foot by six-foot concrete-walled dividing line between general state property and San Quentin's actual prison grounds. A long corridor with a door on either end opening onto the public parking lot and one in the center leading to the visitor processing area, it is the funnel through which all visitors, including attorneys, enter San Quentin. . . . Similar to the standard welfare office waiting room (Jacobs 1966, 74–75; see also Piven and Cloward 1971), the hallway's prime message is one of contemptuous neglect. The Tube is an unheated structure lit by naked, white fluorescent lights. Since the hydraulic hinges on the two exterior doors are broken, the doors must be propped open by garbage cans to prevent them from continually slamming shut; having them simultaneously ajar transforms the Tube into a mini–wind tunnel through which chilly gusts blow throughout the day. The outer wall of the Tube has large windows running its length at shoulder height, and through the scratched glass one can see boats sailing on the San Francisco Bay and stately houses dotting the lush Tiburon Peninsula opposite the prison. . . .

Overall, the atmosphere of the hallway evokes Sykes's (1958) observation that "the physical conditions of life in prison would seem to reflect a sort of half-hearted or indecisive punishment, the imposition of deprivation by indifference or forgetfulness rather than by intent" (p. 8). Miki, a former nurse and current college student who stands in the corridor for hours two or three days a week to visit her husband, offers this unsettling analogy between her predicament and that of her ancestors: "[The Tube] . . . reminds me of a slave-holding tank. Every time I walk in there, and look out the windows at the water, all I can think is a place to hold slaves 'til the ship comes in." There is a conspicuous dearth of amenities in the area, such as adequate seating, a wheelchair ramp, a water fountain, or a clean restroom with a baby-changing facility. The lack of essential facts and tips for visitors is also striking. Despite the plethora of memos, flyers, and signs decorating the corridor, no directions are displayed telling visitors how to enter the prison. There is a "Basic Rules for Visiting" sign hung at the far end of the hallway near the parking lot door briefly listing various stipulations in small, bland typescript:

1. You must be an approved visitor with a valid picture ID
2. Visitors with minors must bring an original or certified birth certificate from the county for each visit
3. No more than $30.00 in currency. No bills larger than $1.00
4. No purses, wallets, pagers, car alarms or electronically controlled devices. Two (2) keys on a simple key ring
5. Visitors shall remain fully clothed in a dress, blouse/shirt with a skirt, pants or shorts

Among uninitiated visitors, these poorly worded rules increase confusion rather than provide answers. Whose birth certificate exactly is required when visiting with a minor? Are coins allowed as well as one-dollar bills? If purses and wallets are forbidden, are diapers, baby formula, sanitary napkins, or prescribed medication permitted? The handwritten admonishments posted around and to the processing area door provide no further enlightenment: **"NO BLUE, NO EXCEPTIONS!" "NO HAIRPIECES, NO WIGS, NO EXCEPTIONS!"** Nowhere among this mosaic of stipulations can new visitors find the instructions they need: fill out a visiting pass, wait on the benches for phone visits until the appointment time is announced, wait in line for contact visits, and turn the processing door handle when the buzzer sounds.

Logistically, the Tube serves as a means of buffering correctional officers from a flood of oncoming visitors: the processing area door is locked from the inside, and officers admit one person at a time by pressing a button that temporarily unlocks the door while emitting a high-pitched whine. Symbolically, the initial containment of people in an excluded zone and the formal, impersonal means of permitting their entry accentuate the tenuous legitimacy of the visitors when on the prison grounds and signal expectations of their deference to authority before they even pass through the door, aptly demonstrating Spain's (1992) claim that "prisons are the clearest example of space being used to reinforce a hierarchy and to assert power" (p. 8). Once inside the processing area, people undergo a rigorous series of identity and security checks. . . . These checks include presenting identification for computerized verification of the right to visit; handing over shoes, coats, belts, jewelry, and other belongings to be placed in a box and sent on a conveyor belt through an X-ray machine; walking through a metal detector while the officers review one's clothing and determine whether one conforms to the visitors' dress code; and having one's hand marked with fluorescent ink—which signals guards at the next checkpoint that one has been properly "processed.". . .

GOING NOWHERE: QUEUING AND WAITING FOR VISITS

> You're stuck in the Tube with a million people and everybody's upset cuz there's only one slob in the processing, children are crying, and you know, you just want to get in there; you got to go back to work tomorrow—I mean, there's so much pressure, and it's easy to get frustrated and upset with other people [that you get to the point where] it's like, *"Why can't that bitch control her child?"* (Sarah, thirty-one-year-old high-tech industry worker)

At a prison, much like at an inner-city emergency room serving a low-income clientele (Abraham 1993, 93–110), the sense of urgency felt by the population trying to get in is unlikely to be matched by the response time of the facility's officials. Although some visitors choose to forfeit a portion of visiting time to avoid extensive waits and long lines in the Tube, the majority arrive during the peak periods—the two hours before a designated area opens for visitation—in an effort to spend as long as possible with their loved ones. As a result, the average visitor passes a significant quantity of time within the corridor's walls before she actually enters the confines of the prison.

On Thursdays and Fridays, "contact" visiting (during which prisoners and their visitors may sit together in a cafeteria-style room) begins at 11:30 in the morning and lasts until 6:30 in the evening, and on Saturdays and Sundays, it starts at 7:30 A.M. and finishes at 2:30 P.M. Miki and Roberta, both of whom visit their husbands two or three days a week, arrive at the Tube between 8:30 and 9:00 A.M. on weekdays and between 5:30 and 6:00 P.M. on weekends to secure the first places in line. They make an odd couple, waiting out their previsit vigils together in this bleak atmosphere. Miki, a sixty-year-old who seems closer in age to her forty-year-old spouse, is the mother of fourteen children and forty-six foster children; her late husband was a Black Panther, and Miki still limps slightly from a leg injury caused by a car bomb planted in 1972 in retaliation for her own political activities. Roberta, who met her husband through a Bible-study class for prisoners, is in her late fifties and wears the sweet, milky expression of a befuddled child, occasionally stroking her blonde tresses and singing out pronouncements like, "I just *really* love sugarplum fairies!" What the two women have in common is that they both are devoted to men with life sentences whom they met and married in prison. Both of them also believe it is worthwhile spending several hours waiting in the Tube before their visit so that they can be at the front of the line and obtain one of the few seats in the visiting room by the windows. As Miki explains,

> There're three window seats in the whole visiting room. And both of us [she and her husband] are *slightly* claustrophobic. So, if I get up there—it's worth it to me to get up there at nine o'clock, *eight-thirty,* just to know that, *I'm* first on-line and *I will get the window seat.* . . . I've always felt like, if you're gonna do something, *do it.* I don't wanna stand on-line, be twenty-fifth on-line, fifteenth on-line, standing there waiting for everybody to get—you know? I'm gonna wait [at] one end or I'm gonna wait [at] this end!

The line that Miki and Roberta lead begins at the processing door and flows through the Tube, continuing as needed through the exit door and down the outside stairs into the parking lot. Since the area closest to the processing door has no benches, the first fifteen to twenty visitors in line are required to stand. On weekdays, an average of twenty people who have contact visits form a queue between 9:30 and 11:30 A.M., while batches of ten to fifteen people who have phone visits (during which the prisoner and his visitors sit separated by a Plexiglas barrier) arrive around forty-five minutes in advance of their appointments, which are scheduled in hour-long segments between 7:30 and 12:00. On weekends and holidays, the corridor swarms with women and children, the line of bodies often streaming down the stairs and onto the asphalt during the hour before visiting begins. Each day there typically are between two and five uninitiated visitors grappling for the first time with San Quentin's environment and procedures; the rest of the people awaiting their turn to walk through the prison's door are all-too-familiar with the grimy concrete and the restless throng in which they must take their place while "doing time" in the Tube.

One of the key issues for those waiting in the corridor is the unpredictability of the precise moment when processing will begin. . . . Regardless of San Quentin's official schedule, the commencement of visiting varies by up to thirty minutes for each group admitted to the prison, and pressure in the Tube regularly mounts and eases in association with these entrance times. There is no announcement made when contact-visitor processing begins; the first signal is the abrupt whine of the door buzzer sometime around 11:30, possibly as late as 11:45. From 11:25 onwards, therefore, the first visitor in line teeters uneasily on the tiny step in front of the processing area door, her hand gripping the handle expectantly. Many people have difficulty opening the door, sometimes because they are elderly, disabled, or holding a baby and cannot muster the strength needed; sometimes because they do not know how to react to the buzzer and think that the door will open automatically; and often because the correctional officers do not activate the buzzer long enough for someone to turn the door handle and push. This last problem causes consternation in the Tube since it is hard to discern whether the officers genuinely cannot calculate how long someone needs to enter the door or whether, as many women suspect, the officers deliberately abbreviate the time they sound the buzzer to "play with" the visitors. . . .

The times of highest tension in the Tube occur when processing is underway for both phone and contact visitors (between 11:30 and 12:30 on Thursdays and Fridays and throughout the morning on Saturdays and Sundays). Correctional officers have no way of viewing the lines in the Tube unless they leave their desks and open the processing area door, and thus they begin calling phone visitors—who are scheduled for "specific" visiting times—without knowledge of the number of people waiting for contact visits. Frequently, therefore, someone at the end of the contact visitor line will just reach the door when an announcement is made for phone visitors, and she then will need to wait an additional fifteen or twenty minutes while the noncontact visitors are admitted to the facility. On busy mornings, phone visitor processing may suspend contact visitor processing multiple times, meaning that someone arriving at 11:00 for 11:30 visiting might be delayed by both the 12:00 and the 12:30 phone visits, not entering the prison until 12:45 or later. With such persistent sluggishness and inefficiency characterizing the entry procedure at San Quentin, it is no wonder that many women sacrifice their early morning "free" hours to the procural of an optimal place in line, thereby losing as few moments as possible of the scarce resource of their time with their incarcerated lovers or relatives.

Even more unpredictable than the morning queues is the period on Thursday and Friday afternoons when entering visitors must wait for "Count" to finish. Prisoners in San Quentin are physically counted multiple times throughout the day to verify that all bodies are present and no one has escaped. Each day there is an institutional Count at 4:00 P.M., in preparation for which all "movement" (the transfer of inmates from one area to another, such as from a cell to the visiting room) ceases at 3:00. This stagnation means that contact visitors must enter the institution before 2:30 so that everyone can be at his or her final destination within the next half hour. Anyone not present before the deadline must wait until the Count "clears" (that is, until the officials are certain all prisoners are on site); swift counts finish within thirty minutes, but typically Count clears between 4:45 and 5:15. Even for women who know about Count, meeting its exigencies is stressful: from 2:00 to 2:30, women race into the Tube directly from work or from their children's schools, swearing at the sluggish traffic or the late buses, perspiring and panting as they frantically dash to the processing door. However, many women, especially new visitors or people who previously have only visited on weekends, do not know about Count and stroll into the Tube from 2:35 onwards, only to be instructed by the correctional officers that they will be admitted "after the four o'clock Count." The imprecision of this starting time is agonizing for people, who stand impotently in the concrete corridor and watch the clock edge closer to 6:30, when visiting ends for the day. . . .

The lengthy and inefficient queues required for visiting a prisoner do not just belittle the worth of his family's and friends' time—they also deprecate the importance of the visit itself, the preciousness of moments spent with those who are otherwise physically barred from one's presence, as argued by Lynn, a thirty-eight-year-old fund-raiser for a nonprofit organization:

> For instance, visiting hours are 7:30 to 2:30. But they don't start processing you until 7:30. And that's a frustration to me in that, "No, I would like to be face-to-face by 7:30, *why can't you start processing* at 7:15? *What is the problem* with the mentality behind starting processing fifteen minutes prior to visiting time?" . . . [Once processing begins] then they take their time, and they have to know that every minute—or maybe they don't. Maybe it's just a matter of not really comprehending, *every minute* is so valuable, you know?

For many women, it is this disparagement of the sanctity of visiting time that wounds most deeply. Indeed, those who arrive hours in advance at the prison gates accept long waits as a logical precondition, part of the "agreement" that must be made when free people wish to enter the institutional walls. Some endorse the authorities' devaluation of their time, asserting, "I don't mind waiting; I have nothing better to do," while others recast their lost hours as investment in their relationships. However, women strongly resent their lack of command over *what* time they sacrifice, and while tempers may be relatively placid when processing is not expected to be underway and people know they are wasting "free" time, tensions soar as soon as women understand that the wait is impinging on potential visiting moments.

"MY PENITENTIARY WARDROBE": THE REGULATION OF APPAREL AND BELONGINGS

There were two visitors in line. The first was an older woman, probably in her late sixties, with a cloud of white hair hovering around her crinkled face. She was wearing an over-sized purple shirt unbuttoned over a thick, white t-shirt and loose black pants. When the buzzer sounded the woman faltered with the heavy door and the second visitor, a middle-age woman dressed in a librarian's prim garb with her hair pinned in a high chignon, assisted her with a strong shove. A minute later we heard raised voices, and the librarian cocked her head to see through the processing window, staring intently at the commotion: "Oh, they're so terrible! That poor woman in there is saying that she can't wear a bra because of a medical condition, and they're telling her she can't come in without a bra. As if *she's* going to try to be sexy! What a dishonorable thing to do to someone!'" The woman watched a few minutes more, spitting with anger: "I wish we didn't feel we were so over a barrel with these people! We have to do everything they say!"

A moment later, the older woman came out of processing. It was a bit strange: she was carrying the wooden tray in which belongings are sent through the X-ray machine. A bra, some jewelry, and her shoes were scattered in the tray, and the woman was in her stocking-feet. She wandered to the end of the Tube, looking a bit dazed, so I went after her. "Can I help you, ma'am?" She quietly asked me where the bathroom was, and I took her around the corner, warning her to watch out for glass shards as we crossed over the asphalt and sidewalk. "This is the worst place I've ever been to," she remarked, with a touch of venom, "thank you, Dear." She went into the dilapidated bathroom, returning to the Tube a few minutes later and then disappearing into the prison once more.

Once they leave the Tube and enter the processing area, visitors commence their official registration as temporary occupants of San Quentin State Prison. . . . Item by item, correctional officers scrutinize people's documents, attire, and belongings to determine whether to permit them direct access to the facility or whether to require a clarification or modification of some sort. Prison officials claim to design the criteria for visitor approval in the interest of institutional safety by attempting to verify that everyone coming into the prison is legally authorized to visit, unarmed, not transporting contraband (defined as any item not explicitly permitted in the prison), and dressed in a nonprovocative manner that can be easily distinguished from prisoners and correctional staff (interview with San Quentin visiting lieutenants, May 10, 2001). . . .

. . . At San Quentin, dress code violations are the most common problem visitors encounter during processing. On average, each day one-third of all visitors are ordered to change some aspect of their attire before they are permitted into the facility; on busy days or days when particularly strict officers are on duty, this number easily rises to one-half or more. One primary reason the dress code causes abundant difficulties is that visitors are not advised of it in advance: when prisoners are told to notify their families and friends of the institution's approval of their visiting privileges, the inmates are not given information about the dress code or visiting hours to pass along to their loved ones. As a result, most people arrive at the prison outfitted in the clothes of everyday life—blue jeans, sleeveless or light-colored T-shirts, thigh-high skirts—and are refused entry based on their apparel.

The fact that the dress code proscribes many ordinary garments, styles, fabrics, and colors makes adherence to it problematic, especially for people on low budgets who cannot afford to augment their wardrobes (and the wardrobes of their children, who must also comply with the rules). . . .

In addition to being awkwardly phrased, the derogatory wording of this list infantilizes visitors by reproaching them as if they were children who needed to be taught the basic rules of civilized life ("Don't expose your genitals!"). The clear targeting of women's sexual expression indicates the assumption of a hyper-sexualized body and the need for a systematic enforcement of "moral" attire. Also, this list does not warn visitors of all of the dress code pitfalls: no bright yellow (the color of prisoners' rain gear), no bright orange (the color of high-security prisoners' jumpsuits), no overalls (the shoulder snaps trigger the metal detector), no hats (considered a security risk), and no shirts displaying any of the shoulder area (considered sexually provocative). Yet it would be impossible to warn visitors of *all* of the rules because they are subject to erratic change without notice. During my observations, several new rules were announced (usually by a handwritten sign taped to the processing door), rigorously implemented for several weeks, and then abandoned for no identifiable reason.

The regulation of garments during visitor processing even penetrates undergarments, and virtually every woman on her first visit is sent away to remove the wire from her underwire bra so that she can pass through the metal detector without triggering the alarm. This causes embarrassment and consternation among visitors, both because of the intimate nature of the offending item (often brought to women's attention by a male correctional officer) and because rectification of the problem involves either wearing a communal soft-cup bra offered by the prison visiting center or ruining one's own bra by cutting the fabric so that the wires can be detached. When someone cannot pass through the metal detector due to her bra, the correctional staff send her to the toilet on the other side of the Tube with a thumbtack to pierce the bra's fabric. However, thumbtacks are too blunt and hard to maneuver when ripping the strong underseam of a bra. After gouging my finger while assisting one woman—who surprised me by handing me the thumbtack, hiking her black T-shirt above her rose-tattooed breast, and expectantly presenting the seam of her lacy bra to me—I started keeping a small pair of sharpnosed scissors in my backpack for women to use. Once they have eviscerated one bra, visitors add it to their San Quentin-designated wardrobe: "I got my regular bras, an' I got my penitentiary bras!" one woman joked.

After a visitor has undergone processing several times, she learns that not only does the official dress code change frequently and unpredictably, but it is irregularly and haphazardly applied. Repeatedly in conversations in the Tube and in interviews, women complained bitterly about certain officers deemed to be stringent to the point of harassment who order women to raise their arms above their heads to determine if their shirts rise unacceptably high, consider "transparent" any apparel that allows the outline of an undergarment to be seen, or deny entry to toddlers wearing blue denim. These officers earn their tough reputations in contrast to their more relaxed colleagues who waive through visitors who are not in flagrant violation of the dress code, overlooking dubious attire or minor infractions. The range in leniency means that people may have a single outfit accepted one day and rejected another, as Fern, a forty-three-year-old substance abuse counselor, observes,

> You wear the same outfit for five or six visits, and all of a sudden it's not appropriate. And so you have to go change. . . . And all that time that you're taking to change, most of that's coming off your visit.

Since there are two processing stations (one on each side of the processing area) in operation most of the day, this spectrum of enforcement also means that visitors being processed simultaneously may experience significantly different treatment, depending on with whom they are interacting. The erratic interpretation of the dress code undermines women's ability to assemble outfits that they know they can "count on" to make it through processing, which in turn disrupts their feelings of mastery over the projection of a persona compatible with their self-image. . . .

Being compelled by correctional staff to modify their attire affronts women, many of whom carefully selected or specifically purchased their garments for their visit. This is a particularly resonant matter for impoverished women, who may invest significant portions of their scarce resources in cultivating and displaying a fashionable "look" that imbues them with a sense of command denied to them in other aspects of their lives. . . . The decision that they are "inappropriate" incenses or humiliates visitors, especially if they are chastised for being too sexually enticing. The combination of not being permitted to dress alluringly for a romantic partner and of having a prison guard criticize one's sexual expression leaves women feeling diminished, shamed, and often frustrated to the point of tears.

Women who are denied entry due to their clothing are referred to the prison visiting center, where they discover a selection of donated, secondhand clothes in outdated or unattractive styles, colors, and fabrics from which they must choose a garment approximately their size. The majority of visitors care deeply about their personal appearances and feel disheartened and self-conscious when instructed to don "'poor' clothes that become associated with personal deficit" (Guy and Banim 2000, 320), and the recognition by other visitors and by prisoners of these clothes as visiting center outfits compounds the demoralization of wearing them, reinforcing women's sense that they must discard their own identities and assume a prescribed carceral character to gain access to the prison. . . .

In addition to the enforced modification of their appearances, visitors must forfeit other "tools" of their "identity kits" to enter San Quentin. There are strict limits on what items people can bring into the prison: no makeup, sunglasses, tampons, sanitary napkins, cigarettes, gum, electronic gadgets, pens, papers, or nonprescription medications are allowed. Visitors are required to present a valid form of identification (driver's license, state- or government-issued identification card, passport, identification card issued by the Mexican consulate) and are permitted to enter the prison with two keys, up to thirty dollars in coins and one-dollar bills, an unopened pack of tissue, a comb or brush, and ten photographs, all of which may be contained in a small, clear plastic purse or bag. Umbrellas are prohibited, and on stormy days visitors make their way along the long walk to and from the visiting areas unprotected from the elements. People with children are allowed to bring six disposable diapers, a factory-sealed pack of baby wipes, two prepared bottles, two jars of factory-sealed baby food, one transparent pacifier, and one baby blanket into the prison but are forbidden to transport strollers, baby seats, toys, or containers of formula onto the grounds. The barring of strollers and baby seats presents distinct difficulties for women, first because the lockers are not large enough to store these items if someone arrived with them on public transportation and second because the visitor (along with the prisoner she is visiting) must then hold her baby for the entire duration of her visit. Restrictions on baby accessories and children's toys also seriously encumber people during family visits, when visitors spend three days and two nights locked in the facility with their incarcerated relatives.

Visitors possessing a prohibited item can return it to their vehicles, secure it in a locker for the price of fifty cents, or leave it on a bench in the Tube with the hope that it will still be there after the visit. Since most people have already placed their shoes in the tray to be sent through the X-ray machine when they are advised that they must discharge an article, they commonly return to the Tube in bare or stocking feet, tiptoeing around the patches of spilled soda and food wrappers as they make their way to the lockers or even the parking lot. One day I observed a mother with an infant, a toddler, and another child parade to and from the lockers three times, prancing high on her red-varnished toes through the filthy corridor. Her first trip was to put her container of baby formula in a locker: "The things they make you do! Baby can't have no formula. I always think I got everything taken care of, but I guess I don't!" Realizing she needed two quarters, she returned to the processing area to retrieve a coin from her purse and then came out and deposited it, taking with her the locker key. A few minutes later she appeared once more with a ten-dollar bill, this time having left her brood behind; unwilling to reopen the locker and necessitate the insertion of two more quarters, she carefully slipped the bill through the crack in the locker door and plucked her way back, shaking her head bemusedly and sidestepping a puddle of Coke. . . .

THE SECONDARY PRISONIZATION OF KIN AND KITH

Altogether, a careful inspection of the "ceremonies" of belittlement (Garfinkel 1968) enacted by the authorities in and around the liminal zone of the Tube reveals the prison apparatus as a machinery for the abridgement of personhood in the purported interest of institutional security. Applying Sykes's (1958, 63-83) notion of "the pains of imprisonment," specifically the "deprivation of autonomy" and the "deprivation of goods and services," to dissect prison visiting procedures suggests that inmates' kin and kith are subjected to *secondary prisonization*, a weakened but still compelling version of the elaborate regulations, concentrated surveillance, and corporeal confinement governing the lives of ensnared felons. As described above, myriad aspects of visitor processing—from the display of pertinent information to the commencement of visiting hours to the implementation of the dress code—are perpetually irregular and subject to change without notice. . . .

This blocking of visitors' capacity to comprehend and thus to contest or remedy the conditions affecting them at the prison along with the disruption of people's control over how they use their time and organize their appearances are features of the "deprivation of autonomy," which engenders feelings of powerlessness and fear among women while locating them in a supplicant relationship with the institution. As Sarah, who has been visiting her husband for two years, remarks,

> That's probably what is the biggest challenge for me, is the fact that nothing stays the same there [at San Quentin]. They're constantly changing the rules. . . . There's *no* consistency, there's *no* stability, nothing stays the same, and that sort of living in the unknown is, is *really* difficult.

The neglect and indignity inflicted on people in the Tube directly connect to another of Sykes's "pains," the "deprivation of goods and services." By failing to provide sufficient amenities to cover visitors' basic physical and hygienic needs and by withholding elementary advice and using designs of "secrecy" to engender feelings of apprehension and helplessness (see Spain 1992, 18–21), officials mark those forced to wait in the corridor as disgraced beings. Furthermore, denying women control over their corporeal self-presentations reinforces their feelings of impotence and subservience in their interactions with the correctional facility, regardless of their cultural or economic capital in the "outside world." Sophia, a thirty-seven-year-old white college graduate, observes,

> I'm articulate and educated and I carry myself with class and all that. However . . . I understand that I'm in a state penitentiary, and I understand that by the law it is a privilege, not a right, that I visit my husband. And with that in mind there are certain guidelines that I have to follow. I have to dress a certain way; I have to conduct myself in a certain manner. And I'm willing to do that.

Women visiting prisoners readily perceive their treatment at the prison as a collapse of institutional differentiation between visitors and inmates. The complaint expressed by Stephanie, a twenty-five-year-old security guard and college student, that the correctional officers "try to make it as hard for them [visitors] as possible . . . you know, *that* is treating the family members as if they're incarcerated too" is commonly heard among women at San Quentin, who feel stigmatized and humiliated by their encounters with the penal arm of the criminal justice system. Through their experiences of the "pains of imprisonment" at the border of the correctional setting, women assume the peculiar status of *quasi-inmates,* people at once legally free and palpably bound. While the ostensible function of the prison when handling visitors is that of a "people-processing organization" (Hasenfeld 1972), the cumulative dishonors it inflicts—the routinization of long and unpredictable waits, containment in an inhospitable and inscrutable environment, interference with self-presentation, the denial of private belongings—make it akin to a "people-*changing* organization" (Hasenfeld 1972, 257–58, emphasis added) that defines and profoundly transforms the public and personal identities of women.

REFERENCES

Abraham, Laurie Kaye. 1993. *Mama might be better off dead: The failure of health care in urban America.* Chicago: University of Chicago Press.

Bauman, Zygmunt. 1995. *Life in fragments: Essays in postmodern morality.* Cambridge, MA: Blackwell.

Beck, Allen J., Jennifer C. Karberg, and Paige M. Harrison. 2002. *Prison and jail inmates at midyear 2001.* Washington, DC: Bureau of Justice Statistics.

Blake, Joe. 1990. *Sentenced by association: The needs of prisoners' families.* London: Save the Children.

Bordo, Susan. 1993. *Unbearable weight: Feminism, western culture, and the body.* Berkeley: University of California Press.

Bourgois, Philippe. 1995. *In search of respect: Selling crack in El Barrio.* Cambridge, UK: Cambridge University Press.

Brubaker, Rogers, and Fred Cooper. 2000. Beyond identity. *Theory and Society* 29:1–47.

Bureau of Justice Statistics. 2002. *Sourcebook of criminal justice statistics.* Washington DC: Bureau of Justice Statistics.

Caddle, Diane, and Debbie Crisp. 1996. *Imprisoned women and mothers.* Home Office Research Study 162. London: Home Office.

California Department of Corrections. 1999. *California Department of Corrections visitors handbook.* Available from http://www.cdc.state.ca.us/facility/visitorhb.htm.

Christie, Nils. 1998. Éléments de géographie pénale (For a penal geography). *Actes de la recherche en sciences sociales* 124:68–74.

Clemmer, Donald. 1940. *The prison community.* Boston: Christopher Publishing House.

Conover, Ted. 2000. *Newjack: Guarding Sing Sing.* New York: Random House.

Douglas, Mary. 1970. *Body symbols.* Oxford, UK: Blackstone.

Fausto-Sterling, Anne. 1995. Gender, race, and nation: The comparative anatomy of "Hottentot" women in Europe, 1815–1817. In *Deviant bodies,* edited by Jennifer Terry and Jacqueline Urla, 19–48. Bloomington: Indiana University Press.

Fishman, Laura T. 1988. Stigmatization and prisoners' wives' feelings of shame. *Deviant Behavior* 9:169–92.

Foucault, Michel. 1977. *Discipline and punish: The birth of the prison.* New York: Vintage.

Garfinkel, Harold. 1968. Conditions of successful degradation ceremonies. In *Prison within society: A reader in penology,* edited by Lawrence Hazelrigg, 68–77. Garden City, NY: Doubleday.

Garland, David, ed. 2001. *Mass imprisonment: Social causes and consequences.* London: Sage.

Goffman, Erving. 1959. *The presentation of self in everyday life.* New York: Anchor.

———. 1961. *Asylums: Essays on the social situation of mental patients and other inmates.* Harmondsworth, UK: Penguin.

———. 1963. *Stigma: Notes on the management of spoiled identity.* New York: Simon & Schuster.

Goodsell, Charles B. 1984. Welfare waiting rooms. *Urban Life* 12:467–77.

Grinstead, Olga, Bonnie Faigeles, and Carrie Bancroft. 2001. The financial cost of prison visiting: A survey of women visitors to a state prison. *Journal of African-American Men* 6:59–70.

Guy, Alison, and Maura Banim. 2000. Personal collections: Women's clothing use and identity. *Journal of Gender Studies* 9:313–27.

Hagan, John, and Ronit Dinovitzer. 1999. The collateral consequences of imprisonment for children, communities, and prisoners. In *Prisons,* edited by Michael Tonry and Joan Petersilia, 121–62. Chicago: University of Chicago Press.

Hairston, Creasie Finney. 1999. Kinship care when parents are incarcerated. In *Kinship care: Improving practice through research,* edited by James P. Gleeson and Creasie Finney Hairston, 189–211. Washington, DC: CWLA Press.

Hasenfeld, Yeheskel. 1972. People processing organizations: An exchange approach. *American Sociological Review* 37:256–63.

Jacobs, P. 1966. *Prelude to riot.* New York: Random House.

Kauffman, Kelsey. 1988. *Prison officers and their world.* Cambridge, MA: Harvard University Press.

Lipsky, Michael. 1980. *Street-level bureaucracy: Dilemmas of the individual in public services.* New York: Russell Sage.

Maksymowicz, Duszka. 2000. *Femme de parloir* (Woman of the visiting room). Paris: L'Esprit frappeur.

Mann, Leon. 1969. Queue culture: The waiting line as a social system. *American Journal of Sociology* 75:340–54.

Owen, Barbara. 1998. *"In the mix": Struggle and survival in a women's prison.* Albany: State University of New York.

Piven, Frances Fox, and Richard Cloward. 1971. *Regulating the poor: The social functions of welfare.* New York: Pantheon.

Schwartz, Barry. 1975. *Queuing and waiting: Studies in the social organization of access and delay.* Chicago: University of Chicago.

Skidmore, Paul. 1999. Dress to impress: Employer regulation of gay and lesbian appearance. *Social & Legal Studies* 8:509–29.

Spain, Daphne. 1992. *Gendered spaces.* Chapel Hill: University of North Carolina Press.

Sykes, Gresham. 1958. *The society of captives: A study of a maximum security prison.* Princeton, NJ: Princeton University Press.

Tonry, Michael. 1995. *Malign neglect: Race, crime, and punishment in America.* New York: Oxford University Press.

Zalba, Serapio R. 1964. *Women prisoners and their families.* Monograph of California Department of Corrections. Clifton Park, NY: Delmar.

REVIEW QUESTIONS

1. The author argues that the rules and their enforcement are gendered in their application and consequences. What is the evidence for this argument?
2. How would a corrections official explain and defend the rules, their enforcement, and the way that the physical structure of the visiting facilities influence the visitation experience?
3. What does the author mean when she argues that the visitation processing experience is a form of prisonization for those who are visiting inmates?

X

AGE-SPECIFIC ISSUES IN CORRECTIONS

READING 25

Moving Beyond the "Pepsi Generation"

The Contemporary Inmate Subculture in Juvenile Correctional Settings

Wilson R. Palacios

This review article explores a host of issues related to inmate subculture within juvenile correctional facilities. Readers are briefed on the recent crackdown against juvenile gangs and a trend toward harsh sentencing practices and how these policy initiatives have impacted juvenile correctional populations. The core components of status hierarchy and conduct norms are reviewed and various criminological theories are presented as vehicles through which to better understand the violent behaviors and norms observed in juvenile facilities. Correctional and law enforcement strategies currently employed in response to the juvenile gang problems are also detailed.

A recent report by the National Center for Juvenile Justice (McCurley and Snyder, 2004) found about 1 in 10 adult victims of violent crime (9%) were preyed upon by a juvenile offender, and about 1 in 2 juvenile victims of violent crime (51%) faced a juvenile offender. Additionally, most (95%) of the victims of sexual assault committed by juveniles were younger than 18, as were 43% of victims of robberies by juveniles, 53% of aggravated assaults, and 61% of simple assaults. In cases where a juvenile committed a simple assault against an adult, more than half (52%) of the victims over the age of 30 were the offender's parent or step-parent. And in sexual assaults, robberies, and aggravated assaults committed by juveniles, 40% of victims were injured, compared with 48% of the victims of the same offenses committed by adults. Sobering statistics such as these have been the catalyst for engineering a juvenile justice system where custody and control override genuine rehabilitative efforts (see Feld, 1998). The outcome of unilateral "get tough" sentencing policies and reforms have been generations of youthful offenders redefining inmate culture across various types of correctional institutions.

Early research indicated that adult inmates ultimately embrace the culture of the prison community by developing inmate social systems (Clemmer, 1940; Sykes, 1958). Various studies have found that the inmate subculture originates because of the stress of confinement (Skyes, 1958), while others have surmised that the subculture is imported from the outside (Irwin, 1981). Regardless of how the subculture evolves, there is empirical evidence that the inmate community can profoundly affect institutional rehabilitative efforts (Clemmer, 1940; Hassine, 1999, 2002; Irwin & Cressy, 1962; Larson, 1983; Rothman, 1971; Sykes, 1958; Taylor & Palacios 2002). Clearly, juvenile correctional facilities are not immune to the notion of an inmate subculture.

CULTURAL NORMS AND VIOLENCE IN JUVENILE CORRECTIONAL FACILITIES

In the United States, juvenile correctional facilities have existed for almost 200 years. Between 1824 and 1853, houses of refuge and reformatories were the first facilities created to house and rehabilitate juvenile delinquents. While attempting to transform juvenile delinquents into worthwhile, productive citizens by using corporal punishment, these institutions encountered individuals with personal histories of physical and sexual abuse, mental health needs, and a multitude of psycho-social problems (Alleman, 2002; Mennel, 1973; Pisciotta, 1994).

During the twentieth century, the facilities began focusing more on a treatment model including psychological treatment and vocational training (Klofas, 2002; Pisciotta, 1994). Despite the expansion of the institutional structure of the juvenile correctional facilities, to include ranches, farms, reception and diagnostic centers, educational programs, training schools, shelters, work camps, and boot camps, juvenile correctional facilities still encounter numerous difficulties and much criticism (Kupchik, 2007; Taylor & Palacios, 2002). The criticisms of the juvenile correctional institutions are associated with the issues of overcrowding, inadequate funding and staffing, violence, and particularly research that supports the theory that incarceration has a negative effect upon self-concept. Some studies have found that the self-concept of boys who are incarcerated, especially, for the first time, is definitely negatively affected, and fostered by an inmate subculture (Armstrong, Gover, & Mackenzie, 2002; Culbertson, 1975; Mennel, 1973; Vito, Tewskbury & Wilson, 1998).

Poole & Regoli (1983), in their research on the inmate subculture, reported that juveniles who exhibit violent behavior prior to imprisonment were most likely to resort to violence while incarcerated. Researchers have constantly questioned the professed goal and the ability of these correctional facilities to rehabilitate (Alleman, 2002; Allen & Simonsen, 1998; Bell, 1990; Hood, 1967; Lee & Haynes, 1980; Reinke, 2006). Among the many reasons for this doubt is the impact of cultural and behavioral norms on violence in juvenile correctional settings.

Juvenile correctional settings, not unlike most social structures, are inherently defined by conflict. It is a social structure by which all relationships therein are defined on the basis of authoritative boundaries and power; authority-subject relationships (Turk, 1969). The cornerstone of these relationships, and much of the resulting conflict, are cultural and behavioral norms. Turk (1969) and other conflict theorists (Chambliss, 1984; Hagan, 1990; Platt, 1975; Quinney, 1975; Sellin, 1938; Vold, 1958) have delineated the personal and social factors that cause friction between authority-subject relationships (in this case, juvenile justice practitioners and juvenile inmates). However, neither these findings nor those of subcultural theorists have been beneficial in the juvenile offender rehabilitation process.

Proponents of subcultural theories, such as Luckenbill and Doyle (1989), Miller (1958), Sampson and Bartusch (1999), and Wolfgang and Ferracuti (1967), have also presented significant findings that are applicable to incarcerated youthful offenders. They consider delinquency to be a concurrent response to society's cultural value system and a bond to group norms. Subcultural theorists contend that delinquency is an expression of principles advocated by one's reference group, such as other members of the subculture, and, therefore, that delinquency comprises behavior compatible with a group of norms.

To this end, several studies that have documented the impact of cultural and behavioral norms on violence in juvenile correctional settings and the corresponding consequences that solid and forceful inmate codes play on the behavior of both inmates and staff (Akers, 2003; Cullen & Agnew, 2003; Zaitzow, 1998).

JUVENILE SOCIAL CODES

Subcultures in juvenile correctional facilities develop independently of administrators and custodians, and juveniles who enter correctional facilities observe a social world of strong inmate codes of behavior that most inmates understand. In their study of an Ohio state institution for boys, Bartollas, Miller, & Dinitz (1976) reported the emergence of a normative informal code consisting of a series of specific principles for daily living that was passed from inmate to inmate. This code had eight elements (see Box 1.1). The values of inmate social systems are embodied in this code, whose violations usually produce sanctions ranging from ostracism and avoidance to physical violence (Sykes & Messinger, 1960:6).

Although this social code appears to unite inmates against the staff, Bartollas, Miller & Dinitz (1976), Poole & Regoli (1983), and Wellford (1967) found that inmates are usually not a cohesive group and typically exploit fragile and new residents. Adult prison inmates often cope with the strict and unforgiving correctional setting by choosing certain social roles to express their individuality (Hassine, 1999; Irwin, 1970; Walker, Spohn & DeLone, 2000). These roles are also characteristic of

BOX 1.1 Juvenile Inmate Social Codes

1. Exploit whomever you can: The conduct norms suggest that the powerless may be victimized in any conceivable way.
2. Don't kiss ass: This tenet warns inmates not to be dependent on staff and to regard youth leaders, social workers, and schoolteachers with distrust and suspicion.
3. Don't rat on your peers: To betray a peer is to break a very serious norm.
4. Don't give up your ass: Since a boy who is sexually exploited often runs the risk of becoming the cottage scapegoat, youths usually fight rather than submit to the pressure.
5. Be cool: This involves not "whining" when things are not going well or not running away from a fight.
6. Don't get involved in another inmate's affairs: This maxim promotes granting as much social distance as self-contained cottage living permits.
7. Don't steal "squares": Stealing cigarettes is a serious offense and youth caught doing it are often seriously assaulted.
8. Don't buy the mind-fucking: Here youth guard against repeated treatment attempts made by staff to modify boys' behaviors and values.

SOURCES: Bartollas, Miller, and Dinitz. *Juvenile Victimization: The Institutional Paradox,* 1976, pp. 105–128; Thornton and Voigt. *Delinquency and Justice,* 1992, p. 428.

BOX 1.2 Institutional Argot: The Social Roles of Juvenile Inmates

1. Heavy: A leader who can maintain power by aggression, or by intelligence and cooperation.
2. Lieutenant: These youths are the heavies' assistants.
3. Slick: Inmates who are highly esteemed by others for their ability to manipulate staff.
4. Booty Bandit: Youths who sexually exploit others.
5. Peddler: Generally, one inmate from a cottage who trades goods from one cottage to another.
6. Messup: Besides making mistakes, violating institutional rules and creating conflict with peers.
7. Thief: In spite of his lowly status, the thief, who steals from other inmates, is found in every cottage.
8. Queen: These are overt homosexuals.
9. Scapegoat: The lowest-ranking social role. A youth who becomes isolated from the group because of his amenability to exploitation, especially sexual exploitation. (pp. 105–128).

SOURCES: Bartollas, Miller, and Dinitz. *Juvenile Victimization: The Institutional Paradox,* 1976, pp. 105–128; Thornton and Voigt. *Delinquency and Justice,* 1992, p. 428; Polsky. *Cottage Six: The Social Systems of Delinquent Boys in Residential Treatment,* 1962.

juvenile correctional facilities, and they frequently identify the types of inmates at the top and bottom of the social system (see Box 1.2).

Bartollas, Miller, and Dintz's (1976) study of exploited inmates at a maximum security juvenile facility for boys classified 90 percent of the inmates as either "exploiters" or victims, of which mostly streetwise African Americans were labeled the former. Schrag (1961) noted in his research on juvenile and adult correctional facilities that male convicts are "labeled in inmate argot as 'square Johns,' 'right guys,' 'outlaws,' or 'politicians,' based on the types of relationships with fellow inmates. The 'right guy' is loyal to his fellow inmates and hostile toward custodians and correctional authorities, while the 'square John' is an outsider in the inmate social network (p. 11)." The formation of social roles plays an important part in the correctional setting (Zaitzow, 1998). Whereas the institution's formal goals focus on treatment, the informal inmate roles, such as the social codes, may sabotage treatment modalities (see Zingraff, 1975). Beyond "square Johns," "outlaws," or "politicians," juvenile correctional settings serve as a center stage for many street gang members, thereby reshaping traditional inmate-convict cultural and behavioral norms into one of a more generalized gang culture.

CONTEMPORARY YOUTH GANG CULTURE AND JUVENILE CORRECTIONS

The law enforcement community and some researchers (see Knox, 1992) commonly refer to contemporary street gangs as "supergangs" or coalitions. Although these "supergangs" have been identified as a major factor in the rising level of drug trafficking and violence in America, the research community is currently engaged in an open debate concerning such a connection (see Howell and Decker, 1999). Nevertheless, Knox (1992, p. 23) defines supergangs as "highly structured, formally organized gangs with numerous chapters, sets, or franchises throughout the United States." Examples of these supergangs or coalitions include the Bloods, Crips, Latin Kings, Vice Lords, Black Guerilla Family, Aryan Brotherhood, El Rukins, the Mexican Mafia, and People and Folk (Knox, 1992; Spergel, 1990).

Most agree that "supergangs" or coalitions compose only a small portion of the youth gang problem in America. Starbuck, Howell, and Lindquist (2001, p. 2–4) argue that the preponderance of contemporary youth gang structure and culture are hybrid manifestations of the more "traditional" American youth gangs from the past. Moreover, they add: "Gang migration, movies, and gangsta music work together to introduce local gangs to large-city gang culture. The lack of existing gang culture allows for modifications and adaptation of the culture of urban gangs." (Starbuck, Howell, and Lindquist, 2001, p. 6) This "cut and paste" gang culture presents unique challenges and issues for judicial, enforcement, and penal institutions (see Coughlin and Venkatesh, 2003) attempting to address corresponding gang migration and proliferation patterns (see Knox, Houston, Tromanhanauer, McCurrie & Laskey, 1996; Maxson, 1998; Maxson, Woods, and Klein, 1995; Moore and Terrett, 1999). Although the primary approach for officials, in dealing with such groups, has been legislative reform and enhanced law enforcement initiatives (Shichor and Sechrest, 1996), it has also inadvertently contributed to the burgeoning gang problem now confronting many correctional administrators and front-line personnel therein.

RESULTS FROM THE WAR ON GANGS

A number of factors have led to the explosion of admissions of juveniles to jails and prisons. These factors include higher levels of violence associated with this particular type of offender group (Curry, Ball & Decker, 1996; Esbensen and Huizinga, 1993; Miller, 2001; Thornberry, 1998; Thornberry, Huizinga, and Loeber, 1995); suppression tactics such as law enforcement antigang units, innovative prosecution tactics (e.g. vertical prosecution); intensive supervision (see R. K. Jackson and McBride, 1996); and legislative initiatives (e.g. mandatory-minimum sentences, extended jurisdiction for juveniles, blended sentencing, truth-in-sentencing statutes), three strikes and you're out, Weed and Seed programs, California's Street Terrorism Enforcement and Prevention Act, and Florida's 1990 Street Terrorism Enforcement and Prevention Act (see Austin, 1996; Gable, 1996; Klein, 1995; Spergel, 1995). Most agree that the war on gangs has created a special population: youthful offenders with street gang affiliations who are not necessarily supervised or managed in the same manner as other groups. This lack of supervision has inadvertently created a problem that has had social, economic, and political consequences for the overburdened, overworked, and understaffed correctional system. Roush and Dunlap (1998) contended that "transferring the problem of the most serious juvenile offenders (including street gang members) to an even more overwhelmed and less effective system makes no sense (p. 15) and that the placement of juveniles in adult prisons reflects a disregard for history, which is replete with examples of how get tough approaches fail" (p. 16). However, Backstrom (1998, p. 14) argued that "we cannot overlook the fact that today's juvenile offenders often are sophisticated, gang-connected juveniles, committing violent crimes, and there are fewer reasons to be concerned about segregating these hard-core juvenile offenders from adults." Although the precise extent of street gang members in correctional facilities, especially juvenile correctional facilities, has been difficult to ascertain, limited national and regional surveys have attempted to fill this void.

THE PREVALENCE OF GANGS IN JUVENILE CORRECTIONAL FACILITIES

A survey by the American Correctional Association (1993) revealed that 40 prison systems were dealing with gangs or, as they are commonly referred to as in this setting, security threat groups. A 1990 Juvenile Correctional Institutions Survey reported that 78% of the responding institutions indicated a recent gang problem, 40% reported the involvement of female inmates in gangs, and approximately one-third reported one or more incidents in which violence involving gang members resulted in serious injuries (Knox, 1992). Jackson and Sharpe's (1997) descriptive analysis of gang activity in 21 eastern North Carolina prisons indicated that about 52% of the participants identified themselves as members of local gangs, such as the Ku Klux Klan, skinheads, posse, bikers, and white pride, and about 18% identified themselves as members of such gang alliances as the Bloods, Crips, and Folks. Jackson and Sharpe stated that "Many urban street gang members are migrating to rural areas as they expand their gangs' recruitment efforts and activities. As we continue to implement major provisions of the crime bill, specifically becoming tougher on gang members and gang activity, there will be increases in the number of arrests and incarcerations of gang members" (p. 6).

As for gang-related violence within juvenile correctional facilities, a survey of 300 state juvenile institutions found that 14% of those that participated reported that gang members have been a problem in terms of assaults on correctional staff, 28% reported more than one incident of aggravated assault, one-third indicated that these assaults on correctional staff were serious enough to warrant hospitalization, and 33% indicated that one or more general incidents of aggravated assaults resulted in serious injuries (Knox, 1992). Furthermore, 9% thought there was a link between the fear of violence from gang members within correctional facilities and staff turnover. Fifty-three percent indicated that juvenile gang members were responsible for vandalism and other types of property damage in juvenile facilities.

How did the juvenile facilities deal with gang members? The survey (Knox, 1992) found that juvenile correctional institutions primarily handled this situation on a case-by-case basis (72%), interrupting communications (32.7%), isolating identified leaders (38.3%), transferring members to other institutions (29%), and imposing institutional lockdowns (22.4%) as control measures. In addition to these methods, state systems like the New York City Department of Corrections use advanced technology in their attempts to control and manage gang members. As of 1996, the New York City Department of Corrections had identified 1,153 inmates as members of 32 gangs and gang-like organizations, both large, well-organized gangs with national reputations and smaller groups (Gaston, 1996). One component of the New York City Department of Corrections Gang Control Program is a database containing an inmate's gang affiliations, status within the organization, arrest history for gang-related incidents, and other institutional information. Another component is a digitized imaging program that allows intake and classification officers to take the complete histories and personal data of gang members, including distinguishing tattoos and other marks. The system is portable and allows for multiple searches on the basis of any data in this file. As Gaston (1996, p. 9) noted, "Every registered person in the entire gang network who fit a description would be displayed on the screen in a photo array—constituting a virtual computerized line-up" (p. 9).

Correctional administrators and front-line personnel have been faced with the realities of a new type of inmate in their facilities. Along these same lines, the prison industrial complex has given way to a new prison culture that many correctional officers, managers, and staff personnel have to maneuver and negotiate on a daily basis. Initially, prison officials adopted a working-with philosophy when they encountered prison gangs, but such an approach led only to quasi-control and stability in many of these institutions (Spergel, 1990). Gido (1991) identified several key issues (such as jail architecture and operations, litigation strategies, lawsuit-prevention programs, and information systems and comparative analyses of populations across jails) pertaining to the establishment of a relevant jail research agenda. The contemporary youth (street) gang member (younger as well as older, with a higher proclivity for violence, female as well as male, and racially and ethnically diverse) presents a new type of jail-prison population. Since get-tough-on crime mandates show no sign of abatement, correctional professionals are faced with finding new and innovative operational practices and inmate management strategies.

SUMMARY

Correctional institutions, by their very nature, are violent social systems. Juveniles entering such total institutions (Goffman, 1961) find themselves in a social reality consisting of cultural norms, values, roles, and jargon that define physical, spatial, and personal boundaries; rejection of such cultural scripts is not an option. The inmate must accept this subculture or be exposed to threatening rejection. The prisoner subculture, carrying its potent theme of violence, evolves somewhat independently from correctional officials but in response to changing prisoner demographics and sentencing policies that sustain a turbulent prison life (Hunt, Riegel, Morales, and Waldorf, 1993).

Gang culture and its concomitant behaviors, attitudes, and beliefs are a present-day reality for most juvenile correctional officials. In the last 17 years, American correctional facilities have experienced a dramatic increase in inmates with gang affiliations, specifically with ties to street gangs (Griffin, 2007). These intricate social processes, its nature, and the cyclical relationship between street-to-prison-to-gang "networks" are of recent emphasis by proponents of offender reentry initiatives (Huebner, Varano, and Bynum, 2007; McGloin, 2007). Unfortunately, contemporary deterrence provisions have inadvertently contributed to this burgeoning institutional gang problem. Many political opponents of the juvenile justice system have been responsible for enacting legislative provisions that have increased the total number of "youthful" offenders now being warehoused in these facilities.

The war on gangs has created a special population, youthful offenders, who are not necessarily supervised or managed in the same manner as other inmate groups (see Griffin and Hepburn 2006 for review). Moreover, a unique inmate social system has evolved around a gang culture; an amorphous social, cultural, and behavioral normative "structure" redefining inmate argot and social codes.

REFERENCES

Akers, R. (2003). "A Social Learning Theory of Crime." In R. Muraskin & Albert R. Roberts (Eds.), *Visions for Change, Crime and Justice in the Twenty-First Century.* (pp. 142–154). Upper Saddle River, NJ: Prentice Hall.

Allen, H.E., & C.E. Simonsen. (1998). *Corrections in America: An Introduction.* Upper Saddle River, NJ: Prentice Hall.

Alleman, T. (2002). "Correctional Philosophies: Varying Ideologies of Punishment." In Rosemary Gido & Ted Alleman (Eds.), *Turnstile Justice: Issues in American Corrections.* 2nd Edition. (pp. 18–37). New York, NY: Prentice-Hall.

American Correctional Association. (1993). *Gangs in Correctional Facilities: A National Assessment.* Washington DC: U.S. Department of Justice, Office of Justice Programs, National Institute of Justice.

Armstrong, G.S., A.R. Gover, and D.L. Mackenzie (2002). "The Development and Diversity of Correctional Boot Camps." In Rosemary Gido & T. Allenman (Eds.), *Turnstile Justice: Issues in American Corrections* 2nd Edition (pp. 115–130). New York, NY: Prentice-Hall.

Austin, J. (1996). "The Effect of Three Strikes and You're Out on Corrections." In D. Shichor and D.K. Sechrest (Eds.), *Three Strikes and You're Out: Vengeance as Public Policy.* (pp. 155–176). Thousand Oaks, CA: Sage.

Backstrom, J.C. (1998). "Housing Juveniles in Adult Facilities: A Commonsense Approach." In *Point Counterpoint: Correctional Issues.* Lanham, MD: American Correctional Association: 13–14.

Bartollas, C., S.J. Miller, and S. Dinitz. (1976). *Juvenile Victimization: The Institutional Paradox.* New York, NY: Wiley.

Bell, J. (1990, April). "Advocates Persevere in Jail Removal Efforts" *Youth Law News,* pp. 10–26.

Chambliss, W.J. (1984). *Criminal Law in Action.* (2nd ed.). New York: John Wiley & Sons.

Clemmer, D. (1940). *The Prison Community,* Boston: Christopher.

Coughlin, B.C. and S.A. Venkatesh (2003). "The Urban Street Gang after 1970." *Annual Review of Sociology* 29:41–64.

Cullen, F.T. and R. Agnew. (2003) *Criminological Theory: Past to Present,* Los Angeles. CA: Roxbury Publishing Co.

Curry, G.D., R.A. Ball, & S.H. Decker, (1996). *Estimating the National Scope of Gang Crime from Law Enforcement Data, Research in Brief.* Washington, DC: U.S. Department of Justice, Office of Justice Programs, National Institute of Justice.

Esbensen, F., and D. Huizinga, (1993). "Gangs, Drugs, and Delinquency in a Survey of Youth." *Criminology* 31:565–589.

Feld, B.C. (1998). "Juvenile and Criminal Justice Systems' Responses to Youth Violence." In Michael Tonry and Mark H. Moore (Eds.), "Youth Violence." *Crime and Justice: A Review of Research,* Volume 24. (pp. 189–261). Chicago: University of Chicago Press.

Gable, R. (1996). *The Juvenile in Adult Jails: Emerging Trends and Concerns.* Longmont, CO: National Institute of Corrections Information Center, Jail Division.

Gaston, A. (1996) "Controlling Gangs through Teamwork and Technology." *Large Jail Network Bulletin.* Washington, DC: U.S. Department of Justice, National Institute of Corrections.

Gido, R. (1991). "A Jail Research Agenda for the 1990s." *Setting the Jail Research for the 1990s.* Washington, DC: U.S. Department of Justice, National Institute of Corrections.

Goffman, E. (1961). *Asylums: Essays on the Social Situation of Mental Patients and Other Inmates.* New York: Doubleday Anchor.

Griffin, M.L. (2007). "Prison Gang Policy and Recidivism: Short-Term Management Benefits, Long-Term Consequences."*Criminology and Public Policy,* 6:223–230.

Griffin, M.L. and J.R. Hepburn (2006). "The Effect of Gang Affiliation on Violent Misconduct among Inmates during the Early Years of Confinement." *Criminal Justice and Behavior,* 33:419–448.

Hagan, J. (1990). *Modern Criminology: Crime, Criminal Behavior, and its Control.* New York: McGraw-Hill.

Hassine, V. (1999). *Life Without Parole: Living in Prison Today.* 2nd Edition. Los Angeles, CA: Roxbury Publishing Company.

———. (2002) "Prison Violence From Where I Stand." In Rosemary Gido & Ted Alleman (Eds.), *Turnstile Justice: Issues in American Corrections,* 2nd Edition. (pp. 38–56). New York, Prentice-Hall.

Howell, J, and S. Decker. (1999). The Youth Gangs, Drugs, and Violence Connection. Juvenile Justice Bulletin, 1999, 1–12. Retrieved from http://www.ncjrs.org/pdfiles/9392pdf

Hood, R.B. (1967). "Research in the Effectiveness of Punishments and Treatments." In *Collected Studies in Criminological Research,* Vol. 1. Strasburg, France: Council of Europe.

Huebner, B.M, S.P. Verano, and T.S. Bynum. (2007). "Gangs, Guns, and Drugs: Recidivism among Serious, Young Offenders." *Criminology and Public Policy,* 6:187–222.

Hunt, G., S. Riegel, T. Morales, and D. Waldorf. (1993). "Changes in Prison Culture: Prison Gangs and the Case of the Pepsi Generation." *Social Problems* 40:398–409.

Irwin, J. (1970). *The Felon.* Englewood Cliffs, NJ: Prentice Hall.

———. (1981). "Sociological Studies of the Impact of Long-term Confinement." In D.A. Ward and K.P. Schoen (Eds.), *Confinement in maximum custody: New last-resort prisons in the United States and Western Europe* (pp. 49–60). Lexington, MA: D.C. Heath.

Irwin, J. and U. Cressy. (1962). "Thieves, Convicts, and Inmate Culture." *Social Problems,* 10:142–155.

Jackson, M.S. & E.G. Sharp. (1997) "Prison Gang Research: Preliminary Findings in Eastern North Carolina." *Journal of Gang Research* 5:1–8.

Jackson, R.K., & W.D. McBride. (1996) *Understanding Street Gangs.* Placerville, CA: Cooperhouse.

Klein, M. (1995). *The American Street Gang: Its Nature, Prevalence, and Control.* New York: Oxford University Press.

Klofas, J.M. (2002). "Outside In: Societal Change and Its Impact on Corrections." In Rosemary Gido & Ted Alleman (Eds.), *Turnstile Justice: Issues in American Corrections.* 2nd Edition. New York: Prentice-Hall.

Knox, G. (1992). *An Introduction to Gangs.* Bristol, IN: Wyndham Hall Press.

Knox, G., J.G. Houston, E.D. Tromanhanauer, T.F. McCurrie, and J. Laskey, (1996). "Addressing and Testing the Gang Migration Issue." In J.M. Miller & J.P. Rush (Eds.), *Gangs: A Criminal Justice Approach.* (pp. 71–83). Cincinnati, OH: Anderson.

Knox, G., T.F. McCurrie, and E.D. Tromanhanauser, (1995). "Findings on African American Female Gang Members Using a Matched-pair Design: A Research Note." *Journal of Gang Research.* 2:61–72.

Kupchik, A. (2007). "The Correctional Experience of Youth in Adult and Juvenile Prisons." *Justice Quarterly.* 24:247–270.

Larson, J. (1983, February). "Rural Female Delinquents' Adaptation to Institutional Life." *Juvenile and Family Court Journal.* 83–92.

Lee, R. and N.M. Haynes. (1980). "Project CREST and the Dual-Treatment Approach to Delinquency: Methods and Research Summarized." In R.R. Ross & P. Gendreah (Eds.), *Effective Correctional Treatment.* (pp. 497–503). Toronto: Butterworth.

Luckenbill, D.F. and D.P. Doyle. (1989) "Structural Position and Violence: Developing a Cultural Explanation." *Criminology* 36: 117–138.

Maxson, C. (1998). *Gang Members on the Move.* Washington, DC: U.S. Department of Justice, Office of Justice Programs, Office of Juvenile Justice and Delinquency Prevention.

Maxson, C., K.J. Woods, and M.W. Klein. (1995). *Street Gang Migration: How Big a Threat?* Washington, DC: U.S. Department of Justice, Office of Justice Programs, National Institute of Justice.

McCurley, C. and H.N. Snyder. (2004). "Victims of Violent Juvenile Crime." *Juvenile Justice Bulletin.* Washington, DC: U.S. Department of Justice, Office of Justice Programs, Office of Juvenile Justice and Delinquency Prevention.

McGloin, J.M. (2007). "The Continued Relevance of Gang Membership." *Criminology and Public Policy,* 6:231–240.

Mennel, R.M. (1973) *Thorns and Thistles: Juvenile Delinquents in the United States*, 1825–1949. Hanover, NH: University Press of New England.

Miller, J. (2001). *One of the Guys: Girls, Gangs, and Gender.* New York, NY: Oxford University Press.

Miller, W.B. (1958). "Lower Class Culture as a Generating Milieu of Gang Delinquency." *Journal of Social Issues.* 15:5–19.

Moore, J.P. and C. Terrett. (1999). "Highlights of the 1997 National Youth Gang Survey." Fact Sheet. Washington, DC: U.S. Department of Justice, Office of Justice Programs, Office of Juvenile Justice and Delinquency Prevention.

Moore, J.W. (1991). *Going Down to the Barrio: Homeboys and Homegirls in Change.* Philadelphia: Temple University Press.

Pisciotta, A. (1994). *Benevolent Repression: Social Control and the American Reformatory-Prison Movement.* New York, NY: New York University Press.

Platt, A.M. (1975). "Prospects for a Radical Criminology in the U.S." In I. Taylor, P. Walton, & J. Young (Eds.), *Critical Criminology.* (pp. 38–46). London: Routledge & Keagan Paul.

Poole, E.D. and R.M. Regoli, (1983) "Violence in Juvenile Institutions: A Comparative Study." *Criminology,* 21:2–3–232.

Quinney, R.A. (1975). *Criminology: An Analysis and Critique of Crime in America.* Boston: Little, Brown.

Reinke, S.J. (2006). "When Worlds Collide, A Case Study of Ethics, Privatization, and Performance in Juvenile Corrections." *Public Performance and Public Review* 29:497–509.

Rothman, D.J. (1971). *The Discovery of the Asylum.* Boston: Little Brown.

Roush, D. and E.L. Dunlap. (1998). "Juveniles in Adult Prisons: A Very Bad Idea." In *Point Counterpoint: Correctional Issues.* Lanham, MD: American Correctional Association: 15–16.

Sampson, R.J. and D.J. Bartusch. (1999) "Attitudes Toward Crime, Police, and the Law: Individual and Neighborhood Differences." *National Institute of Justice Research Preview.* Washington, DC: U.S. Department of Justice, Office of Justice Programs.

Schrag, C. (1961) "A Preliminary Criminal Typology." *The Pacific Sociological Review,* 4:11–16.

Sellin, T. (1938). *Culture Conflict and Crime.* New York: Social Science Research Council.

Shichor, D. and D.K. Sechrest. (1996). *Three Strikes and You're Out: Vengeance as Public Policy.* Thousand Oaks, CA: Sage.

Spergel, I.A. (1990). "Youth Gangs: Continuity and Change." In M. Tonry and N. Morris (Eds.), *Crime and Justice: A Review of Research.* (pp. 171–275). Chicago: The University of Chicago Press.

Spergel, I.A. (1995). *The Youth Gang Problem: A Community Approach.* New York: Oxford University Press.

Starbuck, D., J.C. Howell, and D.J. Lindquist (2001). "Hybrid and Other Modern Gangs." *Juvenile Justice Bulletin.* Washington, DC: U.S. Department of Justice, Office of Justice Programs, Office of Juvenile Justice and Delinquency Prevention.

Sykes, G.M. (1958). *The Society of Captives: A Study of a Maximum Security Prison.* Princeton NJ: Princeton University Press.

Sykes, G.M. and S.L. Messinger. (1960). "The Inmate Social System." In Richard A. Cloward et al. (Eds.), *Theoretical Studies in Social Organization of the Prison.* (pp. 5–19). New York: Social Science Research Council.

Taylor, D.L. and W.R. Palacios. (2002) "The Inmate Subculture in Juvenile Correctional Settings." In Rosemary Gido & Ted Alleman (Eds.), *Turnstile Justice: Issues in American Corrections.* (pp. 57–71). New York: Prentice-Hall.

Thornberry, T.P. (1998). "Membership in Youth Gangs and Involvement in Serious and Violent Offending." In R. Loeber & D.P. Farrington (Eds.), *Serious and Violent Offenders: Risk Factors and Successful Interventions.* (pp. 147–166). Thousand Oaks, CA: Sage.

Thornberry, T.P., D. Huisinga, and R. Loeber. (1995). "The Prevention of Serious Delinquency and Violence: Implications from the Program of Research on the Causes and Correlates of Delinquency." In J.C. Howell, B. Krisber, J.D. Hawkins, & J.J. Wilson (Eds.), *A Sourcebook: Serious, Violent, and Chronic Juvenile Offenders.* (pp. 213–237). Thousand Oaks, CA: Sage.

Turk, A.T. (1969) *Criminality and the Legal Order.* Chicago: Rand McNally.

Vigil, J.D. (1990). "Cholos and Gangs: Culture Change and Street Youths in Los Angeles." In C.R. Huff (Ed.), *Gangs in America.* (pp. 45–62). Newbury Park, CA: Sage.

———. (2003). "Urban Violence and Street Gangs." *Annual Review of Anthropology,* 32:225–242.

Vito, G.F., R. Tewksbury, and D.G. Wilson (1998). *The Juvenile Justice System: Concepts & Issues.* Prospect Heights, Illinois: Waveland Press, Inc.

Vold, G.B. (1958). *Theoretical Criminology.* New York: Oxford University Press.

Walker, S.C., C. Spohn, and M. DeLone (2000). *The Color of Justice.* 2nd Edition. Canada: Wadsworth Thompson Learning.

Wellford, C. (1967) "Factors Associated with the Adoption of the Inmate Code: A Study of Normative Assimilation." *Journal of Criminal Law, Criminology and Police Science,* 56:197–203.

Wolfgang, M.E. and F. Ferracuti, (1967). *The Subculture of Violence: Toward an Integrated Theory of Criminology.* London: Tavistock.

Zaitzow, B.H. (1998). "Doing Time: Everybody's Doing It." *Criminal Justice Policy Review,* 9:13–42.

Zingraff, M.T. (1975). "Prisonization as an Inhibitor of Effective Resocialization." *Criminology,* 13:366–388.

REVIEW QUESTIONS

1. How might the war on gangs be altered to cater to public safety concerns while also making the job of correctional administrators more manageable?
2. What are the unique dimensions to violence and conduct norms within juvenile facilities that can be attributed to the young age of the inmates?
3. What are the important differences between "super-gangs" and "traditional" youth street gangs as they relate to inmate subculture in juvenile facilities?

READING 26

Juveniles in Adult Prisons

Problems and Prospects

Frances P. Reddington

Allen D. Sapp

In this paper, the authors explore the life situations of youthful offenders serving time in adult prisons. The process of transfer of juveniles into adult court is discussed, with an emphasis on how the process may work and why it is done. Additionally, based on survey responses from directors of adult correctional systems, the authors report that these inmates are at significantly greater risk for a range of types of victimization, there is a general lack of safety for these inmates, and programming provided for these inmates is insufficient (and even recognized as such by correctional officials).

INTRODUCTION

The creation of the juvenile court was the culmination of a long term reform movement to remove juvenile offenders from the adult criminal justice system, and to ensure that troubled children were placed in a rehabilitative setting (Krisberg, 1988). The state, under the doctrine of *parens patriae,* acted in the place of a kindly parent towards the child. The juvenile court was a protector of children (Hahn, 1987). Since the creation of the juvenile court, there has been a system "safety valve" through a mechanism within the juvenile court to transfer unsalvageable youth into the adult system (Forst, 1995). However, such drastic measures were at odds with the underpinnings and goals of the juvenile system and were done with a reluctance and an acceptance of impending harm to the child (Sanborn, 1994).

In the late 1970s and early 1980s, many states "got tough" on juvenile crime in response to the public's growing concern and the failure of the juvenile justice system to eradicate juvenile crime or to seemingly even slow it down. The "new" answer was once again to turn to the adult system to deal with those youth who could not be rehabilitated within the juvenile system (Champion, 1989; Feld 1987). The result of this movement was two-fold: first, legislation designed to get tough with juvenile crime focused on ways to expand transfer laws, especially with regards to age, offense requirements and the responsibility of who makes the decision to transfer (National Coalition of State Juvenile Justice Advisory Groups, 1993) and second, more juveniles were being transferred into adult court than at any previous time (Schwartz, 1989).

Transfer has again become the solution to seemingly out of control juvenile crime. The use of transfer, and the consequences of transfer, is one of the most pressing topics concerning juvenile offenders. The embracing of transfer as the answer to the juvenile crime problem raises questions that have been previously asked, though not answered. "The debate over the efficacy of criminal court transfer has been underway for at least 50 years" (Snyder and Sickmund, 1995:156).

Accordingly, in an attempt to examine the issue of transfer, there has been an increase in the philosophical and empirical research concerned with transfer and its processes. Philosophical questions have been raised regarding transformation of the juvenile court into an institution not envisioned by its creators (Feld, 1987). Some researchers posed questions regarding transfer policies (Sanborn, 1994). Empirical studies have included the examination of factors that impact the decision to transfer (Poulos and Orchowsky, 1994; Lee, 1994); dispositions of juveniles transferred to criminal court (Fagan, 1991; Houghtalin, and Mays, 1991; Champion, 1989); differences in the dispositions of certified and noncertified juvenile offenders (Kinder et al, 1995) and the impact of juvenile transfer on violent juvenile crime (Jensen and Metsger, 1994). What is missing from the literature is research designed to determine the impact of juvenile transfer on the adult criminal justice system and an examination of the views of the adult correctional administrators who are faced with the increasing numbers of juveniles in the adult system.

First, this paper presents information about the incidence and reality of juvenile placement into adult facilities. In addition, this paper examines the attitudes of adult correctional administrators towards the transfer of juvenile offenders into adult prisons. These administrators can, in fact, validate if those concerns voiced in the literature about transferring juveniles into the adult system are borne out, as well as provide insight into any unintended results of the transfer movement.

However, before survey results are discussed, it is important to examine how the process of transfer works, how often the process is used, and what generally is the outcome of transfer. Related studies dealing with the treatment of juveniles in the adult system also will be discussed. Finally, the major findings of the present research will be presented and examined. In order to avoid confusion, the term juvenile is used throughout the paper to refer to juveniles who have been transferred by whatever method into the adult court, placed in adult facilities, and are viewed as adults in the eyes of the criminal justice system.

THE TRANSFER PROCESS

There are at least three ways that jurisdiction over juveniles can be waived by juvenile court judges and a juvenile can be processed by criminal courts. These are judicial waivers, prosecutorial waivers, and legislative waivers or automatic waivers or statutory exclusion. Different states may have several methods for transferring juveniles in their juvenile codes.

The Judicial Waiver

Historically, transfer was handled in early juvenile courts by judicial waiver, a practice that continues today in many juvenile courts (Snyder and Sickmund, 1995). The juvenile court Judge makes the decision whether to transfer jurisdiction of the child to the adult system. The Judge examines the individual circumstances of the child's case and makes a decision of transfer based upon that examination. The Supreme Court case, *Kent v. U.S. (1966),* which held that juveniles facing transfer have a right to a transfer hearing, also offered guidelines that judges should consider in the transfer hearing. Consideration is given by judges to the nature of the crime and the potential for rehabilitation within the juvenile justice system.

. . . The request for the transfer hearing may come from a variety of sources, including the juvenile intake division, the prosecutor, and occasionally, the juvenile or their family (Sickmund, 1994). Most state statutes set criteria, usually concerning age and offense, for the use of waiver. However, in the get tough movement of the 1980s and 1990s, many states added or emphasized other provisions in the juvenile statutes which facilitate transfer to the adult system. In both methods described below, the prosecutorial waiver and the legislative waiver or statutory exclusion, the transfer hearing mandated by *Kent* does not have to take place.

The Prosecutorial Waiver

One of the other methods which results in juveniles being handled in the adult court is through the use of prosecutorial discretion. . . . The prosecutor holds concurrent jurisdiction over the juvenile and adult courts. In essence, the prosecutor will make the decision in which court the charges will be filed. Generally, the age of offender and the type of offense that is under the concurrent jurisdiction of the adult and juvenile court is limited by statute, and is often limited to crimes that are violent or serious or where a pattern of repeated criminal activity is established (Sickmund, 1994). Philosophically, this has shifted the responsibility of transfer from a judicial decision based on individual assessment, to a prosecutorial decision based on legal criteria and is in direct opposition to the philosophy of the original juvenile court (Bishop, Frazier, and Henrietta, 1989).

The Legislative Waiver or Statutory Exclusion

The third way that juveniles are handled in criminal court is through legislative statutes. The legislature may define certain criminal acts as automatically under the jurisdiction of the adult court. . . . This process is not "typically" regarded as a type of transfer because the legislatures are in reality sending juveniles to the criminal court by "statutorily excluding them from juvenile court jurisdiction" (Sickmund, 1994:3). In other words, because the juveniles committed certain illegal acts defined as criminal acts and not delinquent acts the offenders are not juveniles in the eyes of the law. Many states have made legislative changes which basically take the decision to transfer out of the judicial system and move it into the legislative arena. . . .

RELATED STUDIES ON THE IMPACT OF WAIVER ON THE JUVENILES IN THE ADULT SYSTEM

This section will examine two major issues regarding the impact of waiver on juveniles which results in incarceration in adult facilities or facilities under the direction of the states department of corrections. These issues are safety issues and future behavior issues.

Safety Issues

Preliminary studies, although few in number, regarding the treatment of juveniles in adult institutions as opposed to those housed in juvenile facilities, indicate that juveniles in adult institutions are at a much greater risk regarding their safety and perceived safety. Research suggests that over fifty percent of youths in prison or in a juvenile facility are victims of property crime during their incarceration (Forst et al., 1989). However, the likelihood of being the victim of a violent crime increased in an adult prison (Forst et al., 1989). "Sexual assault was five times more likely among youth in prison than in training schools, beatings by staff nearly twice as likely, and attacks with weapons nearly 50 percent more common" (Forst et al, 1989:9). In addition, according to Eisikovits et al (1983:9), "[w]hile in prison, youths' major concern was their daily survival among older inmates."

Impact on Future Behavior

Another area of concern is the impact of prison on future behavior of juveniles after release from adult incarceration. One way this can be examined is to look at what types of programs are offered to youthful prisoners. Research suggests that juveniles in adult institutions will give more negative evaluations of the programs they encounter (treatment, training, staff and services in general) than youth in juvenile training schools (Forst et al, 1989). For example, many juveniles in juvenile facilities perceived their health care, family relations programs and counseling services to be of higher quality than did the youths in prison (Forst et al, 1989). According to Eisikovits et al. (1983), where a juvenile is housed will impact how juveniles "do time," and which will most likely impact their future behavior.

METHODOLOGY

This research was designed to examine the attitudes of adult correctional administrators towards the juvenile offenders who are transferred into the adult system, as well as to examine what resources juvenile offenders receive in adult facilities. The survey was conducted through a self-administered questionnaire mailed to the Commissioners or Directors of all state Departments of Corrections in the United States. A total of 44 surveys were returned for a return rate of 88 percent. Since one questionnaire was received after the analysis cut-off date, the results presented are based on the effective return rate of 86 percent. . . .

RESULTS

Two of the major issues in the study focused on safety and future behavior of juveniles incarcerated in adult facilities or facilities under the control of the adult corrections system in the states. Each of these issues involved several parts. When asked what the single biggest problem that juveniles contributed in the adult facilities, prison administrators' most frequent response was *safety issues*. Interestingly, the mean age that respondents cited that juveniles belong in adult facilities is age 17.

Safety Issues

Safety issues can take on a number of meanings. The study attempted to determine the contribution of juveniles in adult facilities to disciplinary problems. Respondents were asked about juveniles' contribution to disturbances as both victims and perpetrators. Results are indicated in Table 1. Responding prison administrators (27.0 percent) indicated that juveniles were the perpetrator of disturbances less often than adult inmates. Other administrators noted that juveniles were the perpetrators more often than adult inmates (21.6 percent) or about the same as adults (16.2 percent). Over one-third (35.2 percent) indicated they did not know.

Administrators reported that juveniles were victimized at about the same rate as adults (37.8 percent). Another 16.2 percent said they were more often the victims in disturbances and only 5.3 percent said juveniles were less often victimized. The lack of separate accounting for juveniles in state prisons contributed to the 40.7 percent who did not know whether juveniles were victimized more often than adults. The distribution of the responses is shown in Table 2.

Respondents were asked about the perception of correctional officers regarding juveniles in the facility. Results are presented in Table 3. More than one-half (52.8 percent) indicated juveniles were harder to deal with than adults and one-third

TABLE 1 Certified Juveniles in Adult Facilities as Perpetrators of Disturbances

More often than adults	21.6%
Less often than adults	27.0%
Same amount as adults	16.2%
Don't know	35.2%

TABLE 2 Certified Juveniles in Adult Facilities as Victims of Disturbances

More often than adults	16.2%
Less often than adults	5.3%
Same amount as adults	37.8%
Don't know	40.7%

TABLE 3 Correctional Officers' Views of Juveniles

The same as adults to deal with	33.3%
Easier than adults to deal with	2.8%
Harder than adults to deal with	52.8%
No response	11.1%

TABLE 4 Reasons for Incarceration of Juveniles in Adult Facilities

Crimes against people	78.4%
Crimes against property	5.4%
Don't know	8.1%
Other	8.1%

(33.3 percent) said they were about the same as adults. Only 2.8 percent suggested that juveniles were easier to deal with than adult inmates. This question was not answered by 11.1 per cent of the respondents. The distribution of the responses is provided in Table 3.

Responses to the question of why the majority of certified juveniles were currently in the facilities were contradictory to the figures usually offered in the literature. The literature suggests that most juveniles transferred to adult correctional facilities are convicted of crimes against property. For example, a Bureau of Justice Statistics Report entitled *National Corrections Reporting Program, 1989*, suggests that that the percentage of juveniles under 18 years of age incarcerated in adult prisons for person crimes was only 38 percent, while property crimes accounted for 41 percent, drugs for 15 percent and other/ unknown for 6 percent (Jones and Krisberg, 1994). The results of this study suggest an overwhelming percentage of the systems responding (78.4 percent) have a majority of their juveniles incarcerated for crimes against people. Only 5.4 percent of the respondents cited that the majority of the juveniles in their system were incarcerated for a crime against property.

When adult correctional administrators were asked what type of juvenile offenders should be held in a juvenile facility until they reached adulthood and then be transferred to an adult facility, there were some significant differences noted. Interestingly, 37.1 percent of the respondents felt that juveniles should be held in the juvenile facility until the age of adulthood for a property crime. The percentage dropped to 17.6 percent for a crime against person and 38.2 percent of the respondents stated that those juveniles belonged in the general population in adult facilities. Three (7.1 percent) of the administrators did not answer this inquiry.

Future Behavior Issues

Respondents were asked a series of questions designed to determine what programming was offered to juveniles in the facilities. Other inquiries were posed about additional programming that should be offered to juveniles because of their age. . . . Juvenile offenders receive additional treatment with career training (10.8 percent), prison survival (5.4 percent) and family counseling (2.7 percent) in only 18.9 percent of the responding adult systems. A total of 30 of the adult prison systems (69.5 percent) did not provide any additional treatment for juveniles incarcerated in adult facilities.

Additional comments indicated two states have special educational programs for youthful offenders, while one system offers alternative to violence workshops and an adjustment group. In one system additional alcohol and drug treatment is offered, and in one system additional counseling is offered to the youth.

Those responses change when asked what additional treatment juveniles *should* receive. Over one-half (54.1 percent) stated that prison survival training was needed and 45.9 percent called for career training. Family counseling was identified as a treatment juveniles should receive by 37.8 percent of the respondents. . . .

Other suggestions for additional treatment ranged from sex offender treatment programs, alternative dispute resolution, education (two respondents), mental health, substance abuse programs (four respondents), counseling for youthful offenders (three respondents), anger management, coping skills, adjustment counseling, values, and fetal alcohol issues.

SUMMARY AND CONCLUSIONS

The number of juveniles being certified and being incarcerated in adult facilities is increasing. In the most recent legislative session, a number of states have again changed their transfer laws by lowering transfer ages, and/or expanding the criminal acts which result in waiver, and/or initiating mandatory waiver laws, and/or expanding those who are given the discretion to determine waiver. Studies have focused on the process of waiver, and the outcome of waiver. This study has shown that correctional administrators do have concerns about both the philosophical underpinnings of transfer and the actual day to day problems of dealing with juveniles in adult facilities. Correctional administrators indicate that juveniles present a number of unique safety issues in the institutions and that juveniles under the age of 17 should not be incarcerated in adult facilities.

Juveniles contribute to overcrowding, which can be viewed as a safety issue, while at the other end of the continuum, juveniles may contribute negatively to the number and severity of confrontations in a facility. To quote one warden during a casual conversation when asked about the juveniles in his facility, he replied that juveniles were difficult to work with because "their mouths run much faster than their asses." Over half of the respondents feel that correctional officers find juveniles more difficult to deal with than adults.

These results also lead one to question if there is an issue here concerning the perception of juvenile offenders. Results indicate that most of the respondents claim that the vast majority of juveniles are in their facilities for violent crimes against people, an assumption not validated in the literature, at least through the numbers represented in judicial waiver. The numbers and crimes for other forms of transfer are not easily assessable. The rate of juveniles transferred for crimes against persons, however, is growing rapidly, which may be an explanation for the results found in this study.

It is also clear that juveniles have special programming needs and that those needs are not being met in most state adult facilities. The implications of incarceration of juveniles in adult prisons, with the resulting safety issues and the lack of needed treatment, does not bode well for the future behavior of those juveniles.

When they are released from incarceration, they are likely to be even less equipped to deal with society than they were when they entered the adult system.

REFERENCES

Bishop, D., C. Frazier and J. Henrietta (1989). "Prosecutorial Waiver: Study of a Questionable Reform." *Crime and Delinquency* 35: 179–201.

Champion, D. (1989). "Teenage Felons and Waiver Hearings: Some Recent Trends, 1980–1988." *Crime and Delinquency* 35: 577–585.

Eisikovits, Z. and M. Baizerman (1983). ""Doin' Time": Violent Youth in a Juvenile Facility and in an Adult Facility." *Journal of Offender Counseling Services and Rehabilitation*. 6: 5–20.

Fagan, J. (1991). *The Comparative Impacts of Juvenile and Criminal Court Sanctions on Adolescent Felony Offenders.* National Institute of Justice, U.S. Department of Justice.

Feld, B. (1987). "Juvenile Court Meets the Principle of Offense: Legislative Changes in Juvenile Waiver Statutes." *Journal of Criminal Law and Criminology* 78:471–533.

Forst, M.L. (1995). *The New Juvenile Justice.* Chicago: Nelson-Hall Publishers.

Forst, M., J. Fagan and Scott (1989). "Youth in Prisons and Training Schools: Perceptions and Consequences of the Treatment—Custody Dichotomy." *Juvenile and Family Court Journal* 4:1–14.

Hahn, Paul (1987). *The Juvenile Offender and the Law.* Ohio: Anderson Publishing Company.

Houghtalin, M and G.L. Mays (1991). "Criminal Dispositions of New Mexico Juveniles Transferred to Adult Court." *Crime and Delinquency.* 37:393–407.

Jensen, E. and L. Metsger (1994). "A Test of the Deterrent Effect of Legislative Waiver on Violent Juvenile Crime." *Crime and Delinquency* 40:69–104.

Jones, M. and B. Krisberg (1994). *Images and Reality: Juvenile Crime, Youth Violence and Public Policy.* National Council on Crime and Delinquency.

Kent v. United States, 383 U.S. 54 (1966).

Kinder, K., C. Veneziano, M. Fichter and H. Azuma (1995). "A Comparison of the Dispositions of Juvenile Offenders Certified an Adults with Juvenile Offenders Not Certified." *Juvenile and Family Court Journal* 37–41.

Krisberg, B. (1988). *The Juvenile Court: Reclaiming the Vision.* National Council on Crime and Delinquency.

Lee, L. (1994). "Factors Determining Waiver in a Juvenile Court." *Journal of Criminal Justice* 22: 329–339.

National Coalition of State Juvenile Advisory Groups (1993). *Myths and Realities: Meeting the Challenge of Serious, Violent and Chronic Juvenile Offenders.* 1992 Annual Report.

Poulos, T. and S. Orchowsky (1994). "Serious Juvenile Offenders: Predicting the Probability of Transfer to Criminal Court." *Crime and Delinquency* 40: 3–17.

Sanborn, J. (1994). "Certification to Criminal Court: The Important Policy Questions of How, When and Why." *Crime and Delinquency* 40:262–281.

Sickmund, M. (1994). *How Juveniles Get to Criminal Court.* Office of Juvenile Justice and Delinquency Prevention, U.S. Department of Justice. Washington, D.C.

Snyder, H. and M. Sickmund (1995). *Juvenile Offenders and Victims: A Focus on Violence.* Office of Juvenile Justice and Delinquency Prevention, U.S. Department of Justice, Washington, D.C.

U.S. Department of Justice. (1995). *Offenders Under Age 18 in Adult Correctional Systems: A National Picture.* Longmont, CO: National Institute of Corrections, Information Center.

REVIEW QUESTIONS

1. What are the advantages and disadvantages of each of the three methods of transferring juveniles to adult court?
2. How safe are juveniles serving sentences in adult prisons? What are the major forms of violence and victimization that juveniles experience?
3. How well are the special needs of juveniles incarcerated in adult prisons being met?

READING 27

Challenges Posed by Older Prisoners

What We Know About America's Aging Prison Population

John J. Kerbs

Jennifer M. Jolley

This article provides a status report on the demographics of America's aging prison population as well as the policy factors that contribute to the recent aging trend. The authors highlight the special needs experienced by older inmates, ranging from health care problems to psychological adjustment and the rigors of re-entry into free society. The article touches upon a host of legal requirements the correctional institutions must meet with respect to older inmates and the various struggles that inevitably occur as prisons jockey to accommodate increasing numbers of older inmates while simultaneously meeting institutional goals and societal expectations. The article concludes with the authors presenting a series of policy suggestions aimed at more effectively and humanely responding to the burgeoning rolls of older inmates.

INTRODUCTION

In 2006, the United States had the highest rate of incarceration in the world (The Sentencing Project, 2008). In June of this same year, federal and state correctional facilities in the United States housed 1,556,518 prisoners; this rate of incarceration set a new recorded high at 497 prisoners per 100,000 U.S. residents (Sabol, Minton, & Harrison, 2007). While most inmates in America's prisons are young, the number of older federal and state prisoners is growing exponentially (Williams, Lindquist, Sudor, Strupp, Willmott, & Walter, 2006). In 1994, there were 50,478 prisoners 50 years of age and older (about 5.9% of the total prison population for 1994) (Camp & Camp, 1994). Since then, Aday (2003) noted that the number of older federal and state prisoners has grown by about 10,000 inmates per year, which suggests that about 11.6% of all federal and state prisoners or 180,000 inmates were 50 years of age or older in 2008. In another 20 years, about one-third of all U.S. prisoners will be age 55 or older (Enders, Paterniti, & Meyers, 2005; Williams, Lindquist, Sudor, Strupp, Willmott, & Walter, 2006).

This publication was made possible by support from East Carolina University's Department of Criminal Justice and the National Institute of Mental Health Training Grant T32-MH19960. All points of view and opinions in this paper are solely those of the author and do not necessarily reflect the official positions or policies of the East Carolina University's Department of Criminal Justice, the National Institute of Mental Health, the George Warren Brown School of Social Work, or the Winterville Police Department.

Dr. John J. Kerbs is an Assistant Professor of Criminal Justice at East Carolina University, Greenville, NC.

Ms. Jennifer M. Jolley is a Doctoral Student with the George Warren Brown School of Social Work, Washington University in St. Louis, in St. Louis, MO.

This dramatic increase in the number and proportion of older inmates stems from the widespread use of federal and state sentencing statutes that generally emphasize longer sentences with fewer (if any) options for early release by restricting or eliminating access to parole and/or good time. Examples of such sentencing strategies include the following: 1) mandatory minimum sentencing strategies, determinate sentencing strategies, and sentencing guidelines that remove flexibility in sentencing by requiring judges to issue sentences that meet outlined length requirements; 2) truth-in-sentencing laws that require convicted offenders to serve the majority of their court-ordered prison sentence (around 85% in most cases); and 3) three-strikes sentencing strategies that require life sentences (often without access to parole) for recidivists (Benekos & Merlo, 1995; Ditton & Wilson, 1999; Turner, Sundt, Applegate, & Cullen, 1995).

While it is not clear if these sentencing strategies have acted as general deterrents and/or reduced crime rates (Austin & Irwin, 2001; Petersilia, 1992; Steffensmeier & Harer, 1993; Turner et al., 1995; Visher, 1987; Zimring & Hawkins, 1991), it is clear that these strategies have increased incarceration rates in the United States and the average length of stay (LOS) in U.S. prisons. Moreover, the increased LOS has led to a graying of the American prison population (Austin & Irwin, 2001; Benekos & Merlo, 1995; Turner, Sundt, Applegate, & Cullen, 1995). Given that around 24% of all federal and state prisoners in 2002 were either serving life sentences or sentences for 20 years or more (Camp, 2003), prison administrators today are facing serious challenges as they try to adapt prison programs to meet aging inmates' developmentally specific service needs for psychological counseling, health care, education, recreation, safety, and vocational training (Aday, 2003, 1994a; Anderson & McGehee, 1994; Chaneles, 1987; Kempker, 2003; Kerbs & Jolley, 2007; Kratcoski & Pownall, 1989; Lemieux, Dyeson, & Castiglione, 2002; Morton, 1993, 1994; Vito & Wilson, 1985; Wilson & Vito, 1986).

Rather than just present a collection of facts about older prisoners, this chapter will place such information within a larger framework that examines how the characteristics of and challenges presented by older inmates relate to their rehabilitative process within today's correctional environment. The examination of inmate rehabilitation is both a philosophical and a pragmatic issue. Thus, the ability to understand the needs of special populations, like older inmates in a rehabilitative context, is important for the critical analysis of correctional systems.

DEFINING THE AGE THAT SEPARATES OLDER PRISONERS FROM YOUNGER PRISONERS

In free society outside of prisons, the most common age that separates younger people from older people is the age of retirement and access to financial benefits that can accompany retirement. For example, access to governmental benefits programs like Medicare and Social Security typically occurs when a citizen reaches the age of 65 or older. In the criminological literature of the 1970s and 1980s, there was no clear consensus, but many researchers considered "55 and over" as old (Fattah & Sacco, 1989; Forsyth & Grambling, 1988; Newman, 1984). Since the 1990s, it seems as if the most commonly used cutoff for defining older prisoners was lowered even further to age 50 for both research and state-level departments of corrections (Aday, 2003; Morton, 1992). This cutoff was largely chosen due to the accelerated aging of older prisoners; in short, people who are chronologically 50 years of age in prison appear physiologically to be 60 to 65 years of age due to health problems (Mitka, 2004).

THE DEMOGRAPHIC CHARACTERISTICS OF OLDER PRISONERS

The national picture for older inmates suggests that they are a diverse group of older offenders, both in terms of their demographic and criminological characteristics. While most prisoners who are 50 years of age and older in federal and state prisons are non-Hispanic Whites, minorities (African Americans, Latinos, and Native Americans) are overrepresented; furthermore, regional variations on a state-by-state basis exist for the proportion of older minorities in departments of corrections (Aday, 2003; Kerbs, 2000a). In terms of gender, about 95% of all older prisoners are male and 5% are female. Additionally, a nationwide increase in the overall number of older inmates is occurring for both men and women (Florida Department of Corrections, 1993; Goetting, 1983; Kratcoski & Babb, 1990; Kratcoski & Pownall, 1989; Lemieux, Dyeson, & Castiglione, 2002; Merianos, Marquart, Damphousse, & Herbert, 1997). Educationally, older prisoners do not fare well. The average older prisoner has around a seventh grade education (Goetting, 1983; Tobin & Metzler, 1983; Wilson & Vito, 1986). In fact, only about 20% of older inmates have high-school educations (Aday, 2003). As for their marital status, a larger proportion of older prisoners (about 34%) as compared to younger prisoners (about 22%) are married (Goetting, 1984); in addition, most state-level studies suggest that a majority of older prisoners are unmarried (Lemieux, Dyeson, & Castiglione, 2002).

With regard to criminological issues, older prisoners are incarcerated for a multitude of offenses, but two offense categories typically define their convictions. First, there is a preponderance of older prisoners convicted of violent offenses (Aday, 1994b). Second, about one-third of all older prisoners are sex offenders, including a number of older inmates convicted of rape and/or sexual assault (Flynn, 1998, 2000).

Beyond offense categories, older prisoners can also be grouped based upon sentencing histories. Detailed discussions of sentencing typologies are not hard to find (see, e.g., Fry, 1987; Goetting, 1983, 1984; Morton, 1992; Teller & Howell, 1981; Tobin & Metzler, 1983). Some typologies are fairly simple in that they identify two types of older prisoners: 1) those incarcerated for the first time, and 2) those incarcerated more than once (Teller & Howell, 1981). Goetting (1984) developed the most advanced typology to date using a national sample from 1979 of 11,397 state prisoners. Within this sample, a total of 248 prisoners were 55 years of age and older, and each of these older prisoners was categorized into one of four groups as follows: 1) about 41% of the sample was categorized as "old first offenders" who were first incarcerated at or above the age of 55; 2) about 2% were "oldtimers" who had entered prison prior to age 55 and served at least 20 continuous years in prison; 3) about 46% were "career criminals" or recidivists, and therefore spent periods of time in and out of prison; and 4) about 11% were "young short-term first offenders" who entered prison before age 55 and served less than two decades in prison (pp. 18–19).

Given the diversity of older prisoners as noted above, there are a few policy issues that deserve mention. To begin with, the largest proportion (about 46%) of older prisoners includes recidivists (career criminals) who potentially represent threats to public safety and who would benefit from effective rehabilitation programming. Older prisoners in this category include offenders who engaged in ongoing criminal activity at different ages; some recidivated while below 50 years of age, while others recidivated closer to or above 50 years of age. As sentencing statutes increasingly punish recidivists with longer sentences as discussed earlier, the number of recidivists will increase and the average age of recidivists will increase as they grow older while serving longer sentences (Kerbs, 2000a). A foremost concern related to the rehabilitation of these inmates includes the potential for them to develop *institutional dependency,* otherwise described as *institutional neurosis* and *prisonization* (Alston, 1986; Fattah & Sacco, 1989).

As applied to aging recidivists, institutional dependency occurs when they serve long sentences and give up on efforts to participate in life outside of prison; hence, they become overly reliant (dependent) upon the prison system to meet their needs. Such a dependency can significantly complicate any attempt at reintegration into society, thus diminishing the potential for successful release (Alston, 1986; Fattah & Sacco, 1989). Unfortunately, institutional dependency is a very real possibility for many aging inmates given the composition of today's inmate population, wherein 24% of all federal and state prisoners are serving life sentences or terms of 20 or more continuous years (Camp, 2003). Correctional personnel must address institutional dependency if society continues to support the practice of incarcerating individuals for extended periods of time.

Finally, as inmates age in prison, their psycho-social development is impacted; inmates are shaped by the environment in which they live as they learn how to adapt to and exist within a social environment over which they have very little control (Byrne & Stowell, 2007; Forst, Fagan & Vivona, 1989; Gilligan & Lee, 2004). As we examine institutional dependency within a context of rehabilitation, it is important to question how the correctional environment affects the older inmate's ability to successfully reenter society and the attendant costs associated with recidivism or unsuccessful rehabilitation. The consequences of recidivism are experienced by the inmate, members of his/her social network, the inmate's local community, and society at large. Some important consequences of ineffective rehabilitation leading to reincarceration include the following: 1) a loss of liberty for the inmate, 2) a loss of contact between the inmate and his/her family members to include spouses, children, and parents; 3) the weakening of social networks within the inmate's local community, 4) the potential for future criminal acts against society because of the inmate's failed ability to successfully adjust to life outside of prison; and 5) rising costs of incarceration borne by society's taxpaying citizens (Hagan & Dinovitzer, 1999). In sum, an astute analysis of the correctional system and the way in which it manages older prisoners includes questions related to the consequences of incarceration and the ways in which inmates and society are affected positively by successful releases and negatively by recidivism.

HEALTH CARE AND OLDER INMATES

Generally speaking, as noted in a study by Maruschak and Beck (2001), older prisoners tend to be in poor health compared to younger prisoners. These researchers analyzed data from the *1997 Survey of Inmates in State and Federal Correctional Facilities* and found that the percentage of state prisoners who reported any health problem increased with age. As one moved up the examined age brackets, the percentage of state prisoners reporting health problems increased from ages 24 or younger (23.8%) to 25–34 years of age (26.8%), to 35–44 years of age (34.0%), and finally to 45 or older (47.6%). Reported health problems included hearing, learning, physical, speech, vision, and mental impairments. The same age-graded pattern emerged for federal prisoners. Again, as one moved up the examined age brackets, the percentage of federal prisoners reporting health problems increased from ages 24 or younger (13.8%) to 25–34 years of age (16.9%), to 35–44 years of age (22.1%), and finally to 45 or older (38.6%).

Such age-graded declines in health are expectable based upon the correctional health-care literature. Rubenstein (1984) noted that older prisoners typically experience a rapid deterioration in their health during incarceration. Fattah and Sacco (1989) suggested that the older prisoners' declining health may be partly due to unhealthy lifestyles before incarceration, unhealthy lifestyles during their incarceration, and/or the stress of incarceration. Fattah and Sacco (1989) also suggested that these factors can act in ways to *aggravate* and *accelerate* the aging process. Consequently, Mitka (2004, p. 423) noted that a "50-year old inmate may have a physiological age that is 10 to 15 years older" than his/her chronological age.

Whereas younger prisoners often experience *acute* health-care problems like colds or flu, older prisoners tend to report having chronic health problems that require ongoing treatment. The scholarly literature suggests that older prisoners experience an average of three serious health problems that can include everything from hypertension and cardio-vascular disease to substance abuse and dependence problems (Chaiklin & Fultz, 1985; Corrections Today, 1990, Kerbs, 2000a; Marquart, Merianos, & Doucet, 2000; Wilson & Vito, 1986). The most commonly reported chronic health problems, according to Loeb and AbuDagga (2006), include arthritis, back problems, cardiovascular diseases, endocrine disorders, psychiatric conditions, respiratory diseases, sensory deficits (vision and hearing problems), and substance abuse problems.

Additionally, gender differences may influence the reporting of health problems by older inmates. In a comprehensive review of the scholarly literature concerning older prisoners, Lemieux, Dyeson, and Castiglione (2002) noted that twice as many older women than men in prison reported degenerative, heart, and respiratory illnesses. Hence, it appears that a larger proportion of older women are in worse health than older men in prison. Given the nature of ailments reported by older women in prison, one might expect a large proportion of them to be disabled.

The best available research to date suggests that this is true. Williams, Lindquist, Sudore, Strupp, Willmott, and Walter (2006) provided an important study examining the relationships among medical conditions reported by women and functional impairment as measured by the ability to complete activities of daily living (ADLs) and in-prison activities of daily living (PADLs). ADLs were defined as: 1) bathing, 2) eating, 3) toileting, 4) dressing, and 5) getting in and out of bed. PADLs were defined as: 1) dropping to the floor for alarms, 2) standing for head count, 3) getting to the dining hall for meals, 4) hearing orders from staff, and 5) climbing on and off the top bunk. Older female inmates who reported having difficulty completing one or more of the ADLs or PADLs were also more likely to report: 1) feeling less healthy, 2) having difficulty in walking by themselves, and 3) having more than one diagnosed medical condition. Additionally, the authors found that older female inmates who had a functional impairment were more likely to report an adverse experience to include: 1) a fall in the previous year, 2) feeling depressed, 3) feeling unsafe in one's cell, and/or 4) physical abuse by another inmate. Finally, 16% of the older female inmates reported experiencing difficulty in completing one or more ADLs, while 69% reported experiencing difficulty in completing one or more PADLs. Therefore, the definition of functional impairment takes on a very different meaning in a prison facility because inmates are required to perform a series of daily acts in prison that they would not otherwise have to perform in the free world. Because prison facilities are generally designed to house young and healthy inmates without ADL and PADL limitations (Williams, Lindquist, Sudore, Strupp, Willmott, & Walter, 2006), older inmates in general and older female inmates in particular may be at an increased risk of medical problems, psychological problems, injury and/or physical abuse. Hence, interventions for older women in prison should focus on preventing these problems by altering their physical environments to decrease functional impairments.

Clearly, aging men and women behind bars will require medical care; but because incarceration blocks the ability of prisoners to care for themselves, the U.S. Supreme Court has ruled that states are required to provide for basic needs such as health care. Failure to provide health care is typically seen as a violation of the Eighth Amendment. For example, in 1976, the U.S. Supreme Court ruled in *Estelle v. Gamble* that "deliberate indifference to serious medical needs of prisoners constitutes the 'unnecessary and wanton infliction of pain' . . . proscribed by the Eighth Amendment" (p. 104). Over a decade later, the U.S. Supreme Court proffered a similar ruling in the case of *DeShaney v. Winnebago County Social Services Department* (1989) and found that when a state simultaneously restrains an individual's liberty and renders a person unable to care for themselves while failing to provide for basic needs such as food, clothing, shelter, medical care, and reasonable safety, the state violates the Eighth Amendment's prohibition against cruel and unusual punishment (Ross, 2005).

As applied to older prisoners, these court cases collectively require prisons to provide a community standard of care for their serious health problems to include acute care, chronic care, dental care, and general medical, nutritional, psychiatric, and long-term care services (Kratcoski & Pownall, 1989). Unfortunately, both the legal and correctional health-care literature suggests that prison hospitals and infirmaries are often inadequate to the task of such treatment. To begin with, medical facilities in prison are more oriented towards the treatment of acute health problems that are more common among younger prisoners (Alston, 1986). Additionally, Lundstrom (1994) suggested that around 90% of all prison hospitals do not meet basic standards of care. Adding to the complexity of problems facing correctional health-care systems is a well-documented history of prison systems hiring doctors with restricted licenses that limit them to work only in prisons due to prior findings of medical negligence and malpractice in the free society (Dabney & Vaughn, 2000; Vaughn & Collins, 2004). Hence, older prisoners with serious medical problems appear to get the worst of two worlds: 1) poorly equipped medical facilities; and 2) incompetent medical personnel. This forces prison systems to send older inmates to community-based hospitals where specialized care is provided at an increased cost due to the requirement of constant supervision that is typically provided by one to two guards at any given time (Kerbs, 2000b; Morton, 2001; Rikard & Rosenberg, 2007). Such outsourcing to community-based hospitals for specialized health-care services is one of the key reasons that the yearly cost of incarceration for older prisoners is three times as much as the cost for younger prisoners (over $60,000/year versus $22,000/year, respectively) (Aday, 2003; Kerbs, 2000b).

Such differential costs associated with an aging prison population have (in part) caused the Federal Bureau of Prisons and state-level departments of correction to significantly increase their correctional health-care budgets. Camp (2003) documented that the aggregate expenditures for federal and state correctional health-care budgets in the United States escalated from 3.17 billion dollars in fiscal year 1999 to 3.87 billion dollars in fiscal year 2002. Since then, federal and state correctional health-care budgets have continued to increase rapidly. For example, the California Department of Corrections and Rehabilitation increased its health-care budget by 263 percent since 2000, to $2.1 billion a year for the fiscal year that ends in July of 2008 (Rau, 2007, December 28). Such expenditures and associated increases are rather dramatic when juxtaposed with the lack of positive results accompanying such expenditures.

In an effort to contain costs associated with outsourcing and escalating correctional health-care budgets, many states have started to provide in-house treatment for chronic conditions (e.g., dialysis services for kidney failure) and terminally ill inmates. To this end, numerous states have opened gero-medical facilities and hospice facilities (Aday, 2003; Beck, 1999). Wright and Bronstein (2007) noted that the "goal of prison hospice programs is to provide the terminally ill inmate with effective pain management during the dying process while also meeting the individual's physical, emotional, social, and spiritual needs" (p. 394). These programs typically operate with a cross-section of paid correctional personnel and prisoner volunteers who receive extensive training. Interestingly, the experience of working in prison hospice appears to have a therapeutic effect on prisoner volunteers because such work gives them the opportunity to reflect on their own lives (Wright & Bronstein, 2007).

Finally, discussions of older prisoners' health care and health problems are incomplete without an examination of the correctional consequences of disabling conditions. In the most extreme cases, older prisoners who are disabled must be hospitalized. Because many conditions experienced by older prisoners are disabling (but not so extreme as to require hospitalization), there are concerns regarding the Americans with Disabilities Act of 1990 (ADA of 1990). As per the 1998 U.S. Supreme Court case of *Pennsylvania v. Yeskey,* the ADA of 1990 was deemed to be unambiguously applicable to federal and state prisoners. Hence, when older prisoners are disabled, prison officials must make reasonable accommodations to provide aging inmates with access to programmatic services (educational, legal, medical, recreational, religious, and social services) and facilities (Atlas & Witke, 2000; Burke, 1999; Lester, 2003; Russell & Stewart, 2001). This legal mandate has forced many prison systems to either retrofit older prisons with handicap-accessible facilities and services or face potential litigation stemming from suits alleging violations of the ADA of 1990. Given that many U.S. prisons were constructed long before 1990 (some in the 1800s), the challenge of retrofitting so many facilities represents a significant obstacle to meeting the rehabilitative needs of older inmates. Clearly, an individual's physical well being is a prerequisite for most tasks in life. Older inmates who suffer from an average of three serious medical conditions will be unable to engage in a meaningful process of rehabilitation without competent medical treatment.

PSYCHOLOGICAL HEALTH OF OLDER PRISONERS

Given the differences in how researchers choose to design and implement their studies, it is inevitable that the literature will provide an array of outcomes for any given research question. An examination of the literature describing the status of mental health for older prisoners is no exception. For example, Rubenstein (1984) examined numerous studies from the 1970s and found differences between the psychological characteristics of younger inmates in comparison with the psychological characteristics of older inmates. The studies collectively described older prisoners as: 1) more introverted and neurotic; 2) more anxious about their physical functioning; 3) more insecure and fearful of authority, guards, illness, pain, the future, and potential homelessness after release; and 4) less active with lower expectations for the future shaped by feelings of helplessness and defeat. In contrast, there were a few studies in the 1980s that described older prisoners as having fewer symptoms of depression, psychic pain (Teller & Howell, 1981), and feelings of loneliness (Fattah & Sacco, 1989) as compared with younger inmates.

However, most studies of U.S. prisons from the 1980s forward have found problems with the psychological well being of older inmates. For example, McCarthy (1983) examined 248 older prisoners in Florida and documented a significant number of older prisoners as reporting "mental health concerns": 24.2% described "life as dull," 25.4% "listed their present life satisfaction as poor," and 34.7% "reported they were not happy" (McCarthy, 1983, p. 65). Additionally, McCarthy reported that almost 30% of the responding inmates felt lonely "quite" often and almost 40% were "sometimes" lonely. Aday (1994b) used a case-study approach with in-depth interviews to examine the psychological problems described by 25 older prisoners who experienced their first incarceration late in life. The average age of the prisoners in this study was 68 and the results showed that the older prisoners' "initial reaction to incarceration later in life was often characterized by family conflict, depression, thoughts of suicide, and a fear of dying in prison" (Aday, 1994b, p. 79). Finally, Colsher, Wallace, Loeffelholz, and Sales (1992) surveyed 119 men (ages 50 and above) in 7 state prisons in Iowa. Most respondents rated their memory and cognitive functions as excellent to good; while approximately 1% of respondents reported psychotic symptoms, a higher proportion of respondents reported symptoms related to worrying too much (16.0%), depression (15.4%), anxiety (8.1%), and loneliness (7.1%).

Based upon the results of such studies with smaller samples from a limited number of prisons, it would appear that many older inmates experience mental health problems, with the most common symptoms reported including feelings of depression, anxiety, and loneliness. However, these studies did not use a common set of definitions or a common scale against which to describe the existence of mental health problems for older inmates. It is important to note that a clear and common set of definitions regarding the kinds of problems that older prisoners face is essential if research is going to be used to assist policymakers and prison administrators in making adjustments to correctional programs in order to better meet the needs of older inmates. In this case, it is clear that older prisoners experience mental health symptoms; furthermore, the presence of mental health symptoms can compromise an inmate's ability to adjust to the prison environment (Wooldredge, 1999) and to prepare for successful community reentry (Blitz, Wolff, Pan, & Pogorzelski, 2005; Pogorzelski, Wolff, Pan, & Blitz, 2005).

More recent studies by Maruschak and Beck (2001) and James and Glaze (2006), using large samples of inmates who were representative of prisoners nationally, have reported on the mental health of older inmates. Maruschak and Beck's study included approximately 13,600 adults, ages 16 and older in federal and state prisons, who were asked to respond to the following question: "Do you have a mental or emotional condition?" (Maruschak & Beck, 2001, p. 2). As the age of the inmates increased, so did the percentage of inmates who responded "yes" to the question. Specifically, 7.8% of state prisoners 16 to 24 years old reported having a mental or emotional condition, while 11.7% of state prisoners 45 or older reported having a mental or emotional condition. Additionally, 4.0% of federal prisoners 16 to 24 years old reported having a mental or emotional condition, while 5.9% of federal inmates 45 or older reported having a mental or emotional condition.

James and Glaze (2006) honed in more specifically on mental health symptoms experienced by older inmates by asking over 18,000 federal and state prisoners to respond to questions based upon diagnostic criteria from the *Diagnostic and Statistical Manual of Mental Disorders (4th Edition).* While this study showed that the presence of mental health symptoms declined with age, the researchers documented a higher percentage of older inmates who experienced mental health symptoms. Specifically, 62.6% of state prisoners ages 24 or younger met criteria for a diagnosable mental health condition; in contrast, 39.6% of state prisoners ages 55 or older met such criteria. A similar pattern also emerged for federal prisoners with 70.3% of federal inmates ages 24 or younger meeting criteria for a diagnosable mental health condition and 52.4% of federal inmates ages 55 or older meeting criteria. Unfortunately, James & Glaze (2006) did not provide more specific information on age-graded differences between younger and older prisoners for any given diagnosis, but future research should examine such issues so prison systems can plan for the delivery of mental health interventions that specifically address those diagnoses reported by an aging prison population.

In addition to describing the proportion of older inmates who experience different types of psychopathological symptoms, it is important to describe the inherent difficulties in adjusting to the harsh realities of the prison environment. Prisons are generally considered to have harmful effects on the mental health of inmates. Fattah and Sacco (1989) noted that deleterious mental health outcomes are "caused by the 'dehumanizing' and 'depersonalizing' characteristics of [the] institutional environment" (p. 88). Although such prison environments can erode the mental health of any prisoner, older inmates appear to be at particular risk of adverse psychological problems. First, research by Silverman and Vega (1990) suggests that older inmates, as compared to younger inmates, are more sensitive to environmental stressors in prison. Second, as compared to younger prisoners, older prisoners are more likely to present a "façade of adjustment . . . which results from a denial and suppression of their feelings [regarding stress and anger]" (Vega & Silverman, 1988, p. 153). Hence, while older prisoners may appear well adjusted, they tend to suppress their emotions.

Unfortunately, suppressing emotions can negatively impact psychological stability and rehabilitation. In fact, research on coping strategies for male inmates has identified adverse psychological and physical consequences for prisoners who choose to use avoidant or passive coping behavior as compared to active coping behavior (Van Harreveld, Van Der Pligt, Claassen, & Van Dijk, 2007). For example, Van Harreveld, Van Der Pligt, Claassen and Van Dijk (2007) described inmates who used a passive coping style as having engaged in the following: "wanting to be left alone, trying to shut out any thoughts, and watching television" (p. 703). In contrast, inmates who used an active coping style were described as having engaged in at least one of two strategies: 1) sharing their feelings with other inmates or family members, and/or 2) cognitively reframing a negative situation by finding something positive to focus upon. Inmates who used a passive style of coping were found to have more negative emotions and fewer positive emotions as compared to inmates who used an active style. Furthermore, the authors found that negative emotions were not only related to the use of a passive coping style, but negative emotions were also associated with psychological stress, depressed mood, and physical distress. Other studies also link negative emotions to the increased prevalence of cardiovascular disease, hypertension, diabetes, asthma, and a compromised immune system (Van Harreveld, Van Der Pligt, Claassen, & Van Dijk, 2007). By implication, these results suggest that older prisoners who suppress their emotions may suffer such psychological and physical consequences.

However, the reduction of psycho-physiological distress for the older inmate may not be as easy as learning how to share one's feelings with another inmate. Van Harreveld et al. (2007) pointed out the importance of examining coping styles within the prison environment and the consequences of choosing one coping style over another. Specifically, given the code of behavior that inmates use to define what kind of behavior is acceptable and what kind of behavior is unacceptable, a coping style that emphasizes the sharing of feelings may make an inmate appear to be weak. Typically, the presentation of self as a tough person within the prison's social environment is critical for maintaining an inmate's safety (Bowker, 1980; Byrne & Stowell, 2007; Edgar & O'Donnell, 1998; Gillian & Lee, 2004). An inmate who wants to avoid being labeled as easy prey needs to be perceived by others as being strong, dangerous, and physically capable. An inmate who is known for sharing his feelings and experiencing distress can be perceived as weak and, therefore, a desirable target for victimization. Hence, older prisoners appear to be experiencing a harmful paradox wherein passive strategies can lead to psychological and physical problems and active strategies can lead to victimization.

While it is important to recognize the negative psychological consequences that inmates face when trying to cope with negative feelings by seeking help from others, it is equally important to acknowledge that inmates who develop a mental disorder require and are legally entitled to psychiatric assistance. To the extent that older inmates are disabled by mental conditions, the ADA of 1990 and the *Pennsylvania v. Yeskey* (1998) decision also require that federal and state prisoners be afforded reasonable accommodations for most psychiatric diagnoses. As for the treatment of psychiatric problems, providing mental-health services to federal and state prisoners is a fundamental responsibility of prison health-care systems (Ross, 2005). Additionally, such treatment can be provided without the prisoner's consent. In the U.S. Supreme Court case of *Washington v. Harper* (1990), the court held that the state can treat prisoners against their will with anti-psychotic drugs if inmates are a danger to self or others and if such treatment is in the prisoner's medical interests (Ross, 2005). Given the aggressive behavioral problems associated with many diagnoses that older people often present (e.g., senile dementia and Alzheimer's disease), *Washington v. Harper* may increasingly be invoked as aging inmates who remain incarcerated require psychiatric treatment due to conditions often linked with the aging process.

Just as in the case of medical conditions, inmates who suffer from psychological conditions require treatment. If an inmate is unable to function due to a cognitive, behavioral, and/or emotional impairment, the inmate's ability to engage in a meaningful process of rehabilitation will be impaired. As Pogorzelski, Wolff, Pan, and Blitz (2005) noted, the process of offender reentry is made difficult enough for the former inmate who faces diminished social support, poor vocational training, limited work experience, low funds, and a criminal record. Adding a mental illness to the mix only serves to complicate matters and to reinforce the existence of the aforementioned deficits. Furthermore, in the case of the older prisoner, the process is compounded by the fact that he/she will experience the effects of ageism and additional disdain for being older and a convicted felon. Given the number and magnitude of the obstacles facing the older inmate upon reentry, mental health treatment should be geared toward (1) treating diagnosed disorders and (2) preparing the inmate for the challenges of reentry along with the likely psychological stress that can accompany such a process.

OLDER INMATES' PSYCHO-SOCIAL ADJUSTMENT TO PRISON

The ability of older prisoners to adjust to life behind bars is a function of individual, social, and environmental factors. For example, at the individual level, Sabath and Cowles (1988) noted that older prisoners with low levels of education and poor health adjust poorly to prison because such problems can block their ability to engage in recreational, social, and work-related activities. This is a problem for their rehabilitation because "inmates are more likely to become angry and disagreeable with others when they have limited assistance for self-improvement or they experience lower levels of activity and social stimulation" (Wooldredge, 1999, p. 235).

Social networks also play a big role in the older prisoner's adjustment to prison. Rubenstein (1984) noted that older prisoners who do not maintain contact with family and friends do not cope as well in prison as those who do maintain such contact. Sabath and Cowles (1988) found that infrequent family visits led to poor adjustment in prison. Results from a study by Wooldredge (1999) also supported the hypothesis that frequent visitation corresponded to healthier attitudes in prison. Of course, the maintenance of external support is not easy for an aging prison population because relationships between inmates and their families and friends can become very strained by incarceration (Aday & Webster, 1979; Rubenstein, 1984). Moreover, their potential isolation can become exacerbated when aging relatives and friends experience illness, disability, and death, all of which can restrict and/or terminate visitation from external contacts (Vega & Silverman, 1988). While irregular visits from family and friends or even a complete cessation of such visits is not uncommon, some older prisoners do maintain external contact via phone calls and letters (Aday, 1994b; Wilson & Vito, 1986). For example, Vega and Silverman (1988) examined a sample of older inmates from two prisons and noted that 57% did not receive visits from family members and 90% did not receive visits from friends; conversely, 90% maintained family contact via phone and mail.

While older inmates' contact with family members and friends may be limited, they must adapt to the challenges of forced contact with other inmates in a physically constrained environment. Contact among inmates can pose a variety of problems to the older prisoner, one of the most serious being an increased likelihood of victimization. For example, Bowker (1980) noted that older inmates can become "easy prey" for predators in prison. Vito and Wilson (1985) argued that, "victimization and fear of victimization by younger, stronger inmates is a serious problem for elderly inmates" (p. 18). Other scholars have also suggested that older prisoners are exploited and easily victimized by other prisoners (Krajick, 1979; Weigand & Burger, 1979). Interestingly, socio-cultural changes in the prison environment over the last three decades may explain why older prisoners appear to be at risk of victimization. Although in past decades they had been given *respect* stemming from their vast criminal experiences (Goetting, 1985), it appears as if their respected status has been eroded by a new generation of younger prisoners who now *disrespect* their elders (Hunt, Riegel, Morales, & Waldorf, 1993). DeLuca (1998) noted that "like the elderly in society, older inmates no longer get the respect once accorded to them, and also similar to their counterparts in free society, they are more likely to be victimized by younger, more aggressive inmates" (p. 211).

Beyond the lack of respect that older inmates might experience at the hands of younger inmates, there is one other key reason to believe that they are at risk of victimization. Given that one-third of all older prisoners are convicted of sex offenses (Flynn, 1998, 2000), they appear to be at risk of inmate-on-inmate victimization because they are stigmatized by their offense. Sex offenders in prison have a very low status in the inmate hierarchy, and they are therefore among the most despised by other inmates (Bowker, 1982; Dumond, 1992).

Recently published research by Kerbs and Jolley (2007) confirms high rates of psychological and economic inmate-on-inmate victimization reported by older male inmates in state prisons. Using a random sample of 65 male inmates ages 50 and older, the researchers reported the rates of victimization over the last 12 months prior to the interview; data were also collected to clarify environmental conditions that were implicated in victimization episodes. Kerbs and Jolley (2007) found that younger inmates were the typical perpetrators of psychological, property, physical, and sexual inmate-on-inmate victimization reported by older male prisoners. Consequently, a majority of the respondents supported age-segregated living arrangements for older prisoners.

When describing instances of psychological victimization, older inmates reported being threatened verbally (16.9%), threatened with fake punches (24.6%), insulted (40%), and/or cut in front of when waiting in lines for food or other services (84.6%). Although such forms of victimization may appear minor, psychological and economic forms of victimization can escalate into more serious types of victimization, thus increasing the likelihood of being victimized in other ways (Bowker, 1980; Edgar & O'Donnell, 1998). Economic victimization was also fairly common, with just under 30% of the older inmates reported that things had been stolen from their cells or that they had been cheated or conned out of their money by another inmate. In regards to physical victimization, 10.8% of older prisoners reported being assaulted without weapons, 6.2% reported being robbed, and 1.5% reported being attacked with weapons. Finally, 10.8% of older inmates reporting being sexually harassed and 1.5% reported being raped.

Collectively, these findings are of concern for the older prisoners' psychosocial adjustment and rehabilitation because victimization and fear of victimization are strong predictors of psychopathology in prison (McCorkle, 1993; Wooldredge, 1999). Such concerns are not likely to vanish anytime soon given the longstanding practice of mainstreaming older inmates into the general prison population with younger inmates. Mainstreaming has been allowed to continue because older prisoners are so well behaved that prison officials see them as *good insurance* against future riots and as *stabilizing, calming* or otherwise *quieting* younger and more aggressive inmates in the general prison population (DeLuca, 1998; Wiegand & Burger, 1979; Wilson & Vito, 1985).

Although there is some research to support such beliefs (Mabli, Holley, Patrick, & Walls, 1979), there is clearly a cost associated with mainstreaming, and the burden of the cost appears to be shouldered by older inmates as they face an increased likelihood of victimization by younger inmates. It is ironic to think that a consistent display of good behavior could lead to increased victimization, as is the case when well-behaved older inmates are deliberately housed with younger inmates who do not, on average, practice the same kind of restraint relative to prison misconduct. Indeed, there is a negative relationship between age and prison misconduct. As age increases, prison misconduct decreases (see, e.g., Cooper & Werner, 1990; Craddock, 1996; Cunningham & Sorensen, 2007; Goetting & Howsen, 1986; Ireland, 2000; Light, 1991; Wooldredge, 1991, 1994; Wooldredge, Griffin, & Pratt, 2001). Thus, it comes as no surprise that less than 10% of all older inmates present serious disciplinary problems (McShane & Williams, 1990). Depending upon the study, it would appear as if desistance from prison misconduct begins in the late twenties (DeLisi, 2003) or mid thirties (Cunningham & Sorensen, 2007).

Such findings are congruent with both the *theoretical* and *empirical* literature concerning criminal careers and age-graded theories of desistance from criminal behavior. *Theoretically,* Laub and Sampson (2001) have created a framework that examines offender behavior across the life-course. Of particular importance to this theory is the role social context plays in the desistance from crime. Aging offenders typically move from a criminal identity that is associated with illegal activities and deviant peers to a law-abiding identity with legal activities and pro-social peers. The dynamic process of desistance is achieved as offenders interact with people, events, and the consequences of their choices within the social environment. The authors identify correlates of this transformative process to include aging; as age increases, so does the potential for meaningful desistance. Given the importance social environments play in the theoretical framework of desistance, it is essential to consider how older inmates who may be attempting to engage in desistance will be affected by a social environment saturated with aggressive younger inmates who may not value desisting behavior. *Empirically,* Sampson and Laub (2003) examined the life-course trajectories of delinquent boys who were followed to age 70. The researchers found that the average age of desistance for all crimes reported by participants in this study was 37. When they examined specific crimes, they found differences for the ages of desistance across property (age 26), violent (age 31), and alcohol/drug crimes (age 37). Such findings suggest that while most younger inmates are probably persisting in their criminal careers, most older prisoners are probably in the process of desisting.

The implications of life-course trajectories suggest that most older prisoners are trying to "go straight" in contrast to younger prisoners who are still misbehaving. Mixing the two groups together appears to do little more than compromise the safety and rehabilitation of older prisoners. Hence, policymakers and correctional personnel might want to reconsider the practice of mainstreaming older inmates into the general prison population. Pragmatically, the time might be right to consider age segregation for those who must stay in prison (Aday, 2003). Alternatively, policymakers may want to consider the selective decarceration (release) of prisoners who are no longer a threat to public safety because of (1) health-related problems that become disabling or (2) age-related desistance (Kerbs, 2000b).

CONCLUSIONS

As America's federal and state prison populations age over the coming decades, pragmatic questions surface regarding the best approaches to handling this special population. While most of this chapter has addressed the medical, psychological, and social issues that face aging inmates in prison, serious questions surface when considering their potential release into the free world given that many older prisoners may be: (1) medically intensive in terms of their health-care needs, (2) psychologically dependent upon the prison to provide for their basic needs, and (3) socially unsupported given the difficulties associated with the maintenance of external support networks during lengthy incarcerations. These three issues loom as significant barriers to successful reintegration into the free world, but these issues are not legitimate reasons to deny release. Hence, policymakers and correctional personnel would be well advised to begin developing programs that aim to successfully reintegrate older inmates.

Although older prisoners present a plethora of problems that complicate their potential release, statistics concerning their rates of recidivism suggest that they are among the best candidates for release. Indeed, their rates of recidivism are far lower than comparable rates for younger inmates. For example, in a recidivism study by Langan and Levin (2002), the data clearly depicted a negative association between age and recidivism; as prisoners aged, they were less likely to be re-arrested, re-convicted, or re-incarcerated within three years of their release. Moreover, the researchers found dramatic differences in the proportions of recidivating inmates who were ages 18 to 24 years old as compared to those who were 45 and older for re-arrest rates (75% versus 45%, respectively), re-conviction rates (52% versus 30%, respectively), and re-incarceration rates (52% versus 40%, respectively) within 3 years. The same negative relationship between age and re-arrest also exists for released sex offenders, and this negative association is present for all types of sex offenders, to include rapists, sexual assaulters, child molesters, and statutory rapists (Langan, Schmitt, & Durose, 2003).

To facilitate the successful re-entry of older prisoners, a few changes need to be made in our correctional systems. First, parole laws need to be revamped. Conceptually, parole is both "a procedure by which a board administratively releases inmates from prison and a provision for postrelease supervision" (Petersilia, 1999, p. 479–480). In past decades, a number of states and the federal government passed sentencing reforms that have restricted and/or abolished access to parole and good time, and this significantly curtailed the capacity of federal and state prison systems to provide aging prisoners with early release options. By the end of 1998, a total of 14 states had eliminated access to parole for all offenders, and a number of other states restricted the use of parole (Petersilia, 1999). By removing and restricting access to parole, America constrained one of the main options for releasing older inmates who no longer posed a threat to society due to age-related desistance and/or medical problems that rendered offenders harmless to society (Kerbs, 2000b). Nonetheless, public safety is advanced by selectively paroling older prisoners who are at low risk of recidivism due to (1) successful rehabilitation within a process of age-graded desistance or (2) health problems that become disabling. Such releases open bed space for younger and more dangerous prisoners who are at greater risk of recidivism. Moreover, the selective decarceration of medically complex inmates can save money because release allows states to circumvent the costs associated with outsourcing medical care with constant supervision from guards. In sum, such gains will not be realized until parole is reinstated and/or revived in states where it was originally abolished or overly restricted to the point of precluding such releases.

Another mechanism for early release is embodied in *compassionate release programs*. Such programs allow for accelerated access to parole while providing case management services to help older prisoners return to the free world. Most of these programs accelerate release in cases involving a medical diagnosis with a poor or terminal prognosis (Morton, 1992). Such releases can save millions of dollars a year for any given state department of corrections (Lundstrom, 1994). While a number of states have such programs (Morton, 1992), they are often less than successful at releasing eligible prisoners due to cumbersome review processes that can result in extensive delays (Beck, 1999). Unfortunately, studies have shown that inmates who are eligible for compassionate release die in prison because of slow review processes and the utilization of prison hospice programs as alternatives to compassionate release programs (Beck, 1999). While compassionate release programs are underutilized, they do represent a cutting-edge approach to cost cutting while enhancing the public safety; to this end, these programs should be used more aggressively in the future.

Finally, there are a number of *reintegration programs* that aim to release prisoners who are at low risk of recidivism, but who need help with employment, financial assistance, and/or housing assistance. Consequently, reintegration programs commonly provide case management services to develop employment plans, residential plans, and supervision plans for prisoners who are either eligible for parole or pre-parole releases (Kerbs, 2000b). One of the more well-known reintegration programs for older inmates is called the Project for Older Prisoners (POPS). Professor Jonathan Turley originally developed POPS in 1989 at Tulane University's Law School. Using law school students as volunteer case managers to cut staffing costs, Professor Turley designed POPS based upon a 4-step process wherein law school students: 1) identify older prisoners who are at low risk of recidivism and whose medical needs are costly; 2) complete all background checks, risk assessments, and interviews; 3) develop release plans supported by residential, financial, and employment options with an eye towards independent living; and 4) write reports for parole boards and/or pardon board reviews. To date, over 200 older prisoners have been released via POPS and not one has been re-incarcerated due to a new offense (Aday, 2003). Hence, it is possible to reintegrate older prisoners while maintaining public safety, a fact that bodes well for the national replication of POPS-like programs.

In summary, older inmates are affected by the psychological and medical consequences of aging within a very unique social environment. It is important for the correctional system to understand the deficits these individuals face along with their potential for rehabilitation. With a thorough understanding of this special population, correctional administrators can design humane and proactive systems to advance the provision of therapeutic environments that offer ethical approaches to confinement while providing programs that promote successful rehabilitation and reentry into the free world.

REFERENCES

Aday, R. H. (2003). *Aging prisoners: Crisis in American corrections.* Westport, CT: Praeger Publishers.

Aday, R. H. (1994a). Golden years behind bars: Special programs and facilities for older inmates. *Federal Probation, 58*(2), 47–54.

Aday, R. H. (1994b). Aging in prison: A case study of new elderly offenders. *International Journal of Offender Therapy and Comparative Criminology, 38*(1), 79–91.

Aday, R. H., & Webster, E. C. (1979). Aging in prison: The development of a preliminary model. *Offender Rehabilitation, 3,* 271–282.

Alston, L. T. (1986). *Crime and Older Americans.* Springfield, IL: Charles C Thomas.

Americans with Disabilities Act of 1990, 42 U.S.C.A. § 12101 et seq. (West 1993).

Anderson, J., & McGehee, R. D. (1994). Incarceration alternatives: A special unit for elderly offenders and offenders with disabilities. *Forum on Corrections Research, 6*(2), 35–36.

Atlas, R., & Witke, L. (2000). ADA: Proposed final regulations for courthouses, jails and prisons. *Corrections Today, 62*(2), 126–131.

Austin, J., & Irwin, J. (2001). *It's about time: America's imprisonment binge* (3rd Edition). Belmont, CA: Wadsworth Publishing Company.

Beck, J. A. (1999). Compassionate release from New York State prisons: Why are so few getting out? *Journal of Law, Medicine, & Ethics, 27,* 216–233.

Benekos, P. J., & Merlo, A. V. (1995). Three strikes and you're out: The political sentencing game. *Federal Probation, 59*(1), 3–9.

Blitz, C.L., Wolff, N., Pan, K., & Pogorzelski, W. (2005). Gender-specific behavioral health and community release patterns among New Jersey inmates: Implications for treatment and community reentry. *American Journal of Public Health, 95*(10), 1741–1746.

Bowker, L. H. (1980). *Prison Victimization.* New York, NY: Elsevier North Holland, Inc.

Bowker, L. H. (1982). Victimizers and victims in American correctional institutions. In R. Johnson & H. Toch (Eds.), *The Pains of Imprisonment* (pp. 63–76). Beverly Hills, CA: Sage.

Burke, C. J. (1999). Winning the battle, losing the war? Judicial scrutiny of prisoners' statutory claims under the Americans with Disabilities Act. *Michigan Law Review, 98,* 482–513.

Byrne, J.M., & Stowell, J. (2007). Examining the link between institutional and community violence: Toward a new cultural paradigm. *Aggression and Violent Behavior, 12,* 552–563.

Camp, C. G. (Ed.). (2003). *The corrections yearbook: Adult corrections 2002.* Middletown, CT: Criminal Justice Institute, Incorporated.

Camp, C. G., & Camp, C. M. (1994). *The corrections yearbook: Adult corrections.* South Salem, NY: Criminal Justice Institute.

Chaiklin, H., & Fultz, L. (1985). Service needs of older offenders. *Justice Professional, 1*(1), 26–33.

Chaneles, S. (1987). Growing old behind bars. *Psychology Today, 21*(10), 47–51.

Colsher, P. L., Wallace, R. B., Loeffelholz, P. L., & Sales, M. (1992). Health status of older male prisoners: A comprehensive survey. *American Journal of Public Health, 82,* 881–884.

Cooper, R., & Werner, P. (1990). Predicting violence in newly admitted inmates. *Criminal Justice and Behavior, 17,* 431–477.

Corrections Today. (1990). The aging prison population: Inmates in gray. *Corrections Today, 52,* 136+.

Craddock, A. (1996). A comparative study of male and female prison misconduct careers. *Prison Journal, 76,* 60–80.

Cunningham, M. D., & Sorensen, J. R. (2007). Predictive factors for violent misconduct in close custody. *The Prison Journal, 87,* 241–253.

Dabney, D. A., & Vaughn, M. S. (2000). Incompetent jail and prison doctors. *The Prison Journal, 80*(2), 151–183.

DeLisi, M. (2003). Criminal careers behind bars. *Behavioral Sciences and the Law, 21,* 653–669.

DeLuca, H.R. (1998). Managing older inmates: It's more than just time. In D.E. Redburn & R.P. McNamara (Eds.), *Social gerontology* (pp. 209–219). Westport, CT: Auburn House.

DeShaney v. Winnebago County Social Services Department, 489 U.S. 189 (1989).

Ditton, P. M., & Wilson, D. J. (1999). *Bureau of Justice Statistics bulletin: Truth in Sentencing in state prisons.* Washington, DC: U.S. Department of Justice.

Dumond, R. W. (1992). The sexual assault of male inmates in incarcerated settings. *International Journal of the Sociology of Law, 20*(2), 135–157.

Edgar, K., & O'Donnell, I. (1998). Assault in prison: The victim's contribution. *British Journal of Criminology, 38,* 635–650.

Enders, S. R., Paterniti, D. A., & Meyers, F. J. (2005). An approach to develop effective health care decision making for women in prison. *Journal of Palliative Medicine, 8*(2), 432–439.

Estelle v. Gamble, 429 U.S. 97 (1976).

Fattah, E. A., & Sacco, V. F. (1989). *Crime and victimization of the elderly.* New York, NY: Springer-Verlag.

Florida Department of Corrections. (1993). *Status report on elderly inmates.* Tallahassee, FL: Author.

Flynn, E. (2000). Elders as perpetrators. In M. Rothman & B. Dunlop (Eds.), *Elders, crime, and the criminal justice system: Myth, perceptions, and reality in the 21st century* (pp. 43–83). New York, NY: Springer.

Flynn, E. (1998). *Managing elderly offenders: A national assessment.* Washington, DC: National Institute of Justice.

Forst, M., Fagan, J., & Vivona, S. T. (1989). Youth in prisons and training schools: Perceptions and consequences of the treatment-custody dichotomy. *Juvenile and Family Court Journal, 40*(1), 1–14.

Forsyth, C. J., & Gramling, R. (1988). Elderly crime: Fact and artifact. In B. R. McCarthy & R. H. Langworthy Eds.), *Older offenders: Perspectives in criminology and criminal justice* (pp. 3–13). New York, NY: Praeger.

Fry, L. J. (1987). Older prison inmate: A profile. *Justice Professional, 2*(1), 1–12.

Gilligan, J., & Lee, B. (2004). Beyond the prison paradigm: From provoking violence to preventing it by creating "anti-prisons" (residential colleges and therapeutic communities). *Annals New York Academy of Sciences, 1036,* 300–324.

Goetting, A. (1985). Racism, sexism, and ageism in the prison community. *Federal Probation, 44*(3), 10–22.

Goetting, A. (1984). Elderly in prison: A profile. *Criminal Justice Review, 9*(2), 14–24.

Goetting, A. (1983). The elderly in prison: Issues and perspectives. *Journal of Research in Crime & Delinquency, 20,* 291–309.

Goetting, A., & Howsen, R. (1986). Correlates of prison misconduct. *Journal of Quantitative Criminology, 2,* 49–67.

Hagan, J., & Dinovitzer, R. (1999). Collateral consequences of imprisonment for children, communities, and prisoners. *Crime and Justice: A Review of Research, 26,* 121–162.

Hunt, G., Riegel, S., Morales, T., & Waldorf, D. (1993). Changes in prison culture: Prison gangs and the case of the "Pepsi Generation." *Social Problems, 40,* 398–409.

Ireland, J.L. (2000). "Bullying" among male prisoners: A review of the research. *Aggression and Violent Behavior, 5,* 201–215.

James, D. J., & Glaze, L. E. (2006). *Bureau of Justice Statistics special report: Mental health problems of prison and jail inmates.* Washington, DC: U.S. Department of Justice.

Kempker, E. (2003). The graying of American prisons: The continued increase in geriatric inmates. *Corrections Compendium, 28*(6), 1–2, 4, 22–26.

Kerbs, J. (2000a). Chapter 10—The older prisoner: Social, psychological, and medical considerations. In B. D. Dunlop & M. B. Rothman (Eds.), *Elders, Crime, and the Criminal Justice System: Myths, Perceptions, and Reality in the 21st Century* (pp. 207–228). New York, NY: Springer Publishing Company.

Kerbs, J. (2000b). Chapter 11—Arguments and Strategies for the Selective-Decarceration of Older Prisoners. In B. D. Dunlop & M. B. Rothman (Eds.), *Elders, Crime, and the Criminal Justice System: Myths, Perceptions, and Reality in the 21st Century* (pp. 229–250). New York, NY: Springer Publishing Company.

Kerbs, J. J., & Jolley, J. M. (2007). Inmate-on-inmate victimization among older male prisoners. *Crime & Delinquency, 53,* 187–218.

Krajick, K. (1979). Growing old in prison. *Corrections Magazine, 5,* 32–46.

Kratcoski, P. C., & Babb, S. (1990). Adjustment of older inmates: An analysis of institutional structure and gender. *Journal of Contemporary Criminal Justice, 6,* 264–281.

Kratcoski, P. C., & Pownall, G. A. (1989). Federal Bureau of Prison programming for older inmates. *Federal Probation, 53*(2), 28–35.

Langan, P. A., & Levin, D. J. (2002). *Bureau of Justice Statistics special report: Recidivism of prisoners released in 1994.* Washington, DC: U.S. Department of Justice.

Langan, P. A., Schmitt, E. L., & Durose, M. R. (2003). *Recidivism of sex offenders released from prison in 1994.* Washington, DC: U.S. Department of Justice.

Laub, J.H., & Sampson, R.J. (2001). Understanding desistance from crime. In M. Tonry (Ed.), *Crime and justice: An annual review of research.* Chicago: University of Chicago Press.

Lemieux, C. M., Dyeson, T. B., & Castiglione, B. (2002). Revisiting the literature on prisoners who are older: Are we wiser? *The Prison Journal, 82*(4), 440–458.

Lester, B. (2003). The Americans with Disabilities Act and the exclusion of inmates from services in prisons: A proposed analytical approach regarding the appropriate level of judicial scrutiny of a prisoners' ADA claim. *North Dakota Law Review, 79,* 83–110.

Light, S.C. (1991). Assault on prison officers: Interactional themes. *Justice Quarterly, 8,* 243–262.

Loeb, S. J., & AbuDagga, A. (2006). Health-related research on older inmates: An integrative review. *Research in Nursing & Health, 29,* 556–565.

Lundstrom, S. (1994). Dying to get out: A study on the necessity, importance, and effectiveness of prison early release programs for elderly inmates suffering from HIV disease and other terminal-centered illnesses. *Brigham Young University Journal of Public Law, 9*(1), 155–188.

Mabli, J., Holley, C. S. D., Patrick, J., & Walls, J. (1979). Age and prison violence: Increasing age heterogeneity as a violence-reducing strategy in prisons. *Criminal Justice & Behavior, 6*(2), 175–186.

Marquart, J. W., Merianos, D. E., & Doucet, G. (2000). The health-related concerns of older prisoners: Implications for policy. *Aging and Society, 20,* 79–96.

Maruschak, L. M., & Beck, A. J. (2001). *Bureau of Justice Statistics special report: Medical problems of inmates, 1997.* Washington, DC: U.S. Department of Justice.

McCarthy, M. (1983). The health status of elderly inmates. *Corrections Today, 45*(Feb), 64–65.

McCorkle, R. C. (1993). Fear of victimization and symptoms of psychopathology among prison inmates. *Journal of Offender Rehabilitation, 19*(1/2), 27–41.

McShane, M. D., & Williams, F. P., III (1990). Old and ornery: The discipl inary experiences of elderly prisoners. *International Journal of Offender Therapy and Comparative Criminology, 34*, 197–212.

Merianos, D. E., Marquart, J. W., Damphouse, K., & Herbert, J. L. (1997). From the outside in: Using public health data to make inferences about older inmates. *Crime & Delinquency, 43*, 298–313.

Mitka, M. (2004). Aging prisoners stressing health care system. *Journal of the American Medical Association (JAMA), 292*(4), 423–424.

Morton, J. B. (2001). Implications for corrections of an aging prison population. *Corrections Management Quarterly, 5*(1), 78–88.

Morton, J. B. (1994). Training staff to work with special needs offenders. *Forum on Corrections Research, 6*(2), 32–34.

Morton, J. B. (1993). Training staff to work with elderly and disabled inmates. *Corrections Today, 55*(1), 42, 44–47.

Morton, J. B. (1992). *An administrative overview of the older inmate.* Washington, DC: U.S. Department of Justice.

Newman, D. J. (1984). Elderly offenders and American crime patters. In E. S. Newman, D. J. Newman, & M. L. Gewirtz (eds.), *Elderly criminals* (pp. 3–16). Boston, MA: Oelgeschlager, Gunn and Hain, Publishers, Inc.

Pennsylvania v. Yeskey, 524 U.S. 206 (1998).

Petersilia, J. (1999). Parole and prisoner reentry in the United States. *Crime and Justice: A Review of Research, 26,* 479–529.

Petersilia, J. (1992). California's prison policy: Causes, costs, and consequences. *Prison Journal, 72,* 8–36.

Pogorzelski, W., Wolff, N., Pan, K., Blitz, C.L. (2005). Behavioral health problems, ex-offender reentry policies, and the "second chance act." *American Journal of Public Health, 95*(10), 1718–1723.

Rau, J. (2007, December 28). Prison healthcare costs outpace California inmate population. *Los Angeles Times.* Retrieved on January 21, 2008, at http://www.boston.com/news/nation/articles/2007/12/28/prison_healthcare_costs_outpace_calif_inmate_population/

Rikard, R. V., & Rosenberg, E. (2007). Aging inmates: A convergence of trends in the American criminal justice system. *Journal of Correctional Health Care, 13*(3), 150–162.

Ross, D. L. (2005). *Civil liability issues in corrections.* Durham, NC: Carolina Academic Press.

Rubenstein, D. (1984). Chapter 10: The elderly in prison—A review of the literature. In E. S. Newman, D. J. Newman & M. L. Gewirtz (Eds.), *Elderly criminals* (pp. 153–168). Boston, MA: Oelgeschlager, Gunn and Hain, Publishers, Inc.

Russell, M., & Stewart, J. (2001). Disablement, prison, and historical segregation. *Monthly Review, 53*(3), 61–75.

Sabath, M. J., & Cowles, E. L. (1988). Factors affecting the adjustment of elderly inmates to prison. In B. R. McCarthy & R. H. Langworthy (Eds.), *Older offenders: Perspectives in criminology and criminal justice* (pp. 178–196). New York, NY: Praeger.

Sabol, W. J., Minton, T. D., & Harrison, P. M. (2007). *Bureau of Justice statistics bulletin: Prison and jail inmates at midyear 2006.* Washington, DC: U.S. Department of Justice.

Sampson, R. J., & Laub, J. H. (2003). Life-course desisters? Trajectories of crime among delinquent boys followed to age 70. *Criminology, 41,* 555–592.

Silverman, M., & Vega, M. (1990). Reactions of prisoners to stress as a function of personality and demographic variables. *International Journal of Offender Therapy and Comparative Criminology, 34*(3), 187–196.

Steffensmeier, D., & Harer, M. D. (1993). Bulging prisons, an aging U.S. population, and the nation's violent crime rate. *Federal Probation, 57*(2), 3–10.

Teller, F. E., & Howell, R. J. (1981). Older prisoner: Criminal and psychological characteristics. *Criminology, 18*, 549–555.

The Sentencing Project (2008). *Facts about prisons and prisoners.* Washington, DC: Author.

Tobin, P., & Metzler, C. (1983). *Typology of older prisoners in Massachusetts state correctional facilities, 1972–1982.* Boston, MA: Massachusetts Department of Corrections.

Turner, M. G., Sundt, J. L., Applegate, B. K., & Cullen, F. T. (1995). "Three strikes and you're out" legislation: A national assessment. *Federal Probation, 59*(3), 16–35.

U.S. Department of Justice. (1997, February 12). *A live satellite video-conference on medical services for geriatric and aging inmates.* Washington, DC: National Institute of Corrections.

Van Harreveld, F., Van Der Pligt, J., Claassen, L., & Van Dijk, W.W. (2007). Inmate emotion coping and psychological and physical well-being: The use of crying over spilled milk. *Criminal Justice and Behavior, 34*, 697–708.

Vaughn, M. S., & Collins, S. C. (2004). Medical malpractice in correctional facilities: State tort remedies for inappropriate and inadequate health care administered to prisoners. *The Prison Journal, 84*(4), 505–534.

Vega, M., & Silverman, M. (1988). Stress and the elderly convict. *International Journal of Offender Therapy and Comparative Criminology, 32*(2), 153–162.

Visher, C. A. (1987). Incapacitation and crime control: Does a "lock 'em up" strategy reduce crime? *Justice Quarterly, 5,* 513–543.

Vito, G. F., & Wilson, D. G. (1985). Forgotten people: Elderly inmates. *Federal Probation, 49*(1), 18–23.

Washington v. Harper, 494 U.S. 210 (1990).

Wiegand, D., & Burger, J. C. (1979). The elderly offender and parole. *Prison Journal, 59,* 48–57.

Williams, B. A., Lindquist, K., Sudore, R. L., Strupp, H. M., Willmott, D. J., & Walter, L. C. (2006). Being old and doing time: Functional impairment and adverse experiences of geriatric female prisoners. *Journal of the American Geriatrics Society, 54*(4), 702–707.

Wilson, D. G., & Vito, G. F. (1986). Imprisoned Elders: The experience of one institution. *Criminal Justice Policy Review, 1,* 399–421.

Wooldredge, J. D. (1999). Inmate experiences and psychological wellbeing. *Criminal Justice and Behavior, 26,* 235–250.

Wooldredge, J.D. (1994). Inmate crime and victimization in a southwestern correctional facility. *Journal of Criminal Justice, 22,* 367–381.

Wooldredge, J.D. (1991). Correlates of deviant behavior among inmates of U.S. correctional facilities. *Journal of Crime and Justice, 14,* 1–25.

Wooldredge, J.D., Griffin, T., & Pratt, T. (2001). Considering hierarchical models for research on inmate behavior: Predicting misconduct with multilevel data. *Justice Quarterly, 18,* 202–232.

Wright, K. N., & Bronstein, L. (2007). An organizational analysis of prison hospice. *The Prison Journal, 87,* 391–407.

Zimring, F. E., & Hawkins, G. (1991). *The scale of imprisonment.* Chicago, IL: University of Chicago Press.

REVIEW QUESTIONS

1. Should prisons be required to provide older inmates with access to life-saving operations such as costly organ transplants?
2. How should prisons deal with older prisoners with terminal illnesses?
3. What are some effective means through which prisons might promote the rehabilitation and safety of older prisoners?
4. What, if any, sorts of special classifications and segregation systems should be used with elderly inmates?
5. What are the pros and cons of the policy proposals detailed in the concluding pages of the article?

XI

GENDER ISSUES IN CORRECTIONS

READING 28

Confronting Problems Faced by Pregnant Inmates in State Prisons

John D. Wooldredge

Kimberly Masters

Women who are pregnant (or who have very recently given birth prior to entering prison) represent one of the frequently forgotten or overlooked segments of the prison population. Pregnant women have a range of unique physical and psychological needs, which are typically not addressed nor served by prison officials. Based on a survey of wardens of prisons for women, this reading shows that few facilities provide basic prenatal care, educational services, or post-birth services that are common and considered basic in the community. The possible consequences of this lack of services and programs are discussed, and clearly suggest serious negative outcomes for both mothers and their children.

Studies have revealed that one out of every four adult women incarcerated in U.S. prisons is pregnant on intake or has given birth at some point during the previous year (Holt 1982; Church 1990). As recently as 1982, the medical resources and programs available to pregnant inmates were inadequate for meeting their special needs. Examples of such inadequacies included an absence of special diets, lighter work assignments, and resources to deal with deliveries, premature births, and miscarriages. This situation often caused tremendous physical stress for pregnant inmates (McHugh 1980; Church 1990; Pollock-Byrne 1990). Further, until recently, the only options available to pregnant inmates included abortion, putting their children up for adoption, releasing them to foster care, or leaving them with relatives (Feinman 1986; Vukson 1988). But the separation of mothers from their newborn children can create severe developmental problems for the infant as well as psychological anguish for the mother (Magid and McKelvey 1987; Catan 1989).

Policy recommendations have been made by various agencies to combat the physical and psychological problems faced by pregnant inmates. These recommendations include prenatal care in prisons, full-time nurses or midwives for pregnant inmates, allowing nursing infants to remain with their mothers during incarceration, extended visiting programs for mothers and their children, and special counseling programs. However, many states have no statutes that define policies for dealing with pregnant inmates, so prison administrators are not obligated to follow these recommendations.

Very little is known about the extent to which prison administrators in the United States have implemented their own policies to combat the problems faced by pregnant inmates. But the implementation of such policies is important for the physical and psychological well-being of pregnant inmates and their subsequently born children. This article presents results from a study of the prevalence and types of policies being implemented voluntarily for the care and support of pregnant inmates in state prisons throughout the United States.

PROBLEMS FACED BY PREGNANT INMATES

Imprisonment can be very stressful for pregnant inmates and those who have recently given birth (McHugh 1980; Greenspan and Greenspan 1985). Pregnant inmates have physical disadvantages that make it more difficult to cope with the physical demands of incarceration. Also, these women sometimes endure psychological stress over whether to have an abortion, what should be done with the child after birth, and how to cope with the separation from their child. Some mothers who have recently given birth while incarcerated also face psychological stress stemming from "separation anxiety" (Greenspan and Greenspan 1985).

The newborn children of incarcerated mothers often face long-term problems of their own. An infant who does not have a continuous, intimate relationship with his or her mother during the first 2 years after birth is more likely to develop one or more of the following traits: psychopathology, inability to relate to others, difficulty with intimacy and assertiveness, lack of trust in others, lack of willpower, indecisiveness, fear of abandonment, fear of new experiences, and poor academic performance (Garbarino 1980; McCarthy 1980; Greenspan and Greenspan 1985; Melina 1986; Magid and McKelvey 1987; Browne 1989; Bradshaw 1990).

The physical problems faced by pregnant inmates cannot be eliminated altogether, short of decarceration, but they can be reduced through a greater availability of medical resources in prison and the implementation of special programs for pregnant inmates. These resources and programs may include a full-time doctor or nurse, an infirmary with beds for overnight stays, easier access to pain killing drugs, special diets, lighter work assignments, and perhaps separate (less crowded) living quarters for pregnant inmates. Recommendations for the improved medical care and treatment of pregnant inmates have been made by the American Correctional Association, the American Public Health Association, and the American Medical Association.

The psychological problems faced by pregnant inmates can be treated, in part, through special counseling programs where psychologists can identify and address the specific needs of these women (Kaplan 1988). However, some of these problems are tied to the issue of separating mothers from their newborn children which, in turn, is related directly to the long-term problems faced by the children themselves. These long-term problems, listed above, are extremely difficult to eliminate once a child enters adulthood (Bradshaw 1990). However, these problems can be prevented altogether with policies designed to maintain contact between incarcerated mothers and their children. Such policies may include nurseries for newborn babies in a prison, and more frequent and/or extended visits with children (Baunach 1985; Feinman 1986; Church 1990). . . . These policies and programs may help to prevent the long-term problems faced by children of incarcerated mothers and simultaneously help to alleviate some of the mothers' psychological stress due to separation anxiety.

The extent to which these recommendations have been adopted by prison administrators across the country remains unknown. Many prison officials have reported that there are not enough incarcerated women with long sentences to justify such resources and programs (Cummings 1979; Snow 1981; Holt 1982).

Further, because these policies are not mandatory, there are tremendous variations in the resources and programs available across states. In short, very little is known about the extent and types of policies which are being used across the United States to deal with the problems faced by pregnant inmates.

DATA AND METHOD

A survey was designed and mailed to all wardens of state prisons for women (including coed facilities) operating in the United States . . . (N = 100). The survey included questions about the types of medical services and programs available to serve the physical and psychological needs of pregnant inmates, and the wardens' perceptions of problems related to the care and support of pregnant inmates. . . .

All of the services and programs available for pregnant inmates were identified. The numbers of facilities with these services and programs were noted and percentages were calculated based on the total number of responses. All of the problems that the wardens observed with the care and support of pregnant inmates were identified as well.

TYPES AND PREVALENCE OF SERVICES AND PROGRAMS FOR PREGNANT INMATES

All facilities in the sample maintain the medical resources and services that are legally required for inmates *in general.* However, in spite of the availability of these general resources and services, only 29 facilities (48%) have written policies related specifically to the medical care of pregnant inmates. These services include the following:

1. Prenatal care (n = 29, or 48%).
2. Networks with community agencies which provide "other" prenatal care (n = 23, or 38%).
3. Lamaze classes (n = 10, or 16%).
4. Special diets and nutritional allowances (n = 9, or 15%).
5. Abortions and abortion counseling (n = 5, or 9%).
6. Full-time nurse or midwife available just for pregnant inmates (n = 5, or 9%).

These types of services represent improvements over what has been offered traditionally. However, note that slightly less than half of the facilities offer any type of prenatal care (48%), and a small minority offer significant improvements beyond prenatal care alone (16%). Further, only 10 facilities (16%) maintain three or more of the six items listed above. Although advancements are being made in the types of medical services available to pregnant inmates, they have yet to be implemented in the vast majority of state prisons housing women.

Regarding special programs for pregnant inmates, those permitting infants to remain in a facility with his or her mother are not available in any of the prisons in the sample. . . .

The available programs designed specifically for pregnant inmates include the following:

1. Prenatal counseling (n = 13, or 21%).
2. Counseling to help mothers find suitable placement for the infant after birth (n = 9, or 15%).
3. Policies for lighter work or no work (n = 9, or 15%).
4. Separate living quarters (n = 8, or 13%).
5. Postnatal counseling (n = 7, or 11%).

Similar to the findings for medical services, these results suggest that there has been an improvement in the types of programs available for pregnant inmates, but these programs are offered in a minority of facilities (21%). Further, three or more of the five programs are available in only nine facilities (15%). It appears that the majority of prison administrators have a long way to go before they meet the special needs of pregnant inmates.

Noticeably absent from the list above are counseling programs designed *specifically* to deal with the psychological problems faced by pregnant inmates. However, some counseling programs that are available to *all* female inmates may also be used for the benefit of this particular group. These programs include the following:

1. Individual and/or group therapy (n = 32, or 52%).
2. Classes in child development and parenting (n = 18, or 30%).
3. Stress management (n = 11, or 18%).
4. Family counseling (n = 6, or 10%).
5. Infant mental health counseling (n = 3, or 5%).

These figures reveal that the programs available to meet the needs of female inmates *in general* are almost as scarce as those for pregnant inmates. For example, incarcerated mothers with children under 18 constitute over 80% of the U.S. female inmate population (Church 1990), but only 18 facilities (30%) offer classes in parenting and only six facilities (10%) offer family counseling. Stress management could be very useful to pregnant inmates, but only 11 facilities (18%) offer such programs. Unfortunately, even though the general programs listed above could serve some of the specific needs of pregnant inmates, they are available only in a small minority of institutions.

PERCEIVED PROBLEMS WITH THE CARE AND SUPPORT OF PREGNANT INMATES

The wardens who responded to the survey observed several problems related to the care and support of pregnant inmates. Only eight respondents did not note *any* related problems whatsoever, but they are all wardens of facilities with the greatest abundance of medical resources, services, and programs for pregnant inmates. Some of the problems noted by the other wardens have already been dealt with in these eight facilities with the programs listed above. However, another set of problems presented by the wardens represent issues which have yet to be dealt with in any of the facilities examined. These problems include the following:

1. Inadequate resources to deal with false labors, premature births, and miscarriages.
2. No maternity clothes.
3. Pregnant inmates are sometimes required to wear belly chains when being transported to the hospital.
4. Minimum security pregnant inmates are sometimes housed in maximum security facilities.
5. No place for a mother and her baby to remain together.
6. No separate visiting areas for mothers and newborn children.
7. Often overcrowded living conditions.

These problems relate to both the physical and psychological needs of pregnant inmates as well as the developmental needs of their subsequently born children. Unfortunately, these problems cannot be alleviated with any of the services and programs that are currently available across the sample. . . .

The wardens' observations indicate that there are many issues related to the physical and psychological welfare of pregnant inmates and their children that have yet to be addressed in most state prisons for women. These observations, combined with previous research findings of the deleterious effects of incarcerating pregnant inmates, provide the foundation for the policy recommendations presented below.

POLICY IMPLICATIONS

The exploratory findings presented here yield four major conclusions regarding available support for pregnant inmates in state prisons. First, in some facilities, improvements in the availability of medical services, counseling programs, and education have been made over time. These improvements may help to alleviate some of the physical and psychological pressures placed on pregnant inmates. Second, a few of these improvements have occurred in about half of all state prisons housing women, but most have occurred in a small minority of institutions. Third, the improvements that have been made are limited not only in their use, but also in their scope. Finally, most wardens of these facilities are dissatisfied with the current state of support for pregnant inmates. In short, policies for the care and support of pregnant inmates are in the processes of improving and expanding, but they have a long way to go before they satisfy the needs of pregnant inmates.

Regarding the educational needs of pregnant inmates, more programs are needed to educate these women about the options available to them, the ramifications of each option, and how to find suitable placement for a newborn child. Classes in parenting skills and child development should also be available to women who choose to keep their children as well as other incarcerated mothers with preschool children.

More administrators need to provide services, implement programs, and create environments that will ease the physical stress of incarceration for pregnant inmates. Policies may include separate living quarters for pregnant inmates and/or the maintenance of less crowded living conditions, special diets, lighter work assignments, permitting maternity clothes to be worn, a greater availability of staff and resources to deal with deliveries, miscarriages, false labors, and premature births, and postnatal care services.

More facilities also need resources and counseling programs that will reduce the psychological stress felt by pregnant inmates. Such resources and programs may include nurseries for newborn children, extended visiting programs for mothers and their children, separate visiting areas for mothers and newborn children, classes in stress management, and family counseling programs.

Needless to say, there are significant barriers to obtaining sufficient resources to implement the recommendations presented above. Following are some recommendations that may be possible in light of the poor economic situations faced by most administrators of state prisons for women:

1. Community-based services that network with a facility's administration could provide many of the counseling, teaching, and advising services for pregnant inmates.
2. The best type of facility presently available to provide the necessary care for pregnant inmates may be the half-way house.
3. As suggested by McHugh (1980), legislation should be enacted that requires that pregnant women be housed in separate facilities that specifically address the special needs of this population.

REFERENCES

Baunach, Phyllis J. 1985. *Mothers in Prison.* New Brunswick, NJ: Transaction Books.

Bradshaw, John. 1990. *Reclaiming and Championing Your Child.* New York: Bantam.

Browne, Dorothy. 1989. "Incarcerated Mothers and Parenting." *Journal of Family Violence* 4:211–21.

Catan, Liza. 1989. "The Development of Young Children in Prison Mother and Baby Units." *Research Bulletin* 26:9–12.

Church, George. 1990. "The View From Behind Bars," *Time* 135:20–22.

Cummings, Patricia. 1979. "The Single Mother as Criminal Defendant: A Practitioner's Guide to the Consequences of Incarceration," *Golden Gate Law Review* 9:507–52.

Feinman, Clarice. 1986. *Women in the Criminal Justice System.* New York: Praeger.

Garbarino, James. 1980. "Changing Hospital Childbirth Practices: A Developmental Perspective on Prevention of Child Maltreatment." *American Journal of Orthopsychiatry* 50:588–97.

Greenspan, Miriam and Nancy, Greenspan. 1985. *First Feelings: Milestones in the Emotional Development of Your Baby and Child.* New York: Penguin.

Holt, Karen. 1982. "Nine Months to Life: The Law and the Pregnant Inmate." *Journal of Family Law* 20:525–43.

Kaplan, Mildred. 1988. "A Peer Support Group for Women in Prison for the Death of a Child." *Journal of Offender Counseling, Services and Rehabilitation* 13:5–13.

Magid, Ken and Carole McKelvey. 1987. *Children Without a Conscience,* New York: Bantam.

McCarthy, Belinda. 1980. "Inmate Mothers: The Programs of Separation and Reintegration." *Journal of Offender Counseling, Services and Rehabilitation* 4:199–212.

McHugh, Gerald. 1980. "Protection of the Rights of Pregnant Women in Prisons and Detention Facilities." *New England Journal of Prison Law* 6:231–63.

Melina, Lois. 1986. *Raising Adopted Children, A Mannual for Adoptive Parents.* New York: Harper & Row.

Pollock-Byrne, Jocelyn. 1990. *Women, Prison, and Crime.* Pacific Grove, CA: Brooks/Cole.

Snow, Charlene. 1981. "Women in Prison." *Clearinghouse Review* 14:1065–68.

Vukson, Todd. 1988. "Inmate Abortion in California: A Constitutional Analysis." *California Western Law Review* 24:107–26.

REVIEW QUESTIONS

1. What are the common physical and psychological problems faced by pregnant inmates?
2. What types of programs and services for pregnant inmates are most common in women's prisons?
3. According to wardens of women's prisons, what are the most commonly perceived problems encountered with providing care and support to pregnant inmates?

READING 29

Gender and Occupational Culture Conflict

A Study of Women Jail Officers

Eric D. Poole

Mark R. Pogrebin

This study considers gender systems that impact work as a correctional officer. Interviews conducted with 108 female correctional officers working in seven institutions are used to illustrate the gender norms and social control mechanisms that are used to subordinate female officers within a male-dominated occupation. The data suggest that male officers treat female jailers as if they are weak, indecisive, and unable to handle the physically and emotionally demanding aspects of the job. The occupational subculture is described as a "cult of masculinity" wherein women are marginalized and degraded. Female officers describe feelings of anger, depression, and powerlessness as a result of the continuous harassment and unequal treatment that they receive. The female officers claim that supervisors provide little relief or intervention in this sexist environment, so the female officers try to manage their emotions internally or through verbal responses. The authors also depict numerous obstacles that hinder female officers from rising to supervisory positions. The article concludes with a discussion of the personal and occupational consequences of an embedded system of institutionalized sexism and some possible means for addressing existing structures and processes.

Since the early 1980s, the number of women working in state and federal jails has grown dramatically. According to the Bureau of Justice Statistics of the U.S. Department of Justice, the number of females employed as correctional officers rose from 16,545 in 1988 to 42,500 in 1999—an increase of 157 percent (Perkins, Stephan, & Beck, 1995; Stephan, 2001). Females now compose 28 percent of the custodial/security staff in jails nationwide. The primary stimulus for the increased employment and utilization of female officers has been the need to comply with federal guidelines on hiring (Equal Opportunity Act of 1972 amending Title VII of the Civil Rights Act of 1964), as well as with various court orders to implement hiring quotas to increase female representation or to rewrite entrance exams and requirements to encourage the employment of women (see Camp, Steiger, Wright, Saylor, & Gilman, 1997). While the initial stimulus for increased hiring of women was prompted by legislative and judicial mandates, several administrative factors have also driven the need for more women employees. First, jails must house both male and female inmates, and women are needed to supervise the female residents. Second, female officers are needed to conduct searches of female visitors. Third, a rapid expansion of the jail work force has increased demand and opened job opportunities for qualified female applicants.

Despite women's increased presence in corrections work, the position of female jail officer is a unique form of non-traditional work for women; it is qualitatively different from other work in that violence is prevalent in the work environment and the job is perceived to be a highly sex-typed male one requiring qualities of dominance, aggressiveness, and authoritativeness (Hemmens, Stohr, Schoeler, & Miller, 2002; Lawrence & Mahan, 1998; Lutze & Murphy, 1999). Female qualities of nurturing, sensitivity, and understanding are thought by many male jail officers not merely unnecessary, but potentially detrimental to job performance. Because female officers are expected to conform to masculine sex-typed work norms, it is likely that the integration problems faced by women entering this occupation are severe; however, little research attention has been focused on female officers working in local jails (see Belknap, 1991; Hogan, Lambert, Hepburn, Burton, & Cullen, 2004; Stohr, Lovrich, & Mays, 1997; Stohr, Lovrich, & Wood, 1996; Stohr, Mays, Beck, & Kelly, 1998).

Based on studies of women working as guards in male correctional facilities, sexism and sexual harassment have emerged as persistent obstacles to workforce integration (Farnworth, 1992; Jurik, 1985; Pogrebin & Poole, 1997; Pollock, 1986; Stohr et al., 1998; Zimmer, 1986;). Women correctional officers experience a hostile work environment where they endure resentment, harassment, and discrimination. The research suggests that male officers seek to maintain male dominance and subordination of female co-workers by sexualizing the prison work environment (Pogrebin & Poole, 1997). What is lacking almost entirely from the research literature is a focus on the impact of the sexualized work environment on women jail officers. The present paper seeks to lay an initial qualitative research foundation upon which this area of concern may be addressed.

We will frame our study by focusing on gender as a normative system, a pervasive network of interrelated norms and sanctions through which female and male behavior is evaluated and controlled (West & Zimmerman, 1987). This conception of gender as a scheme of interpersonal evaluations is, of course, implicit in most critiques of the concepts of "femininity" and "masculinity." Guided by how workplace perceptions and practices bear a close relation to these sociocultural constructions of reality, we will stress what Padavic (1991) has described as the "re-creation of gender in the male workplace" (p. 279) and what Stockard and Johnson (1980) have termed "the reproduction of male dominance in everyday interactions" (p. 10).

Diverse studies of the gender system have irrefutably shown how the subordination of women is sustained through their being socialized for, and restricted to, limited aspirations, options, roles, and rewards (Dworkin, 1974; Hochschild, 1973; Jacobs, 1989; Kosinar, 1981; Laws, 1979; Millet, 1971). The weighty significance of such factors, along with the basic learning processes and major societal institutions that produce and perpetrate them, is unquestionable. Equally important is the role of interpersonal evaluation in ordinary life situations. In particular, informal social control must be recognized as a key mechanism that backs up and enforces many of the restrictions and limitations placed on women. There are various ways, then, in which gender—as a sociocultural complex of meanings, behaviors, and assessments—is instilled and maintained. Hochschild (1973) identifies four main perspectives adopted in studies of women and the gender system. One focuses on the nature of biological and psychological "sex differences"; a second emphasizes "sex roles and the norms which govern them"; a third treats "women as a minority group"; and the fourth—a "politics of caste" outlook—stresses power differentials and exploitation as a tool of control. As Hochschild notes, these alternative approaches reflect different disciplinary traditions, tend to favor different "conceptual vocabularies," and may carry different implications with respect to social change and public policy. In the present work, the first orientation ("sex differences") receives little attention. Each of the other three approaches, however, provides concepts and emphases that are useful for the analysis of women's work experiences. Our central concept of "gender norms" has close ties to the study of "sex roles," even if the focus here on reinforcement in daily interaction departs somewhat from the more usual stress on socialization. In exploring the basic perceptions and responses through which women are devalued, the analogy to deviance labeling and stigmatization will prove valuable. Finally, power and control differentials are going to be critical sensitizing concepts in examining the sexualization of the work setting, in general, and sexual harassment, in particular. In developing an overview of women working in jail it is unnecessary, therefore, and might even prove counterproductive, to attempt to adopt one of these orientations. The sociological penchant for identifying supposedly competing "schools" should not lead us to neglect points on which otherwise different approaches may converge or complement each other. Because the topic of women working in traditional male occupations is highly complex, to study it we may well need a varied arsenal of sociological concepts and outlooks.

Occupational Norms and Workplace Organization

Both early studies and the contemporary literature reveal that women who have entered a variety of traditionally male occupations have faced discriminatory hiring and assignment practices, resistance and opposition from male co-workers, and inadequate on-the-job training (Gray, 1984; Gruber & Bjorn, 1982; Jacobs, 1989; Kanter, 1977; Meyer & Lee, 1978; O'Farrell & Harlan, 1982; Swerdlow, 1989; Walshok, 1981). The experiences of women entering the corrections field are illustrative of these organizational obstacles and challenges to changing occupational norms in a work setting undergoing integration (Belknap, 1991; Bowersox, 1981; Britton, 2003; Carlson, Anson, & Thomas, 2003; Crouch & Alpert, 1982; Farkas, 1999; Fry & Glaser, 1987; Gross, Larson, Urban, & Zupan, 1994; Hemmens et al., 2002; Jenne & Kersting, 1996; Jurik, 1985; Jurik & Halembra, 1984; Jurik & Martin, 2001; Lawrence & Mahan, 1998; Morton, 1991; Petersen, 1982; Savicki, Cooley, & Cjesvold, 2003; Stohr et al., 1998; Wright & Saylor, 1991; Zimmer, 1986, 1987, 1988, 1989; Zupan, 1986, 1992). To understand the persistence of an organizational climate of resentment, skepticism, and hostility toward women working in corrections, we must first examine the nature of the occupational norms that are at stake.

Occupational norms have traditionally been linked to work segregation by sex (Coser & Rokoff, 1971; Jacobs, 1989; Laws, 1979; Stockard & Johnson,

1980). For the most part, the sex typing of specific jobs is arbitrary and follows one basic rule: men and women are different and should be doing different things. Such stereotypical thinking has long sustained the stigmatization of those who violate such norms of occupational segregation, thus reinforcing sex-role typing in the workplace. Sex-role stereotypes function to keep women in ancillary and supportive roles rather than in positions of independence, authority, and leadership (Safilios-Rothschild, 1979). A consequence for women who challenge these sex-role stereotypes is the negative evaluation of their skills, capabilities, and competence. While women in corrections work may perform the job as well as men, they tend not to be seen as being men's equals (Belknap, 1996; Farkas, 1999; Hemmens et al., 1992; Lawrence & Mahan, 1998; Lutze & Murphy, 1999).

Negative reactions to or sanctioning of occupational "deviants" constitutes a powerful social control mechanism in maintaining a polarized male and female work force (Laws, 1979; Schur, 1984). Particularly when women enter what have traditionally been viewed as ultramasculine occupations (such as coal mining, steel manufacturing, firefighting, corrections, etc.), intense reactions are expected to occur (Gray, 1984; Jurik & Martin, 2001; Lutze & Murphy, 1999; Meyer & Lee, 1978; Swerdlow, 1989; Walshok 1981). Several common responses are likely to be found in such situations of female occupational deviance (Schur, 1979). Consciousness of the deviant's femaleness will be heightened. Consciousness of the female's deviance also will be high, and she will be devalued, restricted and otherwise punished for it. Finally, male workers may convince themselves that a woman who commits such occupational deviance deserves whatever she gets. Women come to be viewed as "fair game" for whatever abuses—verbal, emotional, or physical—male co-workers decide to dispense. In such a work situation, then, a specific imputation of deviant identity to the woman is used to rationalize diverse forms of male untoward behavior directed toward her (Schur, 1984). This rationalization suggests that harassment may sometimes implicitly constitute punishment for women's perceived violation of specific gender norms.

Some observers contend that a generalized perception of threat to male power and control on the part of male workers lies behind most harassment in the workplace (Erez & Tontodonato, 1992). It is important, however, to keep in mind that something besides occupational power and control is involved in the harassment phenomenon. As MacKinnon (1979) notes,

> The sense that emerges from incidents of sexual harassment is . . . [that men] want to know that they can go this far this way any time they wish and get away with it. . . . The practice seems an extension of their desire and belief that the woman is there for them, however they may choose to define that. (p. 162)

Harassment functions to sustain both male workplace power and male power to treat women as sexual objects (Stohr et al., 1998; Zimmer, 1988). Workplace harassment, then, is not merely a result of women's violating occupational norms or their being vulnerable as tokens (i.e., being in the numerical minority). On the contrary, it also reflects the socialized and reinforced tendency of male co-workers to view women primarily as visual sexual objects (MacKinnon, 1979). From this standpoint, harassment of women workers has as much to do with the daily harassment they experience in many other contexts as it has to do with the specific features of women's work situations.

The sexualized work environment embodies the treatment of women as objects and a denial of personal autonomy (Farley, 1978). According to MacKinnon (1982), "Sexual objectification is the primary process of the subjection of women" (p. 541). This process is thus central to perceptions of female violations of occupational norms and gender roles, as individual women are submitted to standardized and stereotype-laden categorizations and responses. In this respect the sexualized work environment is the linchpin of occupational inequality (Martin, 1989). The research presented here seeks to explore the dimensions of the sexualized jail setting that women corrections officers face and to understand the significance of gender in their work experiences.

METHOD

Four county jails and three adult detention centers located in four counties in the Denver metropolitan area were selected for the present study. These facilities were managed and staffed by personnel from four sheriffs' departments. Utilizing personnel rosters of deputy sheriffs provided by the respective facilities, we drew a 50% systematic random sample (n = 135) of all female officers from each institution.[1] We contacted sampled officers individually in order to inform them of the purpose of the study, request their participation, and obtain informed consent. A total of 119 women agreed to participate, and interview times were then scheduled. Because of conflicts related to vacation, sick leave, work assignment, transfer, etc., interviews with 11 women could not be conducted. Thus, the present study was based on interview data from 108 women deputies. Their ages ranged from 24 to 51 (median=37), and their length of experience at their present facility ranged from one to fifteen years (median=5).

Interviews were conducted at the respective facilities in private conference rooms, library carrels, or visitation rooms during off hours. Each interview lasted approximately ninety minutes and was tape recorded with the subject's consent. A semi-structured interview format was used, which relied on sequential probes to pursue leads provided by subjects. This allowed the deputies to identify and elaborate on important domains they perceived to characterize their experiences in jail work, rather than the researchers eliciting responses to structured questions.

The interview tapes were transcribed for qualitative data analysis, which involved a search for general relationships among categories of observations. Employing grounded theory techniques similar to those suggested by Glaser and Strauss (1967), we categorized the data into conceptual domains of jail work experiences as identified by the women deputies, as follows: second-class status, occupational subculture, emotion work, and unequal opportunity.

FINDINGS

Second-Class Status

According to Belknap (1991), the conflict between gender-role norms and occupational-role norms in jail work poses unique obstacles for female officers. The traditional male attitude about the inherent masculine nature of the job of jail guard makes the prospect of a female co-worker particularly offensive to some men officers. For example, corrections officers associate masculinity with physical ability and view the use of force as a defining feature of the job (Belknap, 1991). Jurik (1985) reports that male officers believe that women are incapable of exercising sufficient physical force to perform the social control tasks required to control incorrigible inmates; moreover, women are often seen as less reliable in back-up or cover roles when handling violent encounters with inmates. Implicit trust and reliance that an officer will come to another's aid and use any means necessary to protect a peer's life are vital components of the work expectations among corrections officers. Male staff are fearful that the presumed physical limitations of women will place officers at greater risk and make the environment potentially more threatening and dangerous because of the inmates' perception of diminished staff ability to maintain control. Women in line positions are thus regarded as second-class officers, unable to meet reliably job performance criteria of male officers.

Zimmer (1986) reports that female officers are afforded few opportunities to build skills or gain confidence in controlling prisoners in threatening situations. Since women are perceived as weak, indecisive, emotional, and timid, male officers tend to take charge in physical encounters between women deputies and inmates. This action, although necessary in aiding a fellow officer as back-up, reinforces male feelings of physical superiority over women and diminishes the status of female officers. One woman officer describes her experience:

> I've been on many codes [officer back-up] when there is a physical altercation going on and male officers have run in with me and I'm shoved aside so the guys can get in on the fight. . . . I don't know if it's ego. Some of it's patronizing, some protective—"We've got to take care of the little women."

The attitude that female officers need protection from aggressive inmates is also shared by supervisory staff. Instead of developing policy which is inclusive of women in these dangerous encounters, supervisory personnel tend to reinforce the stereotype of women's heightened vulnerability. Two deputies illustrate this problem:

> We had a fight in the girls' pod day room, and there was all this concern all of a sudden that we can't have two female officers in the pod. . . . It's just not safe. The male supervisors think we can't handle it.
>
> [Male supervisors] don't think we can rough it up like the male officers do—that we can't take it like the men, that we are more likely to get injured or something. They don't even want to give us a chance to prove ourselves.

If women corrections officers are not afforded the opportunity to resolve inmate physical altercations, they are restricted in their repertoire of social control techniques. To the extent that supervisory personnel reinforce this subordinate position, women officers will have limited opportunities to demonstrate their physical abilities and gain experience and confidence in the skilled use of force. Such paternalistic treatment thus serves to undermine the authority of women officers and calls in question their ability to perform their job:

> A male deputy . . . in front of some inmates . . . put his arm around me and said, "Dear, I'm going to go to lunch. Can you handle this?"

The paternalistic treatment of women is in itself a denial of their basic role identity as agents of security and control. The notion that women officers can't take care of themselves subjugates them in their work relations with men, as well as imputing diminished capacities in their routine job performance. In her participant observer role as a coal handler in a power plant, Padavic (1991) reports that paternalistic treatment made her "unsure of [her] abilities, afraid of undertaking something new, doing it wrong, and thereby confirming a stereotype" (p. 286). Millett (1971) further notes that while paternalism is held as "a palliative to the injustice of women's social position, chivalry is also a technique for disguising it" (p. 37).

The irony of the self-fulfilling prophecy that operates in the jail setting is two-fold. First, women officers who are subjected to paternalistic protection and control are not given the opportunity to develop or prove their physical skills, which in turn tautologically confirms the male co-workers' stereotypes. Second, when women officers are treated as second-class employees who are perceived in need of protection, they may experience heightened anxiety, exhibit less self-confidence, and even react in inappropriate or unsatisfactory ways. Thus the circle is complete—paternalistic actions serve to foster the stereotypical behavior that in turn confirms the original expectations.

Occupational Subculture

Pollock (1986) notes the guard subculture is an important component of work socialization. Yet male officers tend to adhere to a cult of masculinity that serves to isolate women co-workers as outsiders (Belknap, 1991). By excluding women staff from the informal organizational network of male deputies, the former are often forced to learn much of the job on their own. As a result of this purposive exclusion, women are denied occupational socialization opportunities and a sense of belonging associated with collegial relations. Because much of the job training is done on an informal basis as situations arise, the isolation of female officers undermines their ability to learn the particulars and peculiarities of the job from experienced male colleagues.

Zimmer (1986) reports that female officers are viewed by many of their male peers as being inferior and are therefore denied entree to the officer subculture. One deputy describes her experience of exclusion from informal work networks:

> The male officers go out for drinks after work. Nobody ever bothers to tell me until later on and I find out just in conversation. . . . I once asked a male deputy

> to let me know when the shift goes out and he said that he knows that some of the men bother me, so he didn't ask me along.

The social exclusion of women deputies makes them easy targets for jocular aggression and derogatory nicknames; moreover, male work group solidarity may be enhanced by directing humor at female officers. This "laughter of inclusion" (Dupreel, 1928) affirms the gender distinctions and relative male superiority (Davies, 1982). Innuendo, insinuation, and character assassination are effective strategies in maintaining social distance and social boundaries between the male in-group and the female out-group. As one deputy notes,

> You're always mindful of your position here. You're at work doing your job, but you always feel somehow you don't really belong here.

In short, women officers are often ostracized and belittled by their male co-workers. The male officers view women with a mixture of hostility and resentment, treating them with disdain or simply ignoring them (Jurik, 1985; Van Voorhis, Cullen, Link, & Wolfe, 1991; Zimmer, 1986).

According to Millet (1971), men have a vested interest in sustaining conventional sexual distinctions in role relationships, which reflect a recognition and acceptance of gender-based status and power differentials. In this point we can see a link between gender identity and work role dynamics. Gender norms and work relationships are concerned with maintaining boundaries—moral, social, and psychological. Imputed male work superiority and dominance require female devaluation and subordination. Thus Dworkin (1974) asserts: "The truth of it is that he is powerful . . . when contrasted with her" (p. 44).

Sustaining male workplace superiority dictates that women be isolated so that they cannot compete with males. In this way the strength of women's efforts to compete determines the force required by men to limit or restrict these attempts. Change on one side of the equation invariably affects the other side as well. It is the perception of a threat, regardless of whether that perception is well founded, that constitutes a central basis for resistance to change and triggers the systematic devaluation of women workers (Kanter, 1977).

When male workers' conceptions of their masculinity are closely linked to the nature and conditions of their work (particularly in what have traditionally been viewed as ultramasculine occupations, they are especially likely to feel threatened by female job entrants and resort to more overt subjugation (see Lutze & Murphy, 1999). Of course, if women are cowed into lowering their aspirations or limiting their efforts, it may not matter whether this happens because their workplace threats to men are real or imagined. Either way, the overall subjugation of females would again be taking its toll in lost work contributions and occupational achievements.

Emotion Work

Fox and Hesse-Biber (1984) suggest that certain forms of workplace harassment and abuse are so commonly tolerated that many women have come to regard such activity as inevitable and as virtually a condition of employment. These researchers report that women are reluctant to try to do anything about harassment out of fear of reprisals that may include being fired, demoted, passed over for promotion or a raise, transferred to an undesirable job, or given a poor performance evaluation. In hopes of protecting their job security, female officers often accept and endure the harassment as part of the work environment. Such stressful work conditions often produce feelings of anger, irritability, fear, anxiety, powerlessness, and depression (see Erez & Tontodonato, 1992; Morash & Haar, 1995). Two women deputies describe the types of emotional problems they have had to face:

> . . . I became something of a zombie. I was emotionally numb. I didn't care about anything or anyone and as a result I was very lonely and isolated. Even at parties or at other social occasions I just didn't feel comfortable. . . . People like to talk about work, tell stories, you know. But I couldn't bring myself to talk about what I did at work.
>
> I had trouble sleeping and my home life suffered a lot. . . . I was hurting a lot and pulled back from my own husband. He didn't know what was wrong and I couldn't tell him about it or even explain it myself.

Research in law enforcement agencies and correctional settings has shown that women and minority officers are especially vulnerable to the psychological and physiological disorders associated with sustained exposure to job-related stress (Bartol, Bergen, Volckens, & Knoras, 1992; Cullen, Link, Wolfe, & Frank, 1985; Johnson, 1991; Lovrich & Stohr, 1993; Van Voorhis et al., 1991; Wright & Saylor, 1991; but cf. Carlson et al., 2003). For example, Wexler and Logan's (1983) study of the sources of stress among women officers in a large metropolitan police department indicated that their greatest obstacle was in demonstrating that they could be effective officers without compromising their femininity:

> . . . the most significant stressors seem to be ones in which others were denying them as officers, as women, or both. It is psychologically a very threatening and uncomfortable situation when one's self-perception is substantially different from the perception of others. This is particularly the case when such fundamental identities are at stake as one's gender and profession. (p. 53)

Individuals who feel or know they are deemed marginal employees experience anxiety and are more sensitive about their job performance, often assuming a defensive posture, attempting to overcompensate to prove others wrong in their attitudes, or otherwise reacting in ways that may be perceived as inappropriate or undesirable (Timmins & Hainsworth, 1989; Wright & Saylor, 1991). Two deputies relate their reactions:

> I found that I would lose my temper over the littlest of things. . . . Stupid little things would happen and I would start crying.
>
> I just stayed mad. I became defensive. I had a big chip on my shoulder. I hated the constant abuse and kept thinking that one day I would just kill someone.

The job stress experienced by women working in jails is further exacerbated by their lack of access to the peer-group support structure of fellow male deputies. The informal work subculture often functions to reduce stress, providing individual officers a forum within which they can vent safely. Women deputies' lack of acceptance in this traditional male fraternity thus denies them a critical organizational coping mechanism to mitigate the impact of work-related stress.

Female officers sometimes attempt to deal with their male co-workers by adopting a "give-and-take" approach, a sort of verbal jousting. This tactic, however, is risky, as shown by two women deputies:

> Bantering back and forth with the men takes a lot of stress out of the situation and kind of neutralizes the harassment we experience. But once it goes beyond or crosses the line, there seems to be no course of action for female officers.
>
> I was kidding with a couple of guys out in the parking lot about my pathetic love life and we were talking about going out to get a drink . . . when out of the blue one of them grabbed my head, pulled me up to his face, and stuck his tongue in my mouth. I was shocked and disgusted—just humiliated by that. . . .

Such inability on the part of female deputies to engage in verbal horseplay on an equal footing with male co-workers reflects their lack of acceptance in the work subculture. Pogrebin and Poole (1988) observe that "Joking relations among peers generate feelings of implicit understanding and camaraderie, thus strengthening group norms and bonds" (p. 184). The rub is that women deputies are not accepted as "peers" in the jail work setting; thus, women may find that their attempts to act like "one of the boys" via joking relations are met with "punitive" responses from male co-workers (Seckman & Couch, 1989).

Unequal Opportunity

Women in corrections routinely experience derision, hostility, and exclusion from male supervisors and co-workers. Their attitudes toward job commitment and aspirations to advance in the profession are adversely affected by such treatment (Belknap, 1991). Chapman and her colleagues (1983) report that female corrections officers perceive unequal opportunities and unequal treatment in promotion. Poole and Pogrebin (1988) uncover a similar perception among women police officers; specifically, after only three years on the job, policewomen view their chances of ever being promoted greatly diminished. A veteran officer who had many years working in the patrol side of the sheriff's department tells of her disappointment in not having an opportunity for advancement:

> I came off the street as a road deputy after 12 years on the front lines. I really did think I had the skills to come here and make some rank and do well, but that will never happen.

Jurik (1985) claims that supervisors who are biased against females working as corrections officers use performance evaluations to discourage them and keep them in subordinate positions. Since performance history is a critical criterion in advancement to supervisory ranks, women officers are viewed as less promotable. One deputy notes the nature of the inequality:

> There is one woman who really is an exceptional deputy and I like her a lot. She is really strong and stern and she knows her job very well. If she were a man, they would think she is the best deputy in the world, but because she is female

> they think she is a bitch. But if a male deputy would act like her, they would promote him real fast.

In those rare instances when a female officer receives a choice assignment or a promotion, she is perceived by male staff as not having earned it. For example, females are often teased about trading sexual favors for advancement:

> There are men on this job that think anytime a woman gets ahead the first thing out of their mouth is: "Oh, I wonder who she's sleeping with?" . . . That's their way of dealing with women who're better than them.

Such sexist attributions of female career advancement serve to impede the acceptance of women into the work subculture, which robs them of important training, peer support, sponsorship, and access to inside information for job assignments and promotional opportunities (Zimmer, 1986). If sexist attitudes and actions are allowed to prevail, women officers are unlikely to be seen as capable of becoming supervisors and joining the ranks of the management.

Among those women in our sample who had attained supervisory positions ($n=6$), there was a consensus that they now experience more hostility and resistance than they had encountered when they were line officers. These women perceive greater resentment on the part of not only the male line staff but their fellow male supervisors as well:

> I finally realized after years on the job that I've been playing gin rummy and the men have been playing poker. . . . We are socialized to be a team player and sacrifice for the good of the group. . . . Men are like sharks. Play on a team with sharks, they'll eat you alive.
>
> I'm under the microscope every day of the week, in everything I say and do. Many are just waiting and watching for me to slip up so they can say I can't handle it. . . .
>
> [As a woman supervisor] you're out there on your own. There's no backup, no support, no "Nice job." Well, that's not entirely so. Some will say one thing to your face, then another behind your back.

Supervisory work in many respects is associated with male role characteristics like independence, initiative, forcefulness, competitiveness, and tough-minded objectivity (Kosinar, 1981). Ironically, although the image of the supervisor is one that emphasizes masculine traits, the tasks that the supervisor actually performs are not exclusively those associated with maleness. Compassion, understanding, and interpersonal warmth, traits associated with the female role, have been shown to be just as important to supervisory success as the male qualities (Brown, 1981; Farkas, 1999; Kim, DeValve, DeValve, & Johnson, 2003). Moreover, women in supervisory positions in jail are a new phenomenon, representing a complete reversal of the historically all-male management staff and directly challenging the traditional conceptions of the relationship between sex and power.

Given the greater exclusiveness of supervisory positions, especially the inner circles of upper management, the entry of women into positions of increased status and power may be seen as disruptive and detrimental to the intimacy, solidarity, and informality of the nearly all-male colleague group. And exclusion from this more powerful male management subculture again results in a lack of access to information, contacts, and informal participation, representing yet another barrier to career advancement.

Another source of resistance to women supervisors is the organizational perception that women simply do not make good managers. They are often viewed as overbearing and domineering, as well as inflexible and overly concerned with bureaucratic routines and details (Rosen & Jerdee, 1973; Schein, 1973). The women supervisors in our study do report sex differences in how they do their jobs. And these differences seem to originate in their performance as line officers (see Fry & Glaser, 1987; Stohr, 1997; Zimmer, 1986; Zupan, 1986; but compare Farkas, 1999; Jenne & Kersting, 1996) For example, Worden (1993) reports that women police officers emphasize rules and regulations more and exercise discretion less frequently than do their male counterparts. This is because the standard operating procedures define roles and evaluation criteria, establishing a level playing field with the men. Women jail officers similarly perceive "going by the book" as a safer method of operation, thus avoiding risky discretionary decision making, which may lead to criticism.

> I've learned it's best to know the rules and stick to them in everything you do in here. Someone's always waiting for you to mess up. . . ; so it's better to have rules you can rely on to do your job. . . . Because if a female officer messes up because she wasn't following the rules, then it's made ten times worse.

And most women in our sample also believe that adhering to rules and regulations is a function of their gender socialization:

> Women pay more attention to detail, more strict abidance to the rules. I mean, the rules are the rules, that's the way we've been socialized. We follow the rules or we lose our turn. And we follow the rules well. Even if some rules don't make sense, if it's a rule, we still follow it.

It is likely that women officers who have successfully survived and advanced in the jail organization still embrace these work strategies, tending to rely on what has worked for them in the past. The consequences of employing such a work strategy in the role of a manager, however, are deleterious, if not predictable, as three women supervisors observe:

> I'm firm but fair and run things by the book. For a man, that's OK. For a woman, it's just being a "bitch" . . . . There's definitely a double standard here.
>
> I would say the male supervisors want to be liked and handle things much more loosely . . . [than I do]. They don't want to be seen as the "bad guy." So they'll delegate . . . to others so they don't get criticized. . . . I'm not here to be their buddy. I'm here to do the best job I can. So I can't "loosen up" or "take it easy" or "giv'em a break." That's not my style. Because I'll tell you right now, there's no "good ole gal" network going to back me up or cover for me if I can't do my job. . . .
>
> On my last [performance evaluation] I received several negative comments about how I handle officers. . . . I was criticized for how I write them up. They think I'm too picky and that I demand too much. . . .

Kanter (1977) argues that negative perceptions of women in supervisory positions reflect sex differences in power and influence within organizations. In particular, performance ratings by supervisors are affected by the supervisor's power and influence; and more powerful supervisors generate higher morale, tend to be less rigid and authoritarian, and are generally better liked. Powerless supervisors, on the other hand, are more likely to be controlling in their relationships with subordinates, show favoritism, and generate lower morale. Since men are more likely to be in formal positions of power and authority and to be part of the informal networks of organizational influence, differences in the perception and behavior of female supervisors are more a function of the unequal distribution of organizational power than a reflection of sex differences in managerial or personal style (South, Bonjean, Corder, & Markam, 1982).

DISCUSSION

Women jail deputies find themselves in an occupational dilemma. Many male jail officers harbor negative attitudes toward competent women co-workers because they perceive women who can perform their job-related tasks satisfactorily as threatening. On the other hand, they view female officers who fail to perform the job adequately as confirming the stereotypical "unfitness" of female workers. Thus, the better officers women become, the greater their threat to the male establishment.

Several observers have noted that gender remains the defining or controlling (i.e., master) status in traditionally male occupations, with women treated first on the basis of their sex role and second on the basis of their work role (Reskin & Roos, 1990; Williams, 1989). Hunt (1990) argues that gender-based norms support discriminatory practices and sexual harassment in the work setting, which in turn reinforce and maintain power differentials. The sexualized work environment is intended to keep a woman subservient by making her feel unwelcome, insecure, and fearful. The strategy is to exert control through intimidation and humiliation.

The consequences of institutional sexism may be such as to discourage aspirations and restrict opportunities, or to instill fear of being maligned or punished for even trying. In short, sexism may reduce the efforts of females to demonstrate their full potential. Systematic devaluation of women's work roles easily becomes self-fulfilling and self-perpetrating. It can create and maintain conditions that minimize the need for males to confront evidence contradicting their stereotypes, or to experience dissonance when they demean female co-workers (Schur, 1984).

Sexual harassment represents a violation of Title VII of the U.S. Civil Rights Act, which bans sex-based discrimination (Deitch, 1993). Any conduct that has the purpose or effect of substantially interfering with an individual's work performance or creating an intimidating, hostile or offensive working environment is prohibited; moreover, employers have an affirmative duty to take "all steps necessary" to prevent such conduct and to take remedial actions when it does occur. Yet, we find a great deal of misunderstanding as to what constitutes sex-based discriminatory practices. For example, Gutek and Morasch (1982) note that "men are more likely than women to project sexuality into ambiguous behavior between sexes at work, and to feel that such sexuality is appropriate in the work environment" (p. 59); consequently, what female workers perceive as unwelcome sexual advances may be viewed by male employees as innocent flattery. Konrad and Gutek (1986) further report that males employed in male-dominated jobs are less inclined than men working in gender-integrated jobs to define their gender-based behavior toward women co-workers as sexual harassment. It appears that gender-integrated work settings foster a greater congruence of definitions of acceptable behavior between the sexes, which may serve to reduce the nature and extent of gender-based behavioral misunderstandings.

A complicating factor in effecting change in the jail setting is the social pathology of a male-dominated work culture. The occupational culture of jail work is based on the values and eccentricities of a cult of masculinity, largely exemplified in behaviors such as aggression, taunting, horseplay, and sexually related conversation and innuendo (Belknap, 1991). Despite significant increases in the number of women in local corrections, the generally higher caliber (and more educated) people entering the field, better professional training, and implementation of policies to control sexual harassment and related misconduct, vestiges of the long-established characteristics of the occupational culture still persist (see Belknap, 1995; Lawrence and Mahan, 1998; Stohr et al., 1998). Since survival in the informal organization requires adherence to the subcultural norms, women must develop appropriate adjustment or coping strategies not only in doing their jobs but also in managing their work relations with male officers. Men tend to misinterpret culturally related behaviors of women jail deputies—largely holding them to a double standard—and cannot understand why they are accused of harassment or conduct unbecoming an officer.

The sexualized work environment of the jail is thus grounded in and supported by a combination of structural factors (e.g., occupational segregation, tokenism, hierarchical power arrangements) and cultural themes and processes (e.g., occupational norms, gender-based stereotypes, status inequality) that become manifest in social interaction. Sex discrimination and job segregation regularly place working women under male supervision and control, heavily dependent on males for their economic security. Because of their subordinate economic and occupational situations, most women have neither autonomy nor authority in workplace relations (Kanter, 1977). These consequences of the sexualized work environment thus have implications that go beyond the job itself.

The prevailing opinion of female officers in all seven facilities was that the elimination of harassment in local corrections organizations was dependent on top administrators enforcing policies against sexual harassment. As long as sexist stereotypes are allowed to pervade the work setting, women officers will be viewed and treated as second-class workers. Lovrich and Stohr (1993) further argue that managers and supervisors in corrections need to transform the work environment into one where women officers are recognized and appreciated as valuable resources and are fully integrated into both formal and informal organizational cultures, both of which are intolerant of sexual and gender harassment. Also, there must be a strong advocacy role adopted by jail administrators in order for female deputies to gain equal opportunities for career advancement (Zimmer, 1989).

In order to minimize harassing behavior in the jail setting, administrators need to invest in the career development of all employees, advance the ideals of professionalism, and establish closer linkages to line staff (Belknap, 1996; Stohr et al., 1998; Zimmer, 1989). Such a work climate would help to lower the level of animosity and offensive behavior directed at women officers by male co-workers. The "affirmative duty" of jail management lies not simply in fostering a general atmosphere which will combat harassing behavior but also in implementing proactive mechanisms to monitor and prevent the conditions that give rise to such actions.

The organization of corrections work itself plays a role in producing and reinforcing workplace attitudes and behavior, and thus the extent to which sexism and sexual harassment may be institutionally tolerated. These discriminatory practices and subsequent difficulties faced by women officers can be affected significantly if the organization implements adequate administrative strategies to promote gender integration and institutionalize measures to provide equality of opportunity.

CONCLUSION

The presence of women in what has long been an exclusively male occupation creates a multitude of individual and organizational conflicts. The workplace functions as a complex occupational and organizational entity that shapes workers' perceptions of self and others. The relationship between gender and organizational status reveals that those work roles assigned to women are seen as appropriate extensions of their more diffuse social role of nurturance. These arrangements can act to reflect, magnify, or distort gender differences, which then confirm prevailing stereotypes and organizational norms. This situation has culminated in male co-workers' and supervisors' limited and often inaccurate appraisal of women officers' true potential and capabilities in the field.

To persist in this state of affairs is untenable because evaluating female officers on the basis of male sex-typed norms distracts from the organization's efforts to implement competency-based standards and reduces its ability to analyze work problems and formulate solutions. The jail must demonstrate a philosophical commitment to the thorough integration of women within the formal and informal organizational structure. The more barriers women face in accessing informal channels of information and conflict resolution, the more they are compelled to respond formally with its associated implications of lesser control and power. Jail officers, whether male or female, are less likely to perform effectively if they are not perceived as exercising legitimate authority under conditions of equality.

The nature and scope of jail work continue to increase in complexity, presenting new job expectations and challenges for male and female officers alike. Given the need to adjust and respond to changing organizational demands, it becomes more critical that officers have the opportunity to hone their unique talents and utilize their special skills with greater latitude. Developing alternative or multiple work strategies would thus permit officers to maximize their effectiveness and accomplish tasks otherwise beyond their capacity. An important initiative in realizing such change in organizational culture is to flatten the hierarchical control mechanisms and eliminate the administrative pressures for worker uniformity that have served to reinforce and maintain traditional job stereotypes in the jail setting. Finally, Wexler and Quinn (1985) report that the number of women present in an organization is a critical-mass variable in facilitating gender-integrated work groups. This finding would seem to encourage more aggressive recruitment and retention of women officers who by their sheer numbers may promote the development of an androgynous work culture where an individual officer's success is predicated on ability, rather than sexual physiology.

NOTES

1. Inmate and officer distributions by sex for each facility are shown below, along with the respective sample sizes and number of study participants. Facilities labeled A–D are jails; facilities E–G are detention centers:

	Facility						
	A	B	C	D	E	F	G
Inmates							
Male	279	391	656	1739	218	475	541
Female	18	34	67	172	27	53	35
Officers							
Male	38	158	146	285	105	159	92
Female	21	26	29	81	45	27	36
50% Sample of Female Officers	11	13	15	41	23	14	18
Female Study Participants	10	10	13	30	18	12	15

2. In all seven facilities women officers were assigned to supervise both male and female inmates. The duties of jail deputies were the same for both male and female officers. This is an important occupational issue because many jails in this nation do not permit women officers to work in male inmate housing units, which results in unequal opportunities for women to advance within the organizations.

REFERENCES

Bartol, C.R., Bergen, G.T., Volckens, J.S., & Knoras, K. (1992). Women in small-town policing: Job performance and stress. *Criminal Justice and Behavior, 19,* 240–259.

Belknap, J. (1996). The invisible woman: Gender, crime, and justice. Belmont, CA: Wadsworth.

Belknap, J. (1991). Women in conflict: An analysis of women correctional officers. *Women & Criminal Justice, 2,* 89–115.

Bowersox, M.S. (1981). Women in corrections: Competence, competition, and the social responsibility norm. *Criminal Justice and Behavior, 8,* 491–499.

Britton, D.M. (2003). *At work in the iron cage: The prison as gendered organization.* New York: New York University Press.

Brown, L.K. (1981). *The woman manager in the United States.* Washington, DC: Business and Professional Women's Foundation.

Camp, S.D., Steiger, T.L., Wright, K.N., Saylor, W.G., & Gilman, E. (1997). Affirmative action and the "level playing field": Comparing perceptions of own and minority job advancement opportunities. *Prison Journal, 77,* 313–334.

Carlson, J.R., Anson, R.H., & Thomas, G. (2003). Correctional officer burnout and stress: Does gender matter? *Prison Journal, 83,* 277–288.

Chapman, J.R., Minor, E.K., Rieker, P.P., Mills, T.R., & Bottum, M. (1983). *Women employed in corrections.* Washington, DC: U.S. Department of Justice, National Institute of Justice.

Coser, R.L., & Rokoff, G. (1971). Women in the occupational world: Social disruption and conflict. *Social Problems, 18,* 535–554.

Crouch, B.M., & Alpert, G.P. (1982). Sex and occupational socialization among prison guards: A longitudinal study. *Criminal Justice and Behavior, 9,* 159–176.

Cullen, F.T., Link, B.G., Wolfe, N.T., & Frank, J. (1985). The Social dimensions of correctional officer stress. *Criminal Justice and Behavior, 9,* 159–176.

Davies, C. (1982). Ethnic jokes, moral values, and social boundaries. *British Journal of Sociology, 33,* 383–403.

Deitch, C. (1993). Gender, race, and class politics and the inclusion of women in Title VII of the 1964 Civil Rights Act. *Gender and Society, 7,* 183–203.

Dupreel, E. (1928). Le probleme sociologique du rise. *Revue Philosophique, 106,* 213–260.

Dworkin, A. (1974). *Woman hating.* New York: E.P. Dutton.

Erez, E., & Tontodonato, P. (1992). Sexual harassment in the criminal justice system. In I.L. Moyer (Ed.), *The changing roles of women in the criminal justice system: Offenders, victims, and professionals* (pp. 227–252). Prospect Heights, IL: Waveland Press.

Farkas, M.A. (1999). "Inmate supervisory style: Does gender make a difference?" *Women & Criminal Justice, 10,* 25–45.

Farley, L. (1978). *Sexual shakedown.* New York: McGraw Hill.

Farnworth, L. (1992). Women doing a man's job: Female prison officers working in a male prison. *Australian and New Zealand Journal of Criminology, 25,* 278–296.

Fox, M.F., & Hesse-Biber, S. (1984). *Women at work.* Palo Alto, CA: Mayfield.

Fry, L.J., & Glaser, D. (1987). Gender differences in work adjustment of prison employees. *Journal of Offender Counseling, Services, and Rehabilitation, 12,* 39–52.

Glaser, B.G., & Strauss, A.L. (1967). *The discovery of grounded theory: strategies for qualitative research.* Chicago: Aldine.

Gray, S. (1984). Sharing the shopfloor: Women and men on the assembly line. *Radical America, 18,* 69–88.

Gross, G.R., Larson, S.J., Urban, G.D., & Zupan, L.L. (1994). Gender differences in occupational stress among correctional officers. *American Journal of Criminal Justice, 18,* 219–234.

Gruber, J.E., & Bjorn, L. (1982). Blue-collar blues: The sexual harassment of women autoworkers. *Work and Occupations, 4,* 271–298.

Gutek, B.A., & Morasch, B. (1982). Sex-ratios, sex-role spillover, and sexual harassment of women at work. *Journal of Social Issues, 38,* 55–74.

Hemmens, C., Stohr, M.K., Schoeler, M., & Miller, B. (2002). One step up, two steps back: The progression of perceptions of women's work in prisons and jails. *Journal of Criminal Justice, 30,* 473–489.

Hochschild, A.R. (1973). A review of sex role research. In J. Huber (Ed.), *Changing women in a changing society* (pp. 249–267). Chicago: University of Chicago Press.

Hogan, N.L., Lambert, E.G., Hepburn, J.R., Burton, Jr., V.S., & Cullen, F.T. (2004). Is there a difference? Exploring male and female correctional officers' definition of and response to conflict situations. *Women & Criminal Justice, 15,* 143–165.

Hunt, J. (1990). The logic of sexism among police. *Women & Criminal Justice, 1,* 3–30.

Jacobs, J.A. (1989). *Revolving doors: Sex segregation and women's careers.* Stanford, CA: Stanford University Press.

Jenne, D.L., & Kersting, R.C. (1996). Aggression and women correctional officers in prison. *Prison Journal, 76,* 442–460.

Johnson, L. (1991). Job strain among police officers: Gender comparisons. *Police Studies, 14,* 12–26.

Jurik, N.C. (1985). An officer and a lady: Organizational barriers to women working as correctional officers in men's prisons. *Social Problems, 32,* 375–388.

Jurik, N.C. (1988). Striking a balance: Female correctional officers, gender role stereotypes, and male prisons. *Sociological Inquiry, 58,* 291–305.

Jurik, N.C., & Halembra, G.J. (1984). Gender, working conditions, and the job satisfaction of women in a non-traditional occupation: Female correctional officers in men's prisons. *Sociological Quarterly, 25,* 551–566.

Jurik, N.C., & Martin, S.E. (2001). Femininities, masculinities, and organizational conflict: Women in criminal justice occupations. In C.M. Renzetti & L. Goodstein, L. (Eds.), *Women, crime, and criminal justice* (pp. 264–281). Los Angeles: Roxbury.

Kanter, R.M. (1977). *Men and women of the corporation.* New York: Basic Books.

Kim, A.S., DeValve, M., DeValve, E.Q., & Johnson, W.W. (2003). Female wardens: Results from a national survey of state correctional executives. *Prison Journal, 83,* 406–425.

Kissel, P.J., & Katsampes, P.L. (1980). The impact of women corrections officers on the functioning of institutions housing male inmates. *Journal of Offender Counseling, Services, and Rehabilitation, 4,* 213–231.

Konrad, A.M., & Gutek, B.A. (1986). Impact of work experiences on attitudes toward sexual harassment. *Administrative Science Quarterly, 31,* 422–438.

Kosinar, P. (1981). Socialization and self-esteem: Women and management. In B.L. Forisha & B.H. Goldman (Eds.), Outsiders on the inside: Women and organizations (pp. 31–41). Englewood Cliffs, NJ: Prentice-Hall.

Lawrence, R., & Mahan, S. (1998). Women corrections officers in men's prisons: Acceptance and perceived job performance. *Women & Criminal Justice, 9,* 63–86.

Laws, J.L. (1979). *The second X: Sex role and social role.* New York: Elsevier.

Lovrich, N.P., & Stohr, M.K. (1993). Gender and jail work: Correctional policy implications of perceptual diversity in the work force. *Policy Studies Review, 12,* 66–84.

Lutze, F.E., & Murphy, D.W. (1999). Ultramasculine prison environments and inmates' adjustment: It's time to move beyond the "boys will be boys" paradigm. *Justice Quarterly, 16,* 709–734.

MacKinnon, C.A. (1979). *Sexual harassment of working women.* New Haven, CT: Yale University Press.

MacKinnon, C.A. (1982). Feminism, Marxism, method, and the state: An agenda for theory. *Signs, 7,* 515–544.

Martin, S.E. (1989). Sexual harassment: The link joining gender stratification, sexuality, and women's economic status. In J. Freeman (Ed.), *Women: A feminist perspective* (pp. 57–75). Mountain View, CA: Mayfield.

Meyer, H.H., & Lee, M.D. (1978). *Women in traditionally male jobs: The experiences of ten public utility companies.* Washington, DC: U.S. Department of Labor, Employment and Training Administration.

Millett, K. (1971). *Sexual politics.* New York: Avon Books.

Morash, M., & Haar, R.N. (1995). Gender, workplace problems, and stress in policing. *Justice Quarterly, 12,* 113–140.

Morton, J.B. (1991). *Change, challenge, and choices: Women's role in modern corrections.* Laurel, MD: American Correctional Association.

O'Farrell, B., & Harlan, S. (1982). Craftworkers and clerks: The effect of male coworker hostility on women's satisfaction with nontraditional jobs. *Social Problems, 29,* 252–265.

Padavic, I. (1991). The re-creation of gender in a male workplace. *Symbolic Interaction, 14,* 279–294.

Perkins, C.A., Stephan, J.J., & Beck, A.J. (1995). *Jails and jail inmates 1993–94.* Washington, DC: U.S. Department of Justice, Bureau of Justice Statistics.

Petersen, C.B. (1982). Doing time with the boys: An analysis of women correctional officers in all-male facilities. In B.R. Price & N. Sokoloff (Eds.), *Criminal justice and women* (pp. 437–460). New York: Clark Boardman.

Pogrebin, M.R., & Poole, E.D. (1988). Humor in the briefing room: A study of the strategic uses of humor among police. *Journal of Contemporary Ethnography, 17,* 183–210.

Pogrebin, M.R., & Poole, E.D. (1997). The sexualized work environment: A look at women jail officers. *Prison Journal, 77,* 41–57.

Pollock, J.M. (1986). *Sex and supervision: Guarding male and female inmates.* New York: Greenwood.

Pollock, J.M. (1995). Women in corrections: Custody and the "caring ethic." In A.V. Merlo & J.M. Pollock (Eds.), *Women, law, and social control* (pp. 97–116). Boston: Allyn and Bacon.

Poole, E.D., & Pogrebin, M.R. (1988a). Factors affecting the decision to remain in policing: A study of women officers. *Journal of Police Science and Administration, 16,* 49–55.

Reskin, B.F., & Roos, P.A. (1990). *Job queues, gender queues: Explaining women's inroads into male occupations.* Philadelphia: Temple University Press.

Rosen, B., & Jerdee, T.H. (1973). The influence of sex-role stereotypes on evaluation of male and female supervisory behavior. *Journal of Applied Psychology, 57,* 44–48.

Safilios-Rothschild, C. (1979). *Sex role stereotypes and sex discrimination: A synthesis and critique of the literature.* Washington, DC: U.S. Department of Health, Education, and Welfare, National Institute of Education.

Schein, V.E. (1973). The relationship between sex stereotypes and requisite management characteristics. *Journal of Applied Psychology, 57,* 95–100.

Schur, E.M. (1979). *Interpreting deviance.* New York: Harper & Row.

Schur, E.M. (1984). *Labeling women deviant: Gender, stigma, and social control.* Philadelphia: Temple University Press.

Seckman, M.A., & Couch, C.J. (1989). Jocularity, sarcasm, and relationships. *Journal of Contemporary Ethnography, 18,* 327–344.

South, S.J., Bonjean, C.M., Corder, J., & Markham, W.T. (1982). Sex and power in the federal bureaucracy: A comparative analysis of male and female supervisors. *Work and Occupations, 9,* 233–254.

Stephan, J.J. (2001). *Census of jails, 1999.* Washington, DC: U.S. Department of Justice, Bureau of Justice Statistics.

Stockard, J., & Johnson, M.M. (1980). *Sex roles.* Englewood Cliffs, NJ: Prentice-Hall.

Stohr, M.K. (2006). "Yes, I've paid the price, but look how much I gained": The struggle and status of female correctional officers. In C.M. Renzetti, L. Goodstein, & S.L. Miller (Eds.), *Rethinking gender, crime, and justice: Feminist readings* (pp. 262–277). Los Angeles: Roxbury.

Stohr, M.K., Lovrich, N.P., & Mays, G.L. (1997). Service v. security focus in training assessments: Testing gender differences among women's jail correctional officers. *Women & Criminal Justice, 9,* 65–85.

Stohr, M.K., Lovrich, N.P., & Wood, M. (1996). Service versus security concerns in contemporary jails: Testing general differences in training topic assessments. *Journal of Criminal Justice, 24,* 437–448.

Stohr, M.K., Mays, G.L., Beck, A.C., & Kelly, T. (1998). Sexual harassment in women's jails. *Journal of Contemporary Criminal Justice, 14,* 135–155.

Swerdlow, M. (1989). Men's accommodations to women entering a nontraditional occupation: A case of rapid transit operatives. *Gender & Society, 3,* 373–387.

Timmins, W.M., & Hainsworth, B.E. (1989). Attracting and retaining females in law enforcement. *International Journal of Offender Therapy and Comparative Criminology, 33,* 197–205.

Van Voorhis, P., Cullen, F.T., Link, B.G., & Wolfe, N.T. (1991). The impact of race and gender on correctional officers' orientation to the integrated environment. *Journal of Research in Crime and Delinquency, 28,* 472–500.

Walshok, M.L. (1981). *Blue-collar women: Pioneers on the male frontier.* New York: Anchor Books.

West, C., & Zimmerman, D.H. (1987). Doing gender. *Gender and Society, 1,* 125–151.

Wexler, J.G., & Logan, D.D. (1983). Sources of stress among women police officers. *Journal of Police Science and Administration, 11,* 46–53.

Wexler, J.G., & Quinn, V. (1985). Considerations in the training and development of women sergeants. *Journal of Police Science and Administration, 13,* 98–105.

Williams, C.L. (1989). *Gender differences at work: Women and men in nontraditional occupations.* Berkeley: University of California Press.

Worden, A.P. (1993). The attitudes of women and men in policing: Testing conventional and contemporary wisdom. *Criminology, 31,* 203–237.

Wright, K.N., & Saylor, W.G. (1991). Male and female employees' perceptions of prison work: Is there a difference? *Justice Quarterly, 8,* 505–524.

Zimmer, L.E. (1987). How women reshape the prison guard role. *Gender and Society, 1,* 415–431.

Zimmer, L.E. (1989). Solving women's employment problems in corrections: Shifting the burden to administrators. *Women & Criminal Justice, 1,* 55–80.

Zimmer, L.E. (1988). Tokenism and women in the workplace: The limits of gender-neutral theory. *Social Problems, 35,* 64–73.

Zimmer, L.E. (1986). *Women guarding men.* Chicago: University of Chicago Press.

Zupan, L.L. (1986). Gender-related differences in correctional officers' perceptions and attitudes. *Journal of Criminal Justice, 14,* 349–361.

Zupan, L.L. (1992). The progress of women correctional officers in all-male prisons. In I.L. Moyer (Ed.), *The changing roles of women in the criminal justice system: Offenders, victims, and professionals* (pp. 323–343). Prospect Heights, IL: Waveland Press.

REVIEW QUESTIONS

1. How does sexism experienced by female correctional officers differ from sexism experienced in other occupations?
2. What sorts of effective response strategies can female officers employ to confront the occupational dilemma that they face on a daily basis?
3. What sorts of structural change can be made that would effectively reverse the trend of institutional sexism described in this article?

XII

DEATH ROW

READING 30

The Death Row Community Revisited

Lessons Learned from Community Psychology

Bruce A. Arrigo

Carol Fowler

Kristie R. Blevins

This article theorizes that correctional personnel, condemned inmates, and the affected family/friends coalesce to form what they term an "execution community." In particular, a community psychology framework is used to account for the sense of community that emerges within and across four groups: death-row workers, inmates, the families and loved ones of the inmates, and families and loved ones of the victim. Theoretical consideration is given to the sense of membership (spirit), perceived influence over the execution outcome (trust), reinforcement/fulfillment of needs (trade), and shared emotional commitment (art) experienced within and across these four sets of constituencies. The authors make the argument that a sense of interdependence and interconnectedness exists among the four constituencies and that these relationships constitute a loosely formed death row community.

The modern understanding of capital punishment in the United States has evolved considerably in recent years (e.g., Amnesty International, 1987, 2007; Bedau, 1984, 1987; Bohm, 2007; Garland, 2002, 2005; Haas & Inciardi, 1988; Jones, 1994). Much of this literature raises questions about whether and to what extent executions actually deter crime (Bilionis, 1991; Bohm, Clark, & Aveni, 1991; Shepherd, 2004; Thomson, 1999). Other studies consider whether capital punishment is applied in a discriminatory manner based on race (e.g., Williams & Holcomb, 2001, 2004; Young, 1991), gender (e.g., Rapaport, 1991; Williams & Holcomb, 2004), or socioeconomic status (Mitchell & Sindanius, 1995; Sweeney & Haney, 1992). Overall, there is an abundance of research investigating the purpose and effects of the death penalty, as well as the many issues surrounding differences in the cases in which capital punishment is sought. To date, however, there are only modest assessments of the death row phenomenon and its relationship to capital punishment (cf. Arrigo & Fowler, 2001; Bonta & Gendreau, 1990; Farr, 1998; Smykla, 1987). This lack of research is troubling especially since important social, legal, and psychological connections exist between life on death row and the execution process itself (Johnson, 1998; Keve, 1992).

The length of time in prison while awaiting execution can exceed several years. Typically, prisoners sentenced to die spend over a decade on death row, and some have been awaiting their execution for more than 20 years (Death Penalty Information Center [DPIC], 2007c). During this time on death row, various interpersonal and group dynamics emerge among offenders and prison personnel concerning life on death row and capital punishment (e.g., Arriens, 1997). While extended incarceration, under any circumstances, is an emotionally debilitating process (Bonta & Gendreau, 1990; Haney, 1997, 2006), it is particularly painful and stressful while awaiting execution (Von Drehle, 1996). In fact, psychologists have observed that "protracted periods in the confines of death row can make inmates suicidal, delusional, and insane" and have named such resulting psychological effects "death row syndrome" (DPIC, 2007c: 4). Indeed, several significant constitutional questions exist about the inhumanity of subjecting one to such an ordeal (e.g., Eighth Amendment prohibition against cruel and unusual punishment). These social, psychological, and legal considerations profoundly link the death row phenomenon with the execution process.

One way to understand the linkages between capital punishment and death row is to examine those groups that make up the execution community at any given facility. This is different from presenting aggregate or comparative data on prisoner cohorts; rather, death row groups represent various constituencies. In fact, a variety of non-incarcerated individuals greatly impact and help contribute to the meaning of death row (Smykla, 1987; Vasquez, 1993). Arguably, the death row phenomenon consists not only of death row inmates, but also of those correctional personnel who work with them, as well as the family members of both victims and of the prisoners who are awaiting execution (Cabana, 1996).

This chapter is a modification of an article by Arrigo and Fowler (2001), which explored whether a death row or execution community in fact exists. If such a community can be identified, it sheds greater light on the meaning and practice of capital punishment. Further, understanding this phenomenon may make it possible to humanize the overall practice of capital punishment. For example, by increasing the degree to which the execution experience itself is personalized, given how various groups constituting the death row community are affected by it, important correctional, psychological, and legal implications become much more evident. In addition, if the phenomenon of an execution community informs life on death row, then it suggests that investigating its behavior must extend beyond the limits of criminal justice to the disciplines of psychology, victimology, organizational studies, and other related fields.

One perspective for investigating the notion of a death row community comes from psychology. Psychologists have reexamined what constitutes a community and what a sense of community means (McMillan, 1996; McMillan & Chavis, 1986). Although these observations are largely speculative, considerable room exists in which to apply this model to penal behavior in general and the organization of death row in particular. This chapter relies on the sense of community thesis in order to explore whether an execution community can be identified.

Turning to psychology (and particularly *community* psychology) to explain whether a criminal justice phenomenon exists is not unusual. The disciplines of law, criminal justice, and criminology routinely turn to community-based or humanistic models when evaluating the operation of various facets of the criminal justice system (Territo, Halsted, & Bromley, 1998). In fact, subspecialty areas such as community corrections (Toch, 1998), community policing (Miller & Hess, 2007), community courts (Curtis, 2000; Fletcher, 1995), and community or restorative justice (Van Ness & Strong, 1997; Van Ness, 2006) have become part of popular crime and justice discourse. Therefore, it is feasible that community psychology may facilitate the understanding of death row, its organization, and its membership groups.

The next section of this chapter is a review of the relevant community literature, with a focus on its social and psychological dimensions. We then review the research on death row and capital punishment focusing on those groups or "tiers" impacted by the execution experience. Next, the sense of community model is applied to the behavior of death row groups to ascertain whether and to what extent the construct of community is useful for understanding the death row phenomenon. The chapter concludes with a discussion of implications related to capital punishment and for future research in the area.

WHAT CONSTITUTES A COMMUNITY?

It has been established that there are two basic units of human social organization that are universal: the community and the family (e.g., Durkheim, 1965). Of these two units, community is the older. Indeed, "people lived in groups even before there were families [a]nd will continue to need to maintain communal ties when and if the family, as it is commonly known, disappears" (Rose, 1977: 371). Here, it is important to note that living in groups does not necessarily refer to living within certain geographical boundaries. Rather, a group, or community, may be formed by individuals that are connected in some way, regardless of their physical location (Stein, 1960; see also Stacey, 1969).

While there are several different ways in which "community" may be defined, psychological insights have resulted in one way to understand this oldest of social organizations. Specifically, psychology scholars have reconsidered what a sense of community includes (McMillan, 1996; McMillan & Chavis, 1986). Their research initially resulted in four elements that composed the definition of community: 1) membership; 2) influence; 3) integration and fulfillment of needs; and 4) shared emotional connection (McMillan & Chavis, 1986). In the revision of this formula, the four elements were renamed spirit, trust, trade, and art, respectively (McMillan, 1996). We assert that both the definition and theory of this model will help ground our investigation of death row groups and their behavior.

The first element of community, membership, is "the feeling of belonging or sharing a sense of personal relatedness" (McMillan & Chavis, 1986: 9). Membership also requires boundaries, which signify "that there are people who belong and people who do not" (p. 9). When McMillan (1996) renamed the membership element spirit, he did so to more greatly emphasize the "spark of friendship" that an individual needs in order to "make connections to others so that [each of us has] a setting and an audience to express unique aspects of our personality" (p. 315).

Influence is the second element of community. It refers to "the sense of mattering, of making a difference to a group and of the group mattering to its members" (McMillan & Chavis, 1986: 9). McMillan (1996) later renamed this second principle trust because "[t]he salient element of influence is the development of trust. Trust develops through a community's use of its power" (p. 318).

Integration and fulfillment of needs is the third element of McMillan and Chavis's (1986) sense of community. This element is characterized as reinforcement; that is "the feeling that members' needs will be met by the resources received through their membership in the group" (p. 9). In his revision, McMillan (1996) called this element trade. This more concise term was chosen to represent different types of exchange that may be conducted within a community, starting at a personal level (such as mutual self-disclosure) and expanding to a social, barter, or market economy.

The fourth element is shared emotional connection, which is described as "the commitment and belief that members have shared and will share history, common places, time together, and similar experiences (McMillan & Chavis, 1986: 9). This principle was revised by McMillan (1996) and renamed art to capture what the former term represents. Art consists of differing expressions of shared history, including song, dance, symbols, rituals, holidays, and the like.

McMillan's (1996) revision of the sense of community construct also addressed the interdependence of the four elements. He referred to this interdependence as a "self-reinforcing circle" (p. 323). He also maintained that the interconnectedness of the four elements that make up the sense of community construct functions as follows:

> Spirit with respected authority becomes Trust. In turn, Trust is the basis of creating an economy of social Trade. Together, these elements create a shared history that becomes the community's story symbolized in A[rt] . . . Art supports the Spirit that is in the first element of sense of community (McMillan, 1996: 322–323).

A SOCIAL AND PSYCHOLOGICAL APPRAISAL OF THE DEFINITION OF DEATH ROW

Before attempting to define death row and examining the possible phenomenon of an execution community, it is first necessary to revisit some basic facts about capital punishment in the United States. Capital punishment is the ultimate sanction that can be imposed during criminal sentencing. It has its roots in the retributive philosophy of punishment with its focus on just deserts (Von Hirsch, 1976; Radelet & Akers, 1996). Just deserts is punishment that is deserved and "appropriate to the type and severity of the crime committed" (Schmalleger, 1997: 281; see also, Bedau & Cassell, 2005). The goal of retribution and just deserts, then, is proportionality and equity, and it "is the earliest known rationale for punishment" (Schmalleger, 1997: 280; Von Hirsch, 1976: 15–16). To date, since the death penalty was reinstated in 1976, 1,099 executions have been carried out in the United States. Of these, 929 were by lethal injection, 154 were by electrocution, 11 were by gas, three were by hanging, and two were by firing squad (DPIC, 2007b). As of January 1, 2007, there were 3,350 individuals awaiting execution on death row (DPIC, 2007a).

Some conflicting research exists regarding how death row inmates view their confinement situations. Bonta and Gendreau (1990) reviewed seven different studies conducted between 1962 and 1987. They concluded that, overall, inmates offered mixed opinions related to the physical and mental health effects of prison life while on death row. However, researchers who have interviewed or conducted psychological tests with death row inmates have found evidence of the presence of a range of symptoms (Dicks, 1990; DPIC, 2007c; Johnson, 1979). Common symptoms include insomnia, depression, paranoia, fear, powerlessness, mood lability, and feeling emotionally drained or empty. Further, serious psychological disorders are found more frequently among death row inmates than among the general prison population (Cunningham & Vigen, 2002). Johnson (1998) observes that:

> [d]eath row is the most total of total institutions, the penitentiary most demanding of penitence, the prison most debilitating and disabling in its confinement. On death row the allegorical pound of flesh is just the beginning. Here the whole person is consumed. The spirit is captured and gradually worn down, then the body is disposed of (p. 71).

The fact that death row inmates know they are condemned to die is not the only thing that separates them from inmates in the general prison population. As one might expect, condemned prisoners experience the institution itself differently than other inmates. Because death row inmates are often perceived as having nothing to lose, and therefore more likely to violate the rules or even commit suicide, they are monitored 24 hours a day. This monitoring goes beyond the traditional checks by guards to include closed circuit television and audio recording. They are also housed in individual cells where they are generally unable to see other inmates (though they may be able to hear them). Further, condemned inmates have strict limitations concerning visitation. Besides legal, spiritual, and media visits, most death row facilities allow only one visit per week, and visitors must be immediate family. Consequently, friends or other loved ones may not visit. Showers are allowed only three times per week, and only one hour per day may be spent outside of the cell. If the individual chooses to spend this hour exercising, it must be done at a time when no one else is using the exercise area (Greene, Buckley, Stetler, & Haney, 2003). If nothing else, death row inmates likely spend much more time alone than do inmates in the general prison population (e.g., Chessman, 2006).

Nevertheless, the inmates housed on death row do not make up the entire death row unit. Indeed, there are several other individuals who must be considered among those composing death row (e.g., Dicks, 1990; Johnson, 1998). A second tier of persons composing the death row unit consists of correctional personnel. The correctional officers, administrative staff, medical and mental health personnel, and those persons who provide religious or spiritual services are, arguably, an extension of death row and the inmates located there. As Cabana (1996) asserts, "[e]xecutions do not take place within a vacuum" (p. 45); it must not be taken for granted that the day at the office for these staff can be termed "death work" (p. 45) and as such, the job carries with it the possibility of much stress and distress: moral, physical, psychological, and spiritual.

Participating in the actual execution of another human being may profoundly affect correctional and administrative staff (Brodsky, Zapf, & Boccaccini, 2001;

Keve, 1992; Thigpen, 1993). On many occasions, one's personal religious beliefs must occupy a backseat to the legal sanctioned act of execution (Martin, 1993). Spiritual, medical, and mental health personnel are responsible for promoting human welfare as the basis of their professional ethics, and, on death row, these staff members regularly provide services to condemned men and women (Haney, 2006; Halpern, 2002; Kermani & Drob, 1988). Some of these services (e.g., restoring a death row inmate's psychological competence through the administration of psychotropic medication) can lead directly to execution (Arrigo & Tasca, 1999; Brodsky et al., 2001; Heilbrun, Radelet, & Dvoskin, 1992).

A third tier of individuals impacted by death row consists of family members and loved ones of the victim. Based on the classical model of criminal law and American jurisprudence, justice should be meted out swiftly, surely, and harshly for those found guilty of a crime (Beccaria, 1963; Beirne, 1991; see also Wilson, 1983 for the neoclassical criminological model). In spite of this, for today's crime victims and their families, this ideal has all but disappeared with the many years of arduous appeals. Consequently, the families and loved ones of victims are typically subjected to the lengthy appeal process before there is closure to the violence and brutality they suffered at the hands of the offender (Jones, 1994). However, it should be noted that not all family members and loved ones of victims seek closure in the form of the actual execution. In fact, there are several murder victims' family members that not only oppose capital punishment, but are also active in trying to make their opinions known and abolish the death penalty completely. Besides religious and other personal beliefs against capital punishment, these individuals generally state that killing another individual will not bring back their loved one and would only make another family suffer at the loss of a loved one (Murder Victim's Families for Human Rights [MVFHR], 2007; Murder Victim's Families for Reconciliation, Inc., 2007). Hence, while members of this group all have experienced the murder of a loved one, they may experience the capital punishment process very differently depending on whether or not they support the impending execution of the offender.

The fourth tier of people influenced by death row includes the family and friends of the death row inmate. In the original version of this manuscript (Arrigo & Fowler, 2001) these individuals were included in a single tier along with the loved ones of the victims. However, as will be discussed, additional research has shed light on the effects of capital punishment for family members of the condemned. Therefore, while there may be some overlap among experiences of family members of both the victims and the offenders, enough differences exist such that they can be divided into two separate tiers.

Like the family members of victims, the loved ones of death row inmates also seek resolution to the painful reality they confront. Unable to meaningfully alter or ameliorate their own circumstances, they struggle to endure amidst a climate in which the offender can be counted, at best, among the living dead. As others have observed, the prisoner's loved ones are powerless to change the situation (Cabana, 1996; Smykla, 1987).

A study conducted with family members of inmates on Alabama's death row poignantly reveals the sustained impact of the execution experience for the prisoner's relatives. Smykla (1987) found that "families that faced the threat of a relative's legal execution the longest experienced no meaningful reduction in suffering compared to families that faced that threat for shorter periods of time" (p. 338). "Suffering" was described as including prolonged or distorted grief reactions with symptoms comparable to persons who experienced missing children, had family members who were prisoners of war, or had terminally ill relatives. This and other studies have shown that family members of death row prisoners often suffer from symptoms including lowered self-esteem, self- or other-induced social isolation, feelings of powerlessness, acquisition of medical or mental illnesses, suicidality, and loss of social and intimate relationships (Beck, Blackwell, Leonard, & Mears, 2003; Beck, Britto, & Andres, 2007; Smykla, 1987). These reactions can appear soon after arrest and continue well past the execution.

The offenders' loved ones will also face other challenges. In addition to anticipating the death of a loved one, they will likely be subject to intense media attention throughout the capital punishment process. While the victims' loved ones may face the same amount of media attention, it is different for the family members of the offender because they must also contend with the fact that many members of the general public are in favor of the execution (Beck & Jones, 2007). Further, family members of the condemned often face problems when visiting the prison. First, since states typically have only one death row facility, family members must travel long distances for visitation. Second, conditions for visitation of death row inmates are very impersonal; completely monitored and recorded with no physical contact (see Greene et al., 2003). Such limited contact may lead to family members feeling as though they have already lost their loved one, even though he or she has not yet been executed.

AN APPLICATION OF THE SENSE OF COMMUNITY CONSTRUCT TO DEATH ROW

While various membership groups are certainly involved in and impacted by legal execution, it remains to be seen whether they collectively compose a death row community. To address this question, we use the elements of community as set forth by McMillan and Chavis (1986) and revised by McMillan (1996). They contend that their community model can be generalized in a variety of institutional contexts and that "the definition and theory of sense of community . . . [apply] equally . . . to all types of communities because of their common core (McMillan & Chavis, 1986: 19). They note, however, that the importance of each of the four elements will vary, "depending on the particular community and its membership" (p. 19). Accordingly, their definitional and theoretical typology can be tested by applying it to a broad range of individuals grouped together in some way. Arguably, one such collection of related individuals, brought together by a combination of both location and interests (as described above), includes those composing membership in the four tiers affected by death row. Thus, it may be possible to integrate the sense of community definition and theory with the execution community constituencies.[1] In order to more systematically, though provisionally, apply the sense of community construct to death row and the four membership tiers we identified, McMillan's more recent and concise terminology will be used (see Table 1).

Spirit

There is one common factor that unites all death row constituencies: The eventual execution of a prisoner. Each person, regardless of membership group, has some emotional investment in the government sanctioned death of an inmate. This emotional investment depends, in part, on the person's role with, and relationship to, the prisoner. In the case of an inmate's family member, for example, the execution's impact can have severe emotional consequences (Beck & Jones, 2007; Dicks, 1990; Smykla, 1987). There can also be emotional consequences for the victim's family. Of course, the direction of these consequences (e.g., closure versus sadness or disappointment) differs depending on the perspective of the individual (MVFHR, 2007). The correctional personnel that work on death row may also be affected by the execution. Regardless of whether or not such personnel believe in state-sanctioned death, these employees have come to know these inmates by having work-related contact with them, often for several years. Even death row personnel who are not directly involved in the execution process itself will likely be influenced by the execution (see Pickett & Stowers, 2002). Death row inmates themselves must not only deal with the trauma of their own impending executions, but they routinely live this reality through the experience of capital punishment for others on death row (Chessman, 2006; Parker, 1992).

Admittedly, the emotionally charged relationships found among various death row collectives may not be characterized as friendships; however, there is a distinct boundary present separating the execution community from other types of prisoners and their related staff, victims, and family members. In addition, the spark of "friendship" described by McMillan (1996) refers to a requisite space and audience where connections to others are *possible.* Clearly, the different membership groups composing the execution community have a setting (i.e., the prison) in which to "express unique aspects of their [respective] personalit[ies]" (McMillan, 1996: 318). Thus, the death row community does, in fact, embody a sense of spirit: The relatedness of its tiers and membership in any one of its groups is expressed through the ultimate and most final of all boundaries—death.

Trust

The death penalty in the United States is an ongoing controversy, specifically concerning such issues as cruel and unusual punishment (e.g., *Furman v. Georgia,*

[1]This analysis does not specifically chronicle the reality of death row (Arriens, 1997; Von Drehle, 1996) and does not subsequently link this reality to the psychological sense of community thesis. Instead, this chapter focuses on whether, and to what extent, different collectives, involved in the execution process, function as a cohesive group based on the principles contained in community psychology. Although the former assessment is worthwhile, it is decidedly beyond the scope of the present analysis.

TABLE 1 The Execution Community

Sense of Community Elements	Membership Groups			
	Prisoners	Family Members of the Prisoner	Correctional Personnel	Family Members of the Victim
1. Spirit	Relatedness of the group expressed through death as the ultimate boundary.	Relatedness of the group expressed through death as the ultimate boundary.	Relatedness of the group expressed through death as the ultimate boundary.	Relatedness of the group expressed through death as the ultimate boundary.
2. Trust	Group power is achieved through working through the appellate process.	Group power is achieved through joining activist groups.	Group power is achieved through participation in debriefing and other institution-sponsored programs or identification with professional organizations.	Group power is achieved through utilizing victim advocacy services or and/or joining activist groups.
3. Trade	Information, such as literature, is a traded material resource for the group. Pain is a traded nonmaterial resource exchanged across membership groups.	Information, such as literature, is a traded material resource for the group. Pain is a traded nonmaterial resource exchanged across membership groups.	The value system of rewards is a material resource for the group. Pain is a traded nonmaterial resource exchanged across membership groups.	Information, such as literature, is a traded material resource for the group. Pain is a traded nonmaterial resource exchanged across membership groups.
4. Art	Language symbolizes a shared emotional connection.	Language symbolizes a shared emotional connection.	Language symbolizes a shared emotional connection.	Language symbolizes a shared emotional connection.

1972), execution of the mentally retarded (e.g., *Atkins v. Virginia,* 2002; *Penry v. Lynaugh,* 1989), execution of the mentally incompetent (e.g., *Ford v. Wainwright,* 1986; *Singleton v. Norris,* 2003), and the legal age of execution (e.g., *Eddings v. Oklahoma,* 1982; *Gregg v. Georgia,* 1976). Through the state appellate and United States Supreme Court processes, death row inmates can—and do—exert considerable influence on the outcomes of their respective criminal justice cases. In this context, then, there is a sense of trust for death row inmates: The appeals process is constitutionally ensured, so inmates and their families, as members of the death row community, have an avenue to express some power in the hope of making a difference for those awaiting execution and for the future of capital punishment policy and practice.

A related dimension to the element of trust for prisoners (and their families) awaiting execution comes from participation in activist organizations such as state coalitions to abolish the death penalty, Amnesty International, the Lamp of Hope Project (LHP), and Death Penalty Focus. These types of nonprofit organizations comprise not only death row inmates, but any individuals interested in expressing their concerns about state sanctioned executions (sometimes including victims' families). While these organizations certainly have an interest in abolishing capital punishment as a sanction, they also strive to address other issues including: the overall causes of crime and breaking the cycle of crime in families; informing the public about the death penalty; and improving prison conditions for death row inmates as well as other prisoners (Amnesty International, 2007; Death Penalty Focus, 2007; Pantawapirom, 1997; Tennessee Coalition to Abolish State Killing, 2007).

Organizations like those listed above allow execution community members (especially death row prisoners and their loved ones) to have an outlet to express their viewpoints, advocate for penal reform, and lobby for death penalty abolition. In the context of LHP, its internationally distributed newsletter (*The Texas Death Row Journal*) represents a vehicle to effect these ends or otherwise exercise influence in correctional law, policy, and practice. Similarly, most states distribute newsletters to the members of their coalitions to abolish state killings (e.g., Tennessee's Coalition to Abolish State Killings distributes their quarterly *Lifelines* newsletter).

Family members and loved ones of victims are another important membership group within the execution community. They also experience the sense of community construct through the element of trust. While victims' loved ones do not have direct control over the appellate process, they do experience trust as inmates proceed through this system. For those who support the execution of the offender, they trust that the legal proceedings will ultimately result in execution. For those who do not support the death penalty, they may be trusting that the legal system will eventually overturn the sentence for the condemned. For either subgroup of this tier, they should understand that there is about a 65 percent chance that the capital sentence will be reversed during the appeals process (Gelman, Liebman, West, & Kiss, 2004). Consequently, trust may be experienced differently for members of this tier, depending on their levels of support for the death penalty.

Another example of the element of trust for the loved ones of victims comes from the utilization of victim advocate services. Many victims and their families find that their lives are suspended throughout the execution process with its multiple appeals, stays, new trials, and possible dismissals. The finality of capital punishment can, for some individuals, become an unforeseeable eventuality as several years typically pass before the execution takes place. As Keve (1992) describes, "[victims'] families have a greatly prolonged period of anguish. Through successive appeals, successive execution dates, etc., they are repeatedly interviewed by the news media while their anger and distress are repeatedly revived, sometimes never to be resolved" (p. 14). As a result, their anxiety, frustration, and resentment levels may increase.

Zelenka (1993) describes how the advocacy alternative helps victims and their loved ones deal effectively with their unique and possibly long-term stress. The victim advocate performs various services, which may include keeping clients updated on new developments of the offender's case (e.g., appeal outcomes, incompetency findings, and escapes), and providing referrals for other services such as psychological counseling. The victim advocate fills a void created by an overburdened and beleaguered criminal justice system: The advocate works to meaningfully include victims of crime in legal proceedings, rather than allowing them to wonder about the formal processing of a case that will invariably impact their lives. Through such initiatives as victim advocacy, family members and others brutalized by crime can experience a sense of trust. As members of the execution community, they exercise influence and utilize power when relying on victim advocacy services. These services help ensure that the interests of victims matter.

Similar to offenders and their family members, loved ones of victims may also join activist groups. For those who support the death penalty, several pro-capital punishment organizations exist that they may join. For those against the death penalty, anti-capital punishment organizations now exist designed especially for victims' family members. Organizations such as Murder Victims' Families for Human Rights circulate their *Article 3* newsletter and perform other activities to communicate their position and lobby for condemned prisoners.

As another tier of the death row community, correctional personnel also live the element of trust described by McMillan (1996). Prison staff access trust in two distinct ways. The first method is through programs developed at death row institutions. The second method is through various professional affiliations or through the formal functioning of the criminal justice and legal systems.

One example of programs developed at death row institutions is psychological intervention. Much has been made about the importance of demonstrating competence and compassion during the entire capital punishment process. Interestingly, Martin (1993) maintains that this trend can be explained not simply in relation to benefitting death row inmates but in helping correctional and administrative staff as well. For example, after an execution at the Broad River Correctional Institution in Columbia, South Carolina, members of the execution team are required "to attend individual post-stress debriefings" (Martin, 1993: 62). A similar model was developed at the San Quentin State Prison in California. Using post-traumatic stress disorder as its foundation, the warden and staff psychologist created a pre- and post-trauma intervention program for all correctional and administrative staff (Vasquez, 1993). Similar to the Broad River model, the intent is to prevent psychological injury in the wake of an inmate's legal execution.

What is significant about these types of death row programs is the group cohesion that they stimulate among participants. Johnson (1998) describes the cohesion that execution team members feel while working "together to handle the problems and pressures posed by death work. [There are] essential human needs for purposiveness in action and relationships with others, needs the team members meet through the primary-group relations that exist among them" (p. 135). Where the execution work signals a common project for correctional and administrative personnel, debriefing programs capture the poignancy of staff efforts and the shared emotional trauma they experience. In this context, then, the psychological well-being of correctional personnel is protected. Individual staff members experience a "sense of mattering, of making a difference to a group and of the group mattering to its members" (McMillan & Chavis, 1986: 9).

Another type of program developed for death row correctional personnel involves bifurcating the housing and execution functions. That is, some states (e.g., New York and Texas) have separate facilities for housing death row inmates and carrying out the execution itself. In these situations, the officers involved in the execution process have had no prior personal contact with the prisoner. The idea behind these programs is that they "will minimize the negative effects of execution *on staff* if the two functions are separated" (Greene et al., 2003: 864). In fact, the workers who have had personal contact with these inmates "would just have to say goodbye to a man that never returns" (Greene et al., 2003: 864). Whether these bifurcated systems do reduce the effects of executions on staff has yet to be empirically examined.

Correctional staff members also experience the element of trust through the formal operation of the criminal justice system and their association in professional organizations. One example of this is in the way that mental health personnel are relied upon in the court system. Psychologists and psychiatrists are routinely called upon to testify and clarify aspects of aggravating and mitigating factors in capital cases. According to Kermani and Drob (1988), however, cases involving the death penalty cause a dilemma for these mental health experts, particularly when it comes to the issue of professional ethics (Brodsy et al, 2001; Hensl, 2004). Using psychiatric or psychological testimony in capital cases has been the basis for considerable controversy within the mental health law field (Hensl, 2005; Winnick, 1997). At issue is the "do no harm" provision of the Hippocratic Oath that physicians and health care specialists are mandated to uphold (Arrigo & Tasca, 1999; Hensl, 2004).

Another ethical issue that mental health professionals confront occurs after the capital sentence has been administered and the offender is housed on death row. Correctional mental health professionals assume an important role in determining a prisoner's competence to be executed (Arrigo & Tasca, 1999). Moreover, they assess what medication should be dispensed in order to restore an inmate to competence for purposes of carrying out a capital sentence (*Singleton v. Norris,* 2003; *Washington v. Harper,* 1990). In the latter case, the primary ethical issue is that "the prisoner . . . receive[s] a stay of execution pending restoration of competency" (Heilbrun et al., 1992: 596). Thus, according to some mental health professionals, by medically restoring the inmate to competence the treatment intervention leads directly to the execution of the inmate (Arrigo & Tasca, 1999; Hensl, 2004). This is in direct opposition to the nature of a psychologist's ethical obligation; namely, to "protect the welfare of the people and groups with whom [one] work[s]" (American Psychological Association [APA], 1990: 391; see also, Brodsky et al., 2001; Hensl, 2005).

These (and other similar) ethical dilemmas were, in part, addressed through the APA's 1984 ethical guidelines. As Kermani and Drob (1988) explain, the principles

> Argue that the application of psychiatry in legal settings is always for legal ends and legal purposes and that a professional who has been hired by the prosecution is only obligated to serve his client, the prosecutor, and has essentially *no special obligation with respect to the defendant under examination* (p. 202, emphasis added).

This degree of legal and professional support sustaining the mental health professional's involvement with death row inmates is significant to their identity as a membership group of the execution community. Psychologists, psychiatrists, and related clinical staff experience influence in the capital punishment process. They exercise their will and it is soundly regarded by legal and other correctional personnel. Even when mental health specialists confront professional practice ethical dilemmas, their affiliation with reputable associations or their involvement in the criminal justice system elsewhere, provide guidance to their conduct. Again, there is a sense in which their membership in the death row community matters: What they say or do is of consequence to the group. These are examples of trust.

The distinct membership groups that form the execution community express power differently within the element of trust. For example, the death row inmates influence the execution process primarily by working through the appellate process. Family members of these inmates exert power by joining activist or lobbying associations. Victims and their loved ones may best exert their power through victim advocacy services. Correctional personnel exercise power through their participation in debriefing programs and identifying with professional organizations. This begs the question: How do respective membership groups, constituting an execution community *collectively* experience the psychological element of trust? In other words, how is trust uniformly felt by persons within the individual tiers such that, together, the membership groups form one death row community?

Newbrough and Chavis (1986) maintain that the spirit of community concept is fundamentally psychological. It entails both an "*I-you sense* . . . that differentiates oneself from the collectivity, and a *we sense* of belonging together" (p. 3a). This suggests that power in a community can be distributed differentially among various members or collectives, and that trust is about balancing the emotional leverage any one person or group exercises against other individuals or groups in the community. McMillan and Chavis (1986) refer to this as the "bidirectional" (p. 11) nature of influence or power. Further, McMillan (1996) acknowledges that trust may not be so uniformly embraced or lived out by a community's members. As he describes it:

> Trust develops through a community's use of its power. Who has it? When do they have it? If not present in some members, when don't they have it? For the spirit of community to survive beyond its first initial spark, the community must solve the problems arising from the allocation of power (p. 318).

Understanding or predicting who or what group has the power at any given time in a death row community is difficult at best. For example, while death row prisoners have the right to appeal (seemingly giving them more power than the victim's family at that time), their appellate application might be rejected. If such an appeal is rejected, the inmate's power seems to be reduced. However, this decision does not rest with the immediate members of the death row community. Rather, it lies with the court system, leaving the distribution of power among members of the community in the hands of an outside entity.

Moreover, trust depends on the security individuals or constituencies believe they possess in their respective statuses within a group, and in relation to others who exert influence or power over them. Thus, a diminished or absent level of security for some persons or collectives will minimize their allegiance to a given community (McMillan & Chavis, 1986). This is particularly problematic with the execution experience where various groups feel differently about the type and degree of control they have over the process (Johnson, 1998). As in the example above, members of each tier of the death row community may feel they have differing degrees of control over the capital punishment procedure at different stages in the process.

Therefore, the various groups in the proposed death row community do exercise power distinctively. However, the extent to which they collectively hurdle the distribution of their differential influence "on members . . . to attain uniformity" (McMillan & Chavis, 1986: 11) is uncertain at best. Indeed, trust emerges when individuals understand their relationship to one another in the overall group, and feel secure in that knowledge. "People must know what they can expect from each other in the community (McMillan, 1996: 319). In the case of the death row community, the element of trust, as a component of the sense of community concept, is only partially realized. Membership groups do experience power, but the assorted manifestations of it are not harnessed to produce any semblance of total group conformity.

Trade

Trade within a community encompasses the interchange of reinforcements that draw group members together (McMillan, 1996; McMillan & Chavis, 1986). McMillan and Chavis (1986) argue that "[g]iven the complexity of individuals and groups, however, it [is] impossible to determine all of the reinforcements that bind people together (p. 12). With regard to existing group cohesiveness research, Lott and Lott (1965) contend that "[i]t is taken for granted that individuals are attracted to groups as a direct function of the satisfaction they are able to derive within them (p. 285; see also Greene, 1989; McMillan, 1996). Elaborating on this notion, McMillan (1996) suggests that "[s]ince this premise is widely accepted, there is little empirical evidence to clarify exactly what is reinforcing in a relationship or group membership. Rather, most theory and research in this area only underscore the contention that if people associate together, then it must be reinforcing to do so" (p. 320). The collection of individuals representing a death row constituency is exceedingly diverse and, thus, the reinforcements for different members are bound to be manifold. These observations notwithstanding, essential to the trade element is that members' needs are differentially met and reinforced through the various resources of the group.

To explore the manner in which trade functions in the execution community, we divide the four tiers of the death row constituents into two subgroups. The first of these is composed of prisoners awaiting execution, their loved ones, and the family members of the victims. Individuals in this subgroup appear to lack obvious reinforcements for membership in an execution community. In short, where and how can they experience any sense of group cohesion? Once these individuals find themselves living this execution reality, however, an array of methods is used to adapt cohesively to their situation. Indeed, behaviors are typically modified and different reinforcements surface within the newly imposed environment.

One type of reinforcement for death row prisoners, their loved ones, and the family members of victims is the attempt to generate public awareness of the experience through published articles, essays, and books. While their perspectives may, or may not, be very different, such publications serve to make their viewpoints known, while also letting them learn about the perspectives of others involved in the execution community. Again, the most important feature of trade is its capacity to fill the needs of community participants through their membership in a group.

Abu-Jamal, a prisoner on Pennsylvania's death row, wrote *Live from Death Row* (1995), which may fill a void that other death row inmates confront (see also, Chessman, 2006). Shirley Dicks, the mother of a prisoner awaiting execution in Tennessee, has written several books, including *Death Row: Interviews with Inmates, their Families, and Opponents of Capital Punishment* (1990) and *They're Going to Kill My Son* (1992). These types of books fill a void that other death row inmate parents and family members experience through her writings. Books also exist written for the family members of murder victims. Volumes such as *A Long Journey Home* (Dicks, 2003) and *Life Sentence: Murder Victims and their Families* (Cleary, 2004) are compilations of stories and experiences from the families of murder victims. These writings allow the family members of murder victims to share their experiences and, ultimately, let others in similar situations know that they are not alone in what they are feeling. In these instances, cohesion in the respective subgroups, expressed through the traded resource of information, advances the overall sense of community that death row constituents experience. Additionally, in the examples above, members of the execution community find that their emotional, political, spiritual, social, and other needs are all potentially sustained through the traded resource of literature.

The second subgroup consists of those correctional and administrative staff associated with an execution facility. Reinforcements for this group are much more obvious and abundant than those found in the other subgroup. To illustrate, experiencing financial security, personal status, job satisfaction, collegiality, competence, and so forth are all needs reinforced and met through membership in this subgroup. These needs represent what Rappaport (1977: 18) described as a "person-environment fit." In this instance, the members' professional desires or ambitions direct the available reinforcements. As McMillan and Chavis (1986) explain, "[t]here are many . . . undocumented needs that communities fill, but individual values are the sources of these needs. The extent to which individual values are shared among community members will determine the ability of a community to organize and prioritize its need-fulfillment activities" (p. 13). Thus, what generally binds the death subgroup of correctional and administrative personnel together, as an execution community constituency, is their shared valued system of rewards for work accomplished (see Osofsky, Bandura, & Zimbardo, 2005). It is this need that is cohesively sustained through their membership in this group, even if their work contributes to an execution.

As with our previous analysis on trust, we are led to question how the various tiers representing the execution community collectively tap any shared commodity such that the subgroups are bound together. In other words, what traded resource is reinforcing across the various membership groups making up the death row community? Here, however, it is important to remember that the sense of community concept is essentially psychological. That is, the exchange of reinforcing commodities need not be exclusively material in nature. The economy of trade also includes exchanging feelings, impulses, attitudes, perceptions, judgments, beliefs, and other psychological states. While the subgroups or tiers of the execution community experience "consensual validation" (McMillan & Chavis, 1986: 14) for the values they assign their respective tangible reinforcements, the traded resource that draws all community members together is the pain and despair that comes from the loss of a loved one, the imminent death of another, or engagement with both. This is an intangible reinforcement "represent[ing] a beginning step toward the development of a community economy" (McMillan, 1996: 321).

Further, individuals with primary allegiance to any one membership group, expressed through a social or material economy, may not recognize how their differences can constitute a diverse, and even larger, community (McMillan & Chavis, 1986; Storey, 1991). The same is true of death row and those membership groups representing an execution community. Although the various subgroups experience group cohesion and solidarity for their "similar ways of looking, feeling, thinking, and being" (McMillan, 1996; 321), they are also bound together because of the differential suffering they endure as a shared emotional state. The medium of exchange is self-disclosure (Turner, 1992), and all membership groups uniformly speak about and trade in the discourse of pain, loss, suffering, and despair, both directly and indirectly with one another (Haney, 2006).

The pain and despair stemming from personal loss and the discourse constituting this suffering are psychological exemplars of trade. We note further, however, that they are reinforced over time. Indeed, the period during which the membership groups await execution becomes a unifying dimension where the collectives maintain their allegiance to the death row community. Life on death row means living with the knowledge that one will eventually die. As long as this awareness remains unfulfilled, prospects for inter-group cohesion increase and intensify. Indeed, this knowledge activates and sustains those feelings and that dialogue making the economy of pain, despair, and suffering possible for the various collectives that constitute an execution community. Thus, it follows that trade, as an element of the sense of community concept, is operative both individually and collectively.

Art

The last element in the sense of community definition and theory is art. Art focuses upon those common emotional connections that members live. These connections can be in the form of shared experiences, history, places, and time. McMillan (1996) claims that this "[c]ontact is essential for community building" (p. 322). For everyone involved with a death row inmate or a death row facility, some form of contact is unavoidable. For one group in the death row community, the correctional personnel, the only way to dispense with contact is to give up their jobs at the penal facility. For everyone else involved in the execution community, two ways exist in which to rid themselves of contact. First, and probably less likely, an inmate could win an appeal and subsequently have his or her sentence reduced from death to some other option. As mentioned earlier, this happens in about 65 percent of cases (Gelman et al., 2004). Consequently, the prisoner and his or her loved ones, along with the victim's loved ones, would be removed from the death row community. The second way for them to avoid sustained emotional contact is for the inmate to be executed. In this instance, however, the psychological scarring and bondedness can be so profound that the death of the inmate may actually deepen the connection.

While shared emotional contact is an important factor in linking groups into a community, McMillan (1996) delineates specific factors that influence the quality of those human relationships. Such factors include "closure to events, shared outcome from the event, risk and sacrifice, and honor versus humiliation" (p. 322). These influencing factors are expressions of shared history, time, and space, and are activated through such artifacts as symbols, songs, celebration, rituals, and the like. Both shared emotional contact and the unique quality of those varied connections are facets to what everyone in the execution community experiences. All groups in the execution community are differentially joined by the degree, intensity, duration, and frequency of several shared emotional connections that are associated with the act of capital punishment.

The most significant example of art within the death row community is the use of language as a symbol. As Sykes (1958) explained:

> [t]he development of special languages for special groups organized within the framework of the larger society . . . is a phenomenon common in the social history of language. The argot of inmates in the maximum security prison illustrates this point well (p. 84).

The language shared by a certain group or community can also convey specialized meanings about the quality of the relationships among members of the group. As Sykes (1958) suggested:

> [w]ords in the prison argot, no less than words in ordinary usage, carry a penumbra of admiration and disapproval, of attitude and belief [about enactors of inmate grammar] which channels and controls the behavior of the individual[s] who use them or to whom they are applied (p. 86).

In addition, as Arrigo (1996) argues, particularly in his assessment of confinement for the mentally ill and incarceration for the criminally insane, these specialized meanings are most especially known to those systematically indoctrinated into this grammar or to those well versed in its linguistic coordinates (see also, Arrigo, 2002). Once an individual becomes a member of the death row community, the language specific to this situation is rooted in his or her thoughts, speech, and behavior. Words previously unfamiliar to such membership groups become differentially, though emotionally, impactful for all participants of the execution community. Words or expressions such as *clemency, appellate review, stay of execution, lethal injection,* and *competency to be executed* are symbolic expressions signifying "the part of the community that is transcendent and eternal. They represent . . . values that outlive community members and remain a part of the spirit of the community" (McMillan, 1996: 323). These words or phrases profoundly join the death row constituents representing the execution community and create a shared emotional connection in time, place, history, and experience.

IMPLICATIONS AND CONCLUSIONS

Although speculative and conceptual, this chapter has examined the death row phenomenon by integrating it with principles found in community psychology. The essential thesis was that an execution community or death row community exists, and that its core constituent groups are identifiable. While we have identified four tiers of individuals that compose a death row community, one particular group has received the most attention throughout this chapter—the prisoners awaiting execution. The focus has been on death row inmates because they are, in fact, the locus for all activity. That is, the appellate process outcomes, the stays of execution, the determinations of incompetency, and even the execution itself all begin with the offender on death row. An inmate's experiences initiate a ripple effect that inherently affects all other community members: No individuals in the group remain unaffected. This fact alone suggests that the phenomenon is far-reaching, potentially resulting in reactions from a wide range of citizens. Thus, it followed that some assessment of death row constituency membership and how such membership engendered elements of a sense of community were warranted.

A summary of the relationship between the four membership groups that make up the death row community and the four elements of the sense of community concept are presented in Table 1. We note that a strong association appears in all but the trust element. As previously discussed, individual membership groups uniquely exert influence in the overall execution process. However, the manner in which power is collective channeled and utilized by individual group members across the various tiers is not so easily discernible. Several explanations exist for the absence of a clear relationship between the membership groups and the psychological elements of trust.

First, power is not distributed equally among the various tiers in the execution community. McMillan (1996) asserts that problems stemming from the allocation of power must be resolved before the spark of community can sustain itself. Beyond the legal appeals process, inmates slated for execution have only limited influence when confined in prison (Bohm, 2007). The family members and loved ones of inmates also have a restricted ability to bring about change for the inmate and/or the correctional system. While they often become active in anti-death penalty organizations and support groups, they are often still powerless to directly affect their loved one's case. Loved ones and family members of victims typically have the penal and legal systems on their side, mobilized to carry out the death sentence at the end of the appeals process. Still, they must endure the seemingly endless appeals process, which may leave them feeling powerless during those times. Correctional personnel function as agents of the system. They are entrusted with competently and efficiently directing the administration of all death work. In short, no membership group has complete authority over others; however, the distribution of power is certainly unequal and may vary at different points in the process.

Lawler (1992) notes that when power is unequally distributed within a group, members of the group can develop hostile and ruthless sentiments toward each other. The presence of power differentials among the various tiers in the execution community makes feelings of distrust not only likely but contagious (Cotterell, Eisenberger, & Speicher, 1992). Thus, it follows that in order for the death row community to witness some semblance of collective trust (i.e., exercise a uniform sense of mattering), power would need to be distributed among each tier more evenly, equitably, and equally.

Similarly, there is no agreed upon normative structure for how membership groups in the execution community are to engage one another. The absence of this organizing schema translates into a lack of "social, emotional, and political potential" for the community (McMillan, 1996: 319). Not knowing, for example, how family members or victims are to interact with prisoners or how loved ones of death row inmates are to coexist with correctional personnel undermines opportunities for group cohesion (Bettenhausen & Murnighan, 1992). The membership groups substantially lack this essential feature of social norms and, accordingly, prospects for collective trust are attenuated at best.

Finally, communal trust entails decision making where authority figures ensure that information is appropriately processed and disseminated. In this arrangement, members influence leaders and leaders influence members simultaneously (Miller, 1990). In addition, the reciprocity implied in this relationship helps guarantee the even flow and exchange of power. While leaders may exist among the respective membership groups of the execution community, no authority head symbolically or literally represents the collective community. Thus, trust experienced across the tiers of the death row community is unlikely.

Notwithstanding the less than clear association between the psychological element of trust and the various tiers representing the execution community, the other three constructs informing the sense of community concept do appear to be prominently featured in, and squarely applicable to, our analysis of death row. Thus, in the face of our speculative assessment and given the current political and social climate in support of capital punishment (Bohm, 2007), we contend that a number of areas exist where further examination of the execution community may advance our overall understanding of capital punishment and life on death row.

Although the majority of all Western industrialized nations have discontinued the use of capital punishment, it remains a material force of American correctional justice (Bohm, 2007; Cabana, 1996). Currently practiced in 38 of the 53 jurisdictions across the United States, a closer examination of its use and impact, especially for the most affected by its operation (i.e., the execution community), ostensibly provides greater insight into the underlying strategy of recent tough-on-crime trends. More broadly, however, investigating the death row community phenomenon reminds us of the importance of transcending the limits of existing scholarship within the artificially defined borders of a given discipline. Community psychology is but one avenue by which to advance our knowledge of capital punishment and life on death row. While our comments have been nothing short of conceptual, they do signal a novel direction for those concerned with promoting peace and social justice in corrections. Clearly, these are matters of considerable consequence for those membership groups constituting the execution community.

REFERENCES

Abu-Jamal, M. (1995). *Live from Death Row.* Reading, MA: Addison-Wesley.

American Psychological Association. (1990). Ethical principles of psychologists. *American Psychologist,* 45, 390–395.

Amnesty International. (1987). *The United States of America: The Death Penalty.* London: Author.

Amnesty International. (2007). *Abolish the Death Penalty.* New York: Amnesty International. Available at www.amnestyusa.org.

Arriens, J., ed. (1997). *Welcome to Hell: Letters & Writings from Death Row.* Boston, MA: Northeastern University Press.

Arrigo, B. A. (1996). *The Contours of Psychiatric Justice: A Postmodern Critique of Mental Illness, Criminal Insanity, and the Law.* New York/London: Garland.

Arrigo, B. A. (2002). *Punishing the Mentally Ill: A Critical Analysis of Law and Psychiatry.* Albany, NY: State University of New York Press.

Arrigo, B. A., & Fowler, C. R. (2001). The "death row community": A community psychology perspective. *Deviant Behavior: An Interdisciplinary Journal, 22,* 43–71.

Arrigo, B. A., & Tasca, J. J. (1999). Right to refuse treatment, competency to be executed, and therapeutic jurisprudence: Toward a systematic analysis. *Law and Psychology Review, 23,* 1–47.

Beccaria, C. (1963). *On Crimes and Punishments.* Indianapolis, IN: Bobbs-Merrill.

Beck, E., Britto, S., & Andrews, A. (2007). *In the Shadow of Death Capital: Restorative Justice and Death Row Families.* Oxford: Oxford University Press.

Beck, E., Blackwell, B. S., Leonard, P. B., & Mears, M. (2003). Seeking sanctuary: Interviews with family members of capital defendants. *Cornell Law Review, 88,* 382–418.

Beck, E., & Jones, S. J. (2007). Children of the condemned: Grieving the loss of a father to death row. *Omega: An International Journal for the Study of Dying, Death, Bereavement, Suicide, and Other Lethal Behaviors, 56,* 191–215.

Bedau, H. (1984). *The Case Against the Death Penalty.* New York: American Civil Liberties Union.

Bedau, H. (1987). *Death is Different: Studies in Morality, Law, and Politics of Capital Punishment.* Boston: Northeastern University Press.

Bedau, H. A., & Cassell, P. G. (2005). *Debating the Death Penalty: Should America Have Capital Punishment? The Experts on Both Sides Make their Case.* New York, NY: Oxford University Press.

Beirne, P. (1991). Inventing criminology: The "science of man" in Cesare Beccaria's *Dei Delitti e Delle Pene* 1764. *Criminology, 29,* 777–820.

Bettenhausen, K. L., & Murnighan, J. K. (1992). The development of an intragroup norm and the effects of interpersonal and structural challenges. *Administrative Science Quarterly, 36,* 20–35.

Bilionis, L. D. (1991). Moral appropriateness, capital punishment, and the "Lockett" Doctrine. *Journal of Criminal Law and Criminology 82,* 283–333.

Bohm, R. M., Clark, L. J., & Aveni, A. F. (1991). Knowledge and death penalty opinion: A test of the Marshall Hypotheses. *Journal of Research in Crime and Delinquency 28*:360–387.

Bohm, R. M. (2007). *Deathquest III: An Introduction to the Theory and Practice of Capital Punishment in the United States.* Cincinnati, OH: Anderson Publishing.

Bonta, J., & Gendreau, P. (1990). Reexamining the cruel and unusual punishment of prison life. *Law and Human Behavior 14,* 347–372.

Brodsky, S., Zapf, P., & Boccaccini, M. (2001). The last competency: An examination of legal, ethical, and professional ambiguities regarding evaluations of competence for execution. *Journal of Forensic Psychology Practice, 1,* 1–25.

Cabana, D. A. (1996). *Death at Midnight: The Confession of an Executioner.* Boston: Northeastern University Press.

Calnen, T., & Blackman, L. S. (1992). Capital punishment and offenders with mental retardation: Response to the Penry Brief. *American Journal on Mental Retardation, 96,* 557–564.

Chessman, C. (2006). *Cell 2455, Death Row: A Condemned Man's Own Story.* New York, NY: Carroll & Graf.

Cleary, C. (2004). *Life Sentence: Murder Victims and Their Families.* Dublin, Ireland: O'Brien.

Cotterell, N., Eisenberger, R., & Speicher, H. (1992). Inhibiting effects of reciprocation wariness on interpersonal relationships. *Journal of Personality and Social Psychology, 62,* 658–668.

Cunningham, M. D., & Vigen, M. P. (2002). Death row inmate characteristics, adjustment, and confinement: A critical review of the literature. *Behavioral Sciences and the Law, 20,* 191–210.

Curtis, R. (2000). *Dispensing Justice Locally: The Implementation and Effects of the Midtown Community Court.* New York, NY: Routledge.

Death Penalty Focus. (2007). *About Death Penalty Focus.* San Francisco, CA: Death Penalty Focus. Available at: www.deathpenalty.org.

Death Penalty Information Center. (2007a). *Death Row Inmates by State.* Washington, DC: Death Penalty Information Center. Available at: www.deathpenaltyinfo.org.

Death Penalty Information Center. (2007b). *Executions in the United States.* Washington, DC: Death Penalty Information Center. Available at: www.deathpenaltyinfo.org.

Death Penalty Information Center. (2007c). *Time on Death Row.* Washington, DC: Death Penalty Information Center. Available at: www.deathpenaltyinfo.org.

Dicks, S. (1990). *Death Row: Interviews with Inmates, Their Families and Opponents of Capital Punishment.* Jefferson, NC: McFarland & Company.

Dicks, S. (1992). *They're Going to Kill My Son.* Far Hills, NJ: New Horizon.

Dicks, S. (2003). *A Long Journey Home.* Maryland Heights, MO: Matthews Books.

Durkheim, E. (1965). *The Division of Labor in Society.* G. Simpson, trans. New York: The Free Press.

Farr, K. A. (1997). Aggravating and differentiating factors in the cases of white and minority women on death row. *Crime & Delinquency, 43,* 260–278.

Fletcher, G. P. (1995). *With Justice for Some: Victims' Rights in Criminal Trials.* New York: Addison-Wesley.

Garland, D. W. (2002). The cultural uses of capital punishment. *Punishment and Society, 4,* 459–487.

Garland, D. W. (2005). Capital punishment and the American culture. *Punishment and Society, 7,* 347–376.

Gelman, A., Liebman, J. S., West, V., & Kiss, A. (2004). A broken system: The persistent patterns of reversals of death sentences in the United States. *Journal of Empirical Legal Studies, 1,* 209–261.

Greene, C. N. (1989). Cohesion and productivity in work groups. *Small Group Behavior, 20,* 70–86.

Greene, N. L., Buckley, W. D., Stetler, R., & Haney, C. (2003). Dying twice: Incarceration on death row. *Capital University Law Review, 31,* 853–882.

Haas, K., & Inciardi, J. (1988). *Challenging Capital Punishment.* Newbury Park, CA: Sage.

Halpern, A. L. (2002). Participation in executions. *Internal Medicine News, 35,* 13–14.

Haney, C. (1997). Psychology and the limits of prison pain: Confronting the coming crisis in Eighth Amendment law. *Psychology, Public Policy and Law, 3,* 499–588.

Haney, Craig. 2006. *Reforming Punishment: Psychological Limitations to the Pains of Imprisonment.* Washington, DC: American Psychological Association.

Heilbrun, K., Radelet, M. L., & Dvoskin, J. (1992). The debate on treating individuals incompetent for execution. *American Journal of Psychiatry, 149,* 596–605.

Hensl, K. B. (2004). Restored to health to be put to death: Reconciling the legal and ethical dilemmas of medicating to execute in *Singleton v. Norris. Villanova Law Review, 49,* 291–328.

Hensl, K. B. (2005). Restoring competency for execution: The paradoxical debate continues with the case of *Singleton v. Norris. Journal of Forensic Psychology Practice, 5,* 55–68.

Johnson, R. (1979). Under sentence of death: The psychology of death row confinement. *Law and Psychology Review, 5,* 141–192.

Johnson, R. (1998). *DeathWork: A Study of the Modern Execution Process.* 2nd ed. Belmont, CA: West/Wadsworth.

Jones, P. (1994). It's not what you ask, it's the way that you ask it: Question forum and public opinion on the death penalty. *The Prison Journal, 24,* 32–50.

Karp, D. R. Clear, T. R. (Eds.) (2002). *What Is Community Justice: Cast Studies of Restorative Justice and Community Supervision.* Thousand Oaks, CA: Sage.

Kermani, E. J., & Drob, S. L. (1988). Psychiatry and the death penalty: Dilemma for mental health professionals. *Psychiatric Quarterly, 59,* 193–212.

Keve, P. W. (1992). The costliest punishment—A corrections administrator contemplates the death penalty. *Federal Probation, 56,* 11–15.

Lawler, E. J. (1992). Power processes in bargaining. *Sociological Quarterly, 33,* :17–34.

Lott, A. J., & Lott, B. E. (1965). Group cohesiveness as interpersonal attraction: A review of relationships with antecedent and variables. *Psychological Bulletin, 64,* 259–309.

Martin, G. N. (1993). A warden's reflections: Enforcing the death penalty with competence, compassion. *Corrections Today, 55,* 60–64.

McMillan, D. W. (1996). Sense of community. *Journal of Community Psychology, 24,* 315–325.

McMillan, D. W., & Chavis, D. M. (1986). Sense of community: A definition and theory. *Journal of Community Psychology, 1,* 6–23.

Miller, D. (1990). Organizational configuration, cohesion, change and prediction. *Human Relations, 43,* 771–789.

Miller, L. S., & Hess, K. M. (2007). *Community Policing: Partnerships for Problem Solvingy* (5th ed.). Belmont, CA: Wadsworth Publishing.

Mitchell, M., & Sidanius, J. (1995). Social hierarchy and the death penalty: A social dominance perspective. *Political Psychology, 16,* 591–619.

Murder Victims' Families for Human Rights. (2007). *Victims' Stories.* Cambridge, MA: Murder Victims' Families for Human Rights. Available at: www.mvfhr.org.

Murder Victims' Families for Reconciliation. (2007). *Our Members.* Washington, DC: Murder Victims' Families for Reconciliation. Available at: www.mvfr.org.

Newbrough, J. R., & Chavis, D. M. (1986). Psychological sense of community, I: Foreward. *Journal of Community Psychology, 14,* 3–5.

Osofsky, M. J., Bandura, A., & Zimbardo, P. G. (2005). The role of moral disengagement in the execution process. *Law and Human Behavior, 29,* 371–393.

Pantawapirom, L. (1997). *TX: Death Row Project* [On-line]. Available at: www.igc.org/justice/articles.html.

Parker, T. (1992). Isolated hearts: Welcome to hell: Letters and other writings by prisoners on death row in the United States. *New Statesman & Society, 5,* 37.

Pickett, C., & Stowers, C. (2002). *Within These Walls: Memoirs of a Death House Chaplain.* New York: St. Martin's Press.

Radelet, M. L., & Akers, R. L. (1996). Deterrence and the death penalty: The views of the experts. *Journal of Criminal Law and Criminology, 87,* 1–16.

Rapaport, E. (1991). The death penalty and gender discrimination. *Law and Society Review, 25,* 367–383.

Rappaport, J. (1977). *Community Psychology: Values, Research, and Action.* New York: Rhinehart and Winston.

Rose, P. I. (1977). *The Study of Society: An Integrated Anthology.* 4th ed. New York: Random House.

Schmalleger, F. (1997). *Criminal Justice: A Brief Introduction.* 2nd ed. Upper Saddle River, NJ: Prentice Hall.

Shepherd, J. M. (2004). Murders of passion, execution delays, and the deterrence of capital punishment. *Journal of Legal Studies, 33,* 283–321.

Smykla, J. O. (1987). The human impact of capital punishment: Interviews with families of persons on death row. *Journal of Criminal Justice, 15,* 331–347.

Stacey, M. (1969). The myth of community studies. *The British Journal of Sociology, 20,* 134–147.

Stein, M. (1960). *The Eclipse of Community.* Princeton, NJ: Princeton University Press.

Storey, D. (1991). History and homogeniety: Effects of perceptions of membership groups on interpersonal communication. *Communication Research, 18,* 199–221.

Sweeney, L. T., & Haney, C. (1992). The influence of race on sentencing: A metaanalytic review of experimental studies. *Behavioral Sciences and the Law, 10,* 179–195.

Sykes, G. M. (1958). *The Society of Captives: A Study of a Maximum Security Prison.* Princeton, NJ: Princeton University Press.

Tennessee Coalition to Abolish State Killings. (2007). *Honoring Life by Abolishing the Death Penalty.* Nashville, TN: TCASK. Available at: www.tcask.org.

Territo, L., Halsted, J. B., & Bromley, M. L. (1998). *Crime and Justice in America: A Human Perspective.* Boston, MA: Butterworth-Heinemann.

Thigpen, M. L. (1993). A tough assignment. *Corrections Today, 55,* 56–58.

Thomson, E. (1999). Effects of an execution of homicides in California. *Homicide Studies, 3,* 129–150.

Toch, H. (1998). *Corrections: A Humanistic Perspective.* New York: Harrow and Heston.

Turner, J. H. (1992). The production and reproduction of social solidarity: A synthesis of two rational choice theories." *Journal of the Theory of Social Behavior, 22,* 311–328.

Van Ness, D., & Strong, K. H. (1997). *Restoring Justice.* Cincinnati, OH: Anderson.

Van Ness, D. (2006). *Restoring Justice: An Introduction to Restorative Justice* Cincinnati, OH: LexisNexis/Anderson.

Vasquez, D. B. (1993). Trauma treatment: Helping prison staff handle the stress of an execution. *Corrections Today, 55,* 70–72.

Von Drehle, D. (1996). *Among the Lowest of the Dead: Inside Death Row.* New York: Fawcett Books.

Von Hirsch, A. (1976). *Doing Justice.* New York: Hill and Wang.

Williams, M. R., & Holcomb, J. E. (2001). Racial disparity and death sentences in Ohio. *Journal of Criminal Justice, 29,* 2007–218.

Williams, M. R., & Holcomb, J. E. (2004). The interactive effects of victim race and gender on death sentence disparity findings. *Homicide Studies, 8,* 350–376.

Wilson, J. Q. (1983). *Thinking About Crime.* New York: Vintage.

Winick, B. (1997). *The Right to Refuse Mental Health Treatment.* Washington, DC: American Psychological Association.

Young, R. L. (1991). Race, conceptions of crime and justice, and support for the death penalty. *Social Psychology, 54,* 67–75.

Zelenka, D. J. (1993). South Carolina victim advocate helps address families' concerns. *Corrections Today, 55,* 80–82.

CASES CITED

Atkins v. Virginia, 536 U.S. 304 (2002).

Eddings v. Oklahoma, 455 U.S. 104 (1982).

Ford v. Wainwright, U.S. 82–5542 (1986).

Furman v. Georgia, 408 U.S. 238 (1972).

Gregg v. Georgia, 428 U.S. 1301 (1976).

Penry v. Lynaugh, 109 S. Ct. 2934 (1989).

Perry v. Louisiana, 494 U.S. 1015 (1990).

Singleton v. Norris, 319 F. 3d 1018 (2003).

Washington v. Harper, 494 U.S. 210 (1990).

REVIEW QUESTIONS

1. Referring to the four core constituencies detailed in the text, to what degree does each benefit from a framework that orients to them as being an individualized or collective part of an execution community?
2. What sorts of efforts or initiatives might enhance the collective trust dimension that the authors describe as lacking the execution community?
3. What sorts of research projects might empirically test the theoretical propositions detailed in this article?

READING 31

Humanizing Death Row Inmates

Michael L. Radelet
Department of Sociology
University of Colorado

This article depicts the career-long efforts of one sociologist who has spent work with death row inmates as a means of standing up for his values and making a difference in the lives of those affected by capital punishment. The author frames his work with death row inmates, their advocates, and loved ones as a form of action-oriented work that over time informed his sociological and criminological understandings and eventually inspired an informed commitment to bring about change in our system of capital punishment. A rich biographical account of his experiences, perceptions, and reflections provides the reader with an insider view of the realities of the death penalty process, from the sentencing phase through the aftermath of the actual execution. The article concludes with the author detailing what he sees to be some noteworthy costs and benefits associated with his sustained work against the death penalty and with death row inmates.

POLONIUS: My lord, I will use them
according to their desert.

HAMLET: God's bodkin, man, much better:
Use every many after his own
desert, and who shall scape
whipping? Use them after your
own honor and dignity—the
less they deserve, the more
merit is in your bounty.

Hamlet, Act II, Scene ii

Students enrolled in undergraduate sociology courses are given, at least implicitly, an invitation to do something about a wide array of issues and problems that face our generation. In such courses, students are often encouraged to expand their compassion for those with relatively few resources, their commitment to do something that might improve problematic conditions or address some of the roots of human misery, and their competence to make their work on these issues more effective. It matters little if the student is liberal or conservative or what "side" of controversial issues one finds most palatable. What matters is the willingness to stand up for those values and issues in which she or he believes. And after taking a survey course in Sociology, most students can find at least one issue that attracts their passions and has the potential to be influenced by their unique talents.

An earlier version of this article first appeared as "Humanizing the death penalty," by Michael L. Radelet, in the journal *Social Problems,* Vol. 48:1, 2001, pp. 83–87, published by the University of California Press.

In this essay, I write about my experiences over the past three decades working with death row inmates. My goal is to provide one example of sociologically informed activism and how that "applied sociology" can reciprocally inform academic scholarship. I offer this as one example of taking Sociology into the "real world" and taking the "real world" into Sociology. My point is not at all to debate the death penalty, but rather to give readers a glimpse of how this issue, and others like it, can attract the passions of students and activists. Key to this attraction is acknowledging the humanity of death row inmates and their families, rather than seeing them as examples of sub-human animals.

I focus on two types of action-oriented work. First is the type that deals directly with those who can aptly be described as "Dead M[e]n Walking" (Prejean 1993), as well as their families, attorneys, ministers, and miscellaneous others in their social support circles. A second type of action-oriented work I describe involves using what I have learned from these groups, as well as from sociological and criminological research, in efforts to inform and promote changes in social policy. This work is designed to try to eliminate what Peter Berger called the "monstrous inhumanity" of capital punishment (Berger 1963:161).

While this type of applied work does not usually show up on academic resumes, it is "sociology" in the sense that it uses scholarly research, as well as sociological skills and knowledge needed to apply that research in the complex political environment in which the death penalty is today situated. Admittedly, it is unclear where (or if or why) the line can be drawn between scholarly and more personal endeavors. The former work generally involves objective analysis of the problem under study in a way that allows replication, while the latter is based on an application of that knowledge so that it has a real impact on people's lives. It follows Howard Becker's (1967) invitation for students of social problems to decide "Whose side are we on?"—and the invitation of C. Wright Mills (1959:186–90) to use our sociological imaginations to expose the fallacies of viewing various social failures as the "personal troubles" of a select few. Eliminating murderers one by one will not reduce our country's problems with high rates of criminal violence.

I will proceed first by describing some of this applied work and then I will discuss some of its costs and benefits.

WORKING WITH DEATH ROW INMATES

Soon after I arrived at the University of Florida in 1979, I was asked to analyze a data set that had been assembled to explore the possibility of race effects in the decision to impose death sentences in Florida (Radelet 1981). This was a straightforward quantitative research project, requiring no off-campus work. But the project sparked my curiosity about the death penalty, and soon I was corresponding with a death row inmate who began to teach me what living under a sentence of death was like.

Shortly thereafter I decided to go to the prison and visit, and I did so twice a month for about eighteen months. Our visits took place in a large reconverted cafeteria, and through those visits I met scores of other death row inmates and their visitors. When the inmate I visited took his own life in August 1981, I began to visit another death row inmate, and did so once per month until he was executed in January 1985. By that time there were approximately 225 prisoners awaiting execution on Florida's death row. To varying degrees, I knew several dozen of them. By mid-2007, there were 3,350 inmates under death sentences in the U.S., including 400 in Florida (and one in Colorado, where I now live).

On death row I found a group of men who, together with their families, were far more "human" than most people would realize. For capital punishment to exist, it is necessary to dehumanize those whom we execute. It is not uncommon to see the condemned referred to as subhuman, rabid dogs whose deaths should be treated with no more concern than the death of a moth splattered on a windshield. To be sure, death row inmates have been and can potentially be dangerous, and we can never forget the horror of their crimes and the damage they have done to their victims (and the victims' families, friends, and communities). At the same time, it is equally true these inmates are more than just their crime; more than the worst thing they ever did. It is also true that many have grown considerably since the days of their crimes and are very different people now than they were then. It does not take x-ray vision to find redeeming qualities in each and a humanity that is unique.

After the 1985 execution of the man I was visiting, attorneys for other death row inmates began to ask me to see specific clients as an unpaid legal assistant, rather than as a social visitor. I have continued to do so ever since. Until I left Florida for Colorado in 2001, I visited the prison an average of once per month (and more often in the weeks before an execution), relaying messages, notarizing court papers, counseling, advising, and lending an ear to a wide array of inmates. Since arriving in Colorado I continue to spend three or four hours per week gathering data on new Florida death penalty cases, consulting on three or four Florida cases per year (non-paid), and corresponding with a half-dozen Florida death row prisoners.

Through this I have gotten to know many of the inmates' family members (Radelet, Vandiver, and Berardo 1983). Some have become close friends and, in Florida, stayed with my family and me when visiting their loved ones in prisons. On a dozen occasions the families of inmates stayed in our home at the time of their loved one's execution.

Legal visits with death row inmates have a number of goals, and each person has unique needs. For example, three or four times per year while in Florida I called on a handful of prisoners newly sentenced to death, trying to give them some accurate information about what course their appeals might take. In other cases the inmate simply needed to exchange ideas with someone who had more experience and perspective than his fellow death row inmates. During the summer of 2000, I visited a man a dozen times who refused to see attorneys and who asked to be executed, trying to convince him that his life had some meaning. (He disagreed and was executed in August 2000.) As I write in 2007, I am working with three other prisoners (in three different states) who are considering volunteering for execution. In some cases I have been asked to attempt to convince prisoners awaiting capital murder trials to accept plea bargains giving them life sentences. In addition, I am occasionally asked by attorneys to work directly with inmates with special needs, such as those impaired by mental retardation or mental illness.

Special attention is needed to those inmates whose executions are scheduled in the forthcoming month or two. In part this shares some similarities working with people facing death from natural causes, so in 1985 I took a Hospice "Volunteer Training Course" to learn more about how to deal with these issues. In addition, many inmates need information about progress on their appeals and their chances of success, help in arranging family visits, and even assistance in planning funerals and distributing their box or two of worldly possessions. Through 2001 I was involved in one way or another with almost all of the 50 men and women executed in Florida, and was the "primary care-giver" for about a dozen.

After an execution, there are several tasks that need to be completed: picking up the inmate's property at the prison and distributing it, planning the funeral, arranging for burial or cremation (and soliciting donations for them), and sprinkling the ashes. For example, for two months in 1989 I stored the ashes of serial murder Ted Bundy in my closet until his family was ready to receive them. In another case, an executed inmate's last wish was to have his ashes scattered in Africa. A year after his death, I sprinkled them in the Atlantic Ocean off the coast of Senegal, taking pictures of the area and the ritual, and purchasing necklaces and bracelets from local craftsmen for his wife and daughters as a remembrance of the ceremony (von Drehle 1995:280–81).

In addition to death row inmates and their families, there is one other group with whom I have worked closely that has had a significant impact on my perspective on the death penalty: families of homicide victims. This is a group that has been largely ignored by sociologists and criminologists, not to mention our larger communities. By attending meetings of such groups as Parents of Murdered Children and listening to these families, I have learned that these survivors have much in common with families of death row inmates (Vandiver 1998). I also saw how our failure to deliver needed assistance to these families makes the death penalty so appealing to some of them. I currently serve on the Board of Directors of a group of Colorado families of homicide victims where the murder is unsolved (Radelet and Stanley, 2006; see also www.unresolvedhomicides.org).

One thing I have learned from these families is that the most important thing we can do for families of homicide victims is to find the killer. Yet, between 1961 and 2005, the proportion of homicides in the U.S. that have been cleared by an arrest has decreased from 94 percent to 62 percent. While few people today claim that the death penalty is a stronger deterrent to criminal homicide than other available punishments (in particular, "Life Without Parole," now available in almost every death penalty state), most would agree that increasing the certainty of punishment would indeed be a powerful deterrent to those contemplating committing a homicide.

SOME COSTS AND BENEFITS

Working against the death penalty and working with death row inmates has produced some of the highest highs and lowest lows in my life. On one hand, going through final visits with an inmate scheduled to be killed within hours, comforting his family and attorneys after the visit, and holding a mother's hand as her son is being executed are, to say the least, quite depressing. It is also true that being involved in battles like the fight over the death penalty necessarily attracts a fair share of personal criticism from supporters of the executioner.

Some critics take the stand that personal involvement with death row inmates and taking a stand against the death penalty reflects some lack of integrity and destroys one's credibility as a scholar. Prosecutors and politicians raise this challenge regularly. Such criticism frequently arises when I testify as an expert witness, which I have now done in six dozen cases. It is, of course, a fair question for prosecutors to ask. It is also an easy question to answer. If expert witnesses are asked for an opinion (e.g., Aren't you opposed to the death penalty?), usually they are able to explain *why* they hold that opinion. This opens the door to a conversation about all sorts of issues that normally cannot be discussed in front of juries, such as the issue of racial bias in death sentencing, the regular occurrence of sentencing innocent people to death, and the near-unanimity of opposition to the death penalty by mainstream religious leaders in the U.S. and throughout the world. Generally prosecutors supporting the death penalty do not want academic experts to discuss its merits and shortcomings in front of a jury.

There are also those in the scholarly community who take personal activism by others (usually not by themselves) as a sign of overpowering bias (e.g., Markman and Cassell 1988). The implication of such criticisms is that only those who support the death penalty (or at least those who pretend to have no opinion) are honest and do credible research on the issue. It helps to believe, true or not, that attacks against one's work usually come only when opponents see it as at least potentially effective. In the end, regardless of one's stand, I believe that "objectivity" (in the sense of accurate portrayal of alternative views, perspectives, and interpretations of data) has virtually nothing to do with "neutrality."

Sustained work on long-term social policy change is easier if one works with a group of like-minded people. I have found that the depressing aspects of death penalty work are palatable only because I worked with a small group of activists in Florida (mainly an attorney and a small group of clergy) who are equally involved in anti-death penalty struggles. Together we do some excellent funerals, help each other lick our wounds in our own particular ways, accept each others' periodic needs to retreat and hide, celebrate our victories, and move on to the next battle. Most of us also survive by using a healthy dose of gallows humor (in its most literal sense).

At the same time, in at least two ways this type of activist sociology can be very beneficial to scholarly research. First, working directly with those most involved in the day-to-day struggles can inform one about what research may be helpful to them (either in courtrooms, legislatures, or in the arena of public opinion), and how that research can best be conducted. It can open doors to others with ideas and expertise. It can allow one to transcend "insider" and "outsider" statuses, gaining understanding both from direct experience and from more abstract formulations (Merton 1972:41).

Second, applied research of this sort can be energizing. One never forgets seeing a child saying good-bye to her father on the eve of his execution, and one cannot help but feel empowered by the dream that no other children will have to repeat that experience. A regular feature of funerals of death row inmates is for those in attendance to vow that they will not have died in vain. Like a surgeon, we will lose patients along the way, but we need to learn from each one, and remember that our ultimate goal is to find a cure for the disease.

CONCLUSIONS

By using our sociological imaginations to distinguish personal troubles from public issues, the question of capital punishment becomes much more than the narrow question of whether to execute some low-life who has committed an unusually nasty murder. Instead, it becomes a question that goes to the very core of who we are as a nation and as a people. We cannot debate the question "Who deserves to die?" without also considering the question "Who deserves to kill?" And for the individuals involved on all sides and at all points, this is an issue that goes to the very core of who they are as human beings. That is why viewing the death penalty as a battle between the forces of good versus solitary bad apples—the only viewpoint that can make executions possible—ends up dehumanizing us all.

In the past three decades, as support for the death penalty at times surpassed 80 percent, fighting the executioner has often been frustrating and depressing, and it is often difficult to find reasons for hope or evidence that one's work is making any difference. This gives rise to the question of how prolonged activism on a given issue can be sustained when little or no benefit from the work is perceived.

One response to this question is to note the importance of simply (or not so simply) taking a stand. I remember many years ago standing with a friend outside Florida State Prison in silent vigil as an execution was taking place. A television reporter came forward and, referring to the strong support for the death penalty in the Sunshine State, asked "Do you think your protests are really going to change the world?" My friend responded, "No. We are here to make sure the world does not change us."

A second response to the problem of perceiving little progress in daily efforts to affect massive social problems is to remember that progress can only be measured over decades, not as an outcome of a single day's work. As Mohandas Gandhi reminds us:

> It's the action, not the fruit of the
> action, that's important.
> You have to do the right thing.

It may not be in your power, may not
be in your time,
that there'll be any fruit.
But that doesn't mean you stop doing
the right thing.
You may never know what results
come from your action.
But if you do nothing,
there will be no result.

In short, regardless of the issue, working for widespread value, attitudinal, or policy change need not be fueled by the smell of proximate victory. Being involved in efforts that require investment of the spirit brings its own rewards. From my angle, as the passage from *Hamlet* that prefaces this article suggests, affirming the human worth and dignity of those at the bottom of our stratification ladders uplifts us all.

REFERENCES

Becker, Howard S. 1967. "Whose side are we on?" *Social Problems* 14:239–47.

Berger, Peter L. 1963. *Invitation to Sociology.* Garden City, N.Y.: Anchor Books.

Markman, Stephen J., and Paul Cassell. 1988. "Protecting the innocent: A response to the Bedau-Radelet study." *Stanford Law Review* 41:121–60.

Merton Robert K. 1972. "Insiders and outsiders: a chapter in the sociology of knowledge." *American Journal of Sociology* 78:8–47.

Mills, C. Wright. 1959. *The Sociological Imagination.* N.Y.: Oxford University Press.

Prejean, Helen. 1993. *Dead Man Walking.* N.Y.: Random House.

Radelet, Michael L. 1981. "Racial characteristics and the imposition of the death penalty." *American Sociological Review* 46:918–27.

Radelet, Michael L., Margaret Vandiver, and Felix Berardo. 1983. "Families, prisons, and men with death sentences: The human impact of structured uncertainty." *Journal of Family Issues* 4:593–612.

Radelet, Michael L. and Dawn Stanley. 2006. "Learning from Homicide Co-Victims: A University-Based Project." Pp. 397–409 in James R. Acker and David R. Karp, *Wounds That Do Not Bind: Victim-Based Perspectives on the Death Penalty.* Durham, N.C.: Carolina Academic Press.

Vandiver, Margaret. 1998. "The impact of the death penalty on the families of homicide victims and of condemned prisoners." In *America's Experiment with Capital Punishment,* eds. James R. Acker, Robert M. Bohm, and Charles S. Lanier, 477–505. Durham, N.C.: Carolina Academic Press.

von Drehle, David. 1995. *Among the Lowest of the Dead.* New York: Times Books.

REVIEW QUESTIONS

1. What are the challenges and benefits of humanizing the death row experience?
2. To what degree should scholars impose limits on what Radelet terms action-oriented work as they engage controversial topics such as the death penalty?
3. Identify what you see to be the key ethical dilemmas that the author has had to confront during his career as a death penalty researcher and activist.
4. What sorts of policies and programs can be implemented to address the emotional and practical needs of family members impacted by the death penalty process?

XIII

UNIQUE CHALLENGES

READING 32

A Comparative Evaluation of a New Generation Jail

James L. Williams

Daniel G. Rodeheaver

Denise W. Huggins

This reading presents the results of a comparative evaluation of three types of jails—a traditional linear jail, a dormitory style jail and a direct supervision, and a podular "new-generation" jail. The results show that generally speaking, both inmates and staff perceive the new generation jail as safer and see more positive attributes regarding staffing and staff-inmate interactions in such a facility. The direct supervision facility also positively compares with the other jails in terms of disruptive incidents, disciplinary reports, and staffing, although there does not appear to be a significant cost savings associated with such a jail.

INTRODUCTION

During the late 1970s, the US government developed and implemented a new style of jail characterized by innovative construction and management approaches. These jails are often referred to as "new generation" jails (Bayans, Williams, & Smykla, 1997). By the early 1980s, evaluations of new generation jails began to appear in the correctional literature. . . .

Because of the lingering, deep-seated problems in jails, as well as the crucial importance of improved correctional design and management to state and local governments, there is a need to continue the development, refinement, and implementation of correctional evaluations. There is also a need to develop a more substantial and theoretically informed body of knowledge about the most effective correctional construction and management techniques.

In light of these concerns, the primary purpose of this article is to report findings from a comparative evaluation of a large jail facility in a southwestern state. This evaluation offers an opportunity to examine the impact of three different styles of correctional architecture and management as three physically separate and architecturally distinct facilities are located on the same site. Thus, the opportunity for a naturalistic evaluation is present. . . .

RELATED LITERATURE

. . . New generation (also referred to as "podular direct supervision") jails have been in existence since the late 1970s. . . . The first new generation jails were sponsored and constructed by the Federal Bureau of Prisons in the late 1970s. They represent a significant change in correctional architecture and management.

The typical facility houses up to 48 inmates in large, open living areas, typically called pods. New generation jails forego the use of traditional bars and cells in favor of open living areas. The management philosophy envisions a new mode of interaction between staff and inmates. For example, the staff communicate freely and openly with inmates. The use of coercive measures and labeling of the inmates are absent. Humane, respectful treatment of both inmates and staff is encouraged. In this management style, a correctional officer remains in continual interaction with inmates, monitoring and resolving problems as they occur. This philosophy, usually referred to as direct supervision, has become accepted in an increasing number of jail and correctional facilities. . . .

DATA AND METHODOLOGY

Data Sources and Collection

There were two primary sources of data for this study. The first source was drawn from a questionnaire administered to inmates and staff during June 1995. The purpose of the questionnaire was to measure various aspects of inmate and staff satisfaction with the correctional environment, including perceived safety, security, inmate living conditions, and staff working conditions. . . .

The second source of data encompassed staffing, disciplinary, and maintenance data for each of the three facilities. Specifically, data were collected for each facility for the period March (the month the new generation jail facility opened) to August 1995. Data were collected on staffing patterns of supervisory and line officers for each of the three shifts for each facility. During this period, disciplinary records (incident reports) were collected and disaggregated by category, and average inmate population counts were collected for each facility. The operational data were collected during the period June 1995-September 1995.

. . . The complex consists of three separate jails. One is a traditional linear jail with a capacity of 250 inmates. The second consists of four trailers converted into barracks to house trusties, with a capacity of 160 inmates. The third facility consists of eight pods, each housing 48 inmates, with a capacity of 384 inmates. . . .

. . . A total of 440 questionnaires were distributed to inmates and 249 usable questionnaires were returned, for a response rate of 56%. Of the completed and usable questionnaires returned, 31% were from the linear jail, 23% were from the barracks, and 45% were from the pods.

To limit the evaluation to staff members who had the most direct contact with inmates, only those detention officers at the two lowest ranks were asked to participate. The linear jail employed 51 detention staff (9 supervisors and 42 officers), the barracks employed 39 detention staff (9 supervisors and 30 officers), and the new generation facility employed 72 detention staff (11 supervisors and 61 officers). At the time the data were collected there were a total of 133 line (nonsupervisory) officers employed. At the specific recommendation of the Captain of Jail Operations, we provided a total of 100 questionnaires for nonsupervisory personnel. Those questionnaires were given to the captain, who arranged for the lieutenant in charge of each shift to announce the study at the next two staff briefings.

. . . Usable questionnaires were returned by 53 detention officers, for an overall response rate of 53%. Of the completed questionnaires returned by detention staff, 26% were from the linear jail, 22% from the barracks, and 52% were from the new generation facility. . . .

Inmate Responses: Safety, Security, and Living Conditions

Table 1 illustrates inmate responses to selected items measuring perceptions of facility safety, which suggest that the only significant differences were in terms of inmate perceptions of personal safety and inmate fights. A total of 81% of the respondents in the new generation facility ($\chi 2 = 41.40$, $p < .001$) reported feeling personally safe either always or most of the time, while by contrast only 47% of the inmates in the linear jail reported feeling safe either always or most of the time. This finding is consistent with other evaluations that have indicated that new generation jails are perceived as personally safer environments (Zupan & Menke, 1988).

There were no differences in perceptions of attacks on officers being a problem. Moreover, inmates in each facility did not believe officers had to be careful to protect themselves from harm. Similarly, there were no significant differences by facility in the perceived need for inmates to protect themselves from attacks. The majority of inmates in all facilities almost uniformly denied fearing rape, with no significant differences being reported. To some extent, however, this finding may reflect attitudes among the inmates that make them unwilling to admit to such fears, as to do so may cast doubt on their perceived ability to protect themselves.

Finally, there were significant differences in regard to perceived problems with inmate fights ($\chi 2 = 35.97$, $p < .001$). While the majority of inmates in all facilities reported that inmate fights were not a problem (the percentages ranged from 69% in the linear jail to 84% in the barracks), inmates in the linear jail were the most likely to report that fights were a problem (15% most or all of the time) as compared to inmates in the barracks (5%) or in the new generation facility (8%). In this measure of safety, the barracks were seen as somewhat more effective. This may have been a result of the fact that inmates in the barracks were all low-risk trusties. Overall, the inmates perceived each of the jail facilities as generally safe for officers, for other inmates, and for themselves personally. . . .

Inmate Responses to Open-Ended Items: Likes and Dislikes

The participants were asked to respond to two open-ended items on the survey: (1) to identify positive features of the jail, and (2) to identify things they disliked about the jail. Responses were received from 93% (231) of the inmates. Several interesting differences were noted here. Forty percent (93) of those who responded

TABLE 1 Inmate Perceptions of Facility Safety

Item	Linear		Barracks		Pods	
	N	%	*N*	%	*N*	%
Feel safe here***						
Always	14	18	24	43	52	46
Most of time	22	29	18	32	39	35
Not Sure	6	8	5	9	1	1
Some of time	19	25	8	14	13	12
Never	15	20	1	2	7	6
Attacks on officers a problem						
Always	1	1	0	0	1	1
Most of time	1	1	0	0	1	1
Not Sure	23	30	5	9	17	15
Some of time	4	5	1	2	4	4
Never	46	61	49	88	89	80
Officers have to be careful?						
Always	2	3	1	2	4	4
Most of time	6	78	0	0	2	2
Not Sure	18	23	8	14	14	13
Some of time	9	12	2	4	16	14
Never	41	53	45	80	76	68
Have to protect yourself from attacks?						
Always	17	22	6	11	13	12
Most of time	6	8	3	5	9	8
Not Sure	4	5	5	9	8	7
Some of time	30	39	12	21	34	30
Never	19	25	30	54	48	43
Fear rape?						
Always	2	3	0	0	4	4
Most of time	1	1	0	0	0	0
Not Sure	6	8	5	9	1	1
Some of time	12	15	0	0	8	7
Never	55	72	50	89	98	88
Problems with inmate fights?***						
Always	4	5	2	3	7	6
Most of time	8	11	1	2	2	2
Not Sure	10	13	6	11	11	10
Some of time	39	52	16	29	50	45
Never	13	17	31	55	42	38

*p < .05, **p < .01, ***p < .001

commented on their interactions with officers. Inmates in the new generation facility were substantially more positive toward the officers. One inmate from the new generation facility remarked, "Most officers in the pod treat me with dignity and respect as opposed to being treated like a non-person as in other parts of the jail." Another respondent wrote, "The officers here in the pod are very nice." By contrast, five inmates in the linear jail commented that officers needed to be better trained to handle stress and to learn how to communicate with inmates more effectively. As one inmate wrote, "Some of the officers tend to treat us more as animals or small children than adults."

Seventy-two percent (166) of the inmate respondents commented on the physical facilities of the jail. Thirty-one percent (24) of the inmate respondents in the linear jail and barracks commented critically on such issues as the lack of windows, old mattresses, lack of fresh air and lighting, and the lack of exercise equipment. Comments by inmates in the new generation facility were substantially more positive. None of the inmates in the pods made critical comments about the physical facilities. The favorable comments included positive attitudes about their ability to watch cable TV and to use microwaves, computers, and computer games, as well as a washer and dryer.

Twenty-seven percent (20) of the inmates in the linear jail complained of the lack of things to do, the lack of activities to help them pass the time. As one inmate stated, "We need things to do during the day besides staring at the TV." By contrast, all of the comments from inmates in the new generation facility concerning recreation and the physical facilities were positive.

Seventy-two percent (166) of all the inmates who responded in each facility commented on the overall quality of the jail in which they were housed. While only 25% of the overall comments were negative, all of the negative comments came from the linear jail and barracks. Again, the comments by inmates in the new generation facility were far more positive. One inmate wrote, "As compared to most jails it is a paradise." Another commented, "The pod area is a good thing for the inmates." A third inmate added, "I think (the) sheriff is on to something good; this is the most humane jail I've ever been in."

The open-ended comments from inmates in the new generation facility were overwhelmingly positive, with very few complaints. No inmates complained about the new generation facility. The only complaints concerned food and medical care. In each case, these complaints paralleled those of inmates in the other two facilities.

Staff Responses: Safety, Security, and Working Conditions

Table 2 reports responses to selected measures of facility safety. What is notable in this table is the general uniformity in responses. The majority (over 90%) of staff in each facility feel safe either always or most of the time. The new generation facility was not seen as particularly safer in this respect. No differences were seen regarding inmate fights being a problem. In the perception of problems with attacks on officers, the only difference was that barracks officers reported the least concern (92% never a problem; $\chi 2 = 23.69$, $p < .001$).

There may be several reasons for this uniformity of responses. First, the organizational culture may promote an unwillingness to express fears for personal safety on the part of staff. Second, the items may not have been sensitive or accurate enough to tap actual safety concerns. In addition, a more representative sample may have revealed other differences. . . .

TABLE 2 Staff Perceptions of Facility Safety

Item	Linear		Barracks		Pods	
	N	%	*N*	%	*N*	%
Feel safe here						
Always	7	51	5	42	7	25
Most of time	6	43	6	50	19	68
Not Sure	0	0	0	0	0	0
Some of time	1	7	1	8	1	4
Never	0	0	0	0	1	4
Attacks on officers a problem***						
Always	0	0	0	0	0	0
Most of time	0	0	0	0	0	0
Not Sure	0	0	1	8	4	14
Some of time	9	64	0	0	2	7
Never	5	36	11	92	22	79
Have to protect yourself from attacks?						
Always	6	43	7	58	13	46
Most of time	2	14	1	8	4	14
Not Sure	1	7	0	0	1	4
Some of time	3	21	3	25	4	14
Never	2	14	1	8	6	21
Fear Rape?						
Always	0	0	0	0	2	7
Most of time	0	0	0	0	1	4
Not Sure	0	0	1	8	2	7
Some of time	0	0	2	17	3	11
Never	14	100	9	75	20	71
Problems with inmate fights?***						
Very Often	0	0	0	0	1	4
Often	2	14	0	0	1	4
Some of time	12	86	10	83	25	89
Never	0	0	2	17	1	4

$^{*}p < .05$, $^{**}p < .01$, $^{***}p < .001$

Staff Responses to Open-Ended Items

The staff were also asked to respond to two open-ended items on the survey. These measured positive and negative features of the jail and/or their work environment. A total of 77% (41) of the staff participants responded to these items. The items asked staff to comment on positive and negative features of the jail and/or their work environment. In general, staff responses were similar to those of the inmates. The comments did, however, indicate several differences between the facilities.

One of the most notable differences was related to officer-inmate contact. Officers in the new generation facility seemed to like working individually with many of the inmates and felt more positive about the inmates as persons. For example, one officer stated, "I enjoy working one on one with the inmates. I believe this cuts down a lot on the tension between inmates and officers." It is difficult to discern to what degree this attitude is due to the nature of the working environment in the new generation facility or to personal characteristics of the officers. However, the thrust of other comments of this nature suggests that officer and inmate contact in the new generation facility is less hostile in nature.

Officers in the new generation facility expressed satisfaction with their freedom to work without constant supervision as well as the greater degree of control over inmates that they felt they had. One officer in this facility wrote, "It is clean, quiet, and better controlled than the old style of jail." A second officer commented, "Your supervisors trust you to make your own choices." As another officer stated, "We have full control without being forceful." Another officer wrote, "In the pods there is more control over the inmates' behavior than in other parts of the jail. The officer is in control of the pod whereas in the old jail the inmates control the tanks."

Ten respondents commented positively on the much higher level of cleanliness in the new generation facility. This was in contrast to the comments of four officers in the linear jail who were particularly negative about the lack of cleanliness, fresh air, or adequate temperature control.

Negative comments by staff in the new generation facility paralleled those in the other two jails. Most negative comments centered around working conditions, primarily in the areas of better wages, improvements in morale, additional staffing, higher quality employees, and uniformity of rules. A particular complaint by officers in the linear jail concerned the lack of staffing. One officer commented, "More officers are needed on the floor for support." In contrast to the feelings of positive support from supervisors in the new generation facility were comments by officers in the linear jail and barracks, including one who wrote, "More communication between shifts and officers is needed." Overall, 44% (18) of the respondents expressed positive attitudes toward aspects of their job including the quality of staff and the chance for positive contact with the inmates.

Operational Data by Facility

Incident and Disciplinary Reports Table 3 reports data from incident and disciplinary reports during this period. Because of staffing constraints, these data were provided only for the months of July 1994, January 1995, June 1995, and August 1995. The data are divided into the categories of assaults, incidents (including confrontations and arguments), escape attempts, escape, suicide attempts, possession of contraband, and other (miscellaneous) offenses. Table 3 indicates that the overall number of incidents and disciplinary problems reported in the new generation facility was substantially lower than in the linear jail. This was true even though the overall number of inmates in the new generation facility during this period was higher than in the linear jail. For example, the level of arguments and argument-related incidents varied substantially, from a high of 97 in the linear jail to a low of 61 in the new generation facility.

There were no differences in the number of inmate assaults in the new generation facility and the barracks (12 in each), while in the linear jail the number was nearly three times higher (33). This finding is consistent with Senese (1997),

TABLE 3 Disciplinary Reports Filed by Facility and Type of Report (July 1994–August 1995)

Type	Linear *N*	Barracks *N*	Pods *N*
Assaults			
Inmate-Inmate	33	12	12
Inmate-Officer	3	1	0
Incidents	97	90	61
Escape attempts	0	0	0
Escapes	0	0	0
Suicide attempts	0	0	0
Contraband	18	12	15
Other	12	6	3
Total	163	121	91
Rate of Reports	64	78	29

Note: Data are reported for July 1994, January 1995, June 1995, and August 1995. "Incidents" primarily involve inmate arguments. "Other" represents miscellaneous offenses not otherwise categorized. Rate of reports is calculated by (Total # of reports/average population)*100

who also found lower levels of disciplinary problems in new generation jail facilities. . . .

Staffing Costs Table 4 compares staffing patterns in each of the facilities for 1995, including the average daily inmate population in each facility and the total and average number of supervisors and staff in each facility. The data are divided by shifts. In addition, a staff-inmate ratio was calculated for each facility for this period. While more officers were assigned to the new generation facility, this facility also held more inmates. The staff-inmate ratio was lower in the new generation facility than in the linear jail. In the new generation facility, one staff member supervised six inmates, as compared to one staff member for every eight inmates in the linear jail. The staffing patterns here do not reveal any clear savings in terms of the number of staff assigned to supervise inmates. Thus, these data offer no clear indication that this facility was saving money in staffing costs by using the podular facilities. Our findings differ from those of Horn (1984) and Farbstein and Wener (1989). Horn's (1984) analysis of a direct supervision facility in Miami indicated that staffing requirements were approximately 50% less in the new generation jail than in the existing linear jail. Farbstein and Wener (1989) found that new generation jails required no more staffing overall than traditional jails.

In sum, a review of the operational indicators of incidents, disciplinary reports, and staffing levels suggests the presence of some advantages for the new generation facility. The number of incidents and rate of disciplinary reports were substantially

TABLE 4 Staffing and Population Information by Facility (January 1, 1995–December 31, 1995)

Categories	Linear	Barracks	Pods
Average daily pop.	254	155	311
Supervisors by shift			
Total			
Day	3	3	4
Evening	3	3	4
Night	3	3	3
Average			
Day	2	2	2
Evening	2	2	2
Night	2	2	2
Other Officers			
Total			
Day	14	11	21
Evening	14	10	21
Night	14	9	19
Average			
Day	8	6	15
Evening	8	6	15
Night	7	6	13
Staff/Inmate Ratio	1:8.4	1:6.4	1:6.3

Note: Staff/inmate ratios calculated using average number of officers and average number of supervisors.

lower in the new generation facility during this period, thus achieving one of the goals of lower levels of violence and disciplinary problems, although the new generation facility was not cheaper to staff. When jail officials operate traditional linear facilities, they can supervise more people with fewer staff. However, there appears to be a tradeoff in increased levels of violence and other antisocial behavior. As suggested in the staff comments, use of linear jails also appears to result in many situations where inmates are in effective control of what happens in cell blocks.

CONCLUSIONS

Using traditional criteria of inmate and staff satisfaction, combined with operational data, this study evaluated a new generation jail by comparing it with two other physically adjacent jails: a traditional linear jail and a barracks facility. Data were collected using a survey of inmates and staff combined with operational data on incidents and disciplinary reports and with staffing patterns.

The survey and operational data provide generally positive support for the superiority of the new generation jail. Inmates and staff were much more satisfied with the physical facilities. Staff perceived it as more secure in terms of escape risk. The inmate and staff comments from the new generation facility were substantially more positive in the areas of quality of facilities, inmate-officer relations, and staff control over inmates. Violence and disciplinary problems were significantly lower. No savings in reduced staffing levels or costs were noted. The only differences in job satisfaction were the measure of advancement. Here barracks staff were more optimistic. There were no differences in job satisfaction for staff in the new generation jail. Overall, the staff perceived only limited advantages in safety and security. . . .

REFERENCES

Bayens, G., Williams, J., & Smykla, J. (1997). Jail type and inmate behavior: A longitudinal analysis. *Federal Probation, 61,* 54–62.

Farbstein, J., & Wener, R. (1982). Evaluation of correctional environments. *Environment and Behavior, 14,* 671–694.

Farbstein, J., & Wener, R. (1989). *Comparison of "direct" and "indirect" supervision correctional facilities, final report.* Washington, DC: National Institute of Corrections.

Glaser, D. (1980). The interplay of theory, issues, policy, and data. In M. Klein & K. Teilmann (Eds.), *Handbook of Criminal Justice Evaluation* (pp. 123–142). Newbury Park, CA: Sage.

Horn, S. (1984). *The cost-benefits of podular designed and directly supervised correctional facilities.* Washington, DC: National Institute of Corrections.

Jackson, P., & Stearns, C. (1995). Gender issues in the new generation jails. *Prison Journal, 75,* 203–222.

Nelson, W., & O'Toole, M. (1983). *New generation jails.* Longmont, CO: National Institute of Corrections Information Center.

Nelson, W., & Davis, R. (1995). Podular direct supervision: The first 20 years. *American Jails, 9,* 11–22.

Sechrest, D. (1991). The effects of density on jail assaults. *Journal of Criminal Justice, 19,* 211–223.

Senese, J. (1997). Evaluating jail reform: A comparative analysis of podular/direct and linear jail inmate infractions. *Journal of Criminal Justice, 25,* 73.

Stohr, M., Lovrich, N., & Wilson, G. (1994). Staff stress in contemporary jails: Assessing problem severity and the payoff of progressive personnel practices. *Journal of Criminal Justice, 22,* 313–327.

Stohr, M., Self, R., & Lovrich, N. (1992). Staff turnover in new generation jails: An investigation of its causes and prevention. *Journal of Criminal Justice, 20,* 455–464.

Wener, R., Frazier, W., & Farbstein, J. (1985). Three generations of design and evaluation of correctional facilities. *Environment and Behavior, 17,* 71–95.

Wener, R. (1995). Evaluating the design of direct supervision jails. *Progressive Architecture, 76,* 79–81.

Williams, J., & Sadri, M. (1997, March). Bringing theory into correctional research: Applications to new generation jails. Paper presented at the annual meeting of the Southwestern Sociological Association, New Orleans.

Zimring, C., & Wener, R. (1985). Evaluating evaluation. *Environment and Behavior, 17,* 97–117.

Zupan, L. (1991). *Jails: Reform and the new generation philosophy.* Cincinnati: Anderson.

Zupan, L., & Menke, B. (1988). Implementing organizational change: From traditional to new generation jail operations. *Policy Studies Review, 7,* 615–625.

Zupan, L. & Stohr-Gillmore, M. (1988). Doing time in the new generation jail: inmate perceptions of gains and losses. *Policy Studies Review, 7,* 626–640.

REVIEW QUESTIONS

1. What is the evidence to support the contention that inmates feel safer in the new-generation jail than in the other two types of jails?
2. How are the responses of inmates and staff regarding perceptions of safety in the three types of jails similar and different?
3. Does the study support that new-generation jails save money by lowering staffing levels?

REVIEW QUESTIONS

READING 33

Trauma Exposure, Mental Health Functioning, and Program Needs of Women in Jail

Bonnie L. Green

Jeanne Miranda

Anahita Daroowalla

Juned Siddique

This reading reports on an assessment of the psychological and programming needs of women incarcerated in jail. The study shows that women in jail have significantly greater psychological, emotional, substance use/abuse, sexual, and social problems than women in general. Women report that they recognize their need for educational and intervention programming and generally want to participate in programs while in jail. Overall, women in jail report much higher rates of exposure to a variety of traumatic experiences in life than women in the general population.

The Bureau of Justice recently reported that the nation's jail population has increased more than 40% since 1990 (U.S. Department of Justice, 2003) with rates of incarceration increasing more for women than for men. Since 1995, the male population has risen by 3.8% annually, whereas the female population has risen by 5.9%. This dramatic growth has been attributed to increases in illicit drug use among women along with an increase in drug-related convictions and mandatory sentencing (Covington, 1998; Owen & Bloom, 1995; U.S. Department of Justice, 1999). Even so, women inmates still make up only 12% of the jail population (U.S. Department of Justice, 2003). Perhaps for this reason, relatively little attention has been paid to the needs of this small but growing population (Koons, Burrow, Morash, & Bynum, 1997).

Most incarcerated women are mothers; 7 in 10 women under correctional sanction have minor children (U.S. Department of Justice, 1999). Several studies have examined the impact on children of their mother's incarceration, and the effects are quite negative: These children suffer emotional distress, poor school performance, and aggressive behavior (Greene, Haney, & Hurtado, 2000). Yet little is known about the capabilities of incarcerated women to fulfill their parenting roles once they are released from prison or the vulnerabilities of their children based on previous interactions with these mothers.

Women prisoners have also been shown to have very high exposure to a variety of trauma experiences, especially to interpersonal violence, including childhood physical and sexual abuse (Battle, Zlotnick, Najavits, Gutierrez, & Winsor, 2003; Browne, Miller, & Maguin, 1999; Greene et al., 2000; Jordan, Schlenger, Fairbank, & Caddell, 1996; Owen & Bloom, 1995; Teplin, Abram, & McClelland, 1996). They also have high rates of mental disorders and substance abuse (Battle et al., 2003; Jordan et al., 1996; Sanders, McNeill, Rienzi, & DeLouth, 1997; Teplin et al., 1996). . . . A recent review suggests that exposure to traumatic events is nearly universal among incarcerated women with studies showing ranges of trauma exposure to be between 77% and 90% (Battle et al., 2003), including a range of estimates for each type of trauma, but with all rates well exceeding those in the general population (Kessler, Sonnega, Bromet, Hughes, & Nelson, 1995). Indeed, the experience of trauma is likely a determining factor in the involvement in criminal behavior for women through such mechanisms as child abuse leading to early running away and abuse-related psychopathology like PTSD leading to substance abuse for self-medication purposes, both, in turn, being associated with increased risk for criminal behavior (Battle et al., 2003).

Trauma exposure, especially interpersonal trauma, is also a significant predictor of risky health behaviors including smoking, substance abuse, and risky sexual behavior (Rheingold, Acierno, & Resnick, 2004). . . .

Historically, jail services have been developed for, and are mostly geared toward, male inmates. However, recent studies suggest that the need for services targeting women and their specific issues are increasingly recognized. For example, Koons et al. (1997) did a comprehensive survey of state and federal administrators in settings where women were incarcerated to examine treatment programs in place in their own jurisdictions. The areas covered by these programs included substance abuse education (55%), substance abuse treatment (47%), programs for parenting (44%), life skills (42%), and relationship skills (37%). Programs addressing other areas were available in less than one quarter of the surveyed sites, with programs targeting sexual abuse being identified by only 13% of programs and mental health being targeted by only 7% of participants. Administrators indicated that their programs tended to target five or more areas. Indeed, in spite of various mandates to provide at least basic mental health treatment in the criminal justice system, only a minority of jails offers a comprehensive range of services (Steadman, Barbera, & Dennis, 1994). In a more general survey of mental health services in jails serving both men and women, Morris, Steadman, and Veysey (1997) found that although 50% of the jails they surveyed provided crisis intervention and psychotropic medications, other services were much less common. Only about a third of the sites offered counseling, and only about a quarter reported offering discharge planning—clearly a critical element in a plan to prevent recidivism.

Although services targeting women and acknowledging their gender-specific victimization experiences are becoming more common (Welle, Falkin, & Jainchill, 1998) and a variety of newly developed services targeted at women inmates' particular needs have been proposed (e.g., Covington, 1998; Zlotnick, Najavits, Rohsenow, & Johnson, 2003), these specialized services continue to be the exception rather than the rule. . . .

In this study, we examined trauma exposure, mental health problems, and substance abuse issues among a sample of female jail detainees in a county facility. Each area has strong implications for the development of appropriate services. We also expanded the focus beyond these previously studied variables to include several other areas that have important implications for the economic, social, and family goals described above including risky sexual behavior and parenting capacity.

Finally, we interviewed the women about their own perceptions of need and what services they would find useful while incarcerated.

METHOD

Procedures

A convenience sample of female inmate volunteers at the Prince George's County Correctional Center participated in this project. . . . Approximately 125 women are present in this facility at a given time, housed together in one section, with stays of varying lengths. Some women are pretrial detainees, whereas others are serving sentences following conviction. . . .

Participating women were given a $15 certificate good for purchases in the center store in partial compensation for their time.

The interview took approximately 1.5 to 2 hours to complete. The interviewers were two female clinical psychologists (Ph.D.s) with clinical and research interviewing experience. . . .

RESULTS

Sample

One hundred women participated in this project. . . . The sample was predominantly composed of young, single women with fairly low levels of educational attainment. Nearly half had not completed high school (44%). . . . Participants were predominantly African American with a smaller White/mixed-race sample. Approximately three quarters of the women had children younger than the age of 18. Most women were awaiting trial, although 20% were serving a current sentence. Finally, women were charged with a variety of crimes and sometimes were multiply charged (our categories were not mutually exclusive), but most had relatively brief stays in the jail. . . .

Trauma Exposure

Results of the trauma exposure, substance abuse, and mental health assessment are presented in Table 1. . . . Similar to other studies, rates of lifetime trauma exposure were extremely high. In total, 98% of the women had been exposed to at least one category of trauma. The most common trauma exposure was to violence perpetrated by a husband, partner, or boyfriend with 71% reporting this experience. In total, 62% reported having been exposed to childhood traumas and 90% to at least one type of interpersonal trauma.

Substance Abuse

Substance abuse was common, as can be seen in Table 1. Although one-third of the sample (34%) reported that they do not drink, 32% were classified . . . as

TABLE 1 Trauma, Psychiatric Disorders, and Substance Abuse

	% Affected
Childhood trauma	
Sexually molested	48%
Physically abused	26%
Neglected	25%
Any childhood trauma	62%
Other trauma	
Life-threatening accident	42%
Fire, flood, or natural disaster	9%
Witnessed someone injured or killed	58%
Family member killed	58%
Raped	58%
Physically attacked/abused	57%
Domestic abuse	71%
Threatened with a weapon	55%
At least one trauma	98%
Substance abuse problems[a]	
Alcohol problem	32%
Drug problem	72%
Marijuana	37%
Cocaine, crack, heroin	60%
Hallucinogens	10%
Alcohol or drug problem	74%
Psychiatric disorders	
Current major depressive disorder (MDD)	25%
Dysthymia	12%
Possible bipolar disorder	13%
Current post-traumatic stress disorder (PTSD)	22%
MDD, PTSD, or bipolar	36%

a. Substance abuse assessed for the 6 months preceding incarceration.

having an alcohol problem. Nearly three quarters (72%) reported recent use of an illicit substance, and 74% reported either an alcohol or substance abuse problem.

Mental Health Problems

Although not as frequent as substance abuse problems, rates of the psychiatric disorders studied were higher than would be expected in the community. One fourth of the women reported current MDD and 22% had current PTSD. Twelve percent screened positive for dysthymia and 13% for bipolar disorder. Adding together the three major categories (excluding dysthymia), just more than one third had one of the psychiatric diagnoses.

Sexual and Reproductive Behavior

Women were an average age of 16 at the time of their first voluntary intercourse. Nearly all had been pregnant at least once (92%), many had miscarried (44%), and more than half had undergone at least one abortion (60%). Nearly half reported having had a sexually transmitted disease (STD). The number of lifetime sexual partners averaged 30.4 (range of 2 to 300; 11 women reported 100 or more partners), and, on average, women had 14.4 (range of 0 to 200) sexual partners who became sexual partners on the first encounter. Thirty-six percent reported never, rarely, or only sometimes using condoms, although condom use was not associated with PTSD. . . .

Perceived Program/Service Needs

We asked the women, "Aside from incarceration, what do you see as your biggest problem right now?" The most common response was substance abuse problems (42%), followed by family issues (22%), lack of skills and direction (12%), and lack of a job or appropriate job training (9%). Four women indicated that being in jail was their only problem. The women also reported on the types of programs they would be interested in attending if they were available (Table 2). All possibilities were endorsed by half or more of the respondents except alcohol treatment. Among the most endorsed were job training (93%), problem-solving skills (91%), stress management (88%), and communication-skills training (83%).

We explored the relationships between perceived service needs and identification of problems. The strongest associations were for substance abuse. Those who specified substance abuse as their biggest problem were more interested in drug or alcohol treatment than those who did not. . . . The association between having

TABLE 2 Programs of Interest

If the Following Programs Were Offered	% Interested
Drug education/treatment	75%
Alcohol treatment	45%
General Equivalency Diploma preparation	50%
Stress management	88%
Relationship workshops	82%
Job training	93%
Individual mental health counseling	80%
Group mental health counseling	69%
Anger management	76%
Reading skills	63%
Parenting skills	79%
Communication skills	83%
Problem-solving skills	91%
Health education	82%

a mental disorder and being interested in individual or group treatment came close to being significant ($p < .10$). We did not find associations between expressed problems and perceived service needs in the areas of jobs or parenting.

DISCUSSION

This study replicated findings of high levels of trauma exposure, especially interpersonal trauma, among incarcerated women along with high rates of substance use problems and clinically important levels of depression and PTSD (Battle et al., 2003; Browne et al., 1999; Greene et al., 2000; Jordan et al., 1996; Owen & Bloom, 1995; Sanders et al., 1997; Teplin et al., 1996). Nearly all of the women had been exposed to a traumatic event (98%), 90% reported at least one interpersonal trauma, and 71% reported being exposed to domestic violence. More than one-third (36%) had one of the current mental disorders we assessed with 22% meeting criteria for current PTSD and 25% for current MDD. Thirty-two percent of women were screened as having an alcohol problem, and 72% reported illicit drug use before entering the jail. These figures are similar to those found in other studies. The most comprehensive study of jail detainees (Teplin et al., 1996) found that 60% of the sample had a substance abuse diagnosis, 14% met criteria for current MDD, and 22% met criteria for current PTSD. Although our study found identical rates of PTSD as in Teplin et al. (1996), our higher rates of substance use problems and major depression are likely due to the fact that we used screening rather than diagnostic measures for these constructs. Our PTSD measure, however, was a diagnostic rather than a screening measure. All of the rates observed in this study are higher than those in the general population (Kessler et al., 1994, 1995)

Our findings showed moderate levels of risky sexual behavior, including failure to use condoms and sex with multiple partners, with 43% reporting STDs. A study in a New York jail where women were physically tested for STDs found a rate of 61% at the time of entry into the jail (Richie & Johnson, 1996). Although our figures are not directly comparable, they appear to be in the same range or slightly lower than those from the Hutton et al. (2001) study, which found 56% of women prisoners never or rarely used condoms and that 7% reported 100 or more lifetime sexual partners (11% in the present study). Comparing these figures to a sample of college sophomore women (Green et al., 2004) where we used a similar measure, the college sample was younger (19–20), had more education, and had a similar age at first intercourse (16–17). However, the incarcerated women had much higher rates of high-risk sexual behaviors. . . .

There is an increasing understanding of the fact that many women in prison or jail for committing crimes are crime victims themselves. In particular, they have often been abused sexually and physically in childhood, many have been raped, and exposure to family violence is endemic. Indeed, some of this exposure probably contributes to their involvement in criminal behavior (Battle et al., 2003). Most programs focus heavily on substance abuse (Battle et al., 2003; Welle et al., 1998).

Indeed, substance abuse rates are high, and abuse of substances is a common reason for incarceration. However, there seems to be a growing appreciation that the overwhelming exposure to violence among these women needs to be addressed directly and explicitly. . . .

Programs that provide skills training, particularly in the area of parenting, are needed. Although we did not examine the children of study participants, other studies have suggested that interventions for children of inmates are indicated as well (Greene et al., 2000). . . . A study by Greene et al. (2000) showed that 83% of the children of the incarcerated mothers they interviewed had either been sexually or physically abused or had witnessed violence in their homes. These mothers also reported that the children had seen the people in their households use drugs or alcohol and had seen the mothers under the influence of alcohol or drugs. Greene et al. referred to these findings as the "cycle of pain." Our findings suggest that these women may have quite unrealistic views about what are reasonable expectations for children and what it means to be a parent and that they lack the skills to provide adequate parenting for their children. The combination of the children's exposures and the parenting deficits they experience put them at extremely high risk for continuing the violence cycle and becoming wards of the state themselves in addition to their potential psychological pain and suffering. . . .

The women seemed quite aware of the areas of their own needs, and they expressed strong interest in programs addressing these needs. In regard to their "biggest problem" at present, they identified substance abuse and issues with family and children as the most important problems. They endorsed interest in most of the programs that were hypothetically offered, but the highest endorsements were for problem-solving skills, stress management, and job training—a good fit with their trauma histories, mental health problems, and poverty identified in this study. Almost 80% of the women endorsed programs that taught parenting skills—about the same proportion that had children younger than 18. . . .

Because of the multiple and chronic problems identified in these women and their limited skills for adaptively coping with them, services such as case management may be particularly appropriate adjunct interventions for programs that follow these women into the community. In fact, case managers have been found to be an important component of successful diversion programs (Ventura, Cassel, Jacoby, & Huang, 1998), particularly when case managers are ethnically matched with clients and have a high level of involvement with each client (Steadman, Morris, & Dennis, 1995). Case managers may be needed to work with the women over an extended period of time to help them solve day-to-day life problems, provide assistance with parenting skills, and help women with entitlements.

This raises a larger issue of continuity of psychosocial services once the women have left the jail setting, as well as the broad range of other services needed, although we did not address these in the present study. Because they are going back to the real world, they may need a greater number of continuing services and more support than they did in jail. Yet the jail or prison may be the only place where a larger range of services is available (Osher, Steadman, & Barr, 2003). . . .

REFERENCES

American Psychiatric Association. (1994). *Diagnostic and statistical manual of mental disorders* (4th ed.). Washington, DC: Author.

Bassuk, E. L., & Donelan, B. (2003). Social deprivation. In B. L. Green, M. Friedman, J. de Jong, S. Solomon, T. Keane, J. Fairbank, et al. (Eds.), *Trauma interventions in war and peace: Prevention, practice, and policy* (pp. 33–55). New York: Kluwer.

Battle, C. L., Zlotnick, C., Najavits, L. M., Guttierrez, M., & Winsor, C. (2003). Posttraumatic stress disorder and substance use disorder among incarcerated women. In P. C. Ouimette & P. J. Brown (Eds.), *Trauma and substance abuse: Causes, consequences, and treatment of comorbid disorders* (pp. 209–225). Washington, DC: American Psychological Association.

Bavolek, S. J., & Keene, R. G. (1999). *Adult-Adolescent Parenting Inventory, AAPI-2: Administration and development handbook.* Park City, UT: Family Development Resources.

Browne, A., Miller, B., & Maguin, E. (1999). Prevalence and severity of lifetime physical and sexual victimization among incarcerated women. *International Journal of Law and Psychiatry, 22,* 301–322.

Chan, A. W. K., Pristach, E. A., Welte, J. W., & Russell, M. (1993). Use of the TWEAK test in screening for alcoholism/heavy drinking in three populations. *Alcoholism: Clinical and Experimental Research, 17,* 1188–1192.

Chatterji, S., Saunders, J. B., Vrasti, R., Grant, B. F., Hasin, D., & Mager, D. (1997). Reliability of the alcohol and drug modules of the Alcohol Use Disorder and Associated Disabilities Interview Schedule—Alcohol/Drug-Revised (AUDADIS-ADR): An international comparison. *Drug and Alcohol Dependence, 47,* 171–185.

Covington, S. S. (1998). Women in prison: Approaches in the treatment of our most invisible population. *Women & Therapy, 21,* 141–155.

Green, B. L., Krupnick, J. L., Stockton, P., Goodman, L., Corcoran, C., & Petty, R. (2004). *Effects of adolescent trauma exposure on risky behavior in college women.* Manuscript submitted for publication, Georgetown University Medical Center, Washington, DC.

Greene, S., Haney, C., & Hurtado, A. (2000). Cycles of pain: Risk factors in the lives of incarcerated mothers and their children. *The Prison Journal, 80,* 3–23.

Hammett, T. M., Roberts, C., & Kennedy, S. (2001). Health-related issues in prisoner reentry. *Crime & Delinquency, 47,* 390–409.

Hutton, H. E., Treisman, G. J., Hunt, W. R., Fishman, M., Kendig, N., Swetz, A., et al. (2001). HIV risk behaviors and their relationship to posttraumatic stress disorder among women prisoners. *Psychiatric Services, 52,* 508–513.

Jordan, B. K., Schlenger, W. E., Fairbank, J. A., & Caddell, J. M. (1996). Prevalence of psychiatric disorders among incarcerated women. *Archives of General Psychiatry, 53,* 1048–1060.

Kessler, R. C., McGonagle, K. A., Zhao, S., Nelson, C. B., Hughes, M., Eshleman, S., et al. (1994). Lifetime and 12-month prevalence of DSM-III-R psychiatric disorders in the United States: Results from the National Comorbidity Survey. *Archives of General Psychiatry, 51,* 8–19.

Kessler, R. C., Sonnega, A., Bromet, E., Hughes, M., & Nelson, C. B. (1995). Posttraumatic stress disorder in the National Comorbidity Survey. *Archives of General Psychiatry, 52,* 1048–1060.

Koons, B. A., Burrow, J. D., Morash, M., & Bynum, T. (1997). Expert and offender perceptions of program elements linked to successful outcomes for incarcerated women. *Crime & Delinquency, 43,* 512–532.

Miranda, J., Chung, J. Y., Green, B. L., Krupnick, J., Siddique, J., Revicki, D. A., et al. (2003). Treating depression in predominantly low-income young minority women: A randomized controlled trial. *Journal of the American Medical Association, 290,* 57–65.

Molitor, F., Ruiz, J. D., Klausner, J. D., & McFarland, W. (2000). History of forced sex in association with drug use and sexual HIV risk behaviors, infection with STD's and diagnostic medical care. *Journal of Interpersonal Violence, 15,* 262–278.

Morris, S. M., Steadman, H. J., & Veysey, B. M. (1997). Mental health services in United States jails: A survey of innovative practices. *Criminal Justice and Behavior, 24,* 3–19.

Osher, F., Steadman, H. J., & Barr, H. (2003). A best practice approach to community reentry from jails for inmates with co-occurring disorders: The APIC model. *Crime & Delinquency, 49,* 79–96.

Owen, B., & Bloom, B. (1995). Profiling women prisoners: Findings from national surveys and a California sample. *The Prison Journal, 75,* 165–185.

Rheingold, A., Acierno, R., & Resnick, H. S. (2004). Trauma, PTSD, and health risk behaviors. In P. P. Schnurr & B. L. Green (Eds.), *Trauma and health: Physical health consequences of exposure to extreme stress* (pp. 217–243). Washington, DC: American Psychological Association.

Richie, B. E., & Johnson, C. (1996). Abuse histories among newly incarcerated women in a New York City jail. *Journal of the American Medical Women's Association, 51,* 111–114.

Sanders, J. F., McNeill, K. F., Rienzi, B. M., & DeLouth, T. B. (1997). The incarcerated female felon and substance abuse: Demographics, needs assessment, and program planning for a neglected population. *Journal of Addictions and Offender Counseling, 18,* 41–52.

Spitzer, R. L., Williams, J. B. W., Kroenke, K., Linzer, M., deGruy, F. V., Hahn, S. R., et al. (1994). Utility of a new procedure for diagnosing mental disorders in primary care: The PRIME-MD 1000 study. *Journal of the American Medical Association, 272,* 1740–1756.

Steadman, H. J., Barbera, S. S., & Dennis, D. L. (1994). A national survey of jail mental health diversion programs. *Hospital and Community Psychiatry, 45,* 1109–1113.

Steadman, H. J., Morris, S. M., & Dennis, D. L. (1995). The diversion of mentally ill persons from jails to community-based services: A profile of programs. *American Journal of Public Health, 85,* 1630–1635.

Teplin, L. A., Abram, K. M., & McClelland, G. M. (1996). Prevalence of psychiatric disorders among incarcerated women: 1. Pretrial jail detainees. *Archives of General Psychiatry, 53,* 505–512.

U.S. Department of Justice, Bureau of Justice Statistics. (1999). *Women offenders* (Report NCJ 175688). Washington, DC: Government Printing Office.

U.S. Department of Justice, Bureau of Justice Statistics. (2003). *Prison and jail inmates at midyear 2002* (Report NCJ 198877). Washington, DC: Government Printing Office.

Ventura, L. A., Cassel, C. A., Jacoby, J. E., & Huang, B. (1998). Case management and recidivism of mentally ill persons released from jail. *Psychiatric Services, 49,* 1330–1337.

Veysey, B. M., Steadman, H. J., Morrissey, J. P., & Johnson, M (1997). In search of the missing linkages: Continuity of care in U.S. jails. *Behavioral Sciences and the Law, 15,* 383–397.

Welle, D., Falkin, G. P., & Jainchill, N. (1998). Current approaches to drug treatment for women offenders. *Journal of Substance Abuse Treatment, 15,* 151–163.

World Health Organization. (1997). *Composite International Diagnostic Interview (CIDI): Core version 2.1 interviewer's manual.* Geneva, Switzerland: Author.

Zlotnick, C., Najavits, L. M., Rohsenow, D. J., & Johnson, D. M. (2003). A cognitive-behavioral treatment for incarcerated women with substance abuse disorder and posttraumatic stress disorder: Findings from a pilot study. *Journal of Substance Abuse Treatment, 25,* 99–105.

REVIEW QUESTIONS

1. What are the major problems confronting women incarcerated in jail?
2. What types of services/programs do women in jail report the greatest need/desire for?
3. What might be the anticipated outcomes for women who report having had high and frequent exposure to trauma, coupled with the other experiences frequently reported by women in jail?

READING 34

Incarcerating Ourselves

Tribal Jails and Corrections

Eileen M. Luna-Firebaugh

This article focuses on tribal jails; those correctional facilities located on Native American reservations and that primarily serve a clientele of Native Americans. Because of sovereignty issues, these jails are not regulated by the same laws and standards as other American correctional facilities. Tribal jails tend to be small, inefficient, poorly staffed, and under-resourced facilities where conditions are very bad. Through assessments of three tribal jails, Luna-Firebaugh shows the serious negative conditions and consequences of poorly operated jails.

A study by Lawrence A. Greenfeld and Steven K. Smith (1999) for the Bureau of Justice Statistics (BJS) painted a bleak picture of the American Indian community. This study found that American Indians experience per capita rates of violence that are more than double those of the U.S. population in general, and Indian young adults between the ages of 18 and 24 were the victims of violence at the highest rate of any racial group considered by age, about one violent crime for every four persons of this age.

The violent crime rate among American Indian males aged 12 or older was 153 per 1,000, as compared with 60 per 1,000 for all races. These rates held steady for both urban and rural areas. For urban populations, the rate for all races was 65 per 1,000, whereas the rate for American Indians was 207 per 1,000. The rural rate of violent crime was 37 per 1,000 for all races, as compared to 89 per 1,000 for American Indian men.

The study found that American Indian women are the victims of crime at a rate that is nearly 50% higher than that reported by Black males. Yet another startling fact is that American Indians are usually criminally victimized by someone of another race. At least 70% of the crime experienced by American Indians is interracial, with the criminal perpetrator being White in 60% of the cases.

The incarceration rate for American Indians, reflected in the Greenfeld and Smith (1999) study, is similarly startling. American Indians were held in local jails at the highest rate of any racial group. A second study, *Jails in Indian Country, 1998 and 1999* was published by BJS in July 2000 (Ditton, 2000). This study found that the number of American Indians incarcerated throughout the United States was 19,679 on June 30,1999. Furthermore, on a per capita basis, American Indians were incarcerated in prisons at a rate that was 38% higher than the national rate.

The predominant factor found in the 1999 BJS study was the effect of alcohol consumption. Almost half (46%) of all convicted American Indians in local jails had been under the influence of alcohol when they committed the offense for which they had been convicted. This percentage rises to 70% when only violent crimes are considered (Greenfeld & Smith, 1999). This is in stark contrast with all other racial groups, where only a third or less were reported to be under the influence of alcohol during the commission of nonviolent crimes and 41% for violent crimes.

This high incidence of substance abuse is no longer generally addressed in non-Indian prisons and jails. Thus, Indian people held in non-Indian facilities often do not participate in programs that may assist them in avoiding substance abuse on the outside. This is not the case in jails in Indian Country, where 59 of 69 facilities offered substance abuse programs, and 57 of the 69 offered counseling and education programs (Ditton, 2000).

The crime rates in Indian country create a demand for incarceration and corrections systems that reduce crime. The incarceration of American Indians takes place in different types of facilities. Federal prisons are the place of incarceration for American Indians accused of enumerated felonies covered by the Major Crimes Act (1885), and facilities run by the Bureau of Indian Affairs (BIA) are also prevalent in Indian country. In other instances, particularly in those states covered under Public Law 280 (1953), American Indians are held in state jails and prison systems. In many other cases, tribal jails are the place of incarceration.

The effect of these statistics and the environment they create in Indian country are problems for both tribal governments and tribal law enforcement agencies. The costs attendant to the building and maintenance of jails are extensive. The development and implementation of corrections systems that reduce recidivism and help to heal communities are even more difficult to put into place. However, the human costs of not doing so are even more expensive.

The sovereignty of Indian nations is a concept that can be advanced in legal and/or de facto manners. The establishment of tribal governmental structures and institutions, and the extension of tribal jurisdiction where appropriate, is an effort that expands tribal sovereignty while meeting the needs of tribal members. The establishment and implementation of tribal jails is one such effort. But it does not come without cost. The decisions that must be made, the policies and protocols that must be developed, and the staff that must be recruited and trained are problems that must be overcome if crime and criminality is to ease in Indian country. It is these challenges that are the focus of this article.

TRIBAL JAILS

The 2000 BJS study of Indian detention facilities found that there were 69 jails affiliated with 53 tribes operating in Indian country. These jails were located in 18 states, some of them Public Law 280 states. The jails are run by different agencies, with 48 run by Indian Nations, 20 by the BIA, and 1 run privately. Tribal consortiums jointly run 4 of the jails, whereas a number of the others receive inmates from other tribes on a contract basis. BIA data reported in the study indicate that tribal jails employed 659 persons and had an authorized inmate capacity of approximately 2,100 adults and juveniles. In 1999, the actual jail population in Indian country was almost 1,700 (Ditton, 2000).

Regulatory Rules and Laws

American Indian nations are sovereign. They operate under their own laws and rules and have jurisdiction over their own members and Indians of other tribes.

Absent Public Law 280, American Indian nations are not subject to the laws of the states in which they are located. Furthermore, American Indian nations retain sovereign immunity and may not be sued (*Santa Clara Pueblo v. Martinez,* 1978). However, the operation of tribal jails is subject to the Indian Civil Rights Act of 1968 (ICRA), which provides that no Indian nation exercising self-government shall deny any of its citizens certain rights, among them the right to be free from excessive bond or cruel and unusual punishment. Furthermore, where the wording of ICRA is similar or identical to the wording of the U.S. Constitution, the courts have found that the language in ICRA may be given the interpretation given the Constitution (*United States v. Lester,* 1981).

Under this analysis, the jails of American Indian nations can be held to standards set by the Eighth Amendment to the U.S. Constitution. The Eighth Amendment prohibits confinement of convicted prisoners under substandard conditions that involve unnecessary and wanton infliction of pain (*Rhodes v. Chapman,* 1981). Prisoners must be provided with reasonably adequate food, clothing, shelter, sanitation, medical care, and personal safety (*Ramos v. Lamm,* 1980/1981); they must be confined in an environment that does not result in their degeneration or that threatens their mental and physical well-being (*Ramos v. Lamm,* 1980/1981) and that meets standards that are not "incompatible with the evolving standards of decency that mark the progress of a maturing society" (*Estelle v. Gamble,* 1976).

The issue of overcrowding is yet another instance where the Eighth Amendment may be violated. The courts have held that whether overcrowding of a jail violates the Eighth Amendment depends on the length of time prisoners are held in overcrowded conditions, the level of overcrowding, and whether overcrowding affects sanitation or medical care (*Ruiz v. Estelle,* 1982/1982).

Compliance with Federal Guidelines

Federal guidelines over the operation of jails and prisons are extensive, but they do not necessarily cover tribal jails. Where, however, the tribal jail is operated under a 638 contract (Indian Self-Determination and Education Assistance Act, 1975), the American Indian nation agrees to meet BIA standards. Furthermore, where tribal police are employed pursuant to a 638 contract, they are designated by the BIA to carry out the federal government's responsibilities.

The BIA has formulated minimum standards for detention programs on Indian reservations. These standards include guidelines for medical care, safety of inmates, and numbers of inmates allowed in each cell (Bureau of Indian Affairs, 1991). However, even though these standards are established, they are frequently violated by the conditions that exist in tribal jails.

Cost of Running a Tribal Jail

The cost of nunning a tribal jail is a significant commitment by any law enforcement agency but particularly for one of limited resources. Most tribal police departments run on extremely limited budgets. Almost half of all tribal police agencies (46.6%) have operating budgets of $500,000 or less. These budgets are composed of a bundle of funding. For almost half of the tribal police departments (41.4%), the BIA provides 100% of the funding. Only 17.2% indicate that they receive none of their budget from the BIA. However the departments are funded, the expenditures for incarceration and corrections are a heavy commitment. The question is whether these expenditures bring a level of value to tribal communities, which makes the outlay of funds worthwhile.

Staffing of Tribal Jails

Tribal jails exist throughout Indian country. The jails are generally small and consume a number of staff out of proportion to the rest of tribal law enforcement. The 10 largest jails house approximately 40% of those in custody. These 10 largest jails are all in Arizona, with Gila River's Sacaton Juvenile Detention Facility having a rated capacity of 100 and the Sacaton Adult Detention Facility having a capacity of 86. With their third detention facility, the Gila River facilities have the capacity to house 230 inmates, making this the largest in Indian Country. The Tohono O'odham Detention Center, although rated for 33 adults and 16 juveniles, housed a total of 98 inmates at midyear in 1999. The 8 facilities of the Navajo Nation have a total capacity of 206 detainees. On the other end of the spectrum, 42 of the 69 tribal jails (61%) are rated for fewer than 25 inmates, and 19 of the 69 (27%) are rated for fewer than 10 inmates (Ditton, 2000).

For many tribes, the staffing of a jail is a serious commitment. According to the 2000 BJS study (Ditton, 2000), 66 of the 69 facilities studied asserted that they needed additional jail staff to meet the needs of running the jail, and 67 reported that their staff needed additional training. Most tribal police departments are relatively small. For some of these, staff assigned to run and maintain jail services can adversely affect police services available to the whole tribal community. . . .

The Incarceration of Juveniles in Indian Country

Indian people have had many adverse experiences in jails and prisons run by federal, state, and local governments. These experiences are complicated by the age of the detainee. The number of American Indian youth in custody is on the rise. A recent study found that the number of American Indian youth increased 50% between 1994 and 2000. Throughout Indian country, juveniles account for 16% of the total number in custody (Ditton, 2000). Federal guidelines require that juveniles be kept out of view or hearing of adult prisoners; however, not all tribal jails comply with such rules. Of the 43 facilities eligible to hold juveniles, in 9 facilities juveniles were separated from adults by sight only (21%), and in 4 facilities (9%) juveniles were not separated from adults at all.

The federal government does not own or operate any juvenile detention facilities. Thus, requirements enacted for the safety of juveniles can complicate the situation for youth who are in temporary custody for substance abuse. Ted Quasula, director of BIA Law Enforcement Services, has been quoted as saying, "It's not uncommon for a juvenile to ride around in the back of a squad car until they sober up somewhat, because we simply don't have the facilities" (Coalition for Juvenile Justice, 2000).

This failure of the federal government to own or operate any juvenile detention facilities requires that American Indian youth under federal supervision be incarcerated in public and private jail facilities far from their home communities, thus increasing their alienation from their culture and kinship relations (Coalition for Juvenile Justice, 2000).

Tribal jails have tried to address these problems with incarceration and cultural dislocation through the development of tribal juvenile facilities. There are eight facilities that deal specifically with the incarceration of juveniles, two of which are run by the Navajo Nation. Although tribal jails that house adults routinely exceed their rated capacity, that is not the case with these juvenile facilities. On June 30, 1999, tribal jails housed 197 male and 70 female juvenile inmates. On this same date, only one juvenile facility exceeded its rated capacity (Ditton, 2000).

Tribal Incarceration of Adults

The situation for American Indian youth is echoed in the adult Indian community as well, with members of the Indian community subjected to difficult experiences and cultural dislocation by incarceration within the non-Indian world. Thus, although the development and staffing of tribal jails can be both a financial and operational burden for tribes, they can also bring significant benefits for tribal people. Tribal jails allow tribal members to be housed within or close to their home tribal community, thus increasing the possibility of family and cultural contacts while also holding miscreants directly accountable to the Indian nations themselves, which can be a significant step forward for law and order in Indian country.

Inmates in tribal jails are generally those convicted of misdemeanors. A total of 10 facilities held inmates convicted of felonies, and 9 held only those inmates in detention for less than 72 hours (Ditton, 2000). Tribal jails are routinely overcrowded, with 11 in 1999 under a court order or consent decree that restricted the maximum number of inmates who could be incarcerated.

On June 30, 1999, tribal jails housed 1,354 male inmates and 223 female inmates. More than half of the adult detention facilities operated above 100% capacity, and 15 (22%) operated at above 150% of rated capacity. Approximately 5% of inmates in tribal jails were housed in areas not originally intended for holding prisoners. A total of 11% of inmates in tribal jails were double-bunked in single occupancy cells, and 7% of inmates were housed in holding areas or drunk tanks (Ditton, 2000).

The overcrowding in smaller facilities was worse than in larger ones. In mid-1999, whereas overall Indian country jails were at 108% capacity, the occupancy rate for jails with capacities of fewer than 10 was 161% of capacity and 155% of capacity for those rated to hold up to 24 inmates.

Case Study Examples

During the course of this research, 2000 to 2001, the author conducted site visits and interviews at three tribes. Two tribes, the Tohono O' odham and the Puyallup, operate tribal jails. The Tohono O'odham house only their own prisoners and on occasion provide a holding space for federal detainees. The Puyallup tribe has a regional jail with contractual relationships with a number of tribes in the Pacific Northwest. The third, the Lummi Nation, does not have its own jail but instead has a contract with the county within which the tribe is located. The chiefs of police at each tribe were interviewed, along with jail personnel at Puyallup and Tohono O'odham. The jail director for Whatcom County was interviewed pursuant to Lummi prisoners.

The Tohono O'odham The primary issue for the Tohono O'odham jail is severe overcrowding. The jail is rated for holding 33 adult prisoners. According to jail administrators, the population has often exceeded 130 inmates. The nation does not transport or house any inmates in facilities of another Indian nation, the BIA, or the county due to transportation issues and the costs attendant to house prisoners pursuant to a contract. Due to the overcrowding, there is minimal movement within the jail and limited access to diversion programs, advocacy services, or ceremonies. All of these inmates are members of the O'odham community. The nation does not contract with other Indian nations to house its prisoners, as there are not enough beds.

In 1995, the BIA and the U.S. Department of Justice's National Institute of Corrections conducted a facility review and preliminary assessment of the Tohono O'odham detention facility (Martin & Alese, 1995). This review was requested by the Support Services Commander of the Tohono O'odham Nation Police Department. The review found that there were many facility-related problems, including inefficient design, malfunctioning mechanical systems, and overcrowding. The report further found that overcrowding, inadequate staffing, a lack of written policies and procedures, and a lack of space for effective programs resulted in a number of operational deficiencies. Six years later, the site visit by the author confirmed that these problems continue.

The O'odham jail is supported through tribal funding only. In the past, the nation received funding for the jail from the BIA. Now, due to the overcrowded conditions, federal funding has been largely eliminated, leaving the nation to support the jail mainly through tribal funding. The jail costs $1.2 million to operate, of which $300,000 conies from BIA 638 funding. The nation applied recently for grant funding but was denied. The nation was told it was denied because it is a gaming tribe, placing it very low on the priority list.

The overcrowded conditions are complicated by a number of situations. The jail houses a number of prisoners for long periods of time. Although the average stay is 10 to 15 days, one inmate, for example, is serving a sentence of 12 years. There is one cell used for suicide watch, which is absolutely bare. It is supposed to be used for minimum periods of time; however, due to the overcrowded conditions, individual inmates have remained there for 10 to 15 days at a time. The drunk tank is yet another feature affected by overcrowding. It now contains double bunks but has no bathroom or television. It has been used to house up to 10 inmates at a time.

Yet another issue is the overcrowding that results from tribal police picking up undocumented aliens on tribal land. The traditional lands of the nation are split by the U.S.–Mexico border. The border stretches for more than 75 miles over nation lands. Frequently, the police of the nation apprehend migrants crossing the border illegally. Until recently, these migrants were then transported to the jail and held there until the U.S. Border Patrol picks them up. This often resulted in scores of migrants being held in the yard of the jail for up to 6 hours. The nation provided water and food for these people, whose numbers on some occasions have exceeded 300. The nation was not compensated for the provision of custodial service or food or water; however, the jail staff ensured that the detainees were safe and sheltered.

This practice was a problem for jail personnel as well as for the inmates. The detainees were placed in the jail yard, which is the sole recreation area for inmates and also the location of the classroom where all education, counseling, and programs are held. Advocate services are conducted in the classroom, as are church services and meetings between inmates and their families.

Traditional ceremonies are considered a privilege. There is an average of 15 to 20 inmates who wish to participate in traditional ceremonies, and their participation depends on good behavior and a process of random selection from among those who request to participate. Traditional healers meet with inmates in the yard and a sweathouse is set up there. Some traditional elders have come into the jail to work with individual inmates, and there is a belief that there is a need for more spiritual healing. The nation is largely Roman Catholic; however, church services are also limited. When there were detainees in the yard, all programs were stopped and there was no opportunity for recreation or ceremonies. Given the overcrowded conditions, the ability to move outside is very important. This ability is curtailed when migrants occupied the yard. In 2002, due to the above concerns, the nation discontinued housing Border Patrol detainees.

The Puyallup Unlike the Tohono O'odham, the Puyallup Nation provides a regional jail for the tribes of the Pacific Northwest. The jail has a bed capacity of 25 with an average jail population of 10 to 15. The highest number of inmates has been 23. With this low average population, the Puyallup Nation has been able to enter into contracts with a number of the 12 tribes in the I-5 corridor. At present, 7 of the 12 tribes have contracts with the Puyallup to house their prisoners.

The Puyallup jail houses only Native prisoners. Approximately 40% of the inmates are Puyallup tribal members. The jail admits only misdemeanor offenders with a maximum sentence of 1 year. The average stay is from 7 to 30 days. The jail requires inmates to serve time certain. Absent a tribal court order, it does not allow for early release, which, however, jail staff may request.

The Puyallup jail no longer takes juvenile prisoners. Prior to 1977, the nation housed juveniles; however, issues arose regarding sight and sound separation, so the nation ceased this responsibility. There is now a move to build a juvenile facility.

The jail has recently undergone a complete remodeling to bring it up to federal codes. The cost to complete this upgrading was $350,000. The operational costs per year are approximately $300,000. The costs are primarily borne by the Puyallup Nation, with some federal funding. Additional funding is received from contracting with other tribes to house their prisoners.

The primary issue for the jail, besides meeting the federal requirements, has been staffing. The jail operates in a Public Law 280 state. All jail staff members are state certified and cross-deputized with the state of Washington and with the county. A total of 70% of the staff is Native, with half of those being Puyallup tribal members. Four of the eight staff are female, as is the chief jailer. The chief of police favors the hiring of female staff. He stated that individual inmates open up to female staff in a way that they would not to male staff.

The training level of staff is very high. The Puyallup Nation emphasizes professional staff development with internal and federal training as well as participation in state training programs. The jail staff also conducts training sessions for the staff of surrounding agencies. This highly qualified staff results in a high attrition rate, however, as custodial staff frequently leave for other jurisdictions where the salaries are significantly higher.

The Lummi The Lummi tribe is geographically within Whatcom County, Washington. Washington is a Public Law 280 state, and thus all enumerated major crimes are under state jurisdiction. The Lummi have asserted tribal jurisdiction over all misdemeanors committed by Indians on the reservation and over all juvenile crimes other than homicide. The tribe has its own police department and judicial system but does not maintain its own jail. Rather, the tribe maintains contracts with Whatcom County to house both adult and juvenile tribal prisoners.

The contract is negotiated for 2 years at a time. The 2000 contract is per bed night, with a charge of $90 per night for juveniles and $53 per night for adults. The total cost for 2000 was $60,000 for adults and $13,000 for juveniles. In addition, the tribe is billed separately for any necessary medical services for tribal inmates.

The Lummi tribal court handles all prosecution of charges. However, although a defense attorney is not required under the Indian Civil Rights Act, the state of Washington is a PL 280 state. Thus, the tribal attorney has required that the state laws prevail in this instance, and the tribe must provide a defense attorney for all criminal charges.

This arrangement seems to meet the needs of the Lummi tribe. They report no problems between tribal prisoners and jail personnel. When the Lummi tribe decided that it wanted inmates to serve time certain rather than being allowed to earn early release, the county agreed even though this was contrary to county laws. Another issue was the length of time tribal detainees were incarcerated pending arraignment. Lengthy stays prior to arraignment by tribal courts were a problem for the county jail. Therefore, as a result of negotiations between the county and the tribe, the tribal court now holds a probable cause hearing within 48 hours of arrest.

The issue of access to ceremonies and religious activities has been resolved through agreement. There is no place for ceremonies in the Whatcom County Jail. Instead, when ceremonies are held, the tribal court issues temporary releases and the county releases the prisoners into tribal custody. The prisoner is then escorted to the ceremony by tribal personnel and then returned to county custody.

In the past, the county had limited beds for juveniles, so youth sentenced to detention by the Lummi tribal court were denied entry. The tribe then contracted for a designated bed at the county juvenile facility for tribal youth. However, elders have begun to intercede with minor criminal conduct by juveniles. The tribal court now routinely refers juvenile cases to the Elders Council rather than sentencing them to county juvenile detention. The tribe has found that most juveniles prefer this resolution process. The juvenile must stipulate to the elements of the crime to participate.

Integration of Native Traditions and Customs

Many native people and researchers contend that incarceration within a tribal setting allows the inmate to come to reconciliation with traditional values and thus limits recidivistic tendencies. The author inquired specifically about access and availability of traditional and cultural activities at Puyallup and Tohono O'odham and regarding the arrangements made by Lummi for its prisoners held in county detention.

The Puyallup custodial staff asserted that access to religious and ceremonial activities and sweat lodges was one of the reasons why the nation felt so strongly about the importance of having a tribal jail. The tribal police chief stated that the state of Washington handles incarceration very differently than the Puyallup Nation. The nation emphasizes diversion and treatment and the continuation of family and community connections. Domestic violence and alcohol counseling programs are held at the jail. Ceremonies and sweats are held off-site at the tribal medical building, but inmates may choose to participate as long as the tribal court agrees. When the tribal court wants a prisoner released for participation in a ceremony, the order is faxed to the jail, and jail personnel provide transportation for the prisoner.

The Tohono O'odham jail personnel asserted that few inmates request to participate in traditional ceremonies, as most tribal members are Roman Catholic. However, due to the overcrowded conditions, even church participation is restricted.

There is a sweat lodge set up in the small recreation yard and traditional healers are allowed to enter the jail facilities and work with inmates; however, access is restricted. The nation encourages elders and other community members to come to the jail and meet with inmates, as it is believed that this would help to instruct them in proper O'odham behavior. Some elders have taken the initiative to do this, with the support of jail staff.

The Lummi require that a request for participation in spiritual or ceremonial activities come from the tribal court. The court may make a request to the tribal police department for temporary release of a prisoner. As long as the prisoner is being held solely for tribal charges, the tribal police department notifies the county jail of the temporary release and transports and guards the prisoner during the time of release. The tribe asserts that religious ceremonies are held for all and that there has never been a problem with the attendance of inmates.

Alternatives to Incarceration

Alternatives to incarceration serve a number of purposes in Indian country. They are often perceived as a more culturally compatible approach to punishment for crimes. Incarceration as a punishment was almost nonexistent prior to colonialization. Western society is based on the concept of individual liberty; thus, the deprivation of liberty is seen as the worst punishment that can be imposed. In traditional Indian societies, however, the greatest good is the community. Incarceration was not normally practiced. Rather, restoration of harmony and restitution for the crime was the norm.

Many Indian communities have followed the tradition of compensation for the victim and restoration of harmony for the community. These communities have placed an emphasis on alternatives to incarceration, thus preserving the perpetrator within the community and stressing the need for the perpetrator to accept responsibility for his or her actions. The Ditton (2000) study found that the number of persons in 1999 who were supervised in the communities rather than being incarcerated rose by 8% during 1998. Of those in alternative programs, 19% were electronically monitored, 14% were in home detention, 42% were sentenced to perform community service, 7% were required to report daily, and 15% were sentenced to other alternatives. The fact that almost half of those in alternative systems were required to perform community service underscores the attempt by tribal communities to emphasize restitution and restoration of community harmony.

CONCLUSION

The expansion of tribal sovereignty and the safety of Indian communities are critical priorities for tribal governments, and an essential element of each is the detention and rehabilitation of criminal perpetrators. Detention is an activity done reasonably well by any detention facility, be it federal, state, or tribal. However, rehabilitation is often not a priority in state or federal institutions. Jails in Indian country, on the other hand, give expressed support and some resources to the idea that perpetrators should be reintegrated into their tribal communities and that there should be a restoration of community harmony.

The Puyallup tribal jail is an example of this attempt to rehabilitate criminal perpetrators. The management of the Puyallup tribal jail asserts that inmates frequently request to be held in tribal jail rather than in the county facility, as they contend that they are treated with greater respect there and that the jail personnel work with the inmates and their families in an attempt to restore the family and community harmony. The Puyallup jail has counselors and medical personnel readily available and encourages inmates to seek work release conditions, which helps them to support their families while serving their sentence.

The idea of rehabilitation is one that has largely been replaced in mainstream facilities, where warehousing is the norm. Often, degrading practices are not only engaged in but also supported and encouraged by the community. An example of this is the Maricopa, Arizona, county jail facility run by Sheriff Joseph Arpaio. Sheriff Arpaio houses inmates in large tents in an area where the daytime temperature can exceed 110 degrees, requires them to dress in pink, and feeds them bologna sandwiches that are tinted green. This is defended as a means of discouraging further participation in crime, but few, if any, diversion or counseling programs are available.

Intentional degradation of inmates in tribal custody was not observed during this study. Rather, concern was frequently expressed about the welfare of prisoners and the belief that programs are needed to try to change their misguided behavior. Counseling; diversion programs; drug, alcohol, and domestic violence programs; and religious and ceremonial activities are provided in an attempt to restore the inmate to a higher level of responsibility.

The focus of tribal jails and tribal courts seems to be the welfare of the whole community, of which the inmate is a part. The tribal legal system anticipates and encourages the return of inmates to tribal society on completion of their term of incarceration. The emphasis, both stated and unstated, is that inmates are tribal members and that they have a responsibility to change their pattern of behavior and to take up their role as community members in sovereign communities on their release. The tribal community and the jail staff accept a role in the rehabilitation of the inmate and in the restoration of the inmate to the community when his or her time has been served. However challenged the tribal jails are financially, administratively, or in staffing, this goal of rehabilitation and restoration is a worthy one, and one that should be supported, as it is through the healing of individuals and communities that true sovereignty can flower.

REFERENCES

Bureau of Indian Affairs, 25 CFR sec. 11.305 (1991).

Coalition for Juvenile Justice. (2000, February 16–19.). *Enlarging the healing circle: Ensuring justice for American Indian children.* Report on the 5th Annual Ethnic and Cultural Diversity Training Conference. Washington, DC: Author.

Ditton, P. M. (2000, July). *Jails in Indian country, 1998 and 1999* (NCJ 173410). Washington, DC: U.S. Department of Justice, Office of Justice Programs, Bureau of Justice Statistics.

Estelle v. Gamble, 429 U.S. 97, 102 (1976).

Greenfeld, L. A., & Smith, S. K. (1999, February). *American Indians and crime* (NCJ 173386). Washington, DC: U.S. Department of Justice, Office of Justice Programs, Bureau of Justice Statistics.

Indian Civil Rights Act (ICRA), 82 Stat. 77, 25 U.S.C.A. sec. 1301 *et seq.* (1968).

1975 Indian Self-Determination and Education Assistance Act, Pub. L. 93–638, 88 Stat. 2203 (1975).

Major Crimes Act, 18 U.S.C.A. Sec 1153 (1885).

Martin, M. D., & Alese, J. (1995, February). *A facility review and preliminary assessment of detention needs for the Tohono O'odham Nation* (B.I.A. #95-J4002). Washington, DC: National Institute of Corrections, U.S. Department of Justice, Bureau of Indian Affairs, U.S. Department of Interior Technical Assistance.

Public Law 280, 67 Stat 588 (1953).

Ramos v. Lamm, 639 F.2d 559, 566 (10th Circ. 1980), *cert. den.,* 450 U.S. 1041 (1981).

Rhodes v. Chapman, 452 U.S. 337, 346 (1981).

Ruiz v. Estelle, 666 F. 2d 854 (5th Cir. 1982), *cert. den.,* 460 U.S. 1042 (1982).

Santa Clara Pueblo v. Martinez, 436 U.S. 49, 58 (1978).

United States v. Lester, 647 F. 2d, 869 8th Cir. (1981).

REVIEW QUESTIONS

1. How is the operation and governance of tribal jails different from most American jails?
2. In what ways are conditions in tribal jails better and worse than in most American jails?
3. How do jails operated by tribes tend to differ from other jails for Native Americans?

XIV

CORRECTIONS IN THE COMMUNITY

READING 35

Residential Community Correctional Programs

Edward J. Latessa

Lawrence F. Travis III

Residential community corrections facilities—sometimes referred to as halfway houses—are discussed as a diverse yet important component of American correctional efforts. Such facilities have been a part of the American correctional landscape since at least the mid-1800s. However, the facilities of today are very different from those of the 1800s. As largely misunderstood (or simply not even recognized) aspects of the correctional system, these facilities provide housing, treatment, and supervision of a wide range of types of offenders, in a wide range of settings. Included among the things not known about such facilities is the degree to which they are effective. As outlined here, a number of issues can be assessed when evaluating residential community corrections facilities, what is looked at (and how) may be the most important factor in what an outcome evaluation says about such facilities.

Community residential programs for criminal offenders have a long history in the United States (Allen, Carlson, Parks, & Seiter, 1978; Latessa & Travis, 1986). In the past, the typical use of community residential facilities was as "halfway houses." These programs were designed as transitional placements for offenders to ease the movement from incarceration to life in the free society. In time, some programs developed as alternatives to incarceration, so that the "halfway" aspect could mean either halfway *into* prison, or halfway *out of* prison.

Between 1950 and 1980, the number and use of such halfway houses grew considerably. . . . Increasingly, the population served by these programs has come to include large numbers of probationers and persons awaiting trial. In many jurisdictions, placement in a residential facility is available as a direct sentencing option to the judge. These changes in the role and population of residential programs supported the replacement of the traditional halfway house notion with the broader title of *community corrections residential facility.*

This chapter reviews the history, purposes, and structure of residential community corrections programs. It includes an assessment of the types and effectiveness of programs, and concludes by describing emerging trends and future directions for residential programs.

WHAT'S IN A NAME?

Until recently, community corrections residential programs were subsumed under the general title of halfway houses. This label, however, has proven to be inadequate as a description of the variety of residential programs used with correctional populations today. The International Halfway House Association, founded in

1964, has itself changed its name to reflect more accurately the variety of purposes and persons served by residential programs.

The contemporary name given to such programs, community corrections residential facilities, is a broader title that reflects the role expansion of the traditional halfway house that has occurred in recent years. Rush (1991) defines a residential facility as "a correctional facility from which residents are regularly permitted to depart, unaccompanied by any official, for the purposes of using community resources, such as schools or treatment programs, and seeking or holding employment" (p. 265).

This definition is free of any reference to incarceration that was implicit in the term *halfway.* Further, it does not necessitate the direct provision of any services to residents within the facility, and clearly identifies the program with a correctional mission. Thus, unlike the traditional halfway house, the community residential facility serves a more diverse population and plays a broader correctional role. Traditional halfway houses are included within the category of residential facilities, but their ranks are swelled by newer adaptations, such as community corrections centers, prerelease centers, and restitution centers.

THE DEVELOPMENT OF COMMUNITY RESIDENTIAL PROGRAMS

Halfway houses as transitional programming for inmates released from prisons are not a new phenomenon (Latessa & Allen, 1982). Their origins can be traced at least as far back as the early nineteenth century in England and Ireland (Keller & Alper, 1970). In the United States, the exact origin of halfway houses is not clear, but one such program was started in New York City in 1845, the Isaac T. Hooper Home (Rush, 1991, p. 143). A halfway house for released female prisoners was opened in Boston, Massachusetts, in 1864. For nearly 100 years, halfway houses tended to be operated by charitable organizations for the benefit of released inmates. Halfway house programs did not begin a period of expansion until after World War II (Beha, 1977).

In the 1950s, specialized residential programs designed to deal with substance-abusing offenders were added to the traditional halfway house programs. Residential programs for alcoholic or drug-addicted offenders opened and spread throughout this period, and into the 1960s. For typical criminal offenders, however, halfway house placements were rare.

In the middle 1960s, the President's Commission on Crime and Administration of Justice (1967) signaled a change in correctional philosophy toward the goal of reintegration. Reintegration placed increased emphasis on the role of the community in corrections, and on the value of keeping offenders in the community, rather than in prison, whenever possible. This ideology of community corrections supported the notion of residential placements for convicted offenders, and halfway houses began a period of unprecedented expansion, supported by federal funds from programs as diverse as the Office of Economic Opportunity and the Law Enforcement Assistance Administration (Hicks, 1987, p. 6).

During the early 1980s, however, support for halfway house programs dwindled. The effects of recession, demise of LEAA, and a general hardening of public attitudes toward offenders worked against the continued growth and development of halfway houses or other residential programs. This period of retrenchment was, however, shortlived. The same forces that temporarily halted the growth of residential programs soon added their weight to continued development.

In the last decade, community corrections residential facilities have grown in response to the crisis of prison crowding. Allen et al. (1978, p. 1) attribute an increased use of halfway houses with parole populations to three factors: the philosophy of reintegration, success with such programs in the mental health field, and the lower costs of halfway houses compared with prisons. To these was added the need to respond to prison crowding in the 1980s.

The lack of prison capacity, coupled with an increasing emphasis on risk control and retributive sentencing, spurred a search for intermediate sanctions. Over the last several years, a number of observers have called for the creation of penal sanctions that range in severity between incarceration and traditional probation supervision (McCarthy, 1987). They suggest that such sanctions will allow the correctional system to meet the punitive and risk-control goals of sentencing, especially with those persons diverted from prison or jail because of crowding.

The list of intermediate sanctions includes house arrest, electronic monitoring, and intensive supervision (*Federal Probation,* 1986; Petersilia, 1987). DuPont (1985) explicitly identifies a role for community residential facilities as an adjunct to traditional probation or parole supervision. Such facilities would serve to increase both the punitive severity and public safety of traditional community-based corrections.

In an era when both correctional costs and populations grow yearly, planners, practitioners, and policymakers have supported a wide range of correctional alternatives. As Guynes (1988) has observed, one effect of prison and jail crowding has been a dramatic increase in probation and parole populations. Further, Petersilia (1985), among others, suggests that these larger supervision populations are increasingly made up of more serious and more dangerous offenders. Community residential facilities have come to be seen as an important option for the management and control of these growing and more dangerous offender populations.

A result has been the redefinition of the role of community residential facilities. The traditional role of transitional placement for offenders, or as a response to special needs populations such as substance abusers, has been expanded. Residential placement has emerged as a correctional alternative in its own right.

Hicks (1987) observes that the use of residential placement as an alternative to incarceration or traditional community supervision has engendered some changes in operations and philosophy. She terms this a movement "toward supervision rather than treatment." Thus in many cases residential facilities provide little more than a place to live and access to community resources. The emphasis in these programs is upon custody and control rather than counseling and correction.

PRISON ON THE CHEAP?

Unable or unwilling to underwrite the costs of prison for large numbers of convicted offenders, several jurisdictions have supported community residential facilities. As Hicks (1987) notes, "Budget weary legislators often view halfway houses as an inexpensive lunch" (p. 7). Residential programs, they hope, will provide public safety as well as incarceration, but at a fraction of the cost. As substitute prisons, however, the atmosphere of these programs has changed.

Traditional halfway houses, where staff and programs are designed for the provision of direct services to residents, still continue. These programs provide counseling, substance abuse treatment, educational and vocational training, and a variety of social services. In other, newer programs, especially those operated by corrections departments, the atmosphere is closer to that of a minimum-security prison than a rehabilitative community.

This addition of residential programs as "bed space" to the traditional use of such programs as treatment modalities has led to a schizophrenic field of practice. In most facilities, rules and regulations are stricter, and enforcement more rigid, than in earlier days. Additionally, a number of "large" facilities, housing hundreds of residents, have been added. Typically "prerelease" centers, these larger facilities house prison inmates eligible for parole, or in the final months before their release.

The recent growth in community residential facilities has complicated the picture. These facilities serve a variety of clients, ranging from as-yet-unconvicted offenders diverted from court through prison inmates. Facility sizes range from those housing fewer than 10 residents to those with populations in the hundreds. Treatment services range from programs providing full services to those in which few, if any, direct services are available to residents. The one constant is that residents live in the facilities for a period of time, and are generally free to leave the facilities during approved hours, for approved purposes, without escort.

RESIDENTIAL FACILITIES IN CONTEMPORARY CORRECTIONS

As the foregoing discussion illustrates, it is not possible to describe the average residential facility. Diversity in population, program, size, and structure is the rule. It is, unfortunately, also not possible to know for certain how many such facilities are in operation today, or the number of offenders served by them. As Hicks (1987) observes, "There are no national figures, only educated guesses" (p. 2).

The International Halfway House Association published a directory of residential facilities in 1981 that lists almost 2,300 facilities with a combined capacity of nearly 100,000 beds (Gatz & Murray, 1981), Not all of these facilities, however, serve correctional populations. Five years earlier, Seiter et al. (1977) estimated that approximately 400 facilities existed that served correctional populations, with a capacity of about 10,000 beds. In 1978, a survey of parole authorities revealed the existence of nearly 800 facilities, with almost 15,000 inmates being paroled to halfway house placements. More recently, the National Institute of Corrections supported a survey that identified 641 community corrections residential facilities. The identification was based on the characteristics of residents as under correctional supervision, among other criteria.

While the methods and definitions employed in these different studies varied considerably, the results are fairly consistent. Given these admittedly incomplete data, it is possible to estimate that there are in excess of 600 residential facilities in operation today. Further, it appears that the number of facilities has grown as much as 50% in the last decade.

It is not possible to estimate the number of offenders served by these facilities with any certainty. Length of residence is typically short, on the order of three to four months, meaning that a facility with 50 beds may serve 150 to 200 individuals annually. Based on the probability that a halfway house would serve three to four times as many residents as it has beds in each year, Allen and his colleagues (1978, p. 2) estimate that roughly 10,000 beds equals 30,000 to 40,000 residents each year. Further, many of those in residential facilities are included in the totals of other correctional population counts, such as the number of prison inmates or persons under parole supervision. Still, it is clear that the total number of residents in these facilities each year is substantial.

TYPES OF FACILITIES

The large number of facilities and their differing traditions, populations, and services render it difficult to assess the impact of residential programs. Beyond noting that these programs have played an important role in the provision of services to convicted offenders, and that their importance as alternatives to imprisonment has increased, the variety of facilities means that questions of effectiveness must be narrowly drawn.

Allen and his colleagues (1978), for example, have developed a four-class typology of halfway houses, using two dimensions to yield four possible types of facilities. Halfway houses can be either public or private, and they can be either interventive or supportive in program. Public or private, of course, relates to the organization of the facility as either a government entity or not. Program types are based on whether the services of the facility are designed to intervene in problem areas of the residents' lives, such as substance abuse counseling, or to provide a supportive environment in which residents use community resources.

This simple typology indicates that different facilities must be assessed differently. For example, a residential facility designed to provide supportive services would not be well evaluated on the basis of direct service provision. Similarly, a program aimed at intervention would not be well understood solely in terms of resident length of stay. Rather, the type of program offered in a facility must form an important base of any assessment effort.

WHAT DO WE KNOW ABOUT THE EFFECTIVENESS QUESTION?

Despite the long tradition of residential community correctional programs, the research literature concerned with them is sparse and inconclusive. There appear to be a number of reasons that residential programs have been largely ignored by correctional researchers.

First, residential facilities represent a relatively small part of the correctional system, and, as mentioned above, it is often difficult to distinguish between residential facilities that serve only correctional clientele and those that serve a broader constituency. Second, many programs are operated by private entities, and are either unwilling or unable to facilitate research. Third, generalization is a problem, because these programs are often markedly different from locale to locale, in terms of both the treatment offered and the types of clients they accept. Finally, it is often difficult to develop an adequate comparison group and to conduct a follow-up of residents. Despite these obstacles, there have been some notable attempts to evaluate the effectiveness of residential programs.

As correctional interventions, residential community correctional programs seem to meet two objectives: a reduction in postprogram criminality (recidivism) and an increase in prosocial behavior on the part of clients. Outcome assessments of residential programs then should assess both of these dimensions of program effectiveness. The literature indicates that recidivism has generally been the focus of most outcome evaluations, with varying definitions of recidivism.

In the first systematic evaluation of correctional halfway houses, Allen et al. (1976) reviewed 35 studies of halfway houses. Of these, 17 used quasi-experimental designs in comparing postprogram recidivism rates, 2 utilized true experimental designs, and 16 relied on nonexperimental designs. Based on the experimental and quasi-experimental studies, the researchers concluded that the evidence was about equally divided between lower recidivism rates for halfway house residents and no difference in recidivism rates when compared with a control group. They also found no evidence that halfway houses improved socially acceptable adjustment behaviors of residents, but that they were cheaper to operate than prisons, while more expensive than parole and probation.

Focusing on parolees, Latessa and Allen (1982) reported on evaluations of halfway house programs providing an overview of evaluations of programs throughout the United States. They rated 44 such studies as being characterized by sufficient methodological rigor to allow assessment of postrelease outcome. Of these, only 2 studies were found to have employed true experimental designs, involving random assignment to either an "experimental" (halfway house placement) or "control" (incarceration or other placement) group. Neither study indicated that halfway house clients performed significantly better than did subjects in the control conditions. An additional 23 studies employed quasi-experimental designs. There were also 19 nonexperimental studies that reported outcome data.

In general, the results were mixed, with some reports showing significantly lower recidivism among halfway house residents, some showing no significant differences, and others showing that the halfway house clients did significantly worse on release than did their counterparts in the control groups. In their conclusions, Latessa and Allen suggest that the literature indicates that halfway house programs are at least as effective as parole, especially given that halfway house clients are generally characterized by having higher risk and greater needs than those in a traditional parole population. Similarly, Seiter et al. (1977) conclude that prior evaluations "suggest that halfway house programs may more effectively reintegrate prisoners returning to the community than direct release to parole" (p. 160).

In an attempt to compare "recidivism" rates, some research has indicated that certain social, demographic, and criminal history characteristics must be controlled. Those with less education, who are younger, and who have less successful employment records, longer prior criminal records, and generally less stability in their social and personal lives are more likely to recidivate (Beha, 1977; Beran, McGruder, & Allen, 1974; Donnelly & Forschner, 1984; Dowell, Klein, & Kirchmar, 1985; Moczydlowski, 1980; Moran, Kass, & Muntz, 1977; Seiter, Petersilia, & Allen, 1974).

In a recent study, Donnelly and Forschner (1987) used discriminant function analysis and found that a similar set of factors serve to distinguish between residents who completed or failed to complete a halfway house program. Thus it appears that in order to determine if a residential program has been effective it is necessary to ensure that any differences between the treatment and control groups on these dimensions are known.

In addition to recidivism, however defined, it is important that improved prosocial behavior or social adjustment be measured. One of the earliest examples of this type of measurement was done by Seiter et al. (1974), using a scale of social adjustment. This scale allowed a cumulative score of the subject's involvement in employment, education, residence, interpersonal relations, and the like to be computed. The scale yielded a continuous score for each subject, thereby allowing comparisons. Based on their measure of recidivism *and* social adjustment, Seiter et al. conclude in their study of Ohio halfway houses that "halfway houses are more effective at assisting ex-offenders in their reintegration to the community than traditional modes of assistance."

Several other studies of halfway house program effectiveness have also attempted to address this dimension of outcome. Beck (1979) evaluated federal community treatment centers (CTCs) with measures of both recidivism and social adjustment, measured as days employed and money earned. He concluded that CTC clients fared better in social adjustment than did control subjects. Toborg, Center, Milkman, and Davis (1978) report similar effects in social adjustment in their review and assessment of more than 250 community assistance programs.

Finally, as Donnelly and Forschner (1987) have observed, "The success or failure of a halfway house is often defined in terms of the number or percent of the residents who complete the halfway house program" (p. 5). While they note that completion of the program may not satisfy those who define the "real goal" of correctional intervention as reduced recidivism, they argue that program completion is both an important organizational goal of the halfway house agency and inversely related to recidivism. These characteristics of program completion, they suggest, make it an appropriate criterion of outcome.

In a recent study of halfway house programs that examined both recidivism and social adjustment, we studied 132 probationers who resided in three halfway houses during 1983 (Latessa & Travis, 1986). A comparison group was composed of a sample of 140 felony probationers selected from the county probation department. We conducted a three-year follow-up through the use of official criminal records.

The results of this study illustrate the similarities and differences between the two groups. While there were a number of similarities between the halfway house and probation samples with regard to demographics, criminal history, and special problems/needs, some notable differences existed. Those in the halfway house sample were less educated and less likely to have been married. Those in the probation group had more prior convictions, and the halfway house subjects exhibited more prior involvement in drugs, alcohol treatment, and psychiatric problems. These data support other studies that have found that residential populations are in need of more intensive treatment than regular probationers. We also found that the halfway house group received significantly more services and treatment than the probation sample. This was true in almost every area examined.

Finally, the factors examined for the follow-up showed no significant differences between the two groups in terms of new crime convictions or social adjustment. Simply stated, the halfway house group did no better and no worse than the probation sample with regard to convictions or positive adjustment.

In addition to the outcome analysis, we conducted a discriminant analyses of factors associated with outcome (both recidivism and program completion). The results revealed few surprises. Prior criminal history, measured by the number of prior adult convictions, filing of technical probation violations, and the presence of a drug problem predicted recidivism in expected ways. Similarly, the provision of employment training was associated with fewer new convictions. In regard to program completion, higher scores on a social adjustment scale, enrollment in an educational program, and the absence of drug or psychiatric problems were associated with success. The provision of group counseling, however, was associated with failure.

While further research is required if we are to understand the relationships fully, the data from our study and from the studies of other researchers tend to support the following observations:

1. Residential community correctional groups display greater service needs than do regular probation or parole groups.
2. Many of these needs, such as psychiatric and drug/alcohol abuse history, are related both to positive adjustment and to new criminal convictions.
3. Offenders in residential facilities are more likely to receive a variety of treatment and counseling services.
4. When these observations are combined with the finding of no significant differences in recidivism and social adjustment outcomes between groups, the possibility of a treatment effect is raised. That is, from these studies it would appear that halfway house residents receive services commensurate with their needs.

5. Based on group characteristics at intake, an a priori assumption that the halfway house group would demonstrate a higher rate of recidivism and lower social adjustment seems reasonable. That, generally, no such differences in outcome have been observed and that residential groups have received considerably more treatment interventions may indicate that program participation is beneficial for this group.

The obvious implication of these conclusions is that placement into a residential program should be considered a dispositional option for convicted offenders. A general assessment of risk alone, however, may not adequately identify those most likely to benefit from such placement. That is, rather than viewing residential placement as a punitive (more intrusive) or incapacitative (more controlling) sanction for convicted offenders, placement in a program should be guided by an assessment of an offender's needs. It is possible that residential intervention can reduce the likelihood of negative outcome through meeting the treatment needs of clients.

There is also little evidence that successful completion of a residential program is a prerequisite of successful completion of probation or parole. Indeed, this suggests that residential programs, perhaps by virtue of their more rigorous rules and expectations of program participation, may not be appropriate for some offenders.

Most of the research has revealed that residential placement has been used with those offenders presenting higher needs and a priori risk, in general, than the regular probation/parole population. Even among this group, however, such placement may not always be necessary. Future research should address case classification issues. Such efforts could help identify the types of features within this high-risk/high-needs group who are most likely to benefit from placement in a particular residential program.

As is clear from the evaluation studies summarized above, most of the research on residential facilities has focused on halfway houses or similar placements with an interventive design. As yet, little is known about the use and effects of residential placements in facilities designed to provide closer surveillance of offenders, without interventive treatments. For these programs, the primary criteria of evaluation would appear to be protection of public safety and cost considerations. Extrapolating from what we have learned about interventive programs, it is reasonable to expect that residents in such facilities will pose no greater danger to the community than those under probation or parole supervision. They are no more likely to "recidivate" than those who are imprisoned. And, when compared with imprisonment, residential facility costs should be lower.

THE FUTURE OF RESIDENTIAL FACILITIES

What does the future hold for residential community correctional facilities? First, in many ways they will remain an enigma to correctional researchers. Residential facilities that evolved from traditional halfway houses are now becoming multiservice agencies. The evolution will continue, but, unfortunately, so will our lack of understanding of these facilities, their effectiveness, and their role in the correctional process.

Second, residential community correctional facilities will continue to grow and develop new programs. In large part this will be a response to the crowding of local and state correctional institutions. Many traditional residential facilities will seize the opportunity and will diversify and offer a wider range of programs and services, such as victim assistance programs, family and drug counseling, drunk driver programs, work release centers, and house arrest, electronic monitoring, and day programs for offenders.

Finally, while there has been an increase in public sector operation of residential facilities, particularly prerelease and reintegration centers, it will be the private sector that will continue to play a dominant role in the development and operation of residential correctional programs. A number of arguments support private provision of community-based correctional services. Principal among these is cost-effectiveness. Proponents argue that the private sector will contain costs and thus, for the same dollar amount, provide more, or at least better, service. Government agencies, it is suggested, cannot achieve the same level of cost-efficient operation as can private, especially for-profit, companies.

As Clear, Hairs, and Record (1982) succinctly summarize: "Due to 'domestication' (characterized by a lack of competition and critical self-assessment), corrections officials often are inadvertently rewarded by taking a budget-administration approach rather than a cost-management stance." The attraction of private involvement in community corrections is the promise of a free market, or, as Greenwood (1981) put it, "They would be free to innovate, to use the latest technology and management techniques as in any profit service industry."

Another, perhaps more compelling, reason for the continued development of private community residential programs is that they can offer what Gendreau and Ross (1987) call "therapeutic integrity." That is, because of their accountability to the contractor and the possibility of competition, privately operated programs may provide more intensive and higher-quality service provision than might government agencies. Indeed, many who have studied public community correctional agencies have lamented the increasingly bureaucratic role of the change agent (Clear & Latessa, 1989), noting the large number of staff who are simply "putting in time" for retirement or who are encumbered by paperwork and red tape. It often seems that organizational goals outweigh concerns about effective treatment and service delivery.

Of course, this is really an issue of accountability that involves some nonmonetary value questions. This is one of the fundamental differences between the private and public sectors. Private enterprise often measures outcome in terms of profit, while the public sector measures it in terms of social value and benefits. While there is no empirical evidence that the private sector is "better" at providing services, reducing recidivism, and so forth, there is a growing sentiment that it ought to at least be given a chance. Privately run facilities may also be in a better position to lobby for more services, staff, and programs. One need only look at the typical adult probation department, where caseloads range from 150 to 300, to see how ineffective they have been in garnering additional resources. Private providers may, because of contractual agreements, be better able to advocate for additional support.

Of more importance than the simple dichotomy between public and private operation is the future evolution of the mission of community corrections residential facilities. The traditional halfway house had a charitable, quasi-volunteer, and service-oriented mission (Wilson, 1985). The contemporary multiservice community agency or department of corrections-operated facility is more formal, legalistic, and control oriented. As correctional agencies contract with both new private sector vendors and older, charitable programs, the emphasis in residential facilities may change from treatment to custody. Further, as the importance of correctional contracts for the support and spread of residential facilities grows, the "community" nature of these programs may increasingly be replaced by a more formal, governmental administrative style. That is, the forces that currently support the development of programs may ultimately change them in fundamental ways.

The traditional halfway house operated by a civic-minded reform group for the purpose of assisting offenders may be replaced by a for-profit or nonprofit contractor working for the government. Thus, rather than a focus on the needs and interests of the community and the offender, the emphasis may be placed on the needs of the correctional system for bed space.

Of course, it is also entirely likely that the current confusion in residential programs will continue. There will continue to be traditional halfway houses focused on the needs of residents, with deep roots in the community. There will also be a variety of custody and crowding-control facilities designed to provide minimal direct services. Only time will tell what the future of community corrections residential facilities will be. The one thing that is clear is that some form of such facilities will exist in the future.

REFERENCES

Allen, H. E., Carlson, E. W., Parks, E. C., & Seiter, R. P. (1978). *Program models: Halfway houses.* Washington, DC: U.S. Department of Justice.

Allen, H. E., Seiter, R. P., Carlson, E. W., Bowman, H. H., Grandfield, J. J., & Beran, N. J. (1976). *National Evaluation Program Phase I: Residential inmate aftercare, the state of the art summary.* Columbus: Ohio State University, Program for the Study of Crime and Delinquency.

Beck, J. L. (1979). An evaluation of federal community treatment centers. *Federal Probation, 43*(3), 36–40.

Beha, J. A. (1977). Testing the functions and effects of the parole halfway house: One case study. *Journal of Criminal Law and Criminology, 67,* 335–350.

Beran, N. J., McGruder, J. L., & Allen, H. E. (1974). *The community reintegration centers of Ohio: A second year evaluation.* Columbus: Ohio State University, Program for the Study of Crime and Delinquency.

Clear, T., Hairs, P. M., & Record, A. L. (1982). Managing the cost of corrections. *Prison Journal, 53,* 1–63.

Clear, T., & Latessa, E. J. (1989, March). *Intensive surveillance versus treatment.* Paper presented at the annual meeting of the Academy of Criminal Justice Sciences, Washington, DC.

Donnelly, P. G., & Forschner, B. (1984). Client success or failure in a halfway house. *Federal Probation, 48*(3), 38–44.

Donnelly, P. G., & Forschner, B. (1987). Predictors of success in a co-correctional halfway house: A discriminant analysis. *Journal of Crime and Justice, 10*(2), 1–22.

Dowell, D., Klein, C., & Kirchmar, C. (1985). Evaluation of a halfway house for women. *Journal of Criminal Justice, 13,* 217–226.

DuPont, P. (1985). *Expanding sentencing options: A governor's perspective.* Washington, DC: National Institute of Justice.

Federal Probation. (1986). Intensive probation supervision [Special issue]. Vol. 50, No. 2.

Gatz, N., & Murray, C. (1981). An administrative overview of halfway houses. *Corrections Today, 43,* 52–54.

Gendreau, P., & Ross, R. R. (1987). Revivification of rehabilitation: Evidence from the 1980's. *Justice Quarterly, 4,* 349–407.

Greenwood, P. (1981). *Private enterprise prisons? Why not?* Santa Monica, CA: RAND Corporation.

Guynes, R. (1988). *Difficult clients, large caseloads plague probation, parole agencies.* Washington, DC: U.S. Department of Justice.

Hicks, N. (1987). A new relationship: Halfway houses and corrections. *Corrections Compendium,12*(4), 1, 5–7.

Keller, O. J., & Alper, G. (1970). *Halfway houses: Community centered correction and treatment.* Lexington, MA: D. C. Heath.

Latessa, E. J., & Allen, H. E. (1982). Halfway houses and parole: A national assessment. *Journal of Criminal Justice, 10*(2), 153–163.

Latessa, E. J., & Travis, L. F. (1986, October). *Halfway houses versus probation: A three year follow-up of offenders.* Paper presented at the annual meeting of the Midwestern Criminal Justice Association, Chicago.

McCarthy, B. R. (Ed.). (1987). *Intermediate punishments: Intensive supervision, home confinement, and electronic surveillance.* Monsey, NY: Criminal Justice Press.

Moczydlowski, K. (1980). Predictors of success in a correctional halfway house for youthful and adult offenders. *Corrective and Social Psychiatry and Journal of Behavior Technology, Methods and Therapy, 26,* 59–72.

Moran, E., Kass, W. & Muntz, D. (1977). In-program evaluation of a community correctional agency for high risk offenders. *Corrective and Social Psychiatry and Journal of Behavior Technology, Methods and Therapy, 23,* 48–52.

Petersilia, J. (1985). *Probation and felon offenders.* Washington, DC: U.S. Department of Justice.

Petersilia, J. (1987). *Expanding options for criminal sentencing* (Publication No. R-3544-EMC). Santa Monica, CA: RAND Corporation.

President's Commission on Law Enforcement and Administration of Justice. (1967). *Task force report: Corrections.* Washington, DC: Government Printing Office.

Rush, G. E. (1991). *The dictionary of criminal justice* (3rd ed.). Guilford, CT: Dushkin.

Seiter, R. P., Carlson, E. W., Bowman, H., Grandfield, H., Beran, N. J., & Allen, H. E. (1977). *Halfway houses.* Washington, DC: Government Printing Office.

Seiter, R. P., Petersilia, J. R., & Allen, H. E. (1974). *Evaluation of adult halfway houses in Ohio* (Vol. 2). Columbus: Ohio State University, Program for the Study of Crime and Delinquency.

Toborg, M. A., Center, L. J., Milkman, R. H., & Davis, D. W. (1978). *The transition from prison to employment: An assessment of community-based assistance programs.* (National Evaluation Program Phase I report). Washington, DC: U.S. Department of Justice.

Wilson, G. P. (1985). Halfway house programs for offenders. In L. F. Travis (Ed.), *Probation, parole, and community corrections* (pp. 151–164). Prospect Heights, IL: Waveland.

REVIEW QUESTIONS

1. Why did residential community corrections facilities (e.g. halfway houses) develop and then become less popular in the twentieth century?

2. What has the research evaluating the effectiveness of residential community corrections facilities told us about the "success" of such facilities?

3. According to the authors, what types of offenders are best suited for placement in a residential community corrections facility?

READING 36

A Qualitative Assessment of the Pains Experienced on Electronic Monitoring

Brian K. Payne

Randy R. Gainey

This reading presents the results of a survey of offenders serving sentences on electronic monitoring and home incarceration. The offenders report that they prefer serving their sentences on home incarceration rather than being in jail, yet they also report significant negative experiences with such a sanction. The authors conceptualize the identified negative aspects of electronic monitoring using the "pains of imprisonment" framework of Gresham Sykes. The most commonly reported negative aspects of electronic monitoring and home incarceration are a deprivation of autonomy, a loss of access to goods and services, the financial costs associated with the service, and negative consequences on one's family life.

Overcrowding is one of the most significant issues confronting corrections departments across the United States (Austin, 1995). New methods of sanctioning offenders have been introduced, attempting to deal with the overcrowding problem (Colson & Van Ness, 1989) while punishing offenders (Jolin & Stipak, 1992) and at the same tune reducing the economic costs of imprisonment (Charles, 1989; Clark, 1994; Rackmill, 1994). One such method, electronic monitoring, was started in 1984 in West Palm Beach, Florida (Maxfield & Baumer, 1990), and was "designed as a punishment alternative to help build accountability and responsibility" (Papy & Nimer, 1991, p. 31). Starting with only 94 offenders on electronic monitoring, by the early 1990s it was estimated that more than 12,000 offenders were on electronic monitoring (Clark, 1994, p. 99; Renzema & Skeleton, 1991, p. 6).

Ethical, legal, political, and social questions quickly followed the implementation of these programs (Maineprize, 1992; Schmidt, 1991; Walker, 1990). On one hand, Lilly (1989) pointed out that house arrest acts "as a tool of Big Brotherism because it uses electronic equipment to turn homes into prisons and can widen the criminal justice net" (p. 89). On the other hand, intermediate sanctions are viewed as an "effective and economical alternative to incarceration" (p. 89). Setting the intrusiveness and other legal issues aside, there is still debate concerning the punitiveness of electronic measuring programs. . . .

In this article, we use Gresham Sykes's (1958) typology of the "pains of imprisonment" to assess the "pains of punishment" of electronic monitoring. Sykes's typology outlines five pains resulting from incarceration in a jail or prison: deprivation of autonomy, deprivation of goods and services, deprivation of liberty, deprivation of heterosexual relationships, and deprivation of security.

LITERATURE REVIEW

Although it is clear that many incarcerated offenders experience many of these losses and therefore experience a form of punishment, the scholarly literature and the popular media suggest, in general, that electronic monitoring programs are viewed by members of the public as being too lenient. One writer in the media, for example, points out that local chapters of Mothers Against Drunk Driving (MADD) are against electronic monitoring because they believe it is "not mean enough" (Sullivan, 1990, p. 51). Larivee (1993) points out that all community-based corrections programs "suffer from the public's perception that such programs represent softness toward crime" (p. 20). Alternatively, the public finds favor in the sanction's low cost for the taxpayer (Brown & Elrod, 1995).

Studies on punitiveness and electronic monitoring house arrest programs are rare. Information about the punitiveness of these programs is typically gathered in broader studies focusing on all types of intermediate sanctions. These broader studies have examined three areas: the public's perceptions concerning the punitiveness of community-based sanctions (Brown & Elrod, 1995; Sigler & Lamb, 1995/1996), criminal-justice officials' attitudes toward these programs (Petersilia & Deschenes, 1994b; Sigler & Lamb, 1995/1996), and incarcerated offenders' perceptions concerning the severity of these programs (Apospori & Alpert, 1993; Crouch, 1993; McClelland & Alpert, 1985; Petersilia & Deschenes, 1994a, 1994b; Spelman, 1995).

According to Spelman (1995), "the severity of a punishment is best defined as the pain actually felt by the offender, not the pain intended by the public" (p. 109). Thus, the best way to determine if a sentence is punitive is not to ask the public or justice system employees if they view a punishment as severe, but to ask those who actually receive the punishment their perceptions of severity. However, to date, very little research has focused directly on offenders' perceptions of severity of sanctions (see, e.g., Apospori & Alpert, 1993; Crouch, 1993; McClelland & Alpert, 1985; Petersilia & Deschenes, 1994a, 1994b; Spelman, 1995). Each of these studies show that on some level, inmates prefer incarceration over some of the intermediate sanctions. . . .

Although studies show that offenders prefer certain jail or prison sentences to some forms of intermediate punishments, many members of the public still believe that electronic monitoring programs are less punitive than are prisons. As Lilly and Jenkins (1989) point out, "The trouble is, hardly anyone asks the criminals, or their families, what they do say" (p. 23). These previous studies seem to move toward assessing how offenders view electronic monitoring programs. However, the aim of the previous studies was to determine whether inmates preferred incarceration over various intermediate sanctions. Collectively, these studies suggest that those serving prison or jail terms view intermediate sanctions as punitive and, in fact, at times more punitive than incarceration.

Missing in the scholarly literature are studies asking those who have served or are serving sentences on electronically monitored programs about their perceptions of that aspect of ther sentences. This exploratory study fills that void by surveying offenders who were sentenced to an electronic monitoring program in Norfolk, Virginia. Of primary concern in this article is whether the pains of imprisonment noted previously by Sykes (1958) are similar to the pains experienced by those on electronic monitoring.

METHOD

A survey instrument developed by the authors was administered from April through August 1997 to 29 offenders on electronic monitoring. . . .

The 27 fully completed survey instruments formed our data set. The responses obtained from the instruments were content analyzed using standard forms of thematic and semantic content analysis (Berg, 1995). Following Sykes's (1958) typology, this process involved locating relevant themes and specific terms throughout the 27 instruments and considering both their usual and taken-for-granted meanings. . . .

RESULTS

Generally, we found that the offenders, unlike those in previous studies that focused primarily on incarcerated offenders, preferred electronic monitoring to incarceration. In fact, none of the offenders indicated that they would rather be in jail. Instead, 23 respondents (85.19%) indicated that not being in jail was one of the most attractive aspects of the sanction. Statements such as "Jail is terrible;" "If more people were on this, less would be going to jail;" "It's not as noisy as jail;" "If I go to jail, it would be worse;" and "I would pay twice the amount to stay out of jail" were common responses elicited by the respondents. Some, of course, were more adamant about the advantages they saw. For example, one respondent said, "In jail, you are like a caged animal. All they talk about [in jail] is getting back on the street to cop some and to get laid. For me, being incarcerated would have done more damage." Another respondent summed up her fear of jail more succinctly: "If I had to stay on electronic monitoring the rest of my life, I'd rather be on it than in jail." Offenders on electronic monitoring clearly saw some of the obvious benefits of the sanction (i.e., as compared to jail). As will be shown, keeping their jobs, maintaining family relationships, and avoiding negative associations and dangers in jail were cited as positive aspects of the electronic monitoring sanction.

Although the respondents preferred electronic monitoring to incarceration, this is not to suggest that there are no pains associated with it as a sanction. Rather, many of the same pains experienced as a result of imprisonment in a jail or prison were felt by the offenders sentenced to house arrest. Also, some pains specific to electronic monitoring as a sanction became evident. Table 1 outlines the number of offenders experiencing each of the pains outlined by Sykes (1958) and those specific to offenders receiving electronic monitoring as a sanction.

TABLE 1 Pains Experienced by Participants

	Number	Percentage
Pains of imprisonment		
Deprivation of autonomy	25	92.6
Deprivation of goods and services	23	85.2
Deprivation of liberty	9	33.3
Deprivation of heterosexual relations	8	29.6
Deprivation of security	1	3.7
Additional pains		
Monetary costs	11	40.7
Family effects	11	40.7
Watching others effects	9	33.3
Bracelet effects	7	25.9

Similarities to Pains of Imprisonment

Deprivation of Autonomy According to Sykes (1958), deprivation of autonomy is a pain of imprisonment reflecting a loss of control and freedom for the inmate. Sykes writes that the inmate "is subject to a vast body of rules and commands that are designed to control" (p. 73). As a pain of imprisonment, these rules take away the inmate's sense of self and change the offender from an independent member of society to one with no ability to make choices about daily routines.

Statements made by many of the participants clearly suggest that deprivation of autonomy is a pain felt by those sanctioned to electronic monitoring. In fact, 92.59% (n = 25) of the offenders made comments reflecting a loss of autonomy. Consistently, comments such as "being caged"; "This is jail inside your home;" "The only thing this lacks is bars on windows;" and "The only difference between this and jail is that I'm not in a cell, but in a house" were made by the respondents. Comparing their loss of control to being in jail is noteworthy, particularly considering that most made comments reflecting a preference to electronic monitoring over jail. Also note that most could make this comparison because most spent at least some time incarcerated.

Interestingly, describing the deprivation of autonomy in further detail, Sykes (1958) writes, "Of the many threats which may confront the individual . . . there are few better calculated to arouse acute anxieties than the attempt to reimpose the subservience of youth" (p. 76). Offenders seemed to support this suggestion stating, "It is like being on punishment from my mother and having to give up my allowance" and "This is like when you are a kid and your parents put you on punishment." Another said "I feel like a dog on a leash."

Although the majority of offenders described lack of control and freedom as experiences resulting from the sanction, they also seemed to learn from it. One said, "It has taught me a very valuable lesson that there is nothing like freedom, even if it's just to go to the store or doctor, or out in your yard to do some work." And another said,

> It has taught me a valuable lesson of what it is like to have my freedom taken away from you [sic]. Also, [I learned] not to take anything for granted as so many of us do. You don't realize what you've got until it's gone.

Although deprivation of autonomy was the pain that seemed most significant to the offenders, other pains were apparent as well.

Deprivation of Goods and Services According to Sykes (1958), "The average inmate finds himself in a harshly Spartan environment which he defines as painfully depriving" (p. 68). Like the inmates in jail or prison, those experiencing the sanction of electronic monitoring also defined their punishment as "painfully depriving." A majority of the participants (n = 23 or 85.19%) made comments suggesting that they experienced deprivations of goods and services.

Participants noted that due to the sanction, their abilities to shop, eat out, go to church, work extra hours, and do many of the things others take for granted were limited, if not nonexistent. One participant described the worst part of electronic monitoring as "I can't go shopping." Another said, "At times it can be a hassle. . . . I lose a lot of money having to be back here on time. Used to be, I could stay [at work] until 11:00. It's an inconvenience." Work and shopping were not the only goods and services lacking among the respondents. As one said, "I do not like electronic monitoring because it is summertime and I can't enjoy it. It is like being at the beach and not being able to touch the sand, water, or look at the pretty girls."

Deprivation of Liberty Deprivations of liberty include the restriction of the individual's movements, seclusion from one's significant others, and the loss of certain civil rights (Sykes, 1958). Deprivations of liberty are similar to deprivations of autonomy in that certain freedoms (i.e., movement) or rights are taken away from the offender. The distinction is that whereas deprivations of autonomy yield limited restrictions of freedom, deprivations of liberty entail complete restrictions of freedom and other constitutional rights. The way that electronic monitoring restricts movements was established when autonomy was considered. In fact, offenders would likely argue that some of the deprivations of autonomy noted earlier seem to them to be deprivations of liberty as well. Although deprivations of liberty as restrictions of movement applies to each of the offenders on electronic monitoring, the loss of certain civil rights, such as voting rights, appears to be another deprivation of liberty relevant to electronic monitoring.

An innocuous question regarding political affiliation generated some interesting responses regarding deprivation of liberty. Only 18 participants indicated that they were Democrat, Republican, or Independent. The rest made comments suggesting that they could not participate in elections (n = 9). Some simply said they "can't vote," or "don't vote." A few, however, seemed to experience this loss a little more painfully. One said, "We lose our voting rights forever. But we're still taxed. Yet the constitution says that there shall be no taxation without representation. Could you explain that one to me?" Another said, "Voting is a subject I don't discuss." Although all did not indicate a lack of voting privileges, it could have been due to the fact that some were convicted of misdemeanors, rather than felonies, and would therefore still have this right. Convicted felons in Virginia, however, whether they are on electronic monitoring or in prison, experience this deprivation for life unless their voting privileges are reinstated by the governor.

Deprivation of Heterosexual Relationships Sykes (1958) describes deprivation of heterosexual relationships as including both physical and psychological losses experienced by inmates. Physical losses for inmates are clear and would not necessarily be experienced by those on electronic monitoring who are involved in sexual relationships. If relationships are broadened to include all types of relationships (rather than just sexual relationships), then ways in which electronic monitoring affect psychological aspects of relationships become evident.

It is important to note that these effects can be both positive and negative. Indeed, from a sociological perspective, one could argue that electronic monitoring, by not cutting the offender off from family and prosocial (conventional) friends, is a benefit in and of itself. In all, 13 (48.15%) of the inmates noted that the sanction had a positive effect on their relationships, whereas 8 (29.63%) described negative results. For those who experienced positive results, many suggested that being able to be close to their partners, children, and other significant others was one of the things they liked about the sanction.

Others, however, experienced increased stress in their relationships because of the sanction. One said, "My wife goes out more, leaves me more often, and is more friendly with men. She responds to me hatefully." Others also recognized increased stress in their relationships. It is worth noting that 7 of the 8 respondents who described negative effects in their relationships also described some positive effects from the sanction. The only respondent who noted only negative aspects said of his live-in relatives, "They get a free ride. I have to pay the phone and electric bill. If I don't, I'm back in jail and they know that."

Deprivation of Security Deprivation of security reflects the possibility that inmates live in an environment where they are preyed on by evil guards and fellow inmates. Sykes (1958) cites an inmate who said, "The worst thing about prison is you have to live with other prisoners" (p. 77). Comments by 9 (33.33%) of the respondents support this statement. These comments were usually brief, saying things such as "Serious criminals are in jail" and "What's mine is mine." One respondent was a little more specific, suggesting, "The little things makes [sic] it different from jail. You don't have to go to the bathroom in front of a bunch of guys." Although those who noted security concerns generally noted that they feel safer at home than in jail, one offender said, "Sometimes I become paranoid, but I get over it and can get on with it." This was the only statement reflecting any similarity to deprivation of security as described by Sykes.

Additional Pains

Four pains not discussed by Sykes became evident through the statements made by the respondents. These additional pains are: monetary costs, family effects, watching others effects, and bracelet effects.

Monetary Costs A trend and seeming societal benefit of electronic monitoring involves making the offenders pay fees for being involved in the program. Of the offenders, 11 (40.74%) noted monetary costs as one of the negative aspects of the sanction. Some simply said, "I pay for this," Others seemed to be a little more annoyed with the cost. One, for example, said,

> My lawyer didn't explain how much the program costs. If it weren't for my mother, I would never be able to support myself and I would be forced to go back to jail. I can completely understand how someone who has no real job skills, no other financial support and a felony on their record would have a hard time making ends meet, and pay for the program, even if they can find a job. So, I am not making excuses, but I can see how people may feel trapped and forced to find illegal means to support themselves.

Another said, "The worst part of it all is that it costs me $70 a week."

Although the offenders clearly experience the monetary costs as a pain resulting from the sanction, obvious advantages for the rest of society exist as a result of having the offenders pay for the program. One offender summed it up in this way: "Jail costs the public a lot. Electronic monitoring costs the offender a lot."

Family Effects Of the total offenders, 18 (66.66%) indicated that the sanction affected their families. Of these, 11 (61.11%) described negative results, whereas 7 (38.88%) shared positive family experiences (e.g., sharing time together, helping each other, etc.) because of the sanction.

Beyond the simple inability to spend time with family members in public, ways that the sanction directly affected family members stem from the way the sanction is imposed. That is, the method of monitoring the offender often interfered with the daily routines of family members. One respondent said, "My fiancé is just as much on house arrest as I am." Another said, "I live with my parents and the phone calls wake them up during the middle of the night or early in the mornings." Furthermore, one indicated that "having to adjust the machine when they're on the phone because it sounds off and they have to get off the phone" was a problem for the family members. Thus, for some family members, the sanction directly affected some of the activities others might take for granted.

Roles may also shift for some family members. As one respondent stated, "Electronic monitoring has shifted a great deal of the responsibilities outside the home onto my wife." At least four others noted the negative effects of being forced to become more dependent on their significant others.

Watching Others Effects Inmates in jail or prison are largely isolated, not viewing directly what those on the outside are doing (Rokach, 1997). In some ways, this may isolate them from jealousy, envy, or temptations to beat the system. Based on this possibility, another pain that does not compare easily to Sykes's (1958) pains of imprisonment, which we call watching others effects, arises. Essentially, because of the conditions of the sanction, offenders on electronic monitoring are often forced to watch as others engage in activities that they would like to be involved. One third ($n = 9$) of the respondents made statements suggesting that watching others was a pain associated with the sanction.

Describing this pain, one offender said, "It is difficult due to the fact that you are tempted to leave the house because of all of the direct temptations you encounter." Another said, "It's annoying how some people joke me about not being able to go outside." A third respondent described this pain even more specifically: "It's torture doing it. . . . You have to watch others get ready for the Garth Brooks concert and then they are going out the door and I have to say, 'Have a good time, I'll stay home and baby-sit.'"

Bracelet Effects We refer to the final cost of electronic monitoring as bracelet effects, referring to the impact of wearing the monitor. In all, 7 (25.93%) of the offenders noted problems wearing the monitor. Interestingly, 4 of the 8 (50.00%) females noted problems, whereas only 3 of the 19 (15.79%) males noted this concern. Although the cell frequencies were too small for statistical tests of significance, the verbatim comments in and of themselves suggest potential gender differences regarding how wearing the bracelet is experienced by the offenders. The four women who expressed problems with the bracelet made the following statements: "I need bigger socks to cover it when I work," "I don't like it around my leg," "I have to wear pants all of the time," "It is uncomfortable," and "I have a foreign object attached to my leg." Alternatively, the males said, "I work in boots and it is uncomfortable;" "It's uncomfortable, but the only time I think about it is when I shower and come in here;" and "The strap is very uncomfortable." Inductively, it seems as if the men were more concerned with comfort, whereas the women were more concerned with how the monitor potentially affected their appearances. Although this cannot be tested here, sheer differences in the numbers lend support to the possibility that the monitor affects women differently than it affects men.

DISCUSSION

Table 2 outlines the similarities and differences in the pains experienced in prison or jail and those suggested by the offenders on electronic monitoring. As shown, some of the pains of electronic monitoring are similar to imprisonment. Alternatively, the experiences of those on electronic monitoring are unique and qualitatively different from those who are in jail or prison. Although differences exist, contrary to prior studies on offenders' perceptions about the severity of intermediate sanctions in general and electronic monitoring specifically, our results suggest that these offenders prefer electronic monitoring to jail. However, the offenders in this study were quick to point out that electronic monitoring, as designed, is

TABLE 2 Similarities and Differences in Pains Among Offenders

Pain	Prison/Jail	Electronic Monitoring
Deprivation of autonomy	Yes	Yes
Deprivation of goods and services	Yes	Yes
Deprivation of liberty	Yes	Yes
Deprivation of heterosexual relations	Yes	Yes and No
Deprivation of security	Yes	No
Monetary costs	Yes, but different	Yes
Family effects	Yes, but different	Yes
Watching others effects	No	Yes
Bracelet effects	No	Yes

in many ways equivalent to a jail sentence. Several important implications evolve from these findings.

First, the fact that so many respondents shared a fear of and/or horror stories about jail and prison suggests that incarceration is indeed a sentence feared by this group of offenders. Most of the respondents had spent at least part of their sentences in jail or prison. Thus, they felt, for the most part, lucky to be out of jail. As Sykes (1958) notes, "Imprisonment, then, is painful" (p. 78). It could be that certain groups are more attracted to incarceration and that others would prefer to avoid it at all costs. Such a suggestion is supported by Crouch (1993) who found that older unmarried individuals who have been widely exposed to institutional corrections are more likely to prefer prison to alternative sanctions. Our research, conversely, suggests that those with spouses, families, and jobs see the benefits in their lives of electronic monitoring.

Second, the finding that so many of the offenders, although preferring the sanction to jail, still viewed the sanction as a form of incarceration lends support to the notion that electronic monitoring programs punish offenders. In fact, in many ways, offenders receiving such sanctions experience additional costs such as the monetary costs, family effects, watching others effects, and bracelet effects mentioned by our respondents. Thus, as in previous research, electronic monitoring (as an intermediate sanction) might be perceived as punitive as or even more punitive than jail or prison (Spelman, 1995). To borrow from Sykes (1958), electronic monitoring, then, is painful. According to Turner, Cullen, Sundt, and Applegate (1997),

> The challenge for correctional reformers is to address the public's desire from community-based sanctions that intervene sufficiently in the offenders' lives to exact a measure of retribution, to reduce the risk the offenders pose, and to increase the chances that the offender will not recidivate. (p. 23)

Our research addresses the first area and finds that electronic monitoring punishes offenders and therefore provides a measure of retribution. Note as well that suggestions in the literature support the rehabilitative nature of programs such as these (Lilly, Ball, Curry, & Smith, 1992; Papy & Nimer, 1991).

By meting out punishment and at the same time rehabilitating the offender, the programs benefit society in at least two ways. First, by rehabilitating the offender, both society and the offender should, in theory, benefit from the sanction when it is applied effectively. Second, according to Kant and many others (Dillingham, Montgomery, & Tabor, 1990), retribution is a natural emotion. Electronic monitoring, if it is as punitive as jail or prison, should satisfy the public's need to punish certain types of offenders. As research shows, however, this sanction is often viewed as too lenient by members of society (Larivee, 1993).

Often, such findings are answered by explanations centering on the belief that we live in an overly punitive society. Deflecting the blame to society is a little misleading because very little research has actually examined how punitive electronic monitoring is. How we can expect members of society to make informed choices about the severity of alternative sanctions with so little empirical research is troubling. Note, also, that recent research shows that some members of society actually are starting to support community-based sanctions for some offenders, especially if the sanctions are perceived as cost effective (Brown & Elrod, 1995; Sigler & Lamb, 1995/1996).

Clearly, more attention needs to be given to how offenders experience their sanctions. To do this, academicians, legislatures, practitioners, and members of the public must come to terms with what punishment actually entails. Until this occurs, legislatures will continue to follow the expressed desires of the public which, despite recent changes noted by Brown and Elrod (1995) and Sigler and Lamb (1995/1996), is generally more in favor of severe punishments. The irony is that electronic monitoring, at least according to the offenders in this study, is a severe sanction. Combining this finding with previous studies (Lilly et al., 1992; Papy & Nimer, 1991), the sanction can punish and at the same time treat the offender. To quote Sykes (1958) one last time, "Modern society does expect the tyranny of captivity to serve a useful purpose beyond that of keeping known criminals confined" (p. 132).

This is not to suggest that these results are definitive and that we can start spreading the word about this apparently misinterpreted sanction. The fact that we have used offenders from just one program and have relied solely on exploratory questions of those offenders limits the generalizability of our findings. Instead, more research needs to be done so that the information needed for the public to make informed decisions about these types of sanctions becomes available. Until this information is available, these programs will continue to be viewed as too lenient and will therefore lack the needed support of legislatures.

In closing, the goal of this research was not to evaluate or determine the fate of electronically monitored house arrest programs. Rather, the purpose was to better understand the experience of house arrest and electronic monitoring as a form of punishment. Walker (1990) states that these programs "will remain as a potential tool of corrections in the future since technologies cannot be reinvented, only improved or made obsolete" (p. 16). By using offenders on house arrest as a sample, this research contributes to the literature on perceptions of punishment among offenders. . . .

REFERENCES

Apospori, E., & Alpert, G. (1993). Research note: The role of differential experience with the criminal justice system in changes in perceptions of severity of legal sanctions over time. *Crime and Delinquency, 39*(2), 184–194.

Austin, J. (1995). An overview (correctional options). *Corrections Today, 57*(1), 1–9.

Berg, B. (1995). *Qualitative research methods for the social sciences* (2nd ed.). Boston: Allyn & Bacon.

Brown, M. P., & Elrod, P. (1995). Electronic house arrest: An examination of citizen attitudes. *Crime and Delinquency, 41*(3), 332–346.

Charles, M. T. (1989). The development of a juvenile electronic monitoring program. *Federal Probation, 53*(2), 3–11.

Clark, C. S. (1994). Prison overcrowding: Will building more prisons cut the crime rate? *CQ Researcher, 4*(5), 99–106.

Colson, C., & Van Ness, D. W. (1989). Alternatives to incarceration: A conservative perspective. *Journal of State Government, 62*(2), 59–64.

Crouch, B. M. (1993). Is incarceration really worse: Analysis of offenders' preferences for prison over probation. *Justice Quarterly, 10*(1), 67–88.

Denying ex-cons the vote permanently: What purpose is served? (1996, September 26). *The Virginian-Pilot,* p. A14.

Dillingham, S. D., Montgomery, R. H. Jr., & Tabor, R. W. (1990). *Probation and parole in practice* (2nd ed). Cincinnati: Anderson.

Jolin, A., & Stipak, B. (1992). Drug treatment and electronically monitored home confinement: An evaluation of a community-based sentencing option. *Crime and Delinquency, 38*(2), 158–170.

Larivee, J. J. (1993). Community programs: A risky business. *Corrections Today, 55*(6), 20–24.

Lilly, J. R. (1989). What about house arrest. *Journal of State Government, 62,* 89–91.

Lilly, J. R., Ball, R. A., Curry, G. D., & Smith, R. C. (1992). The Pride, Inc., Program: An evaluation of 5 years of electronic monitoring. *Federal Probation, 56*(4), 42–33.

Lilly, R., & Jenkins, J. (1989, October 6). Life with the tag. *New Statesman and Society, 2*(70), 23–24.

Maineprize, S. (1992, April). Electronic monitoring in corrections: Assessing cost effectiveness and the potential for widening the net of social control. *Canadian Journal of Criminology, 32,* 161–180.

Maxfield, M. J., & Baumer, T. L. (1990). Home detention with electronic monitoring: Comparing pretrial and postconviction programs. *Crime and Delinquency, 36*(4), 521–536.

McClelland, K. A., & Alpert, G. P. (1985). Factor analysis applied to magnitude estimates of punishment seriousness: Patterns of individual differences. *Journal of Quantititative Criminology, 1*(3), 307–318.

Papy, J. E., & Nimer, R. (1991). Electronic monitoring in Florida. *Federal Probation, 55*(1), 31–33.

Petersilia, J., & Deschenes, E. P. (1994a). Perceptions of punishment: Inmates and staff rank severity of prison versus intermediate sanctions. *Prison Journal, 74*(3), 306–329.

Petersilia, J., & Deschenes, E. P. (1994b). What punishes? Inmates rank the severity of prison vs. intermediate sanctions. *Federal Probation, 58*(1), 3–8.

Rackmill, S. J. (1994). An analysis of home confinement as a sanction. *Federal Probation, 58*(1), 45–52.

Renzema, M., & Skeleton, D. (1991). The scope of electronic monitoring today. *Journal of Offender Monitoring, 4*(4), 6–11.

Rokach, A. (1997). Loneliness in jail: Coping strategies. *International Journal of Offender Therapy and Comparative Criminology, 41*(3), 260–271.

Schmidt, A. K. (1991). Electronic monitors: Realistically, what can be expected? *Federal Probation, 55*(2), 47–53.

Sigler, R. T., & Lamb, D. (1996). Community-based alternatives to prison: How the public and court personnel view them. *Journal of Offender Monitoring, 9*(2), 1–8. (Reprinted from *Federal Probation, 59*(2), 3–9, 1995).

Spelman, W. (1995). The severity of intermediate sanctions. *Journal of Research in Crime and Delinquency, 32*(2), 107–135.

Sullivan, R.E. Jr. (1990, November 29). Reach out and guard someone: Using phones and bracelets to reduce prison overcrowding. *Rolling Stone, 592,* 51.

Sykes, G. (1958). *The society of captives.* Princeton, NJ: Princeton University Press.

Turner, M. G., Cullen, F. T., Sundt, J. L., & Applegate, B. (1997). Public tolerance for community based sanctions. *Prison Journal, 77*(1), 6–26.

Walker, J. L. (1990). Sharing the credit, sharing the blame: Managing political risks in electronically monitored house arrest. *Federal Probation, 54*(2), 16–20.

REVIEW QUESTIONS

1. How does the comparison of home incarceration versus jail for the offenders in this sample contrast with similar comparisons of incarceration versus community corrections supervision in other studies? Why would this sample be similar or different than those reported in other studies?
2. What are the major pains of imprisonment reported by these offenders serving sentences on electronic monitoring and home incarceration?
3. What deprivations would you expect to be experienced by offenders on home incarceration and electronic monitoring that is not reported by any/many offenders?

READING 37

Prisoner Reentry

Public Safety and Reintegration Challenges

Joan Petersilia

This reading explores the use of parole in contemporary American corrections. The changes in the legal nature, structure, process, and resources for parole are examined and shown to have led to an infrequent use of parole today. Rather than seeing parole as a way to be "easy" on offenders, Petersilia argues that there are a number of collateral consequences that accompany parole supervision. The position taken in this reading is that parole is important, can have positive effects for offenders and society, but needs to be changed from its current structure and focus.

. . . Virtually no systematic, comprehensive attention has been paid by policy makers to deal with people after they are released, an issue that has been termed *prisoner reentry.* There are a few studies of various parole innovations, some research on distinct populations such as sex offenders, and some evaluations of programs such as drug treatment systems that link prison-based and community-based interventions. But, as a general matter, we know very little about correlates of success and failure in the process of reintegration. Failure to better understand the ingredients of successful integration is critical, and the crime reduction gains made in recent years may erode unless we consider the cumulative impact of tens of thousands of returning felons on families, children, and communities. Failure to pay attention to parole services is unfortunate from another standpoint as well because at the point of release, most inmates have an initial strong desire to succeed.

Of course, inmates have always been released from prison, and officials have long struggled with how to help them succeed. But the current situation is decidedly different. The numbers of releasees dwarf anything in our history, the needs of parolees are more serious, the public and parole system is less tolerant of failures, and the corrections system retains few rehabilitation programs—either in prison or in the community. . . .

PAROLE IN THE UNITED STATES: MANAGING MORE PEOPLE, MANAGING THEM LESS WELL

Changes in sentencing practices, coupled with a decrease in availability of rehabilitation programs, have placed new demands on the parole system. Support and funding have declined, resulting in dangerously high caseloads. Parolees sometimes abscond from supervision, often without consequence. It is not surprising that most parolees fail to lead law-abiding lives and are rearrested.

Determinate Sentencing Means Automatic Release Parole in the United States has changed dramatically since the mid-1970s, when most inmates served open-ended indeterminate prison terms—10 years to life, for example—and a parole board, usually appointed by the governor, had wide discretion to release inmates or keep them behind bars. In principle, offenders were paroled only if they were rehabilitated and had ties to the community—such as a family or a job. This made release from prison a privilege to be earned. If inmates violated parole, they could be returned to prison to serve the balance of their term—a strong incentive not to commit crimes.

Today, indeterminate sentencing and discretionary release have been replaced in 14 states with determinate sentencing and automatic release (Tonry, 1999). For example, in California, where more than 125,000 prisoners are released each year, no parole board asks whether the inmate is ready for release because he or she *must* be released once the prisoner has served the determinate term imposed by the court. Offenders receive fixed terms at the time of their initial sentencing and are automatically released at the end of their prison term, usually with credits for good time. In 1990, 39% of inmates were released to supervision by parole board action and 29% by mandatory release; by 1998, those figures had been reversed, and 26% were released by parole board decision and 40% by mandatory release. With widespread adoption of truth-in-sentencing statutes, we can expect these trends to continue, so that release by the parole board will become a vestige of a bygone era, retained in some states and, in others, reserved for an aging prison cohort sentenced under the old regime.

A parolee must generally be released to the county where he last resided before going to prison. Because offenders overwhelmingly come from poor, culturally isolated, inner-city neighborhoods, those are where they return. The greatly expanded use of incarceration in the United States has a particularly acute impact on communities that are already characterized by great concentrations of disadvantage. According to recent research, in some communities, up to 15% of the young Black males are incarcerated on a given day (Lynch & Sabol, 2001), up to 13% of adult males enter prison or jail in a given year (Center for Alternative Sentencing and Employment Services [CASES], 2000), and up to 2% of all residents enter prison in a given year (Rose, Clear, & Scully, 1999). . . .

More Parolees Have Unmet Needs State and federal incarceration rates quadrupled between 1980 and 1996. . . . The Bureau of Justice Statistics (BJS) has calculated that an African American male has a 29% lifetime chance of serving at least a year in prison—a rate six times higher than for Whites. Sentences for drug offending are the major reason for increases in admissions—accounting for approximately 45% of the growth. Aggravated assault and sexual assault are also major contributors to growth (Blumstein & Beck, 1999). . . .

Increased dollars have funded operating costs for more prisons but *not* more rehabilitation programs. Fewer programs and a lack of incentives for inmates to participate in them mean that fewer inmates leave prison having participated in programs to address work, education, and substance use deficiencies. In-prison substance abuse programs are expanding, but programs are often minimal, and many inmates do little more than serve time before they are released. The Office of National Drug Control Policy reported that 70% to 85% of state prison inmates need substance abuse treatment; however, just 13% receive any kind of treatment in prison (McCaffrey, 1998).

Lynch and Sabol (2000a, 2000b) also compared 1991 and 1997 prison release cohorts in terms of their participation in vocational training, educational programs, and prerelease programs. They found that there had been a decrease in participation in vocational training from around 32% in 1991 to around 27% of the cohort in 1997. Participation in educational programs dropped even more, from around 42% in 1991 to around 34% in 1997. Participation in prerelease programs does not decrease in this period—only about 12% of either the 1991 or 1997 release cohort participated in *any* prerelease program. Lynch and Sabol conclude that neither the resources nor the participation in preparatory programs has kept pace with the quantitative increase in the size of reentry cohorts.

These program reductions come at a time when inmates need *more* help, not less. Many have long histories of crime and substance use, are gang members, and lack marketable skills. Deinstitutionalization has also led to a greater number of mentally ill people being admitted to prisons and jails. A recent survey revealed that nearly one in five U.S. prisoners report having a mental illness (Ditton, 1999). Psychologists warn that overcrowded and larger "supermax" prisons can cause serious psychological problems because prisoners in such institutions spend many hours in solitary or segregated housing, and those who study prison coping have found that greater time in isolation results in depression and heightened anxiety (Bottoms, 1999).

Gangs have become major factors in many prisons, with implications for in-prison and postprison behavior. Racial tensions in prison mean that inmates tend to be more preoccupied with finding a safe niche than with long-term self-improvement. Gang conflicts started (or continued) in prison get settled after release: "There is an awful lot of potential rage coming out of prison to haunt our future" (Abramsky, 1999, p. 33).

Parolee Supervision Replaces Services On release, 80% of parolees are assigned to a parole officer. The remaining 20%—including some of the most serious—will "max out" (e.g., not have received any credits for good time) and will receive no supervision. The offenders *least* willing to engage in rehabilitative programs are often *not* subject to parole supervision and services. About 100,000 parolees (about 1 in 5) left prison in 1998 without any postcustody supervision (Beck, 2000).

Parole officers are charged with enforcing conditions of release, including no drug use, finding and maintaining employment, and not associating with known criminals. The number of parole agents has not kept pace with the increased number of parolees. In the 1970s, one agent ordinarily was assigned 45 parolees; today, caseloads of 70 are common—far higher than the 35 to 50 considered ideal. Eighty percent of all U.S. parolees are supervised on "regular" rather than intensive caseloads, which means less than two 15-minute face-to-face contacts per month (Petersilia, 1999). Despite the evidence that more serious offenders are being released, just 6% of the parole population is on intensive supervision (Beck, 2000). Supervision costs about $2,200 per parolee, per year, compared with about

$22,000 per year, per prisoner. Those arrangements do not permit much monitoring, and the *Los Angeles Times* recently reported that parole agents in California have lost track of about one fourth of the 127,000 parolees they were supposed to supervise in 1999 (Associated Press, 1999). Nationally, about 9% of all parolees have absconded (Bonczar & Glaze, 1999).

Most Parolees Return to Prison Persons released from prison face a multitude of difficulties. They remain largely uneducated, unskilled, and usually without solid family support systems—to which are added the burdens of a prison record. It is not surprising that most parolees fail, and rather quickly—rearrests are most common in the first 6 months after release.

Fully two-thirds of all those released on parole will be rearrested within 3 years. Parole failures now constitute a growing proportion of all new prison admissions. In 1980, parole violators constituted 18% of all admissions, but recent years have seen a steady increase to the point where they constituted 35% of all new admissions in 1997 (Beck & Mumola, 1999).

THE COLLATERAL CONSEQUENCES OF PAROLE RELEASE

Recycling parolees in and out of families and communities has unfortunate effects on community cohesion, employment and economic well-being, democratic participation, family stabilization and childhood development, mental and physical health, and homelessness (Hagan & Dinovitzer, 1999).

Community Cohesion and Social Disorganization The social characteristics of neighborhoods—particularly poverty, ethnic composition, and residential instability—influence crime. There are "tipping points" beyond which communities are no longer able to exert positive influences on the behavior of residents. Norms start to change, disorder and incivilities increase, out-migration follows, and crime and violence increase (Wilson, 1987).

Elijah Anderson (1990) vividly illustrates the breakdown of social cohesion in socially disorganized communities. Moral authority increasingly is vested in "street-smart" young men for whom drugs and crime are a way of life. Attitudes, behaviors, and lessons learned in prison are transmitted into the free society. Anderson concludes that as

> family caretakers and role models disappear or decline in influence, and as unemployment and poverty become more persistent, the community, particularly its children, becomes vulnerable to a variety of social ills, including crime, drugs, family disorganization, generalized demoralization and unemployment. (p. 4)

Prison gangs have growing influence in inner-city communities. Joan Moore (1996) notes that most California prisons are violent and dangerous places, and new inmates search for protection and connections. Many find both in gangs. Inevitably, gang loyalties are exported to the neighborhoods. The revolving prison door strengthens street gang ties. Moore commented, "In California . . . frankly I don't think the gangs would continue existing as they are without the prison scene" (p. 73). Moore also found that state-raised youth, whose adolescence involved recurring trips to California juvenile detection facilities, were the most committed to the most crime-oriented gangs. She warns that as more youth are incarcerated earlier in their criminal careers, larger numbers of youth will come out of prison with hostile attitudes and exert strong negative influences on neighborhoods.

Recently, Rose et al. (1999) explored the direct effects of offenders going to prison and returning to their home community after 1 year in prison. They theorized that the aggregate impact of high levels of incarceration would damage networks of social control and decrease the legitimacy of formal social control. In their model, when public control occurs at high levels, informal controls function less effectively. The result is more crime. They tested their theory in Tallahassee, Florida, and found support for the proposition that spatial concentrations of incarceration promote higher-than-expected rates of crime. Using "neighborhood" as the level of analysis, they found that low rates of prison admissions were associated with no drop in crime the following year, moderate rates of admissions were associated with moderate drops in crime, but higher rates of admission—after a "tipping point" was reached of about 1.5% of the neighborhood's total population—had a strong, positive relationship to crime in the following year. This result supports the idea that high rates of admitting people to prison can destabilize informal networks of social control and lead to increases in crime.

Work and Economic Well-being Most inmates leave prison with no savings, no immediate entitlement to unemployment benefits, and few employment prospects. National statistics indicate that 7 in 10 prison inmates function at the two lowest levels of both prose and numeric literacy, meaning that they are unable to fill out a Social Security or job application, write a business letter, calculate a price discount, read a bus schedule, or perform many other text- and number-based tasks of daily life (National Institute for Literacy, 2001). Therefore, it is not surprising that, 1 year after release, as many as 60% of former inmates are not employed in the regular labor market (California Department of Corrections, 1994).

Incarceration is also stigmatizing, and there is increased reluctance among employers to hire ex-offenders. Evidence for the stigma of conviction was provided by experiments in which employers were sent fictitious letters of job applications containing information about the conviction status of job applicants (Buikhuisen & Dijksterhuis, 1971). Employers were less likely to respond positively to ex-convicts than those who provided no information about past convictions. A survey in five major U.S cities suggests that employers would be more likely to hire welfare recipients or applicants with little work experience than ex-convicts (Holzer, 1996). Holzer also reports that 65% of all employers said they would not knowingly hire an ex-offender (regardless of the offense), and between 30% and 40% had checked the criminal records of their most recent employees.

The "get-tough" movement of the 1980s also increased employment restrictions on parolees. Commonly, a felony record can temporarily disqualify employment in licensed or professional occupations. These prohibitions typically extend beyond the professions to include jobs in health care and skilled trades. In addition, felony status in several states can bar public-sector employment. The severity of civil disabilities varies across states. In California, for example, parolees are barred from law, real estate, medicine, nursing, physical therapy, and education. In Colorado, the jobs of dentist, engineer, nurse, pharmacist, physician, and real estate agent are closed to convicted felons. Their criminal record may also preclude them from retaining parental rights, be grounds for divorce, and bar them from jury service. Although the legal status of ex-felons is well documented (Office of the Pardon Attorney, 1996), little is known about the effects on employment of civil disabilities.

Simon (1993) notes that these disabilities are inherently contradictory. The United States spends millions of dollars to "rehabilitate" offenders, convincing them that they need to obtain legitimate employment, and then frustrates whatever was accomplished by barring them from many kinds of employment and its rewards. Moreover, the loss of a solid industrial base, which has traditionally supplied jobs within poorer inner-city communities, has left urban parolees with few opportunities.

The underemployment of ex-felons has broader economic implications. One reason America's unemployment statistics look so good compared with those of other industrial democracies is that 1.6 million mainly low-skilled workers—precisely the group unlikely to find work in a high-tech economy—have been incarcerated and are thus not considered part of the labor force (Western & Becket, 1999). If they were included, U.S. unemployment rates would be 2% higher. Recycling ex-offenders back into the job market with reduced job prospects will have the effect of increasing unemployment rates in the long run.

Family Stabilization and Childhood Development Women are about 7% of the U.S. prison population, but their incarceration rates are increasing faster than are those for men. About 80% of U.S. female inmates are mothers with, on average, two dependent children; two thirds of their children are younger than age 10 (Snell, 1994). More than half of incarcerated men are parents of children younger than 18 years of age. Altogether, more than 1.5 million children have parents in U.S. prisons, and the number will increase as the proportion of female inmates increases.

We know little about the effects of a parent's incarceration on childhood development, but it is likely to be significant. When mothers are incarcerated, their children are usually cared for by grandparents or other relatives or placed in foster care. One study found that roughly half of these children do not see their mothers the entire time they are in prison (because there are fewer prisons for women, women are often incarcerated further away from their children than are men, making family visits more difficult). The vast majority of imprisoned mothers, however, expect to resume their parenting role and reside with their children after their release, although it is uncertain how many actually do (Bloom & Steinhart, 1993).

Mothers released from prison have difficulty finding services such as housing, employment, and child care, and this causes stress for them and their children.

Children of incarcerated and released parents often suffer confusion, sadness, and social stigma, and these feelings often result in school-related difficulties, low self-esteem, aggressive behavior, and general emotional dysfunction. If the parents are negative role models, children fail to develop positive attitudes about work and responsibility. Children of incarcerated parents are five times more likely to serve time in prison than are children whose parents are not incarcerated (Beck, Gilliard, & Greenfeld, 1993).

We have no data on involvement of parolees in family violence, but it may be significant. Risk factors for child abuse and neglect include poverty, unemployment, alcohol/drug abuse, low self-esteem, and poor health of parents—common attributes of parolees. Concentrated poverty and social disorganization increase child abuse and neglect and other adjustment problems, which in turn constitute risk factors for later crime and violence.

Mental and Physical Health Prisoners have significantly more medical and mental health problems than the general population, due to lifestyles that often include crowded or itinerant living conditions, intravenous drug use, poverty, and high rates of substance abuse. In prisons, 50-year-olds are commonly considered old, in part because the health of the average 50-year-old prisoner approximates that of average persons 10 years older in the free community. While in prison, inmates have access to state-provided health care, but on release, most are unable easily to obtain health care and have the potential for spreading disease (particularly tuberculosis, hepatitis, and HIV) and presenting serious public health risks (McDonald, 1999).

In New York City, a major multi-drug-resistant form of tuberculosis emerged in 1989, with 80% of cases being traced to jails and prisons. By 1991, the Rikers Island Jail had one of the highest TB rates in the nation. In Los Angeles, an outbreak of meningitis in the county jail moved into the surrounding neighborhoods. . . .

Inmates with mental illness also are increasingly being imprisoned—and being released. In 1998, 16% of jail or prison inmates reported either a mental condition or an overnight stay in a mental hospital (Bureau of Justice Statistics, 1999). Even when public mental health services are available, many mentally ill individuals fail to use them because they fear institutionalization, deny they are mentally ill, or distrust the mental health system.

Democratic Participation and Political Alienation An estimated 3.9 million Americans—1 in 50 adults—were in 1998 permanently unable to vote as a result of a felony conviction. Of these, 1.4 million were African American males, representing 13% of all Black men. The numbers will certainly increase. In 1996, a young Black man age 16 had a 28.5% chance of spending time in prison during his life. The comparable figure for White men was 4.4% (Bonczar & Beck, 1997).

Denying large segments of the minority population the right to vote will likely alienate former offenders further. Disillusionment with the political process also erodes citizens' feelings of engagement and makes them less willing to participate in local activities and exert informal social control over residents. This is important because our most effective crime-fighting tools require community collaboration and active engagement.

Housing and Homelessness. The latest census counts about 230,000 homeless in America. In the late 1980s, an estimated quarter of them had served prison sentences. The figure is surely higher now, with many U.S. cities reporting a critical shortage of low-cost housing. California officials report that 10% of the state's parolees remain homeless, but in urban areas such as San Francisco and Los Angeles, the rate has reached 30% to 50% (Legislative Analysts Office, 1999).

Transients, panhandling, and vagrants increase citizens' fears, and that ultimately contributes to increased crime and violence. This is because neighborhood crime often worsens when law-abiding citizens are afraid to go onto streets filled with graffiti, transients, and loitering youth. Fearful citizens eventually yield control of the streets to people who are not frightened by these signs of decay and who often are the people who created the problem in the first place. A vicious cycle begins. Wilson and Kelling (1982) illustrate this by describing how a broken window can influence crime rates. If the first broken window in a building is not repaired, people who like breaking windows may assume no one cares and break some more. Soon, the building will have no windows. As "broken windows" spread—homelessness, prostitution, graffiti, panhandling—businesses and law-abiding citizens move away, and disorder escalates, leading to more serious crime.

RESPONDING TO THE PROBLEM

Government officials voice growing concern about the problem of prisoner reentry. Former Attorney General Janet Reno recently called prisoner reentry "one of the most pressing problems we face as a nation" (Reno, 2000). Federal programs are being developed to encourage responsible fatherhood among offenders, job training for parolees, and establishment of reentry courts. Reentry courts are modeled on "drug courts," which use judges instead of corrections officers to monitor released offenders (Travis, 2000). . . .

Initiatives such as these may or may not prove useful, but often they are not based on thoughtful analysis and debate. It is safe to say that parole has received less research attention in recent years than any other part of the correctional system. A congressionally mandated evaluation of prevention programs included just *one* parole evaluation among hundreds of recent studies that were examined (Sherman et al., 1997). I have spent many years working on *probation* effectiveness but know of no similar body of knowledge on *parole* effectiveness. Without better information, the public is unlikely to give corrections officials the political permission to invest in rehabilitation and job training programs for parolees. With better information, we might be able to persuade voters and elected officials to shift away from solely punitive crime policies and toward policies that balance incapacitation, rehabilitation, and just punishment.

Parole *release* also needs to be reconsidered. In 1977, 72% of all U.S. prisoners were released after appearing before a parole board, but that figure had declined to 26% by 1998, the lowest since the federal government began compiling statistics on the subject.

Parole was abolished because it came to symbolize the alleged leniency of a system in which hardened criminals were "let out" early. If parole were abolished, politicians argued, then parole boards could not release offenders early, and inmates would serve longer terms. However, this has not happened. Stivers (2000) shows that, after controlling for offender and offense characteristics, inmates released in 1995 in nonparole states served 7 months less, on average, than did inmates with the same characteristics released in states using discretionary parole. Similar experiences in Florida, Connecticut, and Colorado caused those states to reinstate discretionary parole after discovering that abolition resulted in shorter terms being served by most offenders.

Parole experts have been saying all along that the public is misinformed when it labels parole as lenient. To the contrary, through their exercise of discretion, parole boards can target more violent and dangerous offenders for longer periods of incarceration. When states abolish parole or reduce parole authorities' discretion, they replace a rational, controlled system of "earned" release for *selected* inmates with "automatic" release for nearly *all* inmates (Burke, 1995). Nonparole systems may sound tough, but they remove an important gate-keeping role that can protect communities and victims.

Parole boards are in a position to demand participation in drug treatment, and research shows that coerced drug treatment is as successful in achieving abstinence as is voluntary participation. Parole boards can also require an adequate plan for a job and residence in the community—and that has the added benefit of refocusing prison staff and corrections budgets on transition planning.

Parole boards can meet personally with the victim. Involving victims in parole hearings has been one of the major changes in parole in recent years. Ninety percent of parole boards now provide information to victims on the parole process, and 70% allow victims to be present during the parole hearing.

Perhaps most important, parole boards can reconsider the tentative release date when more information about the offense and offender has been collected and the offender's behavior in prison has been observed. More than 90% of U.S. offenders receive criminal sentences as a result of pleading guilty to offenses and not as a result of a trial. Usually they plead guilty to a reduced charge. Because there is no trial, there is little opportunity to fully air the circumstances surrounding the crime or the risks presented by the criminal. The parole board can revisit the case to discover how much injury the victim really suffered or whether a gun was involved—even though the offense to which the offender pled, by definition, indicates no weapon was involved. Burke (1995) observes, "In a system which incorporates discretionary parole, the system gets a second chance to make sure it is doing the right thing" (p. 7).

Ironically, "no-parole" systems also significantly undercut postrelease supervision. When parole boards have no ability to select who will be released, they are forced to supervise a more serious parolee population and not one of their own choosing. Parole officers say it is impossible to ensure cooperation of offenders when offenders know they will be released, regardless of their willingness to comply with certain conditions (e.g., get a job). And due to prison crowding, some states are no longer allowing parolees to be returned to prison for technical violations. Parole officers say that parole has lost its power to encourage inmates toward rehabilitation and sanction parole failures. Field supervision tends to be undervalued and, eventually, underfunded and understaffed.

No one would argue for a return to the unfettered discretion that parole boards exercised in the 1960s. That led to unwarranted disparities. Parole release decisions must be principled and incorporate explicit standards and due process protections. Parole guidelines, which are used in many states, can establish uniformity in parole decisions and objectively weigh factors known to be associated with recidivism. Rather than *entitle* inmates to be released at the end of a fixed time period, parole guidelines specify when the offender becomes *eligible* for release.

We also need to rethink who should be responsible for making parole release decisions. In most stales, the chair and all members of the parole board are appointed by the governor; in two thirds of the states, there are no professional qualifications for parole board membership. Although this may increase the political accountability of the parole board, it also makes it highly vulnerable to improper political pressures. In Ohio, by contrast, parole board members are appointed by the director of corrections, serve in civil service positions, and must have an extensive background in criminal justice.

CONCLUDING REMARKS

Parole supervision and release raise complicated issues and deserve more attention than they now get. Nearly 700,000 parolees are doing time on U.S. streets. Most have been released to parole systems that provide few services and impose conditions that almost guarantee parolees' failure. Monitoring systems are getting better, and public tolerance for failure is decreasing. A rising tide of parolees is back in prison, putting pressure on states to build more prisons and, in turn, taking money away from rehabilitation programs that might help offenders stay out of prison. Parolees will continue to receive fewer services to help them deal with their underlying problems, ensuring that recidivism rates and returns to prison remain high—and public support for parole remains low.

This situation represents formidable challenges to policy makers. The public will not support community-based punishments until they have been shown to "work," and they will not have an opportunity to "work" without sufficient funding and research. Spending on parole services in California, for example, was cut 44% in 1997, causing parole caseloads nearly to double (now at a ratio of 82 to 1). When caseloads increase, services decline, and even parolees who are motivated to change have little opportunity to do so. . . .

Given the increasing human and financial costs associated with prison—and all of the collateral consequences parolees pose to families, children, and communities—investing in effective reentry programs may be one of the best investments we make.

REFERENCES

Abramsky, S. (1999). When they get out. *Atlantic Monthly, 283*(6), 33.

Anderson, E. (1990). *Streetwise: Race, class, and change in an urban community.* Chicago: University of Chicago Press.

Associated Press. (1999, August 27). State agencies lost track of parolees. *Santa Barbara News Press,* p. B9.

Beck, A. (2000). *Prisoners in 1999* (Bulletin NCJ 183476). Washington, DC: Bureau of Justice Statistics.

Beck, A., Gilliard, D., & Greenfeld, L. (1993). *Survey of state prison inmates 1991* (NCJ-136949). Washington, DC: Bureau of Justice Statistics.

Beck, A., & Mumola, C. (1999). *Prisoners in 1998* (NCJ 175687). Washington, DC: Bureau of Justice Statistics.

Bloom, B., & Steinhart, D. (1993). *Why punish the children: A reappraisal of the children of incarcerated mothers in America.* San Francisco: National Council on Crime and Delinquency.

Blumstein, A., & Beck, A. J. (1999). Population growth in U.S. prisons, 1980–1996. In M. Tonry & J. Petersilia (Eds.), *Prisons* (Vol. 26, pp. 17–62). Chicago: University of Chicago Press.

Bonczar, T. P., & Beck, A. J. (1997). *Lifetime likelihood of going to state or federal prison* (NCJ 160092). Washington, DC: Bureau of Justice Statistics.

Bonczar, T. P., & Glaze, L. E. (1999). *Probation and parole in the United States.* Washington, DC: U.S. Department of Justice, Bureau of Justice Statistics.

Bottoms, A. (1999). Interpersonal violence and social order in prisons. In M. Tonry & J. Petersilia (Eds.), *Prisons* (Vol. 26, pp. 205–283). Chicago: University of Chicago Press.

Buikhuisen, W., & Dijksterhuis, F.P.H. (1971). Delinquency and stigmatization. *British Journal of Criminology, 11,* 185–187.

Bureau of Justice Statistics. (1999). *Mental health and treatment of inmates and probationers* (NCJ-174463). Washington, DC: Bureau of Justice Statistics.

Burke, P. B. (1995). *Abolishing parole: Why the emperor has no clothes.* Lexington, KY: American Probation and Parole Association.

California Department of Corrections. (1994). *Supervised parole.* Sacramento, CA: Author.

Center for Alternative Sentencing and Employment Services (CASES). (2000). *The community justice project.* New York: Author.

Ditton, P. (1999). *Mental health and treatment of inmates and probationers* (NCJ-174463). Washington, DC: Bureau of Justice Statistics.

Hagan, J., & Dinovitzer, R. (1999). Collateral consequences of imprisonment for children, communities, and prisoners. In M. Tonry & J. Petersilia (Eds.), *Prisons* (pp. 121–162). Chicago: University of Chicago Press.

Holzer, H. J. (1996). *What employers want: Job prospects for less-educated workers.* New York: Russell Sage.

Legislative Analysts Office. (1999). *Crosscutting issues: Judiciary and criminal justice* [Online]. Available: www.lao.ca.gov/analysis.

Lynch, J. P., & Sabol, W. J. (2000a). Prison use and social control. In J. Horney (Ed.), *Policies, processes, and decisions of the criminal justice system* (pp. 7–44). Washington, DC: U.S. Department of Justice.

Lynch, J. P., & Sabol, W. J. (2000b). *Prisoner reentry and the consequences of sentencing reform* [Online]. Available: www.urban.org/news/tuesdays/12–00/lynch.html.

Lynch, J. P., & Sabol, W. J. (2001). *Crime policy report.* Washington, DC: Urban Institute Press.

May, J. P. (2000). Feeding a public health epidemic. In J. P. May (Ed.), *Building violence: How America's rush to incarcerate creates more violence.* Thousand Oaks, CA: Sage.

McCaffrey, B. (1998). *Drug treatment in the criminal justice system.* Washington, DC: Office of National Drug Control Policy.

McDonald, D. C. (1999). Medical care in prisons. In M. Tonry & J. Petersilia (Eds.), *Prisons* (Vol. 26, pp. 427–478). Chicago: University of Chicago Press.

Moore, J. (1996, January). *Bearing the burden: How incarceration weakens inner-city communities.* Paper presented at the Unintended Consequences of Incarceration, New York.

National Institute for Literacy. (2001). *Fact sheet: Correctional education* [Online]. Available: www.nifl.gov/newworld/correct.htm.

Office of the Pardon Attorney. (1996). *Civil disabilities of convicted felons: A state-by-state survey.* Washington, DC: U.S. Department of Justice.

Petersilia, J. (1999). Parole and prisoner reentry in the United States. In M. Tonry & J. Petersilia (Eds.), *Prisons* (pp. 479–529). Chicago: University of Chicago Press.

Reno, J. (2000, February). *Remarks of the Honorable Janet Reno on reentry court initiative.* Presented at John Jay College of Criminal Justice, New York [Online]. Available: http://www.usdoj.gov/ag/speeches/2000/doc2.htm. Retrieved May 19, 2000.

Rose, D., Clear, T., & Scully, K. (1999, November). *Coercive mobility and crime: Incarceration and social disorganization.* Paper presented at the American Society of Criminology, Toronto, Canada.

Sherman, L., Gottfredson, D., Mackenzie, D., Eck, J., Reuter, P., & Bushway, S. (Eds.). (1997). *Preventing crime: What works, what doesn't, what's promising.* College Park: University of Maryland Press.

Simon, J. (1993). *Poor discipline: Parole and the social control of the underclass, 1890–1990.* Chicago: University of Chicago Press.

Snell, T. L. (1994). *Women in prison* (NCJ-145321). Washington, DC: Bureau of Justice Statistics.

Stivers, C. (2000). *Impacts of discretionary parole release on length of sentence served and recidivism.* Unpublished manuscript, School of Social Ecology, University of California, Irvine.

Tonry, M. (1999). *Reconsidering indeterminate and structured sentencing: Issues for the 21st century.* Washington, DC: U.S. Department of Justice, National Institute of Justice.

Travis, J. (2000). *But they all come back: Rethinking prisoner reentry.* Washington, DC: National Institute of Justice.

Western, B., & Beckett, K. (1999). How unregulated is the U.S. labor market? The penal system as a labor market institution. *American Journal of Sociology, 104*(4), 1030–1060.

Wilson, J. Q., & Kelling, G. L. (1982, March). Broken windows. *Atlantic Monthly,* pp. 29–38.

Wilson, W. J. (1987). *The truly disadvantaged: The inner city, the underclass, and public policy.* Chicago: University of Chicago Press.

REVIEW QUESTIONS

1. What are the commonly experienced collateral consequences of being on parole?
2. What arguments does the author make for why offenders should be on parole? What support does she provide for her position?
3. The public often believes that parole is "lenient" or "soft." However, Petersilia argues this is an incorrect perception. Why?

XV

FUTURE DIRECTIONS IN CORRECTIONS

READING 38

Corrections and Sentencing in the Twenty-first Century

Evidence-Based Corrections and Sentencing

Doris Layton MacKenzie

This article reflects upon the changes that occurred in correctional philosophy and practice throughout the twentieth century as a means of forecasting what lies ahead in terms of society's response to crime and criminals. Three primary eras of American corrections are depicted in the twentieth century: a rehabilitation-focused era characterized by individualized sentences and treatment regimens, a retribution-centered era embodied by punitive sentencing and harsh conditions of confinement, and a crime control or incapacitation-focused era emphasizing risk reduction through mass incapacitation. The authors note the core factors that inspired these philosophies and practices and then go on to describe some of the resultant scholarly, institutional, and societal implications. From here, the author highlights a series of debates and a research agenda that promise to inform our correctional understanding and practices during the first several decades of the twenty-first century.

In the past 30 years of the 20th century, major changes occurred in the United States in corrections and sentencing. The strong emphasis on rehabilitation that had existed from the turn of the century gave way to new philosophies of corrections. The new philosophies focused on retribution and crime control. As we move into the 21st century, we see more changes. . . .

INDETERMINATE SENTENCING AND REHABILITATION

From the late 1800s until around 1970, the predominant model of corrections and sentencing in the United States was rehabilitation. Thirty years ago, all states, the federal government, and the District of Columbia had indeterminate sentencing systems. In some states, the indeterminacy of the sentences permitted sufficient leeway to permit courts to sentence offenders to prison for time periods from 1 day to life. Parole boards were assigned the task of determining when the offender had made sufficient progress to be awarded supervised release. After sentencing, decisions were almost totally the prerogative of correctional authorities or parole boards.

Indeterminate sentencing was clearly based on a medical-type model of corrections. The idea behind indeterminate sentencing was individualization of sentences. Judges awarded sentences with a wide range between the minimum and maximum length of time the offender had to serve in prison. Offenders were supposed to be released when they were rehabilitated. Release decisions were the responsibility of prison authorities and the parole board. Correctional officials were given a great deal of discretion to tailor dispositions to the treatment needs of individual offenders.

The strong rehabilitative perspective of the 1960s is reflected in the recommendations made by President Lyndon Johnson's blue-ribbon panel established to "probe fully and deeply into the problems of crime in our Nation" (President's Commission on Law Enforcement and Administration of Justice, 1967, pp. 166–169). Prominent among the recommendations were reduced probation and parole caseloads; increased services for felons, juveniles, and adult misdemeanants who could profit from community treatment; and the training of officers to provide more active interventions. In regard to rehabilitation, the panel recommended model, small-unit correctional institutions for flexible, community-oriented treatment; upgrading of educational and vocational training; modern correctional industries aimed at rehabilitation; and an expansion of graduated release and furlough programs (President's Commission on Law Enforcement and Administration of Justice, 1967, pp. 166–174).

The recommendations of this panel, as well as the indeterminate sentencing structure, clearly demonstrate that the emphasis at the time was on rehabilitation with a focus on community treatment, diversion, reintegration, and education and employment programs. It should be noted that although the philosophical emphasis was on rehabilitation, in actual practice the programs were often poorly implemented and funded.

CHANGING TIMES, 1970–2000

The decade of the 1960s began with great optimism about the promises of a new frontier. By the end of the decade, belief in "The Great Society" had given way to a despairing distrust of the state. The change had a dramatic effect on corrections and sentencing. Inherent in the rehabilitative ideal and indeterminate sentencing was a trust in criminal justice officials to reform offenders.

One of the most visible influences on this change was Martinson's (1974) summary of a more elaborate report by Lipton, Martinson, and Wilks (1975). Martinson's essay described the results of the research team's assessment of 231 evaluations of treatment programs conducted between 1945 and 1967. From this research, Martinson concluded that "with few and isolated exceptions the rehabilitative efforts that have been reported so far have had no appreciable effects on recidivism" (p. 25).

This report was widely interpreted as demonstrating that "nothing works" in rehabilitation (Sechrest, White, & Brown, 1979). Critics argued that Martinson's (1974) conclusions were flawed for two reasons. First, the research methodology of the studies reviewed was so inadequate that only a few studies warranted any unequivocal interpretations. Second, the majority of studies examined programs that were so poorly implemented they would hardly be expected to have an impact on recidivism (Cullen & Gilbert, 1982; Palmer, 1975). Despite the concerns about the conclusions, the phrase "nothing works" became an instant cliché and exerted a powerful influence on popular and professional thinking.

Several factors may explain why Martinson's (1974) conclusions became so widely accepted at that point in time. Some argue that the historical times were ripe for major changes in the criminal justice system (Cullen & Gendreau, 2000).

The decade prior to Martinson's essay was characterized by social turbulence. Protests and riots over civil rights and the war in Vietnam were common occurrences. Within the criminal justice system, the 1971 riot and slaughter of inmates and guards at Attica demonstrated the extent to which government officials would go to suppress offender protests. People began to question whether judges and correctional officials could be trusted to exercise the extreme discretion permitted by indeterminate sentencing.

Some people questioned the unbridled discretion available to criminal justice decision makers that gave preferential sentences to the advantaged and coerced inmates into conformity. Others wanted to return to earlier times when "law and order" reigned in our country, and they called for a "war on crime" to preserve the social order. Both called for changes in the criminal justice system, and a virtual revolution occurred in sentencing and corrections.

RETRIBUTION, CRIME CONTROL, AND DETERMINATE SENTENCING

The first proposed solution to the problems of corrections and sentencing was a return to a justice model; offenders would receive fair and just punishment for their offenses (American Friends Service Committee, 1971; Von Hirsch, 1976). This model was based on retributive notions of deserved punishment; the sentence should fit the crime—nothing more, nothing less. From this perspective, prison should not be used to achieve any utilitarian motive such as rehabilitation or crime control. The relevant factors to consider in sentencing are the crime or crimes of conviction and the offender's past criminal history.

The justice model carried direct implications for public policy. For example, offenders should be given substantial procedural protections at all stages of criminal justice processing. Therefore, the legal rights of inmates became of great importance for the courts and corrections. Perhaps the largest policy impact was the need to change from an indeterminate sentencing model to determinate or "flat" sentencing. Under determinate sentencing, a specific crime would carry a clearly identified sentence length, not a broad minimum and maximum. Parole would be eliminated. Sentence lengths would be determined by guidelines. Offenders would know how much time they had to do in prison; rehabilitation would be voluntary and not coerced.

At almost the same time that some were arguing for a justice model, others were arguing for changes that would increase the crime control aspects of corrections and sentencing through incapacitation and deterrence. In part, support for this perspective was garnered by the rising crime rates that occurred during the decade from 1965 to 1975. The "law and order" advocates attached rehabilitation as being "soft" on crime. They wanted to implement policies that would limit the ability of judges and correctional officials to mitigate the harshness of sanctions. They advocated "get-tough" proposals such as mandatory minimum sentences and lengthy determinate sentences as methods for reducing criminal activities through incapacitation and deterrence.

The concept of incapacitation is simple—although offenders are in prison, they clearly cannot commit crimes outside of prison (Blumstein, Cohen, & Nagin, 1978). Crime is reduced because the imprisoned offenders are prevented from committing crimes. Most people accept the notion that crime prevention through incapacitation is one of the primary justifications of imprisonment (Zimring & Hawkins, 1995). Also generally accepted is the fact that some individuals should be incarcerated for long periods of time as retribution for the seriousness of their offenses and because they pose a threat if released. The questions arise about how broadly the incapacitation strategy should be used. Some ask that prison space should be reserved for only the most serious offenders. Others advocate a general incapacitation strategy that would incarcerate substantial numbers of felons.

Further support for incapacitation came from research demonstrating large differences in the crime rates of individual offenders. Research examining the criminal activities of offenders demonstrated that a small number of very active offenders accounted for a disproportionately large number of the arrests (Wolfgang, Figlio, & Sellin, 1972). Theoretically, if these "career criminals"—the name given to the highly active offenders—could be identified and incapacitated, crime in the community would be reduced (Blumstein, Cohen, Roth, & Visher, 1986). This "selective incapacitation" strategy would identify offenders who are expected to commit the most crimes and the most serious crimes. These offenders would be imprisoned for longer periods of time.

During the period from 1975 to 2000, numerous policies, practices, and laws reflected the crime control perspective. Habitual offenders laws, mandatory sentences, and the more recent three-strikes laws were expected to control crime in the community. The "War on Drugs" expanded criminal sanctions for drug crimes. Increasing the arrests and punishment for drug offenses was expected to be effective in reducing illegal drug use and sales. Intermediate sanctions such as electronic monitoring and intensive supervision combined with urine testing increased the control over offenders in the community. This emphasis on control was a change from the 1960s community corrections programs' focus on rehabilitation (Morris & Tonry, 1990). Truth in sentencing increased the proportion of sentences offenders had to serve in prison before release.

IMPACT OF THE CHANGES

The incarceration rate in the United States was relatively stable from 1930 until 1975. On average, 106 inmates were incarcerated for every 100,000 individuals in the population. The rate fluctuated only slightly, from a low of 93 inmates to a maximum of 137 (*Sourcebook,* 1998). This was the era of rehabilitation and indeterminate sentencing.

Beginning around 1975, the incarceration rate in this country began a dramatic increase that has continued to the present time. By 1985, there were 202 inmates in state or federal prisons for every 100,000 adults in the population; by 1995, the rate increased to 411 inmates. By the end of 1998, more than 1.3 million prisoners were under federal or state jurisdiction; more than 1.8 million were in either jail or prison (Beck & Mumola, 1998).

The increases in rates were not limited to prisons and jails. There were also substantial increases in probation and parole populations. Since 1980, the total correctional populations grew from 1.8 million to 5.9 million in 1998. One in 34 adults or 2.9% of the population were incarcerated or on probation or parole at the end of the year. The increase in rates varied by gender, ethnicity, and race. Although women traditionally make up a relatively small percentage of the correctional population, the increase in female incarceration rates grew more rapidly than the rates did for men. However, the greatest overall rate of incarceration as well as the greatest increases occurred for minority males. The incarceration rates for African Americans were 6,607 and 474 (per 100,000 adult residents) for males and females, respectively. For Whites, the rates were 944 for males and 73 for females (Bonzcar & Glaze, 1999).

The enormous growth in correctional populations led to a rapid increase in expenditures. As an annual cost per U.S. resident, total state correctional spending rose from $53 in 1985 to $103 in 1996. The per year spending for prisons increased at a greater rate than other areas of state budgets (Stephan, 1996).

In an examination of what accounted for the enormous increase in incarceration rates, Blumstein and Beck (1999) concluded that only a small percentage of the increases in incarceration rates resulted from an increased number of offenses being committed (they estimated 12%). According to their analyses, drug offenders were the major component of the overall growth in incarceration. From 1980 until 1996, the drug incarceration rate grew from 15 inmates for every 100,000 adults to 148 inmates. However, if violent offenses are combined (murder, sexual assault, robbery, assault, and other violent crimes), then the growth in the incarceration rate was greater than the growth in the drug incarceration rate.

Furthermore, the factors contributing to the increase in drug offenders in prison differed from those associated with other crime types. The increased number of drug offenders was primarily a result of an increase in the number of arrests for drug offenses. In addition, more of those arrested for drug offenses were sent to prison. By 1998, the most serious offense of approximately 30% of the incoming prisoners was a drug offense, up from 10% in 1980 (Blumstein & Beck, 1999).

EVIDENCE-BASED CORRECTIONS AND SENTENCING

Incapacitation and Deterrence Research Considerable research has focused on understanding sanctioning policies and crime rates. After observing the rising incarceration rate, many people ask what impact this increase has had on public safety. The relationship between crime and incarceration rates is not simple and varies greatly depending on the period examined. For example, although the incarceration rate was stable from 1965 until approximately 1972, crime rates for adults fluctuated during the same period. Most reviews of the literature on the impact of crime control policies (incapacitation and deterrence) conclude that the effect of these policies on crime reduction has been modest (Blumstein et al., 1978; Blumstein et al., 1986; Reiss & Roth, 1993; Spelman, 2000). Most of the research uses complex statistical simulations to estimate the impact of incapacitation policies on crime. It is generally accepted that these policies prevent crime because offenders who are imprisoned do not have the opportunity to commit crimes, but valid estimates of the exact number of crimes prevented are difficult to obtain. Moreover, although there is a consistent finding that a small number of offenders commit a large number of crimes, predicting who these offenders are and incapacitating them have not been particularly successful.

Costs of Incarceration Another controversy arises when people discuss the costs of corrections. The enormous increase in incarceration rates led to overcrowded prisons and greatly increased the costs of corrections. In the early 1980s, Zedlewski (1987) proposed the importance of considering not only the cost of corrections but also the costs that arise when felons are released from prison. According to Zedlewski, when the potential costs are considered, the costs of releasing felons may outweigh the costs of keeping them in prison. For example, there are costs for arrests, revocation hearings, court proceedings, and such things as the costs to victims and additional private security. These costs must be weighted against the cost of keeping someone in prison. Debates exist about how to calculate costs and what should be included in cost calculations. Others argue that it is impossible to adequately identify the costs because costs to the communities and families of prisoners are not considered in the current calculations.

Intermediate Sanctions and Increased Control Intermediate sanctions are one type of correctional program that has been studied extensively. Most of these programs were designed to increase the control over offenders; they did not necessarily increase any type of therapy or treatment. In general, these programs were not found to successfully reduce the recidivism of offenders (MacKenzie, 1997; Tonry, 1996). In fact, in many instances, the increased surveillance associated with the programs resulted in more technical violations and returns to prison.

Rehabilitation Rehabilitation strategies focus on changing individual offenders so they will live crime-free lives. An increasing number of studies have examined the effectiveness of rehabilitation-type programs. Although there is some debate about the effectiveness of rehabilitation programs, recent literature reviews and meta-analyses demonstrate that rehabilitation can effectively change some offenders and reduce their criminal activities (Cullen & Gendreau, 2000). Some treatment programs are clearly better than others, and effective programs follow some basic principles. The programs must address characteristics that can be changed (dynamic factors) and factors that are directly related to criminal behavior (criminogenic factors) (Andrews & Bonta, 1998). Age, gender, and early criminal involvement are risk factors associated with criminal behavior; however, these characteristics are not dynamic criminogenic factors because they cannot be changed through programming. Conversely, antisocial attitudes, drug use, and anger responses are common dynamic, criminogenic factors that can be targeted in treatment.

There is also a concern that programs have "therapeutic integrity" or be implemented in a way that would be consistent with effective rehabilitation programming (e.g., designed by knowledgeable individuals and provided by appropriately educated and experienced staff who use adequately evaluated programs and give appropriate treatment dosage).

Another method for drawing conclusions about the effectiveness of programs is through systematic reviews. My colleagues and I at the University of Maryland have used two methods to assess the effectiveness of programs in reducing recidivism. Using the "count" method, we assessed evaluations for the quality of the science and also the direction and significance of the results (Bouffard, MacKenzie, & Hickman, 2000; Chanhatasilpa, MacKenzie, & Hickman, 2001; MacKenzie, 2000; MacKenzie & Hickman, 1998; Polizzi, MacKenzie, & Hickman, 1999). When there were a sufficient number of evaluations of a particular type of program, we conducted a meta-analysis to examine effectiveness (Gallagher, Wilson, Hirschfield, Coggeshall, & MacKenzie, 1999; Wilson, Gallagher, Coggeshall, & MacKenzie, 1999; Wilson, Gallagher, & MacKenzie, 2000).

Results from these assessments clearly demonstrate that while some correctional programs are effective in reducing recidivism some programs are not, some look promising, and the effectiveness of others is unknown. For example, according to our reviews and decision-making rules, we have found sufficient evidence from rehabilitations to conclude that the following are effective in reducing recidivism of offenders: in-prison therapeutic communities (TC) and in-prison TCs with follow-up community treatment, cognitive-behavioral therapy, non-prison-based sex offender treatment programs, vocational education programs, multicomponent correctional industry programs, and community employment programs. On the other hand, there is no evidence of the effectiveness for increased referral, monitoring, and management in the community; correctional programs that increase control and surveillance in the community; programs emphasizing structure, discipline, and challenge (e.g., boot camps using old-style military models, juvenile wilderness programs); specific deterrence programs (shock probation and Scared Straight); and vague, nondirective, unstructured counseling. Other programs appear promising (e.g., drug courts, juvenile aftercare), or the effect is unknown (anger/stress management programs, life skills training programs), but at this point in time, there is insufficient research to draw conclusions.

EMERGING PARADIGMS

As we move into the 21st century, we still see a tension in correctional goals. Some people continue to argue in support of incapacitation and deterrence as strategies for corrections and sentencing. Debates still continue in many states about whether to abolish parole. Three-strikes laws are still in existence; the war on drugs continues. Others support a move toward more rehabilitation but support more required or coerced change. For example, drug courts operate on the philosophy that the court can coerce individuals to participate in treatment. Community probation and parole programs work with the community to coerce felons to act responsibly. As Cullen and Gendreau (2001) argue, an important change for criminologists is the move from "nothing works" to "what works."

Those who argue for rehabilitation have become concerned about the unintended consequences of the U.S. incarceration policy (Lynch & Sabol, 2000; Rose & Clear, 1998). The increasing number of minorities in correctional populations has resulted in devastation in some inner-city communities as the majority of young males are in prison or under the supervision of correctional authorities. The removal of so many young men from communities, combined with the increasing number of women incarcerated, means that many children have little contact with one or both of their parents. Young men returning to the communities from prison have reduced chances for employment, which further affects the community.

The "new penology" focuses on risk assessment and management of the correctional populations (Feeley & Simon, 1992). Instead of a concern about changing the offender, interest focuses more on managing offenders while they are under correctional control. This is a radical departure from previous philosophies when correctional employees were interested in individuals and their future. The fear is that such a philosophy will set up a "we versus them" mentality that manages offenders but fails to view them as part of the community.

The current interest in restorative and community justice is in direct contrast to the proposed new penology. Simultaneous with tough-on-crime initiatives, restorative and community justice programs have been proliferating across the United States (Bazemore, 2000; Braithwaite, 1996). The programs provide new ways of viewing the justice system. The assumption is that crime damages individuals, communities, and relationships, and justice should repair the harm and heal the wounds resulting from crime. Restorative justice involves the victim, offender, and the community in the search for solutions.

Community corrections, also called "neighborhood probation or parole," "corrections of place," or "police-corrections partnerships," is a new model of community supervision focusing on engaging the community in supervising probationers and parolees. To coerce offenders into changing their behavior, members of the community, the police, and family are called on to help in supervision. At the same time, there is an emphasis on increasing services and treatment for the individual offender. Agents provide more active supervision, problem solve to initiate changes in offenders, and provide offenders with help in obtaining employment, social support, and needed treatment. Thus, it is not just providing the opportunity for services and treatment but also coercing offenders into participating.

Research demonstrating the effectiveness of some treatment programs has led to an emerging interest in treatment. This is demonstrated by many types of programs that are being introduced. An important component of restorative justice and community corrections is the availability of treatment and services for offenders. Many of these new programs combine rehabilitation programs with coercion to force offenders to participate. Specialized courts such as drug courts, mental health courts, reentry courts, and juvenile and family courts emphasize both treatment and control. The reintegration and reentry programs discussed by Petersilia (2001) provide services and treatment within controlled environments.

In summary, in the past 30 years, we have moved from the 1960s' focus on rehabilitation to a philosophy of crime control. As we move into the 21st century, we see another change, but the tension between crime control policies and rehabilitation continues to exist. Two important trends that seem to characterize the new paradigm are evidenced-based corrections and coerced change. The articles in this issue demonstrate the tension of correctional policies—when supermax prisons operate—as the philosophy of criminologists changes to one of what works, systematic reviews emphasize the evidence-based corrections, and reentry programs of coerced change are created.

REFERENCES

American Friends Service Committee. (1971). *Struggle for justice*. Philadelphia: Author.

Andrews, D. A., & Bonta, J. (1998). *The psychology of criminal conduct*. Cincinnati, OH: Anderson.

Bazemore, G. (2000). Community justice and a vision of collective efficacy: The case of restorative conferencing.

Beck, A. J., & Mumola, C. J. (1999). *Prisoners in 1998*. Washington, DC: U.S. Department of Justice, Bureau of Justice Statistics.

Blumstein, A., & Beck, A. J. (1999). Population growth in U.S. prisons, 1990–1996. In M. Tonry & J. Petersilia (Eds.), *Prisons*. Chicago: University of Chicago Press.

Blumstein, A., Cohen, J., & Nagin, D. (Eds.). (1978). *Deterrence and incapacitation*. Washington, DC: National Academy Press.

Blumstein, A., Cohen, J., Roth, J., & Visher, C. (Eds.). (1986). *Criminal careers and "career criminals."* Washington, DC: National Academy Press.

Bonczar, T. P., & Glaze, L. E. (1999). *Probation and parole in the United States, 1998*. Washington, DC: U.S. Department of Justice, Bureau of Justice Statistics.

Bouffard, J., MacKenzie, D. L., & Hickman, L. (2000). Effectiveness of vocational education and employment programs for adult offenders: A methodology-based analysis of the literature. *Journal of Offender Rehabilitation, 31*(2), 1–41.

Braithwaite, J. (1996). Restorative justice. In M. Tonry (Ed.), *The handbook of crime & punishment* (pp. 323–344). New York: Oxford University Press.

Cecil, D. K., Drapkin, D. A., MacKenzie, D. L., & Hickman, L. J. (2000). The effectiveness of adult basic education and life-skills programs in reducing recidivism: A review and assessment of the research. *Journal of Correctional Education, 51*(2), 207–226.

Chanhatasilpa, C., MacKenzie, D. L., & Hickman, L. J. (2001). A methodologically-based review of the effectiveness of community-based programs for chemically-dependent offenders. *Journal of Substance Abuse Treatment, 19,* 383–393.

Cullen, F., & Gendreau, P. (2000). Assessing correctional rehabilitation: Policy, practice, and prospects. In J. Homey, J. Martin, D. L. MacKenzie, R. Peterson, & D. Rosenbaum (Eds.), *Policies, processes, and decisions of the criminal justice system*. Washington, DC: National Institute of Justice, U.S. Department of Justice.

Cullen, F. T., & Gendreau, P. (2001). From nothing works to what works: Changing professional ideology in the 21st century. *The Prison Journal, 81*(3), 312–337.

Cullen, F. T., & Gilbert, K. E. (1982). *Reaffirming rehabilitation.* Cincinnati, OH: Anderson.

Farrington, D. P., Petrosino, A., & Welsh, B. C. (2001). Systematic reviews and cost-benefit analyses of correctional interventions. *The Prison Journal, 81*(3), 338–358.

Feely, M. M. & Simon, J. (1992). The new penology: Notes on the emerging strategy of corrections and its implications. *Criminology, 30,* 449–475.

Gallagher, C. A., Wilson, D. B., Hirschfield, P., Coggeshall, M. B., & MacKenzie, D. L. (1999). The effects of sex offender treatment on sexual reoffending. *Corrections Management Quarterly, 9*(4), 19–29.

Lipton, D., Martinson, R., & Wilks, J., (1975). *The effectiveness of correctional treatment: A survey of correctional treatment evaluations.* New York: Praeger.

Lynch, J. P., & Sabol, W. J. (2000). Prison use and social control. In J. Horney, J. Martin, D. L. MacKenzie, R. Peterson, & D. Rosenbaum (Eds.), *Policies, processes, and decisions of the criminal justice system.* Washington, DC: National Institute of Justice, U.S. Department of Justice.

MacKenzie, D. L. (1997). Criminal justice and crime prevention. In L.W. Sherman, D. Gott-fredson, D. G., MacKenzie, J. Eck, P. Reuter, & S. Bushway (Eds.), *Crime prevention: What works, what doesn't, what's promising* (pp. 9–1–9–76). Washington, DC: National Institute of Justice, U.S. Department of Justice.

MacKenzie, D. L. (2000). Evidence-based corrections: Identifying what works. *Crime & Delinquency, 46*, 457–471.

MacKenzie, D. L., & Hickman, L. (1998). *What works in corrections.* Report to the State of Washington Joint Audit and Review Committee. College Park, MD.

Martinson, R. (1974). What works? Questions and answers about prison reform. *Public Interest, 35*(2), 22–54.

Morris, N., & Tonry, M. (1990). *Between prison and probation: Intermediate punishments in a rational sentencing system.* New York: Oxford University Press.

Palmer, T. (1975). Martinson revisited. *Journal of Research in Crime and Delinquency, 12,* 133–152.

Petersilia, J. (2001). Prisoner reentry: Public safety and reintegration challenges. *The Prison Journal, 81*(3), 359–374.

Polizzi, D. M., MacKenzie, D. L., & Hickman, L. (1999). What works in adult sex offender treatment? A review of prison- and non-prison-based treatment programs. *International Journal of Offender Therapy and Comparative Criminology, 43*(3), 357–374.

President's Commission on Law Enforcement and Administration of Justice. (1967). Washington, DC: U.S. Department of Justice.

Reiss, A., & Roth, J. (1993). *Understanding and control of violence.* Washington, DC: National Academy Press.

Rose, D. R., & Clear, T. R. (1998). Incarceration, social capital, and crime: Implications for social disorganization theory. *Criminology, 36*, 441–479.

Sechrest, L., White, S. O., & Brown, E. D. (Eds.), (1979). *The rehabilitation of criminal offenders: Problems and prospects*. Washington, DC: National Academy of Sciences.

Sourcebook of criminal justice statistics. (1998). Washington, DC: U.S. Department of Justice, Bureau of Justice Statistics.

Spelman, W. (2000). The limited importance of prison expansion. In A. Blumstein & J. Wallman (Eds.), *The crime drop in America* (pp. 97–129). Cambridge, UK: Cambridge University Press.

Stephan, J. J. (1997). *Census of state and federal correctional facilities, 1995*. Washington, DC: U.S. Department of Justice.

Toch, H. (2001). The future of supermax confinement. *The Prison Journal, 81*(3), 375–387.

Tonry, M. (1996). Intermediate sanctions. In M. Tonry (Ed.), *The handbook of crime & punishment* (pp. 683–711). New York: Oxford University Press.

Von Hirsch, A. (1976). *Doing justice*. New York: Hill & Wang.

Wilson, D. B., Gallagher, C., Coggeshall, M. B., & MacKenzie, D. L. (1999). Corrections-based education, vocation, and work programs. *Corections Management Quarterly, 3*(4), 8–18.

Wilson, D. B., Gallagher, C., & MacKenzie, D. L. (2000). A meta-analysis of corrections-based education, vocation, and work programs for adult offenders. *Journal of Research in Crime and Delinquency, 37*(4), 347–368.

Wolfgang, M., Figlio, R. G., & Sellin, T. (1972). *Delinquency in a birth cohort*. Chicago: University of Chicago Press.

Zedlewski, E. (1987). *Making confinement decisions*. Washington, DC: National Institute of Justice.

Zimring, F. E., & Hawkins, G. (1995). *Incapacitation: Penal confinement and the restraint of crime*. New York: Oxford University Press.

REVIEW QUESTIONS

1. What are the primary factors that influenced a shift from rehabilitative philosophies and practices during the first two-thirds of the twentieth century to more punitive and incapacitation focused orientations of the century's closing years?
2. What are the costs and benefits of evidence-based corrections and sentencing?
3. What are the pros and cons associated with our current get-tough orientation toward crime and punishment?
4. What are some of the anticipated policies that follow from the emerging paradigms that MacKenzie forecasts for the twenty-first century?

READING 39

The Future of Supermax Confinement

Hans Toch

One of the most politically popular developments in corrections in the last several decades has been the development of supermax prisons. These institutions, where inmates are essentially completely isolated in cells with little to no human contact, are popularly believed to be effective ways to control the most dangerous individuals in our society. However, as this article points out, numerous problems exist with such a correctional practice, including physical and mental health deterioration of inmates, high levels of violence, exorbitant financial costs, and a significant risk of recidivism once inmates are released. The author identifies a pressing reform agenda for how supermax institutions should be structured and used.

The earliest experiments in supermax confinement were conducted 200 years ago and abandoned in horrified disgust. Pennsylvania and New York independently invented segregated control units. They sequestered offenders in those units who were deemed hard core and recalcitrant. In both settings—one in the Pittsburgh Penitentiary and the other at Auburn Prison—the inmates suffered grievous psychological harm.

Visitors who came to admire and emulate correctional innovations in the United States recoiled in distress after seeing the results of these experiments. The French team de Beaumont and de Tocqueville (1833) had sung many praises of American correctional practices. They drew the line, however, when it came to "the evil effect of total solitude" they had been forced to observe (p. 6).

Unfortunately, the supermax experiments of the 1820s had been conducted on a substantial scale. The Auburn segregation wing that had been established by the New York Legislature contained 80 prisoners—an appreciable number in 1821. de Beaumont and de Tocqueville (1833) dutifully recorded that

> this trial, from which so happy a result had been anticipated, was fatal to the greater part of the convicts: in order to reform them, they had been submitted to complete isolation; but this absolute solitude, if nothing interrupt it, is beyond the strength of man; it destroys the criminal without intermission and without pity; it does not reform, it kills.
>
> The unfortunates, on whom this experiment was made, fell into a state of depression, so manifest, that their keepers were struck with it; their lives seemed in danger, if they remained longer in this situation; five of them, had already succumbed during a single year; (c) their moral state was not less alarming; one of them had become insane; another, in a fit of despair, had embraced the opportunity when the keeper brought him something, to precipitate himself from his cell, running the almost certain chance of a mortal fall. (p. 5)

It also became clear in short order that supermax confinement did not deter reoffending. de Beaumont and de Tocqueville (1833) noted that "this system, fatal to the health of the criminals, was likewise inefficient in producing their reform" (p. 5). In New York, the governor had been forced to pardon 26 unhappy survivors of the experiment. Fourteen recidivated and had to be reconfined. These reconvicted inmates returned to modified conditions of incarceration, which afforded opportunities for congregate programming.

The Pennsylvania supermax setting was established at a new prison in Pittsburgh. As in our modern supermax units, one of the noteworthy features was that segregated prisoners found respite through surreptitious communication with each other, de Beaumont and de Tocqueville (1833) pointed out that "as these criminals did not work, we may say that their sole occupation consisted in mutual corruption . . . [They] spent their whole time in idleness, injurious to themselves, and burthensome to the public treasury" (p. 8)

de Beaumont and de Tocqueville (1833) returned to France as sadder but wiser observers. They had resolved that

> we shall say nothing more of the defective parts in the prison system of the United States; if at some future period France shall imitate the penitentiaries of America, the most important thing for her will be to know those which may serve as models, (p. 15).

I shall suggest in this article that the same resolve might be made by contemporary foreign observers, although they might note that we have a tendency not to learn from our past mistakes. The second question to be considered is that of the impressions to be garnered by future observers of American corrections.

My fond hope is that observers of the future will view today's supermaxes as we have come to view their predecessors such as the penitentiary at Alcatraz. The shells of this redoubtable experiment stand as a titillating tourist attraction to remind us of how uncompromisingly tough we once were in creating offshore dungeons for supergangsters. Ironically, the hero of this supermax experience for most observers is the intrepid convict who swam off into the sunset and sank somewhere in San Francisco Bay.

THE VULNERABILITIES OF SUPERMAX SETTINGS

A particularly ironic aspect of the history of supermax confinement is that today we grapple with the same issue that prominently faced our precursors. Despite advances in our diagnostic acumen and the quality of our mental health care, we are left with the fact that supermax settings remain demonstrably psychologically injurious (Haney & Lynch, 1997). Unmitigated isolation is indisputably stressful, and it reliably overtaxes the resilience of many incarcerated offenders. In the words of the judge in the decisive case involving supermax confinement (*Madrid v. Gomez,* 1995), such segregation "may press the outer borders of what most humans can psychologically tolerate." More specifically, the judge in the case found that the conditions in California's first supermax prison (Pelican Bay) "cause mentally ill inmates to seriously deteriorate; other inmates who are otherwise able to psychologically cope with normal prison routines may also begin decompensating in SHU."

There are several reasons for the immutability of this issue. The most surprising of these reasons is a paradox—the fact that persons who are problems also often have problems. This fact can strike us as counterintuitive because we think of difficult people as being tough and resilient, especially when they project facades of toughness and resilience. We can also come to confuse the effect of problematic behavior—its nuisance value—with its intent, although we ought to recognize that a great deal of acting out consists of helpless outbursts or retaliatory rage. Where noxious behavior is repetitive, its offensiveness increases, but so does the chance that the behavior may be obsessive or blindly self-destructive.

Offenders who are sent to supermax settings because they have problems adjusting to other prisons disproportionately are persons who have had mental health problems in the past (Toch & Adams, 1989). The more problematic the individual offenders are (the closer they come to the "worst of the worst" stereotype of supermax prisoners), the more serious their mental health problems are apt to be (Toch, 1982). The relationship was obvious to the judge in *Madrid v. Gomez* (1995), who wrote that "since inmates suffering from mental illness are more likely to engage in disruptive conduct, significant numbers of mentally ill inmates in the California prison system are ultimately transferred to the Pelican Bay SHU."

It does not help matters that supermax routines contain features serendipitously designed to evoke symptoms of mental illness or to play into such symptoms. This affinity was captured by the Pelican Bay judge when he concluded that segregated confinement was "the mental equivalent of putting an asthmatic in a place with little air to breathe." Supermaxes may differ to some degree, but all are repositories of an anti-humanistic technology. The prisoners in supermax are dealt with by machines orchestrated via computerized consoles. They are communicated with by muffled voices through impermeable partitions, and they are intrusively surveilled. Supermax residents tend to sleep a great deal (especially when no activities are afforded them), but restful regenerative sleep is never attainable. Prison night merges into day (lights never go out in one's cell), and anticipated interruptions are a constant.

During rare respites from isolation, supermax residents are loaded down with hardware that circumscribes movement. Refusal to come out of one's cell—which is a common symptom when someone is mentally ill—brings a phalanx of intruders in spacesuits with gigantic (and sometimes electrified) shields. Such invaders charge in wedge formation and press their targets against the wall or floor with irresistible force. No experience is better calculated to produce panic and an overwhelming sense of helplessness (Haney, 1993).

Most supermax regimes feature gradations of "levels" that offer calibrated increments in amenities. The lowest levels in such sequences are completely stripped down. They provide a condition of drastic understimulation, enforced inactivity, and sensory deprivation. This condition is defined as a baseline or starting point for an incentive system, but the core of the experience is unfreezing or crisis promotive. The fact that it occurs during initiation into the setting can have incalculable adverse effects. The effects can be especially traumatizing for some—for instance, young offenders who are habituated to high levels of activity and conviviality. Although there are no data about differential reactions to enforced inactivity and isolation, observers have described evidence of acute distress among younger inmates:

> It might take a few months, but there was a defining moment when the most youthful prisoners in isolation units regressed into something less than human. "The light went out in their eyes," said Romano, a retired Roman Catholic prison chaplain. "They became like Zombies. I'd talk to them through the food slot, and all I got back was a blank stare." (Grondahl, 2000, p. B8)

For administrators of supermax, the initiation experience can also be counterproductive because persons who have no physical freedom or scope for activities can never manifest differences in behavior (unless they decompensate or explode with blind rage) that can be used as criteria for their "promotion." The whole system is a dispensary of differential stress in which the least tolerable stresses are applied at the most vulnerable juncture.

THE DEPRIVATION OF FAIRNESS

An arguably unfortunate feature of supermax confinement is that it rests on arbitrariness papered over with a veneer of due process. Supermax settings are places of administrative confinement. This means that prisoners are not sent to supermax for something they have done but for something someone thinks they might do because of the type of person someone thinks they are. Such conclusions can be based on events in the person's remote past or on some perceived attribute not under the person's control. The substance of assessments is also unappealable because the subject cannot argue that the nonexistent charges against him have not been proved. Being "the worst of the worst" is an attributed status, and it lies in the eyes of correctional administrators. Due process does not enter here as a vehicle for preventing miscarriages of justice but as a checklist of procedural formalities, as a dotting of "i"s and crossing of "t"s in the inmate's gulag deportation order.

The process whereby inmates are assigned to supermax is reminiscent of traditional inquisitory tribunals. The point is to arrive at lists of stigmata that ratify a reprehensible status—in this case, being "the worst of the worst." A standard example is that of ascribed gang membership, which is a popular criterion for supermax placement. The rationale has to do with gang involvement in drug trafficking, internecine warfare, and forcible recruitment. But individual gang members do not stand accused of such conduct. Instead, they are charged with aggravated gang membership, unregenerate affiliation, or gang activism.

The "evidence" that is invoked consists of information that the person is a presumptive member of an alleged gang. In Arizona, this information is culled via a two-stage sequence, which comprises gang "certification" and "validation" of membership. Validation includes the testimony of uncorroborated informants but also comprises observed association with suspected gang members and "gang tattoos." A profession (confession) of gang membership by the offender is considered desirable but is reportedly hard to come by since the advent of supermax confinement.

The parallel with the workings of inquisitory tribunals becomes particularly blatant after the prisoner is indicted as a gang member:

> Once validated, the inmate can either refuse to renounce his membership or renounce his membership and debrief (tell what he knows about the gang).
>
> Those who refuse to renounce their gang affiliation are sent to the Special Management Unit (super-maximum security) where they will complete the remainder of their sentence. Those who debrief successfully are placed in protective segregation, also in the Special Management Unit, where they will complete the remainder of their sentence. Once released, validated STG members who return to Arizona's prisons will again be confined in the Special Management

> Unit. As of October 20, there have been 58 inmates who have been successfully debriefed and 399 inmates who have refused to renounce. (Palumbo, Hepburn, Griffin, Fischer, & Janisch, 2000, p. 6)

The Arizona program has an evaluation component, which consists of a survey of staff perceptions and opinions (Palumbo et al, 2000, p. 7). No evidence is gathered that might suggest that segregation of "validated" gang members has reduced the prevalence of prison misbehavior in Arizona. Nor would such evidence—if it were available—demonstrate the success of the program because no aggregate statistics can prove that any individual in supermax would have offended if left at large or that less drastic intervention might not have worked equally well.

Moreover, it is just as plausible that supermax confinement may increase the likelihood of future violent behavior. Perception of capricious deprivation and custodial overkill predictably engenders bitterness and alienation. For this reason, supermax prisons may turn out to be crucibles and breeding grounds of violent recidivism. The graduates of such settings (often released directly into the community) may be time bombs waiting to explode. They may become "the worst of the worst" because they have been dealt with as such.

THE SUPERMAX REGIME

The goal of supermax is ostensibly incapacitation. But supermaxes accentuate deprivations of confinement in the name of incapacitation. One hears arguments such as "these men are experiencing the consequences of their actions," and "they have earned their way to supermax, so they have nothing to complain about."

Under an incapacitation regime, rules and strictures have custodial justifications. Prisoners have to be prevented from escaping, accumulating weapons, or importing drugs. In supermaxes, residents are presumptively violence prone, so they have to be kept from assaulting staff or each other. An officer serving meals might be attacked by a prisoner lurking behind his door, ready to launch excrement or wield a sharpened toothbrush. The inmate must therefore be requested to be in view while meals are dispensed.

But custodial measures in supermaxes evolve into caricatures of themselves. The need to see the prisoners while meals are served, for example, has turned into a system that often leaves an inmate hungry if he does not jump to a prespecified location. Provisions such as these lend themselves to selective enforcement, giving rise to allegations of harassment:

> If [prisoners] are not behind the line, they don't get their meal. We don't want people working here who only give the inmate a second to get to the line and walk away, but sometimes that happens. Then the inmate makes a huge deal about it. If the inmate would have followed the rules, he would have gotten his meal. (Vogel, 1998, p. 7)

Over time, custodial measures have also escalated to become redundant. Physical strictures have kept prisoners in cells. Lights are kept on so that inspections can take place. Inspections are designed to ensure that no bundle could be substituted for the recumbent body of an absconded inmate who could not possibly abscond.

Prisoners are carefully shackled to furniture but surveilled by guards. Objects are confiscated in which nonavailable weapons could hypothetically be stored.

Although redundancy can be justified as precautionary ("one can't ever be too careful with this sort of inmate"), there are no equivalent rationales for rules devoid of custodial import, and these strictures include the rationing of basics, such as showers, telephone calls or visits, reading material, and writing paper a prisoner can have. Such strictures are punitive, not custodial, and punitive transfers in prison call for meaningful due process, including proof of culpability.

Psychologically, restrictive regimes invite games of cops and robbers. Rules spark efforts to evade them, and regimentation breeds resistance. When prisoner reactions become overtly hostile or assertive, they tend to be countered with more regimentation and added strictures, leading to a climate of trench warfare. When this is a steady diet, officers and prisoners are situationally dehumanized.

Arguably, the most insidious impact of supermaxes is on the attitudes of their staff. The supermax mission of sequestering "the worst of the worst" can lead staff members to view their charges with trepidation or contempt. The fact that there is no real contact with the inmates converts them into physical objects to be ministered to. The exercise of handmaiden functions (serving food or distributing mail) can be experienced as demeaning. Sometimes this experience can lead to compensatory demonstrations of power ("show the bastards who is in charge"). In turn, capricious exercises of discretion become affronts to the prisoners, who are dependent on and at the mercy of guards. Escalating vindictive interactions result, in which issues of self-esteem are reciprocally raised:

> Let's say you asked for something early in the day, like toilet paper. They wouldn't give it to you or would wait until the end of the day. Dinner would come and you would ask, what happened to my toilet paper? And the guard would say, "Oh, you don't want to eat?" and take your meal away. (Vogel, 1998, p. 14)

The inference is not that psychopathic guards are predisposed to exercises of sadism but that supermax work degrades the workers. Given time, staff who have been prevented from human encounters with their charges become callous and cynical. They are also apt to feel themselves underused. This is not surprising if the only professional development available to them is membership on extraction teams.

THE SURVIVAL OF SUPERMAX

On the face of it, the future of supermax confinement ought to look unpromising. The institution is vulnerable to charges that it impairs the mental health of prisoners and that it makes violent men more dangerous. Some supermax assignment procedures appear arbitrary and unfair. The regime is draconian, redolent with custodial overkill, and stultifying.

Foreign visitors today are no more impressed with what they see than were de Beaumont and de Tocqueville. One observer from Wales (King, 2000) subtitled his report "An American Solution in Search of a Problem?" He wrote that

> where prison regimes are so depriving as those offered in most supermax facilities, the onus is upon those imposing the regimes to demonstrate that this is justified—

> and demonstration goes beyond simply asserting that the recipients are gang members or "the worst of the worst." To the best of my knowledge, no convincing demonstration has yet been provided. (p. 182)

It is unfortunately not incumbent on the custodians of human institutions to "provide convincing demonstrations." Under our own legal system, the onus is on critics to prove that deplorable conditions violate constitutional standards. This task is a daunting one, and the odds have not been overly encouraging.

Supermaxes have physical staying power because of the massive investment in their plants. These singular monuments have no other conceivable uses, including as regular prisons. Moreover, most prison staff have come to see supermaxes as guarantors of safety and as vehicles for achieving peace and tranquility in their systems. In part, this conviction rests on an experience (sometimes referred to as "Marionization") that consisted of gathering problem prisoners in one prison (Marion), where they assaulted each other and attacked members of the staff.

Supermaxes are presumed to be sustained by public sentiment but are in fact favored by risk-aversive correctional administrators, who seek to divest themselves of difficult prisoners. Public support is a late development, generated by propagandistic coverage. King (2000) observes that

> one of the most disturbing sights for a European visitor to American supermax facilities is to watch parties of school children being indoctrinated with the notion that it is somehow necessary and appropriate for dehumanized prisoners to be moved from "living pods" to "dog run" exercise yards in handcuffs, legirons and waist chains. (p. 183)

SUPERMAX REFORM

Although supermax survival is not in immediate question, the future of the institution hinges on the willingness of correctional administrators to consider proactive reforms. There is a great deal of current litigation, and it is only a matter of time before some unregenerate supermax engages the interest of a sympathetic judiciary. In the absence of amelioration, evolving standards of human decency can easily collide with obdurately anachronistic practices.

Mental health–related concerns have already been adjudicated, and the problem must be addressed for supermaxes to withstand scrutiny. Two courses of action are available to mitigate the situation. One option is to screen out of the supermax population any inmates manifesting symptoms of emotional disorders or liable to manifest such symptoms. A second approach consists of an infusion of mental health professionals who can deal with personal crises and difficulties that inmates may experience.

The criteria for screening out vulnerable residents need to be inclusive and subject to review. Diagnostic categories covering major psychiatric disorders fall short of what is required for screening purposes. Supermax confinement is stressful, and the experience is bound to tax persons with limited coping competence. Unfortunately, such breakdowns under stress can never be accurately predicted. One must therefore observe and report any reactions of residents that may indicate the onset of a problem. This is a difficult task because routine prisoner reactions to extreme deprivations are bound to be extreme. Sleeping with a blanket over one's head is standard operating procedure in supermax confinement, but it may also suggest a psychotic break or panic-induced retreat into self-insulation. Angry discourse can indicate a manic episode, or it may be an expression of understandable disgruntlement.

There are predictable hurdles in providing mental health ministrations given the physical strictures of supermax. Therapeutic alliances are not forged through closed doors or telephone connections. Staff who control conditions of confinement (or who fatefully affect them) do not evoke openness and trust.

Of necessity, addressing mental health–related problems in supermax is linked to conditions of confinement because these conditions are the stressors that exacerbate the psychological travails of vulnerable prisoners. One option is to create lower pressure subsettings in supermaxes designed for prisoners who are disturbed but also disruptive enough to require sequestration. A second option is that of an across-the-board amelioration of the supermax regime.

HUMANIZING SUPERMAX

Supermaxes have to justify or modify the draconian strictures that typically prevail at entry into the setting. The argument that such strictures are required as an incentive for promotion to a less sensorily deprived environment is specious because less onerous gradations of conditions would serve the same ends. Moreover, a system that starts at the bottom deprives itself of a backup condition for residents who misbehave, and administrative confinement (purgatory) becomes confusingly indistinguishable from punitive confinement (inferno, aka, the hole). One must keep in mind that supermax placement is not a response to anyone's violent transgression—as is sometimes wrongly implied—but a classificatory decision. Indiscriminable treatment of people who have transgressed and have not transgressed makes no sense. It violates principles of justice to punish a person—however reprehensible he may be—for a predisposition to misbehave.

Most supermax residents will eventually be released—many directly from supermax—and their prospective neighbors have a stake in the level of preparedness of these inmates for civilian life. It would be a disservice to the citizenry for the prison system to operate a setting that increases the violence potential of its residents. Not to do harm, however, is a minimalist goal. Supermax residents have time on their hands, and it makes sense to provide opportunities for these residents to constructively occupy their time and to engage in efforts at self-improvement. The contention that the supermax resident is unreformable is a premise susceptible to disconfirmation.

Some supermaxes provide programming, citing it as an amenity or privilege to be earned. Most supermax programs consist of cell-study assignments purveyed through a mail slot, but as a matter of standard practice, even such modest involvement tends to be prohibited at intake into the setting, where it is most urgently needed. The lack of authorized activity (other than litigation) not only makes the adjustment process excruciatingly difficult for the prisoner but also sends him a strange and counterproductive message. On one hand, we ask the inmate to refrain from misbehavior, and on the other hand, we deprive him of alternative courses of action. The poor prisoner may justly infer that he is expected to spend his life passively vegetating.

Programming could in fact be the core of a supermax regime, starting on the very day the prisoner arrives. Supermax sentence planning at intake could revolve around activities that would be made available to the inmate, and his planned progression could gain content and substance from scintillating sequences of program involvements. Rosters of cell-study, audio, or television-mediated modules can be handed to each incoming prisoner to provide him with the options he could exercise. New inmates would be interviewed by staff members who could plan the experiences of the prisoners based on information about their interests and needs, rather than about their alleged patterns of past transgressions.

There is also classification to be done. The "worst of the worst" is a term of art that describes a motley assortment of people. The category is not a homogeneous aggregate that calls for assembly-line management. Some of the "worst" inmates are "worse"—and pose more physical risk—than others, and they may require a greater measure of custodial restraint. An internal supermax classification system that can distinguish between higher risk and lower risk residents could mitigate the one-fits-all custodial regime and its ritualistic overkill. More exquisitely refined classifications could also permit other interesting variations in dispositions responsive to the unique problems of inmates. Such differences could be accommodated by variations in regime among pods, units, or tiers.

Diversification of programming in supermax can enrich the lives of staff as well as those of prisoners. Officers can become more constructively involved, expanding the range of their contacts with inmates and getting to know them as persons rather than animate objects. The direct participation of supermax officers in program planning and classification can go a long way to reduce any evolving sense of underutilization and may preempt the onset of alienation.

Sometimes it sounds as if the mission of supermax is reintegration. The candidates nominated for residency are presumed to have violence potential. Before these prisoners graduate—unless their release has been mandated—they have to demonstrate that they have changed into less dangerous persons. This transformation is supposed to occur despite the fact that the prisoners have had no leeway for engaging in any behavior—either good or bad—and that the staff have had no opportunity to get to know them and their problems. The treatment strategy that is credited with the transmutation consists of routine diminishments of deprivation.

If supermaxes were to claim reintegration as a real goal, we would have to abandon outlandish presumptions. We would instead have to mobilize substantial, individualized treatment approaches. We would have to furnish avenues for supermax residents to explore their conduct and to evolve less destructive behavior patterns (Toch & Grant, 1997). To introduce such interventions would require a paradigm shift of major proportions.

The reforming of supermax regimes would not do violence to a coherent strategy or preconceived model. Supermax creation is incestuous, in that uniformity is achieved through imitation. Each new supermax prison adopts rules and regulations from its precursors, who acquired them from prior supermaxes. No one along the line has been tempted to second-guess or revise received wisdom. As a result, uniformity of practice has evolved side-by-side with uniformity of physical arrangement.

The haphazardly evolved supermax regime is difficult to justify and invites prevailing criticism and litigation. It may not be obvious, but this development is bound to benefit the supermax. Being sued, or fearing the prospect of being sued, is an unfreezing experience. Some supermaxes may dig in their heels, but others will use the opportunity for a mindful review of prevailing practices. It is hard to predict where this sort of process will lead, but if it is taken seriously, it may help supermaxes to survive, possibly as defensible correctional institutions.

REFERENCES

de Beaumont, G., & de Tocqueville, A. (1833). *On the penitentiary system of the United States, and its application in France; with an appendix on penal colonies, and also, statistical notes.* Philadelphia: Carey, Lea and Blanchard.

Grondahl, P. (2000, March 26). Chaplain himself felt effects of the box. *Albany Times Union,* p. B8.

Haney, C. (1993, Spring). "Infamous punishment": The psychological consequences of isolation. *The National Prison Project Journal,* pp. 3–21.

Haney, C., & Lynch, M. (1997). Regulating prisons of the future: A psychological analysis of supermax and solitary confinement. *New York Review of Law and Social Change, 23,* 477–570.

King, R. D. (2000). The rise and rise of supermax: An American solution in search of a problem? *Punishment and Society, 1*(2), 163–186.

Madrid v. Gomez, 1995 W.I. 17092 (N.D. Cal 1995).

Palumbo, D., Hepburn, J., Griffin, M., Fischer, D., & Janisch, R. (2000). *Taking back the yards: Controlling and managing prison gangs.* Paper presented at annual meeting of the American Society of Criminology, San Francisco.

Toch, H. (1982). The disturbed disruptive inmate: Where does the bus stop? *Journal of Psychiatry and Law, 10,* 227–249.

Toch, H., & Adams, K. (with Grant, J. D.). (1989). *Coping: Maladaptation in prison.* New Brunswick, NJ: Transaction Books.

Toch, H., & Grant, J. D. (1997). Coping with noncoping convicts. In H. Toch (Ed.), *Corrections: A humanistic approach* (pp. 135–146). Guilderland, NY: Harrow and Heston.

Vogel, J. (1998). Behind closed doors. *Seattle Weekly, 23,* 7–17.

REVIEW QUESTIONS

1. Why are supermax prisons considered by the public to be "good" correctional practice?
2. What are the negative outcomes of incarceration in supermax prisons for inmates?
3. In what ways could supermax prisons be modified or reformed so as to alleviate their problems, but still have them achieve their central goals?

READING 40

Public-Private Partnerships in the U.S. Prison System

Anne Larason Schneider

This article considers in detail the role of private industry in America's prison system. The author provides a historical record that details three types of public-private partnerships: private ownership of a prison facility, private for-profit use of inmate labor, and the private management of a prison. Attention is then shifted to contemporary models of public-private partnerships. A model of "private prisons" is described wherein detailed contracts and per diem cost afford a private entity for-profit authority over the daily operations of a privately owned facility filled with state inmates. The recent growth in the popularity of private prisons is linked to a political structure that includes an intricate system of lobbying, law making, and contract bidding and negotiations. The author attributes the surge in prison populations and the resulting demand for private prisons to a series of political choices. The existing studies of private prisons are reviewed as means of assessing the relevant cost, quality of service delivery, and public safety issues. From here, the author sets out to make some predictions about the future use of private prisons and the policy debates that will likely follow.

Public-private partnerships in the operation of prisons have existed from the colonial period to contemporary times, although the extent of reliance on the private sector and the policy design models have varied somewhat. Drawing on ideas from policy design theory (Schneider & Ingram, 1997), this study will identify the characteristics of the partnerships, the reasons for private-sector involvement, the rationales and claims made by competing perspectives, and the consequences of private-sector involvement.

Prison policy differs from other policy arenas in ways that have implications for the appropriate role of the private sector. First, prisons deliver punishment, whereas most policies deliver benefits or regulations. Other policies that impose costs—such as tax policy—may be unwanted or resented, but no other policy arena actually delivers punishment. Second, the target populations of prison policy are vastly different from most target populations—prisoners are not free, they do not make choices about most events in their daily life, they have virtually no political power, and they are socially constructed as deviant or violent by most of the population. Third, although many policy arenas offer some form of political capital for elected officials, few, if any, offer such lucrative possibilities as prisons. By inflicting harsh punishment upon criminals who are socially constructed as deviant, violent, and undeserving, elected officials can gain the accolades of the general public without incurring any noticeable political costs from those actually receiving the punishment. The monetary costs of mandatory long sentences are postponed to the future and spread across all taxpayers. Thus, it may be many years after legislation is passed before the full financial impact is felt. Finally, private-sector involvement in prison policy adds significant new target populations to the political arena by introducing businesses, corporations, and stockholders in publicly traded private prisons into the lobbying milieu. These groups have much to gain from a continued expansion of the number of prisoners available—that is, the prisoner "market."

Because of these differences, the politics of policy making may take on different characteristics, and the criteria by which policy should be evaluated must go beyond the usual reliance on effectiveness or efficiency to include the contributions of policy to justice, citizenship, and democratic institutions. It is one question to ask whether private involvement in prison management is more efficient on a per prisoner basis, but quite another question to ask whether the number of prisoners in society as a whole is efficient, or just, or appropriate in other ways for a democratic society.

THE RISE AND DECLINE OF PUBLIC-PRIVATE PRISON PARTNERSHIPS

The three following basic types of partnerships have been apparent in the history of prisons in the United States: ownership of the facility in which the prisoners are kept; private use of prison labor and taking of profits from their labor; and private management of the facility, including the day-by-day supervision of prisoners.

Case studies of the emergence of prisons in the American states suggest that private involvement began through a convergence of interests among reformers, public officials, and local businesses (Shichor, 1995; Walker, 1980). Humanitarian reformers believed that prisons would be more humane than common forms of punishment in the American colonies—and later in the western frontier—which were death, branding, torture, or other physical punishment. The role of reformers was evident in the founding of the first prison in the Quaker colony of William Penn when the great law of 1682 banned the death penalty for everything except premeditated murder. This prison was a 5 feet by 7 feet cell. Later, the colony rented space from local businesses (Walker, 1980).

Public officials from the colonial period to the early 1900s believed that prisons could be self-supporting or even profitable for the state, and businesses were interested in sharing in those profits. Some states permitted a private individual or firm to build, manage, and handle the day-to-day operation of the prison itself, a system similar to the ones that have generated such intense debate in the 1980s and 1990s. Knepper (1990) reports that in 1825, Kentucky was not making enough money to support its growing prison population and was in desperate financial straits. A businessman, Joel Scott, paid the state $1,000 a year for the work of convicts in a 250-bed facility that he built and operated, with all profits kept for his own company.

In Louisiana (Walker, 1980), the state leased out the entire operation for 5 years and received $50,000 for the lease. Tennessee, in 1866, leased its Nashville prison to a furniture company for 43 cents per day per prisoner, reportedly because it was suffering from severe financial difficulties, and the number of prisoners had greatly expanded after the Civil War ended. California, in 1851, could not keep up with the increased crime attributed to the influx of settlers and was close to bankruptcy (Shichor, 1995), so the state leased its prison for 10 years to two local businessmen.

Oklahoma and Arizona not only viewed the prisons as potential profitmaking entities for the state and for local businesses, but considered prisons to be an important part of the state's economic development program (Conley, 1980, 1981; Knepper, 1990). Oklahoma prisoners actually built McAlister Prison, which included an industrial factory and a 2,000-acre farm. Arizona's first territorial governor, Anson P. K. Safford, believed that a territorial prison would show that the territory was civilized and had a stable social environment sufficient to attract eastern businesses (Knepper, 1990). He was able to exploit the racial characteristics of prisoners—claiming that most of them were wild and dangerous Mexicans who preyed on travelers throughout the state, especially near the Mexican border. He also claimed that it would be the first profit-making state institution and that hard work was good for the health of prisoners (Knepper, 1990). Arizona eventually contracted with a private firm, the Arizona Canal Company, to take over the entire daytime operation of the prison. The prison provided all male convicts to the company for 10 years, for 70 cents per day, in the form of future water rights.

All of these forms of public-private partnerships eventually generated serious problems that produced opposition from business, labor, and humanitarian reformers. In some states, prisoners rioted or protested to such an extent that the partnerships were ended. For example, Tennessee ended its lease arrangement only a year after it began, apparently because the inmates burned the furniture factory. Subsequently, they built branch prisons and leased the prisoners to coal mining companies. In 1891 and 1892, free miners raided the prisons and set the prisoners free, reportedly because the competition was hurting them economically (Knepper, 1990). In Alabama, Knepper reported that opponents were worried that private leasing of prison labor would undermine the fundamental principle of restoring the prisoner's sense of obligation to a just society. They were worried that lessees would try to lengthen the sentences of good workers by giving bad reports about them.

Humanitarian reformers in Texas focused on what they viewed as excessive inmate deaths and injuries that were blamed on the private companies and the prisons they operated. California's contract system was accused of bid rigging, having a corrupt trustee system, selling of pardons, and other issues to the point that the Governor physically took control of San Quentin from the lessee—a former member of the legislature—and used the scandal for political advantage (Shichor, 1995). After a court had ruled that the takeover was illegal, the state had to buy the lease back from the private company for $275,000. In Oklahoma, businesses that did not have contracts joined with labor unions to oppose the prison industry system on the grounds of unfair competition (Conley, 1981).

New York passed legislation in 1842 that restricted the use of prison labor so much that it essentially ended public-private partnerships, and by the turn of the century, most other states had followed suit. Finally, in 1935, the social reform legislation initiated by the Roosevelt administration produced the Hawes-Cooper Act that authorized states to prohibit the entry of prison-made goods produced in other states. In 1936, the Walsh-Healy Act prohibited convict labor on government contracts that exceeded $10,000. In 1940, the Sumners-Ashurst Act made it a federal offense to transport prison-made goods across state borders, regardless of state laws. By the beginning of World War II, public-private partnerships in prisons were virtually nonexistent.

THE REEMERGENCE OF PUBLIC-PRIVATE PARTNERSHIPS: PRIVATE PRISONS

Although prison industries have enjoyed a small resurgence, the most discussed form of public-private partnership today is the one popularly called private prisons, in which a private firm operates (and usually owns) a secure adult facility for prisoners and solicits contracts with local, state, or federal governments.

These relationships are different and far more complex than those in the previously discussed historical period. The 19th century experiments with private involvement almost always involved local businesses. In the 1990s, the businesses are national and international corporations—some of which are publicly traded on one or another of the major stock exchanges. Although some of the private prisons have emerged as a result of contracts with the state in which they are located, the more common situation is that a private firm builds a prison in a state and simultaneously attempts to negotiate contracts with the home state—or any other state, county, or federal entity—for prisoners. The firm is usually paid on a per diem basis, either on the number of prisoners it houses for a particular entity or on the number of places it has reserved for that jurisdiction. In the past, the business paid the state for use of its prisoners; today, the state pays the business to manage the prisoners. Some state contracts, such as Arizona's, require that the Department of Corrections place a monitor on site to make critical decisions about disciplinary matters. Most of the state contracts require that private firms offer the service at 5% to 10% below what it would have cost the state. This, of course, creates complicated cost models involving a delicate balancing act between accounting principles and political realities. In Arizona and some other states, the state law actually includes a detailed description of what is to be counted or not counted in the costs of both private and public prisons (Prison Privatization Act, 1998). Arizona legislation requires that private prisons take out large insurance policies to reimburse state agencies that may have to intervene when an escape is in process or a riot occurs.

The growth of private prisons has been dramatic, as the number of places for prisoners in private facilities has increased from 1,345 (0.5% of all prisoners) in 1985 to 106,940 (8.5% of all prisoners) by December 1997 (Thomas, Bolinger, & Badalamenti, 1998). Thomas, Bolinger, and Badalamenti's *Private Adult Correctional Facility Census,* 10th edition (1997), listed 118 facilities located in 25 different states and Washington, DC; Puerto Rico; Australia; and the United Kingdom. The Private Prison Project at the University of Florida currently shows 162 facilities with 132,346 places (Thomas, 1999). Texas has 19 private prisons, the most of any state by far, as well as having the largest prison capacity and the highest number of actual prisoners held. Most of these prisoners, however, are not from Texas. In

1997, almost 6,000 prisoners from 14 different states were "outsourced" from their home state to a private prison located elsewhere. Most of the privately managed facilities are in the South (with 74, 41% of the total); this is followed by the West (with 32, 27% of the total). There are only 5 in the midwestern states, and only 1 of these has contracts that permit it to take prisoners from the state where it is located. There are only 4 in the Northeast, and none has contracts with its home state. The 5 facilities in the Northeast take local prisoners, federal prisoners, and out-of-state prisoners.

SUBGOVERNMENT POLITICS AND THE GROWTH OF PRIVATE PRISONS

The Corrections Corporation of America (CCA) was the first corporation to enter the private prison business and currently is the largest one. In 1998, CCA officially became Prison Realty Corporation, and it, along with 10 other private prison businesses, is traded on a major stock exchange. The emergence of CCA is well worth describing here, for it is indeed a new model of public-private partnership in the prison business and it offers a fascinating case of subgovernment policy making.

CCA was well connected with political and financial leaders in Tennessee, and it had strong ties to experts in the prison business. One of the founders of Nashville-based CCA was Tom Beasley, a former chair of the Tennessee Republican party, and another was Nashville banker and financier, Doctor R. Crants. Another CCA founder, Don Hutton, was the former head of the American Correctional Association—the association responsible for the accreditation standards of adult prisons (Shichor, 1995). Several high-ranking political officials in Tennessee owned CCA stock, including Honey Alexander (wife of the Governor, Lamar Alexander); the state insurance commissioner, John Neff; and the Speaker of the House of Representatives, Ned McWherter. He and Mrs. Alexander both divested themselves of CCA shares to avoid conflict of interest (Shichor, 1995; American Federation of State, County, and Municipal Employees [AFSCME], 1998).

In 1985, Tennessee reportedly faced a crisis in its criminal justice system (Folz & Scheb, 1989). The state was under a court order to reduce the number of prisoners from 7,700 to 7,019 within 3 months. The previous year, they had the highest rate of inmate-on-inmate violence of any state in the union. To complicate the situation further, Tennessee faced a significant budget shortfall and a rate of 450 new prison admissions for every 250 releases.

Realizing that Tennessee faced this kind of pressure, CCA offered to pay the state $100 million for a 99-year lease to operate the entire adult correctional system. CCA reportedly offered to invest $250 million in new facilities, and to receive $170 million per year to manage the system, which was approximately the size of the current state budget for prisons. According to the case study by Folz and Scheb (1989), Republican Governor Lamar Alexander was very interested, and it appeared that bipartisan support for privatization was substantial. A public opinion poll showed that 40% of the voters favored it, with 32% disapproving. Intense lobbying, however, scuttled the CCA proposal, with the most active opposition from the Tennessee State Employees Association; Tennessee Bar Association; Tennessee Trial Layers; American Civil Liberties Union; and AFSCME (AFSCME, 1998).

A much more modest bill was adopted during the 1986 session and signed into law, permitting private management of one new medium security facility. The restrictions written into this bill, however, were so unfavorable to business that there was only one firm bid on it (CCA declined). The first state contract in Tennessee was not granted until 1992 (to CCA), during the administration of Governor Ned McWherter, who was elected governor after Alexander. This contract was immediately challenged on conflict-of-interest grounds because another firm, U.S. Corrections Corporation, reportedly had submitted a lower bid (AFSCME, 1998).

CCA also contacted Texas officials in 1984 (Ethridge, 1990). Ethridge, in his doctoral dissertation, reports that Governor Mark White, a Democrat, viewed the private prison possibility as an opportunity to direct some business to a particular group of developers, and after CCA agreed to use those developers, White reportedly assisted CCA in gaining financial support from Merrill Lynch. Criticism about his close ties to the developers was deflected, Ethridge reports, by White's claim that private prisons were part of his economic development program for the state. CCA promised, among other things, a 20% savings in the costs of prison construction and operation. The legislation was passed with bipartisan support, according to Ethridge, although it was not passed until after White had left office and was succeeded by Bill Clements.

The policy-making context in Texas also was described as one of crisis and failed criminal justice policy (Ethridge, 1990). The total admissions to prison in Texas were twice the number of releases (Ethridge), the state had been found in contempt of court for not having obeyed previous orders to reduce overcrowding, Governor Clements reportedly faced a $231 million budget deficit for fiscal year 1986, and the estimates were that $400 million was needed to build enough prisons to meet the court mandate. The only person to speak against the legislation was the legislative coordinator for the Texas State Employee Union (Ethridge), who said that it was morally wrong and involved a fundamental conflict of interest because profit motives were not consistent with the best interests of prisons and the public. He was quoted as follows:

> Because prison contracts are structured on a per diem basis, the interests of the corporation will be to increase occupancy rates, to increase profits. . . . There is also a conflict of interest because corporate correctional officers will seek to maintain an ever increasing incarceration population and will lobby for tougher prison sentencing policies. (Ethridge, p. 82)

In 1987, Texas took the additional step of passing legislation that permitted local governments to contract for private facilities without having a vote of the people, which ordinarily would be required for any capital project. This may have contributed to the fact that Texas now has more private facilities (19) than any other state.

Privatization has also sparked old-fashioned partisan politics in some states. Arizona's Republican-controlled legislature passed legislation authorizing private prisons in 1985 and again in 1986, but both bills were vetoed by Democratic

Governor Bruce Babbitt. Another bill was passed in 1987 and signed by Republic Governor, Evan Mecham, but Arizona's public employee union filed suit against the legislation on constitutional grounds and won. Republican-controlled legislatures again passed privatization legislation in 1988 that was vetoed by Democratic Governor, Rose Mofford, who had taken over as Governor after the impeachment of Evan Mecham. Privatization legislation finally succeeded in 1990, when it was approved mainly along party lines in the legislature and signed into law by Republican Governor Fife Symington. The partisan nature of private involvement in prisons is also documented by Gallagher and Edwards (1997), who found that states with Democratic governors and strong labor unions were more resistant to private prison industries.

The private prison subgovernment not only includes business leaders, state-elected officials, political party elites, and correctional experts, but also two influential social science researchers as well. The initial studies by both Logan and Thomas indicated that privatization had reduced the costs of prisons (Logan, 1990, 1996; Logan & McGriff, 1989; Thomas, 1997). Thomas is a member of CCA's Prison Realty Corporation's board of directors, and his center at the University of Florida had been partially funded by the corporation (Thomas, 1999). Academics on the whole have been very cautious about the privatization of prisons, if not opposed to it (McDonald, 1990; Shichor, 1995; Sparks, 1994); thus, the emergence of research by well-respected academics that shows private prisons to be less expensive or higher quality has been important in legitimizing the arguments presented by businesses and policy makers.

THE RHETORIC, CLAIMS, AND SCRIPT OF PRIVATE PRISONS

The most common script offered as an explanation for the growth of private prisons is that increasing crime rates, along with mandatory sentences and longer terms, have produced a rapid increase in prisoners. The increase in prisoners produced extensive overcrowding in secure adult facilities during the 1980s—a time when almost all states were faced with serious financial problems and budget deficits. These factors created a crisis in criminal justice policy, and public officials turned to the private sector to reduce the costs of prison operation.

As plausible as this scenario seems, it is simply inaccurate in some respects. There has been a virtual explosion in the number of persons sentenced to secure state and federal facilities, but it is very difficult to sustain an argument that the increase in prisoners has been the logical result of people committing more crimes than in the past. Data on the rate of imprisonment from 1925 to 1973 show that there was virtually no change in the rate of imprisonment, with the rate hovering around 100 prisoners per 100,000 people (Schneider, 1998). From 1973 to 1997, however, the rate increased to an all time high of 446 prisoners per 100,000 people (Bureau of Justice Statistics, 1998; Maguire & Pastore, 1994, 1996). If this were produced by an increase in crime, then one would expect the rate of crime commission to have increased in a similar way, but, except for drug crimes, this is not the case. In fact, victimization survey data on commission of violent crimes has been going down, not up, since 1973 when the first victimization survey was conducted (Maguire & Pastore, 1994). The uniform crime data on murder, which is the most serious and the most precise in terms of definition—shows an up-and-down pattern, certainly not a steady upward trend that could in any way account for the increase in prisoners (Bureau of Justice Statistics, 1998; Maguire & Pastore, 1995).

The increase in prisoners is accounted for by public policy changes, not changes in the propensity of people to inflict harm on others. The policy changes that produced the increase in incarceration and the overcrowding that results include longer sentences, mandatory sentences, three strikes you're out, no parole, no early release, and the huge increase in penalties for drug offenses. The point here is that turning to the private sector to build more prisons or to manage prisons so that the savings can be used to offset deficits, reduce overcrowding, or permit even more growth in incarceration is a policy choice made by elected public officials. There were other choices that could have been made. By the end of 1996, only 18 states had authorized contracts for private prisons within their state, and 32 had not. It must be emphasized that most states cannot prevent a private business from building a prison in the state and contracting with the federal government or with other states to take their prisoners. Unless a state passes legislation prohibiting the prison business, it is subject to finding one of these within its borders at some point in the future.

The policy choices available to states that are alternatives to privatization include reducing the scope of incarcerative sanctions, increasing the number of community-based alternatives, reducing the length of sentences, increasing the number of early release programs, or investing in prevention programs such as early childhood parenting and education.

The second part of the script is that the increase in prisoners produced overcrowding (which is supported by the evidence), and that overcrowding, combined with tight budgets, led public officials to turn to the private sector to build or manage prisons with the promise of a 5% to 20% savings. This savings, presumably, would permit the state to reduce its overcrowding. To examine this claim, I conducted an analysis in which the number of private prison contracts in the state is regressed on the three following possible explanatory variables: the extent of budget health from 1980 to 1986 (as measured by the difference between revenue one year and expenditures the next year, divided by expenditures; see Berry & Berry, 1992), the extent of overcrowding in the state and local prison systems, and the rate of incarceration (Schneider, 1998). The first two variables reflect the expectation that privatization was produced by the combination of an overcrowded prison system and the budget shortfalls characteristic of the 1980 to 1986 period. The third variable, rate of incarceration per 100,000, is a commonly used indicator for the punitiveness of the criminal justice system in the state.

The results show that budget health is statistically significant, but in the opposite direction of the prediction (beta = .36, t = 2.64, significance = .012). That is, states with larger budget shortfalls were less likely to turn to the private sector. Overcrowding had no significant relationship (beta = −.089, t = −.66). On the other hand, states with higher rates of incarceration were more likely to have private prison contracts (beta = .32, t = 2.4, significance = .02). The conclusion I draw is that increased privatization was driven by the same kinds of value orientations that produce more punitive criminal justice systems—a generalized sort of conservative, antigovernment, law and order ideology.

The purpose of this paper is not to offer a complete predictive model of the growth of private prisons, but only to examine the efficacy of the rationales that have been offered. Increases in the number of prisoners, overcrowding, and tight budgets were not causal factors that forced states to turn to private prison management. Instead, these trends required the states to confront the punitiveness of the criminal justice policies that had been produced in the decades after the 1960s. These trends established a context within which privatization could be promoted as a solution to a problem. In Kingdon's (1984) terms, it opened a window of opportunity in which a solution (privatization) found the problem that it could help solve.

In Schneider and Ingram's (1993, 1997) framework, privatization gave policy makers the opportunity to gain political capital through the appearance of doing something about the failed criminal justice system and simultaneously open up market opportunities for private business. It offered the attractive political opportunity to continue the negative social construction of prisoners and, at the same time, to develop a new positively constructed constituency of businesses, corporations, and stockholders who could profit from prisons. Support for private prisons also permitted officials to take advantage of the positive valance associated with downsizing government through privatization.

Policy makers in some states turned to privatization, others did not—at least not yet. The rationales used in states that adopted privatization could have been used with just as much credibility, if not more credibility, in states that resisted the privatization movement.

ISSUES, COSTS, AND QUALITY OF PUBLIC-PRIVATE PARTNERSHIPS

The media coverage of private prisons has tended toward the dramatic, and it is usually unfavorable. More than one state has had the experience of a riot or escape from a private prison within its borders that houses persons who are from other states entirely. Local police and state highway patrol are expected to help quell the riot or find the escapees—at public expense. Ohio discovered that a private prison within its borders was taking prisoners classified as maximum security when they thought that the prison had agreed to only take minimum and medium security prisoners. However, these kinds of problems—riots, escapes, inmate-on-inmate violence—also occur in publicly managed prisons, and there have been far too few studies making reliable comparisons to draw the conclusion that private prisons are more subject to these sorts of problems than public prisons.

Most of the empirical research on private prisons emphasizes cost differences. Although fraught with methodological problems, the current studies are summarized in Table 1. For the most part, these studies show a slight advantage to the private prisons and illustrate (in Texas, at least) that a state may realize a reduction

TABLE 1 Summary of Cost Studies

	Cost per Inmate per Day			
State	Private	Public	Year (data)	Comment
Texas	$36.76	$42.70 to $43.13	1990	Study conducted by the Texas Sunset Advisory Commission compared four private prerelease minimum security prisons for males with hypothetical operation by the state (operational costs only)
	$33.95 to $33.61	$39.79 to $38.64	1995 to 1996	Texas Criminal Justice Policy Council report to the legislature in January 1997, for prisoners in the Texas Institutional Division (reported in Thomas, 1998)
	$27.91	$28.96	1996	Texas Criminal Justice Policy Council report to the legislature in January 1997, for prisoners in the Texas Jail Division (reported in Thomas, 1998)
California	$42.67	$36.15 to $45.55	1991 to 1992	Sechrest and Shichor (1993) compared three for-profit community correctional facilities, one operated by a private business, one by a local government, and one by a police department, both of the latter on a for-profit basis under contract from the state
Tennessee	$73.50	$77.50	1985 to 1988	Logan and McGriff (1989) compared two privately operated 350-bed facilities in Hamilton County, Tennessee (these cost figures assume full occupancy)
	$35.39	$34.90 to $35.45	1993 to 1994	Tennessee Select Oversight Committee on Corrections, 1995, studied one private, minimum-maximum security facility for men with two similar public facilities (U.S. GAO report considers this study to have the best methodology)
Washington (Tennessee data)	$33.61	$35.82 to $35.28	1993 to 1994	Washington's Department of Corrections Privatization Feasibility Study (Legislative Budget Committee for the State of Washington, 1996) used the same data from the Tennessee study of 1993 to 1994, but adjusted it as if the facilities were at full capacity
(Louisiana data)	$23.75 to $23.34	$23.55	1995 to 1996	Washington's Department of Corrections Privatization Feasibility Study (Legislative Budget Committee for the State of Washington, 1996) compared two private and one public mixed-custody facilities in Louisiana
Louisiana				Archambeault and Deis (1996; quoted in Thomas, 1998) compared three large medium-maximum security prisons in Louisiana over 5 fiscal years, 1992 to 1996, and found cost savings of 11.7% for the 5-year totals
Arizona	$35.90 to $44.37	$43.08	1995 to 1996	Thomas's (1997) study of Arizona's costs produced an estimate of $44.37 for a private, 450-bed dual gender minimum security prison (Marana) when taking into account the state officials located at the site, but arrived at an adjusted cost of $35.90 after amortizing the costs of constructions, not including the taxes paid by the facility and other adjustments

in per inmate cost, over time. It is interesting to note, however, that comparative data are available for only a handful of the private prisons. Following are some of the many methodological issues:

- How should indirect costs be allocated in the public and private facilities?
- Should the cost of the private and public facilities be based on the actual average daily population or on the number of places the facility is built to hold? What should be done if it is more than 100% full?
- Should the state costs associated specifically with privatization (e.g., having monitors on site) be counted as part of the cost of the private prison?
- Should in kind services provided by one public agency to another be added to the cost of the public prison (e.g., health or mental health programs)?
- Should services provided by the public sector to the private prison, such as capturing escapees or prosecuting inmates for violent acts on one another, be added to the private prison's costs?
- Should the taxes paid by private prisons be adjusted out, as Thomas (1997) has done in his cost studies, on the grounds that these are returned to the state?

In addition, the studies virtually never explain how or why the private prison manages to have lower costs even though they have the added responsibility of making a profit. There is a general perception that the reduced costs are at the expense of employee salaries. The methodologies also suffer because the comparisons, due to necessity, are of only one or two institutions and usually cover only 1 year of data. The natural variability in annual expenditures for any particular prison may be rather high from one year to the next, and differences as simple as the average age (experience) of employees may account for sizable cost differences between institutions.

Quality comparisons are even less common than cost analyses, although there have been some researchers who have made concerted efforts to develop a methodology with solid theoretical underpinnings for quality studies. Logan (1996) compared a New Mexico women's prison, operated under private contract with the prison that had previously housed New Mexico's women inmates, with a federal women's prison in West Virginia. He examined eight dimensions of service (security, safety, order, care, activity, justice, conditions, and management), each with six or eight separate indicators. The data included staff and inmate surveys as well as institutional records. He concluded that the private prison, overall, had a higher level of service quality, even though there were some interesting differences between staff and inmate assessments (with staff preferring the private prison and inmates preferring the public one).

Thomas' (1997) study of Arizona included several qualitative comparisons, but the fact that the private facility (Marana) housed a mixed gender population made comparisons risky. On most of the indicators, there were no differences, mainly because the time periods were so short that some of the more serious kinds of incidents (riots, inmate-on-inmate assaults or murders, staff abuse of prisoners) were not reported from any facility. The privately operated facility (Marana) had fewer jobs assigned per inmate than the medium security (level 2) public prisons (52 compared with 83), and was given lower ratings by the state's annual audits on most of the indicators. The private prison had an overall *good* rating, whereas all of the public facilities received an overall *excellent* rating. It is impossible to know whether these audit data reflect real differences in performance or system bias against private prisons.

Lanza-Kaduce, Parker, and Thomas (1999) conducted a comparative recidivism analysis for the Florida state legislature in which they compared the 12-month recidivism records of persons released from two privately operated facilities and those released from public facilities. The research design involved a sample matched-on-offense category (using 53 specific categories), race, number of prior incarcerations, and age. Multiple measures of recidivism were used, including rearrest, reconviction, and resentencing to incarceration as well as an overall indicator of any recidivism. There was a sample size of 198 in each group. With fewer rearrests (96 compared to 192), fewer reincarcerations (101 to 146), and fewer incidents of any form (172 to 237), the results clearly gave the edge to private facilities. There were similar differences in the severity of the recidivism offense. Finally, the study compared persons in the private facility who had completed their assigned programs and those who had not. The lower recidivism rates in the private prison, compared to the public prison, were due almost entirely to the fact that the private facility had more persons who completed their assigned rehabilitative programs. The noncompleters had recidivism rates almost identical to the persons from the public facilities—giving some powerful indication that successful completion of in-prison programs predicts the reduction of subsequent criminal activity.

A study of several Louisiana prisons (Archambeault & Deis, 1996) included a number of qualitative dimensions. The state-operated facilities were found to have higher quality in terms of preventing escapes, preventing sexual offenses, using urine testing, and having a wide scope of educational and job-related programs. The private facilities were found to have fewer critical incidents, a safer work environment for employees and prisoners, more effective discipline, and better access to programs for prisoners.

The design and methodologies of these studies indicate that on a localized, institutional basis, private prisons appear not to damage or harm the criminal justice system capacity of the state, and it may reduce costs without reducing service, or it may even improve service.

Another empirical question that needs analysis is whether public-private partnerships accentuate the pressure for an ever-increasing supply of prisoners, leading to longer sentences and more intrusive criminal justice practices. It would be naive to believe that private prison corporations are not involved in lobbying, and it would be equally naive to expect that they are only interested in capturing a larger market share from the public-sector prisons. In fact, possible conflicts between the two can be avoided if both work to ensure that there is a ready supply of prisoners to be housed. Prison as the punishment of choice has always been politically attractive, but it is limited due to its long-term cost. Even though the public may be easily swayed by the law and order rhetoric into believing that long prison terms are deserved by those who break the law, the public, nevertheless, does not like to spend money on people they perceive as undeserving, such as prisoners and would prefer to allocate those funds to education or other target populations.

Hence, public-private partnerships that permit a large role for the private sector have the potential effect of bringing about a coalition between public and private providers of prisons with both advocating for increasing the scope of duration of prison sentences. Second, private management appears to cost less and therefore can be promoted by elected officials as a way of reducing the costs of the criminal justice system, even though the number of persons imprisoned stays the same or even increases.

The results of a regression analysis (see Schneider, 1998) indicate weak supports for these contentions, although the newness of private prisons and the complexities of the policy-making process are such that caution is in order. The results show that states with more contracts to private prison companies within their jurisdiction in 1996 had higher rates of incarceration per 100,000 in 1997 than states with fewer contracts (beta = .50, t = 3.85, significance = .000), even when budget health was controlled. This conclusion should be taken with caution, however, because the proportion of all prisoners who could be held in private facilities currently under contract or being built is still only about 8%. Furthermore, the time lag in the causal analysis is complicated. Decisions by a state to permit private prisons occur through several legislative sessions and may not result in any private prison contracts for several years after the authorization. The incarceration rate is the product of policy decisions over a long period of time, not simply during 1 year. It is possible that the rate of incarceration and the use of private contracts are both the product of an underlying conservative ideology, but it is also possible that political dynamics are being altered by the presence of private prisons in the state in such a way that the state can continue to increase the proportion of its population it is able and willing to place behind bars.

CONCLUSIONS AND IMPLICATIONS

Public-private partnerships in prison operation is different from most other policy arenas because prisons deliver punishment, and there is no way to turn this into a technical administrative exercise devoid of discretion. When private owners or managers run a prison, they hire the guards and staff, and set the tone for how the prisoners are treated. There is enormous discretion exercised by the caseworkers who are in direct contact with prisoners. There are important differences between delivering service, benefits, treatment, or regulations to a target population and delivering confinement, orders, rules, discipline, and physical pain to a captive population that has no choice and no say in how they are treated.

In terms of the future of public-private partnerships in prisons, I believe this is a policy arena in which we would expect to find pendulum effects similar to those observed during historical experiments with private involvement. Extensive private involvement will give way to public delivery mechanisms that, in turn, will yield to private ones at some future time. A pendulum pattern in public and private delivery systems is expected because prisons are institutions that cannot be managed as effectively as expected by the media, political elites, or general public regardless of whether they are entirely under government control or whether they involve extensive privatization. Perhaps prisons will never be effective enough in producing public safety because public safety is more contingent on societal factors such as families, communities, schools, nonprofits, economic opportunities, and the absence of race and class discrimination. Institutions that cannot produce the level of performance expected and desired by the media, political leaders, and the public will move from the public sector toward partnerships with extensive private involvement, and then back toward the public sector, as the private gives up on them.

REFERENCES

American Federation of State, County, and Municipal Employees (1998). *Corrections corporation of America. Public employee, January, February* [On-line]. Available: http://www.afscme.org/afscme/press/pejf9809.html.

Archambeault, W. G. & Deis, D. R. Jr. (1996). *Private versus public prisons in Louisiana. Report to the National Institute of Justice* [On-line]. Available: http://www.uss.uconn.edu/~wwwsoci.

Berry, F. S. & Berry, W. D. (1992). Tax innovation in the states: Capitalizing on political opportunity. *American Journal of Political Science, 36,* 715–742.

Bureau of Justice Statistics. (1998). *Prisoners and prison capacity* [On-line]. Available: http://www.ojp.usdog.gov/bjs/pub.

Conley, J. A. (1980). Revising conceptions about the origin of prisons: The importance of economic considerations. *Social Science Quarterly, 62,* 249–257.

Conley, J. A. (1981). Prisons, production and profit: Reconsidering the importance of prison industries. *Journal of Social History, 53,* 259–275.

Ethridge, P. A. (1990). *An analysis of the policy process pertaining to the utilization of private prisons in Texas.* Unpublished doctoral dissertation, Sam Houston State University.

Folz, D. H. & Scheb, J. M. (1989). Prisons, profits, and politics: The Tennessee privatization. *Judicature, 73,* 98.

Gallagher, D., & Edwards, M. E. (1997). Prison industries and the private sector. *Atlantic Economic Journal, 25,* 91–98.

General Accounting Office (1997). *Private and public prisons: Studies comparing operational and/or quality of service* (U.S. GAO Letter Rep. GGD-96-158) [On-line]. Available: http://www.securitymanagement.com:80/library/000231.html.

Kingdon, J. (1984). *Agendas, alternatives and public policies.* Boston: Little, Brown.

Knepper, P. E. (1990). *Imprisonment and society in Arizona territory.* Unpublished doctoral dissertation, School of Justice Studies, Arizona State University.

Lanza-Kaduce, L., Parker, K. F. & Thomas, C. W. (1999). A comparative recidivism analysis of releases from private and public prisons. *Crime & Delinquency, 45,* 28–47.

Legislative Budget Committee for the State of Washington. (1996). *Department of Corrections privatization feasibility study.* Olympia, WA: Legislative Budget Committee.

Logan, C. H. (1990). *Private prisons: Pros and cons.* New York: Oxford University Press.

Logan, C. H. (1996). Well kept: Comparing quality of confinement in a public and a private prison. *National Institute of Justice Report* [On-line]. Available: http://www.uc.uconn.edu/~wwwsoci.

Logan, C. H. & McGriff, B. (1989, September/October). *Comparing costs of public and private prisons. A case study* (National Institute of Justice Research in Brief Rep. No. 216). Washington, DC: National Institute of Justice.

Maguire, K., & Pastore, A. L. (Eds.). (1994). *Sourcebook of criminal justice statistics.* Washington, DC: Bureau of Justice Statistics.

Maguire, K., & Pastore, A. L. (Eds.). (1996). *Sourcebook of criminal justice statistics.* Washington, DC: Bureau of Justice Statistics.

McDonald, D. C. (1990). The cost of operating public and private correctional facilities. In D.C. McDonald (Ed.), *Private prisons and the public interest* (pp. 86–106). New Brunswick, NJ: Rutgers University Press.

Prison Privatization Act, 128 Ariz. Rev. Stat. §§ 41–1609, 1681–1684, 1803. (1997).

Schneider, A. (1998, September). *Private prisons as public policy.* Paper presented at the American Political Science Association Annual Conference, Boston.

Schneider, A., & Ingram, H. (1993). Social constructions and target populations: Implications for politics and policy. *American Political Science Review, 87,* 334–347.

Schneider, A., & Ingram, H. (1997). *Policy design for democracy.* Lawrence: University Press of Kansas.

Sechrest, D., & Shichor, D. (1993). Corrections goes public (and private) in California. *Federal Probation, 57,* 3–8.

Shichor, D. (1995). *Punishment for profit: Private prisons/public concerns.* Thousand Oaks: Sage.

Sparks, R. (1994). Can prisons be legitimate? Penal politics, privatization, and the timeliness of an old idea. *British Journal of Criminology, 34,* 14–28.

Tennessee Select Oversight Committee on Corrections. (1995). *Comparative evaluation of privately-managed CCA prison and state-managed prototypical prisons.* Nashville: Tennessee Legislature.

Texas Sunset Advisory Commission. (1991). Information report on contracts for correctional facilities and services. In *Recommendations to the Governor of Texas and members of the seventy-second legislature* (chap. 4). Austin, TX: Author.

Thomas, C. W. (1997). *Comparing the cost and performance of public and private prisons in Arizona.* Phoenix, AZ: Arizona Department of Corrections.

Thomas, C. W. (1998). *Evaluating the potential public policy implication of correctional privatization by the state of Iowa.* Miami: University of Florida.

Thomas, C. W. (1999). *Private prison project* [On-line]. Available: http://web.crim.ufl.edu/pcp/census/.

Thomas, C. W., Bolinger, D., & Badalamenti, J. L. (1997). Private adult correctional facility census (11th ed.). *Private Corrections Project* [On-line]. Available: http://web.crim.ufl.edu/pcp/census/1997.

Thomas, C. W. Bolinger, D., & Badalamenti, J.L. (1998). Private adult correctional facility census (11th ed.). *Private Corrections Project* [On-line]. Available: http://web.crim.ufl.edu/pcp/census/1998.

Walker, S. (1980). *Popular justice: A history of American criminal justice.* New York: Oxford University Press.

REVIEW QUESTIONS

1. What were the costs and benefits of the models of public-private prison partnerships that existed prior to the twentieth century?
2. To what extent have lobbyists and private corporations such as the Corrections Corporation of America shaped our government's response to crime in the past several decades?
3. Describe what, if any, ethical restrictions should be placed on policy makers as they interact with private entities interested in expanding the use of private prisons?
4. What, if any, credence do you place in the author's predictions about a pendulum effect to future public-private prison partnerships?

Acknowledgements

Bruce A. Arrigo, Carol R. Fowler, and Kristie R. Blevins. Essay prepared especially for Prisons & Jails: A Reader.

Mark Blumberg and J. Dennis Laster. Reprinted by permission of Waveland Press, Inc from Blumberg, M. & J.D. Laster. 1999. The impact of HIV/AIDS on corrections. In (K.C. Hassa & G.P. Alpert, Eds.) *The dilemmas in corrections: Contemporary readings,* 4th edition (pp. 574–591). Prospect Heights, IL: Waveland (Long Grove, IL: Waveland Press, Inc., 2006). All rights reserved

Megan L. Comfort. Reprinted from Comfort, M., In the Tube at San Quentin: The "secondary prisonization" of women visiting inmates. *Journal of Contemporary Ethnography* (32:1) pp. 77–107, copyright 2003 by Sage. Reprinted by permission of Sage Publications, Inc.

Francis T. Cullen, Edward J. Latessa, Velmer S. Burton, Jr., and Lucien X. Lombardo. Excerpted article from Cullen, F.T., E.J. Latessa, V.S. Burton Jr. and L.X. Lombardo. 1993. The correctional orientation of prison wardens: Is the rehabilitation idea supported? *Criminology* 31:1, 69–92. Reprinted by permission of the American Society of Criminology.

Dean A. Dabney and Michael S. Vaughn. Excerpted article from Dabney, D.A. and M.S. Vaughn. 2000. Incompetent jail and prison doctors. *The Prison Journal* 80:2, 151–183. Reprinted by permission of the author.

David R. Eichenthal and Laurel Blatchford. Reprinted from Eichenthal, D.R. and L. Blatchford, Prison crime in New York State. *The Prison Journal* (77:4) pp. 456–466, copyright 1997 Sage. Reprinted by permission of Sage Publications, Inc.

Mary Ann Farkas. Reprinted from Farkas, M.A., A typology of correctional officers. *International Journal of Offender Therapy and Comparative Criminology* (44:4) pp. 431–449, copyright 2000 Sage. Reprinted by permission of Sage Publications, Inc.

Peter Finn. Reprinted from Finn, P. 1998. Correctional officer stress: A cause for concern and additional help. Originally published in *Federal Probation* (62:2). Reprinted by permission of the Administrative Office of the U.S. Courts.

Mark Fleisher and Scott H. Decker. Essay prepared especially for Prisons & Jails: A Reader.

Bonnie L. Green, Jeanne Miranda, Anahita Daroowalla, and Juned Siddique. Reprinted from Green, B.L., J. Miranda, and A. Daroowalla, Trauma exposure, mental health functioning and program needs of women in jail. *Crime & Delinquency* (51:1) pp. 133–151, copyright 2005 Sage. Reprinted by permission of Sage Publications, Inc.

Christopher Hensley, Mary Koscheski, and Richard Tewksbury. Reprinted from Hensley, C., M. Koscheski, and R. Tewksbury. 2003. The impact of institutional factors on officially reported sexual assaults in prisons. *Sexuality and Culture* 7:4, 16–26 with kind permission from Springer Science and Business Media.

John J. Kerbs and Jennifer M. Jolley. Essay prepared especially for Prisons & Jails: A Reader. This publication was made possible by support from East Carolina University's Department of Criminal Justice and the National Institute of Mental Health Training Grant T32-MH19960. All points of view and opinions in this paper are solely those of the author and do not necessarily reflect the official positions or policies of the East Carolina University's Department of Criminal Justice, the National Institute of Mental Health, the George Warren Brown School of Social Work, or the Winterville Police Department

Stephen E. Lankenau. Reprinted from Lankenau, S.E., Smoke 'em if you got 'em: Cigarette black markets in US prisons and jails. *The Prison Journal* (81:2) pp. 142–161, copyright 2001 Sage. Reprinted by permission of Sage Publications, Inc.

Edward J. Latessa and Lawrence F. Travis III. Reprinted from Latessa, E.J. and L.F. Travis III. Residential community correctional programs. In (Byrne, J.M., A.L. Lurigio and J. Petersilia, Eds.) *Smart sentencing: The emergence of intermediate sanctions* pp. 166–181, copyright 1992. Reprinted by permission of Sage Publications, Inc.

Carl G. Leukefeld and Frank R. Tims. Reprinted from *Journal of Substance Abuse Treatment,* 10, Leukefeld, C.G. and F.R. Tims, Drug abuse treatment in prisons and jails, pp. 77–84, copyright 1993, with permission from Elsevier.

Eileen M. Luna-Firebaugh. Reprinted from Luna-Firebaugh, E.M., Incarcerating ourselves: Tribal jails and corrections. *The Prison Journal* (83:1) pp. 51–66, copyright 2003. Reprinted by permission of Sage Publications, Inc.

Doris Layton MacKenzie. Reprinted from MacKenzie, D.L., Corrections and sentencing in the 21st century: Evidence-based corrections and sentencing. *The Prison Journal* (81:3) pp. 299–312, copyright 2001 Sage. Reprinted by permission of Sage Publications, Inc.

James W. Marquart. Excerpted article from Marquart, J.W. 1986. Prison guards and the use of physical coercion as a mechanism of prisoner control. *Criminology* 24:2, 347–366. Reprinted by permission of the American Society of Criminology.

James W. Marquart, Dorothy E. Merianos, Jaimie L. Hebert, and Leo Carroll. Reprinted from Marquart, J.W., D.E. Merianos, J.L. Hebert, and L. Carroll, Health condition and prisoners: A review of research and emerging areas of inquiry. *The Prison Journal* (77:2) pp. 184–208, copyright 1997 Sage. Reprinted by permission of Sage Publications, Inc.

Wilson R. Palacios, Ph.D. Essay prepared especially for Prisons & Jails: A Reader.

Brian K. Payne and Randy R. Gainey. Reprinted from Payne, B.K and R.R. Gainey, A qualitative assessment of the pains experienced on electronic monitoring. *International Journal of Offender Therapy and Comparative Criminology* (42:2) pp. 149–162, copyright 2008 Sage. Reprinted by permission of Sage Publications, Inc.

Joan Petersilia. Reprinted from Petersilia, J., Prisoner reentry: Public safety and reintegration challenges. *The Prison Journal* (81:3) pp. 360–375, copyright 2001 Sage. Reprinted by Permission of Sage Publications, Inc.

Eric D. Poole and Mark R. Pogrebin. Essay prepared especially for Prisons & Jails: A Reader.

Michael L. Radelet. Essay prepared especially for Prisons & Jails: A Reader. A version of this article first appeared as, "Humanizing the death penalty," by Michael L. Radelet in the journal, *Social Problems,* vol. 48:1, 2001, pp. 83–87, published by the University of California Press. Copyright 2001 by the Regents of the University of California.

Frances P. Reddington and Allen D. Sapp. Reprinted from Reddington, F.P. and A.D. Sapp. 1997. Juveniles in adult prisons: Problems and prospects. *Journal of Crime and Justice* 22:2, 139–152 with permission. Copyright 1997 Matthew Bender & Company, Inc., a member of the LexisNexis Group. All rights reserved.

Thomas J. Schmid and Richard S. Jones. Reprinted from Schmid, T.J. and R.S. Jones, Ambivelent actions: Prison adaptation strategies of first-time, short-term inmates. *Journal of Contemporary Ethnography* (21:4) pp. 439–463, copyright 1993 Sage. Reprinted by permission of Sage Publications, Inc.

Anne Larason Schneider. Reprinted from Schneider, A.L, Public-private partnerships in the US prison system. *American Behavioral Scientist* (43) pp. 192–208, copyright 1999 Sage. Reprinted by permission of Sage Publications, Inc.

Chris Sigurdson. Reprinted from Sigurdson, C. 2000. The mad, the bad and the abandoned: The mentally ill in prisons and jails. *Corrections Today* 62:7, 70–78. Reprinted with permission of the American Correctional Association, Alexandria, VA.

Jonathan Simon. Reproduced with permission from Simon, J. From the big house to the warehouse: Rethinking prisons and state government in the 20th century. *Punishment and Society* 2:2, 213–234. (© Sage UK, 2000), by permission of Sage Publications Ltd.

Christopher Smith. Reprinted from Smith, C.E. Prisoners' rights in the Rehnquist era. *The Prison Journal* (87:4) pp. 457–476, copyright 2007 by Sage. Reprinted by permission of Sage Publication, Inc.

Richard Tewksbury. Excerpted article from Tewksbury, R. 1993. Motivations of post-secondary correctional educators. *Journal of Criminal Justice Education* 4:1, 115–131. Reprinted by permission of the author.

Richard Tewksbury and Elizabeth Ehrhardt Mustaine. Excerpted article from Tewksbury, R. and E.E. Mustaine. 2005. "Insiders" Views of Prison Amenities: Beliefs and Perceptions of Correctional Staff Members. *Criminal Justice Review,* 30:2,174–188.

Richard Tewksbury and Matthew T. DeMichele. Excerpted article from Tewksbury, R. and M.T. DeMichele. 2003. The good, the bad, and the (sometimes) ugly truths: American penal goals and perspectives. *American Journal of Criminal Justice* 28:1, 1–14. (© Southern Criminal Justice Association, 2003), by permission of the author.

Hans Toch. Reprinted from Toch, H., The future of supermax confinement. *The Prison Journal* (81:3) pp. 376–388, copyright 2001 Sage. Reprinted by permission of Sage Publications, Inc.

Jeremy Travis. Reprinted from Travis, J. 2005. Families and children. In (Travis, J. Ed.) *But they all come back: Facing the challenges of prison reentry.* (pp. 119–150). Washington, D.C.: Urban Institute. Reprinted by permission by the Urban Institute Press.

James L. Williams, Daniel G. Rodeheaver, and Denise W. Huggins. Excerpted article from Williams, J.L., D.G. Rodeheaver and D.W. Huggins. 1999. A comparative analysis of a new generation jail. *American Journal of Criminal Justice* 23:2, 223–246. Reprinted by permission of the Southern Criminal Justice Association.

Nancy Wolff, Cynthia L. Blitz, Jing Shi, Jane Siegel, and Ronet Bachman. Reprinted from Wolf, N., C.L. Blitz, J. Shi, and R. Bachman, Physical violence inside prisons: Rates of victimization. *Criminal Justice & Behavior* (34:5) pp. 588–599, copyright 2007 Sage. Reprinted by permission of Sage Publications, Inc.

John D. Wooldredge and Kimberly Masters. Reprinted from Wooldredge, J.D. and K. Masters, Confronting problems faced by pregnant inmates in state prisons. *Crime & Delinquency* (39:2) pp. 195–203, copyright 1993 Sage. Reprinted by permission of Sage Publications, Inc.

Frank A. Zeigler and Rolando V. Del Carmen. Reprinted from Zeigler, F.A. & R.V. Del Carmen, Constitutional issues arising from "three strikes and you're out legislation." In *Three Strikes and you're out: Vengeance as public policy* pp. 3–23, copyright 1996 by Sage. Reprinted by permission of Sage Publications, Inc.

Franklin E. Zimring. Reproduced with permission from Zimring, F. Imprisonment rates and the new politics of criminal punishment. *Punishment and Society* 3:1, 161–166. (© Sage UK, 2001), by permission of Sage Publications Ltd.